Great Writing

Great Writing:

A Reader for Writers

■

Third Edition

Harvey S. Wiener
Marymount Manhattan College

Nora Eisenberg
CUNY—LaGuardia Community College

Boston   Burr Ridge, IL   Dubuque, IA   Madison, WI   New York
San Francisco   St. Louis   Bangkok   Bogotá   Caracas   Kuala Lumpur
Lisbon   London   Madrid   Mexico City   Milan   Montreal   New Delhi
Santiago   Seoul   Singapore   Sydney   Taipei   Toronto

McGraw-Hill

A Division of The McGraw·Hill Companies

GREAT WRITING: A READER FOR WRITERS
Published by McGraw-Hill, an imprint of The McGraw-Hill Companies, Inc. 1221 Avenue of the
Americas, New York, NY, 10020. Copyright © 2002, 1998 by The McGraw-Hill Companies, Inc.
All rights reserved. No part of this publication may be reproduced or distributed in any form or by
any means, or stored in a database or retrieval system, without the prior written consent of The
McGraw-Hill Companies, Inc., including, but not limited to, in any network or other electronic
storage or transmission, or broadcast for distance learning. Some ancillaries, including electronic and
print components, may not be available to customers outside the United States.

This book is printed on acid-free paper.

2 3 4 5 6 7 8 9 0 FGR/FGR 0 9 8 7 6 5 4 3 2

ISBN 0-07-237064-5

Editorial director: *Phillip A. Butcher*
Executive editor: *Lisa Moore*
Senior marketing manager: *David Patterson*
Project manager: *Diane M. Folliard*
Production supervisor: *Carol A. Bielski*
Media producer: *Gregg Di Lorenzo*
Freelance design coordinator: *Mary L. Christianson*
Supplement producer: *Susan Lombardi*
Freelance cover designer: *e3 design group*
Cover image: *Ginko in Autumn,* ©*Anita Munman, anitamunman@mail.com*
Typeface: *10/12 Times Roman*
Compositor: *Shepherd Incorporated*
Printer: *Quebecor World Fairfield Inc.*

Library of Congress Cataloging-in-Publication Data
Great writing: a reader for writers / [compiled by] Harvey S. Wiener, Nora Eisenberg.—
3rd ed.
　　p. cm.
　ISBN 0-07-237064-5 (alk. paper)
　　1. College readers. 2. English language—Rhetoric—Problems, exercises, etc. 3. Report
writing—Problems, exercises, etc. I. Wiener, Harvey S. II. Eisenberg, Nora, 1946-
PE1417 .G67 2002
808'.0427—dc21　　　　　　　　　　　　　　　　　　　　　　　　2001030917

www.mhhe.com

About the Authors

Harvey S. Wiener is Vice President at Marymount Manhattan College. He has written many books on reading and writing for college students and their teachers, including *The Writing Room* (Oxford, 1981). He has served as chair of the Teaching of Writing Division of the Modern Language Association and as a member of the Executive Committee of the Conference on College Composition and Communication. Dr. Wiener was founding president of the Council of Writing Program Administrators. A Phi Beta Kappa graduate of Brooklyn College, he holds a Ph.D. in Renaissance literature from Fordham University. Dr. Wiener has won grants from the National Endowment for the Humanities, the Fund for the Improvement of Postsecondary Education, and the Exxon Education Foundation.

Nora Eisenberg is a professor of English at LaGuardia Community College of the City University of New York, where she has taught courses in composition, creative writing, and literature. She is the director of the City University Faculty Publication Program and founder of the CUNY Write Safe, an online resouce for students and teachers. Dr. Eisenberg holds a Ph.D. from Columbia University and has taught at Brooklyn College, Stanford University, and Georgetown University. She has published numerous articles on Virginia Woolf and is the coauthor with Harvey Wiener of many books on writing. Dr. Eisenberg is also a fiction writer; her short stories have appeared in such journals as the *Voice Literary Supplement* and *Partisan Review.* Her novel, *The War at Home,* will be published by Leapfrog Press in 2002.

Preface

We believe in a number of important principles about learning to write, and these principles inform this book and establish its content, approach, and format.

We believe first in the primacy of text and in the enduring authority, intelligence, and joy in great writing. When aspiring writers read great writing carefully and attentively, they come close to producing exceptional writing themselves. Aiming for contemporaneity, too many anthologies for writers avoid great writing; they may offer readable, serviceable samples, but they rarely show our language at its very best or address the great intellectual issues of our civilization. To use readings as guides for writing—as exercises in form, as explorations of style, as laboratories for the growth of ideas in words and sentences—students must read the very best our culture has to offer. Shakespeare, Swift, Woolf, Cather, Plato, Hawthorne, Orwell, Mill, Poe, Emerson, Brontë, White, Hughes, Didion, Keats, Joyce, Thoreau, great writers of our civilization, help provide the models that teach the writer's craft.

With a title like *Great Writing* we know that we are going out on a limb, and we want to admit at the outset that our selections unabashedly proclaim our own subjective judgments, tastes, and prejudices. An experienced reader could grumble about our exclusions or could question some of the pieces or authors we chose to include. Still, we strove to make selections that many educated readers would identify as important writing by great figures. You will recognize most of the authors and many of the selections. Our goal was always to choose the most clearly written, the most elegantly and intelligently reasoned, the most sensitive and thought-provoking pieces that suited the rhetorical strategies we believe best organize a course of study. We aimed for ethnic, geographical, and sexual diversity among our authors, and we tried to balance long pieces with short ones, humorous pieces with serious ones, and intense pieces with relaxed ones. We chose excerpts as rarely as possible yet could not always avoid them when we drew from novels, long works of fiction, or long essays. Where excerpts appear, we have explained the context so that what precedes or follows the selection is always clear. Of course, our wish is that students will like so much of what they read here that they will choose to read or reread on their own the full-length works—all of Ovid's *Metamorphoses,* Brontë's *Wuthering Heights,* and Thoreau's *Walden,* to name a few.

We also believe that poets, dramatists, novelists, and short story writers have as much to teach about writing essays as do nonfiction writers. Certainly in regard to description, narration, imagery, style, tone, characterization, symbol, point of view, satire, irony, dialogue, diction, coherence, allusion, and analogy—basic terms that readers and writers use to talk about their efforts—our collection of poems, short stories, and scenes from novels and plays can speak to beginning writers and can teach them. To exclude poetry, fiction, and dramatic literature from a reader is to risk a loss of exposure to great minds at a critical point in a student's growth.

More than offering great ideas and brilliant style, poets, fiction writers, and playwrights grapple with the same kinds of rhetorical principles that many people have too long insisted are the purview of essayists alone. Surely Marvell in "To His Coy Mistress" worked through the familiar conventions of argument and persuasion that face any writer who chooses to take a position and to win supporters. Certainly Carson McCullers in "A Tree. A Rock. A Cloud." faced the same need for clarity and personalized meaning, the same confusions of de-notation and connotation, the same impulse to establish new lexical validity that any writer faces in attempting an important definition. This is not to say, of course, that we are challenging the rightful place of the expository essay in a program for developing writers; rather, we aim to complement that place by es-tablishing for it a larger context that includes great writing in any genre. In fact, you will find many outstanding essays in this book.

Exploring the writer's craft through a consideration of rhetorical patterns is a useful way to study writing. We have chosen to organize this book by means of traditional rhetorical categories: description, narration, exemplification, process analysis, comparison and contrast, classification, causal analysis, defini-tion, and argumentation and persuasion. Our choice of selections demonstrates our conviction that elements of writing in all genres rely on these categories. Every chapter contains poetry, fiction, essays, and occasionally drama—all within familiar rhetorical contexts. We're not offering these examples as pure or absolute models of their type, however. Sometimes the rhetorical strategy is a dominant mode in the selection and is easy to recognize. At other times the strat-egy may be more subtle. A single paragraph or two, even a couple of sentences, may demonstrate some particularly striking application of a rhetorical principle. Sometimes more than one strategy—say, description and narration, causality and process, or definition, illustration, and argumentation—may work hand in hand.

The value in practicing rhetorical patterns is that they point the way to a range of available options for writers. We agree with many critics of rhetorically organized readers—it's the rare writer who chooses a rhetorical strategy and then sets out to fill it with ideas. No one says, "Today I'm going to write a clas-sification essay." Ideas always come first for writers, and as these ideas develop, writers pay attention to audience, purpose, language, style, and all the varied, complex factors that help make an essay successful. Still, as ideas develop, writ-ers cannot help but benefit from knowing rhetorical options and using them cre-atively and intelligently. Thus, if a writer wanted to develop an essay about the Civil War, a knowledge of cause-and-effect strategies would help him or her present clearly a sense of why the war began; a knowledge of descriptive strate-gies would help breathe life into a Union hospital scene; a knowledge of com-parison and contrast strategies would help in a consideration of the relative strengths of the North and the South. The writer would not have to exclude one strategy for the other: Powerful writing often relies on a number of different rhetorical patterns within a single essay. Again, the key is choices. Learning to write within rhetorical contexts expands a writer's choices and, no matter what the assignment, improves dramatically the possible approaches to writing.

We have made significant revisions for this new addition, adding outstanding pieces of great writing to an already noteworthy collection. Drawing from a wide range of cultures and ethnic backgrounds, we continue to offer challenging essays, stories, poems, and plays. Susan Sontag, Jane Smiley, Adam Gopnik, Andrew Sullivan, Annie Dillard, Ian Frazier—these and other renowned writers are just a few of the new voices in the chorus of talent in *Great Writing*. Also new to this edition are samples of student writing. Before the end of each chapter's introduction, we show how one student responded to the rhetorical strategy. Marginal annotations highlight essential elements in the student's draft.

"Summing Up" sections at the end of each chapter's introduction provide useful reviews of the major ideas explored in the chapter. In crystallizing the main points, "Summing Up" will help guide students' thoughtful reading and writing throughout the book. The section at the end of each chapter called "Crossover" taps students' critical thinking skills by asking them to consider linkages among selections that raise similar issues, themes, and ideas.

We want to thank our friends and colleagues who encouraged us to develop this text and who read proposals and early drafts. Don McQuade and Bob Atwan listened to early versions of our thoughts. John Wright saw the goals of our project immediately and gave us the support and energy we needed to carry it through. Elizabeth McMahan (Illinois State University), Lee Jacobus (University of Connecticut), and Gratia Murphey (Youngstown State University) did a thorough, thoughtful job of critiquing an early manuscript. Steven Nardi provided invaluable help in the revision of the manuscript. His sharp intelligence and grace make him a joy to work with. Lisa Moore at McGraw-Hill guided *Great Writing* to, and through, production with affection, respect, and care. To all the people who helped us along, including our families, we are deeply in debt.

Harvey S. Wiener
Nora Eisenberg

Contents

Chapter Two

NARRATION

Chapter Three
EXEMPLIFICATION

Chapter Four
PROCESS ANALYSIS

Chapter Five
COMPARISON AND CONTRAST

Chapter Six

CLASSIFICATION

Chapter Seven
CAUSAL ANALYSIS

Chapter Nine
ARGUMENTATION AND PERSUASION

Thematic Contents

Language and Writing

Education, Science, and Culture

Death, Illness, and Mortality

Race, Gender, and Ethnicity

Work, Professions, and Money

Nature

Great Writing

INTRODUCTION: THE WRITING PROCESS

INTRODUCTION TO THE WRITING PROCESS

All public writing—whether fiction, nonfiction, drama, or poetry—is the end-point of a creative process made permanent by language. Understanding the process of writing, that is, how a piece develops from start to finish, is an essential feature of learning how to write. Yet without digging in diaries, personal journals, biographies, or letters, when we read what great writers have written, we do not see any of that process. We see only a final product. The routes of access to it—the false starts, the wrong turns, the winding roadways—are not open to our inspection as we read.

If they share anything, though, great writers share an elaborate and often agonizing commitment to process. To produce a page of writing they follow a series of irregular, often undefinable steps that, despite some similarities, may differ from task to task and from writer to writer. If this seems paradoxical—writers doing the same thing differently—it is nonetheless true. The steps are different, are taken in no certain sequence, and vary dramatically, yet every writer follows some steps that take him or her from an emerging idea to a piece of finished prose or poetry. Of course, we can rarely arrive at a fully satisfactory response to the age-old question that attentive readers will ask, often incredulously, about the writer of a wonderful essay or story or poem: "How did she do that?" Still, by considering the ways writers get to where they want to go, we can uncover new paths to our own final products.

GETTING STARTED

All writers begin with thinking. They may use pen, pencil, typewriter, or computer to pin down tentatively that thinking in language before making any permanent commitment to an idea with polished, well-crafted sentences. A vague notion about your subject is frequently your only starting point, but you want to sharpen this notion in your own mind before trying to develop it fully in a draft. The point here is that writing even a first draft is an effort you should usually make *after* the idea starts to take its course. The various stages of thinking and writing in advance of a draft are called *prewriting*. Thus, you might prewrite by jotting ideas on a small slip of paper or writing a list of questions or a very rough outline that you'll subject to frequent revision. Some writers who have trouble generating ideas on a subject will try free association. They make a list of everything that enters their minds about the topic, or they write nonstop for a set time period. In either case, they censor nothing. These are useful strategies for bringing unconscious thoughts and ideas to the surface. Looking the list over, a writer can see just how he or she is thinking, can group together related ideas that appear on different parts of the page, or can identify some feature of the topic that limits it and makes it more clearly focused than it was before. To tease this feature out even further, a writer might try list making, outlining, or free association again and again.

You can nurture an emerging idea by holding it up to someone else's thinking. What have others written about the topic? What do trusted people—

a friend, a professor, a parent—believe about the issues? Has a recent television documentary or radio talk show addressed them? Ezra Pound, the great twentieth-century poet who along with T.S. Eliot and a number of others helped usher in the modern age of literature, called poets "the antennae of the race." We extend that neat label to all writers. Put out your antennae, consider how the world is thinking about your concerns, write about them freshly and with your own special insights. And don't hesitate to share your drafts as *drafts* with any sound thinker who will read what you've written. Pound tore apart Eliot's early drafts of *The Wasteland* and with trenchant commentary helped bring great poetry to birth.

THE DRAFTING PROCESS

By the time the first draft appears, then, a writer has already taken a number of definable steps. These steps may be recursive (writers go back and forth from their questions to their outlines to their drafts) and in no logical order, and many writers skip some steps altogether or replace them with other steps. One thing for sure, though, is that the trail leading to the draft and the draft itself are pretty messy affairs. You can always tell how intense the prewriting effort was from the scratch-outs, erasures, insertions, and loops and arrows on a page. A tidy early draft is probably a bad one. You've got to be struggling with word choice, syntax, emphasis, rhythm, and so many other issues that your page is often a battlefield of as many dead words as living ones to take up the charge. Don't aim for neatness. Slash foggy thinking. Snip imprecise words. Trim wordy sentences. Changing words and ideas while you write and after you write is absolutely vital for an emerging creative effort. Look at some of the changes that Virginia Woolf makes in a draft of the first three paragraphs of her brilliant novel *Mrs. Dalloway:*

> Mrs Dalloway said she would buy the flowers herself.
>
> For Lucy had her work cut out for her. The doors would be taken off their hinges; Rumpelmayers men were coming. And then, thought Clarissa, what a day! What an ~~an ecstasy!~~ a ~~miracle!~~ ~~ecstasy~~! lark! What a plunge! For so it had always seemed to her, when, with a little squeak of the hinges which she could hear now, she had burst open the French windows, ~~as and stepped out on to the terrace at Bourton~~, and plunged at Bourton ~~into the terrace~~ into the open air. ~~Like waves, like~~ How fresh, how calm, stiller than this of course, the air was in the early morning; rooks cawing, dogs barking; ~~and the~~—, ~~which naturally one lost later—and then, rooks cawing, dogs barking; and and with it all—but Peter Walsh she would say she~~ like the flap of a wave; like the kiss of a wave; ~~for~~—chill and sharp and yet, (for a girl of eighteen as she was then) ~~how . and~~ a ~~little~~ solemn, ~~yes, solemn~~. Peter Walsh would say—whatever Peter Walsh did say— ~~when he found when he found her~~ "Musing among the vegetables?" Wasn't that it? Peter who didn't know a rose from a cauliflower, and "preferred men to cabbages." She "I prefer men to cabbages." He must have said it at breakfast, for her to be thinking of it on the terrace, in a morning, ~~and then going she had out on to the terrace~~, and she had gone

on to the terrace, as she done over and over again, ~~with to escape, to look, to think it over, what Peter said and how the morning looked~~ and stood there, just for a moment, and felt she could not feel now, ~~at her age~~, that something tremendous was about to happen, but ~~that~~ and so stood, and so looked, at the flowers, at the trees, and wondered why, then, ~~that~~ this young man, whom they hardly knew, should begin like that, to Aunt Helena of all people, at breakfast. ~~Not to like flowers~~! It was very like him. And he would be back from India one of these days, June or July, she forgot which, ~~and to be perfectly honest~~ she ~~had~~ ~~for she~~ never ~~cold not read~~ his letters; they were awfully dry; it was his sayings one remembered, his big pocket knife, his eyes; his ~~charm too~~; and his grumpiness; and ~~when~~ millions of things ~~where~~ had utterly vanished, a few ~~sayin~~things. like this. ~~which brought back to her that~~ about cabbages.*

And that's not all by any means. The final draft shows many changes from the earlier efforts as she struggles to root abstract concepts in sensory diction:

> Mrs. Dalloway said she would buy the flowers herself.
>
> For Lucy had her work cut out for her. The doors would be taken off their hinges; Rumpelmayer's men were coming. And then, thought Clarissa Dalloway, what a morning—fresh as if issued to children on a beach.
>
> What a lark! What a plunge! For so it had always seemed to her, when, with a little squeak of the hinges, which she could hear now, she had burst open the French windows and plunged at Bourton into the open air. How fresh, how calm, stiller than this of course, the air was in the early morning; like the flap of a wave; the kiss of a wave; chill and sharp and yet (for a girl of eighteen as she then was) solemn, feeling as she did, standing there at the open window, that something awful was about to happen; looking at the flowers, at the trees with the smoke winding off them and the rooks rising, falling; standing and looking until Peter Walsh said, "Musing among the vegetables?"—was that it?—"I prefer men to cauliflowers"—was that it? He must have said it at breakfast one morning when she had gone out on to the terrace—Peter Walsh. He would be back from India one of these days, June or July, she forgot which, for his letters were awfully dull; it was his sayings one remembered; his eyes, his pocket-knife, his smile, his grumpiness and, when millions of things had utterly vanished—how strange it was!—a few sayings like this about cabbages.

One only can imagine the emotional energy, the intellectual vigor, the agony of creation at play here as these early paragraphs develop. But there is joy, too, in the process, an excitement of discovery, self-awareness, and pride as the words and sentences finally say what Woolf wants them to say. She reports that joy while writing her book; she reports plunging "deep into the richest strata of my mind. I can write, & write & write now: The happiest feeling in the world." As you write, you too will move from states of frustration and despair to states of exhilaration; that is all part of the roller coaster a writer will ride to a finished draft.

---

*These paragraphs are reproduced from Wallace Hildicks' *Word for Word* (New York: Norton, 1965).

UNITY, COHERENCE, THESIS

Among your most important concerns as you shape your drafts into efforts you'll want to make public is whether your thoughts cohere and whether they are unified. *Unity* and *coherence* are two of the most important aims writers can have for anything they write. Your writing is coherent if one idea leads smoothly and logically to the next. Your writing is unified if each idea relates clearly to your main point and to the other ideas you've presented. Transitional devices, repetitions, a constant focus on your thesis—these can help you produce unified, coherent writing. As you read the selections in this text, pay particular attention to the way great writers achieve the same goals you're after.

One of the surest beacons to unity and coherence in an essay (and most of your college writing, as you probably know, will focus on the expository essay) is a carefully wrought *thesis statement.* What is a thesis? Simply put, a thesis is the main point you wish to make, and like much else in your writing, your thesis will evolve as you develop your drafts. But the thesis is more than just a statement of topic: It represents a conviction that you have about that topic. Thus, the most useful kind of thesis is one that states your topic and your opinion or attitude toward it as well. When James Thurber writes, in "Courtship through the Ages" (see Chapter Three), "For the past ten million years nature has been busily inventing ways to make the male attractive to the female, but the whole business of courtship, from the marine annelids up to man, still lumbers heavily along, like a complicated musical comedy," you know both his topic, *that for ten million years nature has tried ways to make the male attractive to the female,* and his opinion about the topic, *that courtship after ten million years still trudges along clumsily.* In many cases your thesis will declare a generalization that the rest of your essay will develop with specifics. When Langston Hughes opens "Salvation" (see Chapter Two) with "I was saved from sin when I was going on thirteen," he establishes the general theme of the selection. Throughout the piece, Hughes supports his assertion with concrete detail. Although not all writers will state a thesis in their essays, allowing readers on occasion to infer it for the pleasure of arriving at the knowledge on their own, any writer must be able to state the thesis of her or his writing; and it's always a near-perfect check on the essay itself to use the thesis as a touchstone for determining whether you've actually achieved what you set out to do. Students writing to fulfill course requirements find it very productive to include a thesis in their essays.

If you do include a thesis, you'll generally make it the centerpiece of your *introduction*—the first paragraph or two of your written effort. A good introduction aims for one result only: To grab the readers' attention and make it worth their while to read on. Introductions generally are not troublesome: Yes, you must consider issues of length, tone, and style, issues important throughout your writing, but once you have a thesis in mind, you should find that, without any high drama or overwrought writing, the introduction will emerge from that thesis as you set the stage for your topic. Tell a story; explain why the topic is important; give background information; ask questions to stimulate the reader's interest; state contradictory arguments to the one you will propose—you have many options for developing an original introduction.

Your essay will take shape along the rhetorical lines explored in *Great Writing,* and as you'll see in each chapter, we try to help you link what you've read with what you're trying to write so that each paper flowers on its own from your unique ideas, the rhetorical context, and the selections we have presented. Thesis statements and introductions, of course, cut across the various essays you'll have to write—as does the *conclusion* of your paper. A good conclusion does more than just sum up the main point of your essay. Don't accept the maxim of tiresome instruction in conclusion writing: "Just restate the thesis." True, in complex essays, it's often a good idea to remind the reader of what you had planned to do when you started and how you have achieved your intentions. But merely telling your readers that you have told them what you said you were going to tell them at the outset—this is tedious and pointless. Use the opportunity of a concluding paragraph or two to set a new frame of reference for your topic. Make a generalization built on what you've asserted in the essay. State any views that oppose your own, in an effort to acquaint the reader with a spectrum of insights about the subject. Refute those who disagree with your position. Propose a solution to a problem that you have uncovered. The last words the reader sees of your writing are its conclusion, and it's well worth the effort to come up with something fresh and powerful.

But here we must provide an important caution, one we'll repeat through this book. No rhetorical strategy is an end unto itself. No professional writer sits down one day to write a comparison and contrast essay. Your topic always has the final word about which techniques and methods will illuminate your point. The value in studying writing through a rhetorically organized course is that you can see an organized presentation of options available to writers. These are options you should draw on any time you need to write, but you always should feel free to mix rhetorical methods as your topic suggests. Thus, even though you may be asked to write a definition essay for your writing class, for example, to help you develop skill in this particular rhetorical option, be aware that other strategies may serve you well as you write. Let's say that you want to define the term *love.* You might want to compare your definition to a definition of *puppy love* or *brotherly love.* You might explain the causes for your new definition— what led you, for example, to see love as a spiritual union between two people with common beliefs. You might want to classify the different kinds of love in order to make a case for your definition's falling beyond familiar categories. Description and narration could easily come into play—describe a person displaying love as you define it or narrate a moment to capture the meaning you have in mind. And on and on through the various strategies we've identified in *Great Writing.* The point here, of course, is to keep your mind open to possibilities, to realize that no rhetorical strategy excludes others as aids, and to understand that you can enrich your writing by mixing modes as your topic, audience, and purpose dictate.

USING GREAT WRITING

We've structured the chapters in this book and the questioning apparatus to reflect important principles we believe in: a commitment to great writing; enthusiasm for fiction, nonfiction, poetry, and drama as models that developing writers must study; a belief in rhetorical strategies as important and useful approaches to writing exercises; and strong support for attention to the writing process as a means for learning the writer's craft.

First, read the introduction to each chapter. Each introduction provides an overview of the rhetorical strategy at hand by defining it and placing it in the larger context of human thought and expression. In this section we try to point out what you should be looking for in the essays, poems, plays, and stories you will read that will help you with your own writing. The introduction considers the reading selections that follow and calls attention to readers' expectations for the rhetorical mode. In addition, the introduction treats the general issues you must attend to as a writer practicing a particular rhetorical technique. In every chapter the section entitled Purpose and Audience focuses on these major elements in writing. Finally, in the section entitled Process, we try to help you think about how to produce your own writing in the mode we are exploring. Here we make suggestions about steps to take and pitfalls to avoid.

Once you finish the chapter introductions and turn to the selections themselves, you'll find a headnote before each selection. The first paragraph of the headnote provides biographical information on the writer, and the second paragraph provides any important information you might need to know about the selection in order to help you understand or appreciate it better. Study questions appear after each selection. The first group of questions asks you to test your literal understanding of the piece; the next group focuses your attention on the language, form, and structure that help make the piece great; and the final group offers ideas for writing that grow out of what you've read.

"A good book," John Milton wrote in the *Areopagitica* (1644), "is the precious life-blood of a master-spirit, embalmed and treasured up on purpose to a life beyond life." We bring you many of those master spirits in *Great Writing* and wish only that their grand efforts help you develop your own craft and spur you to continue perfecting it.

SUMMING UP: THE WRITING PROCESS

- Think about your subject before you begin to write.

- Use prewriting—the stages of thinking and writing in advance of a draft—to sharpen your tentative thoughts on a topic: Prewriting may include jotting ideas, producing a list of questions, using free association, or making a rough outline.

- Consider what others think or have thought about your subject: Read what others have written; talk to friends; review a film.

- Share your drafts with readers you trust.

- As you revise, slash foggy thinking, cut imprecise words, and trim wordy sentences.

- Observe *unity* and *coherence* as you write. *Unity* means that each idea relates to your main point and the other ideas. *Coherence* means that one idea leads smoothly and logically to the next.

- Produce a thesis that states your main point and your attitude or opinion toward it.

- Transitions, repetitions, and a constant focus on your thesis help you achieve unity and coherence.

- Invent an introduction that draws the reader's attention to the topic.

- Produce a conclusion that goes beyond the mere restatement of your thesis.

Chapter One

■

DESCRIPTION

INTRODUCTION TO DESCRIPTION

In a famous and frequently quoted line, Joseph Conrad, one of the great novelists in the English language, asserts the preeminent role of description in the writer's craft. "My task which I am trying to achieve," he writes in the Preface to *The Nigger of the Narcissus* (1897), "is, by the power of the written word to make you hear, to make you feel—it is before all, to make you *see*. That—and no more, and it is everything."

The senses are the stock in trade for any writer, but particularly for the writer of description. The French novelist George Sand wrote to her friend Flaubert, "I believe that art needs a palette overflowing with colour, soft or violent according to the subject of the painting; that the artist is an instrument on which everything must play before he can play on others." To bring readers to sense what they themselves sense, writers turn to the language of the senses, to words that convey sight, sound, smell, taste, and touch. What, in fact, other than an image—a sketch, a photograph, a painting, a film sequence, a cluster of sentences—immediately links the mind of the creator of the image with the mind of the observer? In any kind of writing an image can create a sudden and immediate illumination that pages and pages of prose that lack sensory detail rarely achieve.

READING DESCRIPTION

Imagery and the Senses

Readers of description acknowledge the power of the image, the phrase or sentence that provides an indelible sensation in language. The image may appeal to the sense of sight with colors and with actions portrayed by energetic verbs. The image may appeal to the sense of sound with one of the multitude of English words that name sounds (onomatopoeia like *ring, whoosh, buzz,* and *roar*) or that describe them (*loud, groaning, shattering, hoarse*). The image may appeal to the sense of touch (*soft, wet, rough*), to the sense of smell (*acrid, perfumed, dusty*), to the sense of taste (*bitter, lemony, sweet*). Often a single image or a combination of images appeals to many senses. Conrad was a master of sensory diction. This brief passage opening Chapter Three of *Lord Jim* is only one of hundreds like it alive in color, action, sound, and touch.

> A marvellous stillness pervaded the world, and the stars, together with the serenity of their rays, seemed to shed upon the earth the assurance of everlasting security. The young moon recurved, and shining low in the west, was like a slender shaving thrown up from a bar of gold, and the Arabian Sea, smooth and cool to the eye like a sheet of ice, extended its perfect level to the perfect circle of a dark horizon. The propeller turned without a check, as though its beat had been part of the scheme of a safe universe; and on each side of the *Patna* two deep folds of water, permanent and somber on the unwrinkled shimmer, enclosed within their straight and diverging ridges a few white swirls of foam bursting in a low hiss, a few wavelets, a few

ripples, a few undulations that, left behind, agitated the surface of the sea for an instant after the passage of the ship, subsided splashing gently, calmed down at last into the circular stillness of water and sky with the black speck of the moving hull remaining everlastingly in its centre.

Conrad does make us hear and feel and above all see. We hear the hissing foam and the gentle splash as the ship passes; we feel the smooth, cool Arabian Sea and the marvelous stillness of the moment; we see the reflecting moon in the dark, the somber folds of water, the ripples and the undulations of the waves. It is Conrad's genius, of course, his photographic eye, as Galsworthy calls it, that records the scene and shapes it for his readers. But his language helps establish some general features to look for as we read description. First, the main goal of description is clarity, and toward that end the writer uses what Flaubert calls *le seul mot juste,* the single correct word. Notice the specificity of Conrad's nouns to signify the texture of the sea's surface—*ridges, swirls, foam, wavelets, ripples, undulations.* Specific words like these as opposed to a more general word like *waves,* for example, compel readers to see exactly what Conrad wants them to see. His modifiers sharpen the meaning of the nouns but do not overwhelm them. Only a fifth of the words in this passage are adjectives. Great writers resist using modifiers when specific nouns can create a clearer picture than any describing words could. Similarly, verbs show remarkable precision here, with minimal help from adverbs: *recurved, thrown up, turned, agitated, subsided, calmed.*

Concrete Details

Among the nouns and verbs you will notice a preponderance of concrete as opposed to abstract words. Conrad does not totally avoid language apart from perceivable experience—"everlasting security" and "safe universe" are abstractions certainly—but his description hangs more on concrete images like the passage of the ship through the water than on these theoretical words and concepts. A writer's purpose may demand a higher degree of abstraction than Conrad allows here, but more often than not the descriptive passage relies heavily on concrete sensory diction. Concrete words make descriptions clear and easy to see in the imagination.

Memorable, accurate description relies on selectivity of detail, perhaps the most difficult goal for a writer. In observing anything, we are bombarded with sensory impressions, hundreds of them, that register on our minds. In re-creating an object, a person, or a scene, what does the writer leave in? What does the writer leave out? Including everything is never the intention; the readers would be overwhelmed and would have no clue to what makes the scene special. The intention is to include only indispensable detail. Paul Claudel, a twentieth-century French writer, insists quite correctly that "nothing unessential is the first condition of art." Leaving out is as important as putting in. When we read, we look for the economy of expression and the originality of thought that immediately make an object clear, sharp, and alive. Being original and conveying that originality at just the right level of detail are part of the genius of the writer and contribute to our judgments about the quality of a piece of prose or poetry.

In reaching for the clear and indelible image, writers often turn to figurative devices. Figurative devices compare. By likening one object in a description to another object, writers can bring an immediately sharp, visual quality to a scene. With Conrad's unusual simile of the moon shining low in the west "like a slender shaving thrown up from a bar of gold" the comparison between the moon and a sliver of gold makes us see this moon as we have seen no other. Similes, metaphors, and personification (and other figures) are powerful descriptive tools, and you should be aware of them as you read.

With description, as with all other writing, readers are right to ask themselves what is the point of the writer's efforts to provide intense sensory details. A travel brochure or a catalogue can afford indulgent particulars, that is, description for its own sake, but serious writers always have a higher purpose than merely describing. In fiction, descriptive details set a scene, limn a character, provide a delectable insight that serves the larger purpose of the piece. In a descriptive essay, a thesis should emerge if the writer does not state one precisely; in other words, you should know why the writer is showing you the picture on which he or she has focused. When Kazin opens his piece with "In Brownsville tenements the kitchen is always the largest room and the center of the household," you can bet that the descriptive details throughout will support that point. Similarly, in E. B. White's essay "Once More to the Lake," you know from the very first paragraph why the writer intends to marshal descriptive details for his readers: The thesis here is very clear, and you could state it easily in your own words.

Showing versus Telling

You should also note a writer's efforts to *show* you a scene, not just tell you about it. Showing means drawing pictures; telling means offering judgments. Telling readers, for example, that a face is beautiful is very much different from showing details of the face so that readers infer its beauty. Critical readers like to draw their own conclusions, and writers can never be sure when they provide judgments that readers will see what the writer sees; in fact, without supporting details, how many people could agree on what a beautiful face was? No descriptive writer avoids judgments entirely, and as in every other case in writing, audience and purpose dictate the degree to which a writer will adhere to any principle, even one as sound as "show—don't tell." Even Conrad provides judgments—note how he starts his paragraph with a generalization that *tells* us about the scene: "A marvellous stillness pervaded the world, and the stars, together with the serenity of their rays, seemed to shed upon the earth the assurance of everlasting security." Yet we are not left to take Conrad's word for it. Every sentence after that judgment supports and enhances it, so that we are helpless to conclude anything other than "marvellous stillness" pervading the world he draws. In description the balance always tips in favor of details that show rather than tell. Similarly, Momaday's description of Rainy Mountain balances skillfully rich natural details of the scene with his judgments of it. As you read the selections in this chapter—selections like Woolf's "Death of the Moth," E. B. White's "Once More to the Lake," and Pastan's "Grudnow"—you will experience what writers of description always strive for: concrete, sensory language that brings a person, an object, a scene immediately to life.

WRITING DESCRIPTION

Description will find its way into much of your writing as a means of supporting your ideas with detail. In papers that narrate, compare and contrast, explain a process, or argue, for example, concrete sensory images will help you make a point with clarity and force. In this chapter, however, we ask you to use description as the dominant mode of your writing so that you can practice a range of strategies that will make your writing clear and original in execution whenever you need to call on your descriptive powers.

PURPOSE AND AUDIENCE

As you choose your topics for description, you must consider your reasons for writing and the people you intend to read your work. A thesis statement can help you immeasurably here: Indicate what you plan to describe, and by stating your opinion or attitude about the topic, you can convey a general sense of purpose.

Subjective and Objective Description

Textbooks often distinguish between *subjective* and *objective* description, and you would choose one or the other of these as a strategy, depending on your purpose and your audience. True, an individual writer's personal perceptions are embedded in the details he or she offers to the reader, and it is therefore hard to make a strong case for an absolute distinction between subjective and objective description. Still, the distinction is worthwhile. Objective descriptions are technical; the details the writer uses are impersonal, at a distance, independent of the perceiving mind. Scientific writing relies on such objective description in one sense so that experiments are replicable. The size and shape of a vein in a dogfish shark dissected in a tray, the color and odor of chemicals in a test tube, the texture of a lesion on human skin—nonsubjective descriptions of these sensory observations help students validate their views as part of a large community of observers who record the details in similar language. Of course, the quality of even the most "objective" observation depends on the observer and his or her past experience, ability to see and to hear, and talent for recognizing those details worth noting and those worth ignoring. Francis Bacon, one of the founders of modern science, acknowledged the difficulties of sensory observation in science: "The subtlety of nature," he writes in *The Great Instauration* (1620), is "greater many times over than the subtlety of the senses and understanding." And he called repeatedly for aids to the senses: "Neither the naked hand nor the understanding left to itself can effect much. It is by instruments and helps that the work is done, which are as much wanted for the understanding as for the hand."

It is not so clear-cut or simple, then, to achieve objective writing. Yet despite difficulties, objective description has its uses, and in areas other than the pure sciences. As we said before, a writer's purpose and the reaction of the audience may demand that he or she keep opinions, impressions, or subjective responses out of the prose. Thus, in describing a bedroom of a nursing home for a report on the aging, your writing would be detached: You would show what you observed, not your reactions to your observations. You'd measure the bed, and, focusing on impressions of sights, you'd measure the length of the window, name the colors of the walls and the ceiling, identify by name and with sensory detail the various pieces of equipment around the room. You'd use language that means just what it says, not language rich in associations and accrued meanings. Certainly, in an objective description you'd avoid stating your opinions: You might think the color of the walls a sickly green, the bed stand dilapidated, the blankets worn and tattered, but none of those impressions should slip into your prose.

If, by contrast, your purpose in writing were to show the deplorable conditions you saw in a nursing home to an audience unfamiliar with those conditions, you'd choose a much more subjective approach, allowing your personal attitudes and impressions to guide your selection of words and shape your construction of images. You'd want people to know how you felt about the scene. You'd select words whose connotations you'd weighed carefully so that readers had precisely the impression you had. You'd be sensitive to shades of meaning. In the simile of the moon and the bar of gold that we commented on earlier, note how Conrad emphasizes the wonderful placid beauty of the moment on the sea with carefully chosen words such as *marvellous, stillness, serenity, slender, smooth,* and *cool.* (Try substituting synonyms for some of these words in the image—*astonishing* for *marvellous, quiet* for *stillness, peacefulness* for *serenity, thin* for *slender, unbroken* for *smooth, moderately cold* for *cool*—to see how they alter the impact of the original.) Note, too, the sound of the words to the ear, the repetition of the word *perfect,* the *s* or *sh* sound at the start of six words in the simile, the three coordinated structures with the word *and.* None of these is accidental. Especially in a subjective description, your words have the potential to compel your reader to see with your eyes, to hear with your ears, to touch with your fingers. All the selections in this chapter are examples of subjective descriptions, and you will see in them the care writers exercise in locating *le seul mot juste.*

PROCESS

Getting Started

To help focus your description, you want to spend some time thinking about purpose and audience. Just what point will you make by means of your description?

What is the overriding impression you wish to create? What will your readers expect to learn from the details you present? Freewriting or brainstorming will help you think on paper about those questions. Conversations with friends who can help you answer some of these questions now will be useful. Once you have selected a subject for description, think about how you will bring it to life. If you choose something that you can visit before you write or that you can observe as you write—a quiet football field, say, or a child at play with her red wagon, or a taco on a paper plate—so much the better. Make lists of sensory images that contribute to the overall effect you are trying to convey; you might even group them in columns—"what I saw," "what I heard," "what I felt," and so on. Don't aim for completeness. You'll have to select carefully among your many sense impressions for those which give the best glimpse of the nature of your subject. If you choose a subject out of your memory of experiences, find some quiet place where you can concentrate and try to imagine your subject in the full richness of its details: the colors, actions, sounds, and smells you associate with it. Listing your sense impressions will be very helpful here too.

Writing Your Draft

When you're ready to write a draft, consider what your thesis is (what you will describe and how you feel about the subject) and how you will arrange the details in your paper. Where do you, the observer, stand in relation to the object? Will you show it to the reader from a fixed position, presenting details spatially from left to right, front to back, top to bottom? Or will you move with the reader as you describe the features of your subject? Will you present details according to importance, building from the least to the most significant? In a subjective description of a ward in a nursing home, for example, you might tour its contents from your entry point at the door, showing what you see and hear as you take the reader around or across the room. But if your interest is to show the run-down conditions of the place, you might show instead the minor inconveniences first, like its threadbare sheets and curtains, peeling paint, and chipped stair rails, and then move to what you consider more serious features of neglect, like lumpy beds, dirty floors, broken nightstands. If you're adventurous, you might trust to an impressionistic portrait, allowing your imagination freedom to both create and organize details. Though this is a tricky and difficult plan to follow, it can sometimes produce a very interesting piece of writing.

Don't ever think of your draft as writing cut in stone. Put down as much as you can in your early efforts, but plan to revise carefully to achieve the goals of accurate description. Revise, edit, rewrite: In producing a public copy of your paper, you must pay attention to these steps that all writers take whenever they write.

Tolstoy writes: "To evoke in oneself a feeling one has once experienced, then by means of movement, lines, colors, sounds, or forms expressed in words, so to transmit that feeling that others experience the same feeling—this is the activity of art." You can carry that activity forward as you write your descriptive paper.

STUDENT WRITING

Look at this selection from a student's essay written for an assignment in descriptive writing. The annotations refer to some of the main principles of descriptive writing established in this chapter.

The Basement

[a]Topic and attitude established in first sentence; personal impressions guide word choice (subjective description); intended main impression: place produces fear in an observer

Everything about the basement in our apartment building on Eastern Parkway frightened me.[a] The pipes hung so low that it was hard, even for a twelve-year old like me at the time, to move around without getting banged on the head. [b]You had to stoop a little and hunch your shoulders forward, a sure way to crick your neck for the rest of the day. The bulbs between the pipes dangled on frayed wires,[c] and I'd always think I heard one starting to[d] sizzle—a crackling cybervoice from beyond? The walls were painted a color somewhere between sullen gray and bleak brown,[c] except where big chunks of plaster were missing. Someone apparently had hung things from the walls in years past. Faded and stiff pieces of Scotch tape made an ugly pattern[e] like pockmarks on an angry face.

[b]Arrangement of details: top to bottom

[c]Visual images and color for concrete sensory detail

[d]Use of sound

[e]Figurative language (simile)

The black holes in the wall scared me the most. I believed someone was hiding in there and would jump out. When I found the courage, I would tiptoe over, stand near the dark space, and listen for sounds. Was that the cry of a tormented soul? The creak of a dead man's shoes[d] behind the walls? Frozen in terror, I stood quaking until I could pull myself back toward the middle of the room.

The basement floors were the same terrible gray-brown as the walls but with drips of oil and mud all around making them look like[g] the surface of a swamp. I imagined that under the floor lay pockets of quicksand that would bubble up from the big drain in the middle of the room and suck me down and away forever.

SUMMING UP: DESCRIPTION

Reading Description

- Look for imagery, the writer's appeal to the five senses.

- Determine the writer's thesis: What point is the writer trying to make through the description?

- Consider the use of precise nouns and verbs as part of the writer's goal of clarity and originality of expression.

- Pay attention to economy of expression: Why does the writer leave out some details and include others?

- Look for figurative expressions, that is, vivid comparisons such as simile, metaphor, and personification.

- Think about how the writer shows you the scene as opposed to telling you about it.

Writing Description

- Considering audience and purpose, distinguish between subjective and objective description.

- Determine the overall impression you wish to create in your description.

- Produce a thesis, or main idea sentence, to identify your topic for description and your attitude toward that topic.

- Do freewriting and (or) brainstorming.

- Produce sensory images to portray your selected subject through concrete details.

- Where appropriate, use figurative language.

- Determine how to arrange the details.

- Produce a draft and revise it.

- Edit your draft and rewrite further as needed.

The Last of the Kiowas

N. Scott Momaday

Born in 1934 of Kiowa and Cherokee descent, N. Scott Momaday now teaches at the University of Arizona. He has been awarded an Academy of American Poets prize and a Guggenheim fellowship.

Momaday says that he writes about "the memories of blood." He is widely respected as an innovator of written forms, and his work is often poetic, autobiographical, and histori- cal, all in service of a central theme. The following selection, from his autobiography, *The Way to Rainy Mountain,* combines myth, history, and personal recollection to tell the story of Momaday's grandmother and the story of the Kiowa tribe.

A single knoll rises out of the plain in Oklahoma, north and west of   1
the Wichita Range. For my people, the Kiowas, it is an old landmark, and they gave it the name Rainy Mountain. The hardest weather in the world is there. Winter brings blizzards, hot tornadic winds arise in the spring, and in summer the prairie is an anvil's edge. The grass turns brittle and brown, and it cracks be- neath your feet. There are green belts along the rivers and creeks, linear groves of hickory and pecan, willow and witch hazel. At a distance in July or August the steaming foliage seems almost to writhe in fire. Great green and yellow grasshoppers are everywhere in the tall grass, popping up like corn to sting the flesh, and tortoises crawl about on the red earth, going nowhere in the plenty of time. Loneliness is an aspect of the land. All things in the plain are isolate; there is no confusion of objects in the eye, but *one* hill or *one* tree or *one* man. To look upon that landscape in the early morning, with the sun at your back, is to lose the sense of proportion. Your imagination comes to life, and this, you think, is where Creation was begun.

I returned to Rainy Mountain in July. My grandmother had died in the   2
spring, and I waited to be at her grave. She had lived to be very old and at last infirm. Her only living daughter was with her when she died, and I was told that in death her face was that of a child.

I like to think of her as a child. When she was born, the Kiowas were liv-   3
ing the last great moment of their history. For more than a hundred years they had controlled the open range from the Smoky Hill River to the Red, from the head-waters of the Canadian to the fork of the Arkansas and Cimarron. In al- liance with the Comanches, they had ruled the whole of the southern Plains. War was their sacred business, and they were among the finest horsemen the world has ever known. But warfare for the Kiowas was preeminently a matter of dispo- sition rather than of survival, and they never understood the grim, unrelenting advance of the U.S. Cavalry. When at last, divided and ill-provisioned, they were driven onto the Staked Plains in the cold rains of autumn, they fell into

panic. In Palo Duro Canyon they abandoned their crucial stores to pillage and had nothing then but their lives. In order to save themselves, they surrendered to the soldiers at Fort Sill and were imprisoned in the old stone corral that now stands as a military museum. My grandmother was spared the humiliation of those high gray walls by eight or ten years, but she must have known from birth the affliction of defeat, the dark brooding of old warriors.

Her name was Aho, and she belonged to the last culture to evolve in North America. Her forebears came down from the high country in western Montana nearly three centuries ago. They were a mountain people, a mysterious tribe of hunters whose language has never been positively classified in any major group. In the late seventeenth century they began a long migration to the south and east. It was a journey toward the dawn, and it led to a golden age. Along the way the Kiowas were befriended by the Crows, who gave them the culture and religion of the Plains. They acquired horses, and their ancient nomadic spirit was suddenly free of the ground. They acquired Tai-me, the sacred Sun Dance doll, from that moment the object and symbol of their worship, and so shared in the divinity of the sun. Not least, they acquired the sense of destiny, therefore courage and pride. When they entered upon the southern Plains they had been transformed. No longer were they slaves to the simple necessity of survival; they were a lordly and dangerous society of fighters and thieves, hunters and priests of the sun. According to their origin myth, they entered the world through a hollow log. From one point of view, their migration was the fruit of an old prophecy, for indeed they emerged from a sunless world.

Although my grandmother lived out her long life in the shadow of Rainy Mountain, the immense landscape of the continental interior lay like memory in her blood. She could tell of the Crows, whom she had never seen, and of the Black Hills, where she had never been. I wanted to see in reality what she had seen more perfectly in the mind's eye, and traveled fifteen hundred miles to begin my pilgrimage.

Yellowstone, it seemed to me, was the top of the world, a region of deep lakes and dark timber, canyons and waterfalls. But, beautiful as it is, one might have the sense of confinement there. The skyline in all directions is close at hand, the high wall of the woods and deep cleavages of shade. There is a perfect freedom in the mountains, but it belongs to the eagle and the elk, the badger and the bear. The Kiowas reckoned their stature by the distance they could see, and they were bent and blind in the wilderness.

Descending eastward, the highland meadows are a stairway to the plain. In July the inland slope of the Rockies is luxuriant with flax and buckwheat, stonecrop amid larkspur. The earth unfolds and the limit of the land recedes. Clusters of trees, and animals grazing far in the distance, cause the vision to reach away and wonder to build upon the mind. The sun follows a longer course in the day, and the sky is immense beyond all comparison. The great billowing clouds that sail upon it are shadows that move upon the grain like water, dividing light. Farther down, in the land of the Crows and Blackfeet, the plain is yellow. Sweet clover takes hold of the hills and bends upon itself to cover and seal the soil. There the Kiowas paused on their way; they had come to the place where they must change their lives. The sun is at home on the plains. Precisely there does it have the certain character of a god. When the Kiowas came to the land of the Crows, they could see the dark lees of the hills at dawn across the Bighorn River, the profusion of light on the grain shelves, the oldest deity ranging after the solstices. Not yet would they veer southward to the caldron of the land that lay below; they must wean their blood from the northern winter and hold the mountains a while longer in their view. They bore Tai-me in procession to the east.

A dark mist lay over the Black Hills, and the land was like iron. At the top of a ridge I caught sight of Devil's Tower upthrust against the gray sky as if in the birth of time the core of the earth had broken through its crust and the motion of the world was begun. There are things in nature that engender an awful quiet in the heart of man; Devil's Tower is one of them. Two centuries ago, because they could not do otherwise, the Kiowas made a legend at the base of the rock. My grandmother said:

> Eight children were there at play, seven sisters and their brother. Suddenly the boy was struck dumb; he trembled and began to run upon his hands and feet. His fingers became claws, and his body was covered with fur. Directly there was a bear where the boy had been. The sisters were terrified; they ran, and the bear after them. They came to the stump of a great tree, and the tree spoke to them. It bade them climb upon it, and as they did so it began to rise into the air. The bear came to kill them, but they were just beyond its reach. It reared against the tree and scored the bark all around with its claws. The seven sisters were borne into the sky, and they became the stars of the Big Dipper.

From that moment, and so long as the legend lives, the Kiowas have kinsmen in the night sky. Whatever they were in the mountains, they could be no more. However tenuous their well-being, however much they had suffered and would suffer again, they had found a way out of the wilderness.

My grandmother had a reverence for the sun, a holy regard that now is all but gone out of mankind. There was a wariness in her, and an ancient awe. She was a Christian in her later years, but she had come a long way about, and she never forgot her birthright. As a child she had been to the Sun Dances; she had taken part in those annual rites, and by them she had learned the restoration of her people in the presence of Tai-me. She was about seven when the last Kiowa Sun Dance was held in 1887 on the Washita River above Rainy Mountain Creek. The buffalo were gone. In order to consummate the ancient sacrifice—to impale the head of a buffalo bull upon the medicine tree—a delegation of old men journeyed into Texas, there to beg and barter for an animal from the Goodnight herd. She was ten when the Kiowas came together for the last time as a living Sun Dance culture. They could find no buffalo; they had to hang an old hide from the sacred tree. Before the dance could begin, a company of soldiers rode out from Fort Sill under orders to disperse the tribe. Forbidden without cause the essential act of their faith, having seen the wild herds slaughtered and left to rot upon the ground, the Kiowas backed away forever from the medicine tree. That was July 20, 1890, at the great bend of the Washita. My grandmother was there. Without bitterness, and for as long as she lived, she bore a vision of deicide.

Now that I can have her only in memory, I see my grandmother in the several postures that were peculiar to her: standing at the wood stove on a winter morning and turning meat in a great iron skillet; sitting at the south window, bent above her beadwork, and afterwards, when her vision failed, looking down for a long time into the fold of her hands; going out upon a cane, very slowly as she did when the weight of age came upon her; praying. I remember her most often at prayer. She made long, rambling prayers out of suffering and hope, having seen many things. I was never sure that I had the right to hear, so exclusive were they of all mere custom and company. The last time I saw her she prayed standing by the side of her bed at night, naked to the waist, the light of a kerosene lamp moving upon her dark skin. Her long, black hair, always drawn and braided in the day, lay upon her shoulders and against her breasts like a shawl. I do not speak Kiowa, and I never understood her prayers, but there was something inherently sad in the sound, some merest hesitation upon the syllabics of sorrow. She began in a high and descending pitch, exhausting her breath to silence; then again and again—and always the same intensity of effort, of something that is, and is not, like urgency in the human voice. Transported so in the dancing light among the shadows of her room, she seemed beyond the reach of time. But that was illusion; I think I knew then that I should not see her again.

Houses are like sentinels in the plain, old keepers of the weather watch. There, in a very little while, wood takes on the appearance of great age. All colors wear soon away in the wind and rain, and then the wood is burned gray and the grain appears and the nails turn red with rust. The windowpanes are black and opaque; you imagine there is nothing within, and indeed there are many ghosts, bones given up to the land. They stand here and there against the sky, and you approach them for a longer time than you expect. They belong in the distance; it is their domain.

Once there was a lot of sound in my grandmother's house, a lot of coming and going, feasting and talk. The summers there were full of excitement and reunion. The Kiowas are a summer people; they abide the cold and keep to themselves, but when the season turns and the land becomes warm and vital they cannot hold still; an old love of going returns upon them. The aged visitors who came to my grandmother's house when I was a child were made of lean and leather, and they bore themselves upright. They wore great black hats and bright ample shirts that shook in the wind. They rubbed fat upon their hair and wound their braids with strips of colored cloth. Some of them painted their faces and carried the scars of old and cherished enmities. They were an old council of warlords, come to remind and be reminded of who they were. Their wives and daughters served them well. The women might indulge themselves; gossip was at once the mark and compensation of their servitude. They made loud and elaborate talk among themselves, full of jest and gesture, flight and false alarm. They went abroad in fringed and flowered shawls, bright beadwork and German silver. They were at home in the kitchen, and they prepared meals that were banquets.

There were frequent prayer meetings, and great nocturnal feasts. When I 13 was a child I played with my cousins outside, where the lamplight fell upon the ground and the singing of the old people rose up around us and carried away into the darkness. There were a lot of good things to eat, a lot of laughter and surprise. And afterwards, when the quiet returned, I lay down with my grandmother and could hear the frogs away by the river and feel the motion of the air.

Now there is a funeral silence in the rooms, the endless wake of some final 14 word. The walls have closed in upon my grandmother's house. When I returned to it in mourning, I saw for the first time in my life how small it was. It was late at night, and there was a white moon, nearly full. I sat for a long time on the stone steps by the kitchen door. From there I could see out across the land; I could see the long row of trees by the creek, the low light upon the rolling plains, and the stars of the Big Dipper. Once I looked at the moon and caught sight of a strange thing. A cricket had perched upon the handrail, only a few inches away from me. My line of vision was such that the creature filled the moon like a fossil. It had gone there, I thought, to live and die, for there, of all places, was its small definition made whole and eternal. A warm wind rose up and purled like the longing within me.

The next morning I awoke at dawn and went out on the dirt road to Rainy 15 Mountain. It was already hot, and the grasshoppers began to fill the air. Still, it was early in the morning, and the birds sang out of the shadows. The long yellow grass on the mountain shone in the bright light, and a scissortail hied above the land. There, where it ought to be, at the end of a long and legendary way, was my grandmother's grave. Here and there on the dark stones were ancestral names. Looking back once, I saw the mountain and came away.

Meaning and Idea

1. What is the main idea of Momaday's essay? How do his descriptions and elaborations make his theme more effective?

2. It seems that Aho, Momaday's grandmother, is "The Last of the Kiowas," but somehow the reader also feels that Momaday himself is the person referred to in the title. How does the writer create this impression?

3. Momaday calls the cricket he sees on the handrail a *fossil*. Is it? How is this brief description evocative of the theme in the selection? What other passages seem *thematic* in this way?

Language, Form, Structure

1. Do you find Momaday's descriptive language effective? Why? Even if you did not know the exact meaning of words he used, did you feel that they still conveyed something? Emotion? Atmosphere?

2. Identify the transition points in the essay where Momaday moves back and forth between describing Aho's world, his own memory of Aho and his own actions around Rainy Mountain, and other literal, topographic descriptions. How do the transitions contribute to the unity and coherence of the selection?

3. Define the following words and use each in a sentence, being sure to incorporate the same definition as the one used by the writer: knoll; writhe; infirm; preeminently; disposition; stature; caldron; reverence; sentinels; abide; ample; nocturnal.

Ideas for Writing

1. Use paragraph 10, beginning "Now that I can have her only in memory," as the model for an essay about a memorable relative or friend. Describe the person "in the several postures that were peculiar to her" or him. Use concrete sensory detail to bring your description to life.

2. Observe closely a painting or photograph of a famous person. Pay careful attention to the setting of the image. What objects surround the subject? What actions are they performing? Now write an essay analyzing what the setting reveals about the subject.

3. Reread "The Last of the Kiowas." How and why is the description within the essay so effective? Why does the essay seem so *thematic?*

Once More to the Lake

E.B. White

Elwyn Brooks White was born in Mount Vernon, New York, in 1899. After graduating from Cornell University, he worked as a reporter, and in 1926, he joined the staff of *The New Yorker*. His delightful and insightful contributions to that magazine in great part helped set its past and present tone. White was a versatile writer whose descriptions have delighted readers of all ages. In addition to his *New Yorker* writing, his legacy includes *One Man's Meat* (1942), *Here Is New York* (1949), *Charlotte's Web* (1952), and the collected *Essays of E.B. White* (1977).

Taken from White's *Essays*, this reflective description of a scene first visited some 37 years in the past amply supports President John Kennedy's evaluation of White as "an essayist whose concise comments on men and places has revealed to yet another age the vigor of the English sentence." His strongly subjective, yet precise, descriptions help bridge the gaps between the actual, physical changes he sees in the place and the emotional, perceptual changes he feels.

AUGUST 1941

*O*ne summer, along about 1904, my father rented a camp on a lake in Maine and took us all there for the month of August. We all got ringworm from some kittens and had to rub Pond's Extract on our arms and legs night and morning, and my father rolled over in a canoe with all his clothes on; but outside of that the vacation was a success and from then on none of us ever thought there was any place in the world like that lake in Maine. We returned summer after summer—always on August 1 for one month. I have since become a salt-water man, but sometimes in summer there are days when the restlessness of the tides and the fearful cold of the sea water and the incessant wind that blows across the afternoon and into the evening make me wish for the placidity of a lake in the woods. A few weeks ago this feeling got so strong I bought myself a couple of bass hooks and a spinner and returned to the lake where we used to go, for a week's fishing and to revisit old haunts.

I took along my son, who had never had any fresh water up his nose and who had seen lily pads only from train windows. On the journey over to the lake I began to wonder what it would be like. I wondered how time would have marred this unique, this holy spot—the coves and streams, the hills that the sun set behind, the camps and the paths behind the camps. I was sure that the tarred road would have found it out, and I wondered in what other ways it would be desolated. It is strange how much you can remember about places like that once you allow your mind to return into the grooves that lead back.

You remember one thing, and that suddenly reminds you of another thing. I guess I remembered clearest of all the early mornings, when the lake was cool and motionless, remembered how the bedroom smelled of the lumber it was made of and of the wet woods whose scent entered through the screen. The partitions in the camp were thin and did not extend clear to the top of the rooms, and as I was always the first up I would dress softly so as not to wake the others, and sneak out into the sweet outdoors and start out in the canoe, keeping close along the shore in the long shadows of the pines. I remembered being very careful never to rub my paddle against the gunwale for fear of disturbing the stillness of the cathedral.

The lake had never been what you would call a wild lake. There were cottages sprinkled around the shores, and it was in farming country although the shores of the lake were quite heavily wooded. Some of the cottages were owned by nearby farmers, and you would live at the shore and eat your meals at the farmhouse. That's what our family did. But although it wasn't wild, it was a fairly large and undisturbed lake and there were places in it that, to a child at least, seemed infinitely remote and primeval.

I was right about the tar: it led to within half a mile of the shore. But when I got back there, with my boy, and we settled into a camp near a farmhouse and into the kind of summertime I had known, I could tell that it was going to be pretty much the same as it had been before—I knew it, lying in bed the first morning smelling the bedroom and hearing the boy sneak quietly out and go off along the shore in a boat. I began to sustain the illusion that he was I, and therefore, by simple transposition, that I was my father. This sensation persisted, kept cropping up all the time we were there. It was not an entirely new feeling, but in this setting it grew much stronger. I seemed to be living a dual existence. I would be in the middle of some simple act, I would be picking up a bait box or laying down a table fork, or I would be saying something and suddenly it would be not I but my father who was saying the words or making the gesture. It gave me a creepy sensation.

We went fishing the first morning. I felt the same damp moss covering the worms in the bait can, and saw the dragonfly alight on the tip of my rod as it hovered a few inches from the surface of the water. It was the arrival of this fly that convinced me beyond any doubt that everything was as it always had been, that the years were a mirage and that there had been no years. The small waves were the same, chucking the rowboat under the chin as we fished at anchor, and the boat was the same boat, the same color green and the ribs broken in the same places, and under the floorboards the same fresh water leavings and débris—the dead helgramite, the wisps of moss, the rusty discarded fishhook, the dried blood from yesterday's catch. We stared silently at the tips of our rods, at the dragonflies that came and went. I lowered the tip of mine into the water, tentatively, pensively dislodging the fly, which darted two feet away, poised, darted two feet back, and came to rest again a little farther up the rod. There had been no years between the ducking of this dragonfly and the other one—the one that was part of memory. I looked at the boy, who was silently watching his fly, and it was my hands that held his rod, my eyes watching. I felt dizzy and didn't know which rod I was at the end of.

We caught two bass, hauling them in briskly as though they were mack-   6
erel, pulling them over the side of the boat in a businesslike manner without any landing net, and stunning them with a blow on the back of the head. When we got back for a swim before lunch, the lake was exactly where we had left it, the same number of inches from the dock, and there was only the merest suggestion of a breeze. This seemed an utterly enchanted sea, this lake you could leave to its own devices for a few hours and come back to, and find that it had not stirred, this constant and trustworthy body of water. In the shallows, the dark, water-soaked sticks and twigs, smooth and old, were undulating in clusters on the bottom against the clean ribbed sand, and the track of the mussel was plain. A school of minnows swam by, each minnow with its small individual shadow, doubling the attendance, so clear and sharp in the sunlight. Some of the other campers were in swimming, along the shore, one of them with a cake of soap, and the water felt thin and clear and unsubstantial. Over the years there had been this person with the cake of soap, this cultist, and here he was. There had been no years.

Up to the farmhouse to dinner through the teeming dusty field, the road   7
under our sneakers was only a two-track road. The middle track was missing, the one with the marks of the hooves and the splotches of dried, flaky manure. There had always been three tracks to choose from in choosing which track to walk in; now the choice was narrowed down to two. For a moment I missed terribly the middle alternative. But the way led past the tennis court, and something about the way it lay there in the sun reassured me; the tape had loosened along the backline, the alleys were green with plantains and other weeds, and the net (installed in June and removed in September) sagged in the dry noon, and the whole place steamed with midday heat and hunger and emptiness. There was a choice of pie for dessert, and one was blueberry and one was apple, and the waitresses were the same country girls, there having been no passage of time, only the illusion of it as in a dropped curtain—the waitresses were still fifteen; their hair had been washed, that was the only difference—they had been to the movies and seen the pretty girls with the clean hair.

Summertime, oh, summertime, pattern of life indelible with fade-proof   8
lake, the wood unshatterable, the pasture with the sweetfern and the juniper forever and ever, summer without end; this was the background, and the life along the shore was the design, the cottages with their innocent and tranquil design, their tiny docks with the flagpole and the American flag floating against the white clouds in the blue sky, the little paths over the roots of the trees leading from camp to camp and the paths leading back to the outhouses and the can of lime for sprinkling, and at the souvenir counters at the store the miniature birch-bark canoes and the postcards that showed things looking a little better than they looked. This was the American family at play, escaping the city heat, wondering whether the newcomers in the camp at the head of the cove were "common" or "nice," wondering whether it was true that the

people who drove up for Sunday dinner at the farmhouse were turned away because there wasn't enough chicken.

It seemed to me, as I kept remembering all this, that those times and those summers had been infinitely precious and worth saving. There had been jollity and peace and goodness. The arriving (at the beginning of August) had been so big a business in itself, at the railway station the farm wagon drawn up, the first smell of the pine-laden air, the first glimpse of the smiling farmer, and the great importance of the trunks and your father's enormous authority in such matters, and the feel of the wagon under you for the long ten-mile haul, and at the top of the last long hill catching the first view of the lake after eleven months of not seeing this cherished body of water. The shouts and cries of the other campers when they saw you, and the trunks to be unpacked, to give up their rich burden. (Arriving was less exciting nowadays, when you sneaked up in your car and parked it under a tree near the camp and took out the bags and in five minutes it was all over, no fuss, no loud wonderful fuss about trunks.)

Peace and goodness and jollity. The only thing that was wrong now, really, was the sound of the place, an unfamiliar nervous sound of the outboard motors. This was the note that jarred, the one thing that would sometimes break the illusion and set the years moving. In those other summertimes all motors were inboard; and when they were at a little distance, the noise they made was a sedative, an ingredient of summer sleep. They were one-cylinder and two-cylinder engines, and some were make-and-break and some were jump-spark, but they all made a sleepy sound across the lake. The one-lungers throbbed and fluttered, and the twin-cylinder ones purred and purred, and that was a quiet sound, too. But now the campers all had outboards. In the daytime, in the hot mornings, these motors made a petulant, irritable sound; at night in the still evening when the afterglow lit the water, they whined about one's ears like mosquitoes. My boy loved our rented outboard, and his great desire was to achieve single-handed mastery over it, and authority, and he soon learned the trick of choking it a little (but not too much), and the adjustment of the needle valve. Watching him I would remember the things you could do with the old one-cylinder engine with the heavy flywheel, how you could have it eating out of your hand if you got really close to it spiritually. Motorboats in those days didn't have clutches, and you would make a landing by shutting off the motor at the proper time and coasting in with a dead rudder. But there was a way of reversing them, if you learned the trick, by cutting the switch and putting it on again exactly on the final dying revolution of the flywheel, so that it would kick back against compression and begin reversing. Approaching a dock in a strong following breeze, it was difficult to slow up sufficiently by the ordinary coasting method, and if a boy felt he had complete mastery over his motor, he was tempted to keep it running beyond its time and then reverse it a few feet from the dock. It took a cool nerve, because if you threw the switch a twentieth of a second too soon you would catch the flywheel when it still had speed enough to go up past center, and the boat would leap ahead, charging bull-fashion at the dock.

We had a good week at the camp. The bass were biting well and the sun shone endlessly, day after day. We would be tired at night and lie down in the accumulated heat of the little bedrooms after the long hot day and the breeze would stir almost imperceptibly outside and the smell of the swamp drift in through the rusty screens. Sleep would come easily and in the morning the red squirrel would be on the roof, tapping out his gay routine. I kept remembering everything, lying in bed in the mornings—the small steamboat that had a long rounded stern like the lip of a Ubangi, and how quietly she ran on the moonlight sails, when the older boys played their mandolins and the girls sang and we ate doughnuts dipped in sugar, and how sweet the music was on the water in the shining night, and what it had felt like to think about girls then. After breakfast we would go up to the store and the things were in the same place—the minnows in a bottle, the plugs and spinners disarranged and pawed over by the youngsters from the boys' camp, the Fig Newtons and the Beeman's gum. Outside, the road was tarred and cars stood in front of the store. Inside, all was just as it had always been, except there was more Coca-Cola and not so much Moxie and root beer and birch beer and sarsaparilla. We would walk out with the bottle of pop apiece and sometimes the pop would backfire up our noses and hurt. We explored the streams, quietly, where the turtles slid off the sunny logs and dug their way into the soft bottom; and we lay on the town wharf and fed worms to the tame bass. Everywhere we went I had trouble making out which was I, the one walking at my side, the one walking in my pants.

One afternoon while we were at that lake a thunderstorm came up. It was like the revival of an old melodrama that I had seen long ago with childish awe. The second-act climax of the drama of the electrical disturbance over a lake in America had not changed in any important respect. This was the big scene, still the big scene. The whole thing was so familiar, the first feeling of oppression and heat and a general air around camp of not wanting to go very far away. In midafternoon (it was all the same) a curious darkening of the sky, and a lull in everything that had made life tick; and then the way the boats suddenly swung the other way at their moorings with the coming of a breeze out of the new quarter, and the premonitory rumble. Then the kettle drum, then the snare, then the bass drum and cymbals, then crackling light against the dark, and the gods grinning and licking their chops in the hills. Afterward the calm, the rain steadily rustling in the calm lake, the return of light and hope and spirits, and the campers running out in joy and relief to go swimming in the rain, their bright cries perpetuating the deathless joke about how they were getting simply drenched, and the children screaming with delight at the new sensation of bathing in the rain, and the joke about getting drenched linking the generations in a strong indestructible chain. And the comedian who waded in carrying an umbrella.

When the others went swimming my son said he was going in, too. He pulled his dripping trunks from the line where they had hung all through the shower and wrung them out. Languidly, and with no thought of going in, I watched him, his hard little body, skinny and bare, saw him wince slightly as he pulled up around his vitals the small, soggy, icy garment. As he buckled the swollen belt, suddenly my groin felt the chill of death.

Meaning and Idea

1. Why does White go to the lake? When was he at the lake before? Whom does he bring with him now? With whom did he go to the lake on his earlier visits?

2. During what season do the visits take place? Describe the weather during White's return.

3. White's essay traces things that have changed at the lake and things that have not changed over the years. Identify what seems not to have changed. Identify the changes that White notes. Why do you think White devotes a paragraph to the change in motorboats? What effect do the new outboard motors have on White's feeling of the years not passing? Why?

4. What understanding does he develop from his trip to the lake as an adult?

Language, Form, Structure

1. In paragraph 1 White writes that he returned to the lake "for a week's fishing and to revisit old haunts." What are the denotations and connotations of the word *haunt?* In what way is "haunt" central to the essay?

2. What illusion does White try to sustain (paragraph 4)? Why is the illusion "creepy" (paragraph 4)? How successful is White in maintaining his illusion? Relate the last line to the rest of the essay.

3. List the images in the essay that most effectively render White's sense of sameness. What senses does White call on in these images? Which images do you find the most compelling?

4. White's use of language invites attention. He refers to his son as "my son" and "my boy." But sometimes he calls him simply "the boy" (paragraphs 4 and 5). What effect does he achieve with this phrasing? How does this choice of words relate to the essay's meaning? White makes use of a simile in his discussion of the storm (paragraph 12). To what event or events does he compare the storm? Do you feel the simile contributes to the essay's meanings about time and change? Why?

5. In this essay about time, White makes use of temporal organization. Consider the sequence of time from paragraph to paragraph and within each paragraph. How does White's organizational pattern add to the essay's ideas?

Ideas for Writing

1. Write a paragraph in which you describe a favorite place—a room, a park, a street, a corner. Choose details that convey the place's special features and qualities. Organize your description spatially, moving from one direction to another.

2. White's essay, which first appeared in 1939, is extremely popular even today. It appears in numerous textbook anthologies and other kinds of essay collections. How do you account for its popularity? Write a paper in which you analyze "Once More to the Lake" to explain why it is so popular as an example of the essay form.

3. Write a paragraph in which you discuss White's language. What phrases most impressed you? What in them seemed special?

Wuthering Heights

Emily Brontë

Born on July 30, 1818, in Yorkshire as the fifth child of the Reverend and Mrs. Patrick Brontë, Emily Brontë attended Roe Head School with her sister Charlotte (author of *Jane Eyre*). Brontë worked as a governess and studied in Brussels, hoping to open a school in Haworth, where the Brontë family lived. In 1846, Emily, Charlotte, and their sister Anne published a collection of their poems under the pseudonyms Currer, Ellis, and Acton Bell. Ellis Bell is the author named for the 1847 edition of *Wuthering Heights*. (In the same year Emily Brontë's sisters published novels too, Charlotte's *Jane Eyre* and Anne's *Agnes Grey*.) Emily Brontë died of consumption at the age of 30.

Although *Wuthering Heights* is in the form of a journal written by the narrator, Mr. Lockwood, the novel provides more than personal thoughts, speculations, and fantasy. Here we read a history of a household society, strange certainly, but so vividly described as to occupy a permanent place in western literature. In this first chapter Brontë pays careful attention to details of place and of people's actions to create a clear picture of some of the characters who dominate the book.

CHAPTER 1

*1*801—I have just returned from a visit to my landlord—the solitary neighbour that I shall be troubled with. This is certainly a beautiful country! In all England, I do not believe that I could have fixed on a situation so completely removed from the stir of society. A perfect misanthropist's Heaven—and Mr. Heathcliff and I are such a suitable pair to divide the desolation between us. A capital fellow! He little imagined how my heart warmed towards him when I beheld his black eyes withdraw so suspiciously under their brows, as I rode up, and when his fingers sheltered themselves, with a jealous resolution, still further in his waistcoat, as I announced my name.

"Mr. Heathcliff?" I said.

A nod was the answer.

"Mr. Lockwood your new tenant, sir—I do myself the honour of calling as soon as possible, after my arrival, to express the hope that I have not inconvenienced you by my perseverance in soliciting the occupation of Thrushcross Grange: I heard, yesterday, you had had some thoughts—"

"Thrushcross Grange is my own, sir," he interrupted wincing, "I should not allow any one to inconvenience me, if I could hinder it—walk in!"

The "walk in," was uttered with closed teeth and expressed the sentiment, "Go to the Deuce!" even the gate over which he leant manifested no sympathizing movement to the words; and I think that circumstance determined me to accept the invitation: I felt interested in a man who seemed more exaggeratedly reserved than myself.

When he saw my horse's breast fairly pushing the barrier, he did pull out   7
his hand to unchain it, and then sullenly preceded me up the causeway, calling,
as we entered the court:

"Joseph, take Mr. Lockwood's horse; and bring up some wine."   8

"Here we have the whole establishment of domestics, I suppose," was the   9
reflection, suggested by this compound order. "No wonder the grass grows up
between the flags, and cattle are the only hedge-cutters."

Joseph was an elderly, nay, an old man, very old, perhaps, though hale   10
and sinewy.

"The Lord help us!" he soliloquised in an undertone of peevish displeas-   11
ure, while relieving me of my horse: looking, meantime, in my face so sourly
that I charitably conjectured he must have need of divine aid to digest his dinner,
and his pious ejaculation had no reference to my unexpected advent.

Wuthering Heights is the name of Mr. Heathcliff's dwelling. "Wuthering"   12
being a significant provincial adjective, descriptive of the atmospheric tumult to
which its station is exposed, in stormy weather. Pure, bracing ventilation they
must have up there, at all times, indeed: one may guess the power of the north
wind, blowing over the edge, by the excessive slant of a few, stunted firs at the
end of the house; and by a range of gaunt thorns all stretching their limbs one
way, as if craving alms of the sun. Happily, the architect had foresight to build it
strong: the narrow windows are deeply set in the wall; and the corners defended
with large jutting stones.

Before passing the threshold, I paused to admire a quantity of grotesque   13
carving lavished over the front, and especially about the principal door, above
which, among a wilderness of crumbling griffins, and shameless little boys, I detected the date "1500," and the name "Hareton Earnshaw." I would have made a
few comments, and requested a short history of the place, from the surly owner,
but his attitude at the door appeared to demand my speedy entrance, or complete
departure, and I had no desire to aggravate his impatience, previous to inspecting the penetralium.

One step brought us into the family sitting-room, without any introduc-   14
tory lobby, or passage: they call it here "the house" preeminently. It includes
kitchen, and parlor, generally, but I believe at Wuthering Heights, the kitchen
is forced to retreat altogether, into another quarter, at least I distinguished a
chatter of tongues, and a clatter of culinary utensils, deep within; and I observed no signs of roasting, boiling, or baking, about the huge fire-place; nor
any glitter of copper saucepans and tin cullenders on the walls. One end, indeed, reflected splendidly both light and heat, from ranks of immense pewter
dishes; interspersed with silver jugs, and tankards, towering row after row, in a
vast oak dresser, to the very roof. The latter had never been under-drawn, its
entire anatomy lay bare to an inquiring eye, except where a frame of wood
laden with oatcakes, and clusters of legs of beef, mutton and ham, concealed
it. Above the chimney were sundry villanous old guns, and a couple of horse-
pistols, and, by way of ornament, three gaudily painted canisters disposed
along its ledge. The floor was of smooth, white stone: the chairs, high-backed,

primitive structures, painted green: one or two heavy black ones lurking in the shade. In an arch, under the dresser, reposed a huge, liver-coloured bitch pointer surrounded by a swarm of squealing puppies, and other dogs, haunted other recesses.

The apartment and furniture would have been nothing extraordinary as belonging to a homely, northern farmer with a stubborn countenance, and stalwart limbs, set out to advantage in knee-breeches, and gaiters. Such an individual, seated in his arm-chair, his mug of ale frothing on the round table before him, is to be seen in any circuit of five or six miles among these hills, if you go at the right time, after dinner. But, Mr. Heathcliff forms a singular contrast to his abode and style of living. He is a dark skinned gypsy, in aspect, in dress, and manners, a gentleman, that is, as much a gentleman as many a country squire: rather slovenly, perhaps, yet not looking amiss, with his negligence, because he has an erect and handsome figure—and rather morose—possibly, some people might suspect him of a degree of under-bred pride—I have a sympathetic chord within that tells me it is nothing of the sort; I know, by instinct, his reserve springs from an aversion to showy displays of feeling—to manifestations of mutual kindliness. He'll love and hate, equally under cover, and esteem it a species of impertinence, to be loved or hated again—No, I'm running on too fast—I bestow my own attributes over liberally on him. Mr. Heathcliff may have entirely dissimilar reasons for keeping his hand out of the way, when he meets a would be acquaintance, to those which actuate me. Let me hope my constitution is almost peculiar: my dear mother used to say I should never have a comfortable home, and only last summer, I proved myself perfectly unworthy of one.

While enjoying a month of fine weather at the sea-coast, I was thrown into the company of a most fascinating creature, a real goddess, in my eyes, as long as she took no notice of me. I "never told my love" vocally; still, if looks have language, the merest idiot might have guessed I was over head and ears: she understood me, at last, and looked a return—the sweetest of all imaginable looks—and what did I do? I confess it with shame—shrunk icily into myself, like a snail, at every glance retired colder and farther; till, finally, the poor innocent was led to doubt her own senses, and, overwhelmed with confusion at her supposed mistake, persuaded her mamma to decamp.

By this curious turn of disposition I have gained the reputation of deliberate heartlessness, how undeserved, I alone can appreciate.

I took a seat at the end of the hearthstone opposite that towards which my landlord advanced, and filled up an interval of silence by attempting to caress the canine mother, who had left her nursery, and was sneaking wolfishly to the back of my legs, her lip curled up, and her white teeth watering for a snatch.

My caress provoked a long, guttural gnarl.

"You'd better let the dog alone," growled Mr. Heathcliff, in unison, checking fiercer demonstrations with a punch of his foot. "She's not accustomed to be spoiled—not kept for a pet."

Then, striding to a side-door, he shouted again.

"Joseph!"   22

Joseph mumbled indistinctly in the depths of the cellar; but, gave no inti-   23
mation of ascending; so, his master dived down to him, leaving me *vis-à-vis* the
ruffianly bitch, and a pair of grim, shaggy sheep dogs, who shared with her a
jealous guardianship over all my movements.

Not anxious to come in contact with their fangs, I sat still—but, imagining   24
they would scarcely understand tacit insults, I unfortunately indulged in winking
and making faces at the trio, and some turn of my physiognomy so irritated
madam, that she suddenly broke into a fury, and leapt on my knees. I flung her
back, and hastened to interpose the table between us. This proceeding roused the
whole hive. Half-a-dozen four-footed fiends, of various sizes, and ages, issued
from hidden dens to the common centre. I felt my heels and coat-laps peculiar
subjects of assault; and, parrying off the larger combatants, as effectually as I
could, with the poker, I was constrained to demand, aloud, assistance from some
of the household, in re-establishing peace.

Mr. Heathcliff and his man climbed the cellar steps with vexatious   25
phlegm. I don't think they moved one second faster than usual, though the
hearth was an absolute tempest of worrying and yelping.

Happily, an inhabitant of the kitchen made more dispatch; a lusty dame,   26
with tucked up gown, bare arms, and fire-flushed cheeks, rushed into the midst
of us flourishing a fryingpan; and used that weapon, and her tongue, to such purpose, that the storm subsided magically, and she only remained, heaving like a
sea after a high wind, when her master entered on the scene.

"What the devil is the matter?" he asked, eyeing me in a manner that I   27
could ill endure after this inhospitable treatment.

"What the devil, indeed!" I muttered. "The herd of possessed swine could   28
have had no worse spirits in them than those animals of yours, sir. You might as
well leave a stranger with a brood of tigers!"

"They won't meddle with persons who touch nothing," he remarked, put-   29
ting the bottle before me, and restoring the displaced table. "The dogs do right to
be vigilant. Take a glass of wine?"

"No, thank you."   30

"Not bitten, are you?"   31

"If I had been, I would have set my signet on the biter."   32

Heathcliff's countenance relaxed into a grin.   33

"Come, come," he said, "you are flurried, Mr. Lockwood. Here take a lit-   34
tle wine. Guests are so exceedingly rare in this house that I and my dogs, I am
willing to own, hardly know how to receive them. Your health, sir!"

I bowed and returned the pledge; beginning to perceive that it would be   35
foolish to sit sulking for the misbehaviour of a pack of curs: besides, I felt loath
to yield the fellow further amusement, at my expense; since his humour took
that turn.

He—probably swayed by prudential considerations of the folly of offending   36
a good tenant—relaxed, a little, in the laconic style of chipping of his pronouns,

and auxiliary verbs; and introduced, what he supposed would be a subject of interest to me, a discourse on the advantages and disadvantages of my present place of retirement.

I found him very intelligent on the topics we touched; and, before I went ₃₇ home, I was encouraged so far as to volunteer another visit, tomorrow.

He evidently wished no repetition of my intrusion. I shall go, notwith- ₃₈ standing. It is astonishing how sociable I feel myself compared with him.

Meaning and Idea

1. Why has Lockwood chosen to live in Thrushcross Grange? Why has he come to visit Heathcliff? What impression does Brontë give us of Heathcliff? Of Joseph? Describe each of these men in your own words.

2. What impression does Brontë create of the narrator Lockwood? Why does he see himself as having the reputation of "deliberate heartlessness"? How do Lockwood and Heathcliff compare in temperament? How does Lockwood feel toward Heathcliff? What is the meaning of the last sentence?

3. Describe the outside and the family sitting room of "Wuthering Heights," Heathcliff's dwelling. Why does Lockwood not ask for a history of the place? Why is "Wuthering Heights" an appropriate name for it?

Language, Form, Structure

1. What is Brontë's purpose in the first chapter of her novel *Wuthering Heights?* In an essay you might expect a thesis to state the main idea of the piece, but not in a novel, certainly. What, however, is the point of this chapter? Write a sentence in which you state the main idea as precisely as you can.

2. Brontë provides a series of outstanding descriptions here—of the house, of Heathcliff and Joseph, of the dogs, of the "lusty dame" from the kitchen. What details stand out particularly? Where does Brontë appeal to the senses of sight, sound, and touch? What does she achieve by using specific words such as *jugs* and *tankards* (instead of *vessels,* say) or *beef, mutton,* and *ham* (instead of *meat*)? In the description of the dwelling, what impression do the details of the scene seem to be creating?

3. Make a list of images that describe actions in this chapter. How appropriate are the words Brontë selects to the impressions she wishes us to have of the characters? How does the sentence that first describes Heathcliff's actions (paragraph 1, sentence 6) serve to establish his character? What is the effect of an image such as "Mr. Heathcliff and his man climbed the cellar steps with vexatious phlegm"? How does the spoken conversation of the men help establish their characters?

4. Reread the paragraph in which the dogs assault Lockwood. Which sensory details make their actions particularly clear and vivid to you? Why does Brontë dwell at such length on the dogs?

5. Use a dictionary to check the meanings of any of the following words that you do not know: desolation; perseverance; sullenly; hale; sinewy; peevish; pious; sundry; stalwart; singular; slovenly; morose; aversion; impertinence; decamp; *vis-à-vis;* physiognomy; prudential.

Ideas for Writing

1. Write a paragraph description of a room in your house or in another house that you know well. Concentrate on rich sensory details of color, action, sound, smell, and touch.

2. Write an essay in which you describe someone in the setting of his or her home or apartment. Use sharp sensory details to paint a picture of the person and the scene. Try to make the details revolve about a single impression you want to give of the person or place. Perhaps, like Brontë, you might wish to show a kind of hostile moroseness, or you might wish to show cheerfulness, neatness, friendliness, indifference, or some other quality.

3. Write a paragraph in which you comment on Brontë's skills as a writer of description. How effective are the images she creates? What patterns, if any, do you discover?

Mantis

Annie Dillard

Annie Dillard was born in Pittsburgh, Pennsylvania, in 1945. Her writing ranges across poetry, fiction, and autobiography, but Dillard is perhaps best known for *Pilgrim at Tinker Creek,* the book which won her a Pulitzer Prize at age 29 in 1975 and from which this selection is taken. She has received many awards besides the Pulitzer, including a Guggenheim fellowship and grants from the National Endowment for the Arts. Dillard often has been compared to Thoreau for her visionary depictions of nature. She has spoken often about the central role of spirituality in her writing.

The intensity with which she observes the mantis in this piece is Dillard's signature style. Dillard makes her reader look again at a world which is nearly always overlooked. To read "Mantis" is to rediscover our intimate relationship with the natural world that surrounds us.

I have just learned to see praying mantis egg cases. Suddenly I see them everywhere; a tan oval of light catches my eye, or I notice a blob of thickness in a patch of slender weeds. As I write I can see the one I tied to the mock orange hedge outside my study window. It is over an inch long and shaped like a bell, or like the northern hemisphere of an egg cut through its equator. The full length of one of its long sides is affixed to a twig; the side that catches the light is perfectly flat. It has a dead straw, deadweed color, and a curious brittle texture, hard as varnish, but pitted minutely, like frozen foam. I carried it home this afternoon, holding it carefully by the twig, along with several others—they were light as air. I dropped one without missing it until I got home and made a count.

Within the week I've seen thirty or so of these egg cases in a rose-grown field on Tinker Mountain, and another thirty in weeds along Carvin's Creek. One was on a twig of tiny dogwood on the mud lawn of a newly built house. I think the mail-order houses sell them to gardeners at a dollar apiece. It beats spraying, because each case contains between one hundred twenty-five to three hundred fifty eggs. If the eggs survive ants, woodpeckers, and mice—and most do—then you get the fun of seeing the new mantises hatch, and the smug feeling of knowing, all summer long, that they're out there in your garden devouring gruesome numbers of fellow insects all nice and organically. When a mantis has crunched up the last shred of its victim, it cleans its smooth green face like a cat.

In late summer I often see a winged adult stalking the insects that swarm about my porch light. Its body is a clear, warm green; its naked, triangular head can revolve uncannily, so that I often see one twist its head to gaze at me as it were over its shoulder. When it strikes, it jerks so suddenly and with such a fearful clatter of raised wings, that even a hardened entomologist like J. Henri Fabre confessed to being startled witless every time.

Adult mantises eat more or less everything that breathes and is small enough   4
to capture. They eat honeybees and butterflies, including monarch butterflies. People have actually seen them seize and devour garter snakes, mice, and even *hum-
mingbirds.* Newly hatched mantises, on the other hand, eat small creatures like
aphids and each other. When I was in elementary school, one of the teachers
brought in a mantis egg case in a Mason jar. I watched the newly hatched mantises
emerge and shed their skins; they were spidery and translucent, all over joints.
They trailed from the egg case to the base of the Mason jar in a living bridge that
looked like Arabic calligraphy, some baffling text from the Koran inscribed down
the air by a fine hand. Over a period of several hours, during which time the
teacher never summoned the nerve or the sense to release them, they ate each
other until only two were left. Tiny legs were still kicking from the mouths of
both. The two survivors grappled and sawed in the Mason jar; finally both died of
injuries. I felt as though I myself should swallow the corpses, shutting my eyes
and washing them down like jagged pills, so all that life wouldn't be lost.

When mantises hatch in the wild, however, they straggle about prettily,   5
dodging ants, till all are lost in the grass. So it was in hopes of seeing an eventual
hatch that I pocketed my jackknife this afternoon before I set out to walk. Now
that I can see the egg cases, I'm embarrassed to realize how many I must have
missed all along. I walked east through the Adams' woods to the cornfield, cutting three undamaged egg cases I found at the edge of the field. It was a clear,
picturesque day, a February day without clouds, without emotion or spirit, like a
beautiful woman with an empty face. In my fingers I carried the thorny stems
from which the egg cases hung like roses; I switched the bouquet from hand to
hand, warming the free hand in a pocket. Passing the house again, deciding not to
fetch gloves, I walked north to the hill by the place where the steers come to
drink from Tinker Creek. There in the weeds on the hill I found another eight egg
cases. I was stunned—I cross this hill several times a week, and I always look for
egg cases here, because it was here that I had once seen a mantis laying her eggs.

It was several years ago that I witnessed this extraordinary procedure, but   6
I remember, and confess, an inescapable feeling that I was watching something
not real and present, but a horrible nature movie, a "secrets-of-nature" short,
beautifully photographed in full color, that I had to sit through unable to look
anywhere else but at the dimly lighted EXIT signs along the walls, and that behind
the scenes some amateur moviemaker was congratulating himself on having
stumbled across this little wonder, or even on having contrived so natural a setting, as though the whole scene had been shot very carefully in a terrarium in
someone's greenhouse.

Meaning and Idea

1. Does Dillard live in the country? the city? the suburbs? How do you know?

2. How much time passes over the course of the essay? Describe each of these
   different times and seasons.

3. What kind of interaction do people and nature have in Dillard's essay? What type of interaction does Dillard seem to wish they had?

4. List some of the characteristics of the praying mantis that capture Dillard's attention. How does she describe those characteristics?

5. What type of person do you think Dillard is? What details tell you how she feels about her surroundings and neighbors?

Language, Form, Structure

1. Analyze the first sentence in Dillard's essay: "I have just learned to see praying mantis egg cases." How does this sentence set the tone for what is to follow?

2. What effect do you think Dillard wishes her essay to have on the reader? Point out details in the essay that you find particularly effective in creating this effect.

3. Write definitions for the following words: organically; entomologist; translucent; Mason jar; terrarium.

Ideas for Writing

1. Describe a pet you have had or an animal you have observed closely. What about that animal caught your attention? Write a short essay in which you describe the animal's actions and your response to it in as much detail as possible.

2. The book that this essay came from is titled *Pilgrim at Tinker Creek.* Make certain that you understand the meaning of the word *pilgrim* thoroughly and then write an essay in which you discuss why Dillard would choose that word to describe her interaction with nature.

3. Write an essay in which you analyze the imagery Dillard has used. How does sensory language contribute to the essay?

Ozymandias

Percy Bysshe Shelley

Percy Bysshe Shelley (1792–1822) is considered among the greatest poets of the romantic era. He was a sensitive nonconformist who as a boy at Eton was nicknamed "Mad Shelley." Later, he was dismissed from Oxford for writing *The Necessity of Atheism.* He was, however, a quiet and modest man. In 1816 he married Mary Gordon, who the next year wrote the classic horror story *Frankenstein.* In 1822 Shelley drowned in a boating accident, and in the romantic fashion, his body was burned on the beach by his friends.

"Ozymandias" displays Shelley's attraction to mythological legend as it combines with his self-proclaimed abhorrence of "religious, political, and domestic oppression." In this poem, he demonstrates the irony of tyrannical bravura while leaving us on a typically romantic landscape.

I met a traveller from an antique land
Who said: Two vast and trunkless legs of stone
Stand in the desert . . . Near them, on the sand,
Half sunk, a shattered visage lies, whose frown,
And wrinkled lip, and sneer of cold command,   5
Tell that its sculptor well those passions read
Which yet survive, stamped on these lifeless things,
The hand that mocked them, and the heart that fed:
And on the pedestal these words appear:
"My name is Ozymandias, king of kings: 10
Look on my works, ye Mighty, and despair!"
Nothing beside remains. Round the decay
Of that colossal wreck, boundless and bare
The lone and level sands stretch far away.

Meaning and Idea

1. Ozymandias is the Greek name for the Egyptian pharaoh Ramses II. According to the description in the poem, what physical characteristics do you know about Ozymandias? From what lines do you learn this? What kind of attitude did he project, according to Shelley's description?

2. What is the "antique land" mentioned here? What, exactly, does the "traveller" describe to the speaker of this poem?

3. Summarize in your own words the statement that appears on the pedestal.

Language, Form, Structure

1. *Irony* refers to the disparity between what is said and what is meant (verbal irony) or what should be and what actually is (situational irony). What is the main situational irony of this poem? What sort of verbal irony exists here as well?

2. Why is *lifeless* a particularly good descriptive word in line 7? Aside from its literal meaning for the poem, what ironic or connotative meanings does it carry here? What are the possible meanings of the word *mocked* in line 8?

3. What are the uses of the verb *survive* in line 7? How does it refer to the phrase that precedes it? How does it refer to the verbal constructions that follow it?

4. What are the special meanings in this poem for the following words: vast; visage; sneer; read; mocked; pedestal; despair; boundless?

Ideas for Writing

1. Choose a situation that you expected to turn out one way but that in fact turned out in some other way. Describe in detail your expectations; then, describe the actual outcome.

2. Write an essay in which you explain the meaning of the words on the pedestal.

3. Write a paragraph in which you discuss the effectiveness of Shelley's use of irony in this poem. How do you think it enhanced or detracted from the impact of the poem?

The Death of the Moth

Virginia Woolf

Virginia Woolf (1882–1941) is now considered one of the most important novelists of the early twentieth century. She is known best for her attempts to portray consciousness through a style that is at once poetic, symbolic, and filled with concrete images and actions. Her most famous novels include *Mrs. Dalloway* (1925), *To the Lighthouse* (1927), and *The Waves* (1931). She also produced two books of very perceptive criticism and voluminous posthumously published diaries.

"The Death of the Moth" illustrates Woolf's ability to see the world as constantly producing profound meaning. Even commonplace events become resonant to the active mind.

*M*oths that fly by day are not properly to be called moths; they do not excite that pleasant sense of dark autumn nights and ivy-blossom which the commonest yellow-underwing asleep in the shadow of the curtain never fails to rouse in us. They are hybrid creatures, neither gay like butterflies nor sombre like their own species. Nevertheless the present specimen, with his narrow hay-coloured wings, fringed with a tassel of the same colour, seemed to be content with life. It was a pleasant morning, mid-September, mild, benignant, yet with a keener breath than that of the summer months. The plough was already scoring the field opposite the window, and where the share had been, the earth was pressed flat and gleamed with moisture. Such vigour came rolling in from the fields and the down beyond that it was difficult to keep the eyes strictly turned upon the book. The rooks too were keeping one of their annual festivities; soaring round the tree tops until it looked as if a vast net with thousands of black knots in it had been cast up into the air; which, after a few moments sank slowly down upon the trees until every twig seemed to have a knot at the end of it. Then, suddenly, the net would be thrown into the air again in a wider circle this time, with the utmost clamour and vociferation, as though to be thrown into the air and settle down upon the tree tops were a tremendously exciting experience.

The same energy which inspired the rooks, the ploughmen, the horses, and even, it seemed, the lean bare-backed downs, sent the moth fluttering from side to side of his square of the windowpane. One could not help watching him. One was, indeed, conscious of a queer feeling of pity for him. The possibilities of pleasure seemed that morning so enormous and so various that to have only a moth's part in life, and a day moth's at that, appeared a hard fate, and his zest in enjoying his meagre opportunities to the full, pathetic. He flew vigorously to one corner of his compartment, and, after waiting there a second, flew across to the other. What remained for him but to fly to a third corner and then to a fourth? That was all he could do, in spite of the size of the downs, the width of the sky, the far-off smoke of houses, and the romantic voice, now and then, of a steamer out at sea. What he could do he did. Watching him, it seemed as if a fibre, very thin but pure, of the enormous energy of the world had been thrust into his frail and diminutive body. As often as he crossed the pane, I could fancy that a threat of vital light became visible. He was little or nothing but life.

Yet, because he was so small, and so simple a form of the energy that was rolling in at the open window and driving its way through so many narrow and intricate corridors in my own brain and in those of other human beings, there was something marvellous as well as pathetic about him. It was as if someone had taken a tiny bead of pure life and decking it as lightly as possible with down and feathers, had set it dancing and zigzagging to show us the true nature of life. Thus displayed one could not get over the strangeness of it. One is apt to forget all about life, seeing it humped and bossed and garnished and cumbered so that it has to move with the greatest circumspection and dignity. Again, the thought of all that life might have been had he been born in any other shape caused one to view his simple activities with a kind of pity.

After a time, tired by his dancing apparently, he settled on the window ledge in the sun, and, the queer spectacle being at an end, I forgot about him. Then, looking up, my eye was caught by him. He was trying to resume his dancing, but seemed either so stiff or so awkward that he could only flutter to the bottom of the windowpane; and when he tried to fly across it he failed. Being intent on other matters I watched these futile attempts for a time without thinking, unconsciously waiting for him to resume his flight, as one waits for a machine, that has stopped momentarily, to start again without considering the reason of its failure. After perhaps a seventh attempt he slipped from the wooden ledge and fell, fluttering his wings, on to his back on the window sill. The helplessness of his attitude roused me. It flashed upon me that he was in difficulties; he could no longer raise himself; his legs struggled vainly. But, as I stretched out a pencil, meaning to help him to right himself, it came over me that the failure and awkwardness were the approach of death. I laid the pencil down again.

The legs agitated themselves once more. I looked as if for the enemy against which he struggled. I looked out of doors. What had happened there? Presumably it was midday, and work in the fields had stopped. Stillness and quiet had replaced the previous animation. The birds had taken themselves off to feed in the brooks. The horses stood still. Yet the power was there all the same, massed outside, indifferent, impersonal, not attending to anything in particular. Somehow it was opposed to the little hay-coloured moth. It was useless to try to do anything. One could only watch the extraordinary efforts made by those tiny legs against an oncoming doom which could, had it chosen, have submerged an entire city, not merely a city, but masses of human beings; nothing, I knew, had any chance against death. Nevertheless after a pause of exhaustion the legs fluttered again. It was superb this last protest, and so frantic that he succeeded at last in righting himself. One's sympathies, of course, were all on the side of life. Also, when there was nobody to care or to know, this gigantic effort on the part of an insignificant little moth, against a power of such magnitude, to retain what no one else valued or desired to keep, moved one strangely. Again, somehow, one saw life, a pure bead. I lifted the pencil again, useless though I knew it to be. But even as I did so, the unmistakable tokens of death showed themselves. The body relaxed, and instantly grew stiff. The struggle was over. The insignificant little creature now knew death. As I looked at the dead moth, this minute wayside triumph of so great a force over so mean an antagonist filled me with wonder. Just as life had been strange a few minutes before, so death was now as strange. The moth having righted himself now lay most decently and uncomplainingly composed. O yes, he seemed to say, death is stronger than I am.

Meaning and Idea

1. What is the setting of this piece?

2. On what details about the moth's struggle with death does Woolf focus? What characteristics do they come to represent for her?

3. What is the "power" that Woolf speaks of in the final paragraph?

Language, Form, Structure

1. What about the moth catches Woolf's attention? At what point in the essay do we become aware that Woolf is thinking about larger issues than an individual moth?

2. Analyze the sound of the first sentence of Woolf's essay. How would you characterize Woolf's language? How do the sound and rhythm contribute to the overall effect of the piece?

3. Write a definition for the following words: sombre; hybrid; specimen; benignant; downs; romantic; garnished; circumspection.

Ideas for Writing

1. Write a close description of the behavior of an insect or animal. Use personification. In your description try to use language that treats the object as noble or admirable.

2. Imagine the moth's death as described by an entomologist (a scientist who studies insects). Write a paragraph considering how a scientific description of the moth's death would differ from Woolf's. What details that Woolf neglects might the entomologist add? What details that she provides might the entomologist omit?

3. Woolf's essay divides into two parts, the first three paragraphs and the last two. Write an essay considering what characterizes each of the two parts and how this division creates the meaning of the essay.

The Kitchen

Alfred Kazin

Alfred Kazin was a literary and social critic who was born in Brooklyn, New York, in 1915 and died in 1998. His studies on American literature included *On Native Grounds* (1942), *Contemporaries* (1962), and *Bright Book of Life* (1973). His various volumes of autobiography provided a valuable social history, particularly of life among Jewish immigrants to this country at the beginning of the century. The most recent, and perhaps the best known, of these volumes was *New York Jew*, published in 1978.

In this touching selection from his 1951 autobiographical work *A Walker in the City*, Alfred Kazin uses precise visual images to recapture "the aliveness of the moment" in his childhood. Through his intimate description of just one room, Kazin evokes all the people and places of the Jewish immigrant section of Brownsville, Brooklyn, as they appeared years ago.

*I*n Brownsville tenements the kitchen is always the largest room and the center of the household. As a child I felt that we lived in a kitchen to which four other rooms were annexed. My mother, a "home" dressmaker, had her workshop in the kitchen. She told me once that she had begun dressmaking in Poland at thirteen; as far back as I can remember, she was always making dresses for the local women. She had an innate sense of design, a quick eye for all the subtleties in the latest fashions, even when she despised them, and great boldness. For three or four dollars she would study the fashion magazines with a customer, go with the customer to the remnants store on Belmont Avenue to pick out the material, argue the owner down—all remnants stores, for some reason, were supposed to be shady, as if the owners dealt in stolen goods—and then for days would patiently fit and baste and sew and fit again. Our apartment was always full of women in their housedresses sitting around the kitchen table waiting for a fitting. My little bedroom next to the kitchen was the fitting room. The sewing machine, an old nut-brown Singer with golden scrolls painted along the black arm and engraved along the two tiers of little drawers massed with needles and thread on each side of the treadle, stood next to the window and the great coalblack stove which up to my last year in college was our main source of heat. By December the two outer bedrooms were closed off, and used to chill bottles of milk and cream, cold borscht and jellied calves' feet.

The kitchen held our lives together. My mother worked in it all day long, we ate in it almost all meals except the Passover *seder*, I did my homework and first writing at the kitchen table, and in winter I often had a bed made up for me on three kitchen chairs near the stove. On the wall just over the table hung a long horizontal mirror that sloped to a ship's prow at each end and was lined in cherry wood. It took up the whole wall, and drew every object in the kitchen to itself.

The walls were a fiercely stippled white-wash, so often rewhitened by my father in slack seasons that the paint looked as if it had been squeezed and cracked into the walls. A large electric bulb hung down the center of the kitchen at the end of a chain that had been hooked into the ceiling; the old gas ring and key still jutted out of the wall like antlers. In the corner next to the toilet was the sink at which we washed, and the square tub in which my mother did our clothes. Above it, tacked to the shelf on which were pleasantly ranged square, blue-bordered white sugar and spice jars, hung calendars from the Public National Bank on Pitkin Avenue and the Minsker Progressive Branch of the Workman's Circle; receipts for the payment of insurance premiums, and household bills on a spindle; two little boxes engraved with Hebrew letters. One of these was for the poor, the other to buy back the Land of Israel. Each spring a bearded little man would suddenly appear in our kitchen, salute us with a hurried Hebrew blessing, empty the boxes (sometimes with a sidelong look of disdain if they were not full), hurriedly bless us again for remembering our less fortunate Jewish brothers and sisters, and so take his departure until the next spring, after vainly trying to persuade my mother to take still another box. We did occasionally remember to drop coins in the boxes, but this was usually only on the dreaded morning of "mid-terms" and final examinations, because my mother thought it would bring me luck. She was extremely superstitious, but embarrassed about it, and always laughed at herself whenever, on the morning of an examination, she counseled me to leave the house on my right foot. "I know it's silly," her smile seemed to say, "but what harm can it do? It may calm God down."

The kitchen gave a special character to our lives; my mother's character. [3] All my memories of that kitchen are dominated by the nearness of my mother sitting all day long at her sewing machine, by the clacking of the treadle against the linoleum floor, by the patient twist of her right shoulder as she automatically pushed at the wheel with one hand or lifted the foot to free the needle where it had got stuck in a thick piece of material. The kitchen was her life. Year by year, as I began to take in her fantastic capacity for labor and her anxious zeal, I realized it was ourselves she kept stitched together. I can never remember a time when she was not working. She worked because the law of her life was work, work and anxiety; she worked because she would have found life meaningless without work. She read almost no English; she could read the Yiddish paper, but never felt she had time to. We were always talking of a time when I would teach her how to read, but somehow there was never time. When I awoke in the morning she was already at her machine, or in the great morning crowd of housewives at the grocery getting fresh rolls for breakfast. When I returned from school she was at her machine, or conferring over *McCall's* with some neighborhood woman who had come in pointing hopefully to an illustration—"Mrs. Kazin! Mrs. Kazin! Make me a dress like it shows here in the picture!" When my father came home from work she had somehow mysteriously interrupted herself to make supper for us, and the dishes cleared and washed, was back at her machine. When I went to bed at night, often she was still there, pounding away at the treadle, hunched over the wheel, her hands steering a piece of gauze under the needle with a finesse that always contrasted sharply with her swollen hands and broken nails. Her left hand had been pierced through when as a girl she had worked in the infamous Triangle Shirtwaist Factory on the East Side. A needle had gone straight through the palm, severing a large vein. They had sewn it up for her so clumsily that a tuft of flesh always lay folded over the palm.

The kitchen was the great machine that set our lives running; it whirred down a little only on Saturdays and holy days. From my mother's kitchen I gained my first picture of life as a white, overheated, starkly lit workshop redolent with Jewish cooking, crowded with women in housedresses, strewn with fashion magazines, patterns, dress material, spools of thread—and at whose center, so lashed to her machine that bolts of energy seemed to dance out of her hands and feet as she worked, my mother stamped the treadle hard against the floor, hard, hard, and silently, grimly at war, beat out the first rhythm of the world for me.

Every sound from the street roared and trembled at our windows—a mother feeding her child on the doorstep, the screech of the trolley cars on Rockaway Avenue, the eternal smash of a handball against the wall of our house, the clatter of *"der Italyéner"*'s cart packed with watermelons, the sing-song of the old-clothes men walking Chester Street, the cries *"Árbes! Árbes! Kinder! Kinder! Heyse gute árbes!"* All day long people streamed into our apartment as a matter of course—"customers," upstairs neighbors, downstairs neighbors, women who would stop in for a half-hour's talk, salesmen, relatives, insurance agents. Usually they came in without ringing the bell—everyone knew my mother was always at home. I would hear the front door opening, the wind whistling through our front hall, and then some familiar face would appear in our kitchen with the same bland, matter-of-fact inquiring look: no need to stand on ceremony: my mother and her kitchen were available to everyone all day long.

At night the kitchen contracted around the blaze of light on the cloth, the patterns, the ironing board where the iron had burned a black border around the tear in the muslin cover; the finished dresses looked so frilly as they jostled on their wire hangers after all the work my mother had put into them. And then I would get that strangely ominous smell of tension from the dress fabrics and the burn in the cover of the ironing board—as if each piece of cloth and paper crushed with light under the naked bulb might suddenly go up in flames. Whenever I pass some small tailoring shop still lit up at night and see the owner hunched over his steam press; whenever in some poorer neighborhood of the city I see through a window some small crowded kitchen naked under the harsh light glittering in the ceiling, I still smell that fiery breath, that warning of imminent fire. I was always holding my breath. What I must have felt most about ourselves, I see now, was that we ourselves were like kindling—that all the hard-pressed pieces of ourselves and all the hard-used objects in that kitchen were like so many slivers of wood that might go up in flames if we came too near the white-blazing filaments in that naked bulb. Our tension itself was fire, we ourselves were forever burning—to live, to get down the foreboding in our souls, to make good.

Twice a year, on the anniversaries of her parents' deaths, my mother placed on top of the ice-box an ordinary kitchen glass packed with wax, the *yortsayt,* and lit the candle in it. Sitting at the kitchen table over my homework, I would look across the threshold to that mourning-glass, and sense that for my mother the distance from our kitchen to *der heym,* from life to death, was only a flame's length away. Poor as we were, it was not poverty that drove my mother so hard; it was loneliness—some endless bitter brooding over all those left behind, dead or dying or soon to die; a loneliness locked up in her kitchen that dwelt every day on the hazardousness of life and the nearness of death, but still kept struggling in the lock, trying to get us through by endless labor.

With us, life started up again only on the last shore. There seemed to be no ₈ middle ground between despair and the fury of our ambition. Whenever my mother spoke of her hopes for us, it was with such unbelievingness that the likes of us would ever come to anything, such abashed hope and readiness for pain, that I finally came to see in the flame burning on top of the ice-box death itself burning away the bones of poor Jews, burning out in us everything but courage, the blind resolution to live. In the light of that mourning-candle, there were ranged around me how many dead and dying—how many eras of pain, of exile, of dispersion, of cringing before the powers of this world!

It was always at dusk that my mother's loneliness came home most to me. ₉ Painfully alert to every shift in the light at her window, she would suddenly confess her fatigue by removing her pince-nez, and then wearily pushing aside the great mound of fabrics on her machine, would stare at the street as if to warm herself in the last of the sun. "How sad it is!" I once heard her say. "It grips me! It grips me!" Twilight was the bottommost part of the day, the chillest and loneliest time for her. Always so near to her moods, I knew she was fighting some deep inner dread, struggling against the returning tide of darkness along the streets that invariably assailed her heart with the same foreboding—Where? Where now? Where is the day taking us now?

Yet one good look at the street would revive her. I see her now, perched ₁₀ against the windowsill, with her face against the glass, her eyes almost asleep in enjoyment, just as she starts up with the guilty cry—"What foolishness is this in me!"—and goes to the stove to prepare supper for us: a moment, only a moment, watching the evening crowd of women gathering at the grocery for fresh bread and milk. But between my mother's pent-up face at the window and the winter sun dying in the fabrics—"Alfred, see how beautiful!"—she has drawn for me one single line of sentience.

Meaning and Idea

1. What is the setting for this description? What is the approximate time period described? How do you know? What is the nature of the environment in which Kazin grew up?

2. What does the kitchen look like? Why does the family have a sewing machine? Why is it in the kitchen?

3. Describe the mother's life. What did she do for a living at home? What did she do for a living earlier in her life? What is the Triangle Shirtwaist Factory? Why is it "infamous"?

4. What is the significance of the two boxes in the kitchen? What are the *yortsayt* candles for?

Language, Form, Structure

1. One of the necessities of good descriptive writing is to maintain a main focus for the description. This allows the writer to keep *unity* within the essay or story. Here, Kazin relies on two interrelated descriptive focuses. What are they? How do they relate to each other? What unifying transition word appears in the first sentence of nearly each paragraph?

2. *Allusions* in writing are figurative devices that make references to historical, cultural, or literary things. In this essay, Kazin makes a great deal of allusions, especially to Jewish culture, as in his allusion to the *seder* (the feast to celebrate the festival of Passover). List and explain at least five other allusions in this essay.

3. Kazin makes use of a number of words or expressions from the Yiddish language in this essay. List them all; then, if you do not know their meanings, write, relying on context clues, what you think the meanings are.

4. Kazin uses some extended images in this essay. Discuss how he uses many images of fire, burning, and light. Which does he use literally? Which metaphorically? How does he use sound imagery literally and metaphorically?

5. In your own words, explain the last sentence in the essay.

6. Write definitions for the following words: innate; baste; stippled; zeal; redolent; ominous; imminent; dispersion; pince-nez; sentience.

Ideas for Writing

1. Describe the kitchen of your own childhood in as much detail as possible. If possible, try to link the physical description to a description of another family member.

2. What is the most important room in a house? Write an essay in which you argue your point with appropriate supporting detail.

3. Kazin's essay is so full of description as to make the reader feel he or she has actually visited this kitchen and felt its many joys and sorrows. In a paragraph, discuss which description had the greatest emotional impact on you. What was that emotional effect? Why was it so strong?

Grudnow

Linda Pastan

Linda Pastan was born in New York City in 1932. She earned a B.A. from Radcliffe in 1954 and an M.A. from Brandeis in 1957. Her first book, *A Perfect Circle of the Sun,* was published in 1971 to solid reviews. Like much of her early poetry, Pastan's first book blurs the border between nature and the human. Her first book to receive truly wide attention and acclaim was the 1975 *Aspects of Eve,* a work that portrays the human condition as one of exile. Other notable books Pastan has published are *The Imperfect Paradise* (1991), *An Early Afterlife* (1995), and *Carnival Evening* (1998).

Pastan is the daughter of immigrant parents, and the themes of exile and an obscure past that permeate "Grudnow" are endemic in her work. The past hangs over the writer, offering both a warm connection to history and a disturbing sense of haunting loss.

*W*hen he spoke of where he came from,
my grandfather could have been
clearing his throat
of that name, that town
sometimes Poland, sometimes Russia,   5
the borders pencilled in
with a hand as shaky as his.
He left, I heard him say,
because there was nothing there.

I understood what he meant   10
when I saw the photograph
of his people standing
against a landscape emptied
of crops and trees, scraped raw
by winter. Everything   15
was in sepia, as if the brown earth
had stained the faces,
stained even the air.

I would have died there, I think
in childhood maybe   20
of some fever,
my face pressed for warmth
against a cow with flanks
like those of the great aunts
in the picture. Or later   25

I would have died of history
like the others, who dug

their stubborn heels into that earth,
heels as hard as the heels
of the bread my grandfather tore   30
from the loaf at supper. He always
sipped his tea through a cube of sugar
clenched in his teeth, the way
he sipped his life here, noisily,
through all he remembered   35
that might have been sweet in Grudnow.

Meaning and Idea

1. What is Grudnow? Why do you think it is, as Pastan writes, "sometimes Poland, sometimes Russia"?

2. What did the grandfather mean when he said there was "nothing there"?

3. What kind of life does Pastan imagine she would have had if she had been born in Grudnow rather than the United States? What details and descriptions let you know?

4. What kind of man was Pastan's grandfather? What details reveal his personality?

Language, Form, Structure

1. What feeling does this poem leave you with? What aspects of the descriptions and details convey this feeling? Refer to specific elements of the poem to support your answer.

2. What is the focus of each individual stanza? How does the meaning change as the poem progresses?

3. How would Pastan's piece be different if it were a prose memoir rather than a poem? What details or descriptions might she have to add?

Ideas for Writing

1. Write a careful description of a photograph that is particularly meaningful to you. Choose details that convey that photo's particularly resonant qualities. Try, as Pastan does, to avoid explicit statements of emotions.

2. Write a paragraph in which you analyze Pastan's use of metaphor and simile. What comparisons particularly impressed you? What details in them seemed particularly unexpected or illuminating? What do the specifics of the comparison she makes add to your understanding of the thing being described?

Ode to Autumn

John Keats

John Keats (1795–1821) was the son of a stable hand and an innkeeper's daughter. Unlike his fellow romantic poets, he was little inclined toward cynical or revolutionary statements; instead, he strove only to capture the "people" in nature and in people. Keats originally studied medicine after being orphaned at age 15. Sadly, he contracted tuberculosis—the same disease that had killed his mother and brother—at age 26. It was from that point on that he wrote some of his masterpieces, including "Ode on a Grecian Urn" and "Ode to a Nightingale."

"Ode to Autumn" exemplifies the lyric mastery with which Keats expressed his devotion to beauty and nature. It is a finely crafted poem rich in picturesque and sensory imagery.

Season of mists and mellow fruitfulness,
    Close bosom-friend of the maturing sun;
Conspiring with him how to load and bless
    With fruit the vines that round the thatch-eves run;
To bend with apples the mossed cottage-trees,   5
    And fill all fruit with ripeness to the core;
        To swell the gourd, and plump the hazel shells
With a sweet kernel; to set budding more,
    And still more, larger flowers for the bees,
    Until they think warm days will never cease,   10
        For summer has o'er-brimmed their clammy cells.

Who hath not seen thee oft amid thy store?
    Sometimes whoever seeks abroad may find
Thee sitting careless on a granary floor,
    Thy hair soft-lifted by the winnowing wind;   15
Or on a half-reaped furrow sound asleep,
    Drowsed with the fume of poppies, while thy hook
        Spares the next swath and all its twined flowers:
And sometimes like a gleaner thou dost keep
    Steady thy laden head across a brook;   20
    Or by a cider-press, with patient look,
        Thou watchest the last oozings hours by hours.

Where are the songs of Spring? Ay, where are they?
    Think not of them, thou hast thy music too,—
While barred clouds bloom the soft-dying day,   25
    And touch the stubble-plains with rosy hue;
Then in a wailful choir the small gnats mourn
    Among the river swallows, borne aloft
        Or sinking as the light wind lives or dies;
And full-grown lambs loud bleat from hilly bourn;   30
    Hedge-crickets sing; and now with treble soft
    The red-breast whistles from a garden-croft;
        And gathering swallows twitter in the skies.

Meaning and Idea

1. The speaker is addressing autumn in the poem. Why does he call autumn a friend of the sun? How do autumn and the sun conspire?

2. Explain stanza 2 in your own words. How is autumn "like a gleaner"?

3. What, according to Keats, is autumn's music?

Language, Form, Structure

1. What is Keats's theme in this poem?

2. What is the focus of imagery in each stanza? How does Keats arrange the imagery within the poem?

3. To which of the five senses does the imagery of this poem appeal? Give an example of an image for each sense you list. Explain each image in your own words.

4. How does Keats use *personification* in the poem? Which stanza makes the most use of personification?

5. Look up the following words in a dictionary: granary; winnowing; furrow; hook; swath; barred; sallow; bleat; bourn; twitter.

Ideas for Writing

1. Write a description, either in prose or in verse, of your favorite season. Try to use images that appeal to each of the five senses.

2. Describe and evaluate the syntax and diction of this nineteenth-century poem.

Snow toward Evening

Melville Cane

Melville Cane (1879–1980) was born in Plattsburg, New York, and educated at Columbia University, where he received his law degree. He was primarily a lawyer yet found enough time to concentrate on his poetry, so that in 1971 he received the Poetry Society of America's gold medal. His collections include *And Pastures New* (1956) and *Snow toward Evening* (1974).

Melville Cane blends direct statement description ("the sky turned gray") with metaphoric description ("From some invisible blossoming tree") to describe a simple, natural event.

*S*uddenly the sky turned gray,
The day,
Which had been bitter and chill,
Grew soft and still.
Quietly   5
From some invisible blossoming tree
Millions of petals cool and white
Drifted and blew,
Lifted and flew,
Fell with the falling night.   10

Meaning and Idea

1. What is the season described in this poem?

2. During what time of day does this poem occur? Aside from the title, what evidence do you have for your answer? How do you know it's not late at night, for example?

Language, Form, Structure

1. This poem is composed of two sentences, each beginning with an adverb. What are these adverbs? How do they help establish the dominant impression in the poem?

2. How does the use of rhyme contribute to the overall feeling of the poem?

3. How does Cane use *metaphor* as a descriptive technique in this poem? What are the "millions of petals"? What is the "invisible blossoming tree"?

Ideas for Writing

1. Describe an evening snow scene that particularly impressed you.

2. Write an essay about the effects of snow on the lives of people and their surroundings. Attempt to use some metaphoric description.

3. Both Cane's poem and Keats's "Autumn" describe seasonal scenes in nature. Which do you find more effective and more evocative? Why?

CROSSOVER

1. Percy Bysshe Shelley, Linda Pastan, John Keats, and Melville Cane bring the poet's eye to the task of description and turn it into a treasure of original phrasing, intense sensory language, and startling insights. Select any two of the poets in this chapter and compare and contrast their strategies for describing the topics of their poems. Which poem has the most memorable phrasing? Which images are most indelible in your mind? Draw liberally from the poets' language to support your point.

2. N. Scott Momaday in "The Last of the Kiowas," E.B. White in "Once More to the Lake," and Alfred Kazin in "The Kitchen" all write about places rooted in memory. How does each writer use memory to contribute to meaning? What does the act of remembering add to the intensity of the descriptions?

Chapter Two

■

NARRATION

INTRODUCTION TO NARRATION

People delight in narratives—whether fiction or fact, imagined or historical. In most cultures we find an exalted place for the story, the narrative with a clear march of scenes that reports a notable sequence of events in vivid language. Stories reflect the reaches of human experience. Even our modern sensibilities, so obviously in flux as a result of the entertainment technologies and the media explosion, show no diminished love of stories. Afternoon soap operas, prime-time comedy and adventure series, and the popular films of our decade build their appeal on narrative frameworks. The fictions we read, too, of course—the novels, short stories, and plays of our age—take much of their life from narrative, as do popular songs and poems. Essays also rely on narrative structures; when Aristotle identified narration as one of the four categories of prose forms (along with description, exposition, and argumentation), it was clearly an acknowledgment of the value of the story for its own sake.

READING NARRATIVE

As speakers, listeners, readers, and writers, we are tireless narrators. We're always telling and listening to stories just for the fun of them. The Canadian novelist Alice Munro identifies this impulse in *Lives of Girls and Women:* "Aunt Elspeth and Auntie Grace told stories. It did not seem as if they were telling them to me, to entertain me, but as if they would have told them anyway, for their own pleasure, even if they had been alone." In this spirit, the narratives in this chapter are appealing because they give pleasure to readers. This is not to say that the narratives here have no further goal. Certainly "A Wagner Matinée," the lead piece in this chapter, delights us by stating the precise sensory details that arouse Aunt Georgiana's joy at hearing a concert after many years, but the dramatic final sentence of the story brings her sacrifices into sudden and shocking perspective. With the contrast between Aunt Georgiana's life of deprivation and a life in which musical performances are familiar ecstasies, Willa Cather is asserting the centrality of art to human experience. Similarly, Raymond Carver's accretion of details in his narrative essay, "My Father's Life," forces us to think again about fate, life, and reminiscence. The essay is great writing because it provides a stirring commentary on human nature, and the narrative structure makes the point more forcefully than any other. All narratives, whether fiction or fact, prose or poetry, share the common bond of purpose. Readers seek out the point of the story and use it as a mark of the story's success. Today's stories may no longer have a moral in the narrow sense, but the effective story will still, at the very least, present an understanding or raise a question, even if it offers no easy solution. "Why is this writer telling us this?" is the most important question we can ask about any piece of narration.

Telling the Story

What in fact does a story do? A story breaks the ice: "It's great being back here talking to this Kiwanis Club in Charleston. Why, twenty years ago, when I was a small girl growing up in Parkersburg, Virginia, I. . . ." A story gives essential information: "My car was parked on the corner of Clark and Wabash, officer, when I saw a man leap out the door of the 7–11 and. . . ." Stories connect us to other people and provide a frame or a mirror to our own lives. Stories prod our imaginations, our consciousness, our humanity. They win us over. They wear us down. Sometimes they push us to action.

Kinds of Narrative

Experienced readers of narrative can identify two general approaches. One is the *narrative summary* where the writer covers large segments of time, skips over some events to highlight others, and aims for broad comprehensive impressions in the minds of readers more than for a highly detailed vision of discrete scenes. Writers of history, memoirs, and biography, as well as news and sports reporters, often do rely on narrative summaries. Essayists, too, use this technique and so do novelists, poets, and short story writers. In this chapter Raymond Carver uses this approach in part. The other approach is the *narrative moment* where the writer chooses a limited time frame and explores all its details for an intense, comprehensive view of a flash of time. Most selections here follow this format. Relying on character, dialogue, plot, and concrete sensory language, the narrative moment is like a sequence of frames on a piece of film that presents carefully chosen details for the viewer. The selection by Langston Hughes, along with others in this chapter, underscores how effective this method is in holding a reader's attention. We're not suggesting any single approach here—writers may use both narrative summary and narrative moments in a novel or poem or story or essay—but as alert readers we want to be aware of how we arrive where writers want to take us. Hence, the distinction between narrative summary and narrative moment is useful.

Time Order

Also when we read, we must be aware of the temporal sequence on which the flesh of the story hangs. Most narratives consist of an orderly *chronology:* First this happened, then that, then some other thing. In using narrative to make a dramatic point, most essayists and fiction writers use this simple arrangement. But experienced writers can and do take great liberties with sequence. A story can begin *in medias res*—in the midst of things—where readers suddenly find themselves in the heat of an event that does not evolve from an orderly march of hours and minutes and seconds. With such stories we often must fill in details on our own, reconstructing pieces as we go along or waiting for information that may be revealed later on about earlier events. Or skillful writers may rely on *flashback,* where they freeze the current narrative, whisking us back in time to explore an earlier event, then returning to the present moment. Yet even in the hands of the most talented writer, the flashback risks confusing readers. Note when you read "A Wagner Matinée" how Cather moves you back and forth in time with great skill but how you must nonetheless concentrate carefully on these temporal shifts in order to keep the story properly focused. The heart of narrative is time—the writer's vision of reality is inseparable from the way he or she views time and its impact on characters, events, and ideas—and you want to pay particular attention to sequence as you read.

WRITING NARRATIVE

To encourage practice in writing narrative, this chapter asks you to concentrate on the story pretty much for its own sake. Later on, you will use narrative as a means for advancing ideas in expository frameworks, but here the story itself is the thing. Your objective is to transform events into clear, vivid prose.

PURPOSE AND AUDIENCE

Stories with a Point

At least once, we have all sat almost transfixed by boredom as we listened to a rambling, pointless story. As soon as someone has to ask about a piece of writing, "What is this all about?" you've exhausted whatever patience your readers may possess. Thus, in choosing your narrative you must be very clear on why you are telling about this particular event. Ask yourself this question as you are brainstorming: "What am I trying to demonstrate with this story?" Write down your answer so that your purpose does not escape you and so that you can see if it holds up. Stating your purpose too generally will not help much: "to answer," "to shock," "to stimulate"—these are not particularly useful statements of purpose because they provide little guidance as you develop the narrative framework. Suppose you saw close up a fire blazing through a section of your town and wanted to write a narrative about it. Notice how each of the purposes below would stimulate a different story line about the same event.

Topic: The October 1984 fire on Walker Street
Purpose:

1. To show the bravery of an understaffed volunteer fire department
2. To follow the actions of a suspicious bystander
3. To show how people clutching their possessions poured from the houses and shops engulfed in flames
4. To trace the events from the first sparks at the corner grocery store to the conflagration that swept through the neighborhood
5. To show the orderly evacuation of 600 children from Birch Lane Elementary School

Not all of these are mutually exclusive. You could combine 1 and 3, for example, or 3 and 4. The point is that your narrative should focus on some purpose that is absolutely clear to you and that you finally make clear to your reader. You might want to state your purpose in a *thesis sentence,* sometimes called a *main idea sentence,* somewhere in your introduction. "Three racing figures in yellow slickers and black boots (this is all there is to the Lewis Valley Volunteer Fire Department) contained the worst fire in our town in twenty years, saving more than a dozen lives before Walker Street lay in a heap of ashes." Or you may choose not to state a thesis or main idea; instead, you may want readers to be able to discover your purpose on their own by concentrating thoughtfully on your story. In either case you must *be able* to state your purpose even if it is just as a check on the integrity of your narrative.

Who Is Your Audience?

Very much related to the purpose of your narrative is the audience you want to read it. Many of the writing exercises in this chapter suggest an audience, and your instructor may define a readership too. But you should be prepared to identify your own audience. For whom are you writing this narrative? If you wrote about the fire in a report to the mayor of Lewis Valley, in a front-page news story for the *Lewis Valley Gazette,* or in a letter to your sister back East, your narrative in each case would differ sharply from the others. Thinking about your audience as you shape your story will help you select appropriate details and eliminate extraneous ones. Also, a good sense of audience will help you develop an appropriate point of view. Would your readers expect you to be as objective as possible? Would they want you to place yourself in the scene as a participant-observer sharing subjective feelings and reactions? Either of these points of view would have a major impact on the tone and structure of your narrative.

PROCESS

Finding a Narrative Topic

Your first step is to find a story worth telling. But it's not accurate to think only in terms of dazzling incidents in the lives of superstars. In simple, everyday activities the sensitive, observing eye can find terrific stories. Walter Prichard Eaton, as a freshman at Harvard more than 30 years ago, recalls how his instructors encouraged him to develop "the daily theme eye." He writes, "It became needful, then, to watch for and treasure incidents that were sharply dramatic or poignant, moods that were clear and definite, pictures that created a single clean impression. . . . By training the daily theme eye, we watched for and found in the surroundings of our life, as it passed, a heightened picturesqueness, a constant wonder, and added significance."

Like Eaton, we remind you to look around for the best stories and to make today the starting point for a fresh view of the events in your life. Also like Eaton, you might wish to keep a notebook of your impressions, jotting down incidents you see that can open a floodgate of narrative when you sit at your chair ready to develop a draft. Selecting a moment you've only recently experienced almost always assures a high level of intensity in your paper: You'll see the events clearly in your mind's eye because they are fresh and vivid to you, and you'll be able to convey that freshness and vividness to your readers. But memorable past events also can etch themselves on your consciousness, and you'll want to comb the past experiences of your life for narrative worth sharing with your readers.

Writing Your Thesis and Developing a Draft

As you think and write with your audience and purpose in mind, produce a thesis statement whether or not you ultimately use it in your essay. Your thesis should state your topic for the narrative and should express your opinion or attitude toward it. Also, be aware of the nature and quantity of detail you need to include. Obviously you cannot cover every minute event in the story you are reporting; such thoroughness would overwhelm your readers. You have to select details carefully so that they reinforce your objective and keep your readers interested. What you learned about concrete sensory detail in the last chapter will be useful here. Much of your narrative will draw on images of sound, color, action, smell, and touch.

You must be particularly attentive to time and sequence when you write narrative. Events should follow each other logically, if not chronologically, and readers should never feel adrift in a sea of unconnected events. If you are bold enough to try flashback, be careful not to bounce back and forth from present to past; it will jar your readers. You might wish to make a time line or a simple list of chronological events so that you have at your fingertips the exact order of actions, no matter how you finally present them.

As you link events together, *transitions* will be very useful. Words such as *then, later, now, before, after, soon, in a moment*—there are hundreds of others—can help you move from beginning to middle to end. But you must use these connectors judiciously and selectively. A clearly told story makes its own internal connections; events flow naturally from one to the other, and a mechanical use of transitions will obstruct that natural flow.

A last point to consider: dialogue. Almost all stories about people draw on the natural conversations among characters in the narrative. Listen to the rhythms in everyday speech, and when your characters speak, make their words sound as if real people spoke them. Dialogue, like other details, requires selectivity. Let all spoken language in your story advance the special point you wish to make.

STUDENT WRITING

In the paper below a student uses narrative strategies such as those we have explored in this chapter and have advanced through the writing assignments that follow the selections. The annotations in the margin highlight important narrative elements.

Buck Fever

One blustery November morning[a] I thought I would experience the thrill of shooting my first deer, but at the last moment I was seized by that dreaded hunter's ailment,[c] buck fever.[b]

    I was staying at my sister's house when the clumping of my brother-in-law Frank's boots on the wooden floors[d] woke me in an instant. Frank whispered,[e] "Do you want to go hunting with me this morning at the farm?" I leapt out of bed and into my gray long johns, my woolen hunting suit, and my orange plastic vest.[d] Soon[f] Frank's Ford pickup lumbered over fifteen miles of slick, ice-covered country roads across the state line to his father's farm. We parked behind the farmhouse and trudged through the snow-covered fields.[g] I heard the wind rustle eerily through the bare birch and poplar trees.

    To encircle the meadow, we split up. Frank turned left, and I went to the right. We had been apart for about fifteen minutes when I saw the soft, brown skin of a deer down in the creek bed at the bottom of the meadow. Cautiously, I tiptoed forward so I wouldn't startle the deer, although I was sure that my heartbeat sounded like cannons firing.[h] The small deer heard me and looked up. I even stopped breathing for fear he would run away. Luckily he lowered his head again and foraged for some sprouts of grass under the snow. At that, I brought my rifle up to my shoulder and took careful aim through the cold, steel sight.

    Then[f] the deer brought his head up again and started right at me. Through the sight I could see drops of moisture at the corners of his eyes. It was at that moment that buck fever struck me,[i] the paralysis that comes when you think too much about the life you are about to take. It's the disease all hunters fear, and it overtook me so suddenly that I started shaking. I dropped the rifle from my shoulder to my side. The thump of the wood and metal slapping against my leg startled the deer, who jumped in surprise and darted away through the woods. I never recovered from buck fever, and I never went hunting again.

[a] Clear narrative moment: "One blustery November morning"

[b] Thesis: deer hunter overcome by fear

[c] Audience awareness: "buck fever" explained

[d] Sensory language

[e] Quotation of exact words spoken

[f] Transition

[g] Clear sequence of events: bedroom, to car, to farm, to fields, and so on

[h] Figurative language: simile

[i] Audience awareness: expanded meaning of buck fever

SUMMING UP: NARRATION

Reading Narrative

- Narrative simply means telling a story—whether fiction or fact, imagined or historical.

- Identify the pleasure-giving qualities of the narrative within the context of the writer's purpose—that is, what entertains you about the writer's story, and what is its point?

- Ask yourself about the narrative: "What is this writer telling me?" What sentence (or sentences) helps you state the writer's thesis, that is, the topic of the narrative and the writer's attitude toward that topic?

- Look for the *narrative summary* approach in which the writer covers large time segments and does not aim to include all the details.

- Look for the *narrative moment* approach in which the writer aims to explore a limited time frame in all its detail.

- Be attentive to the sequence used by the writer, among them *chronology* (exact time order), *in medias res* (a story started in the midst of things), and *flashback* (movement back in time within a current narrative).

Writing Narrative

- Your narrative should transform events into clear, vivid prose that draws on concrete sensory language.

- Produce a thesis so that you will be very clear about why you are relating the event; a carefully developed thesis sentence (or *main idea* sentence) will help you state your topic, your attitude toward it, and your purpose for writing.

- Consider your audience for the narrative and use your sense of audience to help you shape the story, select appropriate details, and eliminate extraneous ones.

- To choose an appropriate narrative, look for stories in the events that surround you. A moment recently experienced often assures a high level of vividness and intensity in your writing; a memorable past event also can stimulate rich, detailed narrative if you concentrate on the event in all its details.

- Use appropriate transitions as needed. Many transitions, such as *now, later,* and *then,* help you move from beginning to middle to end of a narrative.

- Use dialogue—let the characters in your narrative speak—to advance the special point you wish to make in your story.

A Wagner Matinée

Willa Cather

Willa Cather (1876–1947) was amply familiar with the changing social values about which she wrote. Born in Virginia, she was soon on "foreign soil" when her family moved to the Nebraska immigrant town of Red Cloud. There she gained an abiding respect for the land and the people who made something from it. Her best-known novel is *My Antonia* (1918), the story of the struggles of the prairie girl Antonia Shimerda.

In "A Wagner Matinée," Willa Cather tells us the story of a life seemingly fulfilled but inwardly longing. In this story of a woman who appears to have everything, Cather blends flashback with chronological narration to show us what was, what is, and what could have been.

I received one morning a letter, written in pale ink on glossy blue-lined notepaper, and bearing the postmark of a little Nebraska village. This communication, worn and rubbed, looking as if it had been carried for some days in a coat pocket that was none too clean, was from my Uncle Howard, and informed me that his wife had been left a small legacy by a bachelor relative, and that it would be necessary for her to go to Boston to attend the settling of the estate. He requested me to meet her at the station and render her whatever services might be necessary. On examining the date indicated as that of her arrival, I found it to be no later than tomorrow. He had characteristically delayed writing until, had I been away from home for a day, I must have missed my aunt altogether.

The name of my Aunt Georgiana opened before me a gulf of recollection so wide and deep that, as the letter dropped from my hand, I felt suddenly a stranger to all the present conditions of my existence, wholly ill at ease and out of place amid the familiar surroundings of my study. I became, in short, the gangling farm-boy my aunt had known, scourged with chilblains and bashfulness, my hands cracked and sore from the corn husking. I sat again before her parlor organ fumbling the scales with my stiff red fingers, while she, beside me, made canvas mittens for the huskers. The next morning, after preparing my landlady for a visitor, I set out for the station. When the train arrived I had some difficulty in finding my aunt. She was the last of the passengers to alight, and it was not until I got her into the carriage that she seemed really to recognize me. She had come all the way in a day coach; her linen duster had become black with soot and her black bonnet gray with dust during the journey. When we arrived at my boarding house the landlady put her to bed at once and I did not see her again until the next morning.

Whatever shock Mrs. Springer experienced at my aunt's appearance, she considerately concealed. As for myself, I saw my aunt's battered figure with that feeling of awe and respect with which we behold explorers who have left their ears and fingers north of Franz-Joseph Land or their health somewhere along the

Upper Congo. My Aunt Georgiana had been a music teacher at the Boston Conservatory, somewhere back in the later sixties. One summer, while visiting in the little village among the Green Mountains where her ancestors had dwelt for generations, she had kindled the callow fancy of my uncle, Howard Carpenter, then an idle, shiftless boy of twenty-one. When she returned to her duties in Boston, Howard followed her, and the upshot of this infatuation was that she eloped with him, eluding the reproaches of her family and the criticism of her friends by going with him to the Nebraska frontier. Carpenter, who, of course, had no money, took up a homestead in Red Willow County, fifty miles from the railroad. There they had measured off their land themselves, driving across the prairie in a wagon, to the wheel of which they had tied a red cotton handkerchief, and counting its revolutions. They built a dug-out in the red hillside, one of those cave dwellings whose inmates so often reverted to primitive conditions. Their water they got from the lagoons where the buffalo drank, and their slender stock of provisions was always at the mercy of roving Indians. For thirty years my aunt had not been farther than fifty miles from the homestead.

I owed to this woman most of the good that ever came my way in my boyhood, and had a reverential affection for her. During the years when I was riding herd for my uncle, my aunt, after cooking the three meals—the first of which was ready at six o'clock in the morning—and putting the six children to bed, would often stand until midnight at her ironing-board with me at the kitchen table beside her, hearing me recite Latin declensions and conjugations, gently shaking me when my drowsy head sank down over a page of irregular verbs. It was to her, at her ironing or mending, that I read my first Shakespeare, and her old textbook on mythology was the first that ever came into my empty hands. She taught me my scales and exercises on the little parlor organ which her husband had bought her after fifteen years during which she had not so much as seen a musical instrument. She would sit beside me by the hour, darning and counting, while I struggled with the "Joyous Farmer." She seldom talked to me about music and I understood why. Once when I had been doggedly beating out some easy passages from an old score of *Euryanthe* I had found among her music books, she came up to me and, putting her hands over my eyes, gently drew my head back upon her shoulder, saying tremulously, "Don't love it so well, Clark, or it may be taken from you." 4

When my aunt appeared on the morning after her arrival in Boston, she was still in a semi-somnambulant state. She seemed not to realize that she was in the city where she had spent her youth, the place longed for hungrily half a lifetime. She had been so wretchedly train-sick throughout the journey that she had no recollection of anything but her discomfort, and, to all intents and purposes, there were but a few hours of nightmare between the farm in Red Willow County and my study on Newbury Street. I had planned a little pleasure for her that afternoon, to repay her for some of the glorious moments she had given me when we used to milk together in the straw-thatched cowshed and she, because I was more than usually tired, or because her husband had spoken sharply to me, would tell me of the splendid performance of the *Huguenots* she had seen in Paris, in her youth. 5

At two o'clock the Symphony Orchestra was to give a Wagner program, and I intended to take my aunt; though, as I conversed with her, I grew doubtful about her enjoyment of it. I suggested our visiting the Conservatory and the Common before lunch, but she seemed altogether too timid to wish to venture out. She questioned me absently about various changes in the city, but she was chiefly concerned that she had forgotten to leave instructions about feeding half-skimmed milk to a certain weakling calf, "old Maggie's calf, you know, Clark," she explained, evidently having forgotten how long I had been away. She was further troubled because she had neglected to tell her daughter about the freshly opened kit of mackerel in the cellar, which would spoil if it were not used directly. 6

I asked her whether she had ever heard any of the Wagnerian operas, and found that she had not, though she was perfectly familiar with their respective situations, and had once possessed the piano score of *The Flying Dutchman.* I began to think it would be best to get her back to Red Willow County without waking her, and regretted having suggested the concert. 7

From the time we entered the concert hall, however, she was a trifle less passive and inert, and for the first time seemed to perceive her surroundings. I had felt some trepidation lest she might become aware of her queer country clothes, or might experience some painful embarrassment at stepping suddenly into the world to which she had been dead for a quarter of a century. But again, I found how superficially I had judged her. She sat looking about her with eyes as impersonal, almost as stony, as those with which the granite Rameses in a museum watches the froth and fret that ebbs and flows about his pedestal. I have seen this same aloofness in old miners who drift into the Brown Hotel at Denver, their pockets full of bullion, their linen soiled, their haggard faces unshaven; standing in the thronged corridors as solitary as though they were still in a frozen camp on the Yukon. 8

The matinée audience was made up chiefly of women. One lost the contour of faces and figures, indeed any effect of line whatever, and there was only the color of bodies past counting, the shimmer of fabrics soft and fine, silky and sheer; red, mauve, pink, blue, lilac, purple, ecru, rose, yellow, cream, and white, all the colors that an impressionist finds in a sunlight landscape, with here and there the dead shadow of a frock coat. My Aunt Georgiana regarded them as though they had been so many daubs of tube-paint on a palette. 9

When the musicians came out and took their places, she gave a little stir of anticipation, and looked with quickening interest down over the rail at that invariable grouping, perhaps the first wholly familiar thing that had greeted her eye since she had left old Maggie and her weakling calf. I could feel how all those details sank into her soul, for I had not forgotten how they had sunk into mine when I came fresh from plowing forever and forever between green aisles of corn, where, as in a treadmill, one might walk from daybreak to dusk without perceiving a shadow of change. The clean profiles of the musicians, the gloss of their linen, the dull black of their coats, the beloved shapes of the instruments, the patches of yellow light on the smooth, varnished bellies of the 'cellos and the bass viols in the rear, the restless, wind-tossed forest of fiddle necks and 10 bows—I recalled how, in the first orchestra I ever heard, those long bow-strokes seemed to draw the heart out of me, as a conjurer's stick reels out yards of paper ribbon from a hat.

The first number was the *Tannhauser* overture. When the horns drew out the first strain of the "Pilgrims' Chorus," Aunt Georgiana clutched my coat sleeve. Then it was I first realized that for her this broke a silence of thirty years. With the battle between the two motives, with the frenzy of the Venusberg theme and its ripping of strings, there came to me an overwhelming sense of the waste and wear we are so powerless to combat; and I saw again the tall, naked house on the prairie, black and grim as a wooden fortress; the black pond where I had learned to swim, its margin pitted with sun-dried cattle tracks; the rain gullied clay banks about the naked house, the four dwarf ash seedlings where the dishcloths were always hung to dry before the kitchen door. The world there was the flat world of the ancients; to the east, a cornfield that stretched to daybreak; to the west, a corral that reached to sunset; between, the conquests of peace, dearer-bought than those of war.

The overture closed, my aunt released my coat sleeve, but she said nothing. She sat staring dully at the orchestra. What, I wondered, did she get from it? She had been a good pianist in her day, I knew, and her musical education had been broader than that of most music teachers of a quarter of a century ago. She had often told me of Mozart's operas and Meyerbeer's, and I could remember her sing, years ago, certain melodies of Verdi. When I had fallen ill with a fever in her house she used to sit by my cot in the evening—when the cool night wind blew in through the faded mosquito netting tacked over the window and I lay watching a certain bright star that burned red above the cornfield—and sing "Home to our mountain, O let us return!" in a way fit to break the heart of a Vermont boy near dead of homesickness already.

I watched her closely through the prelude to *Tristan and Isolde,* trying vainly to conjecture what that seething turmoil of strings and winds might mean to her, but she sat mutely staring at the violin bows that drove obliquely downward, like the pelting streaks of rain in a summer shower. Had this music any message for her? Had she enough left to at all comprehend this power which had kindled the world since she had left it? I was in a fever of curiosity, but Aunt Georgiana sat silent upon her peak in Darien. She preserved this utter immobility throughout the number from *The Flying Dutchman,* though her fingers worked mechanically upon her black dress, as if, of themselves, they were recalling the piano score they had once played. Poor hands! They had been stretched and twisted into mere tentacles to hold and lift and knead with; on one of them a thin worn band that had once been a wedding ring. As I pressed and gently quieted one of these groping hands, I remembered with quivering eyelids their services for me in other days.

Soon after the tenor began the "Prize Song," I heard a quick drawn breath, and turned to my aunt. Her eyes were closed, but the tears were glistening on her cheeks, and I think, in a moment more, they were in my eyes as well. It never really dies, then—the soul which can suffer so excruciatingly and so interminably; it withers to the outward eye only; like that strange moss which can lie on a dusty shelf half a century, and yet, if placed in water, grows green again. She wept so throughout the development and elaboration of the melody.

During the intermission before the second half, I questioned my aunt and found that the "Prize Song" was not new to her. Some years before there had drifted to the farm in Red Willow County a young German, a tramp cowpuncher, who had sung in the chorus at Bayreuth when he was a boy, along with the other peasant boys and girls. On a Sunday morning he used to sit on his gingham-sheeted bed in the hands' bedroom which opened off the kitchen, cleaning the leather of his boots and saddle, singing the "Prize Song," while my aunt went about her work in the kitchen. She had hovered over him until she had prevailed upon him to join the country church, though his sole fitness for this step, in so far as I could gather, lay in his boyish face, and his possession of this divine melody. Shortly afterward, he had gone to town on the Fourth of July, been drunk for several days, lost his money at a faro table, ridden a saddled Texas steer on a bet, and disappeared with a fractured collarbone. All this my aunt told me huskily, wanderingly, as though she were talking in the weak lapses of illness.

"Well, we have come to better things than the old *Trovatore,* at any rate, Aunt Georgie?" I queried, with a well-meant effort at jocularity.

Her lip quivered and she hastily put her handkerchief up to her mouth. From behind it she murmured, "And you have been hearing this ever since you left me, Clark?" Her question was the gentlest and saddest of reproaches.

The second half of the program consisted of four numbers from the *Ring,* and closed with Siegfried's funeral march. My aunt wept quietly but almost continuously, as a shallow vessel overflows in a rain-storm. From time to time her dim eyes looked up at the lights, burning softly under their dull glass globes.

The deluge of sound poured on and on; I never knew what she found in the shining current of it; I never knew how far it bore her, or past what happy islands. From the trembling of her face, I could well believe that before the last number she had been carried out where the myriad graves are, into the gray, nameless burying grounds of the sea, or into some world of death vaster yet, where, from the beginning of the world, hope has lain down with hope and dream with dream and, renouncing, slept.

The concert was over; the people filed out of the hall chattering and laughing, glad to relax and find the living level again, but my kinswoman made no effort to rise. The harpist slipped the green felt cover over his instrument; the flute-players shook the water from their mouth-pieces; the men of the orchestra went out one by one, leaving the stage to the chairs and music stands, empty as a winter cornfield.

I spoke to my aunt. She burst into tears and sobbed pleadingly. "I don't want to go, Clark, I don't want to go!"

I understood. For her, just outside the concert hall, lay the black pond with the cattle-tracked bluffs; the tall, unpainted house, with weather-curled boards, naked as a tower; the crook-backed ash seedlings where the dishcloths hung to dry; the gaunt, moulting turkeys picking up refuse about the kitchen door.

Meaning and Idea

1. Where was Aunt Georgiana born? Where did she live at the time of the story? For how long? Why did she move there? What is her attitude toward that place? Does that attitude change at all during the course of the story?

2. Why did Aunt Georgiana seldom talk about music?

3. What kind of relationship do you think Aunt Georgiana had with her husband? How can you tell?

4. Who is Wagner? Which of his musical works are played at the matinée? How do Aunt Georgiana's reactions change with each piece? How does Cather use different pieces to further the narrative?

5. At one point Clark states, "I began to think it would be best to get her back to Red Willow County without waking her. . . ." What is the meaning of this statement? Why does he think it?

6. Toward the end of the story the narrator states, "It never really dies, then." What is the "it" in this statement?

Language, Form, Structure

1. To what does Clark compare his aunt's trip? To what does he compare her weeping? How else are comparisons used in this story?

2. What is the conflict in this story? How does Cather develop it? How is it resolved?

3. How is the technique of *flashback* used here? For what purpose? How does Cather maintain narrative unity with the flashbacks?

4. How is color imagery used in the narrative? Give specific examples.

5. Explain each of the following adjectival phrases from the story: reverential affection; gangling farmboy; semi-somnambulant state; wretchedly train-sick; quivering eyelids.

Ideas for Writing

1. Narrate a particularly emotional experience of yours that centered on a musical performance, a play, a film, a poetry reading, or an art or museum exhibition.

2. Write an argumentative essay about the role of art in human life.

3. Write a short commentary on your reaction to Cather's portrayal of the two characters. Do you feel you have sufficient knowledge of either or both of the characters to believe their actions and reactions? Do you have a clear visual impression of the characters? Why?

From *Narrative of the Life of Frederick Douglass, An American Slave*

Frederick Douglass

At the age of 21, Frederick Douglass escaped to the North. Born a slave in Maryland, he had to teach himself to read and write, yet he went on to become a renowned editor, writer, orator, and statesman. He served as a U.S. marshal and as consul general to Haiti, and he had been a counselor to four presidents before he died in 1895.

His autobiography was a firsthand account of slavery; no such narrative had existed before. Leaders of the abolitionist movement quickly saw the appeal of Douglass's involvement in the cause. He was wary at first, concerned that such a bold stance by a runaway slave was dangerous. But he overcame that fear and became one of the most important political voices of his time.

I was born in Tuckahoe, near Hillsborough, and about twelve miles from Easton, in Talbot county, Maryland. I have no accurate knowledge of my age, never having seen any authentic record containing it. By far the larger part of the slaves know as little of their ages as horses know of theirs, and it is the wish of most masters within my knowledge to keep their slaves thus ignorant. I do not remember to have ever met a slave who could tell of his birthday. They seldom come nearer to it than planting-time, harvest-time, cherry-time, spring-time, or fall-time. A want of information concerning my own was a source of unhappiness to me even during childhood. The white children could tell their ages. I could not tell why I ought to be deprived of the same privilege. I was not allowed to make any inquiries of my master concerning it. He deemed all such inquiries on the part of a slave improper and impertinent, and evidence of a restless spirit. The nearest estimate I can give makes me now between twenty-seven and twenty-eight years of age. I come to this, from hearing my master say, some time during 1835, I was about seventeen years old.

My mother was named Harriet Bailey. She was the daughter of Isaac and Betsey Bailey, both colored, and quite dark. My mother was of a darker complexion than either my grandmother or grandfather.

My father was a white man. He was admitted to be such by all I ever heard speak of my parentage. The opinion was also whispered that my master was my father; but of the correctness of this opinion, I know nothing; the means of knowing was withheld from me. My mother and I were separated when I was but an infant—before I knew her as my mother. It is a common custom, in the part of Maryland from which I ran away, to part children from their mothers at a very early age. Frequently, before the child has reached its twelfth month, its mother is taken from it, and hired out on some farm a considerable distance off, and the child is placed under the care of an old woman, too old for field labor. For what this separation is done, I do not know, unless it be to hinder the development of the child's affection toward its mother, and to blunt and destroy the natural affection of the mother for the child. This is the inevitable result.

I never saw my mother, to know her as such, more than four or five times in my life; and each of these times was very short in duration, and at night. She was hired by a Mr. Stewart, who lived about twelve miles from my home. She made her journeys to see me in the night, travelling the whole distance on foot, after the performance of her day's work. She was a field hand, and a whipping is the penalty of not being in the field at sunrise, unless a slave has special permission from his or her master to the contrary—a permission which they seldom get, and one that gives to him that gives it the proud name of being a kind master. I do not recollect of ever seeing my mother by the light of day. She was with me in the night. She would lie down with me, and get me to sleep, but long before I waked she was gone. Very little communication ever took place between us. Death soon ended what little we could have while she lived, and with it her hardships and suffering. She died when I was about seven years old, on one of my master's farms, near Lee's Mill. I was not allowed to be present during her illness, at her death, or burial. She was gone long before I knew any thing about it. Never having enjoyed, to any considerable extent, her soothing presence, her tender and watchful care, I received the tidings of her death with much the same emotions I should have probably felt at the death of a stranger.

Called thus suddenly away, she left me without the slightest intimation of who my father was. The whisper that my master was my father, may or may not be true; and, true or false, it is of but little consequence to my purpose whilst the fact remains, in all its glaring odiousness, that slaveholders have ordained, and by law established, that the children of slave women shall in all cases follow the condition of their mothers; and this is done too obviously to administer to their own lusts, and make a gratification of their wicked desires profitable as well as pleasurable; for by this cunning arrangement, the slaveholder, in cases not a few, sustains to his slaves the double relation of master and father.

I know of such cases; and it is worthy of remark that such slaves invariably suffer greater hardships, and have more to contend with, than others. They are, in the first place, a constant offense to their mistress. She is ever disposed to find fault with them; they can seldom do any thing to please her; she is never better pleased than when she sees them under the lash, especially when she suspects her husband of showing to his mulatto children favors which he withholds from his black slaves. The master is frequently compelled to sell this class of his slaves, out of deference to the feelings of his white wife; and cruel as the deed may strike any one to be, for a man to sell his own children to human flesh-mongers, it is often the dictate of humanity for him to do so; for, unless he does this, he must not only whip them himself; but must stand by and see one white son tie up his brother, of but few shades darker complexion than himself, and ply the gory lash to his naked back; and if he lisp one word of disapproval, it is set down to his parental partiality, and only makes a bad matter worse, both for himself and the slave whom he would protect and defend.

Every year brings with it multitudes of this class of slaves. It was doubtless in consequence of a knowledge of this fact, that one great statesman of the south predicted the downfall of slavery by the inevitable laws of population. Whether this prophecy is ever fulfilled or not, it is nevertheless plain that a very different-looking class of people are springing up at the south, and are now held in slavery, from those originally brought to this country from Africa; and if their increase will do no other good, it will do away the force of the argument, that God cursed Ham, and therefore American slavery is right. If the lineal descendants of Ham are alone to be scripturally enslaved, it is certain that slavery at the south must soon become unscriptural; for thousands are ushered into the world, annually, who, like myself, owe their existence to white fathers, and those fathers most frequently their own masters.

I have had two masters. My first master's name was Anthony. I do not remember his first name. He was generally called Captain Anthony—a title which, I presume, he acquired by sailing a craft on the Chesapeake Bay. He was not considered a rich slaveholder. He owned two or three farms, and about thirty slaves. His farms and slaves were under the care of an overseer. The overseer's name was Plummer. Mr. Plummer was a miserable drunkard, a profane swearer, and a savage monster. He always went armed with a cowskin and a heavy cudgel. I have known him to cut and slash the women's heads so horribly, that even master would be enraged at his cruelty, and would threaten to whip him if he did not mind himself. Master, however, was not a humane slaveholder. It required extraordinary barbarity on the part of an overseer to affect him. He was a cruel man, hardened by a long life of slaveholding. He would at times seem to take great pleasure in whipping a slave. I have often been awakened at the dawn of day by the most heart-rending shrieks of an own aunt of mine, whom he used to tie up to a joist, and whip upon her naked back till she was literally covered with blood. No words, no tears, no prayers, from his gory victim, seemed to move his iron heart from its bloody purpose. The louder she screamed, the harder he whipped; and where the blood ran fastest, there he whipped longest. He would whip her to make her scream, and whip her to make her hush; and not until overcome by fatigue, would he cease to swing the blood-clotted cowskin. I remember the first time I ever witnessed this horrible exhibition. I was quite a child, but I well remember it. I never shall forget it whilst I remember any thing. It was the first of a long series of such outrages, of which I was doomed to be a witness and a participant. It struck me with awful force. It was the blood-stained gate, the entrance to the hell of slavery, through which I was about to pass. It was a most terrible spectacle. I wish I could commit to paper the feelings with which I beheld it.

This occurrence took place very soon after I went to live with my old master, and under the following circumstances. Aunt Hester went out one night,— where or for what I do not know,—and happened to be absent when my master desired her presence. He had ordered her not to go out evenings, and warned her that she must never let him catch her in company with a young man, who was paying attention to her belonging to Colonel Lloyd. The young man's name was Ned Roberts, generally called Lloyd's Ned. Why master was so careful of her, may be safely left to conjecture. She was a woman of noble form, and of graceful proportions, having very few equals, and fewer superiors, in personal appearance, among the colored or white women of our neighborhood.

Aunt Hester had not only disobeyed his orders in going out, but had been so found in company with Lloyd's Ned; which circumstance, I found, from what he said while whipping her, was the chief offence. Had he been a man of pure morals himself, he might have been thought interested in protecting the innocence of my aunt; but those who knew him will not suspect him of any such virtue. Before he commenced whipping Aunt Hester, he took her into the kitchen, and stripped her from neck to waist, leaving her neck, shoulders, and back, entirely naked. He then told her to cross her hands, calling her at the same time a d—d b—h. After crossing her hands, he tied them with a strong rope, and led her to a stool under a large hook in the joist, put in for the purpose. He made her get upon the stool, and tied her hands to the hook. She now stood fair for his infernal purpose. Her arms were stretched up at their full length, so that she stood upon the ends of her toes. He then said to her, "Now, you d—d b—h, I'll learn you how to disobey my orders!" and after rolling up his sleeves, he commenced to lay on the heavy cowskin, and soon the warm, red blood (amid heart-rending shrieks from her, and horrid oaths from him) came dripping to the floor. I was so terrified and horror-stricken at the sight, that I hid myself in a closet, and dared not venture out till long after the bloody transaction was over. I expected it would be my turn next. It was all new to me. I had never seen any thing like it before. I had always lived with my grandmother on the outskirts of the plantation, where she was put to raise the children of the younger women. I had therefore been, until now, out of the way of the bloody scenes that often occurred on the plantation.

My master's family consisted of two sons, Andrew and Richard; one daughter, Lucretia, and her husband, Captain Thomas Auld. They lived in one house, upon the home plantation of Colonel Edward Lloyd. My master was Colonel Lloyd's clerk and superintendent. He was what might be called the overseer of the overseers. I spent two years of childhood on this plantation in my old master's family. It was here that I witnessed the bloody transaction recorded in the first chapter; and as I received my first impressions of slavery on this plantation, I will give some description of it, and of slavery as it there existed. The plantation is about twelve miles north of Easton, in Talbot county, and is situated on the border of Miles River. The principal products raised upon it were tobacco, corn, and wheat. These were raised in great abundance; so that, with the products of this and the other farms belonging to him, he was able to keep in almost constant employment a large sloop, in carrying them to market at Baltimore. This sloop was named Sally Lloyd, in honor of one of the colonel's daughters. My master's son-in-law, Captain Auld, was master of the vessel; she was otherwise manned by the colonel's own slaves. Their names were Peter,

Isaac, Rich, and Jake. These were esteemed very highly by the other slaves, and looked upon as the privileged ones of the plantation; for it was no small affair, in the eyes of the slaves, to be allowed to see Baltimore.

Colonel Lloyd kept from three to four hundred slaves on his home plantation, and owned a large number more on the neighboring farms belonging to him. The names of the farms nearest to the home plantation were Wye Town and New Design. "Wye Town" was under the overseership of a man named Noah Willis. New Design was under the overseership of a Mr. Townsend. The overseers of these, and all the rest of the farms, numbering over twenty, received advice and direction from the managers of the home plantation. This was the great business place. It was the seat of government for the whole twenty farms. All disputes among the overseers were settled here. If a slave was convicted of any high misdemeanor, became unmanageable, or evinced a determination to run away, he was brought immediately here, severely whipped, put on board the sloop, carried to Baltimore, and sold to Austin Woolfolk, or some other slave-trader, as a warning to the slaves remaining.

Here, too, the slaves of all the other farms received their monthly allowance of food, and their yearly clothing. The men and women slaves received, as their monthly allowance of food, eight pounds of pork, or its equivalent in fish, and one bushel of corn meal. Their yearly clothing consisted of two coarse linen shirts, one pair of linen trousers, like the shirts, one jacket, one pair of trousers for winter, made of coarse negro cloth, one pair of stockings, and one pair of shoes; the whole of which could not have cost more than seven dollars. The allowance of the slave children was given to their mothers, or the old women having the care of them. The children unable to work in the field had neither shoes, stockings, jackets, nor trousers, given to them; their clothing consisted of two coarse linen shirts per year. When these failed them, they went naked until the next allowance-day. Children from seven to ten years old, of both sexes, almost naked, might be seen at all seasons of the year.

There were no beds given the slaves, unless one coarse blanket be considered such, and none but the men and women had these. This, however, is not considered a very great privation. They find less difficulty from the want of beds, than from the want of time to sleep; for when their day's work in the field is done, the most of them having their washing, mending, and cooking to do, and having few or none of the ordinary facilities for doing either of these, very many of their sleeping hours are consumed in preparing for the field the coming day; and when this is done, old and young, male and female, married and single, drop down side by side, on one common bed,—the cold, damp floor,—each covering himself or herself with their miserable blankets; and here they sleep till they are summoned to the field by the driver's horn. At the sound of this, all must rise, and be off to the field. There must be no halting; every one must be at his or her post; and woe betides them who hear not this morning summons to the field; for if they are not awakened by the sense of hearing, they are by the sense of feeling: no age nor sex finds any favor. Mr. Severe, the overseer, used to stand by the door of the quarter, armed with a large hickory stick and heavy cowskin, ready to whip any one who was so unfortunate as not to hear, or, from any other cause, was prevented from being ready to start for the field at the sound of the horn.

Mr. Severe was rightly named: he was a cruel man. I have seen him whip   15
a woman, causing the blood to run half an hour at the time; and this, too, in the midst of her crying children, pleading for their mother's release. He seemed to take pleasure in manifesting his fiendish barbarity. Added to his cruelty, he was a profane swearer. It was enough to chill the blood and stiffen the hair of an ordinary man to hear him talk. Scarce a sentence escaped him but that was commenced or concluded by some horrid oath. The field was the place to witness his cruelty and profanity. His presence made it both the field of blood and of blasphemy. From the rising till the going down of the sun, he was cursing, raving, cutting, and slashing among the slaves of the field, in the most frightful manner. His career was short. He died very soon after I went to Colonel Lloyd's; and he died as he lived, uttering, with his dying groans, bitter curses and horrid oaths. His death was regarded by the slaves as the result of a merciful providence.

Mr. Severe's place was filled by a Mr. Hopkins. He was a very different man.   16
He was less cruel, less profane, and made less noise, than Mr. Severe. His course was characterized by no extraordinary demonstrations of cruelty. He whipped, but seemed to take no pleasure in it. He was called by the slaves a good overseer.

The home plantation of Colonel Lloyd wore the appearance of a country   17
village. All the mechanical operations for all the farms were performed here. The shoemaking and mending, the blacksmithing, cartwrighting, coopering, weaving, and grain-grinding, were all performed by the slaves on the home plantation. The whole place wore a business-like aspect very unlike the neighboring farms. The number of houses, too, conspired to give it advantage over the neighboring farms. It was called by the slaves the *Great House Farm.* Few privileges were esteemed higher, by the slaves of the out-farms, than that of being selected to do errands at the Great House Farm. It was associated in their minds with greatness. A representative could not be prouder of his election to a seat in the American Congress, than a slave on one of the out-farms would be of his election to do errands at the Great House Farm. They regarded it as evidence of great confidence reposed in them by their overseers; and it was on this account, as well as a constant desire to be out of the field from under the driver's lash, that they esteemed it a high privilege, one worth careful living for. He was called the smartest and most trusty fellow, who had this honor conferred upon him the most frequently. The competitors for this office sought as diligently to please their overseers, as the office-seekers in the political parties seek to please and deceive the people. The same traits of character might be seen in Colonel Lloyd's slaves, as are seen in the slaves of the political parties.

The slaves selected to go to the Great House Farm, for the monthly al-   18
lowance for themselves and their fellow-slaves, were peculiarly enthusiastic. While on their way, they would make the dense old woods, for miles around, reverberate with their wild songs, revealing at once the highest joy and the deepest sadness. They would compose and sing as they went along, consulting neither time nor tune. The thought that came up, came out—if not in the word, in the

sound;—and as frequently in the one as in the other. They would sometimes sing the most pathetic sentiment in the most rapturous tone, and the most rapturous sentiment in the most pathetic tone. Into all of their songs they would manage to weave something of the Great House Farm. Especially would they do this, when leaving home. They would then sing most exultingly the following words:—

I am going away to the Great House Farm!

O, Yea! O, Yea! O!

This they would sing, as a chorus, to words which to many would seem unmeaning jargon, but which, nevertheless, were full of meaning to themselves. I have sometimes thought that the mere hearing of those songs would do more to impress some minds with the horrible character of slavery, than the reading of whole volumes of philosophy on the subject could do.

I did not, when a slave, understand the deep meaning of those rude and apparently incoherent songs. I was myself within the circle; so that I neither saw nor heard as those without might see and hear. They told a tale of woe which was then altogether beyond my feeble comprehension; they were tones loud, long, and deep; they breathed the prayer and complaint of souls boiling over with the bitterest anguish. Every tone was a testimony against slavery, and a prayer to God for deliverance from chains. The hearing of those wild notes always depressed my spirit, and filled me with ineffable sadness. I have frequently found myself in tears while hearing them. The mere recurrence to those songs, even now, afflicts me; and while I am writing these lines, an expression of feeling has already found its way down my cheek. To those songs I trace my first glimmering conception of the dehumanizing character of slavery. I can never get rid of that conception. Those songs still follow me, to deepen my hatred of slavery, and quicken my sympathies for my brethren in bonds. If any one wishes to be impressed with the soul-killing effects of slavery, let him go to Colonel Lloyd's plantation, and, on allowance-day, place himself in the deep pine woods, and there let him, in silence, analyze the sounds that shall pass through the chambers of his soul,—and if he is not thus impressed, it will only be because "there is no flesh in his obdurate heart." 19

I have often been utterly astonished, since I came to the north, to find persons who could speak of the singing, among slaves, as evidence of their contentment and happiness. It is impossible to conceive of a greater mistake. Slaves sing most when they are most unhappy. The songs of the slave represent the sorrows of his heart; and he is relieved by them, only as an aching heart is relieved by its tears. At least, such is my experience. I have often sung to drown my sorrow, but seldom to express my happiness. Crying for joy, and singing for joy, were alike uncommon to me while in the jaws of slavery. The singing of a man cast away upon a desolate island might be as appropriately considered as evidence of contentment and happiness, as the singing of a slave; the songs of the one and of the other are prompted by the same emotion. 20

Meaning and Idea

1. What is "the inevitable result" of separating a slave mother from her child? What is Douglass referring to when he notes the "glaring odiousness" of how "the children of slave women must follow the condition of their mothers"? Why would these types of measures be a part of slavery?

2. Douglass says his Aunt Hester was consistently whipped by their master and that his own first memory of a whipping was one of these experiences. Why did Master Anthony pick on her? What made the whipping Douglass describes particularly harsh?

3. What was the source for the singing that the slaves often did? Explain the honor and enthusiasm the slaves associated with traveling to Baltimore or the Great House Farm. Why were the singing and enthusiasm especially intense on "allowance" day?

Language, Form, Structure

1. The excerpt from Douglass's autobiography contains detailed descriptions of slave life: clothes, food, bedding, the driver's horn, what the plantation was like. What is the effect of this use of detail? How do the details help flesh out the narrative?

2. Think about what Douglass knows about his own parentage and what he knows about the status and population of mulatto slaves. At times he seems to speak of these and other matters in an impersonal way, and at times he speaks quite personally. What is the effect of this technique? How does he achieve it?

3. Define the following words and use each in a sentence: impertinent; inevitable; duration; intimation; odiousness; ordained; obdurate.

Ideas for Writing

1. Examine a series of related events that you have experienced. First list the events in the order in which they occurred. Now think about why they happened and what they meant to you when they happened. What do they mean to you now? Write an essay that recounts these experiences and feelings. Be sure to create an appropriate introduction and conclusion.

2. Write an argumentative essay about a highly regimented system in which you either defend it or show why it is destructive. You might consider, for example, the army, a strict private school, or a very formal company.

3. The excerpt from Douglass's autobiography shifts back and forth between the detailed recounting of events or circumstances and more stylistic, philosophical examinations of what these things meant. Write an essay that examines why Douglass does this and what the effect is.

There's Been a Death in the Opposite House

Emily Dickinson

"The recluse of Amherst," Emily Dickinson (1830–1886) became one of the world's most renowned poets without ever leaving her home in Amherst, Massachusetts. Critics still argue whether Dickinson, most of whose poems were not published until after her death, wrote from a life fully lived or from one almost fully repressed. She wrote eloquently of love and devotion, yet she did not sustain an intimate romantic relationship or even marry. In all, Dickinson's collected poems leave us a rich expression of universal values and meanings.

Dickinson's "There's Been a Death in the Opposite House" tells readers both of the closeness of death and of the transparency of events in a small, country town. Though a simple narrative, the poem leaves one with a deep feeling and respect for the event.

*T*here's been a death in the opposite house
As lately as today.
I know it by the numb look
Such houses have alway.

The neighbors rustle in and out,   '5
The doctor drives away.
A window opens like a pod,
Abrupt, mechanically;
Somebody flings a mattress out,
The children hurry by;   10
They wonder if it died on that,
I used to when a boy.

The minister goes stiffly in
As if the house were his,
And he owned all the mourners now,   15
And little boys besides;

And then the milliner, and the man
Of the appalling trade,
To take the measure of the house.
There'll be that dark parade   20

Of tassels and of coaches soon;
It's easy as a sign,
The intuition of the news
In just a country town.

Meaning and Idea

1. How does the speaker know that a death has occurred? What images support this knowledge? How does the speaker feel about death?

2. What is a *milliner?* Why is the milliner important to the scene? Who is "the man/Of the appalling trade"?

3. According to the poem, why is it so easy to tell that a death has occurred in a country town?

Language, Form, Structure

1. Who is the audience for this poem? How do you know? The narrative structure here is extraordinarily simple. How does Dickinson take the reader from event to event? What transitions help the narrative movement?

2. Which verbs best convey simple crisp actions? Which adjectives best reflect the issue of death?

3. Contrast the meaning of the word *house* in lines 1 and 19.

4. Which lines in the poem come closest to stating Dickinson's main point?

5. Look up the following words in a dictionary: numb; rustle; flings; measure (noun); intuition.

Ideas for Writing

1. Write a page or two in which you narrate an early experience with death. Try to re-create the scene as clearly as possible.

2. Write an argumentative essay about the rituals surrounding death. Why do we perform these rituals?

3. The speaker of this poem is a man (refer to line 12), yet the poet is a woman. Do you feel Dickinson adequately portrays a man's point of view? Would there by any difference between a man's and a woman's point of view about this scene? In general, do you think writers can easily write through the eyes of a character of the opposite sex? Draw on examples from your reading.

My Father's Life

Raymond Carver

Raymond Carver (1939–1988) was born in Clatskanie, Oregon. He studied at Humboldt State College and the University of Iowa and then worked at a variety of jobs—janitor, stockboy, editor, creative writing instructor—to support his family. All the time, he wrote and began to earn the critical acclaim he now receives. Among other awards, he has been the recipient of a National Endowment for the Arts "Discovery" Award, a Guggenheim fellowship, and the prestigious Strauss Living Award. His poems, essays, and stories have been widely published in magazines, and his narrative sparseness has caused some to compare him to Hemingway. His collections of fiction include *Will You Please Be Quiet, Please* (1976), *What We Talk about When We Talk about Love* (1981), and *Cathedral* (1983).

"My Father's Life" first appeared in the "First Person" column of *Esquire* magazine in September 1984. In it, Carver remembers his father, senses the convergences and divergences of their lives, and at last consigns his father to memory.

*M*y dad's name was Clevie Raymond Carver. His family called him   1
Raymond and friends called him C.R. I was named Raymond Clevie Carver Jr. I hated the "Junior" part. When I was little my dad called me Frog, which was okay. But later, like everybody else in the family, he began calling me Junior. He went on calling me this until I was thirteen or fourteen and announced that I wouldn't answer to that name any longer. So he began calling me Doc. From then until his death, on June 17, 1967, he called me Doc, or else Son.

When he died, my mother telephoned my wife with the news. I was away   2
from my family at the time, between lives, trying to enroll in the School of Library Science at the University of Iowa. When my wife answered the phone, my mother blurted out, "Raymond's dead!" For a moment, my wife thought my mother was telling her that I was dead. Then my mother made it clear *which* Raymond she was talking about and my wife said, "Thank God. I thought you meant *my* Raymond."

My dad walked, hitched rides, and rode in empty boxcars when he went   3
from Arkansas to Washington State in 1934, looking for work. I don't know whether he was pursuing a dream when he went out to Washington. I doubt it. I don't think he dreamed much. I believe he was simply looking for steady work at decent pay. Steady work was meaningful work. He picked apples for a time and then landed a construction laborer's job on the Grand Coulee Dam. After he'd put aside a little money, he bought a car and drove back to Arkansas to help his folks, my grandparents, pack up for the move west. He said later that they were about to starve down there, and this wasn't meant as a figure of speech. It was during that short while in Arkansas, in a town called Leola, that my mother met my dad on the sidewalk as he came out of a tavern.

"He was drunk," she said. "I don't know why I let him talk to me. His   4
eyes were glittery. I wish I'd had a crystal ball." They'd met once, a year or so
before, at a dance. He'd had girlfriends before her, my mother told me. "Your
dad always had a girlfriend, even after we married. He was my first and last. I
never had another man. But I didn't miss anything."

They were married by a justice of the peace on the day they left for Wash-   5
ington, this big, tall country girl and a farmhand-turned-construction worker. My
mother spent her wedding night with my dad and his folks, all of them camped
beside the road in Arkansas.

In Omak, Washington, my dad and mother lived in a little place not much   6
bigger than a cabin. My grandparents lived next door. My dad was still working
on the dam, and later, with the huge turbines producing electricity and the water
backed up for a hundred miles into Canada, he stood in the crowd and heard
Franklin D. Roosevelt when he spoke at the construction site. "He never mentioned those guys who died building that dam," my dad said. Some of his friends
had died there, men from Arkansas, Oklahoma, and Missouri.

He then took a job in a sawmill in Clatskanie, Oregon, a little town along-   7
side the Columbia River. I was born there, and my mother has a picture of my
dad standing in front of the gate to the mill, proudly holding me up to face the
camera. My bonnet is on crooked and about to come untied. His hat is pushed
back on his forehead, and he's wearing a big grin. Was he going in to work or
just finishing his shift? It doesn't matter. In either case, he had a job and a family. These were his salad days.

In 1941 we moved to Yakima, Washington, where my dad went to work   8
as a saw filer, a skilled trade he'd learned in Clatskanie. When war broke out, he
was given a deferment because his work was considered necessary to the war effort. Finished lumber was in demand by the armed services, and he kept his saws
so sharp they could shave the hair off your arm.

After my dad had moved us to Yakima, he moved his folks into the same   9
neighborhood. By the mid-1940s the rest of my dad's family—his brother, his
sister, and her husband, as well as uncles, cousins, nephews, and most of their
extended family and friends—had come out from Arkansas. All because my dad
came out first. The men went to work at Boise Cascade, where my dad worked,
and the women packed apples in the canneries. And in just a little while, it
seemed—according to my mother—everybody was better off than my dad.
"Your dad couldn't keep money," my mother said. "Money burned a hole in his
pocket. He was always doing for others."

The first house I clearly remember living in, at 1515 South Fifteenth   10
Street, in Yakima, had an outdoor toilet. On Halloween night, or just any night,
for the hell of it, neighbor kids, kids in their early teens, would carry our toilet
away and leave it next to the road. My dad would have to get somebody to help
him bring it home. Or these kids would take the toilet and stand it in somebody
else's backyard. Once they actually set it on fire. But ours wasn't the only house
that had an outdoor toilet. When I was old enough to know what I was doing, I
threw rocks at the other toilets when I'd see someone go inside. This was called

bombing the toilets. After a while, though, everyone went to indoor plumbing until, suddenly, our toilet was the last outdoor one in the neighborhood. I remember the shame I felt when my third-grade teacher, Mr. Wise, drove me home from school one day. I asked him to stop at the house just before ours, claiming I lived there.

I can recall what happened one night when my dad came home late to find that my mother had locked all the doors on him from the inside. He was drunk, and we could feel the house shudder as he rattled the door. When he'd managed to force open a window, she hit him between the eyes with a colander and knocked him out. We could see him down there on the grass. For years afterward, I used to pick up this colander—it was as heavy as a rolling pin—and imagine what it would feel like to be hit in the head with something like that.

It was during this period that I remember my dad taking me into the bedroom, sitting me down on the bed, and telling me that I might have to go live with my Aunt LaVon for a while. I couldn't understand what I'd done that meant I'd have to go away from home to live. But this, too—whatever prompted it—must have blown over, more or less, anyway, because we stayed together, and I didn't have to go live with her or anyone else.

I remember my mother pouring his whiskey down the sink. Sometimes she'd pour it all out and sometimes, if she was afraid of getting caught, she'd only pour half of it out and then add water to the rest. I tasted some of his whiskey once myself. It was terrible stuff, and I don't see how anybody could drink it.

After a long time without one, we finally got a car, in 1949 or 1950, a 1938 Ford. But it threw a rod the first week we had it, and my dad had to have the motor rebuilt.

"We drove the oldest car in town," my mother said. "We could have had a Cadillac for all he spent on car repairs." One time she found someone else's tube of lipstick on the floorboard, along with a lacy handkerchief. "See this?" she said to me. "Some floozy left this in the car."

Once I saw her take a pan of warm water into the bedroom where my dad was sleeping. She took his hand from under the covers and held it in the water. I stood in the doorway and watched. I wanted to know what was going on. This would make him talk in his sleep, she told me. There were things she needed to know, things she was sure he was keeping from her.

Every year or so, when I was little, we would take the North Coast Limited across the Cascade Range from Yakima to Seattle and stay in the Vance Hotel and eat, I remember, at a place called the Dinner Bell Cafe. Once we went to Ivar's Acres of Clams and drank glasses of warm clam broth.

In 1956, the year I was to graduate from high school, my dad quit his job at the mill in Yakima and took a job in Chester, a little sawmill town in northern California. The reasons given at the time for his taking the job had to do with a higher hourly wage and the vague promise that he might, in a few years' time, succeed to the job of head filer in this new mill. But I think, in the main, that my dad had grown restless and simply wanted to try his luck elsewhere. Things had gotten a little too predictable for him in Yakima. Also, the year before, there had been the deaths, within six months of each other, of both his parents.

But just a few days after graduation, when my mother and I were packed to move to Chester, my dad penciled a letter to say he'd been sick for a while. He didn't want us to worry, he said, but he'd cut himself on a saw. Maybe he'd got a tiny sliver of steel in his blood. Anyway, something had happened and he'd had to miss work, he said. In the same mail was an unsigned postcard from somebody down there telling my mother that my dad was about to die and that he was drinking "raw whiskey." 19

When we arrived in Chester, my dad was living in a trailer that belonged to the company. I didn't recognize him immediately. I guess for a moment I didn't want to recognize him. He was skinny and pale and looked bewildered. His pants wouldn't stay up. He didn't look like my dad. My mother began to cry. My dad put his arm around her and patted her shoulder vaguely, like he didn't know what this was all about, either. The three of us took up life together in the trailer, and we looked after him as best we could. But my dad was sick, and he couldn't get any better. I worked with him in the mill that summer and part of the fall. We'd get up in the mornings and eat eggs and toast while we listened to the radio, and then go out the door with our lunch pails. We'd pass through the gate together at eight in the morning, and I wouldn't see him again until quitting time. In November I went back to Yakima to be closer to my girlfriend, the girl I'd made up my mind I was going to marry. 20

He worked at the mill in Chester until the following February, when he collapsed on the job and was taken to the hospital. My mother asked if I would come down there and help. I caught a bus from Yakima to Chester, intending to drive them back to Yakima. But now, in addition to being physically sick, my dad was in the midst of a nervous breakdown, though none of us knew to call it that at the time. During the entire trip back to Yakima, he didn't speak, not even when asked a direct question. ("How do you feel, Raymond?" "You okay, Dad?") He'd communicate, if he communicated at all, by moving his head or by turning his palms up as if to say he didn't know or care. The only time he said anything on the trip, and for nearly a month afterward, was when I was speeding down a gravel road in Oregon and the car muffler came loose. "You were going too fast," he said. 21

Back in Yakima a doctor saw to it that my dad went to a psychiatrist. My mother and dad had to go on relief, as it was called, and the county paid for the psychiatrist. The psychiatrist asked my dad, "Who is the President?" He'd had a question put to him that he could answer. "Ike," my dad said. Nevertheless, they put him on the fifth floor of Valley Memorial Hospital and began giving him electroshock treatments. I was married by then and about to start my own family. My dad was still locked up when my wife went into this same hospital, just one floor down, to have our first baby. After she had delivered, I went upstairs to give my dad the news. They let me in through a steel door and showed me where I could find him. He was sitting on a couch with a blanket over his lap. *Hey,* I thought. *What in hell is happening to my dad?* I sat down next to him and 22 told him he was a grandfather. He waited a minute and then he said, "I feel like a grandfather." That's all he said. He didn't smile or move. He was in a big room with a lot of other people. Then I hugged him, and he began to cry.

Somehow he got out of there. But now came the years when he couldn't work and just sat around the house trying to figure what next and what he'd done wrong in his life that he'd wound up like this. My mother went from job to crummy job. Much later she referred to that time he was in the hospital, and those years just afterward, as "when Raymond was sick." The word *sick* was never the same for me again.

In 1964, through the help of a friend, he was lucky enough to be hired on at a mill in Klamath, California. He moved down there by himself to see if he could hack it. He lived not far from the mill, in a one-room cabin not much different from the place he and my mother had started out living in when they went west. He scrawled letters to my mother, and if I called she'd read them aloud to me over the phone. In the letters, he said it was touch and go. Every day that he went to work, he felt like it was the most important day of his life. But every day, he told her, made the next day that much easier. He said for her to tell me he said hello. If he couldn't sleep at night, he said, he thought about me and the good times we used to have. Finally, after a couple of months, he regained some of his confidence. He could do the work and didn't think he had to worry that he'd let anybody down ever again. When he was sure, he sent for my mother.

He'd been off from work for six years and had lost everything in that time—home, car, furniture, and appliances, including the big freezer that had been my mother's pride and joy. He'd lost his good name too—Raymond Carver was someone who couldn't pay his bills—and his self-respect was gone. He'd even lost his virility. My mother told my wife, "All during that time Raymond was sick we slept together in the same bed, but we didn't have relations. He wanted to a few times, but nothing happened. I didn't miss it, but I think he wanted to, you know."

During those years I was trying to raise my own family and earn a living. But, one thing and another, we found ourselves having to move a lot. I couldn't keep track of what was going down in my dad's life. But I did have a chance one Christmas to tell him I wanted to be a writer. I might as well have told him I wanted to become a plastic surgeon. "What are you going to write about?" he wanted to know. Then as if to help me out, he said, "Write about stuff you know about. Write about some of those fishing trips we took." I said I would, but I knew I wouldn't. "Send me what you write," he said. I said I'd do that, but then I didn't. I wasn't writing anything about fishing, and I didn't think he'd particularly care about, or even necessarily understand, what I was writing in those days. Besides, he wasn't a reader. Not the sort, anyway, I imagined I was writing for.

Then he died. I was a long way off, in Iowa City, with things still to say to him. I didn't have the chance to tell him goodbye, or that I thought he was doing great at his new job. That I was proud of him for making a comeback.

My mother said he came in from work that night and ate a big supper. Then he sat at the table by himself and finished what was left of a bottle of whiskey, a bottle she found hidden in the bottom of the garbage under some coffee grounds a day or so later. Then he got up and went to bed, where my mother joined him a little later. But in the night she had to get up and make a bed for herself on the couch. "He was snoring so loud I couldn't sleep," she said. The next morning when she looked in on him, he was on his back with his mouth open, his cheeks caved in. *Gray-looking,* she said. She knew he was dead—she didn't need a doctor to tell her that. But she called one anyway, and then she called my wife.

Among the pictures my mother kept of my dad and herself during those early days in Washington was a photograph of him standing in front of a car, holding a beer and a stringer of fish. In the photograph he is wearing his hat back on his forehead and has this awkward grin on his face. I asked her for it and she gave it to me, along with some others. I put it up on my wall, and each time we moved, I took the picture along and put it up on another wall. I looked at it carefully from time to time, trying to figure out some things about my dad, and maybe myself in the process. But I couldn't. My dad just kept moving further and further away from me and back into time. Finally, in the course of another move, I lost the photograph. It was then that I tried to recall it, and at the same time make an attempt to say something about my dad, and how I thought that in some important ways we might be alike. I wrote the poem when I was living in an apartment house in an urban area south of San Francisco, at a time when I found myself, like my dad, having trouble with alcohol. The poem was a way of trying to connect with him.

Photograph of My Father in His Twenty-Second Year

October. Here in this dank, unfamiliar kitchen
I study my father's embarrassed young man's face.
Sheepish grin, he holds in one hand a string
of spiny yellow perch, in the other a bottle of Carlsberg beer.

In jeans and flannel shirt, he leans against the front fender of a 1934 Ford.
He would like to pose brave and hearty for his posterity,
wear his old hat cocked over his ear.
All his life my father wanted to be bold.

But the eyes give him away, and the hands
that limply offer the string of dead perch
and the bottle of beer. Father, I love you,
yet how can I say thank you, I who can't hold my liquor either
and don't even know the places to fish.

The poem is true in its particulars, except that my dad died in June and not October, as the first word of the poem says. I wanted a word with more than one syllable to it to make it linger a little. But more than that, I wanted a month appropriate to what I felt at the time I wrote the poem—month of short days and failing light, smoke in the air, things perishing. June was summer nights and days, graduations, my wedding anniversary, the birthday of one of my children. June wasn't a month your father died in.

After the service at the funeral home, after we had moved outside, a woman I didn't know came over to me and said, "He's happier where he is now." I stared at this woman until she moved away. I still remember the little knob of a hat she was wearing. Then one of my dad's cousins—I didn't know the man's name—reached out and took my hand. "We all miss him," he said, and I knew he wasn't saying it just to be polite.

I began to weep for the first time since receiving the news. I hadn't been able to before. I hadn't had the time, for one thing. Now, suddenly, I couldn't stop. I held my wife and wept while she said and did what she could do to comfort me there in the middle of that summer afternoon.

I listened to people say consoling things to my mother, and I was glad that my dad's family had turned up, had come to where he was. I thought I'd remember everything that was said and done that day and maybe find a way to tell it sometime. But I didn't. I forgot it all, or nearly. What I do remember is that I heard our name used a lot that afternoon, my dad's name and mine. But I knew they were talking about my dad. *Raymond,* these people kept saying in their beautiful voices out of my childhood. *Raymond.*

Meaning and Idea

1. How did Carver's mother and father meet? What was her reaction to him? How did she feel about him in later life?

2. Why was Carver embarrassed about his home in Yakima?

3. Trace the geographic movement of Carver's father.

4. How does Carver's father get sick? What are the results of that sickness?

5. What parallels between his own life and his father's life does Carver write about? What is his opinion of these similarities?

6. What sort of person was Carver's father? What is your reaction to him? What was Carver's?

Language, Form, Structure

1. How does Carver use *narrative summary* (see page 59) throughout this essay? How does it affect the tone of the writing? How does Carver maintain unity throughout the essay? What words or phrases are often repeated?

2. What is the use of *dialogue* in this essay? How does it enhance the narration?

3. Essentially, this essay is a chronological narrative of the life of Carver's father. Yet the paragraph just after the poem seems to break the chronology momentarily. What is the purpose of this break?

4. What is the effect of the terse line: "Then he died"?

5. Why does Carver include the full text of the poem in this essay? How is its tone different from the narrative tone? Could he have summarized the poem's contents just as easily?

6. Throughout the essay, Carver uses various colloquialisms such as *floozy, raw whiskey,* and *crummy.* Explain the meanings of these terms and find and explain three other colloquialisms.

Ideas for Writing

1. Narrate the history of one of your closest family members. Attempt to follow Carver's pattern of highlighting through narrative summary.

2. Select one incident from the narration you wrote in response to question 1 in this section and expand it to a two- or three-paragraph narration of its own.

3. Write a brief analysis of Carver's style as evidenced in "My Father's Life." Carver, who was primarily a fiction writer, is known for his terse, compact, narrative summary style. Do the same stylistic qualities emerge here? What are the effects of this style on the reader? Draw specific examples from the selection to make your point.

Incident

Countee Cullen

Countee Cullen (1903–1946) was born in New York City. He is considered, along with W. E. B. Du Bois, Langston Hughes, Claude McKay, and Jean Toomer, among the leading writers of the Harlem Renaissance of the 1920s. The Harlem Renaissance was a literary and arts movement that chronicled black life and celebrated black pride. Cullen's contribution was his poetry, in which he intertwined traditional forms with black themes and syntax. Among his best-known volumes of poetry are *Color* (1925) and *Copper Sun* (1927).

In this rhymed, simple three-stanza poem, Countee Cullen tells of a single event which was in fact indicative of a cultural attitude that fostered millions of similar "incidents." As you read, think of how the idea of the poem reflects common moments in our everyday life.

*O*nce riding in old Baltimore
    Heart-filled, head-filled with glee,
I saw a Baltimorean
    Keep looking straight at me.

Now I was eight and very small,   5
    And he was no whit bigger,
And so I smiled, but he poked out
    His tongue, and called me, "Nigger."

I saw the whole of Baltimore
    From May until December;   10
Of all the things that happened there
    That's all that I remember.

Meaning and Idea

1. The "incident" here is very straightforward. Tell what actually happened in a single sentence.

2. About how old was the person who called the narrator "Nigger"? How do you know?

3. What is the effect of the incident on the narrator? What is the immediate change in his attitude? He says he was in Baltimore "From May until December," but how can you tell that the effects were longer lasting than that?

Language, Form, Structure

1. How does stanza 3 differ from the first two stanzas? From what does it derive its effectiveness?

2. Comment on the meaning and tone of the phrase "no whit bigger." What does it tell us about the time frame of this incident?

3. What is the relation between the poem's title and its story? What transitions does the poet use to make the narrative structure clear?

Ideas for Writing

1. Tell of a seemingly simple incident or comment that deeply affected you. What were the circumstances? What were the results?

2. Write an essay on the power of language to affect human emotion.

3. Write a brief paper to explain whether you are satisfied with the format of a poem for telling this story. Do you think it would have been more effective written as a prose narrative? Why or why not?

The Witch's Husband

Judith Ortiz Cofer

Judith Ortiz Cofer was born in Puerto Rico in 1952, and she and her family emigrated to New York in 1956. She received a B.A. from Augusta College in 1974 and went on to earn an M.A. from Florida Atlantic in 1977. She has taught English and Spanish in many parts of Florida and Georgia. Cofer has written several books of poetry and two novels.

The following selection is from *Silent Dancing,* a memoir about her family and their lives in both Puerto Rico and the mainland United States. In this selection she tells how her grandmother's narrative skills kept Cofer from accomplishing a goal.

*M*y grandfather has misplaced his words again. He is trying to find my name in the kaleidoscope of images that his mind has become. His face brightens like a child's who has just remembered his lesson. He points to me and says my mother's name. I smile back and kiss him on the cheek. It doesn't matter what names he remembers anymore. Every day he is more confused, his memory slipping back a little further in time. Today he has no grandchildren yet. Tomorrow he will be a young man courting my grandmother again, quoting bits of poetry to her. In months to come, he will begin calling her Mamá.

I have traveled to Puerto Rico at my mother's request to help her deal with the old people. My grandfather is physically healthy but his dementia is severe. My grandmother's heart is making odd sounds again in her chest. Yet she insists on taking care of the old man at home herself. She will not give up her house, though she has been warned that her heart might fail in her sleep without proper monitoring, that is, in a nursing home or a relative's care. Her response is typical of her famous obstinacy: "*Bueno,*" she says, "I will die in my own bed."

I am now at her house, waiting for my opportunity to talk "sense" into her. As a college teacher in the United States I am supposed to represent the voice of logic; I have been called in to convince *la abuela,* the family's proud matriarch, to step down—to allow her children to take care of her before she kills herself with work. I spent years at her house as a child but have lived in the States for most of my adult life. I learned to love and respect this strong woman who with five children of her own had found a way to help many others. She was a legend in the pueblo for having more foster children than anyone else. I have spoken with people my mother's age who told me that they had spent up to a year at Abuela's house during emergencies and hard times. It seems extraordinary that a woman would willingly take on such obligations. And, frankly, I am a bit appalled at what I have begun to think of as "the martyr complex" in Puerto Rican women, that is, the idea that self-sacrifice is a woman's lot and her privilege. A good woman is defined by how much suffering and mothering she can do in one lifetime. Abuela is the all-time champion in my eyes. Her life has been entirely devoted to others. Not content to bring up two sons and three daughters as the

Depression raged on, followed by the war that took one of her sons, she had also taken on other people's burdens. This had been the usual pattern with one exception that I knew of: the year that Abuela spent in New York, apparently undergoing some kind of treatment of her heart while she was still a young woman. My mother was five or six years old, and there were three other children who had been born by that time, too. They were given into the care of Abuela's sister, Delia. The two women traded places for the year. Abuela went to live in her sister's apartment in New York City, while the younger woman took over Abuela's duties at the house in Puerto Rico. Grandfather was a shadowy figure in the background during that period. My mother doesn't say much about what went on during that year, only that her mother was sick and away for months. Grandfather seemed absent, too, since he worked all of the time. Though they missed Abuela, they were well taken care of.

I am sitting on a rocking chair on the porch of her house. She is facing me   4
from a hammock she made when her first baby was born. My mother was rocked on the hammock. I was rocked on that hammock, and when I brought my daughter as a baby to Abuela's house, she was held in Abuela's sun-browned arms, my porcelain pink baby, and rocked to a peaceful sleep, too. Abuela sits there and smiles as the breeze of a tropical November brings the scent of her roses and her herbs to us. She is proud of her garden. In front of the house she grows flowers and lush trailing plants; in the back, where the mango tree gives shade, she has an herb garden. From this patch of weedy-looking plants came all the remedies of my childhood, for anything from a sore throat to menstrual cramps. Abuela had a recipe for every pain a child could dream up, and she brought it to your bed in her own hands smelling of the earth. For a moment I am content to sit in her comforting presence. She is rotund now—a small-boned brown-skinned earth mother— with a big heart and temper to match. My grandfather comes to stand at the screen door. He has forgotten how the latch works. He pulls at the knob and moans softly, rattling it. With some effort Abuela gets down from the hammock. She opens the door, gently guiding the old man to a chair at the end of the porch. There he begins anew his constant search for the words he needs. He tries various combinations, but they don't work as language. Abuela pats his hand and motions for me to follow her into the house. We sit down at opposite ends of her sofa.

She apologizes to me as if for a misbehaving child.   5

"He'll quiet down," she says. "He does not like to be ignored."   6

I take a deep breath in preparation for my big lecture to Grandmother. This   7
is the time to tell her that she has to give up trying to run this house and take care of others at her age. One of her daughters is prepared to take her in. Grandfather is to be sent to a nursing home. Before I can say anything Abuela says, "*Mi amor,* would you like to hear a story?"

I smile, surprised at her offer. These are the same words that stopped me   8
in my tracks as a child, even in the middle of a tantrum. Abuela could always entrance me with one of her tales.

I nodded. Yes, my sermon could wait a little longer, I thought.   9

"Let me tell you an old, old story I heard when I was a little girl.   10

"There was once a man who became worried and suspicious when he no- ¹¹ ticed that his wife disappeared from their bed every night for long periods of time. Wanting to find out what she was doing before confronting her, the man decided to stay awake at night and keep guard. For hours he watched her every movement through half-closed eyelids with his ears perked up like those of a burro.

"Then just about midnight, when the night was as dark as the bottom of a ¹² cauldron, he felt his wife slipping out of bed. He saw her go to the wardrobe and take out a jar and a little paintbrush. She stood naked by the window, and when the church bells struck twelve, she began to paint her entire body with the paint-brush, dipping it into the jar. As the bells tolled the hour, she whispered these words: *I don't believe in the Church, or in God, or in the Virgin Mary.* As soon as this was spoken, she rose from the ground and flew into the night like a bird.

"Astounded, the man decided not to say anything to his wife the next day, ¹³ but to try to find out where she went. The following night, the man pretended to sleep and waited until she had again performed her little ceremony and flown away, then he repeated her actions exactly. He soon found himself flying after her. Approaching a palace, he saw many other women circling the roof, taking turns going down the chimney. After the last had descended, he slid down the dark hole that led to the castle's bodega, where food and wine were stored. He hid himself behind some cases of wine and watched the women greet each other.

"The witches, for that's what they were, were the wives of his neighbors ¹⁴ and friends, but he at first had trouble recognizing them, for, like his wife, they were all naked. With much merriment, they took the meats and cheeses that hung from the bodega's rafters and laid a table for a feast. They drank the fine wines right from the bottles, like men in a cantina, and danced wildly to eerie music from invisible instruments. They spoke to each other in a language that he did not understand, words that sounded like a cat whose tail has been stepped on. Still, horrible as their speech was, the food they prepared smelled delicious. Cautiously placing himself in the shadows near one of the witches, he extended his hand for a plate. He was given a steaming dish of stewed tongue. Hungrily, he took a bite; it was tasteless. The other witches had apparently noticed the same thing because they sent one of the younger ones to find some salt. But when the young witch came back into the room with a salt shaker in her hand, the man forgot himself and exclaimed, 'Thank God the salt is here.'

"On hearing God's name, all the witches took flight immediately, leaving ¹⁵ the man completely alone in the darkened cellar. He tried the spell for flight that had brought him there, but it did not work. It was no longer midnight, and it was obviously the wrong incantation for going *up* a chimney. He tried all night to get out of the place, which had been left in shambles by the witches, but it was locked up as tight as heaven is to a sinner. Finally, he fell asleep from exhaustion and slept until dawn, when he heard footsteps approaching. When he saw the heavy door being pushed open, he hid himself behind a cask of wine.

"A man in rich clothes walked in, followed by several servants. They ¹⁶ were armed with heavy sticks as if out to kill someone. When the man lit his torch and saw the chaos in the cellar, broken bottles strewn on the floor, meats and cheeses half eaten and tossed everywhere, he cried out in such a rage that the man hiding behind the wine cask closed his eyes and committed his soul to God. The owner of the castle ordered his servants to search the whole bodega, every inch of it, until they discovered how vandals had entered his home. It was a matter of minutes before they discovered the witch's husband, curled up like a stray dog, and—worse—painted the color of a vampire bat, without a stitch of clothing.

"They dragged him to the center of the room and beat him with their sticks 17 until the poor man thought that his bones had been pulverized and he would have to be poured into his grave. When the castle's owner said that he thought the poor wretch had learned his lesson, the servants tossed him naked onto the road. The man was so sore that he slept right there on the public *camino,* oblivious to the stares and insults of all who passed him. When he awakened in the middle of the night and found himself naked, dirty, bloody, and miles from his home, he swore to himself right then and there that he would never, for anything in the world, follow his wife on her nightly journeys again."

"Colorín, colorado." Abuela claps her hands three times, chanting the 18 childhood rhyme for ending a story, *"Este cuento se ha acabado."* She smiles at me, shifting her position on the sofa to be able to watch Grandfather muttering to himself on the porch. I remember those eyes on me when I was a small child. Their movements seemed to be triggered by a child's actions, like those holograms of the Holy Mother that were popular with Catholics a few years ago—you couldn't get away from their mesmerizing gaze.

"Will you tell me about your year in New York, Abuela?" I surprise myself with the question. But suddenly I need to know about Abuela's lost year. It 19 has to be another good story.

She looks intently at me before she answers. Her eyes are my eyes, same 20 dark brown color, almond shape, and the lids that droop a little: called by some "bedroom eyes"; to others they are a sign of a cunning nature. "Why are you looking at me that way?" is a question I am often asked.

"I wanted to leave home," she says calmly, as though she had been expecting the question from me all along. 21

"You mean abandon your family?" I am really taken aback by her words. 22

"Yes, *hija.* That is exactly what I mean. Abandon them. Never to return." 23
"Why?" 24

"I was tired. I was young and pretty, full of energy and dreams." She 25 smiles as Grandfather breaks into song standing by himself on the porch. A woman passing by with a baby in her arms waves at him. Grandfather sings louder, something about a man going to his exile because the woman he loves has rejected him. He finishes the song on a long note and continues to stand in the middle of the tiled porch as if listening for applause. He bows.

Abuela shakes her head, smiling a little, as if amused by his antics, then 26 she finishes her sentence. "Restless, bored. Four children and a husband all demanding more and more from me."

"So you left the children with your sister and went to New York?" I say, 27 trying to keep the mixed emotions I was feeling out of my voice. I look at the serene old woman in front of me and cannot believe that she once left four children and a loving husband to go live alone in a faraway country.

"I had left him once before, but he found me. I came back home, but on the condition that he never follow me anywhere again. I told him the next time I would not return." She is silent, apparently falling deep into thought. 28

"You were never really sick," I say, though I am afraid that she will not resume her story. But I want to know more about this woman whose life I thought was an open book. 29

"I *was* sick. Sick at heart. And he knew it," she says, keeping her eyes on Grandfather, who is standing as still as a marble statue on the porch. He seems to be listening intently for something. 30

"The year in New York was his idea. He saw how unhappy I was. He knew I needed to taste freedom. He paid my sister Delia to come take care of the children. He also sublet her apartment for me, though he had to take a second job to do it. He gave me money and told me to go." 31

"What did you do that year in New York?" I am both stunned and fascinated by Abuela's revelation. 32

"I worked as a seamstress in a fancy dress shop. And. . . . *y pues, hija*"— she smiles at me as if I should know something without being told—"I lived." 33

Why did you come back?" I ask. 34

"Because I love him," she says, "and I missed my children." 35

He is scratching at the door. Like a small child he has traced the sound of Abuela's voice back to her. She lets him in, guiding him gently by the hand. Then she eases him down on his favorite rocking chair. He begins to nod; soon he will be sound asleep, comforted by her proximity, secure in his familiar surroundings. I wonder how long it will take him to revert to infantilism. The doctors say he is physically healthy and may live for many years, but his memory, verbal skills, and ability to control his biological functions will deteriorate rapidly. He may end his days bedridden, perhaps comatose. My eyes fill with tears as I look at the lined face of this beautiful and gentle old man. I am in awe of the generosity of spirit that allowed him to give a year of freedom to the woman he loved, not knowing whether she would ever return to him. Abuela has seen my tears and moves over on the sofa to sit near me. She slips an arm around my waist and pulls me close. She kisses my wet cheek. Then she whispers softly into my ear, "And in time, the husband either began forgetting that he had seen her turn into a witch, or believed that he had just dreamed it." She takes my face into her hands. "I am going to take care of your grandfather until one of us dies. I promised him when I came back that I would never leave home again unless he asked me to: he never did. He never asked any questions." 36

I hear my mother's car pull up into the driveway. She will wait there for me. I will have to admit that I failed in my mission. I will argue Abuela's case without revealing her secret. As far as everyone is concerned she went away to recover from problems with her heart. That part is true in both versions of the story. 37

At the door she gives me the traditional blessing, adding with a wink, *"Colorín, colorado."* My grandfather, hearing her voice, smiles in his sleep. 38

Meaning and Idea

1. Why has Cofer come to Puerto Rico in the first place? Is she surprised when she realizes that instead of convincing her grandmother of something, she herself has become convinced of something? How do you know?

2. Does the grandmother know the granddaughter's topic before she even begins to talk? How do you know? What is the significance of the story of the witch? Does the grandmother know that the story about the witch's husband will be so timely? Why do you think so?

3. This essay contains several narratives. Summarize them briefly. How do they all serve the same purpose or relate to the same theme?

Language, Form, Structure

1. Throughout the beginning of the essay, the writer moves easily between memories of the setting, tales and history regarding her grandmother, the grandfather's state, and the two women moving about the house and then beginning their conversation. How does this flow of subjects affect the reader? What linguistic or rhetorical strategies does Cofer use to help the reader? For example, comment on her use of transitions, thesis statement, and sensory detail.

2. What is the effect of using Spanish words the way Cofer does? Find and define as many of them as you can. Suppose Cofer used only the English equivalents of these words. How would they affect the theme and the atmosphere of the selection?

3. Define the following words: dementia; obstinacy; martyr; tantrum; cauldron; incantation; shambles; oblivious; holograms; mesmerizing; serene; revelation; proximity.

Ideas for Writing

1. Write an essay in which you narrate a story that someone told to you—a family member, a friend, someone you hold dear. Be sure to describe the setting fully, along with the situation in which the person related the tale. Thus, you will be telling two stories: the story that the person told you *and* the story of the person's telling you the story.

2. Write an essay in which you argue for or against young family members assuming responsibility for the care of older relatives.

3. Reread Cofer's essay and write an essay about what she calls the "martyr complex." Use examples you know of or have personally experienced to explain the existence or nonexistence of the martyr complex among women.

The Chimney Sweeper

William Blake

By trade, William Blake (1757–1827) was a painter and an engraver. Yet he was also an eccentric poet; much of his poetry derives from mystical visions and communications which he trusted as much as—or more than—his conscious reality. The "romantic school" shunned him because of his mysticism and abstruseness, and his poetry was all but ignored in his time. Today, however, we count his two major collections of poetry, *Songs of Innocence* (1789) and *Songs of Experience* (1794), among the most lyrical, profound delvings into human existence.

Collected in Blake's second major volume, *Songs of Experience,* "The Chimney Sweeper" is indicative of the poet's indignation at society's treatment of poor and homeless children. Blake's concerns, in general, are with social evils, and these concerns pervade the whole collection.

When my mother died I was very young,
And my father sold me while yet my tongue
Could scarcely cry " 'weep! 'weep! 'weep! 'weep!"
So your chimneys I sweep, and in soot I sleep.

There's little Tom Dacre, who cried when his head,   5
That curled like a lamb's back, was shaved; so I said,
"Hush, Tom! never mind it, for, when your head's bare,
You know that the soot cannot spoil your white hair."

And so he was quiet, and that very night,
As Tom was sleeping, he had such a sight!   10
That thousands of sweepers, Dick, Joe, Ned, and Jack,
Were all of them locked up in coffins of black.

And by came an Angel who had a bright key,
And he opened the coffins and set them all free;
Then down a green plain leaping, laughing, they run,   15
And wash in a river, and shine in the sun.

Then naked and white, all their bags left behind,
They rise upon clouds and sport in the wind;
And the Angel told Tom, if he'd be a good boy,
He'd have God for his father, and never want joy.   20

And so Tom awoke, and we rose in the dark,
And got with our bags and our brushes to work.
Though the morning was cold, Tom was happy and warm;
So if all do their duty they need not fear harm.

Meaning and Idea

1. What do you know about the boy who narrates this poem? What can you discern about his character and his attitude toward life?

2. What is the "sight" of line 10?

3. Summarize the boy's dream (lines 11–20) in your own words.

Language, Form, Structure

1. *Dramatic irony* is the difference between what a narrator says and what the writer intends or knows. How is this poem an example of dramatic irony? How do you interpret the boy's dream? If a *symbol* is something that is both what it is and something else with a larger, more important meaning, how may the dream be viewed as *symbolic?*

2. What is the effect of the repetition of *weep* in line 3?

3. How does Blake use images of lightness and darkness to heighten the drama of this poem?

Ideas for Writing

1. Write a narrative of how a recent dream led you to some resolution of a difficult situation. Be sure to narrate the dream as well.

2. Write an essay about child labor. Should young children be allowed to work? Support your argument with solid details.

3. This poem comes from Blake's *Songs of Experience.* Write a paragraph or two that tell in what ways you might consider this poem a "song." Draw specific examples from "The Chimney Sweeper" to support your point.

Araby

James Joyce

Deservedly considered the writer who forever changed the face of modern fiction, James Joyce (1882–1942) was born into a middle-class family in Dublin, Ireland. Educated at Jesuit boarding schools and later at University College, Dublin, Joyce soon divorced himself physically (though not emotionally) from Irish nationalism and Irish Catholicism. He spent almost all his postcollege years outside Ireland, living and working in such places as Paris, Zurich, and Trieste. His works, some of which are marked by such radical experiments in form and content as "stream of consciousness" narration, include the eloquent *Dubliners* (1914), the semiautobiographical *A Portrait of the Artist as a Young Man* (1916), the monumental *Ulysses* (1922), and the extraordinary (if a little abstruse) *Finnegan's Wake* (1939). Unfortunately, Joyce's creative genius was not justly recognized until after his death.

"Araby" is one of the 15 literary gems that compose Joyce's collection of short stories, *Dubliners,* written between 1904 and 1907. Although some readers may be awed by the creative ambiguities of Joyce's other works, *Dubliners,* his early fiction, is easily accessible. In "Araby" he tells the story of a young man overcome by his confusion of love and infatuation, imagination and reality, freedom and commitment.

*N*orth Richmond Street, being blind, was a quaint street except at the hour when the Christian Brothers School set the boys free. An uninhabited house of two storeys stood at the blind end, detached from its neighbours in a square ground. The other houses of the street, conscious of decent lives within them, gazed at one another with brown imperturbable faces. 1

The former tenant of our house, a priest, had died in the back drawing-room. Air, musty from having been long enclosed, hung in all the rooms, and the waste room behind the kitchen was littered with old useless papers. Among these I found a few paper-covered books, the pages of which were curled and damp: *The Abbott,* by Walter Scott, *The Devout Communicant* and *The Memoirs of Vidocq.* I liked the last best because its leaves were yellow. The wild garden behind the house contained a central apple-tree and a few straggling bushes under one of which I found the late tenant's rusty bicycle-pump. He had been a very charitable priest; in his will he had left all his money to institutions and the furniture of his house to his sister. 2

When the short days of winter came dusk fell before we had well eaten our dinners. When we met in the street the houses had grown sombre. The space of sky above us was the colour of ever-changing violet and towards it the lamps of the street lifted their feeble lanterns. The cold air stung us and we played till our bodies glowed. Our shouts echoed in the silent street. The career of our play brought us through the dark muddy lanes behind the houses where 3 we ran the gauntlet of the rough tribes from the cottages, to the back doors of the dark dripping gardens where odours arose from the ashpits, to the dark odorous stables where a coachman smoothed and combed the horse or shook music from the buckled harness. When we returned to the street light from the kitchen windows had filled the areas. If my uncle was seen turning the corner we hid in the shadow until we had seen him safely housed. Or if Mangan's sister came out on the doorstep to call her brother in to his tea we watched her from our shadow peer up and down the street. We waited to see whether she would remain or go in and, if she remained, we left our shadow and walked up to Mangan's steps resignedly. She was waiting for us, her figure defined by the light from the half-opened door. Her brother always teased her before he obeyed and I stood by the railings looking at her. Her dress swung as she moved her body and the soft rope of her hair tossed from side to side.

Every morning I lay on the floor in the front parlour watching her door. 4 The blind was pulled down to within an inch of the sash so that I could not be seen. When she came out on the doorstep my heart leaped. I ran to the hall, seized my books and followed her. I kept her brown figure always in my eye and, when we came near the point at which our ways diverged, I quickened my pace and passed her. This happened morning after morning. I had never spoken to her, except for a few casual words, and yet her name was like a summons to all my foolish blood.

Her image accompanied me even in places the most hostile to romance. On 5 Saturday evenings when my aunt went marketing I had to go to carry some of the parcels. We walked through the flaring streets, jostled by drunken men and bargaining women, amid the curses of labourers, the shrill litanies of shop-boys who stood on guard by the barrels of pigs' cheeks, the nasal chanting of street-singers, who sang a *come-all-you* about O'Donovan Rossa, or a ballad about the troubles in our native land. These noises converged in a single sensation of life for me: I imagined that I bore my chalice safely through a throng of foes. Her name sprang to my lips at moments in strange prayers and praises which I myself did not understand. My eyes were often full of tears (I could not tell why) and at times a flood from my heart seemed to pour itself out into my bosom. I thought little of the future. I did not know whether I would ever speak to her or not or, if I spoke to her, how I could tell her of my confused adoration. But my body was like a harp and her words and gestures were like fingers running upon the wires.

One evening I went into the back drawing-room in which the priest had 6 died. It was a dark rainy evening and there was no sound in the house. Through one of the broken panes I heard the rain impinge upon the earth, the fine incessant needles of water playing in the sodden beds. Some distant lamp or lighted window gleamed below me. I was thankful that I could see so little. All my senses seemed to desire to veil themselves and, feeling that I was about to slip from them, I pressed the palms of my hands together until they trembled, murmuring: *"O love! O love!"* many times.

At last she spoke to me. When she addressed the first words to me I was 7 so confused that I did not know what to answer. She asked me was I going to

Araby. I forgot whether I answered yes or no. It would be a splendid bazaar, she said she would love to go.

"And why can't you?" I asked. 8

While she spoke she turned a silver bracelet round and round her wrist. 9 She could not go, she said, because there would be a retreat that week in her convent. Her brother and two other boys were fighting for their caps and I was alone at the railings. She held one of the spikes, bowing her head towards me. The light from the lamp opposite our door caught the white curve of her neck, lit up her hair that rested there and, falling, lit up the hand upon the railing. It fell over one side of her dress and caught the white border of a petticoat, just visible as she stood at ease.

"It's well for you," she said. 10

"If I go," I said, "I will bring you something." 11

What innumerable follies laid waste my waking and sleeping thoughts 12 after that evening! I wished to annihilate the tedious intervening days. I chafed against the work of school. At night in my bedroom and by day in the classroom her image came between me and the page I strove to read. The syllables of the word *Araby* were called to me through the silence in which my soul luxuriated and cast an Eastern enchantment over me. I asked for leave to go to the bazaar on Saturday night. My aunt was surprised and hoped it was not some Freemason affair. I answered few questions in class. I watched my master's face pass from amiability to sternness; he hoped I was not beginning to idle. I could not call my wandering thoughts together. I had hardly any patience with the serious work of life which, now that it stood between me and my desire, seemed to me child's play, ugly monotonous child's play.

On Saturday morning I reminded my uncle that I wished to go to the 13 bazaar in the evening. He was fussing at the hallstand, looking for the hat-brush, and answered me curtly:

"Yes, boy, I know." 14

As he was in the hall I could not go into the front parlour and lie at the 15 window. I left the house in bad humour and walked slowly towards the school. The air was pitilessly raw and already my heart misgave me.

When I came home to dinner my uncle had not yet been home. Still it was 16 early. I sat staring at the clock for some time and, when its ticking began to irritate me, I left the room. I mounted the staircase and gained the upper part of the house. The high cold empty gloomy rooms liberated me and I went from room to room singing. From the front window I saw my companions playing below in the street. Their cries reached me weakened and indistinct and, leaning my forehead against the cool glass, I looked over at the dark house where she lived. I may have stood there for an hour, seeing nothing but the brown-clad figure cast by my imagination, touched discreetly by the lamplight at the curved neck, at the hand upon the railings and at the border below the dress.

When I came downstairs again I found Mrs. Mercer sitting at the fire. She 17 was an old garrulous woman, a pawnbroker's widow, who collected used stamps for some pious purpose. I had to endure the gossip of the tea-table. The meal was prolonged beyond an hour and still my uncle did not come. Mrs. Mercer stood up to go: she was sorry she couldn't wait any longer, but it was after eight o'clock and she did not like to be out late, as the night air was bad for her. When she had gone I began to walk up and down the room, clenching my fists. My aunt said:

"I'm afraid you may put off your bazaar for this night of Our Lord."   18

At nine o'clock I heard my uncle's latchkey in the halldoor. I heard him   19 talking to himself and heard the hallstand rocking when it had received the weight of his overcoat. I could interpret these signs. When he was midway through his dinner I asked him to give me the money to go to the bazaar. He had forgotten.

"The people are in bed and after their first sleep now," he said.   20

I did not smile. My aunt said to him energetically: 21

"Can't you give him the money and let him go? You've kept him late   22 enough as it is."

My uncle said he was very sorry he had forgotten. He said he believed in   23 the old saying: "All work and no play makes Jack a dull boy." He asked me where I was going and, when I had told him a second time he asked me did I know *The Arab's Farewell to his Steed.* When I left the kitchen he was about to recite the opening lines of the piece to my aunt.

I held a florin tightly in my hand as I strode down Buckingham Street to-   24 wards the station. The sight of the streets thronged with buyers and glaring with gas recalled to me the purpose of my journey. I took my seat in a third-class carriage of a deserted train. After an intolerable delay the train moved out of the station slowly. It crept onward among ruinous houses and over the twinkling river. At Westland Row Station a crowd of people pressed to the carriage doors; but the porters moved them back, saying that it was a special train for the bazaar. I remained alone in the bare carriage. In a few minutes the train drew up beside an improvised wooden platform. I passed out on the road and saw by the lighted dial of a clock that it was ten minutes to ten. In front of me was a large building which displayed the magical name.

I could not find any sixpenny entrance and, fearing that the bazaar would   25 be closed, I passed in quickly through a turnstile, handing a shilling to a weary-looking man. I found myself in a big hall girdled at half its height by a gallery. Nearly all the stalls were closed and the greater part of the hall was in darkness. I recognised a silence like that which pervades a church after a service. I walked into the centre of the bazaar timidly. A few people were gathered about the stalls which were still open. Before a curtain, over which the words *Café Chantant* were written in coloured lamps, two men were counting money on a salver. I listened to the fall of the coins.

Remembering with difficulty why I had come I went over to one of the   26 stalls and examined porcelain vases and flowered tea-sets. At the door of the stall a young lady was talking and laughing with two young gentlemen. I remarked their English accents and listened vaguely to their conversation.

"O, I never said such a thing!"   27

"O, but you did!"   28

"O, but I didn't!"   29

"Didn't she say that?"   30

"Yes. I heard her."   31

"O, there's a . . . fib!"   32

Observing me the young lady came over and asked me did I wish to buy   33
anything. The tone of her voice was not encouraging; she seemed to have spoken to me out of a sense of duty. I looked humbly at the great jars that stood like
eastern guards at either side of the dark entrance to the stall and murmured:

"No, thank you."   34

The young lady changed the position of one of the vases and went back to   35
the two young men. They began to talk of the same subject. Once or twice the
young lady glanced at me over her shoulder.

I lingered before her stall, though I knew my stay was useless, to make my   36
interest in her wares seem the more real. Then I turned away slowly and walked
down the middle of the bazaar. I allowed the two pennies to fall against the sixpence in my pocket. I heard a voice call from one end of the gallery that the light
was out. The upper part of the hall was now completely dark.

Gazing up into the darkness I saw myself as a creature driven and derided   37
by vanity; and my eyes burned with anguish and anger.

Meaning and Idea

1. Describe the environment in which the narrator lives. What does he find
   special about it? What is the significance of the details he chooses to
   emphasize, especially in the opening paragraphs?

2. What are the narrator's feelings toward Mangan's sister? On what are they
   based? What image of her does his imagination create? How close is it to
   her reality? Why is she always referred to as "Mangan's sister" rather than
   by her own name?

3. Is Mangan's sister older or younger than the narrator? How do you know?

4. What promise does the narrator make to Mangan's sister? Does he keep it?
   Why? Describe what happens. What do you think will be the consequences
   to the narrator?

5. How old do you think the narrator is when he is telling this story? How can
   you tell?

Language, Form, Structure

1. Personification is a figurative technique that attributes human feelings or
   characteristics to inanimate objects. How does Joyce use personification in
   the beginning paragraphs of the story? How does it bear on the narrator's
   character and choices?

2. Trace the uses of color imagery in the story. What are the predominant colors? How do they help set the tone of the story? What is the special significance of the colors used to describe Mangan's sister?

3. Joyce wrote of his stories as having "moments of epiphany"—that is, sudden, great realizations that change the course of the protagonist's actions. What is the "moment of epiphany" in this story? How is it foreshadowed? Imagine this story without its special moment. What does the moment of epiphany contribute to the story as a whole?

4. What is the theme of this story? How does the title support the theme?

5. Select 10 words from this story which were unfamiliar to you and use them in sentences of your own.

Ideas for Writing

1. Write a narrative of a moment in which you felt alone, even though you may have been in the midst of a crowd. Concentrate on details of the environment.

2. Should we always keep our promises? Write an essay in which you set out when you believe that a promise is an absolute obligation and when you might safely break it.

3. In *Dubliners,* the book of stories in which "Araby" was collected, Joyce wanted to write about the "paralysis"—or emotional immobilization—of life in Dublin as he knew it. Write a short analysis of this story in relation to the theme of paralysis. Who or what is paralyzed here?

Salvation

Langston Hughes

Langston Hughes (1902–1967) was one of America's foremost poets, essayists, dramatists, and fiction writers; his self-proclaimed desire as a writer was "to explain and illuminate the Negro condition in America." After being elected class poet in grammar school in
Lincoln, Illinois, Hughes first gained adult recognition as a poet when he was a busboy at
a hotel in Washington, D.C. He left some poems by the plate of the poet Vachel Lindsay,
who fortunately recognized his talent.

"Salvation" is a selection from Hughes's autobiography, *The Big Sea* (1940). In it, he tells
of his "conversion" to Christ in the midst of peer and community pressure. The narrative
informs us of young Hughes's difficult situation, his fanciful reaction to it, and both the
short- and long-term effects of his actions.

I was saved from sin when I was going on thirteen. But not really   1
saved. It happened like this. There was a big revival at my Auntie Reed's
church. Every night for weeks there had been much preaching, singing, praying,
and shouting, and some very hardened sinners had been brought to Christ, and
the membership of the church had grown by leaps and bounds. Then just before
the revival ended, they held a special meeting for children, "to bring the young
lambs to the fold." My aunt spoke of it for days ahead. That night I was escorted
to the front row and placed on the mourners' bench with all the other young sinners, who had not yet been brought to Jesus.

My aunt told me that when you were saved you saw a light, and something   2
happened to you inside! And Jesus came into your life! And God was with you
from then on! She said you could see and hear and feel Jesus in your soul. I believed her. I had heard a great many old people say the same thing and it seemed
to me they ought to know. So I sat there calmly in the hot, crowded church,
waiting for Jesus to come to me.

The preacher preached a wonderful rhythmical sermon, all moans and   3
shouts and lonely cries and dire pictures of hell, and then he sang a song about
the ninety and nine safe in the fold, but one little lamb was left out in the cold.
Then he said: "Won't you come? Won't you come to Jesus? Young lambs,
won't you come?" And he held out his arms to all us young sinners there on the
mourners' bench. And the little girls cried. And some of them jumped up and
went to Jesus right away. But most of us just sat there.

A great many old people came and knelt around us and prayed, old women   4
with jet-black faces and braided hair, old men with work-gnarled hands. And the
church sang a song about the lower lights are burning, some poor sinners to be
saved. And the whole building rocked with prayer and song.

Still I kept waiting to *see* Jesus.   5

Finally all the young people had gone to the altar and were saved, but one   6
boy and me. He was a rounder's son named Westley. Westley and I were surrounded by sisters and deacons praying. It was very hot in the church, and getting late now. Finally Westley said to me in a whisper: "God damn! I'm tired o'
sitting here. Let's get up and be saved." So he got up and was saved.

Then I was left all alone on the mourners' bench. My aunt came and knelt   7
at my knees and cried, while prayers and songs swirled all around me in the little
church. The whole congregation prayed for me alone, in a mighty wail of moans
and voices. And I kept waiting serenely for Jesus, waiting, waiting—but he did-
n't come. I wanted to see him, but nothing happened to me. Nothing! I wanted
something to happen to me, but nothing happened.

I heard the songs and the minister saying: "Why don't you come? My dear   8
child, why don't you come to Jesus? Jesus is waiting for you. He wants you.
Why don't you come? Sister Reed, what is this child's name?"

"Langston," my aunt sobbed.   9

"Langston, why don't you come? Why don't you come and be saved? Oh,   10
Lamb of God! Why don't you come?"

Now it was really getting late. I began to be ashamed of myself, holding   11
everything up so long. I began to wonder what God thought about Westley, who
certainly hadn't seen Jesus either, but who was now sitting proudly on the platform, swinging his knickerbockered legs and grinning down at me, surrounded
by deacons and old women on their knees praying. God had not struck Westley
dead for taking his name in vain or for lying in the temple. So I decided that
maybe to save further trouble, I'd better lie, too, and say that Jesus had come,
and get up and be saved.

So I got up.   12

Suddenly the whole room broke into a sea of shouting, as they saw me rise.   13
Waves of rejoicing swept the place. Women leaped in the air. My aunt threw her
arms around me. The minister took me by the hand and led me to the platform.

When things quieted down, in a hushed silence, punctuated by a few ec-   14
static "Amens," all the new young lambs were blessed in the name of God. Then
joyous singing filled the room.

That night, for the last time in my life but one—for I was a big boy twelve   15
years old—I cried. I cried, in bed alone, and couldn't stop. I buried by head under
the quilts, but my aunt heard me. She woke up and told my uncle I was crying because the Holy Ghost had come into my life, and because I had seen Jesus. But I
was really crying because I couldn't bear to tell her that I had lied, that I had deceived everybody in the church, that I hadn't seen Jesus, and that now I didn't believe there was a Jesus anymore, since he didn't come to help me.

Meaning and Idea

1. In your own words, describe the atmosphere of the revival meeting. What was its purpose?

2. Who are the "lambs" to be saved?

3. Who is most concerned about Langston's "salvation"? Why? Do you think they are sincere?

4. Why does Westley get "saved"? Why does Langston decide to be saved, too?

5. What are the immediate consequences of Langston's actions? What are the long-term consequences?

Language, Form, Structure

1. How do the first two sentences serve as a thesis for this essay? What conflict do they present which must be resolved within the narrative?

2. About midway through the essay, what *allusion* (see page 49) helps place the time period of this narrative? Approximately what time period is it?

3. What is the value of *dialogue* in this selection? Where is it used most effectively? How would paragraph 6, for example, be different if Hughes had omitted Westley's line of dialogue?

4. How is sound imagery used in this essay? Where is it used most vibrantly?

5. How does Hughes slightly change the time frame of the essay in the last sentence?

6. Check the dictionary meanings for the following words: dire; gnarled; rounder; deacons. Use each word in an original sentence.

Ideas for Writing

1. Tell about a time when you told a lie. Be sure to set the situation, tell about the actual event of the lie, and discuss the consequences.

2. Write an essay in which you argue for or against the value of religious experience in our lives.

3. What do you consider the most effective prose narrative techniques in this essay? You might consider, for example, language, sentence structure, temporal sequencing, characterization, or dialogue. In a paragraph or two, explain your choice by analyzing examples from the text.

The Tell-Tale Heart

Edgar Allan Poe

Edgar Allan Poe (1809–1849) was born in Boston. After his mother died when he was only two years old, he was adopted by John Allan of Richmond, Virginia. Poe eventually returned to Boston, then made homes in New York and Baltimore. Known mostly for his macabre and tormented stories and poems, Poe was also a literary critic of some merit. In fact, in one critical essay, he set down guidelines for the writing of the short story which are still relevant well over a hundred years later. In 1835, Poe became editor of the *Southern Literary Messenger* and for much of his life held similar editorial positions. However, his life was beset with difficulties and tragedies: poverty; the illness and death of his 13-year-old bride; bitter personal battles; his own physical and mental dissolution. Poe was found unconscious in a gutter in Baltimore in 1849, where he died soon afterward.

First published in the January 1843 edition of *The Pioneer,* "The Tell-Tale Heart" is Poe's classic gothic horror tale. Colored by the obviously deranged mind of its narrator, this story is a good example of an interior dramatic monologue, in which one character speaks to himself alone.

*T*rue!—nervous—very, very dreadfully nervous I had been and am; but why *will* you say that I am mad? The disease had sharpened my senses—not destroyed—not dulled them. Above all was the sense of hearing acute. I heard all things in the heaven and in the earth. I heard many things in hell. How, then, am I mad? Hearken! and observe how healthily—how calmly I can tell you the whole story.

It is impossible to say how first the idea entered my brain; but once conceived, it haunted me day and night. Object there was none. Passion there was none. I loved the old man. He had never wronged me. He had never given me insult. For his gold I had no desire. I think it was his eye! yes, it was this! One of his eyes resembled that of a vulture—a pale blue eye, with a film over it. Whenever it fell upon me, my blood ran cold; and so by degrees—very gradually—I made up my mind to take the life of the old man, and thus rid myself of the eye for ever.

Now this is the point. You fancy me mad. Madmen know nothing. But you should have seen *me.* You should have seen how wisely I proceeded—with what caution—with what foresight—with what dissimulation I went to work! I was never kinder to the old man than during the whole week before I killed him. And every night, about midnight, I turned the latch of his door and opened it—oh, so gently! And then, when I had made an opening sufficient for my head, I put in a dark lantern, all closed, closed, so that no light shone out, and then I thrust in my head. Oh, you would have laughed to see how cunningly I thrust it in! I moved it slowly—very, very slowly, so that I might not disturb the old man's sleep. It took me an hour to place my whole head within the opening so far that I could see him as he lay upon his bed. Ha!—would a madman have been so wise as this? And then, when my head was well in the room, I undid the lantern cautiously—oh, so cautiously—cautiously (for the hinges creaked)—I undid it just so much that a single thin ray fell upon the vulture eye. And this I did for seven long nights—every night just at midnight—but I found the eye always closed; and so it was impossible to do the work; for it was not the old man who vexed me, but his Evil Eye. And every morning, when the day broke, I went boldly into the chamber, and spoke courageously to him, calling him by name in a hearty tone, and inquiring how he had passed the night. So you see he would have been a very profound old man, indeed, to suspect that every night, just at twelve, I looked in upon him while he slept.

Upon the eighth night I was more than usually cautious in opening the door. A watch's minute hand moves more quickly than did mine. Never before that night had I *felt* the extent of my own powers—of my sagacity. I could scarcely contain my feelings of triumph. To think that there I was, opening the door, little by little, and he not even to dream of my secret deeds or thoughts. I fairly chuckled at the idea; and perhaps he heard me; for he moved on the bed suddenly, as if startled. Now you may think that I drew back—but no. His room was as black as pitch with the thick darkness (for the shutters were close fastened, through fear of robbers), and so I knew that he could not see the opening of the door, and I kept pushing it on steadily, steadily.

I had my head in, and was about to open the lantern, when my thumb slipped upon the tin fastening, and the old man sprang up in the bed, crying out "Who's there?"

I kept quite still and said nothing. For a whole hour I did not move a muscle, and in the meantime I did not hear him lie down. He was still sitting up in the bed listening;—just as I have done, night after night, hearkening to the death watches in the wall.

Presently I heard a slight groan, and I knew it was the groan of mortal terror. It was not a groan of pain or of grief—oh, no!—it was the low stifled sound that arises from the bottom of the soul when overcharged with awe. I knew the sound well. Many a night, just at midnight, when all the world slept, it has welled up from my own bosom, deepening, with its dreadful echo, the terrors that distracted me. I say I knew it well. I knew what the old man felt, and pitied him, although I chuckled at heart. I knew that he had been lying awake ever since the first slight noise, when he had turned in the bed. His fears had been ever since growing upon him. He had been trying to fancy them causeless, but could not. He had been saying to himself—"It is nothing but the wind in the chimney—it is only a mouse crossing the floor," or "it is merely a cricket which has made a single chirp." Yes, he has been trying to comfort himself with these suppositions; but he had found all in vain. *All in vain;* because Death, in approaching him, had stalked with his black shadow before him, and enveloped the victim. And it was the mournful influence of the unperceived shadow that caused him to feel—although he neither saw nor heard—to *feel* the presence of my head within the room.

When I had waited a long time, very patiently, without hearing him lie down, I resolved to open a little—a very, very little crevice in the lantern. So I opened it— you cannot imagine how stealthily, stealthily, until, at length, a single dim ray, like the thread of a spider, shot from out the crevice and full upon the vulture eye.

It was open—wide, wide open—and I grew furious as I gazed upon it. I saw it with perfect distinctness—all a dull blue, with a hideous veil over it that chilled the very marrow in my bones; but I could see nothing else of the old man's face or person: for I had directed the ray as if by instinct, precisely upon the damned spot.

And now have I not told you that what you mistake for madness is but over-acuteness of the senses?—now, I say, there came to my ears a low, dull, quick sound, such as a watch makes when enveloped in cotton. I knew *that* sound well too. It was the beating of the old man's heart. It increased my fury, as the beating of a drum stimulates the soldier into courage.

But even yet I refrained and kept still. I scarcely breathed. I held the lantern motionless. I tried how steadily I could maintain the ray upon the eye. Meantime the hellish tattoo of the heart increased. It grew quicker and quicker, and louder and louder every instant. The old man's terror *must* have been extreme! It grew louder, I say, louder every moment!—do you mark me well? I have told you that I am nervous: so I am. And now at the dead hour of the night, amid the dreadful silence of that old house, so strange a noise as this excited me to uncontrollable terror. Yet, for some minutes longer I refrained and stood still. But the beating grew louder, louder! I thought the heart must burst. And now a new anxiety seized me—the sound would be heard by a neighbor! The old man's hour had come! With a loud yell, I threw open the lantern and leaped into the room. He shrieked once—once only. In an instant I dragged him to the floor, and pulled the heavy bed over him. I then smiled gaily, to find the deed so far done. But, for many minutes, the heart beat on with a muffled sound. This, however, did not vex me; it would not be heard through the wall. At length it ceased. The old man was dead. I removed the bed and examined the corpse. Yes, he was stone, stone dead. I placed my hand upon the heart and held it there many minutes. There was no pulsation. He was stone dead. His eye would trouble me no more.

If still you think me mad, you will think so no longer when I describe the wise precautions I took for the concealment of the body. The night waned and I worked hastily, but in silence. First of all I dismembered the corpse. I cut off the head and the arms and the legs.

I then took up three planks from the flooring of the chamber, and deposited all between the scantlings. I then replaced the boards so cleverly, so cunningly, that no human eye—not even *his*—could have detected any thing wrong. There was nothing to wash out—no stain of any kind—no blood-spot whatever. I had been too wary for that. A tub had caught all—ha! ha!

When I had made an end of these labors, it was four o'clock—still dark as midnight. As the bell sounded the hour, there came a knocking at the street door. I went down to open it with a light heart,—for what had I *now* to fear? There entered three men, who introduced themselves, with perfect suavity, as officers of the police. A shriek had been heard by a neighbor during the night; suspicion of foul play had been aroused; information had been lodged at the police office, and they (the officers) had been deputed to search the premises.

I smiled,—for *what* had I to fear? I bade the gentlemen welcome. The shriek, I said, was my own in a dream. The old man, I mentioned, was absent in the country. I took my visitors all over the house. I bade them search—search *well.* I led them, at length, to *his* chamber. I showed them his treasures, secure, undisturbed. In the enthusiasm of my confidence, I brought chairs into the room, and desired them *here* to rest from their fatigues, while I myself, in the wild audacity of my perfect triumph, placed my own seat upon the very spot beneath which reposed the corpse of the victim.

The officers were satisfied. My *manner* had convinced them. I was singularly at ease. They sat, and while I answered cheerily, they chatted familiar things. But, ere long, I felt myself getting pale and wished them gone. My head ached, and I fancied a ringing in my ears: but still they sat and still they chatted. The ringing became more distinct:—it continued and became more distinct: I talked more freely to get rid of the feeling: but it continued and gained definitiveness—until, at length, I found that the noise was *not* within my ears.

No doubt I now grew *very* pale;—but I talked more fluently, and with a heightened voice. Yet the sound increased—and what could I do? It was *a low, dull, quick sound—much such a sound as a watch makes when enveloped in cotton.* I gasped for breath—and yet the officers heard it not. I talked more quickly—more vehemently; but the noise steadily increased. I arose and argued about trifles, in a high key and with violent gesticulations, but the noise steadily increased. Why *would* they not be gone? I paced the floor to and fro with heavy strides, as if excited to fury by the observation of the men—but the noise steadily increased. Oh God! what *could* I do? I foamed—I raved—I swore! I swung the chair upon which I had been sitting, and grated it upon the boards, but the noise arose over all and continually increased. It grew louder—louder—*louder!* And still the men chatted pleasantly, and smiled. Was it possible they heard not? Almighty God!—no, no! They heard!—they suspected!—they *knew!*—they were making a mockery of my horror!—this I thought, and this I think. But any thing was better than this agony! Any thing was more tolerable than this derision! I could bear those hypocritical smiles no longer! I felt that I must scream or die!—and now—again!—hark! louder! louder! louder! *louder!*—

"Villains!" I shrieked, "dissemble no more! I admit the deed!—tear up the planks!—here, here!—it is the beating of his hideous heart!"

Meaning and Idea

1. If not madness, what does the narrator claim is the effect of his disease? Does he try to convince the reader that he is not mad?

2. Throughout the story, the narrator claims to know well the old man's feelings. How can the narrator actually know those feelings?

3. How does the narrator explain the shriek that brought the police to the house? How does he deal with the police?

4. Given the events as related by the narrator, could he indeed still be haunted by the heart beating? Why? How does this assertion influence one's belief in the rest of the story?

5. In the last paragraph, the narrator describes his actions at trying to drown out the noise of the heart. What does he do? If these actions were true, would the three men still have "chatted pleasantly"? What do you suspect was the truth of the incident? Why?

Language, Form, Structure

1. This story is an example of the *I-narrative* form, or first-person narrative, in which the protagonist tells the events that happen to him and others. Also, this I-narrative is an example of a dramatic monologue. To whom does the narrator address himself? Why?

2. In the first paragraph, the narrator claims, "Above all was the sense of hearing acute." Poe then makes use of numerous auditory images throughout the story. Go through the tale again and list, in order, all the auditory imagery you find. How does this acute sense of hearing eventually cause the narrator's downfall?

3. The narrator's madness causes him to make certain highly ironic statements. Reread the opening three paragraphs, then choose and explain what you consider the most ironic statements.

4. There is a great deal of repetition of words and phrases in this narrative. What is the purpose of these repetitions? What do they indicate about the narrator's emotional state? How do they affect the rhythm of the story?

5. Look up the meanings of the following words: acute; sagacity; stealthily; hideous; vex; waned; suavity; audacity; trifles; gesticulations. Then use each of these words in a sentence of your own.

Ideas for Writing

1. Make up a horror story of your own and narrate it through an unreliable first-person narrator. Try to make it as dramatic as possible.

2. The narrator disputes the charge of madness made against him. How would you define the term? Write an essay in which you set out the characteristics of madness.

3. Write an essay in which you analyze the narrator of "A Tell-Tale Heart." Unlike a third-person narrative where the reader can generally trust the narrator without reservations, in any I-narrative the reader must apply certain tests to the narrator's reliability. For example, we must ascertain

whether the narrator is crazy, drunk, in a heightened emotional state, a habitual liar, and so on. Clearly, the I-narrator in this story is *un*reliable. In that case, what information *can* you obtain from this story? Why would Poe choose to write in this motif? Do you believe any of the story? Which part? Why? What do you suppose *is* the true story here?

In what other stories or books have you questioned the narrator's veracity? How did they compare with this story?

On the Rez

Ian Frazier

Ian Frazier was born in Cleveland in 1951 and now lives in Brooklyn, New York. Frazier came to public attention for the short, satirical pieces he published as a staff writer for *The New Yorker*. His humor, often ensconced in a well-told story, concentrates on a wide variety of subjects. In 1986 several of these vignettes of rural life and observations on contemporary manners were published as *Dating Your Mom*. The title piece, it may be inferred, advises young men that since they universally cite their mom as the best woman they ever knew, they might as well date her. In 1997 he received the inaugural Thurber Prize for American Humor.

It is Frazier's travels in the American West, however, that inspired his most well-known writing. *Great Plains* (1989) came after seven years of exploring the West. Funny and ironic observations coexist with a sadness that the great vistas of the West are disappearing. This selection is taken from his latest book, *On the Rez*, published in 2000.

*E*very summer Pine Ridge opens out in early August like a road   1
map unfolding, as people begin to arrive for the big tribal powwow. First you
see one motor home with an unfamiliar license plate, then you see three, then
ten. They have lawn chairs strapped to the back or the roof, and they're emblazoned with brand names like Tioga or Itasca or HitchHiker or Wanderer. Suddenly the village seems enlarged—a spread-out encampment rather than a small
town. Here and there cars are pulled off the pavement alongside the road, and
people in shorts and carrying cameras or binoculars are stepping through the
sagebrush in the fields. A pale bunch of teenagers sits on the curb outside Big
Bat's licking ice-cream cones, making a row of white knees. At the cement picnic tables west of town a family of seven—two white-haired oldsters, blond dad,
blond mom, and three blond children—carefully lay out seven places for a picnic lunch. Then they sit, hold hands, and all bow their heads in prayer; their
extra-long motor home has Utah plates.

At Yellow Bird's store, cars wait in line for the gas pumps. At the traffic   2
light downtown there's sometimes a mini-traffic jam. It's loud; with plenty of
partly muffled reservation cars in it, a Pine Ridge traffic jam really throbs. The
loudspeakers at the powwow grounds are now on all the time, even though no
events have begun and workmen are only setting up there. A guy is talking on
the public address system as the spirit moves him, commenting on the goings-
on: "Get that sod laid down good and tight, boys. We wouldn't want any of our
fancy dancers to trip and mess up their two-thousand-dollar fancy-dance cos-
tumes . . . And look who's driving up the road now! It's Charlie-Boy Pourier
with the water-sprinkler truck. Good to see you, Charlie—let's see if you can get
that pesky Pine Ridge dust to lay down . . . . ."

Some early arrivals pitch tents and lay out campsites among the trees just west of the powwow grounds. There are two-man and four-man high-tech nylon tents in luminous shades, and old-fashioned canvas wall tents, and several white canvas tipis with pennants of colored cloth hanging from the ends of the tipi poles. People indicate their campsite boundaries with low fences made of wooden stakes connected by twine or strips of yellow plastic tape bearing the words POLICE LINE DO NOT CROSS. Next to many tents are stacks of freshly split firewood logs. The tent neighborhood grows, and soon acquires at least two sketchy streets with many vehicles parked along them. One morning the big tractor-trailer trucks begin to arrive—first the stock trucks with the steers and bucking horses and bulls for the powwow rodeo, and then the long caravan of carnival attractions and rides. The stock trucks park by the rodeo corrals, where the bawling of the animals echoes all around. The carnival trucks assemble in a bunch at another part of the field, sort of like circled wagons. Skinny, muscle-y, bristly-haired carny guys in sleeveless T-shirts get out of the trucks and stretch and smoke and holler remarks at each other. The carny vehicles include three electric generators the size of small boxcars, each with a thick umbilical of cable coming from it. The carny guys begin plugging cables to other cables to yet more cables, until in about an hour the whole carnival encampment is linked to the generators by a web of wires trailing through the dusty grass.

I generally got my breakfast early at Big Bat's, before the morning crowds showed up. The village had a pleasant feeling of expectancy in the cool, just-after-sunup time. One morning as I was staring out the window at the still-empty street and waiting for my Bat's Special Breakfast (two eggs, sausage patty, hash browns, and toast), I noticed Patty Pourier, Bat's wife, sitting two tables away. When my order number was called, I paused by her table, caught her eye, and asked her, "Do you recognize me?" She stared at me for a moment; then the memory of that day when the propane distributorship almost blew up clicked in her eyes. "I thought you looked familiar—we almost died together!" she said. "It's nice to see you here on earth, at Big Bat's, rather than on a cloud someplace in heaven!"

Sometimes when I stopped at Big Bat's, I was hugged by a young man whom I'll call Germaine. He seemed to spend a lot of time at Big Bat's sitting at a table or standing just outside waiting for people to hug. As near as I could tell, he hugged only out-of-towners. His hug was unstudied and unhesitant, like a child's. He went right to the person he intended to hug as if magnetized, and during the embrace he rubbed his forehead on the other person's. The first time he hugged me he took me by surprise and his head knocked my hat to the floor. When I tried to disengage myself after a moment, he made a wordless noise of protest. The next time he hugged me he said, happily, "Remember me?" and of course I did. Usually we have conversations. He would say, "Where're you from? Are you married? I'm single. Do you have any children? I like you." Then he would hug me again.

I noticed that the other people Germaine hugged responded in different ways. A number of Pine Ridge's visitors during powwow season come from foreign countries, and occasionally these visitors reacted to Germaine's hugs with a stiffness suggesting that hugging was not a big part of their culture back home. Indeed, many of the people he hugged seemed surprised and even a bit frightened, as I had been myself the first time. I could imagine that in their years of dreaming in Berlin or Paris about the Oglala Sioux of the American West they had not expected to be nearly tackled in Pine Ridge by one of them the minute they stepped out of their rented camper van. But I noticed, too, that almost all the people soon understood the gesture's gentle spirit, and went along.

The sound of foreign languages on the streets of Pine Ridge—a not uncommon sound during powwow time—raises this place to a category of its own among mid-American towns. It reminds you that Pine Ridge village is also the capital of a nation, one that receives emissaries from far away. The fascination many German people, for example, have with the Oglala had seemed merely odd to me until I saw German and other foreigners at the powwow. They were excited, all eyes and ears and electronic gadgetry, and they made what surrounded them seem exciting, too. I reflected that the moment in history when white people and Native Americans first discovered each other was so momentous and fateful and even thrilling for each culture that some of us feel compelled to reenact it again and again. Nor was the powwow's mood of curiosity about the Other limited to just the visitors' side. One evening during powwow week I went for a walk along a direct road in an out-of-the-way part of the village, and as I came down into a little hollow I met five or six Oglala boys sitting on bicycles. By accident or on purpose they were in a line across the road, blocking it so that I had to stop. Around the road on both sides midsummer foliage screened out all other sights and sounds; we could have been on any creek-bottom road on the Plains. The boys looked at me with unblinking dark eyes. Then the biggest boy, straddling his bicycle and bumping it back and forth between his knees, said to me, "Where did you come from—Europe?"

Most of the time during the week of the powwow I hung out by myself. Le and Floyd John did not seem to be around. Floyd John had left the reservation for Santa Fe or Colorado, depending on which relative I asked. As for Le, all anyone could tell me was that they hadn't seen him. I stopped by Florence's house a couple of times, but no one was there. As I was driving east of Pine Ridge one afternoon, a car came up behind me and blinked its lights and passed, and then arms from the open windows waved me to pull over. I did, and it was Florence and her son Rex and daughter Flora. Florence was on her way to the Porcupine clinic, so sick she looked green. She said she thought Le might be in White Clay, or he might have gone down to Scottsbluff. She said everybody went to the first night of the powwow and I'd surely run into him there. Flora said it was strange that none of us had even seen him walking along the road. I gave them some gas money and went back to Pine Ridge and took a walk on the mown jogging track in the field behind the old IHS hospital. Suddenly from far away I heard a voice shout, *"Hoka hoy!"* A figure was waving at me from the road. I went over toward it and soon recognized Le.

His hair was messed up and he had bags under his eyes. He shook my   9
hand. He was carrying his cowboy boots under one arm and wearing a new pair
of tassel loafers which he said the Porcupine boys had given him, for reasons he
explained to me but I didn't follow. Then he said, "I've been in jail the last five
days. The judge just let me go half an hour ago. They picked me up Thursday
night driving back from White Clay with my niece Verna Yellow Horse. (She's
my niece, but she's only eleven months younger than I am.) We was drinking in
White Clay, and then we came back in her car, and I was driving, and they
pulled me over for not having my headlights on. I thought I'd hit the dimmer,
but I guess I'd turned the lights all the way off. They pulled me out of the car
and tried to give me a Breathalyzer test, and I told the tribal cop who was arresting me that he was a guppy-faced immigrant punk and I'd kick his ass for him
and put him in the hospital. So they locked me up for drunk and disorderly.
They locked Verna up, too. I had to wait to see a judge for a hearing, and the
jailer told me I'd be in until after powwow. I said to him, 'No way.' So this
morning a judge showed up, and when I went before him he said, 'The famous
Mr. Walks Out!' See, he recognized me from your book. He asked me what I
was doin' in there, and then he gave me a new trial date and let me go. As I left I
said to the jailer, 'I told you so.' They're gonna need the room in the jail during
powwow days, anyway."

Le came with me back to the jogging path and we walked a lap together,   10
splashing up grasshoppers at every step. Le said, "They made this path for the
people who worked up at the hospital. The doctors and nurses used to walk on it
and jog on it for exercise. They was always tryin' to get Indian people to exercise more, for their health and especially so they wouldn't develop diabetes.
They didn't persuade too many people, though, so really the only people you
ever saw out here were doctors and nurses. Then the hospital moved to the other
side of town, and not even doctors came here anymore. We still call this the Path
the Doctors Walk On."

At my car I offered to give him a ride to Oglala, where he'd been heading   11
when he called to me. A mile or two from Pine Ridge we passed two women
walking along the road. "Hey—that's Verna!" Le said. "They must've just let her
out, too." We stopped, and Verna, a heavyset woman with long, tangled hair, got
in. Her friend Kay, who was shorter and fatter and had glasses, followed her.
They both seemed to be pretty drunk. Verna told me her name several times, and
said she had been lucky to be in a cell with Kay, because they were old friends.
She told me her age to the month, corroborating Le's story of the difference in
their ages. She said, "I'm so stiff from sleeping on that hard cement floor!" She
and Le talked in English and in Sioux, apparently comparing notes about their arrest and their appearance before the judge. Verna and Kay got out in Oglala by
the post office. Le waited until they had crossed the road, and then he asked me
for some money. I gave him a five, which he pocketed without comment. I asked
him what he was going to do, and he said, "First I'm going to check my mail, and
then I'm going to hitchhike to Oelrichs and buy a gallon of wine." I said I didn't
want to go to Oelrichs. I asked if he would be at the powwow tomorrow night

and he said yes. We said we'd see each other there. He must've been happy to get out of jail; he smiled broadly and waved as I drove away.

By Wednesday afternoon Pine Ridge was jumping. The rodeo was going on—the "Old Man Events," for cowboys forty-five and older—and the powwow would begin that evening. Wherever you looked, near or in the distance, you saw people, and yet somehow at no single place did they constitute a crowd. Many had dressed up specially for the day's events, even more had not. For a while I just went around checking out what people wore. A group of Oglala veterans who would march in the powwow's grand entry parade stood talking by an olive-drab van with white lettering on its sides listing the names of battles in Vietnam. They had on berets, service patches, medals, and feathers; one guy was in crisp jungle-camouflage fatigues, his trousers bloused below the knee into jungle boots of olive nylon and shined black leather. On this head he wore a black baseball cap with a single eagle feather on a leather thong hanging down behind. As I looked at him he nodded back at me and asked if I was a veteran. One of his companions had a clipboard with a list of names; they needed more guys to march in the parade. I said no, I wasn't, and I half-slunk away.

I saw a young woman in dark-purple jeans, silky black blouse, sunglasses, and silver earrings in the shape of baying coyotes, her straight black hair hanging well below her waist and held by a single tie between her shoulder blades; a young man all in denim from his jeans to his sleeveless vest to his oversize Superfly-style denim cap, on which was pinned a large button that read, "I Like A Good Beer Buzz In The Morning"; limping Indian rodeo riders with their identifying numbers still attached to their backs and orthopedic bandages peeking out from their shirts at the wrist or wrapped around the outside of their blue jeans at the knee; a slim young man in a black T-shirt with white lettering that said, "My Heroes Have Always Killed Cowboys"; a one-armed man in a turquoise T-shirt that said "I'm No Wimp"; old Indian men in light-colored Western dress shirts with string ties and their hair slicked back; old Indian women in flouncy, many-colored Spanish-style skirts with their hair held in combs and piled up high; little girls in buckskin dresses decorated with elk's teeth; a big, long-haired man wearing a blue-and-white head rag, narrow reptilian sunglasses, a loud Hawaiian shirt unbuttoned over his stomach, and a heavy chrome-silver watch chain looped from his belt to his right front jeans pocket; and a curly-haired man with a drink-ravaged face, a beaded belt that said "Bull Plume," a yellow straw cowboy hat, pegged jeans, and pointy-toed cowboy boots cut off below the ankles so they resembled slippers with high heels. Of course, most people had on the unusual shorts-T-shirt-and-sneakers combination of the summer fairgoer, which made the exotic getups look even better.

All the activity—the rodeo, the vehicles and horses, the thousands of strolling feet—stirred up a great dust that rose above the village and hung high in the air. Late in the day as the sun declined, it illuminated the dust and gave the sky a reddish tinge. Pinkish-red light glowed on the western sides of the Pine Ridge water towers. The carnival rides began, and neon tubes in soft shades lit up on the whirling armatures of the Tilt-A-Whirl ride and the Mad Hatter's Tea

Party. The carnival's three electric generators roared. Speakers on the façades of the rides played loud rock-and-roll music, and as I stood at a point with speakers on one side and the generators on the other, I decided there wasn't much difference between the two sounds. At sunset storm clouds appeared in the west, and the sky in that direction turned an ominous yellow, and the wind rose. A man named René Shoulders—he had introduced himself to me earlier in the day, not far from the veterans' van, where he, too, had asked if I was a veteran—saw me looking fearfully at the sky. He told me I shouldn't worry. A tornado had been sighted nearby, he said, but the medicine men had prayed and caused the tornado to veer away.

I went into the powwow grounds, passing through a gate in the chain-link 15 fence that surrounded it. Admission was free; among the acts of former tribal chairman Dick Wilson that really irked people back in the seventies was his decision to charge admission to the tribal sun dance. At the center of the powwow grounds, and at the center of the powwow, is an open space about forty steps across where the dancing competitions and other ceremonies and contests are held. A circular structure, poles supporting a roof, encloses this space. The structure includes a raised booth for announcers and officials, with stairs leading to it. Spectators gather under the structure as if at a theater-in-the-round. Some stand or sit on the ground, but most sit on folding lawn chairs they have brought. The best way to observe a powwow is from your own lawn chair, and you may feel a bit unmoored and not-quite-present if you haven't got one. Outside the ring of spectators is a kind of circular promenade lined with booths selling Indian tacos and crafts and lemonade. Many powwow goers occupy this zone, walking round and round.

I did not know for sure what was going on. No program notes had been 16 provided; as at most powwows, events seemed to proceed by spontaneity, with tacit understanding among the main people involved. A tribal official was talking at great length on the loudspeaker, allowing himself many weighty pauses. The spectators remained attentive to the still-empty powwow circle, as if expecting that at any minute something would materalize there. After a while the waiting made me nervous, and I wandered away. When I came back fifteen minutes later, I had just missed the Grand Entry parade. People were refurling flags and folding star quilts and banners. A dozen little girls in jingle dresses ran by, and I saw a young women with lustrous, yard-long hair who had on a sash proclaiming her this year's powwow queen. Dozens of drum groups, from Pine Ridge and other reservations, had arrived. A group of men in matching ribbon shirts carried a flat drum the size of a truck wheel to a place near the announcer's booth, and a minute later they had set it up and had begun to drum and sing.

The men sat on metal folding chairs in a circle around the drum, hitting it 17 hard with leather-wrapped drumsticks and singing a traditional song in loud, high-pitched unison, above which a single higher voice occasionally rose. Full dark had fallen by now, and the overhead lights had come on, but many corners of the powwow grounds were half-lit or in shadow. Shadows made it hard to see all the singers' faces. In a circle around them, intent white people watched and listened, some holding microphones to catch the sound. The observers' faces were wide-eyed, but the singers, as they leaned into the light and back out of it, had their eyes screwed shut and their mouths wide open in song. Some of the singers held a hand to one ear to plug it, the way musicians in recording studios do. They sang at full voice, from deep inside themselves, all of them hitting each note and word with vehemence and at exactly the same time. The singing, a survival from hundreds of years ago, filled the arena and echoed to the prairie sky. [18]

I walked around in the promenade zone looking among the spectators for Le and for Florence's family, but they weren't there. For a while I kept pace with a man named Rick Weiland, a candidate for Congress from that district, who strolled along introducing himself to people in the crowd. He kept meeting powwow fans who would be small help to him at election time; I heard him say, hiding his vexation, "New Zealand! Wow! There are people here from everywhere!" I saw two other journalist-types like me with notebooks and gave them a wide berth. Suddenly out of the shadows a pair of arms reached to embrace me—it was my friend Germaine. "Remember me?" he asked, rubbing his forehead to mine. After he released me he continued around the circle, hugging every stranger he came upon. Those he hugged hugged him back with powwow enthusiasm, happy that someone had welcomed them. Everyone I saw walking away after a hug from Germaine had a smile. [19]

Elaborately feathered dancers entered the powwow circle for the men's Traditional Dance competition. The crowd of spectators standing behind the rows of lawn chairs grew, and those in back couldn't really see. The view from there reminded me of a crowded exhibition of famous paintings I went to once in a museum in New York City: occasionally a gap in the throng would occur, and through it come a dazzling glimpse of color and form; then the ranks would close and all you could see was the backs of people's heads again. At a less crowded spot I worked my way to the front. The dancers were all going counterclockwise, each dancing as if alone, stepping to the drum music, some crouching down low. All of them had numbers pinned on like those worn by rodeo riders or distance racers; the powwow judges would award cash and other prizes to the best dancers in each category and subcategory. A dancer came right by me. He was a big man, and in his costume—turkey-feather bustle three feet across, feathered anklets, feathered gauntlets, beaded headband, tall roach made of a porcupine tail atop his head—he seemed magnified in every dimension, almost a spirit-being. Then I saw the wristwatch he had on beneath the gauntlet, and the sweat on his temple, and the concentration in his eyes. [20]

Now I wanted to be someplace quiet and empty. I maneuvered through the crowd, went by the taco and lemonade stands, out the gate in the chain-link fence, through the field full of parked cars. The carnival had shut down and the rock-and-roll no longer played, and only one generator still purringly ran. I walked to downtown Pine Ridge, past the tribal building, up the hill to the old hospital, and then onto the open field of the Path the Doctors Walk On. I went half a lap around and sat down. The grass was damp; dew had begun to fall. I could hear [21] the amplified voice of the announcer at the powwow. Then his voice stopped, and the only sound was the singing and drumming. It came through the darkness high and strong and wild as if blown on the wind. It could have been ten voices singing or it could have been a thousand. At moments it sounded like other night noises, coyotes or mosquitoes, or like a sound the land itself might make. I imagined what hearing this would have done to me if I were a young man from Bern, Switzerland (say), traveling the prairie wilderness for the first time in 1843. I knew it would have scared and thrilled me to within an inch of my life.

Meaning and Idea

1. In what region does the powwow take place? In what town is it located? Who are the people who gather to watch it?

2. What main events are the spectators waiting for? Where are those events to take place? What other attractions are present? Where are the other events located?

3. Who are the spectators at the powwow? Make a list of different groups represented in the crowd.

Language, Form, Structure

1. Frazier spends a great deal of time describing the people he sees at the powwow. Pick one of the people he describes and consider how that description advances the story Frazier is trying to tell. In only one instance, when he encounters a Native American veteran, do we see Frazier speaking with the people he is observing. In what light does this encounter cast Frazier as a narrator? Why do you think Frazier adds this detail? How does it add to the piece?

2. How would you characterize Frazier's attitude toward the powwow and the people who gather to watch it? In what ways does he view the events and spectators satirically? admiringly? nostalgically? In what ways does his attitude change over the course of the essay? What phrases, details, or descriptions lead you to your conclusion?

3. Look up the word *powwow* in the Oxford English Dictionary. How do the history of the word and the evolution of the current pronunciation and spelling relate to Frazier's essay?

Ideas for Writing

1. Frazier, who is not a Native American, looks on the powwow as an outsider. When have you been a participant or spectator at an event special to a culture of which you are not part? Write an essay describing the event and your experience at it.

2. Look up the Oglala in an encyclopedia or another reference book. What is the history of the tribe? What does your research tell you about its social systems and beliefs? Write an essay filling in the historical background to this piece. How does your new knowledge of Oglala history change your perception of Frazier's essay?

3. Frazier tells his story using a great deal of description and very little interpretation. He carefully describes the German tourists, the Native American veterans, the townspeople, and the other participants but never explicitly says what he thinks of them. Why do you think he withholds his own opinion? Write an essay explaining and interpreting Frazier's use of description rather than interpretation to tell his story.

Graduation

Maya Angelou

Maya Angelou was born in 1928 in a rigidly segregated area of Arkansas. Her early years were extremely difficult, dominated by poverty and personal pain. From these beginnings, Angelou has become an internationally known poet, actor, singer, songwriter, playwright, film director, and civil rights activist. Early in her life she married a South African activist and traveled to Egypt and then Ghana, where she taught and edited several journals. In the 1960s she was active in the civil rights movement, taking a leadership role in Dr. Martin Luther King, Jr.'s, Southern Christian Leadership Conference. Her writing is both critically and popularly acclaimed. In addition to the many literary awards she has won, 10 of her books have been best-sellers. In 1993 she was chosen by President Bill Clinton to write and deliver his presidential inauguration speech.

"Graduation" comes from the autobiographical *I Know Why the Caged Bird Sings,* a harrowing account of Angelou's childhood.

*T*he children in Stamps trembled visibly with anticipation. Some 1
adults were excited too, but to be certain the whole young population had come down with graduation epidemic. Large classes were graduating from both the grammar school and the high school. Even those who were years removed from their own day of glorious release were anxious to help with preparations as a kind of dry run. The junior students who were moving into the vacating classes' chairs were tradition-bound to show their talents for leadership and management. They strutted through the school and around the campus exerting pressure on the lower grades. Their authority was so new that occasionally if they pressed a little too hard it had to be overlooked. After all, next term was coming, and it never hurt a sixth-grader to have a play sister in the eighth grade, or a tenth-year student to be able to call a twelfth-grader Bubba. So all was endured in a spirit of shared understanding. But the graduating classes themselves were the nobility. Like travelers with exotic destinations on their minds, the graduates were remarkably forgetful. They came to school without their books, or tablets or even pencils. Volunteers fell over themselves to secure replacements for the missing equipment. When accepted, the willing workers might or might not be thanked, and it was of no importance to the pregraduation rites. Even teachers were respectful of the now quiet and aging seniors, and tended to speak to them, if not as equals, as beings only slightly lower than themselves. After tests were returned and grades given, the student body, which acted like an extended family, knew who did well, who excelled, and what piteous ones had failed.

Unlike the white high school, Lafayette County Training School distin- 2
guished itself by having neither lawn, nor hedges, nor tennis court, nor climbing ivy. Its two buildings (main classrooms, the grade school and home economics)

were set on a dirt hill with no fence to limit either its boundaries or those of bordering farms. There was a large expanse to the left of the school which was used alternately as a baseball diamond or a basketball court. Rusty hoops on the swaying poles represented the permanent recreational equipment, although bats and balls could be borrowed from the P.E. teacher if the borrower was qualified and if the diamond wasn't occupied.

Over this rocky area relieved by a few shady tall persimmon trees the graduating class walked. The girls often held hands and no longer bothered to speak to the lower students. There was a sadness about them, as if this old world was not their home and they were bound for higher ground. The boys, on the other hand, had become more friendly, more outgoing. A decided change from the closed attitude they projected while studying for finals. Now they seemed not ready to give up the old school, the familiar paths and classrooms. Only a small percentage would be continuing on to college—one of the South's A & M (agricultural and mechanical) schools, which trained Negro youths to be carpenters, farmers, handymen, masons, maids, cooks and baby nurses. Their future rode heavily on their shoulders, and blinded them to the collective joy that had pervaded the lives of the boys and girls in the grammar school graduating class.

Parents who could afford it had ordered new shoes and ready-made clothes for themselves from Sears, Roebuck or Montgomery Ward. They also engaged the best seamstresses to make the floating graduating dresses and to cut down secondhand pants which would be pressed to a military slickness for the important event.

Oh, it was important, all right. Whitefolks would attend the ceremony, and two or three would speak of God and home, and the Southern way of life, and Mrs. Parsons, the principal's wife, would play the graduation march while the lower-grade graduates paraded down the aisles and took their seats below the platform. The high school seniors would wait in empty classrooms to make their dramatic entrance.

In the Store I was the person of the moment. The birthday girl. The center. Bailey had graduated the year before, although to do so he had had to forfeit all pleasures to make up for his time lost in Baton Rouge.

My class was wearing butter-yellow piqué dresses, and Momma launched out on mine. She smocked the yoke into tiny crisscrossing puckers, then shirred the rest of the bodice. Her dark fingers ducked in and out of the lemony cloth as she embroidered raised daisies around the hem. Before she considered herself finished she had added a crocheted cuff on the puff sleeves, and a pointy crocheted collar.

I was going to be lovely. A walking model of all the various styles of fine hand sewing and it didn't worry me that I was only twelve years old and merely graduating from the eighth grade. Besides, many teachers in Arkansas Negro schools had only that diploma and were licensed to impart wisdom.

The days had become longer and more noticeable. The faded beige of former times had been replaced with strong and sure colors. I began to see my classmates' clothes, their skin tones, and the dust that waved off pussy willows. Clouds that lazed across the sky were objects of great concern to me. Their shiftier shapes might have held a message that in my new happiness and with a little bit of time I'd soon decipher. During that period I looked at the arch of heaven so religiously my neck kept a steady ache. I had taken to smiling more often, and my jaws hurt from the unaccustomed activity. Between the two physical sore spots, I suppose I could have been uncomfortable, but that was not the case. As a member of the winning team (the graduating class of 1940) I had outdistanced unpleasant sensations by miles. I was headed for the freedom of open fields.

Youth and social approval allied themselves with me and we trammeled   10 memories of slights and insults. The wind of our swift passage remodeled my features. Lost tears were pounded to mud and then to dust. Years of withdrawal were brushed aside and left behind, as hanging ropes of parasitic moss.

My work alone had awarded me a top place and I was going to be one of   11 the first called in the graduating ceremonies. On the classroom blackboard, as well as on the bulletin board in the auditorium, there were blue stars and white stars and red stars. No absences, no tardinesses, and my academic work was among the best of the year. I could say the preamble to the Constitution even faster than Bailey. We timed ourselves often: "WethepeopleoftheUnitedStatesin ordertoformamoreperfectunion . . ." I had memorized the Presidents of the United States from Washington to Roosevelt in chronological as well as alphabetical order.

My hair pleased me too. Gradually the black mass had lengthened and   12 thickened, so that it kept at last to its braided pattern, and I didn't have to yank my scalp off when I tried to comb it.

Louise and I had rehearsed the exercises until we tired out ourselves.   13 Henry Reed was class valedictorian. He was a small, very black boy with hooded eyes, a long, broad nose and an oddly shaped head. I had admired him for years because each term he and I vied for the best grades in our class. Most often he bested me, but instead of being disappointed I was pleased that we shared top places between us. Like many Southern Black children, he lived with his grandmother, who was as strict as Momma and as kind as she knew how to be. He was courteous, respectful, and soft-spoken to elders, but on the playground he chose to play the roughest games. I admired him. Anyone, I reckoned, sufficiently afraid or sufficiently dull could be polite. But to be able to operate at a top level with both adults and children was admirable.

His valedictory speech was entitled "To Be or Not to Be." The rigid tenth-   14 grade teacher had helped him write it. He'd been working on the dramatic stresses for months.

The weeks until graduation were filled with heady activities. A group of   15 small children were to be presented in a play about buttercups and daisies and bunny rabbits. They could be heard throughout the building practicing their hops and their little songs that sounded like silver bells. The older girls (non-graduates, of course) were assigned the task of making refreshments for the night's festivities. A tangy scent of ginger, cinnamon, nutmeg and chocolate wafted around the home economics building as the budding cooks made samples for themselves and their teachers.

In every corner of the workshop, axes and saws split fresh timber as the woodshop boys made sets and stage scenery. Only the graduates were left out of the general bustle. We were free to sit in the library at the back of the building or look in quite detachedly, naturally, on the measures being taken for our event. [16]

Even the minister preached on graduation the Sunday before. His subject was, "Let your light so shine that men will see your good works and praise your Father, Who is in Heaven." Although the sermon was purported to be addressed to us, he used the occasion to speak to backsliders, gamblers, and general ne'er-do-wells. But since he had called our names at the beginning of the service we were mollified. [17]

Among Negroes the tradition was to give presents to children going only from one grade to another. How much more important this was when the person was graduating at the top of the class. Uncle Willie and Momma had sent away for a Mickey Mouse watch like Bailey's. Louise gave me four embroidered handkerchiefs. (I gave her three crocheted doilies.) Mrs. Sneed, the minister's wife, made me an underskirt to wear for graduation, and nearly every customer gave me a nickel or maybe even a dime with the instruction "Keep on moving to higher ground," or some such encouragement. [18]

Amazingly the great day finally dawned and I was out of bed before I knew it. I threw open the back door to see it more clearly, but Momma said, "Sister, come away from that door and put your robe on." [19]

I hoped the memory of that morning would never leave me. Sunlight was itself still young, and the day had none of the insistence maturity would bring it in a few hours. In my robe and barefoot in the backyard, under cover of going to see about my new beans, I gave myself up to the gentle warmth and thanked God that no matter what evil I had done in my life He had allowed me to live to see this day. Somewhere in my fatalism I had expected to die, accidentally, and never have the chance to walk up the stairs in the auditorium and gracefully receive my hard-earned diploma. Out of God's merciful bosom I had won reprieve. [20]

Bailey came out in his robe and gave me a box wrapped in Christmas paper. He said he had saved his money for months to pay for it. It felt like a box of chocolates, but I knew Bailey wouldn't save money to buy candy when we had all we could want under our noses. [21]

He was as proud of the gift as I. It was a soft-leatherbound copy of a collection of poems by Edgar Allan Poe, or, as Bailey and I called him, "Eap." I turned to "Annabel Lee" and we walked up and down the garden rows, the cool dirt between our toes, reciting the beautifully sad lines. [22]

Momma made a Sunday breakfast although it was only Friday. After we finished the blessing, I opened my eyes to find the watch on my plate. It was a dream of a day. Everything went smoothly and to my credit. I didn't have to be [23] reminded or scolded for anything. Near evening I was too jittery to attend to chores, so Bailey volunteered to do all before his bath.

Days before, we had made a sign for the Store, and as we turned out the lights Momma hung the cardboard over the doorknob. It read clearly: CLOSED, GRADUATION.

My dress fitted perfectly and everyone said that I looked like a sunbeam in it. On the hill, going toward the school, Bailey walked behind with Uncle Willie, who muttered, "Go on, Ju." He wanted him to walk ahead with us because it embarrassed him to have to walk so slowly. Bailey said he'd let the ladies walk together, and the men would bring up the rear. We all laughed, nicely.

Little children dashed by out of the dark like fireflies. Their crepe-paper dresses and butterfly wings were not made for running and we heard more than one rip, dryly, and the regretful "uh uh" that followed.

The school blazed without gaiety. The windows seemed cold and unfriendly from the lower hill. A sense of ill-fated timing crept over me, and if Momma hadn't reached for my hand I would have drifted back to Bailey and Uncle Willie, and possibly beyond. She made a few slow jokes about my feet getting cold, and tugged me along to the now-strange building.

Around the front steps, assurance came back. There were my fellow "greats," the graduating class. Hair brushed back, legs oiled, new dresses and pressed pleats, fresh pocket handkerchiefs and little handbags, all homesewn. Oh, we were up to snuff, all right. I joined my comrades and didn't even see my family go in to find seats in the crowded auditorium.

The school band struck up a march and all classes filed in as had been rehearsed. We stood in front of our seats, as assigned, and on a signal from the choir director, we sat. No sooner had this been accomplished than the band started to play the national anthem. We rose again and sang the song, after which we recited the pledge of allegiance. We remained standing for a brief minute before the choir director and the principal signaled to us, rather desperately I thought, to take our seats. The command was so unusual that our carefully rehearsed and smooth-running machine was thrown off. For a full minute we fumbled for our chairs and bumped into each other awkwardly. Habits change or solidify under pressure, so in our state of nervous tension we had been ready to follow our usual assembly pattern: the American national anthem, then the pledge of allegiance, then the song every Black person I knew called the Negro National Anthem. All done in the same key, with the same passion and most often standing on the same foot.

Finding my seat at last, I was overcome with a presentiment of worse things to come. Something unrehearsed, unplanned, was going to happen, and we were going to be made to look bad. I distinctly remember being explicit in the choice of pronoun. It was "we," the graduating class, the unit, that concerned me then.

The principal welcomed "parents and friends" and asked the Baptist minister to lead us in prayer. His invocation was brief and punchy, and for a second I thought we were getting back on the high road to right action. When the principal came back to the dais, however, his voice had changed. Sounds always affected me profoundly and the principal's voice was one of my favorites. During assembly it melted and lowed weakly into the audience. It had not been in my plan to listen to him, but my curiosity was piqued and I straightened up to give him my attention.

He was talking about Booker T. Washington, our "late great leader," 32 who said we can be as close as the fingers on the hand, etc. . . . Then he said a few vague things about friendship and the friendship of kindly people to those less fortunate than themselves. With that his voice nearly faded, thin, away. Like a river diminishing to a stream and then to a trickle. But he cleared his throat and said, "Our speaker tonight, who is also our friend, came from Texarkana to deliver the commencement address, but due to the irregularity of the train schedule, he's going to, as they say, 'speak and run.' He said that we understood and wanted the man to know that we were most grateful for the time he was able to give us and then something about how we were willing always to adjust to another's program, and without more ado—"I give you Mr. Edward Donleavy."

Not one but two white men came through the door offstage. The shorter 33 one walked to the speaker's platform, and the tall one moved over to the center seat and sat down. But that was our principal's seat, and already occupied. The dislodged gentleman bounced around for a long breath or two before the Baptist minister gave him his chair, then with more dignity than the situation deserved, the minister walked off the stage.

Donleavy looked at the audience once (on reflection, I'm sure that he 34 wanted only to reassure himself that we were really there), adjusted his glasses and began to read from a sheaf of papers.

He was glad "to be here and to see the work going on just as it was in the 35 other schools."

At the first "Amen" from the audience I willed the offender to immediate 36 death by choking on the word. But Amens and Yes, sir's began to fall around the room like rain through a ragged umbrella.

He told us of the wonderful changes we children in Stamps had in store. 37 The Central School (naturally, the white school was Central) had already been granted improvements that would be in use in the fall. A well-known artist was coming from Little Rock to teach art to them. They were going to have the newest microscopes and chemistry equipment for their laboratory. Mr. Donleavy didn't leave us long in the dark over who made these improvements available to Central High. Nor were we to be ignored in the general betterment scheme he had in mind.

He said that he had pointed out to people at a very high level that one of 38 the first-line football tacklers at Arkansas Agricultural and Mechanical College had graduated from good old Lafayette County Training School. Here fewer Amen's were heard. Those few that did break through lay dully in the air with the heaviness of habit.

He went on to praise us. He went on to say how he had bragged that "one 39 of the best basketball players at Fisk sank his first ball right here at Lafayette County Training School."

The white kids were going to have a chance to become Galileos and 40 Madame Curies and Edisons and Gauguins, and our boys (the girls weren't even in on it) would try to be Jesse Owenses and Joe Louises.

Owens and the Brown Bomber were great heroes in our world, but what 41 school official in the white-goddom of Little Rock had the right to decide that those two men must be our only heroes? Who decided that for Henry Reed to become a scientist he had to work like George Washington Carver, as a boot-black, to buy a lousy microscope? Bailey was obviously always going to be too small to be an athlete, so which concrete angel glued to what country seat had decided that if my brother wanted to become a lawyer he had to first pay penance for his skin by picking cotton and hoeing corn and studying correspon-dence books at night for twenty years?

The man's dead words fell like bricks around the auditorium and too many 42 settled in my belly. Constrained by hard-learned manners I couldn't look behind me, but to my left and right the proud graduating class of 1940 had dropped their heads. Every girl in my row had found something new to do with her handker-chief. Some folded the tiny squares into love knots, some into triangles, but most were wadding them, then pressing them flat on their yellow laps.

On the dais, the ancient tragedy was being replayed. Professor Parsons sat, 43 a sculptor's reject, rigid. His large, heavy body seemed devoid of will or willing-ness, and his eyes said he was no longer with us. The other teachers examined the flag (which was draped stage right) or their notes, or the windows which opened on our now-famous playing diamond.

Graduation, the hush-hush magic time of frills and gifts and congratula- 44 tions and diplomas, was finished for me before my name was called. The ac-complishment was nothing. The meticulous maps, drawn in three colors of ink, learning and spelling decasyllabic words, memorizing the whole of *The Rape of Lucrece*—it was for nothing. Donleavy had exposed us.

We were maids and farmers, handymen and washerwomen, and anything 45 higher that we aspired to was farcical and presumptuous.

Then I wished that Gabriel Prosser and Nat Turner had killed all white- 46 folks in their beds and that Abraham Lincoln had been assassinated before the signing of the Emancipation Proclamation, and that Harriet Tubman had been killed by that blow on her head and Christopher Columbus had drowned in the *Santa María.*

It was awful to be Negro and have no control over my life. It was brutal to 47 be young and already trained to sit quietly and listen to charges brought against my color with no chance of defense. We should all be dead. I thought I should like to see us all dead, one on top of the other. A pyramid of flesh with the whitefolks on the bottom, as the broad base, then the Indians with their silly tomahawks and teepees and wigwams and treaties, the Negroes with their mops and recipes and cotton sacks and spirituals sticking out of their mouths. The Dutch children should all stumble in their wooden shoes and break their necks. The French should choke to death on the Louisiana Purchase (1803) while silkworms ate all the Chinese with their stupid pigtails. As a species, we were an abomination. All of us.

Donleavy was running for election, and assured our parents that if he won 48 we could count on having the only colored paved playing field in that part of Arkansas. Also—he never looked up to acknowledge the grunts of acceptance— also, we were bound to get some new equipment for the home economics building and the workshop.

He finished, and since there was no need to give any more than the most 49 perfunctory thank-you's, he nodded to the men on the stage, and the tall white man who was never introduced joined him at the door. They left with the attitude that now they were off to something really important. (The graduation ceremonies at Lafayette Country Training School had been a mere preliminary.)

The ugliness they left was palpable. An uninvited guest who wouldn't 50 leave. The choir was summoned and sang a modern arrangement of "Onward, Christian Soldiers," with new words pertaining to graduates seeking their place in the world. But it didn't work. Elouise, the daughter of the Baptist minister, recited "Invictus," and I could have cried at the impertinence of "I am the master of my fate, I am the captain of my soul."

My name had lost its ring of familiarity and I had to be nudged to go and 51 receive my diploma. All my preparations had fled. I neither marched up to the stage like a conquering Amazon, nor did I look in the audience for Bailey's nod of approval. Marguerite Johnson, I heard the name again, my honors were read, there were noises in the audience of appreciation, and I took my place on the stage as rehearsed.

I thought about colors I hated: ecru, puce, lavender, beige and black. 52

There was shuffling and rustling around me, then Henry Reed was giving 53 his valedictory address, "To Be or Not to Be." Hadn't he heard the whitefolks? We couldn't *be,* so the question was a waste of time. Henry's voice came out clear and strong. I feared to look at him. Hadn't he got the message? There was no "nobler in the mind" for Negroes because the world didn't think we had minds, and they let us know it. "Outrageous fortune"? Now, that was a joke. When the ceremony was over I had to tell Henry Reed some things. That is, if I still cared. Not "rub," Henry, "erase." "Ah, there's the erase." Us.

Henry had been a good student in elocution. His voice rose on tides of 54 promise and fell on waves of warnings. The English teacher had helped him to create a sermon winging through Hamlet's soliloquy. To be a man, a doer, a builder, a leader, or to be a tool, an unfunny joke, a crusher of funky toadstools. I marveled that Henry could go through with the speech as if we had a choice.

I had been listening and silently rebutting each sentence with my eyes 55 closed; then there was a hush, which in an audience warns that something unplanned is happening. I looked up and saw Henry Reed, the conservative, the proper, the A student, turn his back to the audience and turn to us (the proud graduating class of 1940) and sing, nearly speaking,

"Lift ev'ry voice and sing*
Till earth and heaven ring
Ring with the harmonies of Liberty . . ."

It was the poem written by James Weldon Johnson. It was the music composed by J. Rosamond Johnson. It was the Negro national anthem. Out of habit we were singing it.

Our mothers and fathers stood in the dark hall and joined the hymn of encouragement. A kindergarten teacher led the small children onto the stage and the buttercups and daisies and bunny rabbits marked time and tried to follow:

56

"Stony the road we trod
Bitter the chastening rod
Felt in the days when hope, unborn, had died.
'Yet with a steady beat
Have not our weary feet
Come to the place for which our fathers sighed?"

Every child I knew had learned that song with his ABC's and along with "Jesus Loves Me This I Know." But I personally had never heard it before. Never heard the words, despite the thousands of times I had sung them. Never thought they had anything to do with me.

57

On the other hand, the words of Patrick Henry had made such an impression on me that I had been able to stretch myself tall and trembling and say, "I know not what course others may take, but as for me, give me liberty or give me death."

58

And now I heard, really for the first time:

59

"We have come over a way that with tears
has been watered,
We have come, treading our path through
the blood of the slaughtered."

While echoes of the song shivered in the air, Henry Reed bowed his head, said "Thank you," and returned to his place in the line. The tears that slipped down many faces were not wiped away in shame.

60

We were on top again. As always, again. We survived. The depths had been icy and dark, but now a bright sun spoke to our souls. I was no longer simply a member of the proud graduating class of 1940; I was a proud member of the wonderful, beautiful Negro race.

61

Oh, Black known and unknown poets, how often have your auctioned 62
pains sustained us? Who will compute the lonely nights made less lonely by
your songs, or the empty pots made less tragic by your tales?

If we were a people much given to revealing secrets, we might raise mon- 63
uments and sacrifice to the memories of our poets, but slavery cured us of that
weakness. It may be enough, however, to have it said that we survive in exact
relationship to the dedication of our poets (include preachers, musicians and
blues singers).

Meaning and Idea

1. List the two schools discussed in Angelou's piece. Describe the contrast
   between them.

2. How do the graduating seniors stand out from the rest of the students? How
   does Angelou characterize their attitude toward the future?

3. How does Angelou describe her family's reaction to her graduation? How
   does graduation change the way they treat her?

4. Contrast the attitude of the white school administrator Donleavy, who
   comes to visit at graduation, with the attitude of the rest of the town. What
   does he say, and why is it so deflating?

5. What does Angelou mean when she says of the Negro national anthem that
   "I personally had never heard it before"?

Language, Form, Structure

1. The mood of Angelou's essay changes several times. Where do those mood
   changes happen, and what causes them? How does the shift between moods
   make the essay more effective?

2. How aware of segregation in Stamps is Angelou at the beginning of the
   piece? What does it mean to her? What details let you know? How does her
   understanding of her social status change over the course of the essay?
   What details and events are important in helping her develop her
   awareness?

3. Define the following words and use them in original sentences: trammeled;
   heady; mollified; fatalism; dais; piqued; chastening; rod; tread.

Ideas for Writing

1. Write an essay in which you describe your coming into awareness of a
   particular injustice in the world. How did you initially react? What were
   your initial feelings?

2. Look closely at the words of a song or poem that you have known since childhood but to which you have never paid close attention. Write an essay in which you closely analyze the words.

3. Angelou might have chosen to end her essay with the words "I was a proud member of the wonderful, beautiful Negro race," which provide a natural pause. Instead she adds two final paragraphs addressing black poets "known and unknown." Analyze the vocabulary and tone of the final two paragraphs. How do they stand out from the rest of the essay? How do they belong to the essay? Write an essay explaining what these final two paragraphs add to the selection that would have been missing without them.

Wakefield

Nathaniel Hawthorne

Nathaniel Hawthorne (1804–1864) was born in Salem, Massachusetts, the descendant of a long line of Puritan ancestors. His father had been a presiding magistrate at the Salem witch trials. After graduating from college, Hawthorne turned to writing. Until the popular success of *The Scarlet Letter* (1850), his income from writing was not enough to sustain Hawthorne and his family. To make ends meet he worked at several low-level patronage jobs in the Salem Custom House. In the wake of that success Hawthorne wrote most of his best-known books, including *The House of the Seven Gables* (1851). In his later years Hawthorne again accepted a political job, as a consul in Liverpool, which he received for penning a campaign biography for Franklin Pierce. Hawthorne died in 1864 in New Hampshire after a long period of severe illness.

In "Wakefield," there is a great deal of sympathy for the unfortunate title character, who leaves his wife and home for 20 years simply to watch what happens. The mixture of fascination and gentle irony with which Hawthorne treats a hero so unsympathetic might have arisen from his own life experiences of intense loneliness.

*I*n some old magazine or newspaper, I recollect a story, told as   1
truth, of a man—let us call him Wakefield—who absented himself for a long time from his wife. The fact thus abstractedly stated is not very uncommon, nor—without a proper distinction of circumstances—to be condemned either as naughty or nonsensical. Howbeit, this, though far from the most aggravated, is perhaps the strangest instance on record of marital delinquency; and, moreover, as remarkable a freak as may be found in the whole list of human oddities. The wedded couple lived in London. The man, under pretence of going a journey, took lodgings in the next street to his own house, and there, unheard of by his wife or friends, and without the shadow of a reason for such self-banishment, dwelt upwards of twenty years. During that period, he beheld his home every day, and frequently the forlorn Mrs. Wakefield. And after so great a gap in his matrimonial felicity—when his death was reckoned certain, his estate settled, his name dismissed from memory, and his wife, long, long ago, resigned to her autumnal widowhood—he entered the door one evening, quietly, as from a day's absence, and became a loving spouse till death.

This outline is all that I remember. But the incident, though of the purest   2
originality, unexampled, and probably never to be repeated, is one, I think, which appeals to the generous sympathies of mankind. We know, each for himself, that none of us would perpetrate such a folly, yet feel as if some other might. To my own contemplations, at least, it has often recurred, always exciting wonder, but with a sense that the story must be true and a conception of its hero's character. Whenever any subject so forcibly affects the mind, time is well

spent in thinking of it. If the reader choose, let him do his own meditation; or if he prefer to ramble with me through the twenty years of Wakefield's vagary, I bid him welcome; trusting that there will be a pervading spirit and a moral, even should we fail to find them, done up neatly, and condensed into the final sentence. Thought has always its efficacy, and every striking incident its moral.

What sort of a man was Wakefield? We are free to shape out our own idea, and call it by his name. He was now in the meridian of life; his matrimonial affections, never violent, were sobered into a calm, habitual sentiment; of all husbands, he was likely to be the most constant, because a certain sluggishness would keep his heart at rest, wherever it might be placed. He was intellectual, but not actively so; his mind occupied itself in long and lazy musings, that tended to no purpose, or had not vigour to attain it; his thoughts were seldom so energetic as to seize hold of words. Imagination, in the proper meaning of the term, made no part of Wakefield's gifts. With a cold but not depraved nor wandering heart, and a mind never feverish with riotous thoughts, nor perplexed with originality, who could have anticipated that our friend would entitle himself to a foremost place among the doers of eccentric deeds? Had his acquaintances been asked, who was the man in London, the surest to perform nothing to-day which should be remembered on the morrow, they would have thought of Wakefield. Only the wife of his bosom might have hesitated. She, without having analysed his character, was partly aware of a quiet selfishness, that had rusted into his inactive mind,—of a peculiar sort of vanity, the most uneasy attribute about him,—of a disposition to craft, which had seldom produced more positive effects than the keeping of petty secrets, hardly worth revealing,—and, lastly, of what she called a little strangeness, sometimes, in the good man. This latter quality is indefinable, and perhaps non-existent.

Let us now imagine Wakefield bidding adieu to his wife. It is the dusk of an October evening. His equipment is a drab great-coat, a hat covered with an oil-cloth, top-boots, an umbrella in one hand and a small portmanteau in the other. He has informed Mrs. Wakefield that he is to take the night coach into the country. She would fain inquire the length of his journey, its object, and the probable time of his return; but, indulgent to his harmless love of mystery, interrogates him only by a look. He tells her not to expect him positively by the return coach, not to be alarmed should he tarry three or four days; but, at all events, to look for him at supper on Friday evening. Wakefield himself, be it considered, has no suspicion of what is before him. He holds out his hand; she gives her own, and meets his parting kiss, in the matter-of-course way of a ten years' matrimony; and forth goes the middle-aged Mr. Wakefield, almost resolved to perplex his good lady by a whole week's absence. After the door has closed behind him, she perceives it thrust partly open, and a vision of her husband's face, through the aperture, smiling on her, and gone in a moment. For the time, this little incident is dismissed without a thought. But, long afterwards, when she has been more years a widow than a wife, that smile recurs, and flickers across all her reminiscences of Wakefield's visage. In her many musings, she surrounds the original smile with a multitude of fantasies, which make it strange and awful; as, for instance, if she imagines him in a coffin, that parting look is frozen on his pale features; or, if she dreams of him in heaven, still his blessed spirit wears a quiet and crafty smile. Yet, for its sake, when all others have given him up for dead, she sometimes doubts whether she is a widow.

But our business is with the husband. We must hurry after him, along the street, ere he lose his individuality, and melt into the great mass of London life. It would be vain searching for him there. Let us follow close at his heels, therefore, until, after several superfluous turns and doublings, we find him comfortably established by the fireside of a small apartment, previously bespoken. He is in the next street to his own, and at his journey's end. He can scarcely trust his good fortune in having got thither unperceived,—recollecting that, at one time, he was delayed by the throng, in the very focus of a lighted lantern; and, again, there were footsteps, that seemed to tread behind his own, distinct from the multitudinous tramp around him; and, anon, he heard a voice shouting afar; and fancied that it called his name. Doubtless, a dozen busybodies had been watching him, and told his wife the whole affair. Poor Wakefield! Little knowest thou thine own insignificance in this great world! No mortal eye but mine has traced thee. Go quietly to thy bed, foolish man; and, on the morrow, if thou wilt be wise, get thee home to good Mrs. Wakefield, and tell her the truth. Remove not thyself, even for a little week, from thy place in her chaste bosom. Were she, for a single moment, to deem thee dead, or lost, or lastingly divided from her, thou wouldst be woefully conscious of a change in thy true wife, forever after. It is perilous to make a chasm in human affections; not that they gape so long and wide, but so quickly close again!

Almost repenting of his frolic, or whatever it may be termed, Wakefield lies down betimes, and starting from his first nap, spreads forth his arms into the wide and solitary waste of the unaccustomed bed. "No,"—thinks he, gathering the bedclothes about him,—"I will not sleep alone another night."

In the morning, he rises earlier than usual, and sets himself to consider what he really means to do. Such are his loose and rambling modes of thought that he has taken this very singular step, with the consciousness of a purpose, indeed, but without being able to define it sufficiently for his own contemplation. The vagueness of the project, and the convulsive effort with which he plunges into the execution of it, are equally characteristic of a feeble-minded man. Wakefield sifts his ideas, however, as minutely as he may, and finds himself curious to know the progress of matters at home,—how his exemplary wife will endure her widowhood of a week; and, briefly, how the little sphere of creatures and circumstances, in which he was a central object, will be affected by his removal. A morbid vanity, therefore, lies nearest the bottom of the affair. But, how is he to attain his ends? Not, certainly, by keeping close in this comfortable lodging, where, though he slept and awoke in the next street to his home, he is as effectually abroad, as if the stage-coach had been whirling him away all night. Yet, should he reappear, the whole project is knocked on the head. His poor brains being hopelessly puzzled with this dilemma, he at length ventures out, partly resolving to cross the head of the street, and send one hasty glance towards his forsaken domicile. Habit—for he is a man of habits—takes him by the hand, and guides him, wholly unaware to his own door, where, just at the critical moment, he is aroused by the scraping of his foot upon the step. Wakefield! whither are you going?

At that instant, his fate was turning on the pivot. Little dreaming of the doom to which his first backward step devotes him, he hurries away, breathless with agitation hitherto unfelt, and hardly dares turn his head, at the distant corner. Can it be that nobody caught sight of him? Will not the whole household—the decent Mrs. Wakefield, the smart maid-servant, and the dirty little footboy—raise a hue and cry, through London streets, in pursuit of their fugitive lord and master? Wonderful escape! He gathers courage to pause and look homeward, but is perplexed with a sense of change about the familiar edifice, such as affects us all, when, after a separation of months or years, we again see some hill or lake, or work of art, with which we were friends of old. In ordinary cases, this indescribable impression is caused by the comparison and contrast between our imperfect reminiscences and the reality. In Wakefield, the magic of a single night has wrought a similar transformation, because, in that brief period, a great moral change has been effected. But this is a secret from himself. Before leaving the spot, he catches a far and momentary glimpse of his wife, passing athwart the front window, with her face turned towards the head of the street. The crafty nincompoop takes to his heels, scared with the idea, that, among a thousand such atoms of mortality, her eye must have detected him. Right glad is his heart, though his brain be somewhat dizzy, when he finds himself by the coalfire of his lodgings.

So much for the commencement of this long whim-wham. After the initial conception, and the stirring up of the man's sluggish temperament to put it in practice, the whole matter evolves itself in a natural train. We may suppose him, as the result of deep deliberation, buying a new wig, of reddish hair, and selecting sundry garments, in a fashion unlike his customary suit of brown, from a Jew's old-clothes bag. It is accomplished. Wakefield is another man. The new system being now established, a retrograde movement to the old would be almost as difficult as the step that placed him in his unparalleled position. Furthermore, he is rendered obstinate by a sulkiness, occasionally incident to his temper, and brought on, at present, by the inadequate sensation which he conceives to have been produced in the bosom of Mrs. Wakefield. He will not go back until she be frightened half to death. Well, twice or thrice has she passed before his sight, each time with a heavier step, a paler cheek, and more anxious brow; and in the third week of his non-appearance, he detects a portent of evil entering the house, in the guise of an apothecary. Next day, the knocker is muffled. Towards nightfall comes the chariot of a physician, and deposits its big-wigged and solemn burden at Wakefield's door, whence, after a quarter of an hour's visit, he emerges, perchance the herald of a funeral. Dear woman! Will she die? By this time, Wakefield is excited to something like energy of feeling, but still lingers away from his wife's bedside, pleading with his conscience, that she must not be disturbed at such a juncture. If aught else restrains him, he does not know it. In the course of a few weeks, she gradually recovers; the crisis is over; her heart is sad, perhaps, but quiet; and, let him return soon or late, it will never be feverish for him again. Such ideas glimmer through the mist of Wakefield's mind, and render him indistinctly conscious that an almost impassable gulf divides his hired apartment from his former home. "It is but in the next street!" he sometimes says. Fool! it is in another world. Hitherto, he has put off his return from one particular day to another; henceforward, he leaves the precise time undetermined. Not to-morrow,—probably next week,—pretty soon. Poor man! The dead have nearly as much chance of revisiting their earthly homes, as the self-banished Wakefield.

Would that I had a folio to write, instead of an article of a dozen pages! 10 Then might I exemplify how an influence, beyond our control, lays its strong hand on every deed which we do, and weaves its consequences into an iron tissue of necessity. Wakefield is spell-bound. We must leave him, for ten years or so, to haunt around his house, without once crossing the threshold, and to be faithful to his wife, with all the affection of which his heart is capable, while he is slowly fading out of hers. Long since, it must be remarked, he has lost the perception of singularity in his conduct.

Now for a scene! Amid the throng of a London street, we distinguish a 11 man, now waxing elderly, with few characteristics to attract careless observers, yet bearing, in his whole aspect, the handwriting of no common fate, for such as have the skill to read it. He is meagre; his low and narrow forehead is deeply wrinkled; his eyes, small and lustreless, sometimes wander apprehensively about him, but oftener seem to look inward. He bends his head, and moves with an indescribable obliquity of gait, as if unwilling to display his full front to the world. Watch him, long enough to see what we have described, and you will allow, that circumstances—which often produce remarkable men from nature's ordinary handiwork—have produced one such here. Next, leaving him to sidle along the footwalk, cast your eyes in the opposite direction, where a portly female, considerably in the wane of life, with a prayer-book in her hand, is proceeding to yonder church. She has the placid mien of settled widowhood. Her regrets have either died away, or have become so essential to her heart, that they would be poorly exchanged for joy. Just as the lean man and well-conditioned woman are passing, a slight obstruction occurs, and brings these two figures directly in contact. Their hands touch; the pressure of the crowd forces her bosom against his shoulder; they stand, face to face, staring into each other's eyes. After a ten years' separation, thus Wakefield meets his wife!

The throng eddies away, and carries them asunder. The sober widow, re- 12 suming her former pace, proceeds to church, but pauses in the portal, and throws a perplexed glance along the street. She passes in, however, opening her prayer-book as she goes. And the man! with so wild a face, that busy and selfish London stands to gaze after him, he hurries to his lodgings, bolts the door, and throws himself upon the bed. The latent feelings of years break out; his feeble mind acquires a brief energy from their strength; all the miserable strangeness of his life is revealed to him at a glance; and he cries out, passionately, "Wakefield! Wakefield! You are mad!"

Perhaps he was so. The singularity of his situation must have so moulded   13
him to himself, that, considered in regard to his fellow-creatures and the business of life, he could not be said to possess his right mind. He had contrived, or
rather he had happened, to dissever himself from the world,—to vanish,—to
give up his place and privileges with living men, without being admitted among
the dead. The life of a hermit is nowise parallel to his. He was in the bustle of
the city, as of old; but the crowd swept by, and saw him not; he was, we may
figuratively say, always beside his wife, and at his hearth, yet must never feel
the warmth of the one, nor the affection of the other. It was Wakefield's unprecedented fate, to retain his original share of human sympathies, and to be still
involved in human interests, while he had lost his reciprocal influence on them.
It would be a most curious speculation, to trace out the effect of such circumstances on his heart and intellect, separately, and in unison. Yet, changed as he
was, he would seldom be conscious of it, but deem himself the same man as
ever; glimpses of the truth, indeed, would come, but only for the moment; and
still he would keep saying, "I shall soon go back!" nor reflect that he had been
saying so for twenty years.

I conceive, also, that these twenty years would appear, in the retrospect,   14
scarcely longer than the week to which Wakefield had at first limited his absence. He would look on the affair as no more than an interlude in the main
business of his life. When, after a little while more, he should deem it time to
re-enter his parlour, his wife would clap her hands for joy, on beholding the
middle-aged Mr. Wakefield. Alas, what a mistake! Would Time but await the
close of our favourite follies, we should be young men, all of us, and till
doomsday.

One evening, in the twentieth year since he vanished, Wakefield is tak-   15
ing his customary walk towards the dwelling which he still calls his own. It is
a gusty night of autumn, with frequent showers, that patter down upon the
pavement, and are gone, before a man can put up his umbrella. Pausing near
the house, Wakefield discerns, through the parlour windows of the second
floor, the red glow, and the glimmer and fitful flash of a comfortable fire. On
the ceiling appears a grotesque shadow of good Mrs. Wakefield. The cap, the
nose and chin, and the broad waist form an admirable caricature, which
dances, moreover, with the up-flickering and down-sinking blaze, almost too
merrily for the shade of an elderly widow. At this instant, a shower chances to
fall, and is driven, by the unmannerly gust, full into Wakefield's face and
bosom. He is quite penetrated with its autumnal chill. Shall he stand, wet and
shivering here, when his own hearth has a good fire to warm him, and his own
wife will run to fetch the gray coat and small clothes, which doubtless she has
kept carefully in the closet of their bed-chamber? No! Wakefield is no such
fool. He ascends the steps,—heavily!—for twenty years have stiffened his
legs, since he came down,—but he knows it not. Stay, Wakefield! Would you
go to the sole home that is left you? Then step into your grave! The door
opens. As he passes in, we have a parting glimpse of his visage, and recognize
the crafty smile, which was the precursor of the little joke that he has ever

since been playing off at his wife's expense. How unmercifully has he quizzed the poor woman! Well, a good night's test to Wakefield!

This happy event—supposing it to be such—could only have occurred at an unpremeditated moment. We will not follow our friend across the threshold. He has left us much food for thought, a portion of which shall lend its wisdom to a moral, and be shaped into a figure. Amid the seeming confusion of our mysterious world, individuals are so nicely adjusted to a system, and systems to one another, and to a whole, that, by stepping aside for a moment, a man exposes himself to a fearful risk of losing his place for ever. Like Wakefield, he may become, as it were, the Outcast of the Universe.

16

Meaning and Idea

1. Was there really a Wakefield? How do you know?

2. What qualities does Wakefield possess that Hawthorne deprecates? What qualities does Wakefield possess that Hawthorne admires?

3. What does Hawthorne mean when, in the second to last paragraph, he marvels at "how unmercifully he has quizzed the old woman"?

4. Read the last paragraph again carefully. What "moral" does Hawthorne see Wakefield's story as holding?

Language, Form, Structure

1. Hawthorne writes that Wakefield's action, "though of the purest originality" and "probably never to be repeated," still "appeals to the generous sympathies of mankind." Make certain that you understand all of the meanings of "sympathy." What does Hawthorne mean by these words?

2. Hawthorne asks, "What sort of a man was Wakefield?" He then answers that "We are free to shape out our own idea, and call it by his name." What importance does this answer have for understanding Hawthorne's story?

3. Write definitions for the following words: meridian; musing; disposition; portmanteau; indulgent; aperture; superfluous; multitudinous; domicile; sundry; retrograde; throng; meagre; placid; reciprocal.

Ideas for Writing

1. Write a letter to Wakefield in which you express your own reaction to his actions.

2. Write a brief imaginative story about a man who indulges in an absurdly eccentric behavior. Now write a brief analysis of that man's character. Try, like Hawthorne, to imagine how his actions might reveal something about the rest of us.

3. Look back over the story and notice the moments when Hawthorne claims not to know details about the narrative he is recounting. Since Hawthorne has acknowledged that he is re-creating this tale out of his own imagination, why do you think he would stop short of telling the whole story? Write an essay analyzing one of these omissions. How does Hawthorne's silence contribute to the effect of the story as a whole?

CROSSOVER

1. Frederick Douglass, Countee Cullen, and Langston Hughes all provide windows on the experience of growing up as African Americans. Select two of these writers and write an essay that identifies common and differing elements in their portrayed experiences.

2. Judith Ortiz Cofer in "The Witch's Husband," N. Scott Momaday in "The Last of the Kiowas" (Chapter One), and Linda Pastan in "Grudnow" (Chapter One) all write about the influence of a grandparant on the narrator's understanding of his or her personal history. Write an essay exploring each writer's assertion about the grandparent along with your own insight into your own (or one of your friend's) grandmother's or grandfather's life and influence on you or others.

Chapter Three

■

EXEMPLIFICATION

INTRODUCTION TO EXEMPLIFICATION

The process of exemplification is such an essential part of the way we think, the way we talk and argue and respond, that it may seem odd to consider it as a writer's option. Simply put, exemplification means providing examples to illustrate an idea with particulars.

As a case in point, if you wanted to illustrate Dickens's skill at characterization, you could present a single well-developed example—the example of Pip, say, the main character in *Great Expectations.* Or, to make a point about the extraordinary defensive playing by the Yankees and the Braves, you might provide a blow-by-blow retelling of the pitching duel in the last inning of a crucial game between them. In each case, you'd probably infuse the one example with details. In the first, you'd draw on paraphrases and quotations from the novel. In the second, you'd provide concrete sensory images and narrative particulars to bring to life the final breathless moments of play.

A single extended example can make a strong case, yet we are equally impressed with cumulative exemplification. Here, the writer provides a series of illustrations, the accretion of related yet different instances that make the original point grow and solidify. Thus, if you wanted to use *Great Expectations* to demonstrate Dickens's talent for character development, you might deal with Miss Haversham, the convict Magwitch, and Estella as well as with Pip. Similarly, if you were touting the Yankees' defense, you might want to point to instances of skillful fielding by the third baseman, the shortstop, and the right fielder as well as to the masterful job on the mound. Cumulative exemplification provides the reader with many illustrations of the writer's point.

Examples move readers beyond generalizations. As a means for anchoring general ideas in specifics, examples are essential rhetorical strategies to writers of stories, novels, essays, and poems.

READING EXEMPLIFICATION

Examples from Personal Experience

As you read instances to support a writer's position, your critical faculties should engage this question: Are these examples solid illustrations of the point? No matter how clever or amusing they may be, the examples must pertain to the writer's purpose in the essay. Sometimes the writer will list examples, expecting through accumulation of supporting information to win you over, as George Orwell does here in order to persuade us to acknowledge his good memories of Crossgates School:

> I have good memories of Crossgates, among a horde of bad ones. Sometimes on summer afternoons there were wonderful expeditions across the Downs, or to Beachy Head, where one bathed dangerously among the chalk boulders and came home covered with cuts. And there were still more wonderful midsummer evenings when, as a special treat, we were not driven off to bed as usual but

allowed to wander about the grounds in the long twilight, ending up with a plunge into the swimming bath at about nine o'clock. There was the joy of waking early on summer mornings and getting in an hour's undisturbed reading (Ian Hay, Thackeray, Kipling and H.G. Wells were the favourite authors of my boyhood) in the sunlit, sleeping dormitory. There was also cricket, which I was no good at but with which I conducted a sort of hopeless love affair up to the age of about eighteen. And there was the pleasure of keeping caterpillars—the silky green and purple puss-moth, the ghostly green poplar-hawk, the privet hawk, large as one's third finger, specimens of which could be illicitly purchased for sixpence at a shop in the town—and, when one could escape long enough from the master who was "taking the walk," there was the excitement of dredging the dew-ponds on the Downs for enormous newts with orange-coloured bellies. This business of being out for a walk, coming across something of fascinating interest and then being dragged away from it by a yell from the master, like a dog jerked onwards by the leash, is an important feature of school life, and helps to build up the conviction, so strong in many children, that the things you most want to do are always unattainable.

To support the general statement in the first sentence, each subsequent sentence in the paragraph provides a different example. The last sentence develops yet another generalization from the examples. Drawing on personal experiences, Orwell advances his examples with concrete sensory details—"bathed dangerously among the chalk boulders," "in the silent, sleeping dormitory," "the silky green and purple puss-moth"—but he does not expand any one example to any particular degree. Notice how deftly he moves us from one instance to the next. Words and phrases such as "And then there were still more," "there was also," "And then there was" link the instances by repetition and transitions.

In this selection from *Manchild in the Promised Land,* Claude Brown wants to convince us of the strange things he saw down South, but he uses only a few examples, each somewhat more expanded than Orwell's:

Down South seemed like a dream when I was on the train going back to New York. I saw a lot of things down South that I never saw in my whole life before and most of them I didn't ever want to see again. I saw a great big old burly black man hit a pig in the head with the back of an ax. The pig screamed, oink-oinked a few times, lay down, and started kicking and bleeding . . . and died. When he was real little, I used to chase him, catch him, pick him up, and play catch with him. He was a greedy old pig, but I used to like him. One day when it was real cold, I ate a piece of that pig, and I still liked him. One day I saw Grandma kill a rattlesnake with a hoe. She chopped the snake's head off in the front yard, and I sat on the porch and watched the snake's body keep wiggling till it was nighttime. And I saw an old brown hound dog named Old Joe eat a rat one day, right out in the front yard. He caught the rat in the woodpile and started tearing him open. Old Joe was eating everything in the rat. He ate something that looked like the yellow part in an egg, and I didn't eat eggs for a long time after that. I saw a lady rat have a lot of little baby rats on a pile of tobacco leaves. She had to be a lady, because my first-grade teacher told a girl that ladies don't cry about little things, and the rat had eleven little hairless pink rats, and she didn't even squeak about it.

I made a gun down South out of a piece of wood, some tape, a piece of tire-tube rubber, a nail, some wire, a piece of pipe, and a piece of door hinge. And I saw nothing but blood where my right thumbnail used to be after I shot it for the first time. That nail grew back, little by little. I saw a lot of people who had roots worked on them, but I never saw anybody getting roots worked on them.

Down South sure was a crazy place, and it was good to be going back to New York.

Here, too, images of color, sound, and action make the instances come alive. Note how Brown develops the example of the pig by jerking us back and forth in time. In wrenching the chronology, he sustains the shock of the pig's death. The example takes on special significance because of the temporally disconnected memories the writer associates with the murdered animal. Brown uses *and* as a transitional device at the start of several sentences. The repeated phrase "down South" also helps connect the examples smoothly.

Other Kinds of Examples

Both Orwell and Brown write from personal experience and support their examples with concrete sensory details. However, many writers do not call exclusively on events in their lives, and they use other kinds of details to support a point through exemplification. You should be aware of some of these techniques as you read. Writers will draw on facts, the language of numbers, statistics, and cases. They will draw on quotations or paraphrases chosen from experts in the field. They will summarize. They will cite historical or scientific evidence to advance their ideas. Whatever the nature of the details, good writing always provides them, and you should pay careful attention to the kind of concrete support that a writer will use to make the instances come alive. Note the details in this paragraph from Theodore Ziolkowski's "The Existential Anxieties of Engineering":

> Novels portraying the moral anxiety of engineering did not cease to be written after World War I, of course. Literary genres do not disappear so quickly. Some thirty years later Frederick Philip Grove's *Master of the Mill* (1944) recapitulates all the characteristics of the genre. In this powerful Canadian classic, the engineer Samuel Clark learns that his family's milling empire, which supplies 90 percent of the nation's flour, was founded by a criminal act of his father. Clark is unsuccessful in his efforts to assume the responsibility, to compensate for the crime by social welfare, and to protect his own son from the inherited guilt. His plans for social reform fail; the workers are displaced by technology; and his son is shot during a strike of the enraged millers. By the time Clark dies, he realizes that the great pyramidal mill of seventeen stories had always ruled his destiny and determined his every action. "The history of the mill had been his history"—as much so as the submarines, tun-

nels, and bridges of the earlier novels. Having destroyed its creator and disenfranchised its former workers, it survives as a symbol of the engineer's moral anxiety.

In the first two sentences Ziolkowski asserts that post–World War I novels about "the moral anxiety of engineering" did not vanish. As an example, he presents Grove's 1944 *Master of the Mill,* and then, to support the example, he provides specific details from that novel, including a quotation in the next to the last sentence. It is interesting to see here how only one example, richly expanded with detail, serves very nicely to make the point.

Which writer—Orwell, Brown, or Ziolkowski—has used the right number of examples and the appropriate degree of detail? Of course, there is no answer to that question. As a critical reader, you need to decide for yourself whether the examples and supporting details clarify the point. If you're left just short of being convinced or are overwhelmed with more than you need, the writer may have seriously misjudged his or her audience.

In addition to the quantity and quality of the examples, you should look for their manner of arrangement. Does the writer present the instances chronologically—in the order in which they occurred? Does he or she present them according to importance, building from the least to the most significant example? Do you detect any logic in the scheme of arrangement the writer has used? Why are the examples presented in the order in which you see them? As you read the selections in this chapter, in particular Walt Whitman's "There Was a Child Went Forth," Maxine Kingston's "Family Ghosts," and James Thurber's "Courtship through the Ages," you should consider the relation between the examples and their method of arrangement.

WRITING EXEMPLIFICATION

Many topics lend themselves to development through examples, and as you think about your topic, you should be able to list a number of instances to use as possible means of support in your essay. Suppose you wanted to write about the personality of your old family car, an '82 Chevy, with which you associate many happy memories. You could develop an essay through description alone, showing your reader with careful, loving details all the memorable features of this automobile. Or you could narrate one particular trip you took in which your beat-up sedan served as vehicle, living room, dining room, and bedroom on a slow trip to Maine from your home in Dallas. Or, if you wanted to point to a number of pleasant associations, you would reach for exemplification, using two or three instances to show readers the range of memories this car provides for you. The point here is that the topic and your view of how to develop it will suggest an appropriate rhetorical scheme. You start with a sense of your topic and an idea of your purpose in writing about it, and then you consider the strategy that will help you best achieve your goal.

As with all the rhetorical models you're exploring in this book, try not to think of exemplification as an isolated form. Often you see it working hand in hand with description, narration, comparison and contrast, or definition. In writing an exemplification paper about your memories of your old auto, no doubt you'd weave in concrete sensory details. You might tell two or three brief stories about the car, and you might compare and contrast the instances with each other. Again, the rhetorical form you choose should always serve your purpose and suit your intended audience.

PURPOSE AND AUDIENCE

Sources for Your Examples

The nature of the instances you choose for your exemplification paper will depend on what your aim is in your essay and who your intended reader is. As we pointed out earlier, it's hard to find a topic that cannot be approached through exemplification, and so you probably won't have much trouble identifying an appropriate subject and generating examples to support your ideas. Sources for examples are many. The most familiar, of course, is personal experience. Thus, as a start, you might want to search your memory, your own personal past history, to identify instances you could expand with details. Or you could use a topic idea to stimulate new experiences that you could record accurately and share with your readers. To provide examples of the crush of holiday shoppers at a local mall, you could try to recall those harried buyers who'd impressed you during your last shopping spree, but you might tap a fresher source of details if you returned to the mall, pencil in hand, to observe the hustle and bustle around you carefully. Many writers draw on their imaginations for details, spinning hypotheses, metaphors, or analogies to support an issue with a pointed example. Comparing one shopper, as she trails down the aisle in a clothing store, to a long-necked crane poking and pecking and staring at racks of blouses and dresses might make your point creatively and delight your readers.

In addition to personal experience, all you read in books, newspapers, and magazines; all you hear on the radio, in class, and out on the street; and all you see in the movies and on television are remarkable sources for examples to use in your writing. When you have identified a topic, have thought of what you wish to say about it, and have considered what your audience might expect in your essay, don't hesitate to talk your idea over with friends, to watch some local programs on your Public Broadcasting System or on network television, or to check your topic in the card catalogue, the *Readers' Guide for Periodical Literature,* or the *Social Science and Humanities Index* in the library. Your audience might expect solid details drawn from nonexperiential sources, and your own purpose in writing might be served by examples taken from careful investigation. If you wanted to write about those holiday shoppers for the Chamber of Commerce, a group you wanted to convince of the need for a better safety plan during peak shopping hours, you'd want to draw on statistics of accidents and crimes in former years; testimony by store owners, managers, and customers at the mall; and public records of supplemental budgets for part-time police protection in the mall parking lot and in open areas during December. Intent on persuading your readers to take some course of action, and knowing them to respond to hard data, you might be making a mistake to draw only on your own personal experiences to make your point.

PROCESS

Jot down some ideas in a list or a scratch outline to help you decide on a topic and a purpose for writing. With some record of your thoughts on paper, you might find an informal outline or some other grouping system useful before trying a draft. Cluster together any ideas that are related to the same example. As in most writing tasks, a thesis sentence will be very helpful, and you should spend considerable time writing a clear one even though you may decide ultimately not to use it in the final draft. In most cases your thesis will be a generalization that your examples will expand.

Keeping audience and purpose in mind, decide on how many examples you need to hold the readers' attention. Will you offer one single instance expanded with precise and appropriate details? Will you offer three or four examples each with some supporting information? Will you offer a simple listing in which you provide numerous examples, none of which is backed up to any large degree with details? Take into account too the nature of the kinds of examples and the details the essay will require. Will you use images of concrete sensory details to anchor your examples? Will you use statistics, cases, or other data? Will you quote from a book, a television program, or an actual interview? Will you summarize a song or a short story or a lab report? Will you *invent* an example? When you give a draft of your paper to a friend, ask him or her to tell you whether your examples are believable, whether they suit your point, and whether you've developed them with adequate detail.

As we suggested before, you'll have to make a decision about how to arrange the examples for the strongest presentation. If they involve narration, a simple chronological arrangement might serve you best. To build slowly to the most dramatic instance, many writers choose an arrangement by importance, saving the most crucial example for last. Whatever your method of arrangement, aim for coherence by linking your examples so that readers move smoothly from instance to instance. To achieve a coherent essay, you'll find that transitions, used moderately, will be useful, as will other connecting devices, such as pronouns, repetition, and coordinate structures.

Keep in mind that the particulars in your essay will hold your readers' attention. No matter how thoughtful or original or surprising your generalizations may be, specific instances make those generalizations more immediate, interesting, and, finally, understandable.

STUDENT WRITING

In this selection from an essay by a student writer, note how exemplification advances the presentation of the topic.

The Supernatural

aThesis: people turn to the supernatural to have control of their world

bFirst point: older societies turned to supernatural

cSupporting examples drawn from ancient cultures

dSensory details

eTransition

fNext point, "now, in our age" contrasts (see Chapter Five) with point about older cultures

gSupporting examples drawn from today's world

hQuotation from source as supporting detail

Belief in the supernatural gives people a sense of power they feel they've lost in our busy modern lives.[a] Older societies invested heavily in what we call the supernatural.[b] People could do a dance and believe rain would come or stop.[c] They could say a chant to make someone sick or well. Amid the smoke of incense and raging fires[d] clan members could consult the spirits of their ancestors for blessings on crops or hunts.

Now,[e] in our age,[f] science can tell us why it rains or why someone gets sick or well or why animals for food are scarce. Yet very often the reasons science gives are beyond our command. We don't manage barometric pressure. We think we can alter the genetic makeup of crops for a better harvest, but a premature hailstorm or sudden freeze or drought reminds us of how little control we really have. Environmentally caused heat and rain from global warming seem like something we personally can't affect. And, despite medical advances, genetics and environmental conditions such as toxins in the air and food determine much of our health status.[g]

So,[e] many people today turn to the supernatural not to pray for rain or health but to imagine themselves in a world, like that of our ancestors, in which humans think they have more control over their fates. In *Grandmother Moon: Lunar Magic in Our Lives* (1991), for example, Zsuzsanna Emese Budapest tells us all about "the moon's influence" and how we can "tap its power today for creativity, peace, and health."[h] Thus, the supernatural gives us a world in which we can marshal ghosts, witches, and the forces of nature—moon, sun, sky, stars—to sway the course of our existence.

SUMMING UP: EXEMPLIFICATION

Reading Exemplification

- *Exemplification* means the provision of examples to illustrate an idea with particulars.
- Determine whether the writer has provided examples that solidly illustrate the point.
- Determine the writer's thesis and how it lends itself to examples as supporting details.

- Weigh the writer's use of transitional expressions and repetition to connect the examples smoothly.

- Examine the details used to support the point made through exemplification. Writers may use concrete sensory detail, statistics, or cases; they may use quotations or paraphrases from reliable sources; they may summarize or cite historical or scientific evidence.

- Identify how the writer has arranged the details.

Writing Exemplification

- As you define your topic, list a number of instances to use as possible means of support for your essay.

- Consider your aim and your audience, and produce an appropriate thesis that allows the use of exemplification.

- Choose from a variety of sources for examples, depending on your aim. These sources may include personal experience; quotations and paraphrases drawn from books, periodicals, and other media; and statistics and cases.

- Share thoughts and ideas with reliable friends and classmates as you develop your topic.

- Make a scratch outline; group together any ideas related to the same example.

- Determine the number of examples you need to hold your readers' attention.

- Determine the most appropriate method of arranging your examples for the strongest presentation.

- Show an early draft to someone you trust and weigh carefully any advice or recommendations about how to improve your paper.

- To achieve coherence, link your examples so that readers move smoothly from instance to instance; use transitions moderately to connect ideas.

Family Ghosts

Maxine Hong Kingston

Maxine Hong Kingston was born in Stockton, California, in 1940, the daughter of a scholar who has also been a laundry worker and a midwife who has done field work. Kingston's writing, which focuses on the Chinese and Chinese-American experience, has been aptly described by Susan Cinner as a blend of "myth, legend, history and autobiography into a genre of her own invention." Her honors include the National Book Critics' Circle Award in 1976 for *The Woman Warrior,* which was also named by *Time* magazine as among the top 10 nonfiction works of the decade 1970–1980.

In "Family Ghosts," Maxine Hong Kingston uses description, narration, and flashback to set the stage for a ghost story. She derives her tale from ancient Chinese legends of *Sit Dom Kuei*—semimagical words for which she can better give examples than translations or definitions.

When the thermometer in our laundry reached one hundred and eleven degrees on summer afternoons, either my mother or my father would say that it was time to tell another ghost story so that we could get some good chills up our backs. My parents, my brothers, sisters, great-uncle, and "Third Aunt," who wasn't really our aunt but a fellow villager, someone else's third aunt, kept the presses crashing and hissing and shouted out the stories. Those were our successful days, when so much laundry came in, my mother did not have to pick tomatoes. For breaks we changed from pressing to sorting. [1]

"One twilight," my mother began, and already the chills traveled my back and crossed my shoulders; the hair rose at the nape and the back of the legs, "I was walking home after doctoring a sick family. To get home I had to cross a footbridge. In China the bridges are nothing like the ones in Brooklyn and San Francisco. This one was made from rope, laced and knotted as if by magpies. Actually it had been built by men who had returned after harvesting sea swallow nests in Malaya. They had had to swing over the faces of the Malayan cliffs in baskets they had woven themselves. Though this bridge pitched and swayed in the updraft, no one had ever fallen into the river, which looked like a bright scratch at the bottom of the canyon, as if the Queen of Heaven had swept her great silver hairpin across the earth as well as the sky." [2]

One twilight, just as my mother stepped on the bridge, two smoky columns spiraled up taller than she. Their swaying tops hovered over her head like white cobras, one at either handrail. From stillness came a wind rushing between the smoke spindles. A high sound entered her temple bones. Through the twin whirlwinds she could see the sun and the river, the river twisting in circles, the trees upside down. The bridge moved like a ship, sickening. The earth dipped. She collapsed to the wooden slats, a ladder up the sky, her fingers so [3] weak she could not grip the rungs. The wind dragged her hair behind her, then whipped it forward across her face. Suddenly the smoke spindles disappeared. The world righted itself, and she crossed to the other side. She looked back, but there was nothing there. She used the bridge often, but she did not encounter those ghosts again.

"They were Sit Dom Kuei," said Great-Uncle. "Sit Dom Kuei." 4

"Yes, of course," said my mother. "Sit Dom Kuei." 5

I keep looking in dictionaries under those syllables. "Kuei" means 6 "ghost," but I don't find any other words that make sense. I only hear my great-uncle's river-pirate voice, the voice of a big man who had killed someone in New York or Cuba, make the sounds—"Sit Dom Kuei." How do they translate?

When the Communists issued their papers on techniques for combating 7 ghosts, I looked for "Sit Dom Kuei." I have not found them described anywhere, although now I see that my mother won in ghost battle because she can eat anything—quick, pluck out the carp's eyes, one for Mother and one for Father. All heroes are bold toward food. In the research against ghost fear published by the Chinese Academy of Science is the story of a magistrate's servant, Kao Chung, a capable eater who in 1683 ate five cooked chickens and drank ten bottles of wine that belonged to the sea monster with branching teeth. The monster had arranged its food around a fire on the beach and started to feed when Kao Chung attacked. The swan-feather sword he wrested from this monster can be seen in the Wentung County Armory in Shantung today.

Another big eater was Chou Yi-han of Changchow, who fried a ghost. It 8 was a meaty stick when he cut it up and cooked it. But before that it had been a woman out at night.

Chen Luan-feng, during the Yuan Ho era of the T'ang dynasty (A.D. 9 806–820), ate yellow croaker and pork together, which the thunder god had forbidden. But Chen wanted to incur thunderbolts during drought. The first time he ate, the thunder god jumped out of the sky, its legs like old trees. Chen chopped off the left one. The thunder god fell to the earth, and the villagers could see that it was a blue pig or bear with horns and fleshy wings. Chen leapt on it, prepared to chop its neck and bite its throat, but the villagers stopped him. After that, Chen lived apart as a rainmaker, neither relatives nor the monks willing to bring lightning upon themselves. He lived in a cave, and for years whenever there was drought the villagers asked him to eat yellow croaker and pork together, and he did.

The most fantastic eater of them all was Wei Pang, a scholar-hunter of the 10 Ta Li era of the T'ang dynasty (A.D. 766–779). He shot and cooked rabbits and birds, but he could also eat scorpions, snakes, cockroaches, worms, slugs, beetles, and crickets. Once he spent the night in a house that had been abandoned because its inhabitants feared contamination from the dead man next door. A shining, twinkling sphere came flying through the darkness at Wei. He felled it with three true arrows—the first making the thing crackle and flame; the second dimming it; and the third putting out its lights, sputter. When his servant came running in with a lamp, Wei saw his arrows sticking in a ball of flesh entirely covered with eyes, some rolled back to show the dulling whites. He and the servant pulled out the arrows and cut up the ball into little pieces. The servant cooked the morsels in sesame oil, and the wonderful aroma made Wei laugh. They ate half, saving half to show the household, which would return now.

Big eaters win. When other passers-by stepped around the bundle wrapped in white silk, the anonymous scholar of Hanchow took it home. Inside were three silver ingots and a froglike evil, which sat on the ingots. The scholar laughed at it and chased it off. That night two frogs the size of year-old babies appeared in his room. He clubbed them to death, cooked them, and ate them with white wine. The next night a dozen frogs, together the size of a pair of year-old babies, jumped from the ceiling. He ate all twelve for dinner. The third night thirty small frogs were sitting on his mat and staring at him with their frog eyes. He ate them too. Every night for a month smaller but more numerous frogs came so that he always had the same amount to eat. Soon his floor was like the healthy banks of a pond in spring when the tadpoles, having just turned, sprang in the wet grass. "Get a hedgehog to help eat," cried his family. "I'm as good as a hedgehog," the scholar said, laughing. And at the end of the month the frogs stopped coming, leaving the scholar with the white silk and silver ingots.

Meaning and Idea

1. What was the occasion for Kingston's mother telling a ghost story? What was the desired effect? Summarize the ghost story in your own words.

2. Why did her mother "win" the ghost battle? What generalization does Kingston make about those who conquer ghosts? How many examples of "ghost conquerors" does she offer?

3. Not only does Kingston provide examples of "ghost conquerors," within each example she gives instances of different ghost manifestations. List them in the order in which they appear. Where does she provide examples of what the "ghosts" really may have been?

Language, Form, Structure

1. How does Kingston arrange her examples of "heroes" against ghosts? Name the examples she provides.

2. Midway through her mother's story, the narrator shifts. From whom to whom does the narration shift? What is the effect of this change? There is also a significant shift in the time sequence in this essay. Where does it occur? What grammatical change signals the shift? Why does it occur?

3. What transitions appear after each example? How does the first sentence of the last paragraph act as a transition?

4. List and define five unusual animal names used in this essay.

Ideas for Writing

1. What was your favorite kind of story when you were a child? Write an essay in which you exemplify this type of story and the purposes it served for you besides pure enjoyment.

2. How do you account for the increased interest in the supernatural in today's world? Write an essay in which you argue your point with relevant supporting detail.

3. Kingston's writing often demonstrates a clash of cultures, an old-world Chinese culture and a new-world American culture. Using examples drawn from "Family Ghosts," show whether you agree with this point.

The Black Death

Barbara Tuchman

Barbara Tuchman (1912–1989) made history and historical biography an entertaining topic for readers for decades. She attended Radcliffe, where she studied literature and history. Her love of history and of books was what helped her become one of the most prolific and popular historians of the twentieth century.

She received Pulitzer Prizes for *The Guns of August* (1962), about World War I, and for *Stilwell and the American Experience in China* (1971). The following selection comes from *A Distant Mirror: The Calamitous Fourteenth Century* (1978). The detailed and specific way in which she illustrates the Black Plague is a commanding instance of exemplification.

*I*n October 1347, two months after the fall of Calais, Genoese trading ships put into the harbor of Messina in Sicily with dead and dying men at the oars. The ships had come from the Black Sea port of Caffa (now Feodosiya) in the Crimea, where the Genoese maintained a trading post. The diseased sailors showed strange black swellings about the size of an egg or an apple in the armpits and groin. The swellings oozed blood and pus and were followed by spreading boils and black blotches on the skin from internal bleeding. The sick suffered severe pain and died quickly within five days of the first symptoms. As the disease spread, other symptoms of continuous fever and spitting of blood appeared instead of the swellings or buboes. These victims coughed and sweated heavily and died even more quickly, within three days or less, sometimes in 24 hours. In both types everything that issued from the body—breath, sweat, blood from the buboes and lungs, bloody urine, and blood-blackened excrement— smelled foul. Depression and despair accompanied the physical symptoms, and before the end, "death is seen seated on the face."[1]

The disease was bubonic plague, present in two forms: one that infected the bloodstream, causing the buboes and internal bleeding, and was spread by contact; and a second, more virulent pneumonic type that infected the lungs and was spread by respiratory infection. The presence of both at once caused the high mortality and speed of contagion. So lethal was the disease that cases were known of persons going to bed well and dying before they woke, of doctors catching the illness at a bedside and dying before the patient. So rapidly did it spread from one to another that to a French physician, Simon de Covino, it seemed as if one sick person "could infect the whole world."[2] The malignity of the pestilence appeared more terrible because its victims knew no prevention and no remedy.

[1] Anna M. Campbell, *The Black Death and Men of Learning* (New York: Columbia University Press, 1931), 80.
[2] Francis Aidan Gasquet, Abbot, *The Black Death of 1348 and 1349,* 2nd ed. (London, 1908), 41.

The physical suffering of the disease and its aspects of evil mystery were expressed in a strange Welsh lament which saw "death coming into our midst like black smoke, a plague which cuts off the young, a rootless phantom which has no mercy for fair countenance. Woe is me of the shilling in the armpit! It is seething, terrible . . . a head that gives pain and causes a loud cry . . . a painful angry knob. . . . Great is its seething like a burning cinder . . . a grievous thing of ashy color." Its eruption is ugly like the "seeds of black peas, broken fragments of brittle sea-coal . . . the early ornaments of black death, cinders of the peelings of the cockle weed, a mixed multitude, a black plague like half-pence, like berries. . . ."[3]

Rumors of a terrible plague supposedly arising in China and spreading through Tartary (Central Asia) to India and Persia, Mesopotamia, Syria, Egypt, and all of Asia Minor had reached Europe in 1346. They told of a death toll so devastating that all of India was said to be depopulated, whole territories covered by dead bodies, other areas with no one left alive. As added up by Pope Clement VI at Avignon, the total of reported dead reached 23,840,000. In the absence of a concept of contagion, no serious alarm was felt in Europe until the trading ships brought their black burden of pestilence into Messina while other infected ships from the Levant carried it to Genoa and Venice.

By January 1348 it penetrated France via Marseille, and North Africa via Tunis. Shipborne along coasts and navigable rivers, it spread westward from Marseille through the ports of Languedoc to Spain and northward up the Rhone to Avignon, where it arrived in March. It reached Narbonne, Montpellier, Carcassonne, and Toulouse between February and May, and at the same time in Italy spread to Rome and Florence and their hinterlands. Between June and August it reached Bordeaux, Lyon, and Paris, spread to Burgundy and Normandy, and crossed the Channel from Normandy into southern England. From Italy during the same summer it crossed the Alps into Switzerland and reached eastward to Hungary.

In a given area the plague accomplished its kill within four to six months and then faded, except in the larger cities, where, rooting into the close-quartered population, it abated during the winter, only to reappear in spring and rage for another six months.

In 1349 it resumed in Paris, spread to Picardy, Flanders, and the Low Countries, and from England to Scotland and Ireland as well as to Norway, where a ghost ship with a cargo of wool and a dead crew drifted offshore until it ran aground near Bergen. From there the plague passed into Sweden, Denmark, Prussia, Iceland, and as far as Greenland. Leaving a strange pocket of immunity in Bohemia, and Russia unattacked until 1351, it had passed from most of Europe by mid-1350. Although the mortality rate was erratic, ranging from one fifth in some places to nine tenths or almost total elimination in others, the overall estimate of modern demographers has settled—for the area extending from India to Iceland—around the same figure expressed in Froissart's

---

[3]Philip Ziegler, *The Black Death* (New York, 1969), 190.

casual words: "a third of the world died." His estimate, the common one at the time, was not an inspired guess but a borrowing of St. John's figure for mortality from plague in Revelation, the favorite guide to human affairs of the Middle Ages.

A third of Europe would have meant about 20 million deaths. No one knows in truth how many died. Contemporary reports were an awed impression, not an accurate count. In crowded Avignon, it was said, 400 died daily; 7,000 houses emptied by death were shut up; a single graveyard received 11,000 corpses in six weeks; half the city's inhabitants reportedly died, including 9 cardinals or one third of the total, and 70 lesser prelates. Watching the endlessly passing death carts, chroniclers let normal exaggeration take wings and put the Avignon death toll at 62,000 and even at 120,000, although the city's total population was probably less than 50,000.

When graveyards filled up, bodies at Avignon were thrown into the Rhone until mass burial pits were dug for dumping the corpses. In London in such pits corpses piled up in layers until they overflowed. Everywhere reports speak of the sick dying too fast for the living to bury. Corpses were dragged out of homes and left in front of doorways. Morning light revealed new piles of bodies. In Florence the dead were gathered up by the Compagnia della Misericordia—founded in 1244 to care for the sick—whose members wore red robes and hoods masking the face except for the eyes. When their efforts failed, the dead lay putrid in the streets for days at a time. When no coffins were to be had, the bodies were laid on boards, two or three at once, to be carried to graveyards or common pits. Families dumped their own relatives into the pits, or buried them so hastily and thinly "that dogs dragged them forth and devoured their bodies."[4]

Amid accumulating death and fear of contagion, people died without last rites and were buried without prayers, a prospect that terrified the last hours of the stricken. A bishop in England gave permission to laymen to make confession to each other as was done by the Apostles, "or if no man is present then even to a woman," and if no priest could be found to administer extreme unction, "then faith must suffice."[5] Clement VI found it necessary to grant remissions of sin to all who died of the plague because so many were unattended by priests. "And no bells tolled," wrote a chronicler of Siena, "and nobody wept no matter what his loss because almost everyone expected death. . . . And people said and believed, 'This is the end of the world.'"[6]

In Paris, where the plague lasted through 1349, the reported death rate was 800 a day, in Pisa 500, in Vienna 500 to 600. The total dead in Paris numbered 50,000 or half the population. Florence, weakened by the famine of 1347, lost three to four fifths of its citizens, Venice two thirds, Hamburg and Bremen, though smaller in size, about the same proportion. Cities, as centers of transportation, were more likely to be affected than villages, although once a village

[4]Ziegler, *The Black Death*, 58.
[5]Ziegler, *The Black Death*, 125.
[6]Ferdinand Schevill, *Siena: The History of a Medieval Commune* (New York, 1909), 211.

was infected, its death rate was equally high. At Givry, a prosperous village in Burgundy of 1,200 to 1,500 people, the parish register records 615 deaths in the space of fourteen weeks, compared to an average of thirty deaths a year in the previous decade.[7] In three villages of Cambridgeshire, manorial records show a death rate of 47 percent, 57 percent, and in one case 70 percent.[8] When the last survivors, too few to carry on, moved away, a deserted village sank back into the wilderness and disappeared from the map altogether, leaving only a grass-covered ghostly outline to show where mortals once had lived.

In enclosed places such as monasteries and prisons, the infection of one person usually meant that of all, as happened in the Franciscan convents of Carcassonne and Marseille, where every inmate without exception died. Of the 140 Dominicans at Montpellier only seven survived. Petrarch's brother Gherardo, member of a Carthusian monastery, buried the prior and 34 fellow monks one by one, sometimes three a day, until he was left alone with his dog and fled to look for a place that would take him in.[9] Watching every comrade die, men in such places could not but wonder whether the strange peril that filled the air had not been sent to exterminate the human race. In Kilkenny, Ireland, Brother John Clyn of the Friars Minor, another monk left alone among dead men, kept a record of what had happened lest "things which should be remembered perish with time and vanish from the memory of those who come after us." Sensing "the whole world, as it were, placed within the grasp of the Evil One," and waiting for death to visit him too, he wrote, "I leave parchment to continue this work, if perchance any man survive and any of the race of Adam escape this pestilence and carry on the work which I have begun."[10] Brother John, as noted by another hand, died of the pestilence, but he foiled oblivion.

The largest cities of Europe, with populations of about 100,000, were Paris and Florence, Venice and Genoa. At the next level, with more than 50,000, were Ghent and Bruges in Flanders, Milan, Bologna, Rome, Naples, and Palermo, and Cologne. London hovered below 50,000, the only city in England except York with more than 10,000. At the level of 20,000 to 50,000 were Bordeaux, Toulouse, Montpellier, Marseille, and Lyon in France, Barcelona, Seville, and Toledo in Spain, Siena, Pisa, and other secondary cities in Italy, and the Hanseatic trading cities of the Empire. The plague raged through them all, killing anywhere from one third to two thirds of their inhabitants. Italy, with a total population of 10 to 11 million, probably suffered the heaviest toll. Following the Florentine bankruptcies, the crop failures and workers' riots of 1346–47, the revolt of Cola di Rienzi that plunged Rome into anarchy, the plague came as the peak of successive calamities. As if the world were indeed in the grasp of the Evil One, its first appearance on the European

[7]Yves Renouard, *"La Peste noirs de 1348–50,"* *Rev. de Paris* (March, 1959), 111.

[8]John Saltmarsh, "Plague and Economic Decline in England in the Later Middle Ages," *Cambridge Historical Journal,* vol. VII, no. 1, 1941.

[9]Morris Bishop, *Petrarch and His World* (Bloomington: Indiana University Press, 1963), 273.

[10]Ziegler, *The Black Death,* 195.

mainland in January 1348 coincided with a fearsome earthquake that carved a path of wreckage from Naples up to Venice. Houses collapsed, church towers toppled, villages were crushed, and the destruction reached as far as Germany and Greece. Emotional response, dulled by horrors, underwent a kind of atrophy epitomized by the chronicler who wrote, "And in these days was burying without sorrowe and wedding without friendschippe."[11]

In Siena, where more than half the inhabitants died of the plague, work was abandoned on the great cathedral, planned to be the largest in the world, and never resumed, owing to loss of workers and master masons and "the melancholy and grief" of the survivors. The cathedral's truncated transept still stands in permanent witness to the sweep of death's scythe. Agnolo di Tura, a chronicler of Siena, recorded the fear of contagion that froze every other instinct. "Father abandoned child, wife husband, one brother another," he wrote, "for this plague seemed to strike through the breath and sight. And so they died. And no one could be found to bury the dead for money or friendship. . . . And I, Angolo di Tura, called the Fat, buried my five children with my own hands, and so did many others likewise."[12]

There were many to echo his account of inhumanity and few to balance it, for the plague was not the kind of calamity that inspired mutual help. Its loathsomeness and deadliness did not herd people together in mutual distress, but only prompted their desire to escape each other. "Magistrates and notaries refused to come and make the wills of the dying" reported a Franciscan friar of Piazza in Sicily; what was worse, "even the priests did not come to hear their confessions."[13] A clerk of the Archbishop of Canterbury reported the same of English priests who "turned away from the care of their benefices from fear of death."[14] Cases of parents deserting children and children their parents were reported across Europe from Scotland to Russia.[15] The calamity chilled the hearts of men, wrote Boccaccio in his famous account of the plague in Florence that serves as introduction to the *Decameron.* "One man shunned another . . . kinsfolk held aloof, brother was forsaken by brother, oftentimes husband by wife; nay, what is more, and scarcely to be believed, fathers and mothers were found to abandon their own children to their fate, untended, unvisited as if they had been strangers." Exaggeration and literary pessimism were common in the 14th century, but the Pope's physician, Guy de Chauliac, was a sober, careful observer who reported the same phenomenon: "A father did not visit his son, nor the son his father. Charity was dead."[16]

Yet not entirely. In Paris, according to the chronicler Jean de Venette, the nuns of the Hotel Dieu or municipal hospital, "having no fear of death, tended

---

[11]George Deaux, *The Black Death,* 1347 (London, 1969), 143.
[12]Ziegler, *The Black Death,* 58.
[13]Deaux, *The Black Death,* 49.
[14]Ziegler, *The Black Death,* 261.
[15]J. F. C. Hecker, *The Epidemics of the Middle Ages* (London, 1844), 30.
[16]Gasquet, *The Black Death of 1348 and 1349,* 50–51.

the sick with all sweetness and humility." New nuns repeatedly took the places of those who died, until the majority "many times renewed by death now rest in peace with Christ as we may piously believe."[17]

When the plague entered northern France in July 1348, it settled first in Normandy and, checked by winter, gave Picardy a deceptive interim until the next summer. Either in mourning or warning, black flags were flown from church towers of the worst-stricken villages of Normandy. "And in that time," wrote a monk of the abbey of Fourcarment, "the mortality was so great among the people of Normandy that those of Picardy mocked them." The same un-neighborly reaction was reported of the Scots, separated by a winter's immunity from the English. Delighted to hear of the disease that was scourging the "southrons," they gathered forces for an invasion, "laughing at their enemies." Before they could move, the savage mortality fell upon them too, scattering some in death and the rest in panic to spread the infection as they fled.[18]

In Picardy in the summer of 1349 the pestilence penetrated the castle of Coucy to kill Enguerrand's mother, Catherine, and her new husband. Whether her nine-year-old son escaped by chance or was perhaps living elsewhere with one of his guardians is unrecorded.[19] In nearby Amiens, tannery workers, responding quickly to losses in the labor force, combined to bargain for higher wages.[20] In another place villagers were seen dancing to drums and trumpets, and on being asked the reason, answered that, seeing their neighbors die day by day while their village remained immune, they believed that they could keep the plague from en-tering "by the jollity that is in us. That is why we dance."[21] Further north in Tour-nai on the border of Flanders, Gilles li Muisis, Abbot of St. Martin's, kept one of the epidemic's most vivid accounts. The passing bells rang all day and all night, he recorded, because sextons were anxious to obtain their fees while they could. Filled with the sound of mourning, the city became oppressed by fear, so that the authorities forbade the tolling of bells and the wearing of black and restricted fu-neral services to two mourners. The silencing of funeral bells and of criers' an-nouncements of deaths was ordained by most cities. Siena imposed a fine on the wearing of mourning clothes by all except widows.

Flight was the chief recourse of those who could afford it or arrange it. The rich fled to their country places like Boccaccio's young patricians of Flo-rence, who settled in a pastoral palace "removed on every side from the roads" with "wells of cool water and vaults of rare wines." The urban poor died in their burrows, "and only the stench of their bodies informed neighbors of their deaths." That the poor were more heavily afflicted than the rich was clearly

[17]Jean Birdsall, trans., and Richard A. Newhall, ed., *Chronicle of Jean de Venette* (New York: Co-lumbia University Press, 1853), 49.

[18]Gasquet, *The Black Death of 1348 and 1349,* 53, and Ziegler, *The Black Death,* 198.

[19]*L'Art de vérifier les dates des faits historiques,* par un Religieux de la Congregation de St.-Maur, vol. XII (Paris, 1818), 237.

[20]Gasquet, *The Black Death of 1348 and 1349,* 57.

[21]Paulin Paris, ed., *Grandes Croniques de France,* vol. VI (Paris, 1838), 486–87.

remarked at the time, in the north as in the south. A Scottish chronicler, John of Fordun, stated flatly that the pest "attacked especially the meaner sort and common people—seldom the magnates."[22] Simon de Covino of Montpellier made the same observation. He ascribed it to the misery and want and hard lives that made the poor more susceptible, which was half the truth.[23] Close contact and lack of sanitation was the unrecognized other half. It was noticed too that the young died in greater proportion than the old; Simon de Covino compared the disappearance of youth to the withering of flowers in the fields.[24]

In the countryside peasants dropped dead on the roads, in the fields, in their houses. Survivors in growing helplessness fell into apathy, leaving ripe wheat uncut and livestock untended. Oxen and asses, sheep and goats, pigs and chickens ran wild and they too, according to local reports, succumbed to the pest. English sheep, bearers of the precious wool, died throughout the country. The chronicler Henry Knighton, canon of Leicester Abbey, reported 5,000 dead in one field alone, "their bodies so corrupted by the plague that neither beast nor bird would touch them," and spreading an appalling stench.[25] In the Austrian Alps wolves came down to prey upon sheep and then, "as if alarmed by some invisible warning, turned and fled back into the wilderness." In remote Dalmatia bolder wolves descended upon a plague-stricken city and attacked human survivors.[26] For want of herdsmen, cattle strayed from place to place and died in hedgerows and ditches. Dogs and cats fell like the rest.[27]

The dearth of labor held a fearful prospect because the 14th century lived close to the annual harvest both for food and for next year's seed. "So few servants and laborers were left," wrote Knighton, "that no one knew where to turn for help." The sense of a vanishing future created a kind of dementia of despair. A Bavarian chronicler of Neuberg on the Danube recorded that "Men and women . . . wandered around as if mad" and let their cattle stray "because no one had any inclination to concern themselves about the future."[28] Fields went uncultivated, spring seed unsown. Second growth with nature's awful energy crept back over cleared land, dikes crumbled, salt water reinvaded and soured the lowlands. With so few hands remaining to restore the work of centuries, people felt, in Walsingham's words, that "the world could never again regain its former prosperity."[29]

Though the death rate was higher among the anonymous poor, the known and the great died too. King Alfonso XI of Castile was the only reigning

[22]Ziegler, *The Black Death,* 199.
[23]Gasquet, *The Black Death of 1348 and 1349,* 42.
[24]Raymond Cazelles, *"La Peste de 1348–49 en Langue d'oil: épidémic proletarienne et enfantine," Bull philologique et historique* (1962), 293–305.
[25]Ziegler, *The Black Death,* 175.
[26]Ziegler, *The Black Death,* 84, 111.
[27]Gasquet, *The Black Death of 1348 and 1349,* 44, 61.
[28]Ziegler, *The Black Death,* 84.
[29]Henri Denifle, *La Dësolation des églises, monastēres et hopitaux en France pendant la guerre de cent ans,* vol. I (Paris, 1899), 273.

monarch killed by the pest, but his neighbor King Pedro of Aragon lost his wife, Queen Leonora, his daughter Marie, and a niece in the space of six months. John Cantacuzene, Emperor of Byzantium, lost his son. In France the lame Queen Jeanne and her daughter-in-law Bonne de Luxemburg, wife of the Dauphin, both died in 1349 in the same phase that took the life of Enguerrand's mother. Jeanne, Queen of Navarre, daughter of Louis X, was another victim. Edward III's second daughter, Joanna, who was on her way to marry Pedro, the heir of Castile, died in Bordeaux. Women appear to have been more vulnerable than men, perhaps because being more housebound, they were more exposed to fleas. Boccaccio's mistress Fiammetta, illegitimate daughter of the King of Naples, died, as did Laura, the beloved—whether real or fictional—of Petrarch. Reaching out to us in the future, Petrarch cried, "Oh happy posterity who will not experience such abysmal woe and will look upon our testimony as a fable."[30]

In Florence Giovanni Villani, the great historian of his time, died at 68 in the midst of an unfinished sentence: ". . . *e dure questo pistolenza fino a . . .* (in the midst of this pestilence there came to an end . . .).[31] Siena's master painters, the brothers Ambrogio and Pietro Lorenzetti, whose names never appear after 1348, presumably perished in the plague, as did Andrea Pisano, architect and sculptor of Florence. William of Ockham and the English mystic Richard Rolle of Hampole both disappear from mention after 1349. Francisco Datini, merchant of Prato, lost both his parents and two siblings. Curious sweeps of mortality afflicted certain bodies of merchants in London. All eight wardens of the Company of Cutters, all six wardens of the Hatters, and four wardens of the Goldsmiths died before July 1350. Sir John Pulteney, master draper and four times Mayor of London, was a victim, likewise Sir John Montgomery, Governor of Calais.

Among the clergy and doctors the mortality was naturally high because of the nature of their professions. Out of 24 physicians in Venice, 20 were said to have lost their lives in the plague, although, according to another account, some were believed to have fled or to have shut themselves up in their houses. At Montpellier, site of the leading medieval medical school, the physician Simon de Covino reported that, despite the great number of doctors, "hardly one of them escaped."[32] In Avignon, Guy de Chauliac confessed that he performed his medical visits only because he dared not stay away for fear of infamy, but "I was in continual fear."[33] He claimed to have contracted the disease but to have cured himself by his own treatment; if so, he was one of the few who recovered.

Clerical mortality varied with rank. Although the one-third toll of cardinals reflects the same proportion as the whole, this was probably due to their concentration in Avignon. In England, in strange and almost sinister procession,

[30]Ziegler, *The Black Death,* 45.

[31]Frederick Snell, *The Fourteenth Century* (Edinburgh, 1899), 334.

[32]Campbell, *The Black Death and Men of Learning,* 98, 31.

[33]James Westfall Thompson, *Economic and Social History of Europe in the Later Middle Ages* (New York, 1931), 379.

the Archbishop of Canterbury, John Stratford, died in August 1348, his appointed successor died in May 1349, and the next appointee three months later, all three within a year. Despite such weird vagaries, prelates in general managed to sustain a higher survival rate than the lesser clergy. Among bishops the deaths have been estimated at about one in twenty. The loss of priests, even if many avoided their fearful duty of attending the dying, was about the same as among the population as a whole.

Government officials, whose loss contributed to the general chaos, found, on the whole, no special shelter. In Siena four of the nine members of the governing oligarchy died, in France one third of the royal notaries, in Bristol 15 out of the 52 members of the Town Council or almost one third. Tax-collecting obviously suffered, with the result that Philip VI was unable to collect more than a fraction of the subsidy granted him by the Estates in the winter of 1347–48. [26]

Lawlessness and debauchery accompanied the plague as they had during the great plague of Athens of 430 B.C., when according to Thucydides, men grew bold in the indulgence of pleasure: "For seeing how the rich died in a moment and those who had nothing immediately inherited their property, they reflected that life and riches were alike transitory and they resolved to enjoy themselves while they could."[34] Human behavior is timeless. When St. John had his vision of plague in Revelation, he knew from some experience or race memory that those who survived "repented not of the work of their hands. . . . Neither repented they of their murders, nor of their sorceries, nor of their fornication, nor of their thefts." [27]

Meaning and Idea

1. What were the various symptoms of the bubonic plague? Why was the "malignity of the disease" so terrible? How did the survivors dispose of the dead bodies?

2. Give examples of why Tuchman notes that "the plague was not the kind of calamity that inspired mutual help." In what cases *did* people show humanity amid the horrors of the disease? How did the authorities counteract the terrible fear in Tournai? in Siena?

3. What does Tuchman mean by the sentence, "The sense of a vanishing future created a kind of dementia of despair"? What examples does she give to support her observation?

4. Who were some of "the known and the great" who died in the plague? Why was the mortality rate particularly high among doctors and the clergy?

5. Why does Tuchman say in the last paragraph, "Human behavior is timeless"?

---

[34]Raymond Crawfurd, *Plague and Pestilence in Literature and Art* (Oxford, 1914), 30–31.

Language, Form, Structure

1. How do the first two paragraphs serve as a strong introduction to the selection? Which sentence or sentences best express the thesis of the piece? Why do you think that the writer begins with a narrative about the sailors from the Black Sea port of Caffa?

2. Tuchman uses examples throughout the essay to illustrate different aspects of her topic. Which examples are most vivid? How does the piling up of examples serve to convince you of the accuracy of her observations? How does the writer use quotations from other sources to help make her point? Are these quotations tedious and overwhelming, or are they valuable and dramatic? Support your opinion with references to the text.

3. How does the writer use time, particularly dates, as transitions? What other transitional elements does she use? Does the selection, to your mind, achieve the right level of unity and coherence? In what ways other than the use of transitions does Tuchman aim for these important features of writing?

4. How does the last paragraph serve as a fitting conclusion to the selection?

5. Write definitions for the following words: virulent; contagion; malignity; atrophy; truncated; apathy; dearth; dementia.

Ideas for Writing

1. Imagine yourself as an eyewitness to the bubonic plague in the fourteenth century. Write an essay to describe and analyze the events that surround you and your feelings as a surviving observer. Provide examples from Tuchman as well as from your own imagination, trying to achieve as much historical accuracy as you can.

2. Select a cataclysm—that is, a violent natural occurrence—in recent or current history. Do research, if necessary, and write an essay about it, using the principles of exemplification. You might wish to write about AIDS, the eruption of Mount St. Helens, or the San Francisco earthquake, for example.

3. Write a critical essay about how Tuchman's use of examples in this essay advances her thesis. Point out the strongest use of examples and the weakest.

Courtship through the Ages

James Thurber

James Thurber (1894–1961) was perhaps best known and loved by the American public for his stories, essays, and line drawings in *The New Yorker* magazine, where he was employed for many years after being hired by E. B. White in 1925. Thurber always cast a humorously ironic eye on the human condition. His best-known collections include *Is Sex Necessary?* (with E. B. White, 1929), *The Seal in the Bedroom and Other Predicaments* (1932), *The Thurber Carnival* (1945), and *Thurber Country* (1953).

"Courtship through the Ages," Thurber's accumulation of examples of "love displays" by the male toward the opposite sex, first appeared in *The New Yorker* in 1939; that same year it was also collected in Thurber's book *My World—and Welcome to It.*

Surely nothing in the astonishing scheme of life can have non-plussed Nature so much as the fact that none of the females of any of the species she created really cared very much for the male, as such. For the past ten million years Nature has been busily inventing ways to make the male attractive to the female, but the whole business of courtship, from the marine annelids up to man, still lumbers heavily along, like a complicated musical comedy. I have been reading the sad and absorbing story in Volume 6 (Cole to Dama) of the *Encyclopaedia Britannica*. In this volume you can learn all about cricket, cotton, costume designing, crocodiles, crown jewels, and Coleridge, but none of these subjects is so interesting as the Courtship of Animals, which recounts the sorrowful lengths to which all males must go to arouse the interest of a lady.

We all know, I think, that Nature gave man whiskers and a mustache with the quaint idea in mind that these would prove attractive to the female. We all know that, far from attracting her, whiskers and mustaches only made her nervous and gloomy, so that man had to go in for somersaults, tilting with lances, and performing feats of parlor magic to win her attention; he also had to bring her candy, flowers, and the furs of animals. It is common knowledge that in spite of all these "love displays" the male is constantly being turned down, insulted, or thrown out of the house. It is rather comforting, then, to discover that the peacock, for all his gorgeous plumage, does not have a particularly easy time in courtship; none of the males in the world do. The first peahen, it turned out, was only faintly stirred by her suitor's beautiful train. She would often go quietly to sleep while he was whisking it around. The *Britannica* tells us that the peacock actually had to learn a certain little trick to wake her up and revive her interest: he had to learn to vibrate his quills so as to make a rustling sound. In ancient times man himself, observing the ways of the peacock, probably tried vibrating his whiskers to make a rustling sound; if so, it didn't get him anywhere. He had to go in for something else; so, among other things, he went in for gifts.

It is not unlikely that he got this idea from certain flies and birds who were making no headway at all with rustling sounds.

One of the flies of the family Empidae, who had tried everything, finally hit on something pretty special. He contrived to make a glistening transparent balloon which was even larger than himself. Into this he would put sweetmeats and tidbits and he would carry the whole elaborate envelope through the air to the lady of his choice. This amused her for a time, but she finally got bored with it. She demanded silly little colorful presents, something that you couldn't eat but that would look nice around the house. So the male Empis had to go around gathering flower petals and pieces of bright paper to put into his balloon. On a courtship flight a male Empis cuts quite a figure now, but he can hardly be said to be happy. He never knows how soon the female will demand heavier presents, such as Roman coins and gold collar buttons. It seems probable that one day the courtship of the Empidae will fall down, as man's occasionally does, of its own weight.

The bowerbird is another creature that spends so much time courting the female that he never gets any work done. If all the male bowerbirds became nervous wrecks within the next ten or fifteen years, it would not surprise me. The female bowerbird insists that a playground be built for her with a specially constructed bower at the entrance. This bower is much more elaborate than an ordinary nest and is harder to build; it costs a lot more, too. The female will not come to the playground until the male has filled it up with a great many gifts: silvery leaves, red leaves, rose petals, shells, beads, berries, bones, dice, buttons, cigar bands, Christmas seals, and the Lord knows what else. When the female finally condescends to visit the playground, she is in a coy and silly mood and has to be chased in and out of the bower and up and down the playground before she will quit giggling and stand still long enough even to shake hands. The male bird is, of course, pretty well done in before the chase starts, because he has worn himself out hunting for eyeglass lenses and begonia blossoms. I imagine that many a bowerbird, after chasing a female for two or three hours, says the hell with it and goes home to bed. Next day, of course, he telephones someone else and the same trying ritual is gone through again. A male bowerbird is as exhausted as a nightclub habitué before he is out of his twenties.

The male fiddler crab has a somewhat easier time, but it can hardly be said that he is sitting pretty. He has one enormously large and powerful claw, usually brilliantly colored, and you might suppose that all he had to do was reach out and grab some passing cutie. The very earliest fiddler crabs may have tried this, but, if so, they got slapped for their pains. A female crab will not tolerate any caveman stuff; she never has and she doesn't intend to start now. To attract a female, a fiddler crab has to stand on tiptoe and brandish his claw in the air. If any female in the neighborhood is interested—and you'd be surprised how many are not—she comes over and engages him in light badinage, for which he is not in the mood. As many as a hundred females may pass the time of day with him and go on about their business. By nightfall of an average courting day, a fiddler crab who has been standing on tiptoe for eight or ten hours waving a heavy claw in the air is in pretty sad shape. As in the case of the males of all species, however, he gets out of bed next morning, dashes some water on his face, and tries again.

The next time you encounter a male web-spinning spider, stop and reflect that he is too busy worrying about his love life to have any desire to bite you. Male web-spinning spiders have a tougher life than any other males in the animal kingdom. This is because the female web-spinning spiders have very poor eyesight. If a male lands on a female's web, she kills him before he has time to lay down his cane and gloves, mistaking him for a fly or a bumblebee who has tumbled into her trap. Before the species figured out what to do about this, millions of males were murdered by ladies they called on. It is the nature of spiders to perform a little dance in front of the female, but before a male spinner could get near enough for the female to see who he was and what he was up to, she would lash out at him with a flat-iron or a pair of garden shears. One night, nobody knows when, a very bright male spinner lay awake worrying about calling on a lady who had been killing suitors right and left. It came to him that this business of dancing as a love display wasn't getting anybody anywhere except the grave. He decided to go in for web-twitching, or strand-vibrating. The next day he tried it on one of the nearsighted girls. Instead of dropping in on her suddenly, he stayed outside the web and began monkeying with one of its strands. He twitched it up and down and in and out with such a lilting rhythm that the female was charmed. The serenade worked beautifully; the female let him live. The *Britannica*'s spider-watchers, however, report that this system is not always successful. Once in a while, even now, a female will fire three bullets into a suitor or run him through with kitchen knife. She keeps threatening him from the moment he strikes the first low notes on the outside strings, but usually by the time he has got up to the high notes played around the center of the web, he is going to town and she spares his life.

Even the butterfly, as handsome a fellow as he is, can't always win a mate merely by fluttering around and showing off. Many butterflies have to have scent scales on their wings. Hepialus carries a powder puff in a perfumed pouch. He throws perfume at the ladies when they pass. The male tree cricket, Oecanthus, goes Hepialus one better by carrying a tiny bottle of wine with him and giving drinks to such doxies as he has designs on. One of the male snails throws darts to entertain the girls. So it goes, through the long list of animals, from the bristle worm and his rudimentary dance steps to man and his gift of diamonds and sapphires. The golden-eye drake raises a jet of water with his feet as he flies over a lake; Hepialus has his powder puff, Oecanthus his wine bottle, man his etchings. It is a bright and melancholy story, the age-old desire of the male for the female, the age-old desire of the female to be amused and entertained. Of all the creatures on earth, the only males who could be figured as putting any irony into their courtship are the grebes and certain other diving birds. Every now and then a courting grebe slips quietly down to the bottom of a lake and then, with a mighty "Whoosh!," pops out suddenly a few feet from his girl friend, splashing water all over her. She seems to be persuaded that this is a purely loving display, but I like to think that the grebe always has a faint hope of drowning her or scaring her to death.

I will close this investigation into the mournful burdens of the male with the   8
Britannica's story about a certain Argus pheasant. It appears that the Argus displays himself in front of a female who stands perfectly still without moving a
feather. . . . The male Argus the *Britannica* tells about was confined in a cage
with a female of another species, a female who kept moving around, emptying ash-
trays and fussing with lampshades all the time the male was showing off his talents.
Finally, in disgust, he stalked away and began displaying in front of his water
trough. He reminds me of a certain male (*Homo sapiens*) of my acquaintance who
one night after dinner asked his wife to put down her detective magazine so that he
could read her a poem of which he was very fond. She sat quietly enough until he
was well into the middle of the thing, intoning with great ardor and intensity. Then
suddenly there came a sharp, disconcerting *slap!* It turned out that all during the
male's display, the female had been intent on a circling mosquito and had finally
trapped it between the palms of her hands. The male in this case did not stalk away
and display in front of a water trough; he went over to Tim's and had a flock of
drinks and recited the poem to the fellas. I am sure they all told bitter stories of their
own about how their displays had been interrupted by females. I am also sure that
they all ended up singing "Honey, Honey, Bless Your Heart."

Meaning and Idea

1. On what piece of writing does Thurber hinge his essay? Why does he
   use it?

2. In paragraph 2, Thurber gives examples of the things men had to do to
   attract females because their whiskers and mustaches weren't enough. What
   are those other things? What is the ultimate substitute—the "something
   else"—mentioned in that paragraph? What examples of it does Thurber
   include in subsequent paragraphs?

3. Who does Thurber think ultimately has the upper hand in male-female
   relations? How do you know? How does the last sentence of the essay fit in
   with his evaluation?

Language, Form, Structure

1. What is the initial generalization that Thurber sets out to support through
   exemplification? Do you agree with this generalization? Why is
   exemplification a suitable technique for this essay?

2. Thurber tends to use *hyperbole* (the deliberate exaggeration of an idea or
   description) quite freely throughout the essay. Give three examples of the
   most hyperbolic statements. To what purpose does he use hyperbole?

3. An *analogy* is a comparison of two subjects drawn from divergent areas. If
   you showed point by point the similarities between an anthill and a crowded
   train station, you'd be writing an analogy. What is the implicit analogy

throughout this essay? Where in each paragraph is that analogy made most explicitly? What purpose does that explicit analogy serve?

4. How does Thurber arrange his examples in paragraphs 3 through 6? In paragraph 7? Why does he change his arrangement in paragraph 7? Briefly outline Thurber's use of transitions in paragraphs 2 through 7.

5. What is Thurber's attitude toward his topic in this essay? How can you tell? Does he maintain the same attitude throughout the essay?

6. Make certain that you know the meanings of the following words: nonplussed; feats; habitué; badinage; doxies; intoning; ardor.

Ideas for Writing

1. Write a paragraph using examples in which you explain your favorite means of attracting the opposite sex. Which are most effective? Which are least effective?

2. Go to a place where men and women gather socially—a cafeteria, a pub, a lecture hall, for example—and observe their behavior toward each other, especially their means of attracting each other. Write a single generalization about your observation of the scene and support it in an essay of exemplification.

3. Clearly, Thurber uses *irony* here almost to the limits of *sarcasm*. Write a short essay in which you analyze the positive and negative sides of the use of irony in this essay. Support your ideas with specific examples drawn from the text.

Census 2000

William Safire

William Safire has worn many hats: as a political commentator of distinctly libertarian and conservative views, as a functionary in several Republican administrations, and as a writer of spy books and historical novels. Born in 1929, Safire began his career in 1949 as a reporter at the *New York Herald Tribune*. He served in the U.S. Army from 1952 to 1953, after which he became a radio correspondent in Europe and then returned to journalism in New York. In 1968 he was tapped to become a special assistant and a speechwriter to President Richard Nixon. The political connections Safire has acquired over the years have given his political columns a particularly personal edge. Safire consistently subjects hypocrisy within the major parties to ferocious attacks. In 1978 he was awarded the Pulitzer Prize for distinguished commentary.

"Census 2000" is taken from the popular language column Safire writes weekly for *The New York Times Magazine*. Exploring both matters of usage and histories of words, "On Language" tackles vexing questions of grammar, usage, and politics, often drawing vociferous letters to the editor.

*T*en years ago this week, I received in the mail a census form that began, "Please use a black lead pencil only." Naturally, I objected to the loose placement of the *only,* preferring "use only a black lead pencil" or the even more direct and simple "use a black lead pencil." 1

This year, reflecting the leap forward in technology, the United States Census 2000 says, "Please use a black or blue pen." I have a blue pen that writes with black ink; I suppose that's O.K. But I also have a black pen that writes with red ink; is that impermissible? 2

The clear intent is "use black or blue ink." But if the Bureau of the Census, conscious of literal correctness, wrote those words, millions of people unfamiliar with the details of writing instruments would respond: "I don't use ink; I use a ballpoint pen. Does this mean I have to fill this out with a fountain pen? There'll be big inkblots all over the form. What do they want from my life?" 3

Therefore, I give the census-form-writers a little leeway. In return, they try not to make the same mistakes twice. The 1990 form concluded with the admonition "Make sure you have . . . filled this form completely," and I complained that it was possible to fill *in* or fill *out* a form, but not to simply fill a form because a form is not a bucket. In the 2000 form, the error is averted by the adoption of the "Thank you for not smoking" trick: "Thank you for completing your official U.S. Census form." It seems friendlier and is not subject to attack by nitpickers in this space. 4

However, our intrepid people-counters cannot be counted on for the correct use of commas. Turning to the first question in the long form, and aided by 5 my fellow nit-picker Jeff McQuain, we read "people staying here on April 1, 2000 who have no other permanent place to stay. . . ." If a date in midsentence uses a comma, then another comma must follow the year: "on April 1, 2000, who. . . ."

Later, the form directs, "Start with the person, or one of the people living here who owns. . . ." This cries out for a balancing comma: "person, or one of the people living here, who owns. . . ." Better still, forget the commas in that sentence entirely: "Start with the person or one of the people living here who owns. . . ." Use two commas to separate the phrase or no commas if it does not need separation.

This comedy of commas continues with "What is this person's age and what is this person's date of birth?" The two independent clauses call for separation by a comma after "age." (An even better fix is to obviate the need for a comma by shortening it to "What are this person's age and date of birth?")

And the form-writers are tensed up. Right at the start, the past tense is used in "How many people *were* living or staying in this house . . . on April 1, 2000?" Then the tense is switched to the present with instruction to include them "even if they *have* another place to live." Gotta be this or that: *are* and *have* or *were* and *had*.

The Parallel Construction Workers Union should file a grievance about the way a question about occupation is phrased: "patient care, directing hiring policies, supervising order clerks, repairing automobiles, reconciling financial records" are the examples given. The last four of those listed begin with gerunds; why, then, does "patient care" have no "ing"? To be in proper parallel, it should be "caring for patients."

At least that was a series of examples not masquerading as a sentence; correctly, with no verb, no period was placed at the end. However, in what is called the ancestry question (more precisely the lineage question), we read "Italian, Jamaican, African Am., Cambodian, . . . Taiwanese, Ukrainian, and so on." The "and so on" tries to make it all-inclusive, but there is no verb to make it a sentence—and yet in this instance a period is put at the end. No style is followed. And why, when no other group is followed by "Am.," is "African" so designated—and without a hyphen to boot?

Hats off to the writers for sticking to past practice in identifying aboriginal Americans as "American Indians" and not the confusing "Native Americans." That last could mean anyone born in America, in contrast to "Naturalized Americans," citizens born elsewhere. Past designations as Eskimo and Aleut are now lumped together as "Alaska Native."

Thus, the sensitive question of "What is this person's race?" has three main categories: the above "American Indian or Alaska Native," which follows "white" and three choices of names for the other—"Black, African Am., or Negro." The Census Bureau explains that the terminology changes with each generation and that "Negro" was put in so that older members of the group would not feel outdated. What about whites from South Africa? I presume the form presumes that they will choose to describe themselves as white.

In a triumph of inclusive self-differentiation, 11 other racial groups are listed, from "Asian Indian" to "Samoan," with blank space left for anyone to write in "Some other race."

Language has its limitations. In the question about relationships, the form includes, among others, "Husband/wife, Natural-born son/daughter, Adopted son/daughter." That "Natural-born" seems awkward; obviously it is there to distinguish between what the Bible colorfully called "the fruit of one's loins" and an adopted child. But with artificial insemination and test-tube babies in the mix, what is natural and what is not? [13]

The delicious bureaucratic euphemism "POSSLQ" is gone. "Persons of the Opposite Sex Sharing Living Quarters," which appeared in the 1990 census, has been replaced by two categories: "Housemate/Roommate," who shares living quarters "primarily to share expenses," and the new "Unmarried Partner." Says the bureau: "Mark the 'Unmarried Partner' box if the Person is not related to Person 1, shares living quarters, and who [*who* should be dropped] has a close personal relationship with Person 1." [14]

Prediction: In the 2010 census, this last category will be listed as "Lovers." Also, the form-writers will be warier about their use and abuse of commas. [15]

Meaning and Idea

1. What occasion prompted Safire to write this essay?

2. What is wrong with the comma in the census form's citation of the April date?

3. What does Safire mean when he writes, "Language has its limitations"?

4. Identify three instances in which Safire congratulates the census writers on proper grammar or the avoidances of errors.

Language, Form, Structure

1. What is Safire's purpose in writing? What sentence, examples, or details make that purpose clear?

2. There is, of course, no such thing as the "Parallel Construction Workers Union" (paragraph 9). Likewise, a reader might not automatically find the "bureaucratic euphemism" "Persons of the Opposite Sex Sharing Living Quarters" "delicious," as Safire claims to. Analyze the role humor plays in Safire's piece. How does it relate to what you identified as the purpose of the essay?

3. Analyze the two predictions Safire makes in his conclusions. How do these predictions relate to the rest of the essay?

4. Write definitions for the following words: leeway; intrepid; masquerade; aboriginal.

Ideas for Writing

1. Find a piece of bureaucratic writing of the sort Safire criticizes and do a similar analysis. You might want to examine your college catalogue, an application for a loan, or an application for a job. Rewrite some of the sentences to improve the grammar and clarity and analyze the changes you have made.

2. At first some readers might find Safire's grammatical critique nit-picking or pedantic. Write an essay pointing out the larger political issues that Safire leaves for his readers to identify between the lines of his corrections and comments.

What I've Learned from Men

Barbara Ehrenreich

Barbara Ehrenreich was born in Montana in 1941. To the public, she is widely known for her regularly appearing column in *Time* magazine and *The Guardian* of London. Ehrenereich's career, however, has spanned a broad spectrum of areas. In 1968 she earned a Ph.D. in biology, a subject which was the focus of her early writing. Chief among her early concerns was health care. She soon moved beyond that focus, however, and has since tackled a range of subjects linked only by a strong feminism and an abiding concern for the impact of poverty, particularly on women. In 1978 she cowrote *For Her Own Good: One Hundred Fifty Years of the Experts' Advice to Women* with Deirdre English. In 1993 she published her first novel, titled *Kipper's Game.* Her latest book is *Nickle and Dimed: On (Not) Getting By in America* (2001).

"What I've Learned from Men" reflects Ehrenreich's interest both in feminist causes and in the experience of the middle class. The mixture of analysis and personal experience is typical of her work, as is the interest in the impact of confining gender roles on middle-class women.

*F*or many years I believed that women had only one thing to learn from men: how to get the attention of a waiter by some means short of kicking over the table and shrieking. Never in my life have I gotten the attention of a waiter, unless it was an off-duty waiter whose car I'd accidentally scraped in a parking lot somewhere. Men, however, can summon a maître d' just by thinking the word "coffee," and this is a power women would be well-advised to study. What else would we possibly want to learn from them? How to interrupt someone in mid-sentence as if you were performing an act of conversational euthanasia? How to drop a pair of socks three feet from an open hamper and keep right on walking? How to make those weird guttural gargling sounds in the bathroom?

But now, at mid-life, I am willing to admit that there are some real and useful things to learn from men. Not from all men—in fact, we may have the most to learn from some of the men we like the least. This realization does not mean that my feminist principles have gone soft with age: what I think women could learn from men is how to get *tough.* After more than a decade of consciousness-raising, assertiveness training, and hand-to-hand combat in the battle of the sexes, we're still too ladylike. Let me try that again—we're just too *damn* ladylike.

Here is an example from my own experience, a story that I blush to recount. A few years ago, at an international conference held in an exotic and luxurious setting, a prestigious professor invited me to his room for what he said would be an intellectual discussion on matters of theoretical importance. So far, so good. I showed up promptly. But only minutes into the conversation—held in all-too-adjacent chairs—it emerged that he was interested in something more substantial than a meeting of minds. I was disgusted, but not enough to overcome 30-odd years of programming in ladylikeness. Every time his comments took a lecherous turn, I chattered distractingly; every time his hand found its way to my knee, I returned it as if it were something he had misplaced. This went on for an unconscionable period (as much as 20 minutes); then there was a minor scuffle, a dash for the door, and I was out—with nothing violated but my self-esteem. I, a full-grown feminist, conversant with such matters as rape crisis counseling and sexual harassment at the workplace, had behaved like a ninny—or, as I now understand it, like a lady.

The essence of ladylikeness is a persistent servility masked as "niceness." For example, we (women) tend to assume that it is our responsibility to keep everything "nice" even when the person we are with is rude, aggressive, or emotionally AWOL. (In the above example, I was so busy taking responsibility for preserving the veneer of "niceness" that I almost forgot to take responsibility for myself.) In conversations with men, we do almost all the work: sociologists have observed that in male-female social interactions it's the woman who throws out leading questions and verbal encouragements ("So how did you *feel* about that?" and so on) while the man, typically, says "Hmmmm." Wherever we go, we're perpetually smiling—the on-cue smile, like the now-outmoded curtsy, being one of our culture's little rituals of submission. We're trained to feel embarrassed if we're praised, but if we see a criticism coming at us from miles down the road, we rush to acknowledge it. And when we're feeling aggressive or angry or resentful, we just tighten up our smiles or turn them into rueful little moues. In short, we spend a great deal of time acting like wimps.

For contrast, think of the macho stars we love to watch. Think, for example, of Mel Gibson facing down punk marauders in "The Road Warrior". . . John Travolta swaggering his way through the early scenes of "Saturday Night Fever". . . or Marlon Brando shrugging off the local law in "The Wild One." Would they simper their way through tight spots? Chatter aimlessly to keep the conversation going? Get all clutched up whenever they think they might—just might—have hurt someone's feelings? No, of course not, and therein, I think, lies their fascination for us.

The attraction of the "tough guy" is that he has—or at least seems to have—what most of us lack, and that is an aura of power and control. In an article, feminist psychiatrist Jean Baker Miller writes that "a woman's using self-determined power for herself is equivalent to selfishness [and] destructiveness"—an equation that makes us want to avoid even the appearance of power. Miller cites cases of women who get depressed just when they're on the verge of success—and of women who do succeed and then bury their achievement in self-deprecation. As an example, she describes one company's periodic meetings to recognize outstanding salespeople: when a woman is asked to say a few words about her achievement, she tends to say something like, "Well, I really don't know how it happened. I guess I was just lucky this time." In contrast, the men will cheerfully own up to the hard work, intelligence, and so on, to which they owe their success. By putting herself down, a woman avoids feeling brazenly powerful and potentially "selfish"; she also does the traditional lady's work of trying to make everyone else feel better ("She's not really so smart, after all, just lucky").

So we might as well get a little tougher. And a good place to start is by cutting back on the small acts of deference that we've been programmed to perform since girlhood. Like unnecessary smiling. For many women—waitresses, flight attendants, receptionists—smiling is an occupational requirement, but there's no reason for anyone to go around grinning when she's not being paid for it. I'd suggest that we save our off-duty smiles for when we truly feel like sharing them, and if you're not sure what to do with your face in the meantime, study Clint Eastwood's expressions—both of them.

Along the same lines, I think women should stop taking responsibility for every human interaction we engage in. In a social encounter with a woman, the average man can go 25 minutes saying nothing more than "You don't say?" "Izzat so?" and, of course, "Hmmmm." Why should we do all the work? By taking so much responsibility for making conversations go well, we act as if we had much more at stake in the encounter than the other party—and that gives him (or her) the power advantage. Every now and then, we deserve to get more out of a conversation than we put into it: I'd suggest not offering information you'd rather not share ("I'm really terrified that my sales plan won't work") and not, out of sheer politeness, soliciting information you don't really want ("Wherever did you get that lovely tie?"). There will be pauses, but they don't have to be awkward for *you.*

It is true that some, perhaps most, men will interpret any decrease in female deference as a deliberate act of hostility. Omit the free smiles and perky conversation-boosters and someone is bound to ask, "Well, what's come over *you* today?" For most of us, the first impulse is to stare at our feet and make vague references to a terminally ill aunt in Atlanta, but we should have as much right to be taciturn as the average (male) taxi driver. If you're taking a vacation from smiles and small talk and some fellow is moved to inquire about what's "bothering" you, just stare back levelly and say, the international debt crisis, the arms race, or the death of God.

There are all kinds of ways to toughen up—and potentially move up—at work, and I leave the details to the purveyors of assertiveness training. But Jean Baker Miller's study underscores a fundamental principle that anyone can master on her own. We can stop acting less capable than we actually are. For example, in the matter of taking credit when credit is due, there's a key difference between saying "I was just lucky" and saying "I had a plan and it worked." If you take the credit you deserve, you're letting people know that you were confident you'd succeed all along, and that you fully intend to do so again.

Finally, we may be able to learn something from men about what to do   11
with anger. As a general rule, women get irritated: men get *mad.* We make tight little smiles of ladylike exasperation; they pound on desks and roar. I wouldn't recommend emulating the full basso profundo male tantrum, but women do need ways of expressing justified anger clearly, colorfully, and, when necessary, crudely. If you're not just irritated, but *pissed off,* it might help to say so.

I, for example, have rerun the scene with the prestigious professor many   12
times in my mind. And in my mind, I play it like Bogart. I start by moving my chair over to where I can look the professor full in the face. I let him do the chattering, and when it becomes evident that he has nothing serious to say, I lean back and cross my arms, just to let him know that he's wasting my time. I do not smile, neither do I nod encouragement. Nor, of course, do I respond to his blandishments with apologetic shrugs and blushes. Then, at the first flicker of lechery, I stand up and announce coolly, "All right, I've had enough of this crap." Then I walk out—slowly, deliberately, confidently. Just like a man.

Or—now that I think of it—just like a woman.   13

Meaning and Idea

1. Give examples of some of the behaviors women are prone to that Ehrenreich analyzes. What about those behaviors does Ehrenreich find objectionable? How does she contrast them with male behavior?

2. When specific new attitudes and actions does Ehrenreich recommend that women adopt? What consequences does she anticipate will result?

3. What are some of the qualities Ehrenreich claims to admire about men? Do you think this is honest admiration or irony?

Language, Form, Structure

1. What is Ehrenreich's thesis? How does exemplification serve the argument? How does humor serve the thesis?

2. Why do you think Ehrenreich chooses her own experience to be the first example of "ladylike" behavior? Then she returns to it in the conclusion (even though it makes her blush). How does the use of her own experience make the essay more effective?

3. Analyze Ehrenreich's use of slang terms such as *ninny, pissed off,* and *crap.* In each case, how does the use of slang advance her argument?

4. Define the following words and use them correctly in a sentence: lecherous; simper; unconscionable; servility; veneer; taciturn; purveyors; blandishments.

Ideas for Writing

1. Use exemplification to write an essay advocating how men should behave.

2. Observe an example of a woman in a position of power interacting with men and then analyze that interaction in light of Ehrenreich's essay. What examples of "ladylike" behavior did you observe? Did that behavior demonstrate, as Ehrenreich would argue, "persistent servility?"

3. Write an essay in which you evaluate Ehrenreich's examples. Which is the strongest? Which is the weakest? Argue whether her examples are sufficient to support her thesis.

There Was a Child Went Forth

Walt Whitman

Walt Whitman affected American poetry profoundly not only because of his wide-ranging subject matter but also because of his experimental verse. Born on New York's Long Island in 1819, he wrote poems infused with such divergent forces as democratic idealism, opera, Shakespeare, Quaker religious philosophy, sexual openness, and the rhythms of city life. His magnum opus, *Leaves of Grass* (1855), proclaimed the great freedom of the human mind, body, and spirit. Whitman died in 1892.

In this poem Whitman provides a series of indelible images in an effort to define the personality of a child. Critics point to many autobiographical lines in "There Was a Child Went Forth." But the poem goes beyond the concrete experiential world of the poet, a world so vividly re-created here, to a statement on the relation between human character and experience and the unity of all in nature.

*T*here was a child went forth every day,
And the first object he look'd upon, that object he became,
And that object became part of him for the day or a certain part of the day,
Or for many years or stretching cycles of years.

The early lilacs became part of this child.   5
And grass and white and red morning-glories, and white and red clover, and the
      song of the phoebe-bird,
And the Third-month lambs and the sow's pink-faint litter, and the mare's foal
      and the cow's calf,
And the noisy brood of the barnyard or by the mire of the pond-side,
And the fish suspending themselves so curiously below there, and the beautiful
      curious liquid,
And the water-plants with their graceful flat heads, all became part of him.   10
The field-sprouts of Fourth-month and Fifth-month became part of him,
Winter-grain sprouts and those of the light-yellow corn, and the esculent roots of
      the garden,
And the apple-trees cover'd with blossoms and the fruit afterward, and wood-
      berries, and the commonest weeds by the road,
And the old drunkard staggering home from the outhouse of the tavern whence
      he had lately risen,
And the schoolmistress that pass'd on her way to the school,   15
And the friendly boys that pass'd, and the quarrelsome boys,
And the tidy and fresh-cheek'd girls, and the barefoot negro boy and girl,

And all the changes of city and country wherever he went.

His own parents, he that had father'd him and she that had conceiv'd him in her
    womb and birth'd him,

They gave this child more of themselves than that,   20

They gave him afterward every day, they became part of him.

The mother at home quietly placing the dishes on the suppertable,

The mother with mild words, clean her cap and gown, a wholesome odor falling
    off her person and clothes as she walks by,

The father, strong, self-sufficient, manly, mean, anger'd, unjust,

The blow, the quick loud word, the tight bargain, the crafty lure,   25

The family usages, the language, the company, the furniture, the yearning and
    swelling heart,

Affection that will not be gainsay'd, the sense of what is real, the thought if after
    all it should prove unreal,

The doubts of day-time and the doubts of night-time, the curious whether and how,

Whether that which appears so is so, or is it all flashes and specks?

Men and women crowding fast in the streets, if they are not flashes and specks   30
    what are they?

The streets themselves and the facades of houses, and goods in the windows,

Vehicles, teams, the heavy-plank'd wharves, the huge crossing at the ferries,

The village on the highland seen from afar at sunset, the river between,

Shadows, aureola and mist, the light falling on roofs and gables of white or
    brown two miles off,

The schooner near by sleepily dropping down the tide, the little boat slack-tow'd   35
    astern,

The hurrying tumbling waves, quick-broken crests, slapping,

The strata of color'd clouds, the long bar of maroon-tint away solitary by itself,
    the spread of purity it lies motionless in,

The horizon's edge, the flying sea-crow, the fragrance of salt marsh and shore mud,

These became part of that child who went forth every day, and who now goes,
    and will always go forth every day.

Meaning and Idea

1. State in your own words the point Whitman is trying to make in this poem.
   Where does he come closest to stating his purpose? What is the value to the
   poem of the last line in the first stanza (line 4)?

2. What experiences with nature, family, and city are most vivid to you? What
   is the character of the child that Whitman is attempting to draw for us here?

3. What are the doubts and questions aroused by the child's experiences?
   Would you call them typical of a child growing up? Why?

4. Describe the child's father and mother.

Language, Form, Structure

1. Which images are richest in concrete sensory detail? Whitman has a special knack of sketching characters with a series of single words or short phrases. Why are the modifiers describing the father particularly well chosen? What is the effect of placing all the modifiers after the noun *father?*

2. How is this poem an instance of exemplification? Why does Whitman provide a listing of so many details? Why didn't he just choose five or six examples instead of all the ones you see here? How does the use of all these examples reinforce the purpose and meaning of the poem?

3. Why does Whitman repeat the phrase "part of him" (or variations of that phrase) in other lines of the poem? What other words or phrases does he repeat? What is your reaction to the last line of the poem? (Compare its meaning to the meaning of the first stanza.)

4. How has Whitman used sentence structure as a unifying element? What is the advantage of beginning so many sentences with the word *and?* with the word *the?*

5. Explain the meanings of the following words: mire; gainsay'd; facades; aureola; strata. Why has Whitman used the terms "Third-month," "Fourth-month," and "Fifth-month"?

Ideas for Writing

1. Write a paragraph entitled "What Am I?" in which you provide a series of concrete sensory images that show the various experiences that helped shape your personality.

2. Check library resources to investigate the life of a person who interests you. Try to find an identifiable element of character or personality. Then, in an essay, use exemplification to show how experiences in that person's life demonstrate that element of character.

3. A critic of nineteenth-century American literature, F. O. Matthiessen, writes about Whitman: "He understood that language was not 'an abstract construction' made by the learned, but that it had arisen out of the work and needs, the joys and struggles and desires of long generations of humanity, and that it had 'its bases broad and low, close to the ground.' Words are not arbitrary inventions, but the product of human events and customs, the progeny of folkways." Consider the validity of this statement in regard to "There Was a Child Went Forth." Use specific examples from the poem to support your point.

We Real Cool

Gwendolyn Brooks

Gwendolyn Brooks was born in 1917 and moved to Chicago at a very early age. Her deceptively simple, powerful poetry is a lyrical voice for the black and inner-city cultures of Chicago's South Side. Brooks's mother, a former teacher, encouraged her daughter's literary interests. The poet's father provided a central image for her work: a capable and dignified but quite ordinary black man.

In 1950, Brooks became the first African-American woman to win the Pulitzer Prize. She was named poet laureate of Illinois in 1969, a post she still holds. The easy flow of her words and the way she is inspired by rhythm are well suited to her subjects and themes, but sometimes this poetic skill hides a beguiling, ironic aspect. "We Real Cool" is an example of this.

*T*he Pool Players Seven at the Golden Shovel

We real cool. We
Left school. We

Lurk late. We
Strike straight. We   5

Sing sin. We
Thin gin. We

Jazz June. We
Die soon.   10

Meaning and Idea

1. What is the theme of the poem? Who are "We"? How many of them are there? Does the poet think they are truly "cool"? How can you tell?

2. What examples in the poem indicate the lifestyles the speakers lead? What do "Jazz June," "Thin gin," and those other expressions mean?

3. Is the last sentence of the poem, "We / Die soon," coming from the same point of view as the previous line? Whose or what kind of awareness does the poet express in these last words? It may be useful to count the number of *We*'s and the number of "players."

Language, Form, Structure

1. Think about the rhythm of the poem. Speak the poem aloud if you have not already actually *listened* to it. What special elements do you note about the rhythm? How does the poet achieve this rhythm? Why has she chosen this rhythm?

2. Can you tell what the poet's attitude toward the pool players is? Which of the following best describes that attitude: *admiration, contempt, pity, irony?* What does the reader *know* about the speakers based on what they say and/or their attitudes?

3. Be sure you know all the possible meanings for *lurk, thin,* and *jazz.*

Ideas for Writing

1. Think of a person who you feel is or was misdirected or misguided. Write an essay that presents examples to explain what caused this misdirection. Don't forget to include what you feel results from this person's lifestyle.

2. Think of a person who you feel is "trouble." Why do you feel this way? What are the examples that brought you to your point of view? Now, using the examples to support your point, create an essay on the topic.

3. What elements of the poem do you find the strongest? In an essay, explain what the theme of the poem is, why the poem's elements work so well, and how they reveal and support that theme.

My Last Duchess

Robert Browning

Along with Tennyson, Robert Browning (1812–1889) is considered a shining poet of the late Victorian period. He was raised in an artistic and cultured family of nonconformists—a sort of "pre-Bohemian" English intellectual group. Browning's education was excellent and well rounded, and in his early teens he began to write poetry, heavily influenced by Shelley. Browning is considered the master of the dramatic monologue, and his three most popular poems in this vein are *My Last Duchess, Fra Lippo Lippi,* and *Andrea Del Sarto.* His other well-known works include *Rabbi Ben Ezra* (1864) and the popular children's classic *The Pied Piper of Hamelin* (1842). He was happily married to the poet Elizabeth Barrett Browning.

Browning's "My Last Duchess" is considered one of the best-crafted and most consistent revelations of character in all of English poetry. Browning has the Duke of Ferrara (a man probably as powerful as a monarch in sixteenth-century Italy) choose just the right descriptive details and examples to reveal to us the full extent of his massive egotism.

FERRARA

*T*hat's my last duchess painted on the wall,
Looking as if she were alive. I call
That piece a wonder, now; Fra Pandolf's hands
Worked busily a day, and there she stands.
Will't please you sit and look at her? I said   5
"Fra Pandolf" by design, for never read
Strangers like you that pictured countenance,
The depth and passion of its earnest glance,
But to myself they turned (since none puts by
The curtain I have drawn for you, but I)   10
And seemed as they would ask me, if they durst,
How such a glance came there; so, not the first
Are you to turn and ask thus. Sir, 'twas not
Her husband's presence only, called that spot
Of joy into the Duchess' cheek; perhaps   15
Fra Pandolf chanced to say, "Her mantle laps
Over my lady's wrist too much," or, "Paint
Must never hope to reproduce the faint
Half-blush that dies along her throat." Such stuff
Was courtesy, she thought, and cause enough   20
For calling up that spot of joy. She had
A heart—how shall I say?—too soon made glad,

Too easily impressed; she liked whate'er
She looked on, and her looks went everywhere.
Sir, 'twas all one! My favor at her breast,   25
The dropping of the daylight in the West,
The bough of cherries some officious fool
Broke in the orchard for her, the white mule
She rode with round the terrace—all and each
Would draw from her alike the approving speech,   30
Or blush, at least. She thanked men—good! but thanked
Somehow—I know not how—as if she ranked
My gift of a nine-hundred-years-old name
With anybody's gift. Who'd stoop to blame
This sort of trifling? Even had you skill   35
In speech—which I have not—to make your will
Quite clear to such an one, and say, "Just this
Or that in you disgusts me; here you miss,
Or there exceed the mark"—and if she let
Herself be lessoned so, nor plainly set   40
Her wits to yours, forsooth, and made excuse—
E'en then would be some stooping; and I choose
Never to stoop. Oh, sir, she smiled, no doubt,
Whene'er I passed her; but who passed without
Much the same smile? This grew; I gave commands;   45
Then all smiles stopped together. There she stands
As if alive. Will't please you rise? We'll meet
The company below, then. I repeat,
The Count your master's known munificence
Is ample warrant that no just pretense   50
Of mine for dowry will be disallowed;
Though his fair daughter's self, as I avowed
At starting, is my object. Nay, we'll go
Together down, sir. Notice Neptune, though,
Taming a sea-horse, thought a rarity,   55
Which Claus of Innsbruck cast in bronze for me.

Meaning and Idea

1. "My Last Duchess" is considered one of the foremost examples of dramatic monologue in English. A *dramatic monologue* is a form of lyric poetry in which a character reveals—to another person, but without dialogue—his or her inner self at a particular moment and situation. What is the situation in this monologue? To whom is the Duke of Ferrara speaking? What does the duke reveal about himself to the speaker?

2. What does the duke think was *right* about his duchess? What does he think was *wrong* with her?

3. What is the meaning of lines 21–23: "She had / A heart—how shall I say?—too soon made glad, / Too easily impressed"? How does the duke support his allegation?

4. Within the poem's dramatic context, what do you suppose were the "commands" of line 45? Why did all smiles stop after their fulfillment?

5. What, according to the duke, was his ultimate gift to the duchess? How did she receive it?

Language, Form, Structure

1. Within the dramatic context of the monologue, what is the duke's purpose in relating this story? Do you think he has any ulterior motives? What are they? What is the significance of the word *last* in the first line of the poem?

2. How does *exemplification* operate in this poem? How are the examples important in revealing the meaning?

3. What is the use of *dramatic irony* in this poem? (*Dramatic irony* refers to a situation in which the reader knows the truth to be other than what is presented.)

4. Write dictionary definitions for the following words: countenance; durst; mantle; bough; officious; lessoned; munificence; pretense; dowry.

Ideas for Writing

1. Choose a nonabstract painting that you enjoy and make a narrative generalization about it. Then describe the painting in a paragraph that supports your generalization with examples drawn from the painting.

2. Write a paragraph in which you attempt to convince someone of the rightness or wrongness of an action by using exemplification as your support technique.

3. What kind of woman is Ferrara's last duchess? Write an essay in which you attempt to analyze her true character.

Good Times

Lucille Clifton

Lucille Clifton was born in 1936 in upstate New York and graduated from Howard University. She is the recipient of a National Endowment for the Arts grant, among other awards, and has taught at the Columbia University School of the Arts. She says of herself, "I am a black woman poet, and I sound like one." Her poetry is characterized by understatement and succinctness, and although her poems often deal with the nitty-gritty difficulties of life, they are essentially affirmative and optimistic. Clifton's collections of poetry include *Good Times* (1969), *Good News about the Earth* (1972), and *An Ordinary Woman* (1974).

Lucille Clifton's "Good Times" is ultimately a social commentary in which the examples are often ironically double-edged.

*M*y Daddy has paid the rent
and the insurance man is gone
and the lights is back on
and my uncle Brud has hit
for one dollar straight   5
and they is good times
good times
good times

My Mama has made bread
and Grampaw has come   10
and everybody is drunk
and dancing in the kitchen
and singing in the kitchen
oh these is good times
good times   15
good times

oh children think about the
good times

Meaning and Idea

1. In a single sentence, state the main point of this poem. Is Clifton writing about good times or their opposite?

2. What is the meaning of the lines "and my uncle Brud has hit / for one dollar straight"?

3. What examples of "good times" does the speaker give? How do the examples convey the social status of the speaker?

4. At the end of the poem, why does the speaker tell the children to "think about the / good times"?

Language, Form, Structure

1. What is the general tone of this poem? Does that tone seem to contradict the title? How?

2. What is the significance of the stanza divisions of this poem? How does it allow Clifton to arrange her examples?

3. Is there irony in this poem? If so, what kind of irony is it? How does the poet achieve it? What is its purpose?

4. What is the role of repetition in this poem? What does it contribute to the poem's meaning? Notice how the only transition is the word *and*. Why does Clifton use this word eight times? What is the purpose of repeating the words *good times* seven times?

Ideas for Writing

1. Write an exemplification essay called "Good Times" or "Bad Times." Draw on your own experiences to illustrate your point.

2. Write an essay in which you give examples to explain "success." Attempt to be ironic, and end your paragraph with a caution to your readers.

3. This poem is written in very colloquial language. Some "purist" readers of poetry still object to such "unexalted" language being used for poetry. In general, how do you react to poetry of this sort? What else have you read with similar language use (either poetry or prose)? In your answer, make specific references to this and other works.

Clutter

William Zinsser

William Zinsser was born in New York in 1922 and received an A.B. degree from Princeton in 1944. He served in North Africa in World War II, and worked as a journalist and an editor for many years before he began to teach. He has said, "The only way to learn to write is to force yourself to produce a certain number of words on a regular basis," and that is just what he has done. He has produced some 20 books and countless articles over the years.

On Writing Well, the source for this selection, is an important and commonly used work on the art of expository writing. By instruction and example, Zinsser show us exactly what uncluttered writing is.

*F*ighting clutter is like fighting weeds—the writer is always slightly behind. New varieties sprout overnight, and by noon they are part of American speech. Consider what President Nixon's aide John Dean accomplished in just one day of testimony on TV during the Watergate hearings. The next day everyone in American was saying "at this point in time" instead of "now."

Consider all the prepositions that are draped onto verbs that don't need any help. We no longer head committees. We head them up. We don't face problems anymore. We face up to them when we can free up a few minutes. A small detail, you may say—not worth bothering about. It *is* worth bothering about. Writing improves in direct ratio to the number of things we can keep out of it that shouldn't be there. "Up" in "free up" shouldn't be there. To write clean English you must examine every word you put on paper. You'll find a surprising number that don't serve any purpose.

Take the adjective "personal," as in "a personal friend of mine," "his personal feeling" or "her personal physician." It's typical of hundreds of words that can be eliminated. The personal friend has come into the language to distinguish him or her from the business friend, thereby debasing both language and friendship. Someone's feeling *is* that person's personal feeling—that's what "his" and "her" mean. As for the personal physician, that's the man or woman summoned to the dressing room of a stricken actress so she won't have to be treated by the impersonal physician assigned to the theater. Someday I'd like to see that person identified as "her doctor." Physicians are physicians, friends are friends. The rest is clutter.

Clutter is the laborious phrase that has pushed out the short word that means the same thing. Even before John Dean, people had stopped saying "now." They were saying "currently," or "at the present time," or "presently" (which means "soon"). Yet the idea can always be expressed by "now" to mean the immediate moment ("Now I can see him"), or by "today" to mean the historical present ("Today prices are high"), or simply by a form of the verb "to be" ("It is raining"). There's no need to say, "At the present time we are experiencing precipitation."

Speaking of which, we are experiencing considerable difficulty getting *that* word out of the language. Even your dentist will ask if you are experiencing any pain. If he had his own kid in the chair he would say, "Does it hurt?" He would, in short, be himself. By using a more pompous phrase in his professional role, he not only sounds more important; he blunts the painful edge of truth. It's the language of the flight attendant demonstrating the oxygen mask that will drop down if the plane should run out of air. "In the unlikely possibility that the aircraft should experience such an eventuality," she begins—a phrase so oxygen-depriving in itself that we are prepared for any disaster. As for her request to "kindly extinguish all smoking materials," I often wonder what materials are smoking. It's a terrifying sentence.

Clutter is the ponderous euphemism that turns a slum into a depressed socioeconomic area, a salesman into a marketing representative, garbage collectors into waste-disposal personnel and the town dump into the volume reduction unit. I think of Bill Mauldin's cartoon of two hoboes riding a freight car. One of them says, "I started as a simple bum, but now I'm hard-core unemployed." Clutter is political correctness gone amok. I saw an ad for a boys' camp designed to provide "individual attention for the minimally exceptional."

Clutter is the official language used by corporations to hide their mistakes. When the Digital Equipment Corporation recently eliminated 3,000 jobs, its statement didn't mention layoffs; those were "involuntary methodologies." When an Air Force missile crashed, it "impacted with the ground prematurely." When General Motors had a plant shutdown, that was a "volume-related production-schedule adjustment." Today a company that goes belly-up has "a negative cash-flow position."

Clutter is the language of the Pentagon throwing dust in the eyes of the populace by calling an invasion a "reinforced protective reaction strike" and by justifying its vast budgets on the need for "counterforce deterrence." How can we grasp such vaporous double-talk? As George Orwell pointed out in "Politics and the English Language," an essay written in 1946 but cited frequently during the Vietnam and Cambodia years of Presidents Johnson and Nixon, "Political speech and writing are largely the defense of the indefensible. . . .Thus political language has to consist largely of euphemism, question-begging and sheer cloudy vagueness." Orwell's warning that clutter is not just a nuisance but a deadly tool has come true in the recent decades of American military adventurism in Southeast Asia, Central America and other parts of the world.

Verbal camouflage reached new heights during General Alexander Haig's tenure as secretary of state during the Reagan administration. Before Haig, nobody had thought of saying "at this juncture of maturization" to mean "now." He told the American people that he saw "improved pluralization" in El Salvador, that terrorism could be fought with "meaningful sanctionary teeth" and that intermediate nuclear missiles were "at the vortex of cruciality." As for any worries the public might harbor, his message—reduced to one-syllable words—was "leave it to Al." What he actually said was, "We must push this to a lower decibel of public fixation. I don't think there's much of a learning curve to be achieved in this area of content."

I could go on quoting examples from various fields—every profession has its growing arsenal of jargon to fire at the layman and hurl him back from its walls. But the list would be tedious. The point of raising it now is to serve notice that clutter is the enemy, whatever form it takes. It slows the reader and makes the writer seem pretentious.

Beware, then, of the long word that's no better than the short word: "assistance" (help), "numerous" (many), "facilitate" (ease), "individual" (man or woman), "remainder" (rest), "initial" (first), "implement" (do), "sufficient" (enough), "attempt" (try), "referred to as" (called), and hundreds more. Beware of all the slippery new fad words for which the language already has equivalents: overview and quantify, paradigm and parameter, optimize and maximize, prioritize and potentialize. They are all weeds that will smother what you write. Don't dialogue with someone you can talk to. Don't interface with anybody.

Just as insidious are the little word clusters with which we explain how we propose to go about our explaining, or which inflate a simple preposition or conjunction into a whole windy phrase. "I might add," "It should be pointed out," "It is interesting to note"—how many sentences begin with these dreary clauses announcing what the writer is going to do next? If you might add, add it. If it should be pointed out, point it out. If it is interesting to note, *make* it interesting. Being told that something is interesting is the surest way of tempting the reader to find it dull; are we not all stupefied by what follows when someone says, "This will interest you"? As for the windy inflations, they are the countless phrases like "with the possible exception of" (except), "due to the fact that" (because), "he totally lacked the ability to" (he couldn't), "until such time as" (until), "for the purpose of" (for).

Is there any way to recognize clutter at a glance? Here's a device my students at Yale found helpful. I would put brackets around any component in a piece of writing that wasn't doing useful work. Often just one word got bracketed: the unnecessary preposition appended to a verb ("order up"), or the adverb that carries the same meaning as the verb ("smile happily"), or the adjective that states a known fact ("tall skyscraper"). Often my brackets surrounded the little qualifiers that weaken any sentence they inhabit ("a bit," "sort of"), or announcements like "I'm tempted to say," or phrases like "in a sense," which don't mean anything. Sometimes my brackets surrounded an entire sentence—the one that essentially repeats what the previous sentence said, or that says something readers don't need to know or can figure out for themselves. Most first drafts can be cut by 50 percent. They are swollen with words and phrases that do no new work.

My reason for bracketing superfluous words instead of crossing them out was to avoid violating the students' sacred prose. I wanted to leave the sentence intact for them to analyze. I was saying, "I may be wrong, but I think this can be deleted and the meaning won't be affected. But *you* decide: read the sentence without the bracketed material and see if it works." In the early weeks of the term I handed back papers that were festooned with brackets. Entire paragraphs were bracketed. But soon the students learned to put mental brackets around their own clutter, and by the end of the term their papers were almost clean. Today many of those students are professional writers, and they tell me, "I still see your brackets—they're following me through life."

You can develop the same eye. Look for the clutter in your writing and prune it ruthlessly. Be grateful for everything you can throw away. Reexamine each sentence you put on paper. Is every word doing new work? Can any thought be expressed with more economy? Is anything pompous or pretentious or faddish? Are you hanging on to something useless just because you think it's beautiful?   15

Simplify, simplify.   16

Meaning and Idea

1. Zinsser's thesis is quite obvious. When a room or a house is filled with "clutter," what does it look like? What is Zinsser saying about language that suffers from clutter?

2. What examples does the writer provide to help you see what he means by clutter? What is the *ponderous euphemism*?

3. How do corporations and the government contribute to clutter?

4. Answer the question Zinsser raises: "Is there any way to recognize clutter at a glance?"

5. Considering the title of Zinsser's book, *On Writing Well,* what do you think of the tactic he espouses?

Language, Form, Structure

1. What is the effect of the simile in the opening sentence? What other figures of speech lend clarity and focus to Zinsser's piece?

2. How does the use of the many examples he provides strengthen Zinsser's argument? How does Zinsser himself avoid clutter?

3. What does Zinsser gain by talking about small amounts of clutter (unnecessary prepositions and then self-evident adjectives) before he begins to discuss more "substantial" examples?

4. Comment on the last line—two words, really, that serve as the closing of the selection. In what ways is this the perfect conclusion to the topic Zinsser has selected?

5. Define the following words and use each in a sentence: debasing; laborious; pompous; ponderous; euphemism; amok; vaporous; fixation; jargon; tedious; pretentious; insidious; stupefied; superfluous.

Ideas for Writing

1. Find an example in a newspaper or a magazine of the kind of "clutter" Zinsser criticizes and rewrite it to state more clearly what the writer intended.

2. Write an essay called "Simplify, Simplify" in which you use examples to propose ways to streamline some element of your life—your eating or study habits, getting to school or work, or your own writing, for example.

3. Paying special attention to paragraphs 7 and 8, write an essay in which you discuss the uses and abuses of the kind of language Zinsser discusses.

CROSSOVER

1. Barbara Tuchman in "The Black Death" (this chapter) and Susan Sontag in "Two Diseases" (Chapter Five) explore the physical and social repercussions of epidemic disease. Which examples of different aspects of disease seem most powerful to you? Why? What techniques seem most effective?

2. Maxine Hong Kingston in "Family Ghosts" (this chapter) and Langston Hughes in "Salvation" (Chapter Two) consider powerful childhood experiences in potent communities. How does each author characterize his or her community? What specific details contribute to the overall characterization?

Chapter Four

■

PROCESS ANALYSIS

INTRODUCTION TO PROCESS ANALYSIS

In early recorded literature we can identify the impulse to explain and to understand how to perform a task. "Make thee an ark of gopher wood," proclaims the voice of the Lord of the Old Testament to Noah; "rooms shalt thou make in the ark, and shalt pitch it within and without with pitch."

> And this is how thou shalt make it: the length of the ark three hundred cubits, the breadth of it fifty cubits, and the height of it thirty cubits. A light shalt thou make to the ark, and to a cubit shalt thou finish it upward; and the door of the ark shalt thou set in the side thereof; with lower, second, and third stories shalt thou make it. And I, behold, I do bring the flood of waters upon the earth, to destroy all flesh, wherein is the breath of life, from under heaven; every thing that is in the earth shall perish. But I will establish My covenant with thee; and thou shalt come into the ark, thou, and thy sons, and thy wife, and thy sons' wives, with thee. And of every living thing of all flesh, two of every sort shalt thou bring into the ark, to keep them alive with thee; they shall be male and female. Of the fowl after their kind, and of the cattle after their kind, of every creeping thing of the ground after its kind, two of every sort shall come unto thee, to keep them alive. And take thou unto thee of all food that is eaten and gather it to thee; and it shall be for food for thee, and for them. Thus did Noah; according to all that God commanded him, so did he.

Certainly, the simplicity of language and the precise sequence of events belie the complexity of the tasks here—it would be no easy task to make an ark simply by following these instructions—but this explanation from the Book of Genesis provides a striking example of *process analysis* as a key element in early creative literature.

What Is Analysis?

Simply put, the general concept of analysis is the attempt to break something down into parts in an effort to make the whole clear and understandable. When you analyze a novel or a poem, for example, you look carefully at the words and sentences, the chapters or stanzas to give you insights into the total work. Sometimes *causal analysis* motivates your exploration; when you examine a historical event—the Boxer Rebellion, say, or the invasion of Cambodia—you may be looking for the chain of causes and effects that make the situation comprehensible (see Chapter Seven). *Process analysis* states and explains the steps required to do or to make something or to show how something is (or was) done or is (or was) made.

READING PROCESS ANALYSIS

The distinction above between learning how to do or make something and learning how it is done or made is not simply semantic. Rather, the distinction lies at the heart of process analysis as a reflection of thought and as a means of broadening knowledge for readers.

The "How-to" Obsession

The modern reading public has an ongoing love affair with "how-to" books; these books line shelf after shelf in trade book stores everywhere. The cover of an issue of *Publisher's Weekly,* the journal of the book industry, showed for one publisher more than 20 "do-it-yourself" volumes issued in a single year: how to design and build deck patios, basic remodeling techniques, how to build and use greenhouses, and how to design and install outdoor lighting, just to name a few. As a further indication of our seemingly endless attraction to books on process, the *New York Times* Book Review now includes the category "Advice, How-to, and Miscellaneous" in the list of weekly best sellers, a list that for years and years reported on only the two familiar groups, "Fiction" and "Nonfiction." We all want instructions on how to perform some process so that we ourselves can perform it in our backyards, under the hoods of our automobiles, in the solitude of our homes. When Hemingway writes to his 1920 *Toronto Star* readers (see pages 212 to 214), he tells them exactly what steps to take in order to camp out successfully. Even today we can follow the process and duplicate it. Hemingway wrote this piece so that anyone interested in a short stay in the great outdoors could get the most out of it.

Yet as readers we are equally interested in learning about processes that we have no intention of duplicating. We simply want to see a thing from the inside out, so to speak. We read with rapt attention about how homemade bombs are built or about how flappers made bathtub gin, never thinking for a moment to try schemes like these ourselves. When we read about how music boxes work, how the FBI captured one of its most wanted criminals, or how a woman born in the slums of Chicago became a multimillionaire as a banker, we are seeking information for its own sake; our joy here lies simply in learning the steps that produced some situation that fascinates us. Thoreau's goal in the selection from *Walden* reprinted here is to tell you how, not how to. Similarly, Ovid explains step-by-step procedures without the slightest interest in getting his readers to try to copy them. Sometimes writers explain a process so clearly that it could be copied even if the author had not so intended it.

Readers' Expectations

Despite the array of topics that face a reader interested in processes, good "how-to" writing shares a common ground, and alert readers have certain expectations. Perhaps the first here (as for all writing) is clarity. Do you understand the point of the process essay? In other words, can you determine the thesis? And does the writer make the steps comprehensible? An omitted step, an undefined term, an inappropriate assumption of the reader's prior knowledge can turn a process into mayhem. What frustration is greater than trying to put together a utility cabinet, a gas grill, or a motorized toy from accompanying instructions and finding some abstruse technical term at a critical stage in the assembly? Or wondering with consternation how anyone other than a genius in engineering could advance from one step to the next simply by following the available instructions?

Readers of process analysis, like readers of narrative, usually expect to find a clear chronological sequence, although there are other possibilities. If we expect to carry out the steps ourselves, the relation of the steps to each other is especially important. When we read about process for pleasure and for information—as opposed to reading simply as the fastest and most efficient way to do something (the way we read recipes, for example, or instructions for assembling a stereo)—we also expect the writing to be interesting. Often a writer will depart from chronology to give an example, to provide some relevant background details, to define terms, or to give a lively example. But no matter how much the narrative sequence may recede, its framework is usually there as a necessary guide to the steps being explained.

WRITING PROCESS ANALYSIS

In writing process analysis, perhaps more than in any other kind of writing, you, the writer, become a teacher, and you have to be as well informed about your subject as the best teacher always is. When you explain how something is done or made, you are showing the complexities of an operation to someone who may have little knowledge about your subject. Thus, if you're revealing a process that you know how to perform quite well, have performed often, and hope to stimulate someone else to duplicate, your experience should shine in your prose. Readers should recognize with ease how much you are a master of this process. If you're analyzing a process you've investigated but have not ever attempted, readers should have no questions about your authority to write. Your explanations must be securely grounded in relevant, up-to-date, comprehensive information. In advance of selecting a topic to explore through process analysis, then, you should address these questions:

1. What process can I perform well enough to explain to people who might want to try it themselves or who might want to know how the process is carried out?
2. What process interests me enough to make me want to research it adequately and present it clearly in an explanation readers can follow easily?

PURPOSE AND AUDIENCE

Considering Your Options

You have options in regard to your purpose for writing as you consider a topic for development through process analysis. You should decide whether you want primarily to give instructions or to give information. Certainly these two purposes overlap, but it's important to acknowledge some differences. Giving instructions implies a desire on behalf of reader and writer alike to take action. If you're explaining how to plant a garden of perennials, for example, you'd want the reader to be able to follow your directions on a piece of land in his or her own backyard, and the reader would have the same expectations. If you're writing essentially to give information, however, you'll be explaining a process you probably would not expect anyone to act on. Nevertheless, your reader should see easily how this process is achieved and should understand fully how an orderly procedure leads to a realistic end. A consideration of your purpose in writing a process paper is incomplete without considerable thought about your audience. It's comfortable, and sometimes accurate, to assume that anyone who chooses to read *instructions* has a need or a desire for them, and so the writer can count on the readers' loyal interest in the subject right from the start. It's true that most people who choose to read a book called *How to Build a Deck Patio* would have ambitions in the future for expanding their outdoor living space. Such people want to build a deck, and, already motivated and charged with self-interest, they turn to a book for help in realizing their goal.

But it's not always true that instructions are read by captive audiences only. Assume for a moment that you're leafing through a popular magazine and come across a piece called "How to Tune Up Your Car: Ten Simple Steps for People with Ten Thumbs and Two Left Hands." Being unmechanical, you might be one of those who ordinarily shiver and turn the page when you see anything that requires taking things apart and putting them together. But this essay, from its title at least, may be talking your language. You're fed up with the high costs of car maintenance at a service station, and you'll take a chance on reading this essay to see if in fact even a clod like you can follow the process and master it. Here, then, the writer would have been wrong to assume only a captive readership. A good part of this essay would have to go toward capturing and engaging the reader. It's certain that a writer who chose a title like the one we've mentioned above knows how little his audience understands about tuning cars and how important it is to woo that audience from the start.

Furthermore, assuming that you have only an eager, dedicated audience for your instructions can make for sloppy writing. In some cases the easiest way to present a set of instructions is just to number and list them briefly with accompanying illustrations and be done with it. But if you've ever struggled with supposedly simple lists and pictures on the cartons of do-it-yourself products, you know what it means to long for fuller explanations—complete sentences, detailed paragraphs!—when there is no slot into which an equally nonexistent Flap A must fit or when four nuts and three bolts remain to complete a unit that demands three nuts and four bolts. Even interested readers deserve clear, careful prose. Besides, for the kind of process paper that you will write to give instructions at school or on the job, the real audience—your instructor, your fellow classmates, or your coworkers—will almost certainly not have a passion for or an interest in your essay topic. You might be able to tick off 15 quick steps for curing ich in tropical fish, and if you were writing for an amateur collector who had lost a tank of mollies and swordtails to the disease, she might be reading your essay with rapt attention. But if your teacher or the fellow in the next row has no interest in home aquariums, your essay will have to win these people over as much as it will have to teach them how to carry out those basic steps for bacteria-free fish. Although *your* purpose might be to give directions, readers who have no special interest in advance of following them may, despite your goals, be reading only information. Your paper should acknowledge both reader-ships by avoiding complacency at all costs.

Drawing the Reader In

When you analyze a process essentially to convey information, as opposed to writing essentially to give directions, you should always work to draw the reader in, and that rule of thumb should guide a process essay of any kind. You should be weighing the audience's stake in reading your paper. What chord can you strike that will hold your reader's interest? How can you convince your readers that what you say will amuse or inform or surprise them to a high enough degree to warrant their taking the time to read?

Consideration of (and for) your audience raises another question that you must face as you plan and develop your paper. How much can you assume that the audience knows about your topic? This is an important question because the response will guide your level of vocabulary and the scope and depth of detail you must include. Suppose you wanted to explain a quick method you'd devel-oped for adding cuffs to trouser legs or coat sleeves. If your intended audience were a group of young, single males or females who had never held a needle in their hands, you'd have to consider as technical vocabulary some of the basic language required to explain the process, words like *hem, hemline, basting, thimble, finish,* and *blind stitch,* to name a few. If you didn't provide definitions at least for some of these, you couldn't be sure that your readers would under-stand what you were talking about. And for such an audience you couldn't as-sume much advance knowledge of any steps in the process. You'd have to spell out everything from how to hold the garment to how to knot the thread at the end of the needle. However, for an audience of experienced homemakers who had sewn lots of hems and seams before, you could assume a thorough working knowledge of sewing vocabulary and could skip the most elementary steps, fairly confident that your readers knew the basics of needlework.

You can see even from this brief section how complex an issue audience is for the writer of process analysis. It's never easy to know exactly what your au-dience is like, even when you might know pretty well who they are—your teacher, say, or the group of cowriters with whom you've been working in class. Professional writers have similar problems: For example, a writer doing a piece for *Mademoiselle,* a magazine ostensibly for fashion-conscious, upper-middle-class young women, has no guarantee that every reader is equal in knowledge, language, and background to understand an article on the use of weight ma-chines to firm up flabby muscles, or on the process of buying good wines, or on planting a window garden. Some writers of process, then, will define their own audience and refer overtly to it in the paper, weaving their assumptions about the readership into the essay itself. Hemingway makes clear in the first couple of paragraphs of "Camping Out" that he is writing not to experienced campers and fishing enthusiasts but to bona fide amateurs. The writer whose title is "How to Tune Up Your Car: Ten Simple Steps for People with Ten Thumbs and Two Left Hands" has defined his audience directly in the title. The strategy of naming your audience for all to see can help you draw in otherwise reluctant readers. Your audience may not in fact be the audience you've defined, but once they know exactly for whom you're aiming, they may be willing to suspend disbelief, so to speak, and join temporarily the group you're trying to reach. Aware of the readers Hemingway is addressing, even longtime fishermen could enjoy the good-humored recommendations the writer offers to novices.

PROCESS

Finding a Topic

Spend some time identifying a process you want to write about by considering the two questions raised on page 198. If you choose to give directions for a process you know how to do well, you'll have to reflect for a while on the various steps required to carry it out. The more experienced you are, the more automatic your actions become; you may have to bring to a level of conscious thought some of the steps you haven't dwelled on for years. If you choose to give information about a process that interests you, you may have to spend some time in the library looking at books and magazines that will fill in any gaps of knowledge.

Once you have a topic and have duly considered audience and purpose, perhaps the best way to begin is to make a rough list of all the steps required in the process. Once you have your list, look it over carefully. Be sure that you have not left anything out. Are there preparatory steps to take, for example? Is there equipment that must be gathered together before beginning? Should objects be measured or counted beforehand? Should you provide an overview or some background information, including, perhaps, a history of the process, the reasons for your interest in it, the ultimate goals of the process, or your intention to examine in great detail only certain phases of the analysis?

You'll also need to examine as objectively as you can the terminology that appears on your list. Identify specialized terms and plan to define them for your readers.

Exploring Sequence

Look too with special attention at the sequence of steps you've listed. Do they follow each other chronologically? Most process analyses proceed through an orderly sequence of time: Readers have to know what to do first, what to do next, and what to do after that. But you do have other options, and you might want to rearrange the steps on your list. In explaining how you clean a six-room apartment efficiently, you might reject the apparent chronological sequence— "First I clean the bedrooms. . . . Then I wash the bathroom floor. . . . Last I do the kitchen." Instead you might arrange information by importance or by level of difficulty. "The easiest part of the job is vacuuming the carpet on all the floors. . . . The most difficult task is dusting the top corners in the rooms with high ceilings." (This order may be chronological as well, that is, if you do the simple work first and the tough work last, but it does not have to be.)

Another option is to arrange the information in order of physical location. Here you'd move the reader from place to place in the house, with your organizing principle based on the spatial relation of the rooms. Or you could decide on some other logical sequence, sorting information according to an interesting scheme you've worked out. "I have learned that cleaning a six-room house should proceed only in one of these ways: the 'once-over-lightly' approach, the 'I'm starting to get serious about this mess' approach, and the 'pull out the stops because the folks are coming tonight' approach." Whatever order you choose should be meaningful, however, and should help the reader understand the process. A revised version of your list should guide you as you develop your drafts.

Your Thesis

The sample sentence in the paragraph directly above helps illustrate once again the all-important thesis, the one sentence that states the main point of your essay. Notice how the writer draws you into his unusual approach to housecleaning through an amusing set of options. Whether or not you are interested in housecleaning (high on almost everyone's most-tedious-things-to-do list), you'd probably want to read an essay that stated its thesis in such an offbeat way. Further to the point, whether the writer ultimately uses this draft thesis sentence in the essay or uses instead some other version of it edited for brevity, or whether the writer decides not to use a thesis sentence at all, counting instead on the readers' ability to determine the thesis on their own, is irrelevant. The fact that the writer can *produce* a thesis, however, is a sure step toward a successful paper. Keeping the thesis in mind helps the writer stay on task and unify the various ideas in the essay around the main point.

Holding the Reader's Interest

Remember that you're trying to engage your reader's interest, and so you should resist writing your process paper as a mere list of steps. You might relate a personal incident that sheds light on why you chose to analyze this particular process or that taught you the quickest and simplest way to do the job. You might investigate the effects or consequences of the process. You might draw on concrete sensory language to give immediacy and drama to the steps you're explaining. You might insist on the importance of knowing how to master this process or of understanding how it is achieved. You might develop an appropriate comparison or analogy. You might provide diagrams, drawings, photographs, maps, charts, or graphs to illustrate the text of your essay.

And don't ignore your style. Prune from early drafts any details that risk making your paper wordy or unnecessarily complicated. Check your vocabulary for jargon, excessively technical terms, or key words that you failed to define. Pay particular attention to transitions. It's easy to overdo time or step markers—*"first* do this, *then* do that, *next* do something else"—but you will need some of them to help your readers know when one step ends and another begins.

STUDENT WRITING

In this humorous process essay, note how the student writer observes the basic principles of process analysis to make clear—and replicable—her point about doing nothing.

The Do-Nothing Kid

My favorite vacation activity is doing nothing. I will go with my family to the beach. I will go with my friends to a ball game. But in everything I do, my purpose is to do as little as possible. Doing nothing might sound like the easiest thing in the world, but to do it really well you have to do it right.[a,b]

No matter where you are, the first step[c] in doing nothing is deciding on your position. Whether you're sitting or lying down, you will want to make sure that you are in the most comfortable pose possible. That means quickly surveying the place and running for the best seat or patch of sand. A little fast action at the start will give you a site from which you will not have to move for the rest of your stay. Once you get to your chosen spot, quickly wave to your friends or family so that they will think you ran ahead to claim a place for them all.[d]

After[c] you determine and assume your position, to do nothing well you need to delegate. Again a survey is essential. Look at your human resources. Who of the people with you is most interested in food? Who cares most about scorecards or programs? But don't delegate directly. This might lead to resentment. Flatter those you want to have do things for you while you do nothing. "Becca, no one knows better than you how to load up a hot dog with the right fixings," you might say, and watch your younger sister dash off proudly to the hot dog stand. The Do-Nothing[c] Kid strikes again![e]

Once the group activity is under way, to do nothing[f] successfully you have to hide what you're doing, or rather not doing. But you don't want your deception to wear you out. I've found having a list of usable phrases very effective. From behind my sunglasses, my eyes closed, I mutter, "What water!" "What a throw!" "What flavor!"—as appropriate. Or if keeping track of the specifics of place, actions, and people is too much, you can just mutter every now and then, "Great . . . great . . . It's great."

[a]Thesis: "doing nothing" has to be done right

[b]Audience awareness: everyone knows how to do nothing, but writer suggests that readers may not be doing it right

[c]Effective use of transition: "firststep"

[d]Process gives instructions rather than information

[e]Steps in the process identified and stated clearly so that reader, if so inclined, can duplicate it

[f]Repetition of phrase "do nothing" helps achieve coherence

I've been so successful with my do-nothingness[f] that I intend to spread it to all walks of my life. I'll start my academic application of this skill with my next essay-writing assignment. I wonder how it will go over with Professor Chen. Doing nothing,[f] that is.

SUMMING UP: PROCESS ANALYSIS

Reading Process Analysis

- Process analysis states and explains the steps required to do or make something or to show how something is (or was) done or is (or was) made.

- Examine the writer's thesis for its relation to a rhetorical approach based on process analysis.

- Consider all the steps included in the process analysis: Are they clear, complete, and comprehensible?

- Pay attention to new terms.

- Examine the sequence: Has the writer provided a clear chronology of steps (when appropriate) and linked the steps logically?

- Identify the elements that hold your interest: What aspects of language and presentation does the writer use to engage your attention?

- If the writer expects you to duplicate the process, identify the elements that will allow you to achieve that goal.

Writing Process Analysis

- Understand your role as a teacher when your write process analysis; your writing must show mastery or authority over the process you are explaining.

- Ground your explanations of the process in relevant, up-to-date, comprehensive information.

- To identify a topic for process analysis, look for an activity that you can perform well enough to explain how someone can duplicate it or simply how someone might want to know how to carry out the process, or look for an interesting process that you might want to research and present clearly for readers to follow easily.

- Decide on whether you want to give instructions or information.

- Thoroughly consider the audience you are writing for; win them over to your topic even though they might not have any intrinsic interest in it.

- Produce a thesis that carefully defines the parameters of your intentions in writing your process analysis paper.

- Determine how much your audience needs to know about the topic and direct your writing to fulfilling those needs by defining key terms, spelling out essential steps in the process, and drawing on clear language and sentence style.

On Keeping a Notebook

Joan Didion

Born in Sacramento, California, in 1934, Joan Didion is a novelist, a screenwriter, and a film critic, but she has also won acclaim as an essayist. Her dry style prompted the novelist James Dickey to call her "the finest woman prose stylist writing in English today." She is not a baby boomer, but her cool detachment often links her to that generation. She won the Vogue Prix de Paris award in 1956 with an essay she wrote during her last year at Berkeley and has been writing professionally ever since.

The following essay, from *Slouching towards Bethlehem* (1968), is a fine example of the shrewd, incisive writing she produces and of the process she goes through as she creates it.

" '*T*hat woman Estelle,' " the note reads, " 'is partly the reason why George Sharp and I are separated today.' *Dirty crepe-de-Chine wrapper, hotel bar, Wilmington RR, 9:45 A.M. August Monday morning.*"

Since the note is in my notebook, it presumably has some meaning to me. I study it for a long while. At first I have only the most general notion of what I was doing on an August Monday morning in the bar of the hotel across from the Pennsylvania Railroad station in Wilmington, Delaware (waiting for a train? missing one? 1960? 1961? why Wilmington?), but I do remember being there. The woman in the dirty crepe-de-Chine wrapper had come down from her room for a beer, and the bartender had heard before the reason why George Sharp and she were separated today. "Sure," he said, and went on mopping the floor. "You told me." At the other end of the bar is a girl. She is talking, pointedly, not to the man beside her but to a cat lying in the triangle of sunlight cast through the open door. She is wearing a plaid silk dress from Peck & Peck, and the hem is coming down.

Here is what it is: the girl has been on the Eastern Shore, and now she is going back to the city, leaving the man beside her, and all she can see ahead are the viscous summer sidewalks and the 3 A.M. long-distance calls that will make her lie awake and then sleep drugged through all the steaming mornings left in August (1960? 1961?). Because she must go directly from the train to lunch in New York, she wishes that she had a safety pin for the hem of the plaid silk dress, and she also wishes that she could forget about the hem and the lunch and stay in the cool bar that smells of disinfectant and malt and make friends with the woman in the crepe-de-Chine wrapper. She is afflicted by a little self-pity, and she wants to compare Estelles. That is what that was all about.

Why did I write it down? In order to remember, of course, but exactly what was it I wanted to remember? How much of it actually happened? Did any of it? Why do I keep a notebook at all? It is easy to deceive oneself on all those scores. The impulse to write things down is a peculiarly compulsive one, inexplicable to those who do not share it, useful only accidentally, only secondarily, in the way that any compulsion tries to justify itself. I suppose that it begins or does not begin in the cradle. Although I have felt compelled to write things down since I was five years old, I doubt that my daughter ever will, for she is a singularly blessed and accepting child, delighted with life exactly as life presents itself to her, unafraid to go to sleep and unafraid to wake up. Keepers of private notebooks are a different breed altogether, lonely and resistant rearrangers of things, anxious malcontents, children afflicted apparently at birth with some presentiment of loss.

My first notebook was a Big Five tablet, given to me by my mother with   5
the sensible suggestion that I stop whining and learn to amuse myself by writing down my thoughts. She returned the tablet to me a few years ago; the first entry is an account of a woman who believed herself to be freezing to death in the Arctic night, only to find, when day broke, that she had stumbled onto the Sahara Desert, where she would die of the heat before lunch. I have no idea what turn of a five-year-old's mind could have prompted so insistently, "ironic" and exotic a story, but it does reveal a certain predilection for the extreme which has dogged me into adult life; perhaps if I were analytically inclined I would find it a truer story than any I might have told about Donald Johnson's birthday party or the day my cousin Brenda put Kitty Litter in the aquarium.

So the point of my keeping a notebook has never been, nor is it now, to   6
have an accurate factual record of what I have been doing or thinking. That would be a different impulse entirely, an instinct for reality which I sometimes envy but do not possess. At no point have I ever been able successfully to keep a diary; my approach to daily life ranges from the grossly negligent to the merely absent, and on those few occasions when I have tried dutifully to record a day's events, boredom has so overcome me that the results are mysterious at best. What is this business about "shopping, typing piece, dinner with E, depressed"? Shopping for what? Typing what piece? Who is E? Was this "E" depressed, or was I depressed? Who cares?

In fact I have abandoned altogether that kind of pointless entry; instead I   7
tell what some would call lies. "That's simply not true," the members of my family frequently tell me when they come up against my memory of a shared event. "The party was *not* for you, the spider was *not* a black widow, *it wasn't that way at all.*" Very likely they are right, for not only have I always had trouble distinguishing between what happened and what merely might have happened, but I remain unconvinced that the distinction, for my purposes, matters. The cracked crab that I recall having for lunch the day my father came home from Detroit in 1945 must certainly be embroidery, worked into the day's pattern to lend verisimilitude; I was ten years old and would not now remember the cracked crab. The day's events did not turn on cracked crab. And yet it is precisely that fictitious crab that makes me see the afternoon all over again, a home movie run all too often, the father bearing gifts, the child weeping, an exercise in family love and guilt. Or that is what it was to me. Similarly, perhaps it never

did snow that August in Vermont; perhaps there never were flurries in the night wind, and maybe no one else felt the ground hardening and summer already dead even as we pretended to bask in it, but that was how it felt to me, and it might as well have snowed, could have snowed, did snow.

How it felt to me: that is getting closer to the truth about a notebook. I sometimes delude myself about why I keep a notebook, imagine that some thrifty virtue derives from preserving everything observed. See enough and write it down, I tell myself, and then some morning when the world seems drained of wonder, some day when I am only going through the motions of doing what I am supposed to do, which is write—on that bankrupt morning I will simply open my notebook and there it will all be, a forgotten account with accumulated interest, paid passage back to the world out there: dialogue overheard in hotels and elevators and at the hat-check counter in Pavillon (one middle-aged man shows his hat-check to another and says, "That's my old football number"); impressions of Bettina Aptheker[1] and Benjamin Sonnenberg[2] and Teddy ("Mr. Acapulco") Stauffer;[3] careful *aperçus* about tennis bums and failed fashion models and Greek shipping heiresses, one of whom taught me a significant lesson (a lesson I could have learned from F. Scott Fitzgerald, but perhaps we all must meet the very rich for ourselves) by asking, when I arrived to interview her in her orchid-filled sitting room on the second day of a paralyzing New York blizzard, whether it was snowing outside.

I imagine, in other words, that the notebook is about other people. But of course it is not. I have no real business with what one stranger said to another at the hat-check counter in Pavillon; in fact I suspect that the line "That's my old football number" touched not my own imagination at all, but merely some memory of something once read, probably "The Eighty-Yard Run." Nor is my concern with a woman in a dirty crepe-de-Chine wrapper in a Wilmington bar. My stake is always, of course, in the unmentioned girl in the plaid silk dress. *Remember what it was to be me:* that is always the point.

It is a difficult point to admit. We are brought up in the ethic that others, any others, all others, are by definition more interesting than ourselves; taught to be diffident, just this side of self-effacing ("You're the least important person in the room and don't forget it," Jessica Mitford's[4] governess would hiss in her ear on the advent of any social occasion; I copied that into my notebook because it is only recently that I have been able to enter a room without hearing some such phrase in my inner ear.) Only the very young and the very old may recount their dreams at breakfast, dwell upon self, interrupt with memories of beach picnics and favorite Liberty lawn dresses and the rainbow trout in a creek near Colorado Springs. The rest of us are expected, rightly, to affect absorption in other people's favorite dresses, other people's trout.

[1]A leader of the free speech movement at Berkeley in the 1960s.
[2]Public relations expert.
[3]Band leader who opened his own nightclub as a retiree in Acapulco.
[4]British writer who investigates unethical practices in government and business.

And so we do. But our notebooks give us away, for however dutifully we record what we see around us, the common denominator of all we see is always, transparently, shamelessly, the implacable "I." We are not talking here about the kind of notebook that is patently for public consumption, a structural conceit for binding together a series of graceful *pensées,* we are talking about something private, about bits of the mind's string too short to use, an indiscriminate and erratic assemblage with meaning only for its maker.

And sometimes even the maker has difficulty with the meaning. There does not seem to be, for example, any point in my knowing for the rest of my life that, during 1964, 720 tons of soot fell on every square mile of New York City, yet there it is in my notebook, labeled "FACT." Nor do I really need to remember that Ambrose Bierce liked to spell Leland Stanford's name "£eland $tanford" or that "smart women almost always wear black in Cuba," a fashion hint without much potential for practical application. And does not the relevance of these notes seem marginal at best?:

> In the basement museum of the Inyo County Courthouse in Independence, California, sign pinned to a mandarin coat: "This MANDARIN COAT was often worn by Mrs. Minnie S. Brooks when giving lectures on her TEAPOT COLLECTION."

> Redhead getting out of car in front of Beverly Wilshire Hotel, chinchilla stole, Vuitton bags with tags reading:

> MRS LOU FOX
>
> HOTEL SAHARA
>
> VEGAS

Well, perhaps not entirely marginal. As a matter of fact, Mrs. Minnie S. Brooks and her MANDARIN COAT pull me back into my own childhood, for although I never knew Mrs. Brooks and did not visit Inyo County until I was thirty, I grew up in just such a world, in houses cluttered with Indian relics and bits of gold ore and ambergris and the souvenirs my Aunt Mercy Farnsworth brought back from the Orient. It is a long way from that world to Mrs. Lou Fox's world, where we all live now, and is it not just as well to remember that? Might not Mrs. Minnie S. Brooks help me to remember what I am? Might not Mrs. Lou Fox help me to remember what I am not?

But sometimes the point is harder to discern. What exactly did I have in mind when I noted down that it cost the father of someone I know $650 a month to light the place on the Hudson in which he lived before the Crash? What use was I planning to make of this line by Jimmy Hoffa[5]: "I may have my faults, but being wrong ain't one of them"? And although I think it interesting to know where the girls who travel with the Syndicate have their hair done when they find themselves on the West Coast, will I ever make suitable use of it? Might I not be better off just passing it on to John O'Hara?[6] What is a recipe

---

[5]United States labor leader who disappeared mysteriously in 1971.
[6]American novelist who died in 1970.

for sauerkraut doing in my notebook? What kind of magpie keeps this note-book? *"He was born the night the Titanic went down."* That seems a nice enough line, and I even recall who said it, but is it not really a better line in life than it could ever be in fiction?

But of course that is exactly it: not that I should ever use the line, but that I should remember the woman who said it and the afternoon I heard it. We were on her terrace by the sea, and we were finishing the wine left from lunch, trying to get what sun there was, a California winter sun. The woman whose husband was born the night the *Titanic* went down wanted to rent her house, wanted to go back to her children in Paris. I remember wishing that I could afford the house, which cost $1,000 a month. "Someday you will," she said lazily. "Someday it all comes." There in the sun on her terrace it seemed easy to believe in someday, but later I had a low-grade afternoon hangover and ran over a black snake on the way to the supermarket and was flooded with inexplicable fear when I heard the checkout clerk explaining to the man ahead of me why she was finally divorcing her husband. "He left me no choice," she said over and over as she punched the register. "He has a little seven-month-old baby by her, he left me no choice." I would like to believe that my dread then was for the human condition, but of course it was for me, because I wanted a baby and did not then have one and be-cause I wanted to own the house that cost $1,000 a month to rent and because I had a hangover.

It all comes back. Perhaps it is difficult to see the value in having one's self back in that kind of mood, but I do see it; I think we are well advised to keep on nodding terms with the people we used to be, whether we find them attractive company or not. Otherwise they turn up unannounced and surprise us, come ham-mering on the mind's door at 4 A.M. of a bad night and demand to know who de-serted them, who betrayed them, who is going to make amends. We forget all too soon the things we thought we could never forget. We forget the loves and the betrayals alike, forget what we whispered and what we screamed, forget who we were. I have already lost touch with a couple of people I used to be; one of them, a seventeen-year-old, presents little threat, although it would be of some interest to me to know again what it feels like to sit on a river levee drinking vodka-and-orange-juice and listening to Les Paul and Mary Ford and their echoes sing "How High the Moon" on the car radio. (You see I still have the scenes: but I no longer perceive myself among those present, no longer could even improvise the dia-logue.) The other one, a twenty-three-year-old, bothers me more. She was always a good deal of trouble, and I suspect she will reappear when I least want to see her, skirts too long, shy to the point of aggravation, always the injured party, full of recriminations and little hurts and stories I do not want to hear again, at once saddening me and angering me with her vulnerability and ignorance, an appari-tion all the more insistent for being so long banished.

It is a good idea, then, to keep in touch, and I suppose that keeping in touch is what notebooks are all about. And we are all on our own when it comes to keeping those lines open to ourselves: your notebook will never help me, nor mine you. *"So what's new in the whiskey business?"* What could that possibly mean to you? To me it means a blonde in a Pucci bathing suit sitting with a couple of fat men by the pool at the Beverly Hills Hotel. Another man approaches, and they all regard one another in silence for a while. "So what's new in the whiskey business?" one of the fat men finally says by way of welcome, and the blonde stands up, arches one foot and dips it in the pool, looking all the while at the cabaña where Baby Pignatari is talking on the telephone. That is all there is to that, except that several years later I saw the blonde coming out of Saks Fifth Avenue in New York with her California complexion and a voluminous mink coat. In the harsh wind that day she looked old and irrevocably tired to me, and even the skins in the mink coat were not worked the way they were doing them that year, not the way she would have wanted them done, and there is the point of the story. For a while after that I did not like to look in the mirror, and my eyes would skim the newspapers and pick out only the deaths, the cancer victims, the premature coronaries, the suicides, and I stopped riding the Lexington Avenue IRT because I noticed for the first time that all the strangers I had seen for years—the man with the seeing-eye dog, the spinster who read the classified pages every day, the fat girl who always got off with me at Grand Central—looked older than they once had.

It all comes back. Even that recipe for sauerkraut: even that brings it back. I [18] was on Fire Island when I first made that sauerkraut, and it was raining, and we drank a lot of bourbon and ate the sauerkraut and went to bed at ten, and I listened to the rain and the Atlantic and felt safe. I made the sauerkraut again last night and it did not make me feel any safer, but that is, as they say, another story.

Meaning and Idea

1. Why does Didion keep a notebook? Is it to capture something? Truth? Reality? Something else?

2. What did her very first notebook entry, done as a child, indicate about the kind of notebook she was likely to keep?

3. Didion says that her "approach to daily life ranges from the grossly negligent to the merely absent." What is your sense of this insight? Does Didion's habit of keeping a notebook imply negligence or absence? Why do you think so?

4. "I suppose that keeping in touch is what notebooks are all about," writes Didion. What does she mean by this comment?

Language, Form, Structure

1. What is the thesis of this piece? How did you determine it?

2. If you wanted to follow Didion's example of keeping a notebook, what specific steps explained here could you take? Or is this essay an example of explaining "how" rather than "how to"? Explain your answer.

3. Didion calls her entries "bits of the mind's string too short to use." What does she mean? Reexamine the essay and find the transition points between the "bits" and what she expands them to.

4. In the first sentence of the last paragraph, "It all comes back," what is "It"? The sentence seems quite ambiguous, yet somehow it is not. Why? What is your reaction, in general, to the concluding paragraph?

5. Define the following words and use each in a sentence: crepe-de-Chine; viscous; predilection; implacable; *pensées;* ambergris; recriminations; diffident; assemblage; malcontents; presentiment; verisimilitude; *aperçus.*

Ideas for Writing

1. Think of a process that has long and regularly been a part of your life but also has evolved over time. Write an essay about this process and its evolution. For instance, you might choose something like doing homework, playing a musical instrument, or cooking for large holiday parties.

2. Think about the process you follow in writing an essay for your English or composition class. Do you make false starts? Do you have good ideas, which somehow never appear in the final draft? Write an essay about your process of writing an essay, complete with descriptions of what makes writing difficult and with sample experiences.

3. Is Didion's essay only for other keepers of notebooks, other writers? Write an essay to analyze what you think Didion's purposes are in recounting her habits to a public audience.

Camping Out

Ernest Hemingway

Ernest Hemingway (1898–1961) is perhaps America's best-known and most widely read modern writer. He was born in Oak Park, Illinois, and started his career as a journalist for the *Kansas City Star.* Wounded while serving as a volunteer ambulance driver in France, Hemingway became part of the "lost generation" of American expatriate writers in Paris in the 1920s. Nick Adams, his alter-ego fictional hero, first appeared in Hemingway's collection of stories *In Our Time* in 1924. That book was followed by, among others, *The Sun Also Rises* (1926), *A Farewell to Arms* (1929), *For Whom the Bell Tolls* (1940), and *The Old Man and the Sea* (1952)—all characterized by Hemingway's renowned crisp simplicity. After leaving Paris, Hemingway lived, wrote, hunted, and caroused in Key West, Cuba, Montana, and Africa. He received the Nobel Prize for Literature in 1954. A despondent Hemingway shot himself in 1961.

This piece originally appeared in the *Toronto Star,* for which Hemingway was the Paris correspondent, in the 1920s *before* he established himself as a major writer. In this process analysis, we can observe the roots of the author's well-known fascination with outdoor life and his use of simplicity in writing.

*T*housands of people will go into the bush this summer to cut the high cost of living. A man who gets his two weeks' salary while he is on vacation should be able to put those two weeks in fishing and camping and be able to save one week's salary clear. He ought to be able to sleep comfortably every night, to eat well every day and to return to the city rested and in good condition.

But if he goes into the woods with a frying pan, an ignorance of black flies and mosquitoes, and a great and abiding lack of knowledge about cookery the chances are that his return will be very different. He will come back with enough mosquito bites to make the back of his neck look like a relief map of the Caucasus. His digestion will be wrecked after a valiant battle to assimilate half-cooked or charred grub. And he won't have had a decent night's sleep while he has been gone.

He will solemnly raise his right hand and inform you that he has joined the grand army of never-agains. The call of the wild may be all right, but it's a dog's life. He's heard the call of the tame with both ears. Waiter, bring him an order of milk toast.

In the first place he overlooked the insects. Black flies, no-see-ums, deer flies, gnats and mosquitoes were instituted by the devil to force people to live in cities where he could get at them better. If it weren't for them everybody would live in the bush and he would be out of work. It was a rather successful invention.

But here are lots of dopes that will counteract the pests. The simplest perhaps is oil of citronella. Two bits' worth of this purchased at any pharmacist's will be enough to last for two weeks in the worst fly and mosquito-ridden country.

Rub a little on the back of your neck, your forehead and your wrists before you start fishing, and the blacks and skeeters will shun you. The odor of citronella is not offensive to people. It smells like gun oil. But the bugs do hate it.

Oil of pennyroyal and eucalyptol are also much hated by mosquitoes, and with citronella they form the basis for many proprietary preparations. But it is cheaper and better to buy the straight citronella. Put a little on the mosquito netting that covers the front of your pup tent or canoe tent at night, and you won't be bothered.

To be really rested and get any benefit out of a vacation a man must get a good night's sleep every night. The first requisite for this is to have plenty of cover. It is twice as cold as you expect it will be in the bush four nights out of five, and a good plan is to take just double the bedding that you think you will need. An old quilt that you can wrap up in is as warm as two blankets.

Nearly all outdoor writers rhapsodize over the browse bed. It is all right for the man who knows how to make one and has plenty of time. But in a succession of one-night camps on a canoe trip all you need is level ground for your tent floor and you will sleep all right if you have plenty of covers under you. Take twice as much cover as you think that you will need, and then put two-thirds of it under you. You will sleep warm and get your rest.

When it is clear weather you don't need to pitch your tent if you are only stopping for the night. Drive four stakes at the head of your made-up bed and drape your mosquito bar over that, then you can sleep like a log and laugh at the mosquitoes.

Outside of insects and bum sleeping the rock that wrecks most camping trips is cooking. The average tyro's idea of cooking is to fry everything and fry it good and plenty. Now, a frying pan is a most necessary thing to any trip, but you also need the old stew kettle and the folding reflector baker.

A pan of fried trout can't be bettered and they don't cost any more than ever. But there is a good and bad way of frying them.

The beginner puts his trout and his bacon in and over a brightly burning fire, the bacon curls up and dries into a dry tasteless cinder and the trout is burned outside while it is still raw inside. He eats them and it is all right if he is only out for the day and going home to a good meal at night. But if he is going to face more trout and bacon the next morning and other equally well-cooked dishes for the remainder of two weeks he is on the pathway to nervous dyspepsia.

The proper way is to cook over coals. Have several cans of Crisco or Cotosuet or one of the vegetable shortenings along that are as good as lard and excellent for all kinds of shortening. Put the bacon in and when it is about half cooked lay the trout in the hot grease, dipping them in corn meal first. Then put the bacon on top of the trout and it will baste them as it slowly cooks.

The coffee can be boiling at the same time and in a smaller skillet pan-   15
cakes being made that are satisfying the other campers while they are waiting
for the trout.

With the prepared pancake flours you take a cupful of pancake flour and   16
add a cup of water. Mix the water and flour and as soon as the lumps are out it is
ready for cooking. Have the skillet hot and keep it well greased. Drop the batter
in and as soon as it is done on one side loosen it in the skillet and flip it over.
Apple butter, syrup or cinnamon and sugar go well with the cakes.

While the crowd have taken the edge from their appetites with flapjacks   17
the trout have been cooked and they and the bacon are ready to serve. The trout
are crisp outside and firm and pink inside and the bacon is well done—but not
too done. If there is anything better than that combination the writer has yet to
taste it in a lifetime devoted largely and studiously to eating.

The stew kettle will cook you dried apricots when they have resumed their   18
predried plumpness after a night of soaking, it will serve to concoct a mulligan
in, and it will cook macaroni. When you are not using it, it should be boiling
water for the dishes.

In the baker, mere man comes into his own, for he can make a pie that to   19
his bush appetite will have it all over the product that mother used to make, like
a tent. Men have always believed that there was something mysterious and difficult about making a pie. Here is a great secret. There is nothing to it. We've
been kidded for years. Any man of average office intelligence can make at least
as good a pie as his wife.

All there is to a pie is a cup and a half of flour, one-half teaspoonful of   20
salt, one-half cup of lard and cold water. That will make pie crust that will bring
tears of joy into your camping partners' eyes.

Mix the salt with the flour, work the lard into the flour, make it up into a good   21
workmanlike dough with cold water. Spread some flour on the back of a box or
something flat, and pat the dough around a while. Then roll it out with whatever kind
of round bottle you prefer. Put a little more lard on the surface of the sheet of dough
and then slosh a little flour on and roll it up and then roll it out again with the bottle.

Cut out a piece of the rolled out dough big enough to line a pie tin. I like   22
the kind with holes in the bottom. Then put in your dried apples that have
soaked all night and been sweetened, or your apricots, or your blueberries, and
then take another sheet of the dough and drape it gracefully over the top, soldering it down at the edges with your fingers. Cut a couple of slits in the top dough
sheet and prick it a few times with a fork in an artistic manner.

Put it in the baker with a good slow fire for forty-five minutes and then   23
take it out and if your pals are Frenchmen they will kiss you. The penalty for
knowing how to cook is that the others will make you do all the cooking.

It is all right to talk about roughing it in the woods. But the real woodsman   24
is the man who can be really comfortable in the bush.

Meaning and Idea

1. Explain in your own words the overall process that Hemingway analyzes in this essay. What subprocesses does he explain as parts of the overall process? Choose one of those subprocesses and explain it fully.

2. According to the essay, what are some of the advantages of spending your vacation camping out?

3. What are the best ways "to counteract the pests"?

4. What are the bad and good ways to cook trout? What other cooking preparations does Hemingway explain?

5. Is Hemingway in favor of "roughing it"? How do you know? Analyze the first and last paragraphs in light of your answer.

Language, Form, Structure

1. Which sentences best state Hemingway's purpose in this essay? Where does he define his audience?

2. How do the first two paragraphs establish the organization of this process analysis? Where does the process analysis actually begin? What is the purpose of the writing up to that point?

3. How does Hemingway use exemplification in this essay? How does he use description?

4. Write sentences that show that you know the meaning of the following words: assimilate; valiant; requisite; rhapsodize; tyro; dyspepsia; mulligan; concoct; soldering.

Ideas for Writing

1. What is your favorite vacation activity? Write a process analysis telling others how to enjoy a similar vacation experience.

2. Choose a common activity—commuting to work, studying, working out, making a pie crust—and write an essay that tells how to do it correctly as opposed to how to do it incorrectly.

3. The intended audience for "Camping Out" was originally urban newspaper readers in the 1920s. Write an essay in which you analyze Hemingway's use of language. Is the word choice appropriate to his audience? How appropriate is the style of the essay to a 1990s newspaper readership? Would you suggest any modifications if the essay were to be published in a newspaper today?

Behind the Formaldehyde Curtain

Jessica Mitford

Dubbed "Queen of the Muckrakers" by *Time* magazine, Jessica Mitford (1917–1996) was always closely aligned with the radical left. Born in England, Mitford ran away to support Loyalist Spain during the Spanish civil war. After World War II she found a job working in the *San Francisco Chronicle* classifieds department, but she was later fired for her communist affiliations. In the wake of her *Chronicle* experiences Mitford took up writing because, she says, it required no training and no skills. Her subsequent career was spent hunting for targets. Persistent but sensible, thorough, and a master of the biting remark, Mitford became a journalist who skewered everything from snooty restaurants to obstetricians. As a reviewer at *Esquire* notes, Mitford may not have changed the world, but she embarrassed a lot of guilty people in it.

This selection is taken from Mitford's best-known work, the 1963 *American Way of Death*. This book was written as an exposé of the business of funeral homes and morticians, and the year after it was published, it was held responsible for a reduction of 10 percent in the National Casket Company's gross take. In 1996, at the end of a long struggle with cancer, Mitford made arrangements for a $475 cremation. She died a month later.

The drama begins to unfold with the arrival of the corpse at the mortuary.   1

Alas, poor Yorick! How surprised he would be to see how his counterpart   2
of today is whisked off to a funeral parlor and is in short order sprayed, sliced, pierced, pickled, trussed, trimmed, creamed, waxed, painted, rouged, and neatly dressed—transformed from a common corpse into a Beautiful Memory Picture. This process is known in the trade as embalming and restorative art, and is so universally employed in the United States and Canada that the funeral director does it routinely, without consulting corpse or kin. He regards as eccentric those few who are hardy enough to suggest that it might be dispensed with. Yet no law requires embalming, no religious doctrine commends it, nor is it dictated by considerations of health, sanitation, or even of personal daintiness. In no part of the world but in Northern America is it widely used. The purpose of embalming is to make the corpse presentable for viewing in a suitably costly container; and here too the funeral director routinely, without first consulting the family, prepares the body for public display.

Is all this legal? The processes to which a dead body may be subjected are   3
after all to some extent circumscribed by law. In most states, for instance, the signature of next of kin must be obtained before an autopsy may be performed, before the deceased may be cremated, before the body may be turned over to a

medical school for research purposes; or such provision must be made in the decedent's will. In the case of embalming, no such permission is required nor is it ever sought. A textbook, *The Principles and Practices of Embalming,* comments on this: "There is some question regarding the legality of much that is done within the preparation room." The author points out that it would be most unusual for a responsible member of a bereaved family to instruct the mortician, in so many words, to "embalm" the body of a deceased relative. The very term *embalming* is so seldom used that the mortician must rely upon custom in the matter. The author concludes that unless the family specifies otherwise, the act of entrusting the body to the care of a funeral establishment carries with it an implied permission to go ahead and embalm.

Embalming is indeed a most extraordinary procedure, and one must wonder at the docility of Americans who each year pay hundreds of millions of dollars for its perpetuation, blissfully ignorant of what it is all about, what is done, how it is done. Not one in ten thousand has any idea of what actually takes place. Books on the subject are extremely hard to come by. They are not to be found in most libraries or bookshops. 4

In an era when huge television audiences watch surgical operations in the comfort of their living rooms, when, thanks to the animated cartoon, the geography of the digestive system has become familiar territory even to the nursery school set, in a land where the satisfaction of curiosity about almost all matters is a national pastime, the secrecy surrounding embalming can, surely, hardly be attributed to the inherent gruesomeness of the subject. Custom in this regard has within this century suffered a complete reversal. In the early days of American embalming, when it was performed in the home of the deceased, it was almost mandatory for some relative to stay by the embalmer's side and witness the procedure. Today, family members who might wish to be in attendance would certainly be dissuaded by the funeral director. All others, except apprentices, are excluded by law from the preparation room. 5

A close look at what does actually take place may explain in large measure the undertaker's intractable reticence concerning a procedure that has become his major *raison d'être.* Is it possible he fears that public information about embalming might lead patrons to wonder if they really want this service? If the funeral men are loath to discuss the subject outside the trade, the reader may, understandably, be equally loath to go on reading at this point. For those who have the stomach for it, let us part the formaldehyde curtain. . . . 6

The body is first laid out in the undertaker's morgue—or rather, Mr. Jones is reposing in the preparation room—to be readied to bid the world farewell. 7

The preparation room in any of the better funeral establishments has the tiled and sterile look of a surgery, and indeed the embalmer-restorative artist who does his chores there is beginning to adopt the term *dermasurgeon* (appropriately corrupted by some mortician-writers as "demi-surgeon") to describe his calling. His equipment, consisting of scalpels, scissors, augers, forceps, clamps, needles, pumps, tubes, bowls, and basins, is crudely imitative of the surgeon's, as is his technique, acquired in a nine- or twelve-month post-high-school course 8 in an embalming school. He is supplied by an advanced chemical industry with a bewildering array of fluids, sprays, pastes, oils, powders, creams, to fix or soften tissue, shrink or distend it as needed, dry it here, restore the moisture there. There are cosmetics, waxes, and paints to fill and cover features, even plaster of Paris to replace entire limbs. There are ingenious aids to prop and stabilize the cadaver: a Vari-Pose Head Rest, the Edwards Arm and Hand Positioner, the Repose Block (to support the shoulders during the embalming), and the Throop Foot Positioner, which resembles an old-fashioned stocks.

Mr. John H. Eckels, president of the Eckels College of Mortuary Science, thus describes the first part of the embalming procedure: "In the hands of a skilled practitioner, this work may be done in a comparatively short time and without mutilating the body other than by slight incision—so slight that it scarcely would cause serious inconvenience if made upon a living person. It is necessary to remove the blood, and doing this not only helps in the disinfecting, but removes the principal cause of disfigurements due to discoloration." 9

Another textbook discusses the all-important time element: "The earlier this is done, the better, for every hour that elapses between death and embalming will add to the problems and complications encountered. . . ." Just how soon should one get going on the embalming? The author tells us, "On the basis of such scanty information made available to this profession through its rudimentary and haphazard system of technical research, we must conclude that the best results are to be obtained if the subject is embalmed before life is completely extinct—that is, before cellular death has occurred. In the average case, this would mean within an hour after somatic death." For those who feel that there is something a little rudimentary, not to say haphazard, about this advice, a comforting thought is offered by another writer. Speaking of fears entertained in early days of premature burial, he points out, "One of the effects of embalming by chemical injection, however, has been to dispel fears of live burial." How true; once the blood is removed, chances of live burial are indeed remote. 10

To return to Mr. Jones, the blood is drained out through the veins and replaced by embalming fluid pumped in through the arteries. As noted in *The Principles and Practices of Embalming,* "every operator has a favorite injection and drainage point—a fact which becomes a handicap only if he fails or refuses to forsake his favorites when conditions demand it." Typical favorites are the carotid artery, femoral artery, jugular vein, subclavian vein. There are various choices of embalming fluid. If Flextone is used, it will produce a "mild, flexible rigidity. The skin retains a velvety softness, the tissues are rubbery and pliable. Ideal for women and children." It may be blended with B. and G. Products Company's Lyf-Lyk tint, which is guaranteed to reproduce "nature's own skin texture . . . the velvety appearance of living tissue." Suntone comes in three separate tints: Suntan; Special Cosmetic Tint, a pink shade "especially indicated for female subjects"; and Regular Cosmetic Tint, moderately pink. 11

About three to six gallons of a dyed and perfumed solution of formaldehyde, glycerin, borax, phenol, alcohol, and water is soon circulating through Mr. Jones, whose mouth has been sewn together with a "needle directed upward 12 between the upper lip and gum and brought out through the left nostril," with the corners raised slightly "for a more pleasant expression." If he should be buck-toothed, his teeth are cleaned with Bon Ami and coated with colorless nail pol-ish. His eyes, meanwhile, are closed with flesh-tinted eye caps and eye cement.

The next step is to have at Mr. Jones with a thing called a trocar. This is a 13 long, hollow needle attached to a tube. It is jabbed into the abdomen, poked around the entrails and chest cavity, the contents of which are pumped out and replaced with "cavity fluid." This done, and the hole in the abdomen sewn up, Mr. Jones's face is heavily creamed (to protect the skin from burns which may be caused by leakage of the chemicals), and he is covered with a sheet and left unmolested for a while. But not for long—there is more, much more, in store for him. He has been embalmed, but not yet restored, and the best time to start the restorative work is eight to ten hours after embalming, when the tissues have be-come firm and dry.

The object of all this attention to the corpse, it must be remembered, is to 14 make it presentable for viewing in an attitude of healthy repose. "Our customs require the presentation of our dead in the semblance of normality . . . un-marred by the ravages of illness, disease, or mutilation," says Mr. J. Sheridan Mayer in his *Restorative Art.* This is rather a large order since few people die in the full bloom of health, unravaged by illness and unmarked by some disfigure-ment. The funeral industry is equal to the challenge: "In some cases the grue-some appearance of a mutilated or disease-ridden subject may be quite discour-aging. The task of restoration may seem impossible and shake the confidence of the embalmer. This is the time for intestinal fortitude and determination. Once the formative work is begun and affected tissues are cleaned or removed, all doubts of success vanish. It is surprising and gratifying to discover the results which may be obtained."

The embalmer, having allowed an appropriate interval to elapse, returns 15 to the attack, but now he brings into play the skill and equipment of sculptor and cosmetician. Is a hand missing? Casting one in plaster of Paris is a simple matter. "For replacement purposes, only a cast of the back of the hand is neces-sary; this is within the ability of the average operator and is quite adequate." If a lip or two, a nose, or an ear should be missing, the embalmer has at hand a variety of restorative waxes with which to model replacements. Pores and skin texture are simulated by stippling with a little brush, and over this cosmetics are laid on. Head off? Decapitation cases are rather routinely handled. Ragged edges are trimmed, and head joined to torso with a series of splints, wires, and sutures. It is a good idea to have a little something at the neck—a scarf or a high collar—when time for viewing comes. Swollen mouth? Cut out tissue as needed from inside the lips. If too much is removed, the surface contour can easily be restored by padding with cotton. Swollen necks and cheeks are re-duced by removing tissue through vertical incisions made down each side of the neck. "When the deceased is casketed, the pillow will hide the suture inci-sions . . . as an extra precaution against leakage, the suture may be painted with liquid sealer."

The opposite condition is more likely to present itself—that of emacia-tion. His hypodermic syringe now loaded with massage cream, the embalmer seeks out and fills the hollowed and sunken areas by injection. In this proce-dure the backs of the hands and fingers and the under-chin area should not be neglected. 16

Positioning the lips is a problem that recurrently challenges the ingenuity of the embalmer. Closed too tightly, they tend to give a stern, even disapproving expression. Ideally, embalmers feel, the lips should give the impression of being ever so slightly parted, the upper lip protruding slightly for a more youthful ap-pearance. This takes some engineering, however, as the lips tend to drift apart. Lip drift can sometimes be remedied by pushing one or two straight pins through the inner margin of the lower lip and then inserting them between the two front upper teeth. If Mr. Jones happens to have no teeth, the pins can just as easily be anchored in his Armstrong Face Former and Denture Replacer. An-other method to maintain lip closure is to dislocate the lower jaw, which is then held in its new position by a wire run through holes which have been drilled through the upper and lower jaws at the midline. As the French are fond of say-ing, *il faut souffrir pour être belle.*[1] 17

If Mr. Jones has died of jaundice, the embalming fluid will very likely turn him green. Does this deter the embalmer? Not if he has intestinal fortitude. Masking pastes and cosmetics are heavily laid on, burial garments and casket in-teriors are color-correlated with particular care, and Jones is displayed beneath rose-colored lights. Friends will say "How *well* he looks." Death by carbon monoxide, on the other hand, can be rather a good thing from the embalmer's viewpoint: "One advantage is the fact that this type of discoloration is an exag-gerated form of a natural pink coloration." This is nice because the healthy glow is already present and needs but little attention. 18

The patching and filling completed, Mr. Jones is now shaved, washed, and dressed. Cream-based cosmetic, available in pink, flesh, suntan, brunette, and blond, is applied to his hands and face, his hair is shampooed and combed (and, in the case of Mrs. Jones, set), his hands manicured. For the horny-handed son of toil special care must be taken; cream should be applied to remove ingrained grime, and the nails cleaned. "If he were not in the habit of having them mani-cured in life, trimming and shaping is advised for better appearance—never questioned by kin." 19

Jones is now ready for casketing (this is the present participle of the verb "to casket"). In this operation his right shoulder should be depressed slightly "to turn the body a bit to the right and soften the appearance of lying flat on the back." Positioning the hands is a matter of importance, and special rubber posi-tioning blocks may be used. The hands should be cupped slightly for a more life-like, relaxed appearance. Proper placement of the body requires a delicate sense of balance. It should lie as high as possible in the casket, yet not so high that the 20

[1]To be beautiful, one must suffer.—Eds.

lid, when lowered, will hit the nose. On the other hand, we are cautioned, placing the body too low "creates the impression that the body is in a box."

Jones is next wheeled into the appointed slumber room where a few last touches may be added—his favorite pipe placed in his hand or, if he was a great reader, a book propped into position. (In the case of little Master Jones a Teddy bear may be clutched.) Here he will hold open house for a few days, visiting hours 10 A.M. to 9 P.M. 21

All now being in readiness, the funeral director calls a staff conference to make sure that each assistant knows his precise duties. Mr. Wilber Kriege writes: "This makes your staff feel that they are a part of the team, with a definite assignment that must be properly carried out if the whole plan is to succeed. You never heard of a football coach who failed to talk to his entire team before they go on the field. They have drilled on the plays they are to execute for hours and days, and yet the successful coach knows the importance of making even the bench-warming third-string substitute feel that he is important if the game is to be won." The winning of *this* game is predicated upon glass-smooth handling of the logistics. The funeral director has notified the pallbearers whose names were furnished by the family, has arranged for the presence of clergyman, organist, and soloist, has provided transportation for everybody, has organized and listed the flowers sent by friends. In *Psychology of Funeral Service* Mr. Edward A. Martin points out, "He may not always do as much as the family thinks he is doing, but it is his helpful guidance that they appreciate in knowing they are proceeding as they should. . . . The important thing is how well his services can be used to make the family believe they are giving unlimited expression to their own sentiment." 22

The religious service may be held in a church or in the chapel of the funeral home; the funeral director vastly prefers the latter arrangement, for not only is it more convenient for him but it affords him the opportunity to show off his beautiful facilities to the gathered mourners. After the clergyman has had his say, the mourners queue up to file past the casket for a last look at the deceased. The family is *never* asked whether they want an open-casket ceremony; in the absence of their instruction to the contrary, this is taken for granted. Consequently well over 90 per cent of all American funerals feature the open casket— a custom unknown in other parts of the world. Foreigners are astonished by it. An English woman living in San Francisco described her reaction in a letter to the writer: 23

> I myself have attended only one funeral here—that of an elderly fellow worker of mine. After the service I could not understand why everyone was walking towards the coffin (sorry, I mean casket), but thought I had better follow the crowd. It shook me rigid to get there and find the casket open and poor old Oscar lying there in his brown tweed suit, wearing a suntan makeup and just the wrong shade of lipstick. If I had not been extremely fond of the old boy, I have a horrible feeling that I might have giggled. Then and there I decided that I could never face another American funeral—even dead.

The casket (which has been resting throughout the service on a Classic   24
Beauty Ultra Metal Casket Bier) is now transferred by a hydraulically operated
device called Porto-Lift to a balloon-tired, Glide Easy casket carriage which will
wheel it to yet another conveyance, the Cadillac Funeral Coach. This may be
lavender, cream, light green—anything but black. Interiors, of course, are color-
correlated, "for the man who cannot stop short of perfection."

At graveside, the casket is lowered into the earth. This office, once the   25
prerogative of friends of the deceased, is now performed by a patented mechanical lowering device. A "Lifetime Green" artificial grass mat is at the ready to
conceal the sere earth, and overhead, to conceal the sky, is a portable Steril
Chapel Tent ("resists the intense heat and humidity of summer and the terrific
storms of winter . . . available in Silver Gray, Rose, or Evergreen"). Now is the
time for the ritual scattering of earth over the coffin, as the solemn words "earth
to earth, ashes to ashes, dust to dust" are pronounced by the officiating cleric.
This can today be accomplished "with a mere flick of the wrist with the Gordon
Leak-Proof Earth Dispenser. No grasping of a handful of dirt, no soiled fingers.
Simple, dignified, beautiful, reverent! The modern way!" The Gordon Earth
Dispenser (at $5) is of nickel-plated brass construction. It is not only "attractive
to the eye and long wearing"; it is also "one of the 'tools' for building better
public relations" if presented as "an appropriate non-commercial gift" to the
clergyman. It is shaped something like a saltshaker.

Untouched by human hand, the coffin and the earth are now united.   26

It is in the function of directing the participants through this maze of gad-   27
getry that the funeral director has assigned to himself his relatively new role of
"grief therapist." He has relieved the family of every detail, he has revamped the
corpse to look like a living doll, he has arranged for it to nap for a few days in a
slumber room, he has put on a well-oiled performance in which the concept of
death has played no part whatsoever—unless it was inconsiderately mentioned
by the clergyman who conducted the religious service. He has done everything
in his power to make the funeral a real pleasure for everybody concerned. He
and his team have given their all to score an upset victory over death.

Meaning and Idea

1. List some of the steps a funeral home takes to prepare a body for burial.
   What is the purpose of each of those steps?

2. Mitford says that the purpose of the process of treating the dead is to
   transform the body from "a common corpse to a Beautiful Memory
   Picture." Analyze this statement. What does she mean by this comment?

3. Mitford draws attention to the frequent use of *euphemism* in the funeral home.
   The process of preparing the body is known as the "restorative art," the
   preparers call themselves "dermasurgeons," and the bodies, once ready for

viewing, are taken to a "slumber room." What does each of these euphemisms really mean, and what does the use of each euphemism conceal?

4. In what ways has the funeral industry reformed its practices since Mitford wrote this in 1963?

Language, Form, Structure

1. Of embalming, Mitford writes, "A close look at what does actually take place may explain in large measure the undertaker's intractable reticence concerning a procedure that has become his major *raison d'être*." Look up the French term in a good English dictionary. What point is Mitford making about the undertaker's work?

2. Mitford warns her readers that the details she is going to relate are not for the faint of heart. How does her focus on detailing the gruesome particulars of the process serve the purpose of her essay?

3. In a long passage Mitford compares the coordination of the funeral to a high school coach preparing his team for a big game. Analyze this comparison. Why does Mitford choose it?

4. In the third to last paragraph, Mitford intersperses the product descriptions of the funerary implements with a description of the burial. Why does she do this?

5. Define each of the following words and then use it in an original sentence: bereavement; docility; perpetuation; dissuade; distend; rudimentary; emaciation.

Ideas for Writing

1. Write a process analysis that sanitizes a process that you or others find distasteful. You might want to write about cleaning a birdcage or a fish tank, milking cows, or cleaning a basement. Try to imitate some of the techniques Mitford describes to disguise some of the unavoidable portions of the process, for example, euphemism, advertising language, and technical language.

2. Find a description or advertisement in a newspaper or magazine that uses techniques similar to those Mitford describes to conceal unpleasant or inconvenient facts. Write an analysis in which you point out the risks and realities the advertisement is trying to conceal and analyze the method by which that concealment is accomplished.

3. What is Mitford's argument in this essay? Look back over the essay and identify passages where she makes her arguments explicit. Write an essay analyzing Mitford's style of argumentation. What techniques does she use to make her argument convincing?

The Creation

Ovid

Ovid, the name by which we know Publius Ovidius Naso, was born to a wealthy family in the hill country outside Rome in 43 B.C. He began writing verse at age 12 and a few years later moved to Rome. In the year A.D. 8, Emperor Augustus exiled Ovid to a small town on the Black Sea for various scandalous indiscretions. Ovid died in that town in A.D. 18, survived by his third wife and his writings, among them *The Art of Love, Heroines, On Make-Up,* and the *Metamorphoses.*

This selection, translated by Rolfe Humphries, is the opening poem of Book I of Ovid's *Metamorphoses,* or *Stories of Changing Forms,* which is a novel-length series of poems described by John Crowe Ransom as "a key to the literary and religious culture of the ancients." This selection describes the most fundamental process of all, a version of which appears in every mythology and culture.

*B*efore the ocean was, or earth, or heaven,
Nature was all alike, a shapelessness,
Chaos, so-called, all rude and lumpy matter,
Nothing but bulk, inert, in whose confusion
Discordant atoms warred: there was no sun   5
To light the universe; there was no moon
With slender silver crescents filling slowly;
No earth hung balanced in surrounding air;
No sea reached far along the fringe of shore.
Land, to be sure, there was, and air, and ocean,   10
But land on which no man could stand, and water
No man could swim in, air no man could breathe,
Air without light, substance forever changing,
Forever at war: within a single body
Heat fought with cold, wet fought with dry, the hard   15
Fought with the soft, things having weight contended
With weightless things.
       Till God, or kindlier Nature,
Settled all argument, and separated
Heaven from earth, water from land, our air   20
From the high stratosphere, a liberation
So things evolved, and out of blind confusion
Found each its place, bound in eternal order.
The force of fire, that weightless element,
Leaped up and claimed the highest place in heaven;   25

Below it, air; and under them the earth
Sank with its grosser portions; and the water,
Lowest of all, held up, held in, the land.

Whatever god it was, who out of chaos
Brought order to the universe, and gave it   30
Division, subdivision, he molded earth,
In the beginning, into a great globe,
Even on every side, and bade the waters
To spread and rise, under the rushing winds,
Surrounding earth; he added ponds and marshes,   35
He banked the river-channels, and the waters
Feed earth or run to sea, and that great flood
Washes on shores, not banks. He made the plains
Spread wide, the valleys settle, and the forest
Be dressed in leaves; he made the rocky mountains   40
Rise to full height, and as the vault of Heaven
Has two zones, left and right, and one between them
Hotter than these, the Lord of all Creation
Marked on the earth the same design and pattern.
The torrid zone too hot for men to live in,   45
The north and south too cold, but in the middle
Varying climate, temperature and season.
Above all things the air, lighter than earth,
Lighter than water, heavier than fire,
Towers and spreads; there mist and cloud assemble,   50
And fearful thunder and lightning and cold winds,
But these, by the Creator's order, held
No general dominion; even as it is,
These brothers brawl and quarrel; though each one
Has his own quarter, still, they come near tearing   55
The universe apart. Eurus is monarch
Of the lands of dawn, the realms of Araby,
The Persian ridges under the rays of morning.
Zephyrus holds the west that glows at sunset,
Boreas, who makes men shiver, holds the north,   60
Warm Auster governs in the misty southland,
And over them all presides the weightless ether,
Pure without taint of earth.
          These boundaries given,
Behold, the stars, long hidden under darkness,   65
Broke through and shone, all over the spangled heaven,
Their home forever, and the gods lived there,
And shining fish were given the waves for dwelling

And beasts the earth, and birds the moving air.
But something else was needed, a finer being,   70
More capable of mind, a sage, a ruler,
So Man was born, it may be, in God's image,
Or Earth, perhaps, so newly separated
From the old fire of Heaven, still retained
Some seed of the celestial force which fashioned   75
Gods out of living clay and running water.
All other animals look downward; Man,
Alone, erect, can raise his face toward Heaven.

Meaning and Idea

1. Paraphrase Ovid's description of the universe before creation.

2. Describe the process of chaos becoming order as it is presented in this
   poem.

3. What was the relationship among universal opposing forces before the
   creation? What examples does Ovid provide to support this theory? How
   does that condition change after the creation? What brought about the
   change?

4. Identify the following Roman gods to whom Ovid alludes: Eurus;
   Zephyrus; Boreas; Auster.

5. What, according to the poem, was the purpose for humankind in the
   creation? At what point in the creation does humanity appear?

Language, Form, Structure

1. In a four-line preface to the *Metamorphoses,* Ovid wrote:

   > My intention is to tell of bodies changed
   > To different forms; the gods, who made the changes,
   > Will help me—or I hope so—with a poem
   > That runs from the world's beginning to our own days.

   How does this short poem serve as an appropriate beginning to the process
   described in "The Creation"?

2. What is the use of description and narration in this poem? How do they
   enhance the process analysis?

3. Look up the following words in a dictionary: rude; inert; fringe;
   stratosphere; bade; torrid; dominion; ether; taint; celestial.

Ideas for Writing

1. Write an essay that analyzes a creative process with which you are familiar. Attempt to use imagery as much as possible.

2. Select a natural process (leaves turning color, for example) and write an analysis explaining it to readers.

3. Write a prose version of Ovid's "The Creation" for a modern audience, paying particular attention to the "how-this-was-done" elements.

On Economy

Henry David Thoreau

Henry David Thoreau (1817–1862) along with Ralph Waldo Emerson helped move the mid-nineteenth-century American literary center from New York to Boston. Thoreau was a man of deeds, a nonconformist, a social critic. He graduated from Harvard, though he eschewed the professional opportunities that education provided him, choosing instead a quiet life in Concord, Massachusetts, where he was born. His most famous writings are *Walden* (1854), his account of natural living at Walden Pond, and the essay "Civil Disobedience," which significantly influenced the philosophy and tactics of Mahatma Ghandi.

In *Walden* Thoreau describes his experiment in living a solitary, self-sufficient, somewhat ascetic life at Walden Pond. In this selection from that book, he addresses the processes by which he learned to live a life of fiscal and emotional economy. He readily admits personal pride in his accomplishments but also hopes that what he learned will benefit his readers.

*N*ear the end of March, 1845, I borrowed an axe and went down to   1
the woods by Walden Pond, nearest to where I intended to build my house, and began to cut down some tall, arrowy white pines, still in their youth, for timber. It is difficult to begin without borrowing, but perhaps it is the most generous course thus to permit your fellow-men to have an interest in your enterprise. The owner of the axe, as he released his hold on it, said that it was the apple of his eye; but I returned it sharper than I received it. It was a pleasant hillside where I worked, covered with pine woods, through which I looked out on the pond, and a small open field in the woods where pines and hickories were springing up. The ice in the pond was not yet dissolved, though there were some open spaces, and it was all dark-colored and saturated with water. There were some slight flurries of snow during the days that I worked there; but for the most part when I came out on to the railroad, on my way home, its yellow sand-heap stretched away gleaming in the hazy atmosphere, and the rails shone in the spring sun, and I heard the lark and pewee and other birds already come to commence another year with us. They were pleasant spring days, in which the winter of man's discontent was thawing as well as the earth, and the life that had lain torpid began to stretch itself. One day, when my axe had come off and I had cut a green hickory for a wedge, driving it with a stone, and had placed the whole to soak in a pond-hole in order to swell the wood, I saw a striped snake run into the water, and he lay on the bottom, apparently without inconvenience, as long as I stayed there, or more than a quarter of an hour; perhaps because he had not yet fairly come out of the torpid state. It appeared to me that for a like reason men remain in their present low and primitive condition; but if they should feel the influence of the spring of springs arousing them, they would of necessity rise to a higher and more ethereal life. I had previously seen the snakes in frosty mornings in my path with portions of their bodies still numb and inflexible, waiting for the sun

to thaw them. On the 1st of April it rained and melted the ice, and in the early part of the day, which was very foggy, I heard a stray goose groping about over the pond and cackling as if lost, or like the spirit of the fog.

So I went on for some days cutting and hewing timber, and also studs and rafters, all with my narrow axe, not having many communicable or scholar-like thoughts, singing to myself,—

> Men say they know many things;
> But lo! they have taken wings,—
> The arts and sciences,
> And a thousand appliances:
> The wind that blows
> Is all that anybody knows.

I hewed the main timbers six inches square, most of the studs on two sides only, and the rafters and floor timbers on one side, leaving the rest of the bark on, so that they were just as straight and much stronger than sawed ones. Each stick was carefully mortised or tenoned by its stump, for I had borrowed other tools by this time. My days in the woods were not very long ones; yet I usually carried my dinner of bread and butter, and read the newspaper in which it was wrapped, at noon, sitting amid the green pine boughs which I had cut off, and to my bread was imparted some of their fragrance, for my hands were covered with a thick coat of pitch. Before I had done I was more the friend than the foe of the pine tree, though I had cut down some of them, having become better acquainted with it. Sometimes a rambler in the wood was attracted by the sound of my axe, and we chatted pleasantly over the chips which I had made.

By the middle of April, for I made no haste in my work, but rather made the most of it, my house was framed and ready for the raising. I had already bought the shanty of James Collins, an Irishman who worked on the Fitchburg Railroad, for boards. James Collins' shanty was considered an uncommonly fine one. When I called to see it he was not at home. I walked about the outside, at first unobserved from within, the window was so deep and high. It was of small dimensions, with a peaked cottage roof, and not much else to be seen, the dirt being raised five feet all around as if it were a compost heap. The roof was the soundest part, though a good deal warped and made brittle by the sun. Doorsill there was none, but a perennial passage for the hens under the door-board. Mrs. C came to the door and asked me to view it from the inside. The hens were driven in by my approach. It was dark, and had a dirt floor for the most part, dank, clammy, and aguish, only here a board and there a board which would not bear removal. She lighted a lamp to show me the inside of the roof and the walls, and also that the board floor extended under the bed, warning me not to step into the cellar, a sort of dust hole two feet deep. In her own words, they were "good boards overhead, good boards all around, and a good window,"—of two whole squares originally, only the cat had passed out that way lately. There was a stove, a bed, and a place to sit, an infant in the house where it was born, a silk parasol, gilt-framed looking-glass, and a patent new coffee-mill nailed to an oak sapling, all told. The bargain was soon concluded, for James had in the meanwhile returned. I to pay four dollars and twenty-five cents to-night, he to vacate at five to-morrow morning, selling to nobody else meanwhile: I to take possession at six. It were well, he said, to be there early, and anticipate certain indistinct but wholly unjust claims on the score of ground rent and fuel. This he assured me was the only encumbrance. At six I passed him and his family on the road. One large bundle held their all,—bed, coffee-mill, looking-glass, hens,—all but the cat; she took to the woods and became a wild cat, and as I learned afterward, trod in a trap set for woodchucks, and so became a dead cat at last.

I took down this dwelling the same morning, drawing the nails, and removed it to the pond-side by small cartloads, spreading the boards on the grass there to bleach and warp back again in the sun. One early thrush gave me a note or two as I drove along the woodland path. I was informed treacherously by a young Patrick that neighbor Seeley, an Irishman, in the intervals of the carting, transferred the still tolerable, straight, and drivable nails, staples, and spikes to his pocket, and then stood when I came back to pass the time of day, and look freshly up, unconcerned, with spring thoughts, at the devastation; there being a dearth of work, as he said. He was there to represent spectatordom, and help make this seemingly insignificant event one with the removal of the gods of Troy.

I dug my cellar in the side of a hill sloping to the south, where a woodchuck had formerly dug his burrow, down through sumach and blackberry roots, and the lowest stain of vegetation, six feet square by seven deep, to a fine sand where potatoes would not freeze in any winter. The sides were left shelving, and not stoned; but the sun having never shone on them, the sand still keeps its place. It was but two hours' work. I took particular pleasure in this breaking of ground, for in almost all latitudes men dig into the earth for an equable temperature. Under the most splendid house in the city is still to be found the cellar where they store their roots as of old, and long after the superstructure has disappeared posterity remark its dent in the earth. The house is still but a sort of porch at the entrance of a burrow.

At length, in the beginning of May, with the help of some of my acquaintances, rather to improve so good an occasion for neighborliness than from any necessity, I set up the frame of my house. No man was ever more honored in the character of his raisers than I. They are destined, I trust, to assist at the raising of loftier structures one day. I began to occupy my house on the 4th of July, as soon as it was boarded and roofed, for the boards were carefully feather-edged and lapped, so that it was perfectly impervious to rain, but before boarding I laid the foundation of a chimney at one end, bringing two cartloads of stones up the hill from the pond in my arms. I built the chimney after my hoeing in the fall, before a fire became necessary for warmth, doing my cooking in the meanwhile out of doors on the ground, early in the morning: which mode I still think is in some respects more convenient and agreeable than the usual one. When it stormed before my bread was baked, I fixed a few boards over the fire, and sat under them to watch my loaf, and passed some pleasant hours in that way. In those days, when my hands were much employed, I read but little, but the least scraps of paper which lay on the ground, my holder, or tablecloth, afforded me as much entertainment, in fact answered the same purpose as the Iliad.

It would be worth the while to build still more deliberately than I did, considering, for instance, what foundation a door, a window, a cellar, a garret, have in the nature of man, and perchance never raising any superstructure until we found a better reason for it than our temporal necessities even. There is some of the same fitness in a man's building his own house that there is in a bird's building its own nest. Who knows but if men constructed their dwellings with their own hands, and provided food for themselves and families simply and honestly enough, the poetic faculty would be universally developed, as birds universally sing when they are so engaged? But alas! we do like cowbirds and cuckoos, which lay their eggs in nests which other birds have built, and cheer no traveler with their chattering and unmusical notes. Shall we forever resign the pleasure of construction to the carpenter? What does architecture amount to in the experience of the mass of men? I never in all my walks came across a man engaged in so simple and natural an occupation as building his house. We belong to the community. It is not the tailor alone who is the ninth part of a man; it is as much the preacher, and the merchant, and the farmer. Where is this division of labor to end? and what object does it finally serve? No doubt another *may* also think for me; but it is not therefore desirable that he should do so to the exclusion of my thinking for myself.

True, there are architects so called in this country, and I have heard of one at least possessed with the idea of making architectural ornaments have a core of truth, a necessity, and hence a beauty, as if it were a revelation to him. All very well perhaps from his point of view, but only a little better than the common dilettantism. A sentimental reformer in architecture, he began at the cornice, not at the foundation. It was only how to put a core of truth within the ornaments, that every sugarplum, in fact, might have an almond or caraway seed in it,— though I hold that almonds are most wholesome without the sugar,—and not how the inhabitant, the indweller, might build truly within and without, and let the ornaments take care of themselves. What reasonable man ever supposed that ornaments were something outward and in the skin merely,—that the tortoise got his spotted shell, or the shell-fish its mother-o'-pearl tints, by such a contract as the inhabitants of Broadway their Trinity Church? But a man has no more to do with the style of architecture of his house than a tortoise with that of its shell: nor need the soldier be so idle as to try to paint the precise *color* of his virtue on his standard. The enemy will find it out. He may turn pale when the trial comes. This man seemed to me to lean over the cornice, and timidly whisper his half truth to the rude occupants who really knew it better than he. What of architectural beauty I now see, I know has gradually grown from within outward, out of the necessities and character of the indweller, who is the only builder,—out of some unconscious truthfulness, and nobleness, without ever a thought for the appearance; and whatever additional beauty of this kind is destined to be produced will be preceded by a like unconscious beauty of life. The most interesting dwellings in this country, as the painter knows, are the most unpretending, humble log huts and cottages of the poor commonly; it is the life of the inhabitants whose shells they are, and not any peculiarity in their surfaces merely, which makes them *picturesque;* and equally interesting will be the citizen's suburban box, when his life shall be as simple and as agreeable to the imagination, and there is as little straining after effect in the style of his dwelling. A great proportion of architectural ornaments are literally hollow, and a September gale would strip them off, like borrowed plumes, without injury to the substantials. They can do without *architecture* who have no olives nor wines in the cellar. What if an equal ado were made about the ornaments of style in literature, and the architects of our Bibles spent as much time about their cornices as the architects of our churches do? So are made the *belles-lettres* and the *beaux-arts* and their professors. Much it concerns a man, forsooth, how a few sticks are slanted over him or under him, and what colors are daubed upon his box. It would signify somewhat, if, in any earnest sense, *he* slanted them and daubed it; but the spirit having departed out of the tenant, it is of a piece with constructing his own coffin,—the architecture of the grave,—and "carpenter" is but another name for "coffin-maker." One man says, in his despair or indifference to life, take up a handful of the earth at your feet, and paint your house that color. Is he thinking of his last and narrow house? Toss up a copper for it as well. What an abundance of leisure he must have! Why do you take up a handful of dirt? Better paint your house your own complexion; let it turn pale or blush for you. An enterprise to improve the style of cottage architecture! When you have got my ornaments ready, I will wear them.

Before winter I built a chimney, and shingled the sides of my house, which were already impervious to rain, with imperfect and sappy shingles made of the first slice of the log, whose edges I was obliged to straighten with a plane. 9

I have thus a tight shingled and plastered house, ten feet wide by fifteen long, and eight-feet posts, with a garret and a closet, a large window on each side, two trap-doors, one door at the end, and a brick fireplace opposite. The exact cost of my house, paying the usual price for such materials as I used, but not counting the work, all of which was done by myself, was as follows; and I give the details because very few are able to tell exactly what their houses cost, and fewer still, if any, the separate cost of the various materials which compose them:— 10

Boards	$8 03½,	mostly shanty boards
Refuse shingles for roof and sides	4 00	
Laths.	1 25	
Two second-hand windows with glass . . .	2 43	
One thousand old brick	4 00	
Two casks of lime	2 40	That was high.
Hair	0 31	More than I needed.
Mantle-tree iron.	0 15	
Nails.	3 90	
Hinges and screws	0 14	
Latch.	0 10	
Chalk	0 01	{ I carried a good part
Transportation	1 40	on my back
In all.	$28 12½	

These are all the materials, excepting the timber, stones, and sand, which I 11 claimed by squatter's right. I have also a small woodshed adjoining, made chiefly of the stuff which was left after building the house.

I intend to build me a house which will surpass any on the main street in 12 Concord in grandeur and luxury, as soon as it pleases me as much and will cost me no more than my present one.

I thus found that the student who wishes for a shelter can obtain one for a 13 lifetime at an expense not greater than the rent which he now pays annually. If I seem to boast more than is becoming, my excuse is that I brag for humanity rather than for myself; and my shortcomings and inconsistencies do not affect the truth of my statement. Notwithstanding much cant and hypocrisy,—chaff which I find it difficult to separate from my wheat, but for which I am as sorry as any man,—I will breathe freely and stretch myself in this respect, it is such a relief to both the moral and physical system; and I am resolved that I will not through humility become the devil's attorney. I will endeavor to speak a good word for the truth. At Cambridge College the mere rent of a student's room, which is only a little larger than my own, is thirty dollars each year, though the corporation had the advantage of building thirty-two side by side and under one roof, and the occupant suffers the inconvenience of many and noisy neighbors, and perhaps a residence in the fourth story. I cannot but think that if we had more true wisdom in these respects, not only less education would be needed, because, forsooth, more would already have been acquired, but the pecuniary expense of getting an education would in a great measure vanish. Those conveniences which the student requires at Cambridge or elsewhere cost him or somebody else ten times as great a sacrifice of life as they would with proper management on both sides. Those things for which the most money is demanded are never the things which the student most wants. Tuition, for instance, is an important item in the term bill, while for the far more valuable education which he gets by associating with the most cultivated of his contemporaries no charge is made. The mode of founding a college is, commonly, to get up a subscription of dollars and cents, and then, following blindly the principles of a division of labor to its extreme,—a principle which should never be followed but with circumspection,—to call in a contractor who makes this a subject of speculation, and he employs Irishmen or other operatives actually to lay the foundations, while the students that are to be are said to be fitting themselves for it; and for these oversights successive generations have to pay. I think that it would be *better than this,* for the students, or those who desire to be benefited by it, even to lay the foundation themselves. The student who secures his coveted leisure and retirement by systematically shirking any labor necessary to man obtains but an ignoble and unprofitable leisure, defrauding himself of the experience which alone can make leisure fruitful. "But," says one, "you do not mean that the students should go to work with their hands instead of their heads?" I do not mean that exactly, but I mean something which he might think a good deal like that; I mean that they should not *play* life, or *study* it merely, while the community supports them at this expensive game, (but earnestly *live* it from beginning to end). How could youths better learn to live than by at once trying the experiment of living? Methinks this would exercise their minds as much as mathematics. If I wished a boy to know something about the arts and sciences, for instance, I would not pursue the common course, which is merely to send him into the neighborhood of some professor, where anything is professed and practiced but the art of life;—to survey the world through a telescope or a microscope, and never with his natural eye; to study chemistry, and not learn how his bread is made, or mechanics, and not learn how it is earned; to discover new satellites to Neptune, and not detect the motes in his eyes, or to what vagabond he is a satellite himself; or to be devoured by the monsters that swarm all around him, while contemplating the monsters in a drop of vinegar. Which would have advanced the most at the end of a month,—the boy who had made his own jackknife from the ore which he had dug and smelted, reading as much as would be necessary for this—or the boy who had attended the lectures on metallurgy at the Institute in the meanwhile, and had received a Rodgers penknife from his father? Which would be most likely to cut his fingers? . . . To my astonishment I was informed on leaving college that I had studied navigation!—why, if I had taken one turn down the harbor I should have known more about it. Even the *poor* student studies and is taught only *political* economy, while that economy of living which is synonymous with philosophy is not even sincerely professed in our colleges. The consequence is, that while he is reading Adam Smith, Ricardo, and Say, he runs his father in debt irretrievably.

As with our colleges, so with a hundred "modern improvements;" there is an illusion about them; there is not always a positive advance. The devil goes on exacting compound interest to the last for his early share and numerous succeeding investments in them. Our inventions are wont to be pretty toys, which distract our attention from serious things. They are but improved means to an unimproved end, an end which it was already but too easy to arrive at; as railroads lead to Boston or New York. We are in great haste to construct a magnetic telegraph from Maine to Texas; but Maine and Texas, it may be, have nothing important to communicate. Either is in such a predicament as the man who was earnest to be introduced to a distinguished deaf woman, but when he was presented, and one end of her ear trumpet was put into his hand, had nothing to say. As if the main object were to talk fast and not to talk sensibly. We are eager to tunnel under the Atlantic and bring the Old World some weeks nearer to the New; but perchance the first news that will leak through into the broad, flapping American ear will be that the Princess Adelaide has the whooping cough. After all, the man whose horse trots a mile a minute does not carry the most important messages; he is not an evangelist, nor does he come round eating locusts and wild honey. I doubt if Flying Childers ever carried a peck of corn to mill. 14

One says to me, "I wonder that you do not lay up money; you love to travel; you might take the cars and go to Fitchburg today and see the country." But I am wiser than that. I have learned that the swiftest traveller is he that goes afoot. I say to my friend, Suppose we try who will get there first. The distance is thirty miles; the fare ninety cents. That is almost a day's wages. I remember when wages were sixty cents a day for laborers on this very road. Well, I start 15 now on foot, and get there before night; I have travelled at that rate by the week together. You will in the meanwhile have earned your fare, and arrive there sometime to-morrow, or possibly this evening, if you are lucky enough to get a job in season. Instead of going to Fitchburg, you will be working here the greater part of the day. And so, if the railroad reached round the world, I think that I should keep ahead of you; and as for seeing the country and getting experience of that kind, I should have to cut your acquaintance altogether.

Such is the universal law, which no man can ever outwit, and with regard   16
to the railroad even we may say it is as broad as it is long. To make a railroad round the world available to all mankind is equivalent to grading the whole surface of the planet. Men have an indistinct notion that if they keep up this activity of joint stocks and spades long enough all will at length ride somewhere, in next to no time, and for nothing; but though a crowd rushes to the depot, and the conductor shouts "All aboard!" when the smoke is blown away and the vapor condensed, it will be perceived that a few are riding, but the rest are run over,—and it will be called, and will be, "A melancholy accident." No doubt they can ride at last who shall have earned their fare, that is, if they survive so long, but they will probably have lost their elasticity and desire to travel by that time. This spending of the best part of one's life earning money in order to enjoy a questionable liberty during the least valuable part of it reminds me of the Englishman who went to India to make a fortune first, in order that he might return to England and live the life of a poet. He should have gone up garret at once. "What!" exclaim a million Irishmen starting up from all the shanties in the land, "is not this railroad which we have built a good thing?" Yes, I answer, *comparatively* good, that is, you might have done worse; but I wish, as you are brothers of mine, that you could have spent your time better than digging in this dirt.

Before I finished my house, wishing to earn ten or twelve dollars by some   17
honest and agreeable method, in order to meet my unusual expenses, I planted about two acres and a half of light and sandy soil near it chiefly with beans, but also a small part with potatoes, corn, peas, and turnips. The whole lot contains eleven acres, mostly growing up to pines and hickories, and was sold the preceding season for eight dollars and eight cents an acre. One farmer said that it was "good for nothing but to raise cheeping squirrels on." I put no manure whatever on this land, not being the owner, but merely a squatter, and not expecting to cultivate so much again, and I did not quite hoe it all once. I got out several cords of stumps in plowing, which supplied me with fuel for a long time, and left small circles of virgin mould, easily distinguishable through the summer by the greater luxuriance of the beans there. The dead and for the most part unmerchantable wood behind my house, and the drift wood from the pond, have supplied the remainder of my fuel. I was obliged to hire a team and a man for the plowing, though I held the plow myself. My farm outgoes for the first season were, for implements, seed, work, etc., $14.72 ½. The seed corn was given me. This never costs anything to speak of unless you plant more than enough. I got twelve bushels of beans, and eighteen bushels of potatoes, beside some peas and

sweet corn. The yellow corn and turnips were too late to come to anything. My whole income from the farm was

---

Deducting the outgoes $23 44
                                  14 72½
                                  ‾‾‾‾‾‾
There are left . . . . $ 8 71½,

---

beside produce consumed and on hand at the time this estimate was made of the value of $4.50,—the amount on hand much more than balancing a little grass which I did not raise. All things considered, that is, considering the importance of a man's soul and of to-day, notwithstanding the short time occupied by my experiment, nay, partly even because of its transient character, I believe that that was doing better than any farmer in Concord did that year.

The next year I did better still, for I spaded up all the land which I required, about a third of an acre, and I learned from the experience of both years, not being in the least awed by many celebrated works on husbandry, Arthur Young among the rest, that if one would live simply and eat only the crop which he raised, and raise no more than he ate, and not exchange it for an insufficient quantity of more luxurious and expensive things, he would need to cultivate only a few rods of ground, and that it would be cheaper to spade up that than to use oxen to plow it, and to select a fresh spot from time to time than to manure the old, and he could do all his necessary farm work as it were with his left hand at odd hours in the summer; and thus he would not be tied to an ox, or horse, or cow, or pig, as at present. I desire to speak impartially on this point, and as one not interested in the success or failure of the present economical and social arrangements. I was more independent than any farmer in Concord, for I was not anchored to a house or farm, but could follow the bent of my genius, which is a very crooked one, every moment. Beside being better off than they already, if my house had been burned or my crops had failed, I should have been nearly as well off as before.   18

I am wont to think that men are not so much the keepers of herds as herds are the keepers of men, the former are so much the freer. Men and oxen exchange work; but if we consider necessary work only, the oxen will be seen to have greatly the advantage, their farm is so much the larger. Man does some of his part of the exchange work in his six weeks of haying, and it is no boy's play. Certainly no nation that lived simply in all respects, that is, no nation of philosophers, would commit so great a blunder as to use the labor of animals. True, there never was and is not likely soon to be a nation of philosophers, nor am I certain it is desirable that there should be. However, *I* should never have broken a horse or bull and taken him to board for any work he might do for me, for fear I should become a horse-man or a herds-man merely; and if society seems to be the gainer by so doing, are we certain that what is one man's gain is not another's loss, and that the stable-boy has equal cause with his master to be satisfied? Granted that some public works would not have been constructed without this aid, and let man   19 share the glory of such with the ox and horse; does it follow that he could not have accomplished works yet more worthy of himself in that case? When men begin to do, not merely unnecessary or artistic, but luxurious and idle work, with their assistance, it is inevitable that a few do all the exchange work with the oxen, or, in other words, become the slaves of the strongest. Man thus not only works for the animal within him, but, for a symbol of this, he works for the animal without him. Though we have many substantial houses of brick or stone, the prosperity of the farmer is still measured by the degree to which the barn overshadows the house. This town is said to have the largest houses for oxen, cows, and horses hereabouts, and it is not behindhand in its public buildings; but there are very few halls for free worship or free speech in this county. It should not be by their architecture, but why not even by their power of abstract thought, that nations should seek to commemorate themselves? How much more admirable the Bhagvat-Geeta than all the ruins of the East! Towers and temples are the luxury of princes. A simple and independent mind does not toil at the bidding of any prince. Genius is not a retainer to any emperor, nor is its material silver, or gold, or marble, except to a trifling extent. To what end, pray, is so much stone hammered? In Arcadia, when I was there, I did not see any hammering stone. Nations are possessed with an insane ambition to perpetuate the memory of themselves by the amount of hammered stone they leave. What if equal pains were taken to smooth and polish their manners? One piece of good sense would be more memorable than a monument as high as the moon. I love better to see stones in place. The grandeur of Thebes was a vulgar grandeur. More sensible is a rod of stone wall that bounds an honest man's field than a hundred-gated Thebes that has wandered farther from the true end of life. The religion and civilization which are barbaric and heathenish build splendid temples; but what you might call Christianity does not. Most of the stone a nation hammers goes toward its tomb only. It buries itself alive. As for the Pyramids, there is nothing to wonder at in them so much as the fact that so many men could be found degraded enough to spend their lives constructing a tomb for some ambitious booby, whom it would have been wiser and manlier to have drowned in the Nile, and then given his body to the dogs. I might possibly invent some excuse for them and him, but I have no time for it. As for the religion and love of art of the builders, it is much the same all the world over, whether the building be an Egyptian temple or the United States Bank. It costs more than it comes to. The mainspring is vanity, assisted by the love of garlic and bread and butter. Mr. Balcom, a promising young architect, designs it on the back of his Vitruvius, with hard pencil and ruler, and the job is let out to Dobson & Sons, stonecutters. When the thirty centuries begin to look down on it, mankind begin to look up at it. As for your high towers and monuments, there was a crazy fellow once in this town who undertook to dig through to China, and he got so far that, as he said, he heard the Chinese pots and kettles rattle; but I think that I shall not go out of my way to admire the hole which he made. Many are concerned about the monuments of the West and the East,—to know who built them. For my part, I should like to know who in those days did not build them,—who were above such trifling. But to proceed with my statistics.

By surveying, carpentry, and day-labor of various other kinds in the vil- 20
lage in the meanwhile, for I have as many trades as fingers, I had earned
$13.34. The expense of food for eight months, namely, from July 4th to March
1st, the time when these estimates were made, though I lived there more than
two years,—not counting potatoes, a little green corn, and some peas, which I
had raised, nor considering the value of what was on hand at the last date,—
was

Rice	$1 73½	
Molasses	1 73	Cheapest form of the saccharine.
Rye meal	1 04¾	
Indian meal	0 99¾	Cheaper than rye.
Pork	0 22	⎰ Costs more than Indian meal, both
Flour	0 88	⎱ money and trouble.
Sugar	0 80	
Lard	0 65	
Apples	0 25	
Dried apple	0 22	
Sweet potatoes . . .	0 10	
One pumpkin	0 6	
One watermelon . . .	0 2	
Salt	0 3	

Yes, I did eat $8.74, all told; but I should not thus unblushingly publish my
guilt, if I did not know that most of my readers were equally guilty with myself,
and that their deeds would look no better in print. The next year I sometimes
caught a mess of fish for my dinner, and once I went so far as to slaughter a
woodchuck which ravaged my bean-field,—effect his transmigration, as a Tartar
would say,—and devour him, partly for experiment's sake; but though it afforded me a momentary enjoyment, notwithstanding a musky flavor, I saw that
the longest use would not make that a good practice, however it might seem to
have your woodchucks ready dressed by the village butcher.

Clothing and some incidental expenses within the same dates, though little 21
can be inferred from this item, amounted to

	$8 40¾
Oil and some household utensils	2 00

So that all the pecuniary outgoes, excepting for washing and mending, which for
the most part were done out of the house, and their bills have not yet been

received,—and these are all and more than all the ways by which money necessarily goes out in this part of the world,—were

House	$28 12½
Farm one year	14 72½
Food eight months	8 74
Clothing, etc., eight months	8 40¾
Oil, etc., eight months	2 00
	$61 99¾

I address myself now to those of my readers who have a living to get. And to meet this I have for farm produce sold

Earned by day-labor	$23 44
	13 44
In all	$36 78,

which subtracted from the sum of the outgoes leaves a balance of $25.21¾ on the one side,—this being very nearly the means with which I started, and the measure of expenses to be incurred,—and on the other, beside the leisure and independence and health thus secured, a comfortable house for me as long as I choose to occupy it.

These statistics, however accidental and therefore uninstructive they may appear, as they have a certain completeness, have a certain value also. Nothing was given me of which I have not rendered some account. It appears from the above estimate, that my food alone cost me in money about twenty-seven cents a week. It was, for nearly two years after this, rye and Indian meal without yeast, potatoes, rice, a very little salt pork, molasses, and salt; and my drink, water. It was fit that I should live on rice, mainly, who loved so well the philosophy of India. To meet the objections of some inveterate cavillers, I may as well state, that if I dined out occasionally, as I always had done, and I trust shall have opportunities to do again, it was frequently to the detriment of my domestic arrangements. But the dining out, being, as I have stated, a constant element, does not in the least affect a comparative statement like this.

I learned from my two years' experience that it would cost incredibly little trouble to obtain one's necessary food, even in this latitude; that a man may use as simple a diet as the animals, and yet retain health and strength. I have made a satisfactory dinner, satisfactory on several accounts, simply off a dish of purslane (*Portulaca oleracea*) which I gathered in my cornfield, boiled and salted. I give the Latin on account of the savoriness of the trivial name. And pray what more can a reasonable man desire, in peaceful times, in ordinary noons, than a sufficient number of ears of green sweet corn boiled, with the addition of salt? Even the little variety which I used was a yielding to the demands of appetite, and not of health. Yet men have come to such a pass that they frequently starve, not for want of necessaries, but for want of luxuries; and I know a good woman who thinks that her son lost his life because he took to drinking water only.

The reader will perceive that I am treating the subject rather from an economic than a dietetic point of view, and he will not venture to put my abstemiousness to the test unless he has a well-stocked larder. 24

Bread I at first made of pure Indian meal and salt, genuine hoe-cakes, 25 which I baked before my fire out of doors on a shingle or the end of a stick of timber sawed off in building my house; but it was wont to get smoked and to have a piny flavor. I tried flour also; but have at last found a mixture of rye and Indian meal most convenient and agreeable. In cold weather it was no little amusement to bake several small loaves of this in succession, tending and turning them as carefully as an Egyptian his hatching eggs. They were a real cereal fruit which I ripened, and they had to my senses a fragrance like that of other noble fruits, which I kept in as long as possible by wrapping them in cloths. I made a study of the ancient and indispensable art of bread-making, consulting such authorities as offered, going back to the primitive days and first invention of the unleavened kind, when from the wildness of nuts and meats men first reached the mildness and refinement of this diet, and travelling gradually down in my studies through that accidental souring of the dough which, it is supposed, taught the leavening process, and through the various fermentations thereafter, till I came to "good, sweet, wholesome bread," the staff of life. Leaven, which some deem the soul of bread, the *spiritus* which fills its cellular tissue, which is religiously preserved like the vestal fire,—some precious bottleful, I suppose, first brought over in the Mayflower, did the business for America, and its influence is still rising, swelling, spreading, in cerealian billows over the land,—this seed I regularly and faithfully procured from the village, till at length one morning I forgot the rules, and scalded my yeast; by which accident I discovered that even this was not indispensable,—for my discoveries were not by the synthetic but analytic process,—and I have gladly omitted it since, though most housewives earnestly assured me that safe and wholesome bread without yeast might not be, and elderly people prophesied a speedy decay of the vital forces. Yet I find it not to be an essential ingredient, and after going without it for a year am still in the land of the living; and I am glad to escape the trivialness of carrying a bottleful in my pocket, which would sometimes pop and discharge its contents to my discomfiture. It is simpler and more respectable to omit it. Man is an animal who more than any other can adapt himself to all climates and circumstances. Neither did I put any sal-soda, or other acid or alkali, into my bread. It would seem that I made it according to the recipe which Marcus Porcius Cato gave about two centuries before Christ. "Panem depsticium sic facito. Manus mortariumque bene lavato. Farinam in mortarium indito, aquae paulatim addito, subigitoque pulchre. Ubi bene subegeris, defingito, coquitoque sub testu." Which I take to mean, "Make kneaded bread thus. Wash your hands and trough well. Put the meal into the trough, add water gradually, and knead it thoroughly. When you have kneaded it well, mould it, and bake it under a cover," that is, in a baking-kettle. Not a word about leaven. But I did not always use this staff of life. At one time, owing to the emptiness of my purse, I saw none of it for more than a month.

Every New Englander might easily raise all his own breadstuffs in this land of rye and Indian corn, and not depend on distant and fluctuating markets for them. Yet so far are we from simplicity and independence that, in Concord, fresh and sweet meal is rarely sold in the shops, and hominy and corn in a still coarser form are hardly used by any. For the most part the farmer gives to his cattle and hogs the grain of his own producing, and buys flour, which is at least no more wholesome, at a greater cost, at the store. I saw that I could easily raise my bushel or two of rye and Indian corn, for the former will grow on the poorest land, and the latter does not require the best, and grind them in a hand-mill, and so do without rice and pork; and if I must have some concentrated sweet, I found by experiment that I could make a very good molasses either of pumpkins or beets, and I knew that I needed only to set out a few maples to obtain it more easily still, and while these were growing I could use various substitutes beside those which I have named. "For," as the Forefathers sang,— 26

> we can make liquor to sweeten our lips
> Of pumpkins and parsnips and walnut-tree chips.

Finally, as for salt, that grossest of groceries, to obtain this might be a fit occasion for a visit to the seashore, or, if I did without it altogether, I should probably drink the less water. I do not learn that the Indians ever troubled themselves to go after it.

Thus I could avoid all trade and barter, so far as my food was concerned, and having a shelter already, it would only remain to get clothing and fuel. The pantaloons which I now wear were woven in a farmer's family,— thank Heaven there is so much virtue still in man; for I think the fall from the farmer to the operative as great and memorable as that from the man to the farmer;—and in a new country, fuel is an encumbrance. As for a habitat, if I were not permitted still to squat, I might purchase one acre at the same price for which the land I cultivated was sold—namely, eight dollars and eight cents. But as it was, I considered that I enhanced the value of the land by squatting on it. 27

There is a certain class of unbelievers who sometimes ask me such questions as, if I think that I can live on vegetable food alone; and to strike at the root of the matter at once,—for the root is faith,—I am accustomed to answer such, that I can live on board nails. If they cannot understand that, they cannot understand much that I have to say. For my part, I am glad to hear of experiments of this kind being tried; as that a young man tried for a fortnight to live on hard, raw corn on the ear, using his teeth for all mortar. The squirrel tribe 28 tried the same and succeeded. The human race is interested in these experiments, though a few old women who are incapacitated for them, or who own their thirds in mills, may be alarmed.

Meaning and Idea

1. What does Thoreau mean by *economy?* (You may want to check a dictionary definition of the word and compare Thoreau's use of it.) Briefly summarize what Thoreau considers the importance of economy.

2. What is the "experiment" Thoreau mentions? What does Thoreau identify as the nonmonetary personal gains of his experiment?

3. Toward the end of the essay Thoreau claims, "Thus I could avoid all trade and barter, so far as my food was concerned." Describe the process by which he achieved this condition. What are Thoreau's general suggestions to his audience about economizing on food?

4. What is the writer's attitude toward modernization? How does he exemplify his attitude?

5. Thoreau writes in this essay that "my discoveries were not by the synthetic but analytic process." Interpret the meaning of this statement in light of your reading of the essay.

Language, Form, Structure

1. What is the main process which Thoreau explains in this essay? Outline the steps he describes. How does he accomplish the transitions between these steps? How does he arrange them? What is the time span covered by the essay? What stages of the overall process occur at different points in this time span?

2. What is the overall purpose of this selection? In other words, what is Thoreau trying to teach his audience about the process of their lives? Into what categories of daily life and necessities does he divide his overall process analysis?

3. How does Thoreau use description in this essay? Which descriptive details do you find freshest? Which sensory appeals are particularly vivid? Where does Thoreau use data to support his point? Why do you think he uses data?

4. Throughout the essay, Thoreau makes numerous comparisons of the steps of his process to the processes of nature. Identify some of these comparisons. What do they add to the tone and style of the essay? He also makes several comparisons to Greek mythology. Identify them and explain their purpose.

5. How does Thoreau analyze the process of human beings becoming subservient to their work animals? How might this section be read metaphorically?

6. Identify the meanings of 10 of the following words from the essay. Then add five more definitions of words unfamiliar to you in the reading that do not appear on this list: ethereal; perennial; dank; dearth; posterity; revelation; dilettantism; ado; *belles-lettres;* cant; pecuniary; coveted; perpetuate; heathenish; transmigration.

Ideas for Writing

1. Write about a long-term project that you attempted either recently or in the past. Analyze the process by which you approached and carried out this project.

2. In the form of a letter, write to a friend who has trouble managing money and propose a process by which he or she could be more financially responsible.

3. In an essay respond to the following question: Would you classify "economy" as a *how* or a *how-to* process analysis? Support your answer with specific references to Thoreau's essay.

The Rocking-Horse Winner

D. H. Lawrence

D. H. Lawrence was born in 1885 in the English Midlands coal-mining town of Eastwood, the son of a coal miner. Lawrence was ambivalent about his background—he found it overly materialistic and repressive, yet he used it as the basis for nearly all his fiction. In 1912 he ran off with his wife-to-be, Frieda, and they lived outside of England for most of their lives—in Australia, Italy, Germany, Mexico, and the United States. Lawrence's fiction—including *Sons and Lovers* (1913), *The Rainbow* (1915), *Women in Love* (1920), and *Lady Chatterley's Lover* (1928)—created a great uproar for its literary daring and so-called immorality. Lawrence, who was also a prolific critical and travel writer, died of tuberculosis in southern France in 1930; his ashes rest in Taos, New Mexico.

"The Rocking-Horse Winner" shows us how need—real or imagined—can sometimes overcome life itself. Notice how Lawrence uses processes of both building up and deterioration to develop the narrative line.

*T*here was a woman who was beautiful, who started with all the advantages, yet she had no luck. She married for love, and the love turned to dust. She had bonny children, yet she felt they had been thrust upon her, and she could not love them. They looked at her coldly, as if they were finding fault with her. And hurriedly she felt she must cover up some fault in herself. Yet what it was that she must cover up she never knew. Nevertheless, when her children were present, she always felt the centre of her heart go hard. This troubled her, and in her manner she was all the more gentle and anxious for her children, as if she loved them very much. Only she herself knew that at the centre of her heart was a hard little place that could not feel love, no, not for anybody. Everybody else said of her: "She is such a good mother. She adores her children." Only she herself, and her children themselves, knew it was not so. They read it in each other's eyes.

There were a boy and two little girls. They lived in a pleasant house, with a garden, and they had discreet servants, and felt themselves superior to anyone in the neighbourhood.

Although they lived in style, they felt always an anxiety in the house. There was never enough money. The mother had a small income, and the father had a small income, but not nearly enough for the social position which they had to keep up. The father went into town to some office. But though he had good prospects, these prospects never materialised. There was always the grinding sense of the shortage of money, though the style was always kept up.

At last the mother said: "I will see if *I* can't make something." But she did not know where to begin. She racked her brains, and tried this thing and the other, but could not find anything successful. The failure made deep lines come into her face. Her children were growing up, they would have to go to school. There must be more money, there must be more money. The father, who was always very handsome and expensive in his tastes, seemed as if he never *would* be able to do anything worth doing. And the mother, who had a great belief in herself, did not succeed any better, and her tastes were just as expensive.

And so the house came to be haunted by the unspoken phrase: *There must be more money! There must be more money!* The children could hear it all the time, though nobody said it aloud. They heard it at Christmas, when the expensive and splendid toys filled the nursery. Behind the shining modern rocking-horse, behind the smart doll's house, a voice would start whispering: "There *must* be more money! There *must* be more money!" And the children would stop playing, to listen for a moment. They would look into each other's eyes, to see if they had all heard. And each one saw in the eyes of the other two that they too had heard. "There *must* be more money! There *must* be more money!"

It came whispering from the springs of the still-swaying rocking-horse, and even the horse, bending his wooden, champing head, heard it. The big doll, sitting so pink and smirking in her new pram, could hear it quite plainly, and seemed to be smirking all the more self-consciously because of it. The foolish puppy, too, that took the place of the teddy-bear, he was looking so extraordinarily foolish for no other reason but that he heard the secret whisper all over the house: "There *must* be more money!

Yet nobody ever said it aloud. The whisper was everywhere, and therefore no one spoke it. Just as no one ever says: "We are breathing!" in spite of the fact that breath is coming and going all the time.

"Mother," said the boy Paul one day, "Why do we always use uncle's, or else a taxi?"

"Because we're the poor members of the family," said the mother.

"But why *are* we, mother?"

"Well—I suppose," she said slowly and bitterly, "it's because your father has no luck."

The boy was silent for some time.

"Is luck money, mother?" he asked, rather timidly.

"No, Paul. Not quite. It's what causes you to have money."

"Oh!" said Paul vaguely. "I thought when Uncle Oscar said *filthy lucker,* it meant money."

"*Filthy lucre* does mean money," said the mother. "But it's lucre, not luck."

"Oh!" said the boy. "Then what *is* luck, mother?"

"It's what causes you to have money. If you're lucky you have money. That's why it's better to be born lucky than rich. If you're rich, you may lose your money. But if you're lucky, you will always get more money."

"Oh! Will you? And is father not lucky?"

"Very unlucky, I should say," she said bitterly.

The boy watched her with unsure eyes.

"Why?" he asked.

"I don't know. Nobody ever knows why one person is lucky and another unlucky." 23

"Don't they? Nobody at all? Does *nobody* know?" 24

"Perhaps God. But He never tells." 25

"He ought to, then. And aren't you lucky either, mother?" 26

"I can't be, if I married an unlucky husband." 27

"But by yourself, aren't you?" 28

"I used to think I was, before I married. Now I think I am very unlucky indeed." 29

"Why?" 30

"Well—never mind! Perhaps I'm not really," she said. 31

The child looked at her to see if she meant it. But he saw, by the lines of her mouth, that she was only trying to hide something from him. 32

"Well, anyhow," he said stoutly, "I'm a lucky person." 33

"Why?" said his mother, with a sudden laugh. 34

He stared at her. He didn't even know why he had said it. 35

"God told me," he asserted, brazening it out. 36

"I hope He did, dear!" she said, again with a laugh, but rather bitter. 37

"He did, mother!" 38

"Excellent!" said the mother, using one of her husband's exclamations. 39

The boy saw she did not believe him; or rather, that she paid no attention to his assertion. This angered him somewhat, and made him want to compel her attention. 40

He went off by himself, vaguely, in a childish way, seeking for the clue to "luck." Absorbed, taking no heed of other people, he went about with a sort of stealth, seeking inwardly for luck. He wanted luck, he wanted it, he wanted it. When the two girls were playing dolls in the nursery, he would sit on his big rocking-horse, charging madly into space, with a frenzy that made the little girls peer at him uneasily. Wildly the horse careened, the waving dark hair of the boy tossed, his eyes had a strange glare in them. The little girls dared not speak to him. 41

When he had ridden to the end of his mad little journey, he climbed down and stood in front of his rocking-horse, staring fixedly into its lowered face. Its red mouth was slightly open, its big eye was wide and glassy-bright. 42

"Now!" he would silently command the snorting steed. "Now, take me to where there is luck! Now take me!" 43

And he would slash the horse on the neck with the little whip he had asked Uncle Oscar for. He *knew* the horse could take him to where there was luck, if only he forced it. So he would mount again and start on his furious ride, hoping at last to get there. He knew he could get there. 44

"You'll break your horse, Paul!" said the nurse. 45

"He's always riding like that! I wish he'd leave off!" said his elder sister Joan. 46

But he only glared down on them in silence. Nurse gave him up. She could make nothing of him. Anyhow, he was growing beyond her. 47

One day his mother and his Uncle Oscar came in when he was on one of his furious rides. He did not speak to them. 48

"Hallo, you young jockey! Riding a winner?" said his uncle. 49

"Aren't you growing too big for a rocking-horse? You're not a very little boy any longer, you know," said his mother. 50

But Paul only gave a blue glare from his big, rather close-set eyes. He would speak to nobody when he was in full tilt. His mother watched him with an anxious expression on her face. 51

At last he suddenly stopped forcing his horse into the mechanical gallop and slid down. 52

"Well, I got there!" he announced fiercely, his blue eyes still flaring, and his sturdy long legs straddling apart. 53

"Where did you get to?" asked his mother. 54

"Where I wanted to go," he flared back at her. 55

"That's right, son!" said Uncle Oscar. "Don't you stop till you get there. What's the horse's name?" 56

"He doesn't have a name," said the boy. 57

"Gets on without all right?" asked the uncle. 58

"Well, he has different names. He was called Sansovino last week." 59

"Sansovino, eh? Won the Ascot. How did you know this name?" 60

"He always talks about horse-races with Bassett," said Joan. 61

The uncle was delighted to find that his small nephew was posted with all the racing news. Bassett, the young gardener, who had been wounded in the left foot in the war and had got his present job through Oscar Cresswell, whose batman he had been, was a perfect blade of the "turf." He lived in the racing events, and the small boy lived with him. 62

Oscar Cresswell got it all from Bassett. 63

"Master Paul comes and asks me, so I can't do more than tell him, sir," said Bassett, his face terribly serious, as if he were speaking of religious matters. 64

"And does he ever put anything on a horse he fancies?" 65

"Well—I don't want to give him away—he's a young sport, a fine sport, sir. Would you mind asking him himself? He sort of takes a pleasure in it, and perhaps he'd feel I was giving him away, sir, if you don't mind." 66

Bassett was serious as a church. 67

The uncle went back to his nephew and took him off for a ride in the car. 68

"Say, Paul, old man, do you ever put anything on a horse?" the uncle asked. 69

The boy watched the handsome man closely. 70

"Why, do you think I oughtn't to?" he parried. 71

"Not a bit of it! I thought perhaps you might give me a tip for the Lincoln." 72

The car sped on into the country, going down to Uncle Oscar's place in Hampshire. 73

"Honour bright?" said the nephew. 74

"Honour bright, son!" said the uncle. 75

"Well, then, Daffodil." 76

"Daffodil! I doubt it, sonny. What about Mirza?" 77

"I only know the winner," said the boy. "That's Daffodil."   78

"Daffodil, eh?"   79

There was a pause. Daffodil was an obscure horse comparatively.   80

"Uncle!"   81

"Yes, son?"   82

"You won't let it go any further, will you? I promised Bassett."   83

"Bassett be damned, old man! What's he got to do with it?"   84

"We're partners. We've been partners from the first. Uncle, he lent me   85
my first five shillings, which I lost. I promised him, honour bright, it was
only between me and him; only you gave me that ten-shilling note I started
winning with, so I thought you were lucky. You won't let it go any further,
will you?"

The boy gazed at his uncle from those big, hot, blue eyes, set rather close   86
together. The uncle stirred and laughed uneasily.

"Right you are, son! I'll keep your tip private. Daffodil, eh? How much   87
are you putting on him?"

"All except twenty pounds," said the boy. "I keep that in reserve."   88

The uncle thought it a good joke.   89

"You keep twenty pounds in reserve, do you, you young romancer? What   90
are you betting, then?"

"I'm betting three hundred," said the boy gravely. "But it's between you   91
and me, Uncle Oscar! Honour bright?"

The uncle burst into a roar of laughter.   92

"It's between you and me all right, you young Nat Gould," he said, laugh-   93
ing. "But where's your three hundred?"

"Bassett keeps it for me. We're partners."   94

"You are, are you! And what is Bassett putting on Daffodil?"   95

"He won't go quite as high as I do, I expect. Perhaps he'll go a hundred   96
and fifty."

"What, pennies?" laughed the uncle.   97

"Pounds," said the child, with a surprised look at his uncle. "Bassett keeps   98
a bigger reserve than I do."

Between wonder and amusement Uncle Oscar was silent. He pursued the   99
matter no further, but he determined to take his nephew with him to the Lincoln races.

"Now, son," he said, "I'm putting twenty on Mirza, and I'll put five on for   100
you on any horse you fancy. What's your pick?"

"Daffodil, uncle."   101

"No, not the fiver on Daffodil!"   102

"I should if it was my own fiver," said the child.   103

"Good! Good! Right you are! A fiver for me and a fiver for you on Daffodil."   104

The child had never been to a race-meeting before, and his eyes were blue   105
fire. He pursed his mouth tight and watched. A Frenchman just in front had put
his money on Lancelot. Wild with excitement, he flayed his arms up and down,
yelling "*Lancelot! Lancelot!*" in his French accent.

Daffodil came in first, Lancelot second, Mirza third. The child, flushed 106
and with eyes blazing, was curiously serene. His uncle brought him four five-
pound notes, four to one.

"What am I to do with these?" he cried, waving them before the boy's eyes. 107

"I suppose we'll talk to Bassett," said the boy. "I expect I have fifteen 108
hundred now; and twenty in reserve; and this twenty."

His uncle studied him for some moments. 109

"Look here, son!" he said. "You're not serious about Bassett and that fif- 110
teen hundred, are you?"

"Yes, I am. But it's between you and me, uncle. Honour bright?" 111

"Honour bright all right, son! But I must talk to Bassett." 112

"If you'd like to be a partner, uncle, with Bassett and me, we could all be 113
partners. Only, you'd have to promise, honour bright, uncle, not to let it go beyond us three. Bassett and I are lucky, and you must be lucky, because it was
your ten shillings I started winning with. . . ."

Uncle Oscar took both Bassett and Paul into Richmond Park for an after- 114
noon, and there they talked.

"It's like this, you see, sir," Bassett said. "Master Paul would get me talk- 115
ing about racing events, spinning yarns, you know, sir. And he was always keen
on knowing if I'd made or if I'd lost. It's about a year since, now, that I put five
shillings on Blush of Dawn for him: and we lost. Then the luck turned, with that
ten shillings he had from you: that we put on Singhalese. And since that time,
it's been pretty steady, all things considering. What do you say, Master Paul?"

"We're all right when we're sure," said Paul. "It's when we're not quite 116
sure that we go down."

"Oh, but we're careful then," said Bassett. 117

"But when are you *sure?*" smiled Uncle Oscar. 118

"It's Master Paul, sir," said Bassett in a secret, religious voice. "It's as if 119
he had it from heaven. Like Daffodil, now, for the Lincoln. That was as sure
as eggs."

"Did you put anything on Daffodil?" asked Oscar Cresswell. 120

"Yes, sir. I made my bit." 121

"And my nephew?" 122

Bassett was obstinately silent, looking at Paul. 123

"I made twelve hundred, didn't I, Bassett? I told uncle I was putting three 124
hundred on Daffodil."

"That's right," said Bassett, nodding. 125

"But where's the money?" asked the uncle. 126

"I keep it safe locked up, sir. Master Paul he can have it any minute he 127
likes to ask for it."

"What, fifteen hundred pounds?" 128

"And twenty! And *forty,* that is, with the twenty he made on the course." 129

"It's amazing!" said the uncle. 130

"If Master Paul offers you to be partners, sir, I would, if I were you: if 131
you'll excuse me," said Bassett.

Oscar Cresswell thought about it.   132

"I'll see the money," he said.   133

They drove home again, and, sure enough, Bassett came round to the   134
garden-house with fifteen hundred pounds in notes. The twenty pounds reserve
was left with Joe Glee, in the Turf Commission deposit.

"You see, it's all right, uncle, when I'm *sure!* Then we go strong, for all   135
we're worth. Don't we, Bassett?"

"We do that, Master Paul."   136

"And when are you sure?" said the uncle, laughing.   137

"Oh, well, sometimes I'm *absolutely* sure, like about Daffodil," said the   138
boy; "and sometimes I have an idea; and sometimes I haven't even an idea, have
I, Bassett? Then we're careful, because we mostly go down."

"You do, do you! And when you're sure, like about Daffodil, what makes   139
you sure, sonny?"

"Oh, well, I don't know," said the boy uneasily. "I'm sure, you know,   140
uncle; that's all."

"It's as if he had it from heaven, sir," Bassett reiterated.   141

"I should say so!" said the uncle.   142

But he became a partner. And when the Leger was coming on Paul was   143
"sure" about Lively Spark, which was a quite inconsiderable horse. The boy insisted on putting a thousand on the horse, Bassett was for five hundred, and
Oscar Cresswell two hundred. Lively Spark came in first, and the betting had
been ten to one against him. Paul had made ten thousand.

"You see," he said, "I was absolutely sure of him."   144

Even Oscar Cresswell had cleared two thousand.   145

"Look here, son," he said, "this sort of thing makes me nervous."   146

"It needn't, uncle! Perhaps I shan't be sure again for a long time."   147

"But what are you going to do with your money?" asked the uncle.   148

"Of course," said the boy, "I started it for mother. She said she had no luck,   149
because father is unlucky, so I thought if *I* was lucky, it might stop whispering."

"What might stop whispering?"   150

"Our house. I *hate* our house for whispering."   151

"What does it whisper?"   152

"Why—why"—the boy fidgeted—"why, I don't know. But it's always   153
short of money, you know, uncle."

"I know it, son, I know it."   154

"You know people send mother writs, don't you, uncle?"   155

"I'm afraid I do," said the uncle.   156

"And then the house whispers, like people laughing at you behind your   157
back. It's awful, that is! I thought if I was lucky—"

"You might stop it," added the uncle.   158

The boy watched him with big blue eyes, that had an uncanny cold fire in   159
them, and he said never a word.

"Well, then!" said the uncle. "What are we doing?"   160

"I shouldn't like mother to know I was lucky," said the boy.   161

"Why not, son?"   162

"She'd stop me."   163

"I don't think she would."   164

"Oh!"—and the boy writhed in an odd way—"I *don't* want her to know,   165
uncle."

"All right, son! We'll manage it without her knowing."   166

They managed it very easily. Paul, at the other's suggestion, handed over   167
five thousand pounds to his uncle, who deposited it with the family lawyer, who
was then to inform Paul's mother that a relative had put five thousand pounds
into his hands, which sum was to be paid out a thousand pounds at a time, on the
mother's birthday, for the next five years.

"So she'll have a birthday present of a thousand pounds for five successive   168
years," said Uncle Oscar. "I hope it won't make it all the harder for her later."

Paul's mother had her birthday in November. The house had been "whis-   169
pering" worse than ever lately, and, even in spite of his luck, Paul could not bear
up against it. He was very anxious to see the effect of the birthday letter, telling
his mother about the thousand pounds.

When there were no visitors, Paul now took his meals with his parents, as   170
he was beyond the nursery control. His mother went into town nearly every day.
She had discovered that she had an odd knack of sketching furs and dress materials, so she worked secretly in the studio of a friend who was the chief "artist"
for the leading drapers. She drew the figures of ladies in furs and ladies in silk
and sequins for the newspaper advertisements. This young woman artist earned
several thousand pounds a year, but Paul's mother only made several hundreds,
and she was again dissatisfied. She so wanted to be first in something, and she
did not succeed, even in making sketches for drapery advertisements.

She was down to breakfast on the morning of her birthday. Paul watched   171
her face as she read her letters. He knew the lawyer's letter. As his mother read
it, her face hardened and became more expressionless. Then a cold, determined
look came on her mouth. She hid the letter under the pile of others, and said not
a word about it.

"Didn't you have anything nice in the post for your birthday, mother?"   172
said Paul.

"Quite moderately nice," she said, her voice cold and absent.   173

She went away to town without saying more.   174

But in the afternoon Uncle Oscar appeared. He said Paul's mother had had   175
a long interview with the lawyer, asking if the whole five thousand could not be
advanced at once, as she was in debt.

"What do you think, uncle?" said the boy.   176

"I leave it to you, son."   177

"Oh, let her have it, then! We can get some more with the other," said   178
the boy.

"A bird in the hand is worth two in the bush, laddie!" said Uncle Oscar.   179

"But I'm sure to *know* for the Grand National; or the Lincolnshire; or else   180
the Derby. I'm sure to know for *one* of them," said Paul.

So Uncle Oscar signed the agreement, and Paul's mother touched the whole five thousand. Then something very curious happened. The voices in the house suddenly went mad, like a chorus of frogs on a spring evening. There were certain new furnishings, and Paul had a tutor. He was *really* going to Eton, his father's school, in the following autumn. There were flowers in the winter, and a blossoming of the luxury Paul's mother had been used to. And yet the voices in the house, behind the sprays of mimosa and almond blossom, and from under the piles of iridescent cushions, simply trilled and screamed in a sort of ecstasy: "There *must* be more money! Oh-h-h; there *must* be more money. Oh, now now-w! Now-w-w—there *must* be more money!—more than ever! More than ever!" 181

It frightened Paul terribly. He studied away at his Latin and Greek with his tutor. But his intense hours were spent with Bassett. The Grand National had gone by: he had not "known," and had lost a hundred pounds. Summer was at hand. He was in agony for the Lincoln. But even for the Lincoln he didn't "know," and he lost fifty pounds. He became wild-eyed and strange, as if something were going to explode in him. 182

"Let it alone, son! Don't you bother about it!" urged Uncle Oscar. But it was as if the boy couldn't really hear what his uncle was saying. 183

"I've got to know for the Derby! I've got to know for the Derby!" the child reiterated, his big blue eyes blazing with a sort of madness. 184

His mother noticed how overwrought he was. 185

"You'd better go to the seaside. Wouldn't you like to go now to the seaside, instead of waiting? I think you'd better," she said, looking down at him anxiously, her heart curiously heavy because of him. 186

But the child lifted his uncanny blue eyes. 187

"I couldn't possibly go before the Derby, mother!" he said. "I couldn't possibly!" 188

"Why not?" she said, her voice becoming heavy when she was opposed. "Why not? You can still go from the seaside to see the Derby with your Uncle Oscar, if that's what you wish. No need for you to wait here. Besides, I think you care too much about these races. It's a bad sign. My family has been a gambling family, and you won't know till you grow up how much damage it has done. But it has done damage. I shall have to send Bassett away, and ask Uncle Oscar not to talk racing to you, unless you promise to be reasonable about it: go away to the seaside and forget it. You're all nerves!" 189

"I'll do what you like, mother, so long as you don't send me away till after the Derby," the boy said. 190

"Send you away from where? Just from this house?" 191

"Yes," he said, gazing at her. 192

"Why, you curious child, what makes you care about this house so much, suddenly? I never knew you loved it." 193

He gazed at her without speaking. He had a secret within a secret, something he had not divulged, even to Bassett or to his Uncle Oscar. 194

But his mother, after standing undecided and a little bit sullen for some ₁₉₅ moments, said:

"Very well, then! Don't go to the seaside till after the Derby, if you don't ₁₉₆ wish it. But promise me you won't let your nerves go to pieces. Promise you won't think so much about horse-racing and *events,* as you call them!"

"Oh no," said the boy casually. "I won't think much about them, mother. ₁₉₇ You needn't worry. I wouldn't worry, mother, if I were you."

"If you were me and I were you," said his mother, "I wonder what we ₁₉₈ *should* do!"

"But you know you needn't worry, mother, don't you?" the boy repeated. ₁₉₉

"I should be awfully glad to know it," she said wearily. ₂₀₀

"Oh, well, you *can,* you know. I mean, you *ought* to know you needn't ₂₀₁ worry," he insisted.

"Ought I? Then I'll see about it," she said. ₂₀₂

Paul's secret of secrets was his wooden horse, that which had no name. ₂₀₃ Since he was emancipated from a nurse and a nursery-governess, he had had his rocking-horse removed to his own bedroom at the top of the house.

"Surely you're too big for a rocking-horse!" his mother had remonstrated. ₂₀₄

"Well, you see, mother, till I can have a *real* horse, I like to have *some* sort ₂₀₅ of animal about," had been his quaint answer.

"Do you feel he keeps you company?" she laughed. ₂₀₆

"Oh yes! He's very good, he always keeps me company, when I'm there," ₂₀₇ said Paul.

So the horse, rather shabby, stood in an arrested prance in the boy's ₂₀₈ bedroom.

The Derby was drawing near, and the boy grew more and more tense. He ₂₀₉ hardly heard what was spoken to him, he was very frail, and his eyes were really uncanny. His mother had sudden strange seizures of uneasiness about him. Sometimes, for half an hour, she would feel a sudden anxiety about him that was almost anguish. She wanted to rush to him at once, and know he was safe.

Two nights before the Derby, she was at a big party in town, when one of ₂₁₀ her rushes of anxiety about her boy, her first-born, gripped her heart till she could hardly speak. She fought with the feeling, might and main, for she believed in common sense. But it was too strong. She had to leave the dance and go downstairs to telephone to the country. The children's nursery-governess was terribly surprised and startled at being rung up in the night.

"Are the children all right, Miss Wilmot?" ₂₁₁

"Oh yes, they are quite all right." ₂₁₂

"Master Paul? Is he all right?" ₂₁₃

"He went to bed as right as a trivet. Shall I run up and look at him?" ₂₁₄

"No," said Paul's mother reluctantly. "No! Don't trouble. It's all right. ₂₁₅ Don't sit up. We shall be home fairly soon." She did not want her son's privacy intruded upon.

"Very good," said the governess. ₂₁₆

It was about one o'clock when Paul's mother and father drove up to their ₂₁₇ house. All was still. Paul's mother went to her room and slipped off her white fur cloak. She had told her maid not to wait up for her. She heard her husband downstairs, mixing a whisky and soda.

And then, because of the strange anxiety at her heart, she stole upstairs to ₂₁₈ her son's room. Noiselessly she went along the upper corridor. Was there a faint noise? What was it?

She stood, with arrested muscles, outside his door, listening. There was a ₂₁₉ strange, heavy, and yet not loud noise. Her heart stood still. It was a soundless noise, yet rushing and powerful. Something huge, in violent, hushed motion. What was it? What in God's name was it? She ought to know. She felt that she knew the noise. She knew what it was.

Yet she could not place it. She couldn't say what it was. And on and on it ₂₂₀ went, like a madness.

Softly, frozen with anxiety and fear, she turned the doorhandle. ₂₂₁

The room was dark. Yet in the space near the window, she heard and saw ₂₂₂ something plunging to and fro. She gazed in fear and amazement.

Then suddenly she switched on the light, and saw her son, in his green py- ₂₂₃ jamas, madly surging on the rocking-horse. The blaze of light suddenly lit him up, as he urged the wooden horse, and lit her up, as she stood, blonde, in her dress of pale green and crystal, in the doorway.

"Paul!" she cried. "Whatever are you doing?" ₂₂₄

"It's Malabar!" he screamed in a powerful, strange voice. "It's Malabar!" ₂₂₅

His eyes blazed at her for one strange and senseless second, as he ceased ₂₂₆ urging his wooden horse. Then he fell with a crash to the ground, and she, all her tormented motherhood flooding upon her, rushed to gather him up.

But he was unconscious, and unconscious he remained, with some brain- ₂₂₇ fever. He talked and tossed, and his mother sat stonily by his side.

"Malabar! It's Malabar! Bassett, Bassett, I *know!* It's Malabar!" ₂₂₈

So the child cried, trying to get up and urge the rocking-horse that gave ₂₂₉ him his inspiration.

"What does he mean by Malabar?" asked the heart-frozen mother. ₂₃₀

"I don't know," said the father stonily. ₂₃₁

"What does he mean by Malabar?" she asked her brother Oscar. ₂₃₂

"It's one of the horses running for the Derby," was the answer. ₂₃₃

And, in spite of himself, Oscar Cresswell spoke to Bassett, and himself put ₂₃₄ a thousand on Malabar: at fourteen to one.

The third day of the illness was critical: they were waiting for a change. ₂₃₅ The boy, with his rather long, curly hair, was tossing ceaselessly on the pillow. He neither slept nor regained consciousness, and his eyes were like blue stones. His mother sat, feeling her heart had gone, turned actually into a stone.

In the evening, Oscar Cresswell did not come, but Bassett sent a message, ₂₃₆ saying could he come up for one moment, just one moment? Paul's mother was very angry at the intrusion, but on second thoughts she agreed. The boy was the same. Perhaps Bassett might bring him to consciousness.

The gardener, a shortish fellow with a little brown moustache and sharp   237
little brown eyes, tiptoed into the room, touched his imaginary cap to Paul's
mother, and stole to the bedside, staring with glittering, smallish eyes at the tossing, dying child.

"Master Paul!" he whispered. "Master Paul! Malabar came in first all right, a   238
clean win. I did as you told me. You've made over seventy thousand pounds, you
have; you've got over eighty thousand. Malabar came in all right, Master Paul."

"Malabar! Malabar! Did I say Malabar, mother? Did I say Malabar? Do   239
you think I'm lucky, mother? I knew Malabar, didn't I? Over eighty thousand
pounds! I call that lucky, don't you, mother? Over eighty thousand pounds! I
knew, didn't I know I knew? Malabar came in all right. If I ride my horse till
I'm sure, then I tell you, Bassett, you can go as high as you like. Did you go for
all you were worth, Bassett?"

"I went a thousand on it, Master Paul."   240

"I never told you, mother, that if I can ride my horse, and *get there,* then   241
I'm absolutely sure—oh absolutely! Mother, did I ever tell you? I *am* lucky!"

"No, you never did," said his mother.   242

But the boy died in the night.   243

And even as he lay dead, his mother heard her brother's voice saying to   244
her: "My God, Hester, you're eighty-odd thousand to the good, and a poor devil
of a son to the bad. But, poor devil, poor devil, he's best gone out of a life where
he rides his rocking-horse to find a winner."

Meaning and Idea

1. Describe Paul's character. How does his home environment affect him?
   What does he hope to accomplish in this story? Does he manage it? How
   and why does he die?

2. Who are the other main characters in this story? How does each of them
   contribute to the overall process of the story?

3. According to Paul's mother, what is the relation between luck and money?
   What process derives from that relation?

4. What do the voices in the house say? Why? How do they change after the
   first windfall of money? Why?

Language, Form, Structure

1. What is the overall process described in this story? Who is most responsible
   for enacting that process? What are his or her motivations to follow through
   on that process?

2. What is the theme of this story? What is its tone? Describe the relation
   between theme and tone here. Why is process analysis used as one of the
   organizing techniques?

3. The overall process here is divided into smaller processes, among them Paul's ritual on the rocking horse and the process of placing bets. Describe these two processes. What other smaller processes help form the overall process? Describe at least two of them.

4. How does repetition function in this story?

5. Write meanings for each of the following figurative expressions from this story: racked her brains; *filthy lucre;* unsure eyes; compel her attention; brazening it out; in full tilt; spinning yarns; an arrested prance. Then use each phrase in a sentence of your own.

Ideas for Writing

1. Explain a process that you used in order to get something you wanted very much. Be sure to indicate your motivations for beginning the process and tell whether you actually got what you wanted.

2. Describe a process by which you solved a major problem for yourself or someone else. Use narration and dialogue to enhance your analysis.

3. In interpreting this story, critics have often read the overall process involved as a metaphor either for Paul's "coming of age" (that is, his adolescence) or for what Lawrence viewed as the corruption in the society in which it takes place. What is your response to these interpretations? Do you think either, or both, is valid? If so, in what ways? If not, why? Do you think there are any other metaphoric values attached to the processes of the story? Write an essay in which you address some of these issues.

The Baby Myna

Ved Mehta

Ved Mehta was born in Lahore, India (now Pakistan), in 1934 and became an American citizen in 1975. Educated at Oxford and Harvard, Mehta began his education at schools for the blind in Bombay, India, and Little Rock, Arkansas, where his father had sent him to escape the life of degradation and poverty so often the fate of Asian blind children. The main part of Mehta's essay and story writing was accomplished while he was a contributing editor to *The New Yorker* magazine. His explanations of Indian lifestyles are collected in such works as *Walking the Indian Streets* (1960), the biographical *Daddyji* (1972) and *Mamaji* (1979), *The Photographs of Chachji* (1980), and the autobiographical *Vedi* (1982). Among Mehta's honors are a Guggenheim fellowship and a Ford Foundation grant.

In this vignette from his autobiographical *Vedi*, Ved Mehta skillfully blends description and narration to explain the various processes involved in his getting, training, and ultimately losing his pet mynah bird, Sweetie.

*O*ne day, Sher Singh returned from leave in his village in the Kangara District, in the hills, with a baby myna for me. "I have brought you a friend," he said. "It's a baby myna. It's one of the only birds in the world that can talk. It's just the right age to learn to talk."

I was excited. I went with Sher Singh to the Mozang Chowk and bought a wire cage with a door, a metal floor, and a little swing. The cage had a hook at the top, and I hung it in my room. (We were temporarily living in our own house, at 11 Temple Road.) I got a couple of brass bowls—one for water, the other for grain—and filled them up and put them in the cage. I got a brush for cleaning out the cage. I named the myna Sweetie. The name came to me just out of the sky.

"How do you catch a baby myna?" I asked Sher Singh.

"It's difficult, Vedi Sahib. There are very few of them around, and you have to know where a baby myna is resting with her mother. You have to slip up on them in the middle of the night, when they are sleeping in their nest, and throw a cover over them and hope that you catch the baby, because only baby myna can learn to talk. Sometimes the mother myna will nip at your finger, and there are people in my village who are constantly getting their fingers nipped at because they have been trying to catch a baby myna."

At first, Sweetie was so small that she could scarcely fly even a few inches. I would sit her on my shoulder and walk around the room. She would dig her nervous, trembling claws through my shirt and into my shoulder as she tried to keep her balance, fluttering around my ear and sending off little ripples of air. But Sweetie grew fast, and soon she was flying around my room. Before I opened her cage to fill up the bowls or clean the floor, I would have to shut the door. She would often nip at my finger and escape from the cage. She would go and perch on the mantelpiece. When I ran to the mantelpiece to catch her, she would fly up to the curtain rod. When I climbed up onto the windowsill and shook the curtain, she would fly back to the mantelpiece. Sometimes she would be so silent that I would wonder if she was still in the room. Other times, I would hear her flying all around the room—now she would be by the window, now by the overhead light, her wings beating against the pane and the lampshade. I would make kissing sounds, as I had heard Sher Singh make them. I would call to her—"Sweetie! Sweetie!" I would whistle affectionately. I would run frenetically from one end of the room to the other. I would scream with rage. But she wouldn't come to me. I would somehow have to summon Sher Singh through the closed door, and then give him a cue to come in when I thought she wasn't near the door, and he would have to prance around the room and somehow catch her with his duster.

"She's a real hill girl, all right, flying around like that," he would say. 6

When we had finally got her back in the cage, I would scold her roundly, but it didn't seem to do much good. 7

"Vedi Sahib, you'll lose her, like your eyes, if you don't keep her always in the cage," Sher Singh said. 8

"But then how can I feed her? How can I clean out her cage?" 9

"I will do all that, Vedi Sahib. And, because I can see, I can watch her." 10

"But I like looking after her," I said. 11

"You'll lose her, Vedi Sahib," he said. "And mind your finger. She's getting big." 12

I devised a way of filling her bowls and cleaning some of the cage's floor by surreptitiously sticking my fingers between the wires. But now and again I would want to feel her on her swing or take her out and hold her, and then she would nip at my finger and sometimes draw blood. She would escape and give me a real run around the room. 13

Every time I passed Sweetie's cage, I would say "Hello, Sweetie," and wait for her to talk. But she would only flutter in the cage or, at most, make her swing squeak. 14

"Are you sure Sweetie can talk?" I asked Sher Singh. 15

"All baby mynas from Kangara can learn to talk," he said. 16

"Are you sure she is from Kangara?" 17

"Only mynas from Kangara have a black patch on the throat. You can feel it, and you can ask anyone—it's as black as coal." 18

I took Sweetie out of her cage. I held her tight in one hand and tried to feel the patch on her throat with the other. She screamed and tried to bite my finger, but I finally found the patch. It was a little soft, downy raised circle that throbbed with her pulse. 19

"What do mynas sound like when they talk?" I later asked Sher Singh. 20

"They have the voice of the Kangara, of a Kangara hill girl." 21

"What is that?" 22

"The Punjab hills, the leaves in the wind, the waterfall on a mountainside—you know, Vedi Sahib, it's the sound of a peacock spreading its wings in Kangara at dawn." 23

One day, I passed her cage and said, "Hello, Sweetie."   24

"Hello, Sweetie," she answered.   25

I jumped. I don't know how I had expected her voice to sound, but it was   26
thin, sharp, and defiant—at once whiny and abrasive—like three treble notes on
the harmonium played very fast. Her words assaulted my ears—"Sweetie" was
something that film stars called each other on the screen, and sounded very
naughty.

I had scarcely taken in the fact that Sweetie could really speak when she   27
repeated "Hello, Sweetie." She kept on repeating it, hour after hour. "Hello,
Sweetie" would suddenly explode into the air like a firecracker.

Try as I would, I couldn't teach her to say anything else. All the same,   28
there was something thrilling and comforting in having my own film star in the
cage, and I got so used to her enticing outbursts that I missed them when she
kept quiet or was dozing.

Every evening, at the time when my big sisters and my big brother went   29
to play hockey or some other game with their school friends, it was Sher
Singh's duty to take me for a walk to Lawrence Gardens. There I would ride
the merry-go-round—a big, creaky thing with wooden seats and a metal railing—while Sher Singh ran alongside. It would revolve and lurch, tipping this
way and that way, filling me with terror and excitement. On the ground, I
would throw off my shoes and run up and down the hillocks. They were covered with damp, soft grass and occasional patches of dead grass. The grass
would caress, tickle, and prick my feet. All around, there were the light, cheerful sounds of sighted children running and playing and of birds flying and
perching and calling. In the distance, there was the solitary, mournful song of a
nightingale.

I felt sorry that Sweetie, shut up in the house, couldn't enjoy the company   30
of other birds, and one evening I insisted that we take her along in her cage and
let her enjoy the fresh air and the life of Lawrence Gardens, even if it was only
through the wires of her cage.

"But don't let her out of the cage," Sher Singh said. "She is a spirit from   31
the hills. She will fly back to Kangara."

"Fly all the way to Kangara! She would die without food or water. Be-   32
sides, she is my friend. She wouldn't leave me."

"Vedi Sahib, you know how loyal Kangara servants are?"   33

"No one could be more loyal than you, Sher Singh."   34

"Well, Kangara mynas are as disloyal as Kangara servants are loyal. You   35
can love a beloved myna all you want to, give her all the grain to eat you want
to, give her all the water to drink you want to, and at the first opportunity she
will nip at your finger and fly away. But you can kick a servant from Kangara
and he will still give you first-class service."

"Why is that?"   36

"Because servants from Kangara, like mynas, have breathed the Hi-   37
malayan air and are free spirits. A Kangara servant is a servant by choice—but
no myna is in a cage by choice."

I couldn't follow exactly what Sher Singh was saying, but I laughed. Anyway, I insisted that we take Sweetie with us. 38

At Lawrence Gardens, I had no intention of taking Sweetie out of her cage, but when she heard the other birds she set up such a racket that children and servants who usually took little notice of me wandered toward us to find out what I was doing to the poor myna. They said all kinds of things: 39

"She is lonely." 40

"He's keeping her a prisoner." 41

"Tch, tch! He can't play with other children, so he won't let his myna play with other birds." 42

"She'll fly away to Kangara!" I cried. 43

People laughed, hooted, and jeered. "She's so small she probably can't even fly up to that tree." 44

"Why are you pointing? He doesn't know how high that tree is." 45

I suddenly got an idea. I had with me a ball of strong, fortified string that Brother Om used for flying kites. I took Sweetie out of the cage and, while I held her screaming and biting in my hands, I had Sher Singh tie up her legs with the string. Then I caught hold of the ball and let her go, and the people about us clapped and cheered. I started giving her string, and she flew high up and pulled and tugged. I gave her more string and let her lead me where she would around the grass. I thought it was a wonderful game. Before I knew what had happened, her weight at the end of the string was gone, and the limp string had fluttered down on me. 46

"She's bitten through the string! Look, she's bitten through the string!" everyone shouted, running away. 47

"Sher Singh, catch her! Catch her!" I cried. "Bring Sweetie back!" 48

"I think I see her!" he called, running off. 49

A few minutes later, Sher Singh came back. "She's nowhere to be found, Vedi Sahib. She's gone, Sahib—gone straight back to Kangara. You will now have to get along without Sweetie." 50

Sher Singh and I looked for her all over Lawrence Gardens, calling "Sweetie! Sweetie!" until it was dark and everyone had left. Then Sher Singh and I walked home with the empty cage. 51

Meaning and Idea

1. What is a mynah? Why would it be a particularly attractive pet for a child?

2. What problems does the blind child Vedi have with the infant bird? What advice does Sher Singh give him? Why is Vedi reluctant to accept it?

3. How does Sher Singh's description of what the bird's voice would sound like compare with what Vedi actually hears once Sweetie learns to talk?

4. What plan does Vedi put into action for releasing Sweetie at Lawrence Gardens? How does it fail?

Language, Form, Structure

1. How does Ved Mehta use narration as the organizing technique for this selection? How does narration enhance the analysis of the various processes?

2. What is the main point of the selection? As part of a chapter from a long book, "The Baby Myna" understandably lacks a thesis sentence. What might a thesis sentence for this selection include? Write one that you think would be appropriate.

3. What does the tone of this essay tell you about Mehta's feelings about his childhood? How?

4. Write meanings for the following words: frenetically; prance; roundly; surreptitiously; defiant; abrasive; harmonium; enticing; lurch; fortified.

Ideas for Writing

1. Explain the process by which a pet should be trained to do something.

2. Using narration as your organizing principle, write a process analysis of how you learned to do something during your childhood.

3. Ved Mehta has been blind since his childhood. How does this knowledge affect your reading of this selection? Does it make you reevaluate the descriptive passages or the overall tone and development of the process analysis? What other famous writers can you think of who were blind? How do you think their blindness affected their writing?

The Gold Worker

Camara Laye

Camara Laye (1928–1980) was born the son of a goldsmith in Kouroussa, French
Guinea. His writings focus on the sharp contrast between traditional rural culture and
modern urban lifestyles, a relationship that mirrors his own experience of leaving a tribal
system to study and work in Paris. Among his best-known works are *The Dark Child*
(1953) and *A Dream of Africa* (1971). Laye was also a contributor to numerous African,
European, and American journals.

In *The Dark Child*, drawn from his childhood memory, Camara Laye explains the "magical" process of his father's work as a goldsmith. Technical process, though easily identifiable in this selection, is artfully crafted into a vivid narration.

*O*f all the different kinds of work my father engaged in, none fasci-   1
nated me so much as his skill with gold. No other occupation was so noble, no
other needed such a delicate touch. And then, every time he worked in gold it
was like a festival—indeed it *was* a festival—that broke the monotony of ordinary working days.

So, if a woman, accompanied by a go-between, crossed the threshold of   2
the workshop, I followed her in at once. I knew what she wanted: she had
brought some gold, and had come to ask my father to transform it into a trinket.
She had collected it in the placers of Siguiri where, crouching over the river for
months on end, she had patiently extracted grains of gold from the mud.

These women never came alone. They knew my father had other things to   3
do than make trinkets. And even when he had the time, they knew they were not
the first to ask a favor of him, and that, consequently, they would not be served
before others.

Generally, they required the trinket for a certain date, for the festival of   4
Ramadan or the Tabaski or some other family ceremony or dance.

Therefore, to enhance their chances of being served quickly and to more   5
easily persuade my father to interrupt the work before him, they used to request
the services of an official praise-singer, a go-between, arranging in advance the
fee they were to pay him for his good offices.

The go-between installed himself in the workshop, tuned up his *cora,*   6
which is our harp, and began to sing my father's praises. This was always a
great event for me. I heard recalled the lofty deeds of my father's ancestors and
their names from the earliest times. As the couplets were reeled off it was like
watching the growth of a great genealogical tree that spread its branches far and
wide and flourished its boughs and twigs before my mind's eye. The harp played
an accompaniment to this vast utterance of names, expanding it with notes that
were now soft, now shrill.

I could sense my father's vanity being inflamed, and I already knew that [7] after having sipped this milk-and-honey he would lend a favorable ear to the woman's request. But I was not alone in my knowledge. The woman also had seen my father's eyes gleaming with contented pride. She held out her grains of gold as if the whole matter were settled. My father took up his scales and weighed the gold.

"What sort of trinket do you want?" he would ask. [8]

"I want. . . ." [9]

And then the woman would not know any longer exactly what she wanted [10] because desire kept making her change her mind, and because she would have liked all the trinkets at once. But it would have taken a pile of gold much larger than she had brought to satisfy her whim, and from then on her chief purpose in life was to get hold of it as soon as she could.

"When do you want it?" [11]

Always the answer was that the trinket was needed for an occasion in the [12] near future.

"So! You are in that much of a hurry? Where do you think I shall find [13] the time?"

"I am in a great hurry, I assure you." [14]

"I have never seen a woman eager to deck herself out who wasn't in a [15] great hurry! Good! I shall arrange my time to suit you. Are you satisfied?"

He would take the clay pot that was kept specially for smelting gold, and [16] would pour the grains into it. He would then cover the gold with powdered charcoal, a charcoal he prepared by using plant juices of exceptional purity. Finally, he would place a large lump of the same kind of charcoal over the pot.

As soon as she saw that the work had been duly undertaken, the woman, [17] now quite satisfied, would return to her household tasks, leaving her go-between to carry on with the praise-singing which had already proved so advantageous.

At a sign from my father the apprentices began working two sheepskin [18] bellows. The skins were on the floor, on opposite sides of the forge, connected to it by earthen pipes. While the work was in progress the apprentices sat in front of the bellows with crossed legs. That is, the younger of the two sat, for the elder was sometimes allowed to assist. But the younger—this time it was Sidafa—was only permitted to work the bellows and watch while waiting his turn for promotion to less rudimentary tasks. First one and then the other worked hard at the bellows: the flame in the forge rose higher and became a living thing, a genie implacable and full of life.

Then my father lifted the clay pot with his long tongs and placed it on [19] the flame.

Immediately all activity in the workshop almost came to a halt. During the [20] whole time that the gold was being smelted, neither copper nor aluminum could be worked nearby, lest some particle of these base metals fall into the container which held the gold. Only steel could be worked on such occasions, but the men, whose task that was, hurried to finish what they were doing, or left it abruptly to join the apprentices gathered around the forge. There were so many, and they crowded so around my father, that I, the smallest person present, had to come near the forge in order not to lose track of what was going on.

If he felt he had inadequate working space, my father had the apprentices stand well away from him. He merely raised his hand in a simple gesture: at that particular moment he never uttered a word, and no one else would: no one was allowed to utter a word. Even the go-between's voice was no longer raised in song. The silence was broken only by the panting of the bellows and the faint hissing of the gold. But if my father never actually spoke, I know that he was forming words in his mind. I could tell from his lips, which kept moving, while, bending over the pot, he stirred the gold and charcoal with a bit of wood that kept bursting into flame and had constantly to be replaced by a fresh one.

What words did my father utter? I do not know. At least I am not certain what they were. No one ever told me. But could they have been anything but incantations? On these occasions was he not invoking the genies of fire and gold, of fire and wind, of wind blown by the blast-pipes of the forge, of fire born of wind, of gold married to fire? Was it not their assistance, their friendship, their espousal that he besought? Yes. Almost certainly he was invoking these genies, all of whom are equally indispensable for smelting gold.

The operation going on before my eyes was certainly the smelting of gold, yet something more than that: a magical operation that the guiding spirits could regard with favor or disfavor. That is why, all around my father, there was absolute silence and anxious expectancy. Though only a child, I knew there could be no craft greater than the goldsmith's. I expected a ceremony; I had come to be present at a ceremony; and it actually was one, though very protracted. I was still too young to understand why, but I had an inkling as I watched the almost religious concentration of those who followed the mixing process in the clay pot.

When finally the gold began to melt I could have shouted aloud—and perhaps we all would have if we had not been forbidden to make a sound. I trembled, and so did everyone else watching my father stir the mixture—it was still a heavy paste—in which the charcoal was gradually consumed. The next stage followed swiftly. The gold now had the fluidity of water. The genies had smiled on the operation!

"Bring me the brick!" my father would order, thus lifting the ban that until then had silenced us.

The brick, which an apprentice would place beside the fire, was hollowed out, generously greased with Galam butter. My father would take the pot off the fire and tilt it carefully while I would watch the gold flow into the brick, flow like liquid fire. True, it was only a very sparse trickle of fire, but how vivid, how brilliant! As the gold flowed into the brick the grease sputtered and flamed and emitted a thick smoke that caught in the throat and stung the eyes, leaving us all weeping and coughing.

But there were times when it seemed to me that my father ought to turn this task over to one of his assistants. They were experienced, had assisted him hundreds of times, and could certainly have performed the work well. But my father's lips moved and those inaudible, secret words, those incantations he addressed to one we could not see or hear, was the essential part.

Calling on the genies of fire, of wind, of gold and exorcising the evil spirits—this was a knowledge he alone possessed.

By now the gold had been cooled in the hollow of the brick, and my father began to hammer and stretch it. This was the moment when his work as a gold-smith really began. I noticed that before embarking on it he never failed to stroke the little snake stealthily as it lay coiled up under the sheepskin. I can only assume that this was his way of gathering strength for what remained to be done, the most trying part of his task.

But was it not extraordinary and miraculous that on these occasions the lit-tle black snake was always coiled under the sheepskin? He was not always there. He did not visit my father every day. But he was always present whenever there was gold to be worked. His presence was no surprise to *me*. After that evening when my father had spoken of the guiding spirit of his race I was no longer as-tonished. The snake was there intentionally. He knew what the future held. Did he tell my father? I think that he most certainly did. Did he tell him everything? I have another reason for believing firmly that he did.

The craftsman who works in gold must first of all purify himself. That is, he must wash himself all over and, of course, abstain from all sexual commerce during the whole time. Great respecter of ceremony as he was, it would have been impossible for my father to ignore these rules. Now, I never saw him make these preparations. I saw him address himself to his work without any apparent preliminaries. From that moment it was obvious that, forewarned in a dream by his black guiding spirit of the task which awaited him in the morning, my father must have prepared for it as soon as he arose, entering his workshop in a state of purity, his body smeared with the secret potions hidden in his numerous pots of magical substances; or perhaps he always came into his workshop in a state of ritual purity. I am not trying to make him out a better man than he was—he was a man and had his share of human frailties—but he was always uncompromising in his respect for ritual observance.

The woman for whom the trinket was being made, and who had come often to see how the work was progressing, would arrive for the final time, not wanting to miss a moment of this spectacle—as marvelous to her as to us—when the gold wire, which my father had succeeded in drawing out from the mass of molten gold and charcoal, was transformed into a trinket.

There she would be. Her eyes would devour the fragile gold wire, follow-ing it in its tranquil and regular spiral around the little slab of metal which sup-ported it. My father would catch a glimpse of her and I would see him slowly beginning to smile. Her avid attention delighted him.

"Are you trembling?" he would ask.

"Am I trembling?"

And we would all burst out laughing at her. For she would be trembling! She would be trembling with covetousness for the spiral pyramid in which my father would be inserting, among the convolutions, tiny grains of gold. When he had finally finished by crowning the pyramid with a heavier grain, she would dance in delight.

No one—no one at all—would be more enchanted than she as my father ₃₆ slowly turned the trinket back and forth between his fingers to display its perfection. Not even the praise-singer whose business it was to register excitement would be more excited than she. Throughout this metamorphosis he did not stop speaking faster and ever faster, increasing his tempo, accelerating his praises and flatteries as the trinket took shape, shouting to the skies my father's skill.

For the praise-singer took a curious part—I should say rather that it was ₃₇ direct and effective—in the work. He was drunk with the joy of creation. He shouted aloud in joy. He plucked his *cora* like a man inspired. He sweated as if he were the trinket-maker, as if he were my father, as if the trinket were his creation. He was no longer a hired censer-bearer, a man whose services anyone could rent. He was a man who created his song out of some deep inner necessity. And when my father, after having soldered the large grain of gold that crowned the summit, held out his work to be admired, the praise-singer would no longer be able to contain himself. He would begin to intone the *douga,* the great chant which is sung only for celebrated men and which is danced for them alone.

But the *douga* is a formidable chant, a provocative chant, a chant which ₃₈ the praise-singer dared not sing, and which the man for whom it is sung dared not dance before certain precautions had been taken. My father had taken them as soon as he woke, since he had been warned in a dream. The praise-singer had taken them when he concluded his arrangements with the woman. Like my father he had smeared his body with magic substances and had made himself invulnerable to the evil genies whom the *douga* inevitably set free; these potions made him invulnerable also to rival praise-singers, perhaps jealous of him, who awaited only this song and the exaltation and loss of control which attended it, in order to begin casting their spells.

At the first notes of the *douga* my father would arise and emit a cry in ₃₉ which happiness and triumph were equally mingled; and brandishing in his right hand the hammer that was the symbol of his profession and in his left a ram's horn filled with magic substances, he would dance the glorious dance.

No sooner had he finished, than workmen and apprentices, friends and ₄₀ customers in their turn, not forgetting the woman for whom the trinket had been created, would flock around him, congratulating him, showering praises on him and complimenting the praise-singer at the same time. The latter found himself laden with gifts—almost his only means of support, for the praise-singer leads a wandering life after the fashion of the troubadours of old. Aglow with dancing and the praises he had received, my father would offer everyone cola nuts, that small change of Guinean courtesy.

Now all that remained to be done was to redden the trinket in a little water ₄₁ to which chlorine and sea salt had been added. I was at liberty to leave. The festival was over! But often as I came out of the workshop my mother would be in the court, pounding millet or rice, and she would call to me:

"Where have you been?" although she knew perfectly well where I had been. ₄₂

"In the workshop." ₄₃

"Of course. Your father was smelting gold. Gold! Always gold!"   44

And she would beat the millet or rice furiously with her pestle.   45

"Your father is ruining his health!"   46

"He danced the *douga*."   47

"The *douga!* The *douga* won't keep him from ruining his eyes. As for you,   48
you would be better off playing in the courtyard instead of breathing dust and
smoke in the workshop."

My mother did not like my father to work in gold. She knew how danger-   49
ous it was: a trinket-maker empties his lungs blowing on the blowpipe and his
eyes suffer from the fire. Perhaps they suffer even more from the microscopic
precision which the work requires. And even if there had been no such objections involved, my mother would scarcely have relished this work. She was suspicious of it, for gold can not be smelted without the use of other metals, and my
mother thought it was not entirely honest to put aside for one's own use the gold
which the alloy had displaced. However, this was a custom generally known,
and one which she herself had accepted when she took cotton to be woven and
received back only a piece of cotton cloth half the weight of the original bundle.

Meaning and Idea

1. What function does the official praise-singer serve in negotiations between
   the woman and the narrator's father? How does the praise-singer continue
   to participate in the creation of the trinket?

2. Why is there "absolute silence and anxious expectancy" in the workshop?

3. When does the work of the skillful goldsmith really begin? How does the
   snake figure in the work?

4. What elements of ceremony and superstition do you note here? Why does
   the narrator say that his father "was always uncompromising in his respect
   for ritual observance"? How, in fact, is the day for working the gold "like a
   festival"?

5. What is the *douga?* How does the father prepare himself for it?

Language, Form, Structure

1. How does the writer make this highly technical process lively and enjoyable
   for his readers?

2. How does the first paragraph serve as an appropriate introduction to the
   selection? Which sentence in the introduction might be considered a thesis
   sentence?

3. How do description and narration serve as transitional devices here? What
   transitional words and phrases help link the elements of the selection
   together?

4. Explain the following simile from the essay: "As the couplets were reeled off it was like watching the growth of a great genealogical tree." Explain the following metaphor: "after having sipped this milk-and-honey, he would lend a favorable ear to the woman's request." Find and explain at least two other metaphors and two other similes in the selection.

5. Choose 10 of the following words and write definitions for them: trinket; shrill; vanity; smelting; apprentices; bellows; rudimentary; incantations; invoke; espousal; inaudible; covetousness; metamorphosis; intone.

Ideas for Writing

1. Describe the process by which you learned to do something in your childhood. Try to include how your perception of the process now is different from what it was then.

2. Write an essay in which you explain a technical process with which you are familiar. Use narration and description to make the process analysis lively.

3. This selection is a childhood memory explained from the perspective of an adult. In an essay, evaluate Laye's ability to connect those two perspectives.

How to Become a Better Writer

Lorrie Moore

Born in 1957 in Glen Falls, New York, and educated at Sarah Lawrence and Cornell, Lorrie Moore teaches English at the University of Wisconsin at Madison and has published three books and several articles.

She writes the following selection, which comes from her novel *Self Help,* mockingly in the second person. Moore set out to appropriate the "how-to" form for fiction: "I was interested in whatever tensions resulted when a writer foisted the fictional experience of the 'I' of the first person." We can easily read her short story as a process essay describing "how not to."

*F*irst, try to be something, anything, else. A movie star/astronaut. A movie star/missionary. A movie star/kindergarten teacher. President of the World. Fail miserably. It is best if you fail at an early age—say, fourteen. Early, critical disillusionment is necessary so that at fifteen you can write long haiku sequences about thwarted desire. It is a pond, a cherry blossom, a wind brushing against sparrow wing leaving for mountain. Count the syllables. Show it to your mom. She is tough and practical. She has a son in Vietnam and a husband who may be having an affair. She believes in wearing brown because it hides spots. She'll look briefly at your writing, then back up at you with a face blank as a donut. She'll say: "How about emptying the dishwasher?" Look away. Shove the forks in the fork drawer. Accidentally break one of the freebie gas station glasses. This is the required pain and suffering. This is only for starters.

In your high school English class look at Mr. Killian's face. Decide faces are important. Write a villanelle about pores. Struggle. Write a sonnet. Count the syllables: nine, ten, eleven, thirteen. Decide to experiment with fiction. Here you don't have to count syllables. Write a short story about an elderly man and woman who accidentally shoot each other in the head, the result of an inexplicable malfunction of a shotgun which appears mysteriously in their living room one night. Give it to Mr. Killian as your final project. When you get it back, he has written on it: "Some of your images are quite nice, but you have no sense of plot." When you are home, in the privacy of your own room, faintly scrawl in pencil beneath his black-inked comments: "Plots are for dead people, pore-face."

Take all the babysitting jobs you can get. You are great with kids. They love you. You tell them stories about old people who die idiot deaths. You sing them songs like "Blue Bells of Scotland," which is their favorite. And when they are in their pajamas and have finally stopped pinching each other, when they are fast asleep, you read every sex manual in the house, and wonder how on earth anyone could ever do those things with someone they truly loved. Fall asleep in a chair reading Mr. McMurphy's *Playboy*. When the McMurphys come home, they will tap you on the shoulder, look at the magazine in your lap, and grin. You will want to die. They will ask you if Tracey took her medicine all right. Explain, yes, she did, that you promised her a story if she would take it like a big girl and that seemed to work out just fine. "Oh, marvelous," they will exclaim.

Try to smile proudly.   4

Apply to college as a child psychology major.   5

As a child psychology major, you have some electives. You've always liked   6
birds. Sign up for something called "The Ornithological Field Trip." It meets Tuesdays and Thursdays at two. When you arrive at Room 134 on the first day of class, everyone is sitting around a seminar table talking about metaphors. You've heard of these. After a short, excruciating while, raise your hand and say diffidently, "Excuse me, isn't this Birdwatching One-oh-one?" The class stops and turns to look at you. They seem to all have one face—giant and blank as a vandalized clock. Someone with a beard booms out, "No, this is Creative Writing." Say: "Oh—right," as if perhaps you knew all along. Look down at your schedule. Wonder how the hell you ended up here. The computer, apparently, has made an error. You start to get up to leave and then don't. The lines at the registrar this week are huge. Perhaps you should stick with this mistake. Perhaps your creative writing isn't all that bad. Perhaps it is fate. Perhaps this is what your dad meant when he said, "It's the age of computers, Francie, it's the age of computers."

Decide that you like college life. In your dorm you meet many nice peo-   7
ple. Some are smarter than you. And some, you notice, are dumber than you. You will continue, unfortunately, to view the world in exactly these terms for the rest of your life.

The assignment this week in creative writing is to narrate a violent hap-   8
pening. Turn in a story about driving with your Uncle Gordon and another one about two old people who are accidentally electrocuted when they go to turn on a badly wired desk lamp. The teacher will hand them back to you with comments: "Much of your writing is smooth and energetic. You have, however, a ludicrous notion of plot." Write another story about a man and a woman who, in the very first paragraph, have their lower torsos accidentally blitzed away by dynamite. In the second paragraph, with the insurance money, they buy a frozen yogurt stand together. There are six more paragraphs. You read the whole thing out loud in class. No one likes it. They say your sense of plot is outrageous and incompetent. After class someone asks you if you are crazy.

Decide that perhaps you should stick to comedies. Start dating someone   9
who is funny, someone who has what in high school you called a "really great

sense of humor" and what now your creative writing class calls "self-contempt giving rise to comic form." Write down all of his jokes, but don't tell him you are doing this. Make up anagrams of his old girlfriend's name and name all of your socially handicapped characters with them. Tell him his old girlfriend is in all of your stories and then watch how funny he can be, see what a really great sense of humor he can have.

Your child psychology advisor tells you you are neglecting courses in 10 your major. What you spend the most time on should be what you're majoring in. Say yes, you understand.

In creative writing seminars over the next two years, everyone continues 11 to smoke cigarettes and ask the same things: "But does it work?" "Why should we care about this character?" "Have you earned this cliché?" These seem like important questions.

On days when it is your turn, you look at the class hopefully as they scour 12 your mimeographs for a plot. They look back up at you, drag deeply, and then smile in a sweet sort of way.

You spend too much time slouched and demoralized. Your boyfriend sug- 13 gests bicycling. Your roommate suggests a new boyfriend. You are said to be self-mutilating and losing weight, but you continue writing. The only happiness you have is writing something new, in the middle of the night, armpits damp, heart pounding, something no one has yet seen. You have only those brief, frag- ile, untested moments of exhilaration when you know: you are a genius. Under- stand what you must do. Switch majors. The kids in your nursery project will be disappointed, but you have a calling, an urge, a delusion, an unfortunate habit. You have, as your mother would say, fallen in with a bad crowd.

Why write? Where does writing come from? These are questions to ask 14 yourself? They are like: Where does dust come from? Or: Why is there war? Or: If there's a God, then why is my brother now a cripple?

These are questions that you keep in your wallet, like calling cards. These 15 are questions, your creative writing teacher says, that are good to address in your journals but rarely in your fiction.

The writing professor this fall is stressing the Power of the Imagination. 16 Which means he doesn't want long descriptive stories about your camping trip last July. He wants you to start in a realistic context but then to alter it. Like re- combinant DNA. He wants you to let your imagination sail, to let it grow big- bellied in the wind. This is a quote from Shakespeare.

Tell your roommate your great idea, your great exercise of imaginative 17 power: a transformation of Melville to contemporary life. It will be about mono- mania and the fish-eat-fish world of life insurance in Rochester, New York. The first line will be "Call me Fishmeal," and it will feature a menopausal suburban husband named Richard, who because he is so depressed all the time is called

"Mopey Dick" by his witty wife Elaine. Say to your roommate: "Mopey Dick, get it?" Your roommate looks at you, her face blank as a large Kleenex. She comes up to you, like a buddy, and puts an arm around your burdened shoulders. "Listen, Francie," she says, slow as speech therapy. "Let's go out and get a big beer."

The seminar doesn't like this one either. You suspect they are beginning to feel sorry for you. They say: "You have to think about what is happening. Where is the story here?"   18

The next semester the writing professor is obsessed with writing from personal experience. You must write from what you know, from what has happened to you. He wants deaths, he wants camping trips. Think about what has happened to you. In three years there have been three things: you lost your virginity; your parents got divorced; and your brother came home from a forest ten miles from the Cambodian border with only half a thigh, a permanent smirk nestled into one corner of his mouth.   19

About the first you write: "It created a new space, which hurt and cried in a voice that wasn't mine, 'I'm not the same anymore, but I'll be okay.' "   20

About the second you write an elaborate story of an old married couple who stumble upon an unknown land mine in their kitchen and accidentally blow themselves up. You call it: "For Better or for Liverwurst."   21

About the last you write nothing. There are no words for this. Your typewriter hums. You can find no words.   22

At undergraduate cocktail parties, people say, "Oh, you write? What do you write about?" Your roommate, who has consumed too much wine, too little cheese, and no crackers at all, blurts: "Oh, my god, she always writes about her dumb boyfriend."   23

Later on in life you will learn that writers are merely open, helpless texts with no real understanding of what they have written and therefore must half-believe anything and everything that is said of them. You, however, have not yet reached this stage of literary criticism. You stiffen and say, "I do not," the same way you said it when someone in the fourth grade accused you of really liking oboe lessons and your parents really weren't just making you take them.   24

Insist you are not very interested in any one subject at all, that you are interested in the music of language, that you are interested in—in—syllables, because they are the atoms of poetry, the cells of the mind, the breath of the soul. Begin to feel woozy. Stare into your plastic wine cup.   25

"Syllables?" you will hear someone ask, voice trailing off, as they glide slowly toward the reassuring white of the dip.   26

Begin to wonder what you do write about. Or if you have anything to say. Or if there even is such a thing as a thing to say. Limit these thoughts to no more than ten minutes a day; like sit-ups, they can make you thin.   27

You will read somewhere that all writing has to do with one's genitals.   28
Don't dwell on this. It will make you nervous.

Your mother will come visit you. She will look at the circles under your   29
eyes and hand you a brown book with a brown briefcase on the cover. It is entitled: *How to Become a Business Executive.* She has also brought the *Names for
Baby* encyclopedia you asked for; one of your characters, the aging clown-
school teacher, needs a new name. Your mother will shake her head and say:
"Francie, Francie, remember when you were going to be a child psychology
major?"

Say: "Mom, I like to write."   30

She'll say: "Sure you like to write. Of course. Sure you like to write."   31

Write a story about a confused music student and title it: "Schubert Was   32
the One with the Glasses, Right?" It's not a big hit, although your roommate
likes the part where the two violinists accidentally blow themselves up in a
recital room. "I went out with a violinist once," she says, snapping her gum.

Thank god you are taking other courses. You can find sanctuary in   33
nineteenth-century ontological snags and invertebrate courting rituals. Certain
globular mollusks have what is called "Sex by the Arm." The male octopus, for
instance, loses the end of one arm when placing it inside the female body during
intercourse. Marine biologists call it "Seven Heaven." Be glad you know these
things. Be glad you are not just a writer. Apply to law school.

From here on in, many things can happen. But the main one will be this: 34
you decide not to go to law school after all, and, instead, you spend a good, big
chunk of your adult life telling people how you decided not to go to law school
after all. Somehow you end up writing again. Perhaps you go to graduate school.
Perhaps you work odd jobs and take writing courses at night. Perhaps you are
working on a novel and writing down all the clever remarks and intimate personal confessions you hear during the day. Perhaps you are losing your pals,
your acquaintances, your balance.

You have broken up with your boyfriend. You now go out with men who,   35
instead of whispering "I love you," shout: "Do it to me, baby." This is good for
your writing.

Sooner or later you have a finished manuscript more or less. People look   36
at it in a vaguely troubled sort of way and say, "I'll bet becoming a writer was
always a fantasy of yours, wasn't it?" Your lips dry to salt. Say that of all the
fantasies possible in the world, you can't imagine being a writer even making
the top twenty. Tell them you were going to be a child psychology major. "I
bet," they always sigh, "you'd be great with kids." Scowl fiercely. Tell them
you're a walking blade.

Quit classes. Quit jobs. Cash in old savings bonds. Now you have time 37
like warts on your hands. Slowly copy all of your friends' addresses into a new
address book.

Vacuum. Chew cough drops. Keep a folder full of fragments. 38

An eyelid darkening sideways.
World as conspiracy.
Possible plot? A woman gets on a bus.
Suppose you threw a love affair and nobody came.

At home drink a lot of coffee. At Howard Johnson's order the cole 39
slaw. Consider how it looks like the soggy confetti of a map: where you've
been, where you're going—"You Are Here," says the red star on the back of
the menu.

Occasionally a date with a face blank as a sheet of paper asks you whether 40
writers often become discouraged. Say that sometimes they do and sometimes
they do. Say it's a lot like having polio.

"Interesting," smiles your date, and then he looks down at his arm hairs 41
and starts to smooth them, all, always, in the same direction.

Meaning and Idea

1. This selection is about the process of becoming a writer or the process of
   not becoming one, depending on how you look at the piece. What are the
   basic elements in the process Moore describes? If you wanted to be a writer,
   which of her recommendations would you attempt to practice? Why?

2. How do the adverse experiences of the narrator affect her? In what way do
   they skew her vision of the writer's craft? What is the most humorous detail
   here in the catalogue of steps to take to become a better writer?

3. Are we supposed to take Moore's advice seriously? How can you tell? Why
   has she chosen a humorous form of presentation as opposed to a more
   serious one?

Language, Form, Structure

1. Why does Moore choose to write this fictional piece in the second person—
   as advice to "you"?

2. How does the writer achieve the humorous effects here? How does she use
   irony, exaggeration, one-liners, non sequiturs, and other devices to make
   readers laugh?

3. What is your reaction to the first line of the selection? How does it relate to
   the title? How do the first line and the rest of the first paragraph establish
   the humorous dimensions of the piece?

4. Moore writes a number of brief or one-sentence paragraphs. Why does she do so, do you think? What do they contribute to her overall intent? How do they affect the process being described?

5. How do the last two paragraphs provide an appropriate conclusion for this fictional piece? Why does the date smooth his arm hairs? What does this gesture tell you about Moore's view of what the world thinks of the writer's struggles?

6. Define the following words and use each one in a sentence: thwarted; diffidently; ludicrous; demoralized; recombinant; monomania; woozy; sanctuary; ontological.

Ideas for Writing

1. Using the second person, explain a frustrating process as an essay of advice to someone. You may choose, in fact, to make this a how-*not*-to essay.

2. Write an essay that attempts to answer one or both of these two questions from Moore's essay: "Why write? Where does writing come from?" Draw on the strategies of process analysis to develop your paper.

3. Write a critical essay in which you analyze the comic effects in this selection. Draw liberally from the piece to illustrate how Moore made you laugh.

CROSSOVER

1. Ernest Hemingway in "Camping Out" (this chapter), E. B. White in "Once More to the Lake" (Chapter One), and Jack London in "To Build a Fire" (Chapter Seven) offer reflections on nature. How do their views of the natural world differ? Which essay engages you the most with the powers of living things? What techniques does the writer use to affect you? Write an essay to explore these questions.

2. In this chapter, Joan Didion in "On Keeping a Notebook" and Lorrie Moore in "How to Become a Better Writer" tell about how they approach aspects of writing. Which selection makes writing more attractive? Which selection makes writing less attractive? What elements of writing does each piece stress to make its point? Write an essay to explore these questions.

Chapter Five

COMPARISON AND CONTRAST

INTRODUCTION TO COMPARISON AND CONTRAST

Where would we be without the ability to see things in relation to other things? Making comparisons, seeing similarities or differences (or both), is essential for making the judgments we live by. Is he large or small, beautiful or ugly, kind or cruel? Is she attentive or blasé, energetic or lethargic, coy or ostentatious? To answer such questions intelligently we often ask another question: *"Compared to whom?"* Making comparisons allows us to think more deeply. Indeed, thought without comparisons is not really thought as we know it. A mind overtaken by an obsession, for example, is a mind stuck in a single vision, unable to look about with an eye open to relationships and comparisons.

Comparative thinking is a particularly human gift that enables us to organize experience and make the serious and fanciful connections that help us evaluate the conditions of our daily lives.

READING COMPARISON AND CONTRAST

Careful readers know that for the best writers, the comparative faculty is a steady apparatus. The writer of fiction or drama develops one character with another in mind and depends on readers or viewers seeing those created people in relation to one another. We appreciate the nobility of an Othello, for example, more clearly in relation to the vile actions of a Iago or the vulnerable youth of Romeo and Juliet in relation to their ruling elders.

The Importance of Comparisons and Contrasts

The worlds of comedy and tragedy alike are populated with characters meant for the reader to compare—Mutt and Jeff, Felix and Oscar, Lenny and George, and the list goes on—clear opposites meant to illuminate each other. Many writers, then, make generous use of explicit and implicit comparisons. This is as true for the writer of essays as for the writer of imaginative literature. Patterns emerge and generalizations come forth as the essayist in "Once More to the Lake" (see Chapter One) considers subjects relatively. E.B. White's trip to the lake with his son gains meaning for both the writer and the reader as White *compares* the stay to those of his childhood. Without the pressure of these other memories, White's descriptions might have evoked a sense of place but could never have conveyed the rich sense of time and of life passing by. Similarly, readers confronted with Susan Sontag's comparison in this chapter between the public's perceptions about cancer and tuberculosis learn much about our entrenched habits in thinking about and dealing with disease. The primitive dread, shame, and disgust that for centuries marked attitudes toward TB have attached themselves in the modern age to our attitude toward cancer and cancer patients. Sontag's comparison urges us to review our thinking, cast off old prejudices and phobias, and assume the enlightened consciousness and behavior permitted by the advancing science of our era. Her historical perspective allows us to view cancer with increased hope as well. Like TB, so long the dreaded "killer," cancer can be understood and conquered, both mentally and physically. The essay deepens from the apt comparison.

In reading poetry, we are confronted again and again with comparisons. Poets can structure their poems with comparisons, exploring two subjects at once. Such basic comparisons appear in poems such as "The Naked and the Nude" (Chapter Eight) and "Richard Cory" (Chapter Seven). These comparisons help readers see subjects dynamically—Nakedness versus Nudity, town patrician versus town folk. But poets work in fanciful comparisons as well, comparing a lover to a summer's day, home life to a hag-ridden dream, an unfulfilled dream to a raisin in the sun.

Figurative Language

Figurative devices help us compare things in an imaginative fashion. Poems, like our daily lives, are filled with metaphors (a thing is said to be something it really is not—but really *is* if you think about it) and similes (a thing is said to be *like* something it really is not—but really *is* if you think about it). In poetry, as in life, these comparisons can be fresh. Or they can be overused—big as a house, long as the day, eats like a bird, he's a monster, he's an animal, and so on. The similes and metaphors that we use daily may be trite, but they reflect nonetheless our very human desire to see elements in our lives comparatively. In the comparisons offered by figurative language (metaphor, simile, and others) the writer sets something from one class of things (or people or ideas) against something from another class of things. Such comparisons are the opposites of the comparisons we spoke of earlier in which two or more things of the *same* class are compared—two trips, two diseases, two people, two newspapers. Hence, with figurative language a person is compared to an animal—a horse, let's say, because of the quality shared with horses—largeness, endurance, strength, appetite, range of emotions. Or a person is compared to something superhuman in order to emphasize some extraordinary features—she sings like an angel, he's built like a god, and so on. There is pleasure in breaking down barriers between classifications in order to see our world more vividly: combs have teeth, shoes have tongues, corn grows in ears, trees have arms. The metaphors and similes we use again and again in our daily lives may show wear from overuse, but they reflect our desire to see comparisons, to make connections, to play with seeing and saying.

Reading good poetry gives us the chance to enjoy unique comparisons—the poet's similes and metaphors. Langston Hughes's "Dream Deferred," a poem you will read in Chapter Seven, is a prime example of the use of a figurative device to shock us into awareness about both language and the human condition. Who would ever think, for example, of a deferred dream as being like an infected wound? And yet by making this comparison and others equally startling in their originality, Hughes makes us see its validity and makes us see as well the ability of language to transport us to new areas of feeling and thought.

The comparisons presented in this chapter are both sensible—comparing within classes—and fanciful—comparing things from different classes. Each in its way will help you see subjects freshly with the understanding that comes from comparative thinking.

WRITING COMPARISON AND CONTRAST

In writing comparisons, more perhaps than in any other writing, you must plan with care. The comparison paper presents you with a double challenge: to discuss two things at once. Therefore, as you approach your discussion of these two things—two ideas, two people, two places—you must reflect at length on matters such as purpose, audience, and organization.

PURPOSE AND AUDIENCE

Weighing Likenesses and Differences

Often as you write in college, the assignment itself will clarify your purpose. Indeed, some instructors use the term *compare* to mean "to state likenesses" and the term *contrast* to mean "to state differences." For our purpose, however, we are using the term *compare* to mean both or either (similarities and differences), depending on your subject and your thinking.

When the two items in your comparison are very different on the surface—separated by time, nationality, or what have you—stressing likenesses would seem more appropriate because the differences are already so apparent. A paper comparing horses and humans would require little attention to the contrasting features of the animals. Everyone knows the two differ dramatically; what readers want to know is what the writer sees as similarities.

But when the two items you wish to compare are on the surface very similar, stressing differences makes for a more enlightening discussion. In comparing old-fashioned manual typewriters and the electric typewriters that replaced them before word processing, you would spend most of your time detailing the differences between the old and the new technologies. But there are no absolutes. If your employer asked you to compare IBM and Apple computers, you would probably pay careful attention to likenesses as well as differences.

Often, however, subjects are both alike and not alike. Rock groups like the Beatles and the Rolling Stones, for example, share much—the time they began, their popularity, the death of group members, and so on. However, the groups are very different in tone, image, and style. To give your writing a purpose, you must decide which way to go. If you stress differences, it does not mean you will not deal with likenesses at all, only that you won't dwell on them. Perhaps an introductory paragraph can state the obvious similarities and the rest of the paper can explore distinctions. Or, if you find similarities more interesting, you may wish to consider obvious differences first in a paragraph or two and then move on to your main concern and purpose: that the two groups, for example, had more in common than they knew they had, that each in its own way, however unwittingly, fell prey to the violence of the times.

Purpose, Audience, and Comparisons

An effective, persuasive comparison paper must have a purpose—to show likenesses or differences *primarily*. Without this purpose, you risk providing a mere catalogue of features and qualities to no good end. And you want to consider the value of expressing the purpose of your comparison paper in an original statement of thesis. For example, the comparison paper built on thesis statements, such as "There are many similarities between X and Y but also many differences," may be a clear enough paper but one bound to bore the reader. The paper that rests on a daring thesis like Sontag's, for example—that our *similar* responses to two very *different* diseases reflect a continuing negative impulse in our psyche and culture—grabs the reader's attention and holds it. The purpose of comparison, then, is to stress similarities *or* differences *in order to make a point*. It's the additional point that distinguishes the humdrum sorting of qualities from the engaging essay.

As for audience—again, as in other kinds of essays, the reader makes a big difference for the writer. How much does the reader know about the subject? How much background must you give? What are the readers' social, political, or aesthetic inclinations? What are their cultural backgrounds? How old are they? For example, your analysis of the continuing popularity of the Beatles and the Rolling Stones for a teenage or a British audience would be very different from your analysis of them for a middle-aged audience. Your analysis will differ, too, depending on whether the reader was listening to pop music when these groups were in their heydey or whether the reader was "tuned in to" other music at the time or was possibly not yet alive!

PROCESS

First determine what two subjects you wish to compare in your paper. As you consider your subjects, make sure that you have a sound basis for comparison. Ask yourself, are they of the same class of things—two music groups, two plays, two heroes, two books, two treaties? If you find that the subjects you're thinking of comparing are *not* of the same class, then ask yourself if the "stretch" pays off. Does the fanciful comparison allow you to present something in a new light, or is it simply the result of a quick or an idiosyncratic idea?

Making a Grid

Once you have two items for your comparison and have assured yourself that you have a sound basis for comparison, you are ready to identify the features to consider in the comparison. Some writers find a grid a useful tool for this stage of prewriting. Use a grid like the accompanying one or another note-taking system that allows you to generate the points in your comparison and the details and examples that develop or illustrate these points.

Topics for Comparison

A. _____   B. _____

Points
of
Comparison

Next, look over the notes on your grid to see what you can say about your two topics. Where you have the most detail should give you a clue about where you have the most to say.

Thesis and Organization

Formulate a thesis sentence that joins the two subjects in an interesting formulation: "Despite obvious differences . . . X and Y's similarities show them both to be expressions of popular urges" or some such sentence.

With your thesis and your points of comparison developed, you are ready to organize the essay. Organization is critical for any essay, but in the comparison essay it is doubly important. Without careful planning, your essay can end up being an analysis of one of your subjects on a few points and then an analysis of the other on some other points—two separate analyses with no comparisons drawn. Or your essay, without proper planning, can easily become a lopsided affair, with ample discussion of one subject and a race through the next.

The effective comparison paper is balanced and consistent. If you discuss the history of one subject, you should discuss the history of the other; if you discuss the appearance of one subject, you should discuss the appearance of the other.

As you plan, you must decide on an appropriate scheme. Do you wish to discuss one subject covering all the points of comparison and then go on to the next subject covering the same points? Then your paper might look like this:

A.

1.
2.
3.

B.

1.	
2.	
3.	

Or do you wish to allow the points of comparison to structure your discussion? Then your paper might look like this:

1. History	A.
	B.
2. Appearance	A.
	B.
3. Sound	A.
	B.

The first way allows for a fuller presentation of each of the topics on its own terms and for a more inductive approach. The second permits a more dynamic discussion with the relationship being stated throughout. If you choose the first arrangement, you will need to plan to make some more explicit statements of comparison at the end of the essay once you have laid out the different points for each of the two subjects.

Finally, as you write your comparison paper, you will want to make use of the transitional phrases that ease movement from one topic to the other—*similarly, likewise, in contrast, on the other hand, however,* and so on. These phrases will help you and the reader navigate the complicated process of comparative analysis.

STUDENT WRITING

In the essay below, the student writer draws heavily on comparison and contrast strategies to produce an analysis of Seamus Heaney's poem "Digging" (page 313). The poem is about similarities and differences—between and among men of different generations in the speaker's family. Note how the writer navigates the inherent comparisons and contrasts in the poem and uses them to make her own assertions about similarities and differences that she sees in the situations and characters presented by Heaney.

The Poet and His Living Roots

[a]Terms of comparison clear

[b]Thesis: poet moves from view of sharp differences to view of common ground

[c]Transition

[d]Repetition of words *comparison, contrast, differences,* etc. contributes to essay's coherence

[e]Quotations support writer's assertions

[f]Audience awareness: poem summaries help those who may not have read the poem as well as those who have read it but benefit nonetheless from seeing how the student writer reached conclusions

[g]Repetition of "digging" helps achieve coherence

[h]Comparisons and contrasts made point by point: differences in tools used for work, differences between past and present, similarities and differences between digging and writing poetry

[i]Conclusion: sums up both the writer's view of the poem's meaning and the assertions made in the essay

Them and me, then and now—all of us think about these comparisons and differences as we look at our own lives and those of our parents and their parents before them. In "Digging" Seamus Heaney sets his speaker's life against that of his father[a] and in the process says much about poetry and existence. Sharp contrasts fill the poem, but by the end the speaker in Heaney's poem has moved from an appreciation of sharp differences to an appreciation of common ground.[b]

The poem begins with differences. The speaker, a poet, and his father are in different places, doing different work, with different kinds of tools. The poet up in his room sees his father below. The poet is involved in the intellectual work of writing. The father below is digging in the earth. The poet's pen feels like a "gun" in his hands. Below the father holds a "spade." The gun can destroy things, and the speaker is apparently inclined toward destruction. Maybe he has a mental block and cannot write. In contrast,[c,d] the father's shovel is digging in the living earth to make things grow.[h]

After contrasting[c] himself with his father, the speaker establishes another contrast[d]—the present time with twenty years before.[h] Back then the speaker was more connected to his father and his grandfather, sharing much. The men worked their spades to dig in the earth for potatoes, and the boy helped, bringing milk and planting. But now in adulthood he is apart from his father, watching him from a window, thinking, as the father digs below.[f]

How can he reconnect with his father and his grandfather? That's the challenge for the speaker, who has "no spade to follow men like them." The answer lies in another comparison[d]—between digging and writing.[h] At the start of the poem[c] the two activities are markedly different.[d] The pen is like a gun. At the end of the poem, the "squat pen rests" in the speaker's hand, likened to a spade. "I'll dig with it," the speaker writes. For the poet is a "digger" too, and his pen is his tool. Through his mental digging, the poet like his grandfather goes "down and down." Reawakened in him as he does his mental burrowing is the "smell of potato mould," the "squelch and slap/Of soggy peat," the "curt cuts of an edge/Through living roots."[e,g]

Digging back in memory to find his own "roots," the poet heals his anger. His pen is no longer a "gun." Digging[g]

up the authentic traditions of family and history is the poet's job, "Digging" seems to say. When the pen feels like a "gun," the poet cannot write. He is separate from the positive forces of life. In the act of remembering, the poet moves beyond the contrasts at the poem's beginning, and moving through his own "living roots," he arrives at the shared sense of love.[i]

SUMMING UP: COMPARISON AND CONTRAST

Reading Comparison and Contrast

- To use comparison and contrast means to show similarities and differences between objects and ideas.

- Be attentive to the terms of the writer's comparison—that is, be clear about what is being compared to what.

- Identify the writer's thesis: What is her reason for making the comparison? What is her opinion about or attitude toward the topic she has chosen to explore through comparison and contrast strategies?

- Look for the writer's use of figurative expressions, which often help him compare things in an imaginative fashion. Simile, metaphor, personification—these and other figurative devices, by expressing ideas in comparative terms, help readers see issues freshly and vividly.

Writing Comparison and Contrast

- Decide on the two objects or ideas you wish to present together and weigh your audience and your purpose carefully, as well as your method of organization.

- Generally, comparison papers deal with both similarities and differences, yet with one taking the primary spotlight.

- If the two items you want to compare in your paper are very different on the surface, stress their likenesses; the differences will already be quite apparent. If you wish to compare items that are very similar on the surface, stress the differences.

- Develop a thesis statement that tells readers the purpose of your paper to stress similarities or differences. Join the two topics in an interesting formulation as you state your topic clearly; as you indicate the primary focus of your topic, make sure the reader knows that you are using the comparison strategy *to make a point.*

- Determine your intended audience and, considering what your reader knows about the topic, provide appropriate detail.

- In your prewriting on the topic, generate a list of the points you wish to make in the comparison and of the details and examples that develop or illustrate these points.

- Balance your presentation by considering points in relation to *both* topics, not just one.

- Decide on an appropriate scheme for organization:

  Treat each subject separately, presenting all the points of comparison for one of the items of your topic and then covering the same points for the second item

  OR

  Treat each point of the comparison, presenting the two items in relation to each point

- Use transitional phrases carefully to help you move from one aspect of the topic to another. Words and phrases like *similarly, in contrast,* and *on the other hand* help you connect ideas smoothly.

Shakespeare's Gifted Sister

Virginia Woolf

Virginia Woolf (1882–1941) is today considered one of the most important writers in the development of modernist fiction. She lived with her husband, the editor and publisher Leonard Woolf, her sister Vanessa (a painter), and Vanessa's husband Clive Bell (an art critic) as a part of the famous Bloomsbury group in England. This group was to include people such as novelist E.M. Forster, poet T.S. Eliot, art historian Roger Fry, and economist John Maynard Keynes, all of whom became renowned, in one way or another, for their progressive thought and lifestyles. Virginia and Leonard founded the Hogarth Press, which published her work, Eliot's, and Freud's (the first editions in English), among the works of other great writers. Her widely admired fiction includes *Mrs. Dalloway* (1925), *To the Lighthouse* (1927), *Orlando* (1928), and *The Waves* (1931). She also left a rich repository of essays. After years of battling mental illness, she committed suicide in 1941.

This selection, from her 1929 book *A Room of One's Own,* sets an imaginative, fictional context that allows Woolf to explore the inequality between men and women. Notice how she manages to balance description and exemplification of the real with the abstract as she looks at Elizabethan literature.

For it is a perennial puzzle why no woman wrote a word of that extraordinary literature when every other man, it seemed, was capable of song or sonnet. What were the conditions in which women lived, I asked myself; for fiction, imaginative work that is, is not dropped like a pebble upon the ground, as science may be; fiction is like a spider's web, attached ever so lightly perhaps, but still attached to life at all four corners. Often the attachment is scarcely perceptible; Shakespeare's plays, for instance, seem to hang there complete by themselves. But when the web is pulled askew, hooked up at the edge, torn in the middle, one remembers that these webs are not spun in mid-air by incorporeal creatures, but are the work of suffering human beings, and are attached to grossly material things, like health and money and the houses we live in. . . .

But what I find deplorable . . . is that nothing is known about women before the eighteenth century. I have no model in my mind to turn about this way and that. Here am I asking why women did not write poetry in the Elizabethan age, and I am not sure how they were educated; whether they were taught to write; whether they had sitting-rooms to themselves; how many women had children before they were twenty-one; what, in short, they did from eight in the morning till eight at night. They had no money, evidently; according to Professor Trevelyan they were married whether they liked it or not before they were out of the nursery, at fifteen or sixteen very likely. It would have been extremely odd, even upon this showing, had one of them suddenly written the plays of Shakespeare. I concluded, and I thought of that old gentleman, who is dead now, but was a bishop, I think, who declared that it was impossible for any woman, past, present, or to come, to have the genius of Shakespeare. He wrote to the papers about it. He also told a lady who applied to him for information that cats do not as a matter of fact go to heaven, though they have, he added, souls of a sort. How much thinking those old gentlemen used to save one! How the borders of ignorance shrank back at their approach! Cats do not go to heaven. Women cannot write the plays of Shakespeare.

Be that as it may, I could not help thinking, as I looked at the works of Shakespeare on the shelf, that the bishop was right at least in this; it would have been impossible, completely and entirely, for any woman to have written the plays of Shakespeare in the age of Shakespeare. Let me imagine, since facts are so hard to come by, what would have happened had Shakespeare had a wonderfully gifted sister, called Judith, let us say. Shakespeare himself went, very probably—his mother was an heiress—to the grammar school, where he may have learnt Latin—Ovid, Virgil and Horace—and the elements of grammar and logic. He was, it is well known, a wild boy who poached rabbits, perhaps shot a deer, and had, rather sooner than he should have done, to marry a woman in the neighbourhood, who bore him a child rather quicker than was right. That escapade sent him to seek his fortune in London. He had, it seemed, a taste for the theatre; he began by holding horses at the stage door. Very soon he got work in the theatre, became a successful actor, and lived at the hub of the universe, meeting everybody, knowing everybody, practising his art on the boards, exercising his wits in the streets, and even getting access to the palace of the queen. Meanwhile his extraordinarily gifted sister, let us suppose, remained at home. She was as adventurous, as imaginative, as agog to see the world as he was. But she was not sent to school. She had no chance of learning grammar and logic, let alone of reading Horace and Virgil. She picked up a book now and then, one of her brother's perhaps, and read a few pages. But then her parents came in and told her to mend the stockings or mind the stew and not moon about with books and papers. They would have spoken sharply but kindly, for they were substantial people who knew the conditions of life for a woman and loved their daughter—indeed, more likely than not she was the apple of her father's eye. Perhaps she scribbled some pages up in an apple loft on the sly, but was careful to hide them or set fire to them. Soon, however, before she was out of her teens, she was to be betrothed to the son of a neighbouring wool-stapler. She cried out that marriage was hateful to her, and for that she was severely beaten by her father. Then he ceased to scold her. He begged her instead not to hurt him, not to shame him in this matter of her marriage. He would give her a chain of beads or a fine petticoat, he said; and there were tears in his eyes. How could she disobey him? How could she break his heart? The force of her own gift alone drove her to it. She made up a small parcel of her belongings, let herself down by a rope one summer's night and took the road to London. She was not seventeen. The birds that sang in the hedge were not more musical than she was. She had the quickest fancy, a gift like her brother's, for the tune of words. Like him, she had a taste for the theatre. She stood at the stage door; she wanted to act, she said. Men laughed in her face. The manager—a fat, loose-lipped man—guffawed. He bellowed something about poodles dancing and women acting—no woman, he said, could possibly be an actress. He hinted—you can imagine what. She could get no training in her craft. Could she even seek her dinner in a tavern or roam the streets at midnight? Yet her genius was for fiction and lusted to feed abundantly upon the lives of men and women and the study of their ways. At last—for she was very young, oddly like Shakespeare the poet in her face, with the same grey eyes and rounded brows—at last Nick Greene the actor-manager took pity on her; she found herself with child by that gentleman and so—who shall measure the heat and violence of the poet's heart when caught and tangled in a woman's body?—killed herself one winter's night and lies buried at some cross-roads where the omnibuses now stop outside the Elephant and Castle.

That, more or less, is how the story would run, I think, if a woman in   4
Shakespeare's day had had Shakespeare's genius. But for my part, I agree with the deceased bishop, if such he was—it is unthinkable that any woman in Shakespeare's day should have had Shakespeare's genius. For genius like Shakespeare's is not born among labouring, uneducated, servile people. It was not born in England among the Saxons and the Britons. It is not born today among the working classes. How, then, could it have been born among women whose work began, according to Professor Trevelyan, almost before they were out of the nursery, who were forced to it by their parents and held to it by all the power of law and custom? Yet genius of a sort must have existed among women as it must have existed among the working classes.

Meaning and Idea

1. What is Woolf's specific thesis about Shakespeare and his imaginary sister? How is that specific thesis indicative of her overall thesis comparing the lives and creative endeavors of men and women? Summarize briefly what that overall thesis says.

2. What is Woolf's opinion of the contrast between scientific and creative works?

3. How do Woolf's references to the "deceased bishop" exemplify her views concerning how men generally think about women? What other specific examples of such thinking does she offer?

4. What is the Elephant and Castle? What does the last line of the third paragraph indicate about Shakespeare's sister's relative importance?

5. Why does Woolf agree that it would have been "unthinkable" for a woman in Elizabethan times to have achieved Shakespeare's genius? How is she using the term *genius?* Is this a conclusion with which she is happy?

Language, Form, Structure

1. Which developmental pattern for a comparison essay does Woolf follow here? How does she balance the two sides of her comparison? Prepare a point-by-point outline of Woolf's comparison between William and "Judith" Shakespeare. What does she say about their comparative schooling? Writing? Marriages? Results of creative impulses?

2. What generally is Woolf's tone in this essay—sorrowful, angry, comic, sarcastic, ironic? Find three examples from the essay which contribute to that tone.

3. Interpret the following lines as a generalization of Woolf's attitude about the relationship between men and women throughout the ages: "at last Nick Greene the actor-manager took pity on her; she found herself with child by that gentleman and so—"

4. Identify the paragraphs which constitute the introduction, body, and conclusion to this essay.

5. Look up definitions for the following words: perennial; perceptible; askew; incorporeal; poached; escapade; hub; guffawed; betrothed; lusted; servile. Now choose any five and use them in original sentences.

Ideas for Writing

1. Write an essay in which you compare the life and achievements of a famous man with the life and achievements of his imaginary sister. Use the block method of organization, taking care to balance both sections.

2. Write a short essay in which you compare how you and your best friend approach a similar task.

3. Virginia Woolf wrote this piece in the 1920s, whereas Shakespeare wrote in the late 1500s to the early 1600s. How does Woolf make her ideas apply to twentieth-century life? Do you feel that her analysis is relevant to the relations between women and men today? Explain.

Two Kinds

Amy Tan

Born in Oakland, California, in 1952 soon after her parents arrived in the United States, Amy Tan has a sensibility that is resonant with that of many first-generation immigrant Americans, neither Chinese nor American but identifying strongly with both. Tan's first novel, *The Joy Luck Club* (1989), wrestled with those themes.

The novel, composed of 16 interconnected stories narrated by four Chinese-born mothers and their four American-born daughters, is deeply concerned with issues of love, loss, identity, and growth. Jing-mei (June) Woo is one of the daughters in the book. In the following selection, she and her mother embark on a classic family struggle.

*M*y mother believed you could be anything you wanted to be in   1
America. You could open a restaurant. You could work for the government and get good retirement. You could buy a house with almost no money down. You could become rich. You could become instantly famous.

"Of course you can be prodigy, too," my mother told me when I was nine.   2
"You can be best anything. What does Auntie Lindo know? Her daughter, she is only best tricky."

America was where all my mother's hopes lay. She had come here in 1949   3
after losing everything in China: her mother and father, her family home, her first husband, and two daughters, twin baby girls. But she never looked back with regret. There were so many ways for things to get better.

We didn't immediately pick the right kind of prodigy. At first my mother   4
thought I could be a Chinese Shirley Temple. We'd watch Shirley's old movies on TV as though they were training films. My mother would poke my arm and say, "*Ni Kan*"—You watch. And I would see Shirley tapping her feet, or singing a sailor song, or pursing her lips into a very round O while saying, "Oh my goodness."

"*Ni kan*," said my mother as Shirley's eyes flooded with tears. "You al-   5
ready know how. Don't need talent for crying!"

Soon after my mother got this idea about Shirley Temple, she took me to a   6
beauty training school in the Mission district and put me in the hands of a student who could barely hold the scissors without shaking. Instead of getting big fat curls, I emerged with an uneven mass of crinkly black fuzz. My mother dragged me off to the bathroom and tried to wet down my hair.

"You look like Negro Chinese," she lamented, as if I had done this on   7
purpose.

The instructor of the beauty training school had to lop off these soggy   8
clumps to make my hair even again. "Peter Pan is very popular these days," the instructor assured my mother. I now had hair the length of a boy's, with

straight-across bangs that hung at a slant two inches above my eyebrows. I liked the haircut and it made me actually look forward to my future fame.

In fact, in the beginning, I was just as excited as my mother, maybe even more so. I pictured this prodigy part of me as many different images, trying each one on for size. I was a dainty ballerina girl standing by the curtains, waiting to hear the right music that would send me floating on my tiptoes. I was like the Christ child lifted out of the straw manger, crying with holy indignity. I was Cinderella stepping from her pumpkin carriage with sparkly cartoon music filling the air.

In all of my imaginings, I was filled with a sense that I would soon become *perfect.* My mother and father would adore me. I would be beyond reproach. I would never feel the need to sulk for anything.

But sometimes the prodigy in me became impatient. "If you don't hurry up and get me out of here, I'm disappearing for good," it warned. "And then you'll always be nothing."

Every night after dinner, my mother and I would sit at the Formica kitchen table. She would present new tests, taking her examples from stories of amazing children she had read in *Ripley's Believe It or Not,* or *Good Housekeeping, Reader's Digest,* and a dozen other magazines she kept in a pile in our bathroom. My mother got these magazines from people whose houses she cleaned. And since she cleaned many houses each week, we had a great assortment. She would look through them all, searching for stories about remarkable children.

The first night she brought out a story about a three-year-old boy who knew the capitals of all the states and even most of the European countries. A teacher was quoted as saying the little boy could also pronounce the names of the foreign cities correctly.

"What's the capital of Finland?" my mother asked me, looking at the magazine story.

All I knew was the capital of California, because Sacramento was the name of the street we lived on in Chinatown. "Nairobi!" I guessed, saying the most foreign word I could think of. She checked to see if that was possibly one way to pronounce "Helsinki" before showing me the answer.

The tests got harder—multiplying numbers in my head, finding the queen of hearts in a deck of cards, trying to stand on my head without using my hands, predicting the daily temperatures in Los Angeles, New York, and London.

One night I had to look at a page from the Bible for three minutes and then report everything I could remember. "Now Jehoshaphat had riches and honor in abundance and . . . that's all I remember, Ma," I said.

And after seeing my mother's disappointed face once again, something inside of me began to die. I hated the tests, the raised hopes and failed expectations. Before going to bed that night, I looked in the mirror above the bathroom sink and when I saw only my face staring back—and that it would always be this ordinary face—I began to cry. Such a sad, ugly girl! I made high-pitched noises like a crazed animal, trying to scratch out the face in the mirror.

And then I saw what seemed to be the prodigy side of me—because I had   19
never seen that face before. I looked at my reflection, blinking so I could see
more clearly. The girl staring back at me was angry, powerful. This girl and I
were the same. I had new thoughts, willful thoughts, or rather thoughts filled
with lots of won'ts. I won't let her change me, I promised myself. I won't be
what I'm not.

So now on nights when my mother presented her tests, I performed list-   20
lessly, my head propped on one arm. I pretended to be bored. And I was. I got so
bored I started counting the bellows of the foghorns out on the bay while my
mother drilled me in other areas. The sound was comforting and reminded me of
the cow jumping over the moon. And the next day, I played a game with myself,
seeing if my mother would give up on me before eight bellows. After a while I
usually counted only one, maybe two bellows at most. At last she was beginning
to give up hope.

Two or three months had gone by without any mention of my being a   21
prodigy again. And then one day my mother was watching "The Ed Sullivan
Show" on TV. The TV was old and the sound kept shorting out. Every time my
mother got halfway up from the sofa to adjust the set, the sound would go back
on and Ed would be talking. As soon as she sat down, Ed would go silent again.
She got up, the TV broke into loud piano music. She sat down. Silence. Up and
down, back and forth, quiet and loud. It was like a stiff embraceless dance between her and the TV set. Finally she stood by the set with her hand on the
sound dial.

She seemed entranced by the music, a little frenzied piano piece with this   22
mesmerizing quality, sort of quick passages and then teasing lilting ones before
it returned to the quick playful parts.

"*Ni kan,*" my mother said, calling me over with hurried hand gestures.   23
"Look here."

I could see why my mother was fascinated by the music. It was being   24
pounded out by a little Chinese girl, about nine years old, with a Peter Pan haircut. The girl had the sauciness of a Shirley Temple. She was proudly modest like
a proper Chinese child. And she also did this fancy sweep of a curtsy, so that the
fluffy skirt of her white dress cascaded slowly to the floor like the petals of a
large carnation.

In spite of these warning signs, I wasn't worried. Our family had no piano   25
and we couldn't afford to buy one, let alone reams of sheet music and piano lessons. So I could be generous in my comments when my mother bad-mouthed the
little girl on TV.

"Play note right, but doesn't sound good! No singing sound," complained   26
my mother.

"What are you picking on her for?" I said carelessly. "She's pretty good.   27
Maybe she's not the best, but she's trying hard." I knew almost immediately I
would be sorry I said that.

"Just like you," she said. "Not the best. Because you not trying." She gave   28
a little huff as she let go of the sound dial and sat down on the sofa.

The little Chinese girl sat down also to play an encore of "Anitra's Dance" by Grieg. I remember the song, because later on I had to learn how to play it.   29

Three days after watching "The Ed Sullivan Show," my mother told me what my schedule would be for piano lessons and piano practice. She had talked to Mr. Chong, who lived on the first floor of our apartment building. Mr. Chong was a retired piano teacher and my mother had traded housecleaning services for weekly lessons and a piano for me to practice on every day, two hours a day, from four until six.   30

When my mother told me this, I felt as though I had been sent to hell. I whined and then kicked my foot a little when I couldn't stand it anymore.   31

"Why don't you like me the way I am? I'm *not* a genius! I can't play the piano. And even if I could, I wouldn't go on TV if you paid me a million dollars!" I cried.   32

My mother slapped me. "Who ask you be genius?" she shouted. "Only ask you be your best. For your sake. You think I want you be genius? Hnnh! What for! Who ask you!"   33

"So ungrateful," I heard her mutter in Chinese. "If she had as much talent as she has temper, she would be famous now."   34

Mr. Chong, whom I secretly nicknamed Old Chong, was very strange, always tapping his fingers to the silent music of an invisible orchestra. He looked ancient in my eyes. He had lost most of the hair on top of his head and he wore thick glasses and had eyes that always looked tired and sleepy. But he must have been younger than I thought, since he lived with his mother and was not yet married.   35

I met Old Lady Chong once and that was enough. She had this peculiar smell like a baby that had done something in its pants. And her fingers felt like a dead person's, like an old peach I once found in the back of the refrigerator; the skin just slid off the meat when I picked it up.   36

I soon found out why Old Chong had retired from teaching piano. He was deaf. "Like Beethoven!" he shouted to me. "We're both listening only in our head!" And he would start to conduct his frantic silent sonatas.   37

Our lessons went like this. He would open the book and point to different things, explaining their purpose: "Key! Treble! Bass! No sharps or flats! So this is C major! Listen now and play after me!"   38

And then he would play the C scale a few times, a simple chord, and then, as if inspired by an old, unreachable itch, he gradually added more notes and running trills and a pounding bass until the music was really something quite grand.   39

I would play after him, the simple scale, the simple chord and then I just played some nonsense that sounded like a cat running up and down on top of garbage cans. Old Chong smiled and applauded and then said, "Very good! But now you must learn to keep time!"   40

So that's how I discovered that Old Chong's eyes were too slow to keep up with the wrong notes I was playing. He went through the motions in half-time. To help me keep rhythm, he stood behind me, pushing down on my right shoulder for   41 every beat. He balanced pennies on top of my wrists so I would keep them still as I slowly played scales and arpeggios. He had me curve my hand around an apple and keep that shape when playing chords. He marched stiffly to show me how to make each finger dance up and down, staccato like an obedient little soldier.

He taught me all these things, and that was how I also learned I could be lazy and get away with mistakes, lots of mistakes. If I hit the wrong notes because I hadn't practiced enough, I never corrected myself. I just kept playing in rhythm. And Old Chong kept conducting his own private reverie.

So maybe I never really gave myself a fair chance. I did pick up the basics pretty quickly, and I might have become a good pianist at that young age. But I was so determined not to try, not to be anybody different that I learned to play only the most ear-splitting preludes, the most discordant hymns.

Over the next year, I practiced like this, dutifully in my own way. And then one day I heard my mother and her friend Lindo Jong both talking in a loud bragging tone of voice so others could hear. It was after church, and I was leaning against the brick wall wearing a dress with stiff white petticoats. Auntie Lindo's daughter, Waverly, who was about my age, was standing farther down the wall about five feet away. We had grown up together and shared all the closeness of two sisters squabbling over crayons and dolls. In other words, for the most part, we hated each other. I thought she was snotty. Waverly Jong had gained a certain amount of fame as "Chinatown's Littlest Chinese Chess Champion."

"She bring home too many trophy," lamented Auntie Lindo that Sunday. "All day she play chess. All day I have no time do nothing but dust off her winnings." She threw a scolding look at Waverly, who pretended not to see her.

"You lucky you don't have this problem," said Auntie Lindo with a sigh to my mother.

And my mother squared her shoulders and bragged: "Our problem worser than yours. If we ask Jing-mei wash dish, she hear nothing but music. It's like you can't stop this natural talent."

And right then, I was determined to put a stop to her foolish pride.

A few weeks later, Old Chong and my mother conspired to have me play in a talent show which would be held in the church hall. By then, my parents had saved up enough to buy me a secondhand piano, a black Wurlitzer spinet with a scarred bench. It was the showpiece of our living room.

For the talent show, I was to play a piece called "Pleading Child" from the Schumann's *Scenes from Childhood*. It was a simple, moody piece that sounded more difficult than it was. I was supposed to memorize the whole thing, playing the repeat parts twice to make the piece sound longer. But I dawdled over it, playing a few bars and then cheating, looking up to see what notes followed, I never really listened to what I was playing. I daydreamed about being somewhere else, about being someone else.

The part I liked to practice best was the fancy curtsy: right foot out, touch the rose on the carpet with a pointed foot, sweep to the side, left leg bends, look up and smile.

My parents invited all the couples from the Joy Luck Club to witness my debut. Auntie Lindo and Uncle Tin were there. Waverly and her two older brothers had also come. The first two rows were filled with children both younger and older than I was. The littlest ones got to go first. They recited simple nursery rhythms, squawked out tunes on miniature violins, twirled Hula Hoops, pranced in pink ballet tutus, and when they bowed or curtsied, the audience would sigh in unison, "Awww," and then clap enthusiastically.

When my turn came, I was very confident. I remember my childish excitement. It was as if I knew, without a doubt, that the prodigy side of me really did exist. I had no fear whatsoever, no nervousness. I remember thinking to myself, This is it! This is it! I looked out over the audience, at my mother's blank face, my father's yawn, Auntie Lindo's stiff-lipped smile, Waverly's sulky expression. I had on a white dress layered with sheets of lace, and a pink bow in my Peter Pan haircut. As I sat down I envisioned people jumping to their feet and Ed Sullivan rushing up to introduce me to everyone on TV.

And I started to play. It was so beautiful. I was so caught up in how lovely I looked that at first I didn't worry how I would sound: So it was a surprise to me when I hit the first wrong note and I realized something didn't sound quite right. And then I hit another and another followed that. A chill started at the top of my head and began to trickle down. Yet I couldn't stop playing, as though my hands were bewitched. I kept thinking my fingers would adjust themselves back, like a train switching to the right track. I played this strange jumble through two repeats, the sour notes staying with me all the way to the end.

When I stood up, I discovered my legs were shaking. Maybe I had just been nervous and the audience, like Old Chong, had seen me go through the right motions and had not heard anything wrong at all. I swept my right foot out, went down on my knee, looked up and smiled. The room was quiet, except for Old Chong, who was beaming and shouting, "Bravo! Bravo! Well done!" But then I saw my mother's face, her stricken face. The audience clapped weakly, and as I walked back to my chair, with my whole face quivering as I tried not to cry, I heard a little boy whisper loudly to his mother, "That was awful," and the mother whispered back, "Well, she certainly tried."

And now I realized how many people were in the audience, the whole world it seemed. I was aware of eyes burning into my back. I felt the shame of my mother and father as they sat stiffly throughout the rest of the show.

We could have escaped during intermission. Pride and some strange sense of honor must have anchored my parents to their chairs. And so we watched it all: the eighteen-year-old boy with a fake mustache who did a magic show and juggled flaming hoops while riding a unicycle. The breasted girl with white makeup who sang from *Madama Butterfly* and got honorable mention. And the eleven-year-old boy who won first prize playing a tricky violin song that sounded like a busy bee.

After the show, the Hsus, the Jongs, and the St. Clairs from the Joy Luck Club came up to my mother and father.

"Lots of talented kids," Auntie Lindo said vaguely, smiling broadly.

"That was somethin' else," said my father, and I wondered if he was referring to me in a humorous way, or whether he even remembered what I had done. 60

Waverly looked at me and shrugged her shoulders. "You aren't a genius like me," she said matter-of-factly. And if I hadn't felt so bad, I would have pulled her braids and punched her stomach. 61

But my mother's expression was what devastated me: a quiet, blank look that said she had lost everything. I felt the same way, and it seemed as if everybody were now coming up, like gawkers at the scene of an accident, to see what parts were actually missing. When we got on the bus to go home, my father was humming the busy-bee tune and my mother was silent. I kept thinking she wanted to wait until we got home before shouting at me. But when my father unlocked the door to our apartment, my mother walked in then went to the back, into the bedroom. No accusations. No blame. And in a way, I felt disappointed. I had been waiting for her to start shouting, so I could shout back and cry and blame her for all my misery. 62

I assumed my talent-show fiasco meant I never had to play the piano again. But two days later, after school, my mother came out of the kitchen and saw me watching TV. 63

"Four clock," she reminded me as if it were any other day. I was stunned, as though she were asking me to go through the talent-show torture again. I wedged myself more tightly in front of the TV. 64

"Turn off TV," she called from the kitchen five minutes later. 65

I didn't budge. And then I decided. I didn't have to do what my mother said anymore. I wasn't her slave. This wasn't China. I had listened to her before and look what happened. She was the stupid one. 66

She came out from the kitchen and stood in the arched entryway of the living room. "Four clock," she said once again, louder. 67

"I'm not going to play anymore," I said nonchalantly. "Why should I? I'm not a genius." 68

She walked over and stood in front of the TV. I saw her chest was heaving up and down in an angry way. 69

"No!" I said, and I now felt stronger, as if my true self had finally emerged. So this was what had been inside me all along. 70

"No! I won't!" I screamed. 71

She yanked me by the arm, pulled me off the floor, snapped off the TV. She was frighteningly strong, half pulling, half carrying me toward the piano as I kicked the throw rugs under my feet. She lifted me up and onto the hard bench. I was sobbing by now, looking at her bitterly. Her chest was heaving even more and her mouth was open, smiling crazily as if she were pleased I was crying. 72

"You want me to be someone that I'm not!" I sobbed. "I'll never be the kind of daughter you want me to be!" 73

"Only two kinds of daughters," she shouted in Chinese. "Those who are obedient and those who follow their own mind! Only one kind of daughter can live in this house. Obedient daughter!" 74

"Then I wish I wasn't your daughter. I wish you weren't my mother," I ₇₅
shouted. As I said these things I got scared. I felt like worms and toads and
slimy things were crawling out of my chest, but it also felt good, as if this awful
side of me had surfaced, at last.

"Too late change this," said my mother shrilly. ₇₆

And I could sense her anger rising to its breaking point. I wanted to see it ₇₇
spill over. And that's when I remembered the babies she had lost in China, the
ones we never talked about. "Then I wish I'd never been born!" I shouted. "I
wish I were dead! Like them."

It was as if I had said the magic words. Alakazam!—and her face went ₇₈
blank, her mouth closed, her arms went slack, and she backed out of the room,
stunned, as if she were blowing away like a small brown leaf, thin, brittle, lifeless.

It was not the only disappointment my mother felt in me. In the years that ₇₉
followed, I failed her so many times, each time asserting my own will, my right
to fall short of expectations. I didn't get straight A's. I didn't become class president. I didn't get into Stanford. I dropped out of college.

For unlike my mother, I did not believe I could be anything I wanted to be. ₈₀
I could only be me.

Meaning and Idea

1. What is this selection about? What is the basic comparison that Tan draws?
   What other comparisons are in the piece?

2. What is a prodigy? Why does the narrator's mother want her to be a
   prodigy? How does the Chinese girl on "The Ed Sullivan Show" contribute
   to the levels of comparison here?

3. The mother explains what she sees as the two kinds of daughters. What is
   the child's response to her mother? Who is right, do you think?

4. Explain the meaning of the sentences, "For unlike my mother, I did not
   believe I could be anything I wanted to be. I could only be me." How are
   these two lines together both hopeful and hopeless? Do you agree with the
   sentiment expressed here? Or do you agree with the mother? Why?

Language, Form, Structure

1. How does the title of the selection help establish the rhetorical pattern of the
   piece? What do you think "two kinds" refers to—the daughter and some
   imagined perfect child, the daughter and the musical prodigy on "The Ed
   Sullivan Show," the daughter and the mother, all of these? Defend your answers.

2. Identify the various transition points in the selection where the time seems
   to shift. How does Tan achieve the necessary coherence? Where does she
   use narrative elements in this piece?

3. Tan uses a number of figures of speech here. Identify several that you find vivid. How do they help you visualize the scene? What other imagery does Tan use?

4. Define the following words and use each one in a sentence: prodigy; indignity; listlessly; bellows; embraceless; sauciness; cascaded; sonatas; arpeggios; reverie; petticoats; squabbling; spinet; moody; dawdled; stricken.

Ideas for Writing

1. Recount an event from your childhood or youth which you held in one perspective at the time but hold in a different perspective now. Write a comparison of the two attitudes and explain the changes.

2. What should be the appropriate role for a parent or another relative in requiring a child to learn something? Write an essay in which you argue your point with strong supporting detail.

3. Reread the Tan selection and look for and list as many elements of similarity and difference between the mother and daughter as possible. Now think about all the different pairs of people who are compared throughout the essay. How many "twos" are there? Write an essay in which you discuss the many possible meanings of Tan's title.

Like a King

Adam Gopnik

Adam Gopnik is best known as a contributor to *The New Yorker*. His "Paris Journal," the series from which "Like a King" is taken, was a fixture in *The New Yorker's* pages for several years. The series is at times funny and at times serious but always illuminating about both France and Gopnik's native America. Gopnik's interests tend toward both art and photography. He has contributed numerous introductions and edited several collections of criticism. His memoir *From Paris to the Moon,* also including this essay, appeared in 2000.

When we discovered that the child we were going to have in Paris last fall would be a girl—we already have a boy—everybody told us that we had been blessed with the "*choix du roi,*" the king's choice. "Why, it's the *choix du roi!*" the technician said as she looked at the sonogram, more or less in the tone of the host on "Jeopardy" announcing the daily double. "It's the *choix du roi!*" said the woman in the two-hour-photo place on the Rue du Bac when we told her. "A little girl coming after a little boy?" said my friend Pascal, the philosopher, with evident pleasure. "Why, then, it's the *choix du roi!*"

My wife, Martha, was delighted to be having a girl, however the king felt about it. She had always wanted a son and a daughter, and, as she only now explained to me, one of the reasons she had been so eager to leave New York four years earlier, just after the birth of our son, was that all her friends there who had two children had two boys, and she was starting to believe that two boys was just one of the things that happened to women in New York, "like high-intensity step classes and vanilla Edensoy," as she put it. Also, she said, she was worried about having to succumb to the New York social law that compels you nowadays to name your sons exclusively after the men your grandfather used to take a shvitz* with. In our New York circle of under-tens, we already had, in addition to the requisite Maxes, a Harry, a Joe, a Sam, an Otto, and a Charlie—the whole senior staff of Benny's Market: Lowest Prices in Town. "Even if I had had another boy, at least in Paris I wouldn't have had to call him Moe," she explained.

I was pleased by the news, too, of course, but a little mystified by the expression. To be brutally frank, what mystified me was why a king would choose to have any girls at all. If I were a king, I would want only boys, so that the succession would never be challenged by the sinister uncle with a mustache lurking behind my throne. Or only girls, and an immortality pill. What puzzled me even more was the way the phrase, though you heard it on Parisian lips, had a slightly disconcerting air of peasants-in-the-spring ecstasy about it—the kind of thing ("*C'est le choix du roi!*") you would expect to hear set to a Trenet tune and sung by the villagers in a Pagnol film when the baker's daughter gives birth to little Lisette.

*Yiddish for *steam bath.*

I soon sensed, though, that, while people meant it, they also didn't mean it—that it was a thing you said both as a joke and not as a joke. After four years in Paris, I have come to realize that this is where the true cultural differences reside: not in those famous moments when you think that a joke was meant straight ("My goodness, the *dessert grand-mère* is not made by grandmother!"), or you misunderstand something that was meant straight as a joke ("The *tête de veau* is actually the head of a calf!"), but in those moments when you are confronted with something that is meant both as a joke and seriously. This zone of kidding overlaid with not kidding is one that we know at home. When a New Yorker passes out cigars in the office after the birth of his child, for instance, he is both making a joke about passing out cigars—with unspoken but quickly grasped reference to all the episodes of "Bewitched" and "I Love Lucy" in which Darrin or Desi or some other fifties-ish father passed out cigars—and sincerely celebrating the birth of his child. (The proof of this doubleness is that the cigars he passes out will actually be good to smoke, while mockery would make do with a bad or unsmokable cigar. Nobody tried to eat Warhol's soups.)

In Paris, the obstetricians all wear black. When your wife goes to be examined, the doctor who comes out into the waiting room is not a smart Jewish girl in a lab coat, as in New York, but a man with a day's growth of beard, who is wearing black jeans and a black silk shirt, like a character in a David Mamet play about Hollywood producers.

I first became aware of this when we went to get the first of many sonograms of the new baby. The sonogramist we had been sent to performs in a nineteenth-century apartment in the Sixth Arrondissement, with wainscoting and ceiling moldings and windows that open like doors. A curtain was drawn across one half of the living room, and couples sat on two sofas in the other half, turning the pages of *Elle* (*Elle* is a weekly in France) and waiting to be called.

After about ten minutes, the curtain parted and the sonogram specialist came into the room. He had on black jeans and a black silk shirt, open at the front and plunging down toward his navel, sleeves rolled up to the elbows. A day-old growth of beard covered his face. He smiled at us, and asked us to come in. We sat down in front of a handsome Louis XV desk—the sonogram equipment was over in the other corner of the office—and he asked us when the baby had been conceived. My wife gave him the likely date.

"Was that at night or early the next day?" he asked. It took me a moment to realize that he was kidding, and then another moment to realize that he was not, and then still another moment—the crucial cultural-gap moment—to realize that he was neither kidding nor not kidding. That is to say, he was kidding—he knew that it didn't matter—but he was not kidding in the sense that he was genuinely interested, considered that it was part of his profession to view that precise moment of passion or lust with a special tenderness. The moment of conception, the sexual act, was, in his schema, not incidental information to be handled discreetly, or pushed aside altogether, as American obstetricians do—all American "What to Expect" books begin with the Test, not the Act—but the prime moment, the hallowed moment, the first happy domino that, falling, caused all the other dominoes that had brought the three of us together to fall, and (his eyes implied) it was our special shared knowledge that that domino had not in fact fallen but had been nudged, deliberately, and by us. Then he asked Martha to get undressed. There was, to my surprise, no changing room or even a curtain, so she did, like that. (I was the only embarrassed person in the room.) The elaborate hospital rigmarole of American hygiene and American obstetrics—the white coats, the dressing rooms, the lab gowns—is dispensed with. They make no sense, since a pregnant woman is not only not sick but in a sense has doubled the sum of her health.

We looked at the baby on the sonar screen, as though she were a character   9
in a Tom Clancy novel. "She's pretty," he said at last. Then we got a package of fifteen or so pictures of our daughter in embryo, full of allure, as the receptionist said. The pictures were stapled, in neat ruffled rows, into a little wallet, with sans-serif lowercase type, like an E. E. Cummings poem.

"In New York, the obstetricians all wear white and they all have books   10
out," Martha said to me one afternoon. She had called up an obstetrician in New York that day, before her appointment with her French doctor. "She covered me with congratulations, and then she told me all these tests I ought to take. Week ten the CVS, then in week fourteen an early amnio, and then in weeks eighteen to twenty a targeted ultrasound to test for neural-tube defects, and then I'm supposed to get genetic-carrier blood tests for all these other things."

"What did the French obstetrician say when you told her that?"   11

"She made that 'oh' face—you know, that lips-together, 'How naïve can   12
one be?' face—said that it was far too dangerous to do the CVS, and then she prescribed a lot of drugs for pain. I've got anti-spasmodics, anti-nausea drugs, pain-killers, and some other ones, too. Then she told me I could drink red wine and absolutely not to eat any raw vegetables. She keeps asking me if I've had any salad. She says 'salad' the way the doctors in New York say 'uninsured.' "

French doctors like to prescribe drugs as much as New York doctors like   13
to publish books. I suppose that it fulfills a similar need for self-expression with a pen, without having to go to the trouble of having your photograph taken with a professional yet humane grin. You cannot go into a French doctor's office for a cinder in your eye and emerge without a six-part prescription, made up of pills of different sizes to be taken at irregular intervals.

I wanted to meet Martha's doctor, who would be delivering the baby while   14
I "coached"—I am of the Phil Jackson school as a coach; you might not actually see me doing much, but I contribute a lot to the winning atmosphere—and so I accompanied her to the next appointment. We sat in the waiting room and read *Elle* some more. By now, Martha was nervous. An American friend who lives in Normandy had gone into labor a few days before, only to find that all the anesthesiologists had gone out on strike that morning. She had delivered the baby, her second, without any epidural.

"I want to go to a place where the anesthesiologists are scabs," Martha   15
said. "Or nuns, or something. I don't want to go to a place where the man with the epidural is on a picket line."

While we were in the waiting room, a man in black jeans and a black silk [16] shirt with the sleeves rolled up, and with a Pat Riley hair style, peeked in and mischievously summoned one of the women in the waiting room.

"Who's that?" I asked. [17]

"The other obstetrician," Martha said. [18]

"Does he always dress like that?" I demanded. [19]

"Oh, yes. He's very nice. He examined me last time." [20]

Martha's doctor was wearing black stretch slacks, a black tank top, and a [21] handsome gold necklace. She is very exacting about appearances. "You have gained too much weight," she said to Martha, who had in fact gained less than with her first pregnancy. "Start swimming, stop eating." (Martha says that a friend who went for an appointment two months after the birth of her second baby was told by the same doctor, "You look terrible. And do something about your hair.") We did another sonogram. "Look at her, she's pretty," the doctor said as we looked at the sonogram. "There's her *fille,*" she said, pointing to the sex. Then she again counselled Martha to swim more, and gave her a prescription for sleeping pills. We talked a bit about the approach of those hard, exhausting first weeks with a newborn. "Get a night nurse," she advised, "Go out with your husband. Be happy again."

In New York, in other words, pregnancy is a medical condition that, after [22] proper care by people in white coats and a brief hospital stay, can have a "positive outcome." In Paris, it is something that has happened because of sex, which, with help and counsel, can end with your being set free to go out and have more sex. In New York, pregnancy is a ward in the House of Medicine; in Paris, it is a chapter in a sentimental education—a strange consequence of the pleasures of the body.

In America, we have managed to sexualize everything—cars, refrigera- [23] tors, computers, Congress—except the natural consequences of sex. Though it is de rigueur for every pregnant supermodel to have her picture taken when she is full-bellied, it is always the same picture. She covers her breasts, she is swaddled below in some way, and she looks off into the middle distance, not dreamily, as she might when wearing lingerie, but slightly anxiously, as though she could not remember if she had left her husband's electric guitar turned on. The subject, the hidden subject, is not the apotheosis of sexuality but its transcendence into maternal instinct—babe into mother by way of baby.

In France, though, a pregnant woman is alive, since she has demonstrated [24] both her availability and her fecundity: We Have a Winner. Though Lamaze-method childbirth began here, it remains cultish and sectarian. Most women nurse for three months, no more. (It shrinks your breasts, and gives you an uncomfortable accessory.) And, when the anesthesiologists are not striking, they are, as our babysitter says, fully busy. (Two French friends of ours talk about natural childbirth: "What is the English for *accouchement sans douleur?*" one asks. "A lie," the other answers.)

The prohibition on uncooked vegetables, by the way, turns out to have a [25] solid scientific basis. Toxoplasmosis—a mild parasitic infection that is devastating to unborn children—though it's rare in America (it's that thing you can get from cat litter), is common in France. Red wine is recommended, in turn, because it is high in iron and acts as an effective anti-spasmodic.

By law, a French woman who is going to have a baby is guaranteed—not merely allowed but pretty much compelled—to stay four or five nights in a clinic or a hospital. In New York, when our son, Luke, was born—in the Klingenstein Pavilion of Mount Sinai Hospital—we had two days to have the baby, bond, and get out. French law is specific and protective about the rights of pregnant women. If you are a salaried employee, you get six weeks of prenatal leave and ten weeks of paid leave after the baby is born. For a third child, you get eight weeks off and eighteen more, and if you have three at once you get, in all, forty-six weeks of paid leave. (The leave is paid, through a complicated formula, by your employer and the state.) The law is as finely tuned as a viola d'amore. There is even a beautiful added *remarque,* right there on the government document: "*Les artistes du specta-cle, les mannequins des maisons de couture,*" and others who do work that is plainly incompatible with the state of pregnancy (i.e., a bigger belly) are assured of paid leave after the twenty-first week. In France, Cindy and Paulina and the rest would not just be having their pictures taken. They would already be on the dole. 26

The system, Martha's doctor observed once during a visit, is "royal for the users, good for the doctors, and expensive for the society." There are many rational arguments to be made about whether or not the outcomes justify the expenditures, and, in any case, the level of care that the French have insisted on may be unsustainable. But the people who are being treated "royally" are ordinary people—everybody. For many, perhaps most, French people, life at the end of the century in the American imperium may look a bit like a typical transatlantic flight, with the airless, roomless, comfortless coach packed as tight as possible, so that the maximum dollars can be squeezed out of every seat, with a few rich people up front. I am American enough to understand that this is, so to speak, one of the prices of mass travel—that there is no such thing as a free lunch, or clinic—and yet have become French enough to feel, stubbornly, that legroom and a little air should not be luxuries for the rich, and that in a prosperous society all pregnant women should have three sonograms and four nights in a hospital, if they want to. It doesn't seem particularly royal to have four nights in a clinic when you have a baby, or aristocratically spoiled to think that a woman should keep her job and have some paid leave afterward—even sixteen weeks, if she happens to be a mannequin in an haute-couture house. All human desires short of simple survival are luxurious, and a mother's desire to have a slightly queenly experience of childbirth—a lying in rather than a pushing out and a going home—seems as well worth paying for as a tobacco subsidy or another tank. 27

In preparation for our own four-night stay, we had first to search for the right clinic. Friends recommended two: the Clinique Sainte-Isabelle, in the leafy suburb of Neuilly, and the Clinique Belvedere, in Boulogne-Billancourt. We went to tour them. Both clinics had a pastoral, flower-bed, medical but not quite 28 hospital feel, like the sanitarium where they pack off Nicole in "Tender Is the Night." I liked the Belvedere best. The rooms there had a nice faded-white and pale-blue look, like the room in "Madeline" where she goes to have her appendix taken out and sees the crack in the ceiling that had a habit of sometimes looking like a rabbit. The cracks in the ceiling at the Belvedere were expressive, too, and, for a premium, you could have a room with French doors leading out onto the garden. (The ordinary rooms were less grand, though they mostly had garden views, too.) But what I really liked about the place was the clippings in the formal salon—the waiting room—downstairs, which was filled with dusty silk roses and blue-and-gold Louis XVI furniture. The clippings chronicled the birth of minor nobility in the halls of the Belvedere. A Bonapartist pretender had been born there, I remember, and also I think a Prince of Yugoslavia. I liked the kingly company, particularly since it was such cheesy kingly company.

Martha, though, as we toured the clinics, kept asking gentle, pointed questions about labor relations with the anesthesiologists. Now, the anesthesiologists here—were they unionized? Did they have enough vacation time? Would the clinic manager say that they were happy with their working conditions? How long had it been since they signed a contract? Were there any, well, radicals among them—the kind of ex-Trotskyite *soixante-huitards* who might suddenly call for mass action by the workers? Eventually, we settled on the Clinique Sainte-Isabelle, which seemed to be the sensible, primly bourgeois choice of all our friends, and which had a couple of full-time anesthesiologists on call, neither of whom looked like a sansculotte.   29

Everything was going along fine, in fact, until our meeting with the *sage-femme,* the "wise woman," or, in American, the midwife. She was in yet another of the suburban clinics, an odd Jacques Tati modern place. This meeting was brisk, and it concentrated on two essential points: breathing and lying. The breathing bit we had heard about before—you are supposed to breathe from the diaphragm—but she emphasized that it was just as important, for a happy birth, to remember never to tell a taxi-driver that you are in labor. Whatever you do, she said, don't say that you're in labor, or might be in labor, because no taxi-driver in Paris will take a pregnant woman to her clinic, for fear of her having the baby in his car. (You can't call an ambulance, because an ambulance won't go over the city line, and our clinic was out in Neuilly.)   30

Then how were we going to get to the clinic? Martha asked. (We don't have a car.) It's no problem, I interrupted, we'll simply walk over to the taxi stand. (You can't call a taxi, because there is a stand right across the street from our apartment.)   31

"I won't be able to stroll across the street and stand in line if I'm in labor," she objected. "I'll wait in the courtyard. Just get him to do the *demi-tour.*"   32

At these words, my heart was stricken. *Demi-tour* means, literally, a U-turn, but in Paris it is also a half-metaphysical possibility that exists on the Boulevard Saint-Germain just across the street from our apartment building. The boulevard itself runs one-way, from east to west. There is, however, a narrow lane carved out on it, for buses and taxis, that runs the other way, toward the   33

Place de la Concorde and the Quai d'Orsay and, eventually, if you turn right over a bridge, toward Neuilly and the clinic, too. Leading off this lane, at a single light about a hundred feet from our building, there is a small, discreet curved arrow marked on the asphalt. This arrow means that a taxicab—and only a taxicab—can make a U-turn there and go the other way, with the rest of the traffic. In principle, I could get a cab going against the traffic, have him do the *demi-tour,* pick up my pregnant wife, and then go back against the traffic. The trouble is that, though I have sometimes succeeded in persuading taxi-drivers, when we arrive from the airport, to make the *demi-tour,* I have just as often failed. "It's impossible," they will tell you, when you ask them to do it. "No, there is an arrow printed on the pavement that advertises the possibility of this maneuver," I will say. (When I'm under stress, my French becomes very abstract.)

"I've been driving a taxi for twenty years, and it doesn't exist," the cabbie   34
will say. Then you either give up or get hot under the collar, and neither approach helps.

If I asked a Paris cabdriver to attempt the *demi-tour* at, say, five in the   35
morning, to pick up a very pregnant-looking woman, he would know that the only reason was that she was in labor, and to the insult of being instructed would come the injury of being asked to ruin his cab.

For the next few weeks, I became obsessed by the logic and strategies of   36
the *demi-tour.* What if I couldn't pull it off? The only thing to do was to rehearse, just as we had done in New York in the Lamaze class. So I began walking over to the taxi station at all hours of the day and night, getting in a cab, asking the driver to make the *demi-tour,* and then going, well, someplace or other. Then I walked home. Sometimes the driver made the *demi-tour,* and sometimes he didn't. I was determined to keep practicing, until it felt as natural as breathing.

We still hadn't got to the bottom of the whole *choix du roi* thing. Martha   37
had decided to give in to the obstetrician's insistence that she start swimming, and one day, with Luke, we got into a cab to go to the pool. The taxi-driver was wearing a short-sleeved shirt, and had gray hair and a lot of metal teeth. Suddenly, he chuckled and said, of Luke, "Why, he speaks so well. Tell me, is it a little sister or a brother?" A sister, we said, and I grimaced and tightened inside as I prepared myself for the response, which, of course, came on cue.

"Ah," he said, slapping the steering wheel. "*C'est le choix du roi!*"   38

I was so fed up that I said, Please explain it to me. It was an ironic, rhetori-   39
cal question. But he didn't miss a beat.

"I will be happy to explain it," he said, and he actually pulled over to the   40
curb, near the Crillon hotel, so that he could speak in peace. "In Latin countries, we have what we call Salic law—which means that only your son can inherit the throne. You Anglo-Saxons, you don't follow Salic law." I let the Anglo-Saxon thing go by. "For your Anglo-Saxon royal families, it doesn't matter if the king has a *nana* or a *mec.*" A *nana* is a doll and a *mec* is a guy. "But, you see, a French king, under Salic law, had to consolidate his hold on the throne by having a boy. And he had to have a girl, so that she could be offered in marriage to another king, and in this way the royal possessions would be expanded, since the

daughter's son would be a king, too. He," he said gesturing toward Luke in the back seat, "is your strong piece to be kept in reserve, while she"—he gestured toward Martha's belly—"is your pawn to build your empire. That's why it's the king's choice: first a boy to hold the throne, then a girl to get another. *Tendresse* has nothing to do with it. That's why it is the *choix du roi.*"

"It is very odd," he went on expansively, "because in the Hundred Years' War, the King of England, as Duc de Guyenne, a title he had inherited from his grandfather, was subject to Salic law, too. The story of how this worked itself out in the making of the two monarchies is a passionately interesting piece of history. I recommend the series 'Les Rois Maudits' "—the damned or cursed kings—"which is a fascinating study of this history, particularly of the acts of John the Good and what he did as an act of policy to accommodate the Salic principle. The books are by Maurice Druon, of the Academie Française, and I heartily recommend them. Passionately interesting."

We sat in stunned silence.

"Ask him does he do *demi-tours,*" said Martha.

"You're wearing stripes?" she asked. I had put on a striped shirt a few minutes before, in the excitement, but I quickly changed it. I put on a suit and tie, in fact—a nice *marron* cotton number—thinking that, though my New York child had been born with me watching in jeans and a collarless shirt, my French kid ought to see a dad who had a touch more finish.

The drama had begun a few hours earlier, in the middle of the night, and now it was five o'clock and we were on our way to the clinic. At five-thirty, with a babysitter for Luke and a suitcase in hand, we were out on the boulevard. I walked to the curb, held my breath, saw that there were cabs at the taxi stand, and, head down, told Martha to wait where she was while I started across the street, preparing to ask a taxi-driver to make the *demi-tour,* my moment come at last.

Far down the boulevard, a single cab with a firelight light appeared. Martha stepped out into the street, just as though it were five-thirty in the evening on Sixth Avenue, got her right hand up in that weird New York–Nazi taxi salute, and cried, "Taxi!" The guy came skidding to a stop. She got in, and I followed.

"Twenty-four Boulevard du Château in Neuilly," I commanded, my voice pitched a little too high (as it also tends to get in French). "Just cross the street and make the *demi-tour,*" I added, fairly casually, and docilely, at five-thirty in the morning, as he swung the cab over to the taxi lane, on other side of the street, and did a full U-turn. He flew along the boulevard. I took the hand of my Queen.

"You've got him going the wrong way," she whispered.

He was, too. I waited a few blocks, and then told him that I had made a mistake, could he turn around and go the other way. He shrugged, and did.

When we got to the clinic, it was shut tight, no lights on at all. The advantages of a big hospital up on Madison Avenue became a little clearer. No one was answering the door, a thing I doubt happens much at Mount Sinai. We banged and cried out, "*Allô!* Is anybody there?" Finally, an incredibly weary-looking *sage-femme*— not our own—wearing sweater and slippers, sighed, let us in, hooked Martha up to an I.V., and asked to see our papers. She shuffled through them.

"Where is your blood test for the dossier?" she asked at last.   51

"The doctor has it," I said. "She'll be here soon."   52

"That the doctor has it is of no consequence," the nurse said. "If your wife   53
wishes to have an epidural, she must have that paper."

"It's all the way back home," I protested, but, of course, nothing doing. It   54
looked as though Martha's epidural, having escaped French syndicalism, were
about to be done in by French bureaucracy. Having lived in France long enough
to know there was no choice, I found another taxi, rushed all the way home, ran
upstairs, tore open the filing cabinet, found the paper, and then took a taxi back,
setting some kind of land-speed record for trips from central Paris to Neuilly.
The *sage-femme* slipped the paper into the dossier, yawned, put the dossier
down on a radiator, and nobody ever looked at it or referred to it again.

The labor got complicated, for various reasons—basically, the baby at the   55
last moment decided to turn sideways—and Martha's doctor, acting with the quiet
sureness that is the other side of Parisian insouciance, did an emergency cesarean.
It turned out that behind a small, quaint-looking white door down in the basement
there was a *bloc*—a warren of blindingly white-lit, state-of-the-art operating and
recovery rooms. They hadn't shown it to us when we toured the clinic, of course.
It seemed very French, the nuclear power plant hidden in the *bocage*.

The baby came out mad, yelling at the top of her lungs. In New York, the   56
nurses had snatched the baby and taken him off to be washed behind a big glass
nursery window, and then had dressed him in prison garb, the same white night-
shirt and cap that the hundred other babies in the nursery had on. (The next day,
there was also an elaborate maximum-security procedure of reading off the
bracelet numbers of mother and child whenever either one wanted to nurse.)
Here, after the *sage-femme* and I gave her a bath, and the *sage-femme* taped her
umbilical remnant, the *sage-femme* turned to me.

"Where are her clothes?" she asked. I said I didn't know, upstairs in the   57
suitcase, I guessed, and she said you better get them, so I ran up, and came back
down to the *bloc* with the white onesie and a lovely white-and-pink-trimmed
baby-style cat suit, which her mother had bought at Bonpoint a few days before.
All by myself, I carefully dressed the five-minute-old squalling newborn, and
took her back to her mother, in the recovery room. A day later, I would walk the
six blocks to the Mairie, the City Hall, of Neuilly-sur-Seine, and register her
birth. The New York birth certificate had been a fill-in-the-blanks, choose-one-
box business, which we had filled in on our way out of the hospital. The French
birth certificate was like the first paragraph of a nineteenth-century novel, with
the baby's parents' names, their occupations, the years of their birth and of their
emigration, their residence, and her number, baby number 2365 born in Neuilly
in 1999. (It's got a big hospital, too.) After that, of course, would come the
weeks of exhaustion and 3 A.M. feedings, which are remarkably alike from place
to place.

But just then, looking at the sleeping mom and the tiny newborn in her   58
arms, I had a genuine moment of what I can only call revelation, religious vision. When people talk about what it is to have a baby, they usually talk about

starting over, a clean slate, endless possibility, a new beginning, but I saw that that is not it at all. A birth is not a rebirth. It's a weighty event. In a telescopic universe, we choose to see microscopically, and the blessing is that what we see is not an illusion but what is really there: a singularity in the cosmos, another baby born in a Paris suburb. The world is a meaningless place, and we are weird, replicating mammals on its surface, and yet the whole purpose of the universe since it began was, in a way, to produce this baby, who is the tiny end point of a funnel that goes back to the beginning of time—a singularity that history was pointing toward from the start. That history didn't know it was pointing toward Olivia—and, of course, toward Salome over in the other corner of the nursery and little François just arrived, not to mention Max and Otto and possibly even Moe, just now checking in at Mount Sinai—doesn't change the fact that it was. We didn't know we were pointing to her, either, until she got here. The universe doesn't need a purpose, if life goes on. You sink back and hear the nurse cooing in French to the mother and child (*"Ah, calme-toi, ma biche, ma biche,"* she says. "Be calm, my doe, my doe," but which one is she talking to?) and feel as completely useless as any other male animal after a birth and, at the same time, somehow serenely powerful, beyond care or criticism, since you have taken part in the only really majestic choice we get to make in life, which is to continue it.

Meaning and Idea

1. What is this selection about? What is Gopnik's basic comparison? What other comparisons arise?

2. What does the phrase "*choix du roi*" literally mean in English? What does it mean to the French?

3. "In America," Gopnik writes, "we have managed to sexualize everything—cars, refrigerators, computers, Congress—except the natural consequences of sex." Explain what Gopnik means by these words.

4. At the end of the essay Gopnik describes having a "revelation," or "religious vision." What is the substance of that vision? Why do you think he chooses a religious vocabulary to describe it?

Language, Form, Structure

1. Analyze a single passage in which Gopnik compares the French and American approaches to a process or an event. What language does he use to make the comparison vivid? What metaphors or similes does he choose? What do those figures of speech add to the comparison?

2. Gopnik frequently refers to his wife's reactions as well as to his own. How are her reactions different from his? How do her reactions add to the essay's effectiveness?

3. Gopnik often continues to use the French term for something even after he has supplied an English equivalent. In addition to *choix du roi,* for example, he uses *sage-femme* instead of midwife and *demi-tour* instead of U-turn. How does this translation/nontranslation add to his comparison of the French and American cultures?

4. How does Gopnik's perception of the French change over the course of the essay? List the principal events or discoveries that deepen his understanding of the French. How does Gopnik's changing appreciation for the French change his understanding of American culture?

Ideas for Writing

1. Write an essay in which you describe an encounter with a process, setting, or culture that is completely alien to you. How did you begin to understand and negotiate the differences? What did this encounter teach you about yourself or the world with which you are familiar?

2. Given Gopnik's description, which culture's treatment of pregnancy and childbirth do you think is closer to the ideal? Write an essay giving specific reasons why you would prefer one to the other, drawing on Gopnik's essay and perhaps also your own research or experience.

3. Write an essay in which you consider the humor in this piece. Who are the objects of Gopnik's humor? How does Gopnik use humor to make his comparison more telling and memorable for the reader?

The Ruined Maid

Thomas Hardy

Thomas Hardy (1840–1928) was born in Dorset, Wessex, England, and received a liberal education with a special concentration in Latin and Greek. His father having been a master mason, Hardy chose architecture as his intended profession and moved to London in 1862 to apprentice. He practiced as an architect until 1874, when his first critically acclaimed novel, *Far from the Madding Crowd,* appeared. His four best and most widely read novels followed closely: *The Return of the Native* (1878), *The Mayor of Casterbridge* (1886), *Tess of the D'Urbervilles* (1891), and *Jude the Obscure* (1896). Unfortunately, the strongly passionate *Jude* shocked Victorian critical circles, and Hardy's response was to abandon writing novels in favor of composing poetry. He is buried in "Poets' Corner" in Westminster Abbey in London.

In "The Ruined Maid" Hardy uses dialogue to express two views of what, because of moral considerations, is an ambiguous condition. As you finish this poem, consider whether the two speakers' opinions are ultimately more the same or more different.

"*O*'Melia, my dear, this does everything crown!
Who could have supposed I should meet you in Town?
And whence such fair garments, such prosperi-ty"—
"Oh didn't you know I'd been ruined?" said she.

—"You left us in tatters, without shoes or socks,   5
Tired of digging potatoes, and spudding up docks;
And now you've gay bracelets and bright feathers three!"—
"Yes: that's how we dress when we're ruined," said she.

—"At home in the barton you said 'thee' and 'thou,'
And 'thik oon,' and 'theäs oon,' and 't'other'; but now   10
Your talking quite fits 'ee for high compa-ny!"—
"Some polish is gained with one's ruin," said she.

—"Your hands were like paws then, your face blue and bleak
But now I'm bewitched by your delicate cheek,
And your little gloves fit as on any la-dy!"—   15
"We never do work when we're ruined," said she.

—"You used to call home-life a hag-ridden dream,
And you'd sigh, and you'd sock; but at present you seem
To know not of megrims or melancho-ly!"—
"True. One's pretty lively when ruined," said she.   20

—"I wish I had feathers, a fine sweeping gown,
And a delicate face, and could strut about Town!"—
"My dear—a raw country girl, such as you be,
Cannot quite expect that. You ain't ruined," said she.

Meaning and Idea

1. What is the setting for this conversation? Who are the two speakers? What is their relation?

2. What is the first speaker's attitude toward 'Melia! What is 'Melia's attitude toward the speaker? Where and how do we learn of these attitudes?

3. Why does 'Melia call herself "ruined"? How is the term ironic? How do her old and new lives compare? What is Hardy's attitude toward her "ruination"? What is his attitude toward the first speaker?

Language, Form, Structure

1. How is comparison an appropriate format for the theme of this poem? Why is dialogue an effective means to support the comparison? What main point does the poem make?

2. What words suggest 'Melia's newfound sophistication? What words suggest that this sophistication is only a veneer?

3. See if you can find meanings for the following words. Use a collegiate-sized dictionary, since several have archaic, specialized, or dialectical meanings: crown; spudding up docks; barton; sock; megrims.

Ideas for Writing

1. Write a short essay in which you discuss the friend you've known longest in terms of how he or she has changed since five (more or less) years ago. You should include two specific bases of comparison.

2. Write an essay in which you explain each of the views expressed by the speakers in the poem. Be sure to keep a consistent point of view throughout.

3. In this poem, Hardy expresses a comparison in dialogue. Do you feel that dialogue adequately supports the theme here? Making allowances for the fact that the poem was written almost a hundred years ago, how realistic do you find the dialogue? Write an essay that addresses these questions.

Digging

Seamus Heaney

Seamus Heaney was born in 1939 in County Derry and attended Queen's University in Belfast. He has taught extensively in Ireland and the United States and currently works at Harvard, where he spends half his time. The rest of the year he is in Belfast. He is both critically acclaimed and well known by the public at large, quite a feat considering his subject matter and political interests.

His fluid yet muscular style smoothly elaborates the topic at hand without covering it in sticky, overwrought language. Critic Richard Ellman has said that Heaney "does not overwhelm his subjects; rather he allows them a certain freedom from him, and his sharp conjunctions with them leave their authority and his undiminished."

*B*etween my finger and my thumb
The squat pen rests; snug as a gun.

Under my window, a clean rasping sound
When the spade sinks into gravelly ground.
My father, digging. I look down   5

Till his straining rump among the flowerbeds
Bends low, comes up twenty years away
Stooping in rhythm through potato drills
Where he was digging.

The coarse boot nestled on the lug, the shaft   10
Against the inside knee was levered firmly.
He rooted out tall tops, buried the bright edge deep
To scatter new potatoes that we picked
Loving their cool hardness in our hands.

By God, the old man could handle a spade.   15
Just like his old man.

My grandfather cut more turf in a day
Than any other man on Toner's bog.
Once I carried him milk in a bottle
Corked sloppily with paper. He straightened up   20
To drink it, then fell to right away

Nicking and slicing neatly, heaving sods
Over his shoulder, going down and down
For the good turf. Digging.

The cold smell of potato mould, the squelch and slap   25
Of soggy peat, the curt cuts of an edge
Through living roots awaken in my head.
But I've no spade to follow men like them.

Between my finger and my thumb
The squat pen rests.   30
I'll dig with it.

Meaning and Idea

1. How many generations does the poem present? Why does the speaker bring in both his grandfather and his father? What does the poet achieve here?

2. What is actually being compared in the poem other than the three men and what they do? How does the comparison both delight and instruct the reader? In what ways can a pen and a shovel be thought of as related tools? Avoiding the obvious, how are they both similar and different? How is a writer like a digger?

3. Why does the speaker admire his father and his grandfather so much? Why does he not follow in their footsteps? What is the meaning of the line "But I've no spade to follow men like them"?

Language, Form, Structure

1. The poet jumps back and forth in time in this short poem. How does he move the reader smoothly from one time frame to another? How do transitions help him achieve the movement? What does narrative structure contribute to the poem?

2. Heaney uses a staccato style of short, direct sentences throughout. How does this stylistic approach help convey the poem's meaning? In what ways does the style duplicate the actual act of digging in the ground?

3. Why does Heaney avoid describing in detail the work of a poet? Although writing poetry may not seem a physical, strenuous act, how does the poet manage to convey its physicality and its validity? Remember that in fact, the only way we get to see the generations of men here is through the poem itself!

4. What does the simile in the second line, "snug as a gun," contribute to the poem? Why has the poet used such an image—he never again takes up the

comparison and what it implies. How is a pen like a gun? And why does the poet twice use the word *squat* to describe the pen?

5. What would you say is the main point of the poem? Write a single sentence to state it.

6. Define the following words and use each one in a sentence: squat; lug; bog; sods; squelch; peat; curt.

Ideas for Writing

1. Write a paper in which you compare and contrast the work of a member of your family with your own kind of work.

2. Write an essay in which you compare writing to another physical act. Search for similarities and differences beyond the apparent.

3. Write an essay that evaluates Heaney's use of comparisons and use of sensory language. Which images do you find most original? most shocking?

Two Diseases

Susan Sontag

Susan Sontag, born in New York City in 1933, is known for her astute writings about contemporary culture. She has continually surprised readers and critics alike with her range of subject and interpretation, which defy any one "label." Her work has taken the form of fiction, essays, and films. Sontag's fiction includes the novels *The Benefactor, Death Kit,* and, most recently, *Volcano Lover,* as well as the short-story collection *I, etcetera.* Her essay collections include *Against Interpretation* (1966), *About Photography* (1977), *Illness as Metaphor* (1978), and *Under the Sign of Saturn* (1980).

In "Two Diseases" (taken from Chapters 1 and 2 of *Illness as Metaphor*) Sontag uses comparison and contrast techniques to challenge the "trappings of metaphor" which have surrounded two of the worst killers of this era and past centuries—cancer and tuberculosis. Pay close attention to the ways in which Sontag uses historical development, allusions, and exemplification.

Two diseases have been spectacularly, and similarly, encumbered   1
by the trappings of metaphor: tuberculosis and cancer.

The fantasies inspired by TB in the last century, by cancer now, are re-   2
sponses to a disease thought to be intractable and capricious—that is, a disease
not understood—in an era in which medicine's central premise is that all diseases can be cured. Such a disease is, by definition, mysterious. For as long as
its cause was not understood and the ministrations of doctors remained so ineffective, TB was thought to be an insidious, implacable theft of a life. Now it is
cancer's turn to be the disease that doesn't knock before it enters, cancer that
fills the role of an illness experienced as a ruthless, secret invasion—a role it
will keep until, one day, its etiology becomes as clear and its treatment as effective as those of TB have become.

Although the way in which disease mystifies is set against a backdrop of   3
new expectations, the disease itself (once TB, cancer today) arouses thoroughly
old-fashioned kinds of dread. Any disease that is treated as a mystery and
acutely enough feared will be felt to be morally, if not literally, contagious.
Thus, a surprisingly large number of people with cancer find themselves being
shunned by relatives and friends and are the object of practices of decontamina-
tion by members of their household, as if cancer, like TB, were an infectious
disease. Contact with someone afflicted with a disease regarded as a mysterious
malevolency inevitably feels like a trespass; worse, like the violation of a taboo.
The very names of such diseases are felt to have a magic power. In Stendhal's
Armance (1827), the hero's mother refuses to say "tuberculosis," for fear that
pronouncing the word will hasten the course of her son's malady. And Karl
Menninger has observed (in *The Vital Balance*) that "the very word 'cancer' is

said to kill some patients who would not have succumbed (so quickly) to the malignancy from which they suffer." This observation is offered in support of anti-intellectual pieties and a facile compassion all too triumphant in contemporary medicine and psychiatry. "Patients who consult us because of their suffering and their distress and their disability," he continues, "have every right to resent being plastered with a damning index tab." Dr. Menninger recommends that physicians generally abandon "names" and "labels" ("our function is to help these people, not to further afflict them")—which would mean, in effect, increasing secretiveness and medical paternalism. It is not naming as such that is pejorative or damning, but the name "cancer." As long as a particular disease is treated as an evil, invincible predator, not just a disease, most people with cancer will indeed be demoralized by learning what disease they have. The solution is hardly to stop telling cancer patients the truth, but to rectify the conception of the disease, to demythicize it.

When, not so many decades ago, learning that one had TB was tantamount   4
to hearing a sentence of death—as today, in the popular imagination, cancer equals death—it was common to conceal the identity of their disease from tubercular and, after they died, from their children. Even with patients informed about their disease, doctors and family were reluctant to talk freely. "Verbally I don't learn anything definite," Kafka wrote to a friend in April 1924 from the sanatorium where he died two months later, "since in discussing tuberculosis . . . everybody drops into a shy, evasive, glassy-eyed manner of speech." Conventions of concealment with cancer are even more strenuous. In France and Italy it is still the rule for doctors to communicate a cancer diagnosis to the patient's family but not to the patient; doctors consider that the truth will be intolerable to all but exceptionally mature and intelligent patients. (A leading French oncologist has told me that fewer than a tenth of his patients know they have cancer.) In America—in part because of the doctors' fear of malpractice suits—there is now much more candor with patients, but the country's largest cancer hospital mails routine communications and bills to outpatients in envelopes that do not reveal the sender, on the assumption that the illness may be a secret from their families. Since getting cancer can be a scandal that jeopardizes one's love life, one's chance of promotion, even one's job, patients who know what they have tend to be extremely prudish, if not outright secretive, about their disease. And a federal law, the 1966 Freedom of Information Act, cites "treatment for cancer" in a clause exempting from disclosure matters whose disclosure "would be an unwarranted invasion of personal privacy." It is the only disease mentioned.

All this lying to and by cancer patients is a measure of how much harder it   5
has become in advanced industrial societies to come to terms with death. As death is now an offensively meaningless event, so that disease widely considered a synonym for death is experienced as something to hide. The policy of equivocating about the nature of their disease with cancer patients reflects the conviction that dying people are best spared the news that they are dying, and that the good death is the sudden one, best of all if it happens while we're

unconscious or asleep. Yet the modern denial of death does not explain the extent of the lying and the wish to be lied to; it does not touch the deepest dread. Someone who has had a coronary is at least as likely to die of another one within a few years as someone with cancer is likely to die soon from cancer. But no one thinks of concealing the truth from a cardiac patient: there is nothing shameful about a heart attack. Cancer patients are lied to, not just because the disease is (or is thought to be) a death sentence, but because it is felt to be obscene—in the original meaning of that word: ill-omened, abominable, repugnant to the senses. Cardiac disease implies a weakness, trouble, failure that is mechanical; there is no disgrace, nothing of the taboo that once surrounded people afflicted with TB and still surrounds those who have cancer. The metaphors attached to TB and to cancer imply living processes of a particularly resonant and horrid kind.

Throughout most of their history, the metaphoric uses of TB and cancer crisscross and overlap. The *Oxford English Dictionary* records "consumption" in use as a synonym for pulmonary tuberculosis as early as 1398. (John of Trevisa: "Whan the blode is made thynne, soo folowyth consumpcyon and wastying.") But the pre-modern understanding of cancer also invokes the notion of consumption. The OED gives as the early figurative definition of cancer: "Anything that frets, corrodes, corrupts, or consumes slowly and secretly." (Thomas Paynell in 1528: "A canker is a melancolye impostume eatynge partes of the bodye.") The earliest literal definition of cancer is a growth, lump, or protuberance, and the disease's name—from the Greek *karkinos* and the Latin *cancer,* both meaning crab—was inspired, according to Galen, by the resemblance of an external tumor's swollen veins to a crab's legs, not, as many people think, because a metastatic disease crawls or creeps like a crab. But etymology indicates that tuberculosis was also once considered a type of abnormal extrusion: the word tuberculosis—from the Latin *tuberculum,* the diminutive of *tuber,* bump, swelling—means a morbid swelling, protuberance, projection, or growth. Rudolf Virchow, who founded the science of cellular pathology in the 1850s, thought of the tubercle as a tumor.

Thus, from late antiquity until quite recently, tuberculosis was—typologically—cancer. And cancer was described, like TB, as a process in which the body was consumed. The modern conceptions of the two diseases could not be set until the advent of cellular pathology. Only with the microscope was it possible to grasp the distinctiveness of cancer, as a type of cellular activity, and to understand that the disease did not always take the form of an external or even palpable tumor. (Before the mid-nineteenth century, nobody could have identified leukemia as a form of cancer.) And it was not possible definitively to separate cancer from TB until after 1882, when tuberculosis was discovered to be a bacterial infection. Such advances in medical thinking enabled the leading metaphors of the two diseases to become truly distinct and, for the most part, contrasting. The modern fantasy about the cancer could then begin to take shape—a fantasy which from the 1920s on would inherit most of the problems dramatized by the fantasies about TB, but with the two diseases and their symptoms conceived in quite different, almost opposing, ways.

TB is understood as a disease of one organ, the lungs, while cancer is un-   8
derstood as a disease that can turn up in any organ and whose outreach is the
whole body.

TB is understood as a disease of extreme contrasts: white pallor and red   9
flush, hyperactivity alternating with languidness. The spasmodic course of the
disease is illustrated by what is thought of as the prototypical TB symptom,
coughing. The sufferer is wracked by coughs, then sinks back, recovers breath,
breathes normally; then coughs again. Cancer is a disease of growth (sometimes
visible; more characteristically, inside), of abnormal, ultimately lethal growth
that is measured, incessant, steady. Although there may be periods in which
tumor growth is arrested (remissions), cancer produces no contrasts like the oxy-
morons of behavior—febrile activity, passionate resignation—thought to be typical of TB. The tubercular is pallid some of the time; the pallor of the cancer patient is unchanging.

TB makes the body transparent. The X-rays, which are the standard diag-   10
nostic tool, permit one, often for the first time, to see one's insides—to become
transparent to oneself. While TB is understood to be, from early on, rich in visible symptoms (progressive emaciation, coughing, languidness, fever), and can
be suddenly and dramatically revealed (the blood on the handkerchief), in cancer
the main symptoms are thought to be, characteristically, invisible—until the last
stage, when it is too late. The disease, often discovered by chance or through a
routine medical checkup, can be far advanced without exhibiting any apprecia-
ble symptoms. One has an opaque body that must be taken to a specialist to find
out if it contains cancer. What the patient cannot perceive, the specialist will determine by analyzing tissues taken from the body. TB patients may see their X-
rays or even possess them: the patients at the sanatorium in *The Magic Mountain*
carry theirs around in their breast pockets. Cancer patients don't look at their
biopsies.

TB was—still is—thought to produce spells of euphoria, increased ap-   11
petite, exacerbated sexual desire. Part of the regimen for patients in *The Magic
Mountain* is a second breakfast, eaten with gusto. Cancer is thought to cripple
vitality, make eating an ordeal, deaden desire. Having TB was imagined to be an
aphrodisiac, and to confer extraordinary powers of seduction. Cancer is considered to be de-sexualizing. But it is characteristic of TB that many of its symptoms are deceptive—liveliness that comes from enervation, rosy cheeks that
look like a sign of health but come from fever—and an upsurge of vitality may
be a sign of approaching death. (Such gushes of energy will generally be self-
destructive, and may be destructive of others; recall the Old West legend of Doc
Holliday, the tubercular gunfighter released from moral restraints by the ravages
of his disease.) Cancer has only true symptoms.

TB is disintegration, febrilization, dematerialization; it is a disease of   12
liquids—the body turning to phlegm and mucus and sputum and, finally, blood—
and of air, of the need for better air. Cancer is degeneration, the body tissues turning to something hard. Alice James, writing in her journal a year before she died
from cancer in 1892, speaks of "this unholy granite substance in my breast." But

this lump is alive, a fetus with its own will. Novalis, in an entry written around 1798 for his encyclopedia project, defines cancers, along with gangrene, as "full-fledged *parasites*—they grow, are engendered, engender, have their structure, secrete, eat." Cancer is a demonic pregnancy. St. Jerome must have been thinking of a cancer when he wrote: "The one there with his swollen belly is pregnant with his own death" ("*Alius tumenti aqualiculo mortem parturit*"). Though the course of both diseases is emaciating, losing weight from TB is understood very differently from losing weight from cancer. In TB the person is "consumed," burned up. In cancer, the patient is "invaded" by alien cells, which multiply, causing an atrophy or blockage of bodily functions. The cancer patient "shrivels" (Alice James's word) or "shrinks" (Wilhelm Reich's word).

TB is a disease of time; it speeds up life, highlights it, spiritualizes it. In both English and French, consumption "gallops." Cancer has stages rather than gaits; it is (eventually) "terminal." Cancer works slowly, insidiously: the standard euphemism in obituaries is that someone has "died after a long illness." Every characterization of cancer describes it as slow, and so it was first used metaphorically. "The word of hem crepith as a kankir," Wyclif wrote in 1382 (translating a phrase in II Timothy 2:17); and among the earliest figurative uses of cancer are as a metaphor for "idleness" and "sloth." Metaphorically, cancer is not so much a disease of time as a disease or pathology of space. Its principal metaphors refer to topography (cancer "spreads" or "proliferates" or is "diffused"; tumors are surgically "excised"), and its most dreaded consequence, short of death, is the mutilation or amputation of part of the body. [13]

TB is often imagined as a disease of poverty and deprivation—of thin garments, thin bodies, unheated rooms, poor hygiene, inadequate food. The poverty may not be as literal as Mimi's garret in *La Bohème;* the tubercular Marguerite Gautier in *La Dame aux camélias* lives in luxury, but inside she is a waif. In contrast, cancer is a disease of middle-class life, a disease associated with affluence, with excess. Rich countries have the highest cancer rates, and the rising incidence of the disease is seen as resulting, in part, from a diet rich in fat and proteins and from the toxic effluvia of the industrial economy that creates affluence. The treatment of TB is identified with the stimulation of appetite, cancer treatment with nausea and the loss of appetite. The undernourished nourishing themselves—alas, to no avail. The overnourished, unable to eat. [14]

The TB patient was thought to be helped, even cured, by a change in environment. There was a notion that TB was a wet disease, a disease of humid and dank cities. The inside of the body became damp ("moisture in the lungs" was a favored locution) and had to be dried out. Doctors advised travel to high, dry places—the mountains, the desert. But no change of surroundings is thought to help the cancer patient. The fight is all inside one's own body. It may be, is increasingly thought to be, something in the environment that has caused the cancer. But once cancer is present, it cannot be reversed or diminished by a move to a better (that is, less carcinogenic) environment. [15]

TB is thought to be relatively painless. Cancer is thought to be, invariably, excruciatingly painful. TB is thought to provide an easy death, while cancer is the [16] spectacularly wretched one. For over a hundred years TB remained the preferred way of giving death a meaning—an edifying, refined disease. Nineteenth-century literature is stocked with descriptions of almost symptomless, unfrightened, beatific deaths from TB, particularly of young people, such as Little Eva in *Uncle Tom's Cabin* and Dombey's son Paul in *Dombey and Son* and Smike in *Nicholas Nickleby,* where Dickens described TB as the "dread disease" which "refines" death.

> if its grosser aspect . . . in which the struggle between soul and body is so gradual, quiet, and solemn, and the result so sure, that day by day, and grain by grain, the mortal part wastes and withers away, so that the spirit grows light and sanguine with its lightening load. . . .

Contrast these ennobling, placid TB deaths with the ignoble, agonizing cancer deaths of Eugene Gant's father in Thomas Wolfe's *Of Time and the River* and of the sister in Bergman's film *Cries and Whispers.* The dying tubercular is pictured as made more beautiful and more soulful; the person dying of cancer is portrayed as robbed of all capacities of self-transcendence, humiliated by fear and agony.

Meaning and Idea

1. What two diseases does the essay explore? How does Sontag characterize each of them?

2. What is Sontag's main point about the relation between the two diseases?

3. How, according to Sontag, have we formed our ideas about these diseases? What do you think she hopes to accomplish with this essay?

4. What does Sontag say about the realities of the relation between social standing or economic condition and the two diseases she is exploring? What does she say about the images we have of these relations? What is the common connection among cancer, death, and dying in our society?

5. What, if anything, can you generalize from this essay to another terrible disease—AIDS, multiple sclerosis, or muscular dystrophy, for example?

Language, Form, Structure

1. As you know, this essay comes from Sontag's book *Illness as Metaphor.* Explain how the title of the book could apply to this selection.

2. How does Sontag move back and forth between her two subjects? She uses few transitional expressions, yet the essay holds together. How do you explain this coherence?

3. Throughout the essay Sontag uses numerous historical references and literary allusions. Identify a few of them. How are they selected? What is their nature? For what purpose does Sontag include them? Which do you consider more effective, the literary or the statistical allusions?

4. Sontag calls attention to the metaphoric uses of the terms *tuberculosis* and *cancer*. Why?

5. What is the meaning of Sontag's final sentences (after the Dickens quote)? How do they serve as a fitting conclusion?

6. Make a list of any unfamiliar words you find in this essay and write definitions for them.

Ideas for Writing

1. Write a comparison of the two things you fear most. Describe how they affect you and attempt to blend both similarities and differences without losing your focus.

2. Select a social condition (for example, poverty, gentrification, child abuse) about which you have firsthand knowledge or have acquired firsthand experience over the past 5 to 10 years. Compare the manifestations and processes of that condition as it existed 5 to 10 years ago with its present existence. In your essay, make the process of change (or lack of change) clear to the reader.

3. Sontag's essay is very complete, almost encyclopedic. What might that completeness say about her attitude toward the subject? Bear in mind that Sontag herself had recently fought cancer when she wrote this essay. Does that fact color your opinion of this essay? How?

The Allegory of the Cave

Plato

The Greek philosopher Plato (427?–347 B.C.) is considered to be among the greatest world philosophers and the ancestor of much of modern philosophy. He was a student of Socrates, and his dialogues—including *Phaedo, Symposium,* and *Phaedrus*—are thought to be records of his conversations with Socrates and other students.

"The Allegory of the Cave" comes from the *Republic,* Plato's work about an ideal world. This allegory relies on the traditional Socratic method of a dialectic—that is, a questioning dialogue—aimed at arriving at a general truth, or a Platonic Form (an ideal truth). Notice how, through comparison, Plato attempts to make that ideal part of the world of "human affairs" as well as of "the upper world."

And now, I said, let me show in a figure how far our nature is en- 1
lightened or unenlightened: Behold! human beings living in an underground den, which has a mouth open towards the light and reaching all along the end; here they have been from their childhood, and have their legs and necks chained so that they cannot move, and can only see before them, being prevented by the chains from turning round their heads. Above and behind them a fire is blazing at a distance, and between the fire and the prisoners there is a raised way; and you will see, if you look, a low wall built along the way, like the screen which marionette players have in front of them, over which they show the puppets.

I see. 2

And do you see, I said, men passing along the wall carrying all sorts of 3
vessels, and statues and figures of animals made of wood and stone and various materials, which appear over the wall? Some of them are talking, others silent.

You have shown me a strange image, and they are strange prisoners. 4

Like ourselves, I replied; and they see only their own shadows, or the 5
shadows of one another, which the fire throws on the opposite wall of the cave?

True, he said; how could they see anything but the shadows if they were 6
never allowed to move their heads?

And of the objects which are being carried in like manner they would only 7
see the shadows?

Yes, he said. 8

And if they were able to converse with one another, would they not sup- 9
pose that they were naming what was actually before them?

Very true. 10

And suppose further that the prison had an echo which came from the 11
other side, would they not be sure to fancy when one of the passers-by spoke that the voice which they heard came from the passing shadow?

No question, he replied. 12

To them, I said, the truth would be literally nothing but the shadows of the 13
images.

That is certain. 14

And now look again, and see what will naturally follow if the prisoners are 15
released, and disabused of their error. At first, when any of them is liberated and
compelled suddenly to stand up and turn his neck round and walk and look towards the light, he will suffer sharp pains; the glare will distress him and he will
be unable to see the realities of which in his former state he had seen the shadows; and then conceive some one saying to him, that what he saw before was an
illusion, but that now, when he is approaching nearer to being and his eye is
turned towards more real existence, he has a clearer vision—what will be his
reply? And you may further imagine that his instructor is pointing to the objects
as they pass and requiring him to name them—will he not be perplexed? Will he
not fancy that the shadows which he formerly saw are truer than the objects
which are now shown to him?

Far truer. 16

And if he is compelled to look straight at the light, will he not have a pain 17
in his eyes which will make him turn away to take refuge in the objects of vision
which he can see, and which he will conceive to be in reality clearer than the
things which are now being shown to him?

True, he said. 18

And suppose once more, that he is reluctantly dragged up a steep and 19
rugged ascent, and held fast until he is forced into the presence of the sun himself, is he not likely to be pained and irritated? When he approaches the light his
eyes will be dazzled and he will not be able to see anything at all of what are
now called realities.

Not all in a moment, he said. 20

He will require to grow accustomed to the sight of the upper world. And 21
first he will see the shadows best, next the reflections of men and other objects
in the water, and then the objects themselves; then he will gaze upon the light of
the moon and the stars and the spangled heaven; and he will see the sky and the
stars by night better than the sun or the light of the sun by day?

Certainly. 22

Last of all he will be able to see the sun, and not mere reflections of him in 23
the water, but he will see him in his own proper place, and not in another; and he
will contemplate him as he is.

Certainly. 24

He will then proceed to argue that this is he who gives the season and the 25
years, and is the guardian of all that is in the visible world, and in a certain way
the cause of all things which he and his fellows have been accustomed to behold?

Clearly, he said, he would first see the sun and then reason about him. 26

And when he remembered his old habitation, and the wisdom of the den 27
and his fellow-prisoners, do you not suppose that he would felicitate himself on
the change, and pity them?

Certainly, he would. 28

And if they were in the habit of conferring honors among themselves on those who were quickest to observe the passing shadows and to remark which of them went before, and which followed after, and which were together; and who were therefore best able to draw conclusions as to the future, do you think that he would care for such honors and glories, or envy the possessors of them? Would he not say with Homer,

> Better to be the poor servant of a poor master,

and to endure anything, rather than their manner?

Yes, he said, I think that he would rather suffer anything than entertain these false notions and live in this miserable manner.

Imagine once more, I said, such a one coming suddenly out of the sun to be replaced in his old situation; would he not be certain to have his eyes full of darkness?

To be sure, he said.

And if there were a contest, and he had to compete in measuring the shadows with the prisoners who had never moved out of the den, while his sight was still weak, and before his eyes had become steady (and the time which would be needed to acquire this new habit of sight might be very considerable) would he not be ridiculous? Men would say to him that up he went and down he came without his eyes; and that it was better not even to think of ascending; and if any one tried to loose another and lead him up to the light, let them only catch the offender, and they would put him to death.

No question, he said.

This entire allegory, I said, you may now append, dear Glaucon, to the previous argument; the prison-house is the world of sight, the light of fire is the sun, and you will not misapprehend me if you interpret the journey upwards to be the ascent of the soul into the intellectual world according to my poor belief, which, at your desire, I have expressed—whether rightly or wrongly God knows. But, whether true or false, my opinion is that in the world of knowledge the idea of good appears last of all, and is seen only with an effort; and, when seen, is also inferred to be the universal author of all things beautiful and right, parent of light and of the lord of light in this visible world, and the immediate source of reason and truth in the intellectual; and that this is the power upon which he who would act rationally either in public or private life must have his eye fixed.

I agree, he said, as far as I am able to understand you.

Moreover, I said, you must not wonder that those who attain to this beatific vision are unwilling to descend to human affairs; for their souls are ever hastening into the upper world where they desire to dwell; which desire of theirs is very natural, if our allegory may be trusted.

Yes, very natural.

And is there anything surprising in one who passes from divine contemplations to the evil state of man, misbehaving himself in a ridiculous manner; if, while his eyes are blinking and before he has become accustomed to the surrounding darkness, he is compelled to fight in courts of law, or in other places, about the images or the shadows of images of justice, and is endeavouring to meet the conceptions of those who have never yet seen absolute justice?

Anything but surprising, he replied. 40

Any one who has common sense will remember that the bewilderments of 41 the eyes are of two kinds, and arise from two causes, either from coming out of the light or from going into the light, which is true of the mind's eye, quite as much as of the bodily eye; and he who remembers this when he sees any one whose vision is perplexed and weak, will not be too ready to laugh; he will first ask whether that soul of man has come out of the brighter life, and is unable to see because unaccustomed to the dark, or having turned from darkness to the day is dazzled by excess of light. And he will count the one happy in his condition and state of being, and he will pity the other; or, if he have a mind to laugh at the soul which comes from below into the light, there will be more reason in this than in the laugh which greets him who returns from above out of the light into the den.

That, he said, is a very just distinction. 42

Meaning and Idea

1. Who is speaking to whom in this selection? What are they talking about? Do the two speakers maintain similar or dissimilar opinions?

2. Describe the conditions and activities of the prisoners in the cave. What is the contrast in perceptions of things between remaining prisoners and newly released ones? Between prisoners and those who have been outside the cave for a while? Compare the attitude of a prisoner toward his fellow prisoners before and after leaving the cave.

3. How, according to Plato, does someone learn truth?

4. Toward the end of this allegory, with what are the two realms compared or contrasted? How does Plato compare the process of coming out of the light to going into the light? Which does he feel is preferable? Why?

Language, Form, Structure

1. Plato makes use of *allegory* in this selection. What is an allegory? How is this dialogue allegorical?

2. In what ways does Plato use process analysis to serve his comparison here? Briefly outline the processes described. Which is, overall, the most important process?

3. Look up the meanings of the following words: enlightened; glare; perplexed; ascent; dazzled; felicitate; append; misapprehend; rationally; endeavoring.

Ideas for Writing

1. Write a dialogue in which two speakers argue opposing sides of an issue. Write only in dialogue, with no authorial commentary or analysis.

2. Choose an abstract concept—love, art, fear, intelligence, for example—and write a comparison essay in which you explore two points of view concerning that abstraction.

3. How effective is the allegory in helping Plato make his point? Write an analysis in which you draw on specific references to the text.

My Mistress' Eyes Are Nothing Like the Sun

William Shakespeare

The world's most acknowledged literary figure is William Shakespeare (1564–1616). Born in Stratford-on-Avon, England, on April 26, 1564, he never attended university and was, by his own admission, a poor and unmotivated student. After moving to London with his wife, Ann Hathaway, Shakespeare became involved as a dramatist and actor with the Globe Theatre there and was extremely popular in his day. He was somewhat careless with the manuscripts of his now invaluable plays and sonnets. In fact, if not for the efforts of his friends, we might not today have many of his masterpieces, which include, of course, *Hamlet, Macbeth, King Lear, Othello, The Comedy of Errors, The Merchant of Venice, Romeo and Juliet,* and *The Tempest*—the list goes on and on! Shakespeare returned to Stratford-on-Avon at the age of 50 and died there two years later.

In this love sonnet, Shakespeare uses comparison in such a way that we might at first think of it as a "hate sonnet." Notice how he begins to change course in lines 11–12 and then makes his purpose clear in lines 13–14.

*M*y mistress' eyes are nothing like the sun;
Coral is far more red than her lips' red:
If snow be white, why then her breasts are dun;
If hairs be wires, black wires grow on her head.
I have seen roses damasked, red and white,   5
But no such roses see I in her cheeks;
And in some perfumes is there more delight
Than in the breath that from my mistress reeks.
I love to hear her speak, yet well I know
That music hath a far more pleasing sound: 10
I grant I never saw a goddess go,—
My mistress, when she walks, treads on the ground.
     And yet, by heaven, I think my love as rare
     As any she belied with false compare.

Meaning and Idea

1. Who is the speaker of the poem? To whom is he speaking?

2. About whom does the speaker speak? What qualities of that person does he stress?

Language, Form, Structure

1. In this sonnet does Shakespeare rely primarily on similarities or on differences? How does the speaker arrange his descriptive comparisons of his mistress? What is the nature of most of the comparisons?

2. What do the last two lines of the sonnet say about Shakespeare's reasoning in the poem? For what purpose did he use the comparisons which preceded the last two lines?

3. How does Shakespeare use negatives to make what is ultimately a highly positive statement?

4. To learn the meanings of some of the following words, it may be necessary to consult a dictionary such as the *Oxford English Dictionary,* since some of the meanings are archaic: dun; damasked; reeks; grant; belied.

Ideas for Writing

1. Write a description of a person you like very much, but develop your description by using negative comparisons of that person's features to other objects. Be sure that at the end of the description your real purpose is clear.

2. In a paragraph, describe the ugliest person you know (either physically or emotionally ugly). Then, in another paragraph, describe that person through the eyes of someone who loves him or her.

3. Some commentators on this poem have suggested that Shakespeare wrote the sonnet not to his mistress but with a more metaphoric idea in mind. Write a piece in which you explore another meaning or value of the poem. Support your response with specific analyses of references in the poem.

Fire and Ice

Robert Frost

Although Robert Frost is well known as a New England poet, he was in fact born in San Francisco in 1874. After a brief stay in England (1912–1914), where he first gained fame as a poet, Frost settled in New Hampshire, where he lived most of his days, until his death in 1963. Frost the poet is sometimes deceptively simple; underlying his dramatic accounts of the New England people and landscape, there is often deep symbolism and lyricism. His collected poems were published posthumously in 1967; he received four Pulitzer Prizes for poetry, in 1924, 1931, 1937, and 1943.

In this short, almost deceptively singsong poem, Robert Frost compares two notions of the way the world will end.

Some say the world will end in fire,
Some say in ice.
From what I've tasted of desire
I hold with those who favor fire.
But if it had to perish twice,   5
I think I know enough of hate
To say that for destruction ice
Is also great
And would suffice.

Meaning and Idea

1. Who, literally, are those who "say the world will end in fire"? Who are those who say "in ice"? Which group does Frost favor? Why?

2. What impossible occurrence does the poet describe? Why?

3. State, in a single sentence, Frost's meaning in this poem.

Language, Form, Structure

1. Refer back to your answer to question 1 in the Meaning and Idea section above. Then state how Frost uses the two groups to symbolize other things. Explain this symbolic meaning.

2. This poem is quite sparse, yet Frost implicitly creates very graphic images. Describe them and explain how he creates them.

3. What special meanings does Frost employ when he writes "tasted" and "hold with"?

Ideas for Writing

1. What do you consider the most negative social trend that affects you and your peers? Write an essay in which you compare two ways in which this trend manifests itself.

2. Write a paragraph in which you compare two methods of doing something creative—either a natural process (such as growing sprouts) or an abstract process (such as writing a poem).

3. The Bauhaus school of design is famous for its edict: "Less is more." Write a short essay in which you respond to Frost's poem within the context of the Bauhaus statement.

Grant and Lee:
A Study in Contrasts

Bruce Catton

Bruce Catton (1899–1978) was America's acknowledged expert on the Civil War. As a child he recreated historic battles on the playgrounds and fields of Benzonia, Michigan. World War I interrupted his studies at Oberlin, however, and he never returned to finish his bachelor's degree. Instead he pursued a career as a journalist. It was not until later in life that he began to produce the work for which he became famous, 17 of his 18 books were published after he had turned 50. Of those, the most famous is *A Stillness at Appomattox* (1953), which won the Pulitzer Prize and the National Book Award. After his death in 1978 Catton was awarded the Medal of Freedom by President Gerald Ford for his accomplishments.

"Grant and Lee: A Study in Contrasts" portrays not only two men with different backgrounds and temperaments but also the very different traditions that the two men represented.

W̄hen Ulysses S. Grant and Robert E. Lee met in the parlor of a   1
modest house at Appomattox Court House, Virginia, on April 9, 1865, to work out the terms for the surrender of Lee's Army of Northern Virginia, a great chapter in American life came to a close, and a great new chapter began.

These men were bringing the Civil War to its virtual finish. To be sure, other   2
armies had yet to surrender, and for a few days the fugitive confederate government would struggle desperately and vainly, trying to find some way to go on living now that its chief support was gone. But in effect it was all over when Grant and Lee signed the papers. And the little room where they wrote out the terms was the scene of one of the poignant, dramatic contrasts in American history.

They were two strong men, these oddly different generals, and they repre-   3
sented the strengths of two conflicting currents that, through them, had come into final collision.

Back of Robert E. Lee was the notion that the old aristocratic concept   4
might somehow survive and be dominant in American life.

Lee was tidewater Virginia, and in his background were family, culture,   5
and tradition . . . the age of chivalry transplanted to a New World which was making its own legends and its own myths. He embodied a way of life that had come down through the age of knighthood and the English country squire. America was a land that was beginning all over again, dedicated to nothing much more complicated than the rather hazy belief that all men had equal rights, and should have an equal chance in the world. In such a land Lee stood for the feeling that it was somehow of advantage to human society to have a pronounced inequality in the social structure. There should be a leisure class,

backed by ownership of land; in turn, society itself should be keyed to the land as the chief source of wealth and influence. It would bring forth (according to this ideal) a class of men with a strong sense of obligation to the community; men who lived not to gain advantage for themselves, but to meet the solemn obligations which had been laid on them by the very fact that they were privileged. From them the country would get its leadership; to them it could look for the higher values—of thought, of conduct, of personal deportment—to give it strength and virtue.

Lee embodied the noblest elements of this aristocratic ideal. Through him, the landed nobility justified itself. For four years, the Southern states had fought a desperate war to uphold the ideals for which Lee stood. In the end, it almost seemed as if the Confederacy fought for Lee; as if he himself was the Confederacy . . . the best thing that the way of life for which the Confederacy stood could ever have to offer. He had passed into legend before Appomattox. Thousands of tired, underfed, poorly clothed Confederate soldiers, long-since past the simple enthusiasm of the early days of the struggle, somehow considered Lee the symbol of everything for which they had been willing to die. But they could not quite put this feeling into words. If the Lost Cause, sanctified by so much heroism and so many deaths, had a living justification, its justification was General Lee.

Grant, the son of a tanner on the Western frontier, was everything Lee was not. He had come up the hard way, and embodied nothing in particular except the eternal toughness and sinewy fiber of the men who grew up beyond the mountains. He was one of a body of men who owed reverence and obeisance to no one, who were self-reliant to a fault, who cared hardly anything for the past but who had a sharp eye for the future.

These frontier men were the precise opposites of the tidewater aristocrats. Back of them, in the great surge that had taken people over the Alleghenies and into the opening Western country, there was a deep, implicit dissatisfaction with a past that had settled into grooves. They stood for democracy, not from any reasoned conclusion about the proper ordering of human society, but simply because they had grown up in the middle of democracy and knew how it worked. Their society might have privileges, but they would be privileges each man had won for himself. Forms and patterns meant nothing. No man was born to anything, except perhaps to a chance to show how far he could rise. Life was competition.

Yet along with this feeling had come a deep sense of belonging to a national community. The Westerner who developed a farm, opened a shop, or set up in business as a trader could hope to prosper only as his own community prospered—and his community ran from the Atlantic to the Pacific and from Canada down to Mexico. If the land was settled, with towns and highways and accessible markets, he could better himself. He saw his fate in terms of the nation's own destiny. As its horizons expanded, so did his. He had, in other words, an acute dollars-and-cents stake in the continued growth and development of his country.

And that, perhaps, is where the contrast between Grant and Lee becomes   10
most striking. The Virginia aristocrat, inevitably, saw himself in relation to his own
region. He lived in a static society which could endure almost anything except
change. Instinctively, his first loyalty would go to the locality in which that society
existed. He would fight to the limit of endurance to defend it, because in defending
it he was defending everything that gave his own life its deepest meaning.

The Westerner, on the other hand, would fight with an equal tenacity for   11
the broader concept of society. He fought so because everything he lived by was
tied to growth, expansion, and a constantly widening horizon. What he lived by
would survive or fall with the nation itself. He could not possibly stand by un-
moved in the face of an attempt to destroy the Union. He would combat it with
everything he had, because he could only see it as an effort to cut the ground out
from under his feet.

So Grant and Lee were in complete contrast, representing two diametri-   12
cally opposed elements in American life. Grant was the modern man emerging;
beyond him, ready to come on the stage, was the great age of steel and machin-
ery, of crowded cities and a restless, burgeoning vitality. Lee might have ridden
down from the old age of chivalry, lance in hand, silken banner fluttering over
his head. Each man was the perfect champion of his cause, drawing both his
strengths and his weaknesses from the people he led.

Yet it was not all contrast, after all. Different as they were—in back-   13
ground, in personality, in underlying aspiration—these two great soldiers had
much in common. Under everything else, they were marvelous fighters. Furthermore, their fighting qualities were really very much alike.

Each man had, to begin with, the great virtue of utter tenacity and fidelity.   14
Grant fought his way down the Mississippi Valley in spite of acute personal discouragement and profound military handicaps. Lee hung on in the trenches at
Petersburg after hope itself had died. In each man there was an indomitable
quality . . . the born fighter's refusal to give up as long as he can still remain on
his feet and lift his two fists.

Daring and resourcefulness they had, too; the ability to think faster and move   15
faster than the enemy. These were the qualities which gave Lee the dazzling cam-
paigns of Second Manassas and Chancellorsville and won Vicksburg for Grant.

Lastly, and perhaps greatest of all, there was the ability, at the end, to turn   16
quickly from war to peace once the fighting was over. Out of the way these two
men behaved at Appomattox came the possibility of a peace of reconciliation. It
was a possibility not wholly realized, in the years to come, but which did, in the
end, help the two sections to become one nation again . . . after a war whose
bitterness might have seemed to make such a reunion wholly impossible. No
part of either man's life became him more than the part he played in their brief
meeting in the McLean house at Appomattox. Their behavior there put all succeeding generations of Americans in their debt. Two great Americans, Grant and
Lee—very different, yet under everything very much alike. Their encounter at
Appomattox was one of the great moments of American history.

Meaning and Idea

1. How does Catton describe the character of Robert E. Lee and Ulysses S. Grant? What qualities in each man does Catton see as fundamental? What greater historical forces does each represent?

2. What characteristics, according to Catton, do Lee and Grant have in common? Which qualities does Catton regard as the most important of all?

3. Catton describes the meeting in Appomattox Court House as "one of the great moments of American history." Why does he make such a strong statement? How does this short piece justify those grand terms?

Language, Form, Structure

1. Most of this essay is given over to the contrasts between Grant and Lee, yet Catton's most important point is their similarities. Why do you think Catton chooses to write his piece this way, reserving the comparison for the final paragraphs? In what way do the contrasts between Grant and Lee anticipate the similarities?

2. Missing from Catton's brief account of the meeting between these two generals is the important historical fact that at Appomattox Lee was the defeated party and Grant was the victorious one. Why do you think Catton deemphasizes this fact? How does that shift in emphasis increase the interest of his piece and serve his argument?

3. Define the following words and use each one in a sentence: poignant; squire; tanner; sinewy; obeisance; indomitable.

Ideas for Writing

1. Using Catton's description of the two men and some independent research, write an imaginative re-creation of the scene in the Appomattox Court House where these two generals meet.

2. Write a description of an important historical figure with whom you are familiar. Try to relate this historical figure to the broader context of the times he or she lived in.

3. Look back over the essay, paying careful attention to Catton's writing style. How would you characterize it? Write an essay analyzing this style and remarking on how it adds interest to his subject.

A Slow Walk of Trees

Toni Morrison

Toni Morrison, an editor at Random House and a much admired novelist, was born near Cleveland in 1931. In 1953 she received her B.A. from Howard University, and in 1955 she earned her M.A. at Cornell. Her novels focus on the black experience, historical and modern, using a unique blend of historical fact and personal mythos. She has also written or edited several works of nonfiction. In 1993 she won the Nobel Prize for literature.

In this 1976 essay, Morrison shows that Grandmother Ardelia Willis had one set of beliefs, grandfather John Solomon Willis another. This contrast between Morrison's forebears helped formulate her views on the historical and modern-day fortunes and misfortunes of black people in America. Notice how the author keeps offering yet "another slant" on this issue.

*H*is name was John Solomon Willis, and when at age 5 he heard   1
from the old folks that "the Emancipation Proclamation was coming," he crawled under the bed. It was his earliest recollection of what was to be his habitual response to the promises of white people: horror and an instinctive yearning for safety. He was my grandfather, a musician who managed to hold on to his violin but not his land. He lost all 88 acres of his Indian mother's inheritance to legal predators who built their fortunes on the likes of him. He was an unreconstructed black pessimist who, in spite of or because of emancipation, was convinced for 85 years that there was no hope whatever for black people in this country. His rancor was legitimate, for he, John Solomon, was not only an artist but a first-rate carpenter and farmer, reduced to sending home to his family money he made playing the violin because he was not able to find work. And this during the years when almost half the black male population were skilled craftsmen who lost their jobs to white ex-convicts and immigrant farmers.

His wife, however, was of a quite different frame of mind and believed   2
that all things could be improved by faith in Jesus and an effort of the will. So it was she, Ardelia Willis, who sneaked her seven children out of the back window into the darkness, rather than permit the patron of their sharecropper's existence to become their executioner as well, and headed north in 1912, when 99.2 percent of all black people in the U.S. were native-born and only 60 percent of white Americans were. And it was Ardelia who told her husband that they could not stay in the Kentucky town they ended up in because the teacher didn't know long division.

They have been dead now for 30 years and more and I still don't know   3
which of them came closer to the truth about the possibilities of life for black people in this country. One of their grandchildren is a tenured professor at Princeton. Another, who suffered from what the Peruvian poet called "anger that

breaks a man into children," was picked up just as he entered his teens and emotionally lobotomized by the reformatories and mental institutions specifically designed to serve him. Neither John Solomon nor Ardelia lived long enough to despair over one or swell with pride over the other. But if they were alive today each would have selected and collected enough evidence to support the accuracy of the other's original point of view. And it would be difficult to convince either one that the other was right.

Some of the monstrous events that took place in John Solomon's America ⁴ have been duplicated in alarming detail in my own America. There was the public murder of a President in a theater in 1865 and the public murder of another President on television in 1963. The Civil War of 1861 had its encore as the civil-rights movement of 1960. The torture and mutilation of a black West Point Cadet (Cadet Johnson Whittaker) in 1880 had its rerun with the 1970's murders of students at Jackson State College, Texas Southern and Southern University in Baton Rouge. And in 1976 we watch for what must be the thousandth time a pitched battle between the children of slaves and the children of immigrants— only this time, it is not the New York draft riots of 1863, but the busing turmoil in Paul Revere's home town, Boston.

Hopeless, he's said. Hopeless. For he was certain that white people of ⁵ every political, religious, geographical and economic background would band together against black people everywhere when they felt the threat of our progress. And a hundred years after he sought safety from the white man's "promise," somebody put a bullet in Martin Luther King's brain. And not long before that some excellent samples of the master race demonstrated their courage and virility by dynamiting some little black girls to death. If he were here now, my grandfather, he would shake his head, close his eyes and pull out his violin—too polite to say, "I told you so." And his wife would pay attention to the music but not to the sadness in her husband's eyes, for she would see what she expected to see—not the occasional historical repetition, but, *like the slow walk of certain species of trees from the flatlands up into the mountains,* she would see the signs of irrevocable and permanent change. She, who pulled her girls out of an inadequate school in the Cumberland Mountains, knew all along that the gentlemen from Alabama who had killed the little girls would be rounded up. And it wouldn't surprise her in the least to know that the number of black college graduates jumped 12 percent in the last three years; 47 percent in 20 years. That there are 140 black mayors in this country; 14 black judges in the District Circuit, 4 in the Courts of Appeals and one on the Supreme Court. That there are 17 blacks in Congress, one in the Senate; 276 in state legislatures—223 in state houses, 53 in state senates. That there are 112 elected black police chiefs and sheriffs, 1 Pulitizer Prize winner; 1 winner of the Prix de Rome; a dozen or so winners of the Guggenheim; 4 deans of predominently white colleges. . . . Oh, her list would go on and on. But so would John Solomon's sweet sad music.

While my grandparents held opposite views on whether the fortunes of ⁶ black people were improving, my own parents struck similarly opposed postures, but from another slant. They differed about whether the moral fiber of white people would ever improve. Quite a different argument. The old folks argued about how and if black people could improve themselves, who could be counted on to help us, who would hinder us and so on. My parents took issue over the question of whether it was possible for white people to improve. They assumed that black people were the humans of the globe, but had serious doubts about the quality and existence of white humanity. Thus my father, distrusting every word and every gesture of every white man on earth, assumed that the white man who crept up the stairs one afternoon had come to molest his daughters and threw him down the stairs and then our tricycle after him. (I think my father was wrong, but considering what I have seen since, it may have been very healthy for me to have witnessed that as my first black-white encounter.) My mother, however, *believed* in them—their possibilities. So when the meal we got on relief was bug-ridden, she wrote a long letter to Franklin Delano Roosevelt. And when white bill collectors came to our door, it was she who received them civilly and explained in a sweet voice that we were people of honor and that the debt would be taken care of. Her message to Roosevelt got through—our meal improved. Her message to the bill collectors did not always get through and there was occasional violence when my father (self-exiled to the bedroom for fear he could not hold his temper) would hear that her reasonableness had failed. My mother was always wounded by these scenes, for she thought the bill collector knew that she loved good credit more than life and that being in arrears on a payment horrified her probably more than it did him. So she thought he was rude because he was white. For years she walked to utility companies and department stores to pay bills in person and even now she does not seem convinced that checks are legal tender. My father loved excellence, worked hard (he held three jobs at once for 17 years) and was so outraged by the suggestion of personal slackness that he could explain it to himself only in terms of racism. He was a fastidious worker who was frightened of one thing: unemployment. I can remember now the doomsday-cum-graveyard sound of "laid off" and how the minute school was out he asked us, "Where you workin'?" Both my parents believed that all succor and aid came from themselves and their neighborhood, since "they"—white people in charge and those not in charge but in obstructionist positions—were in some way fundamentally, genetically corrupt.

So I grew up in a basically racist household with more than a child's share of contempt for white people. And for each white friend I acquired who made a small crack in that contempt, there was another who repaired it. For each one who related to me as a person, there was one who in my presence at least, became actively "white." And like most black people of my generation, I suffer from racial vertigo that can be cured only by taking what one needs from one's ancestors. John Solomon's cynicism and his deployment of his art as both weapon and solace, Ardelia's faith in the magic that can be wrought by sheer effort of the will; my mother's openmindedness in each new encounter and her habit of trying reasonableness first; my father's temper, his impatience and his efforts to keep "them" (throw them) out of his life. And it is out of these learned and selected attitudes that I look at the quality of life for my people in this country now. These widely disparate and sometimes conflicting views, I suspect, were held not only by me, but by most black people. Some I know are clearer in their positions, have not sullied their anger with optimism or dirtied their hope with despair. But most of us are plagued by a sense of being worn shell-thin by constant repression and hostility as well as the impression of being buoyed by visible testimony of tremendous strides. There *is* repetition of the grotesque in our history. And there *is* the miraculous walk of trees. The question is whether our walk is progress or merely movement. O.J. Simpson leaning on a Hertz car *is* better than the Gold Dust Twins on the back of a soap box. But is "Good Times" better than Stepin Fetchit? Has the first order of business been taken care of? Does the law of the land work for us?

Are white people who murder black people punished with at least the same dispatch that sends black teen-age truants to Coxsackie? Can we relax now and discuss "The Jeffersons" instead of genocide? Or is the difference between the two only the difference between a greedy pointless white life-style and a messy pointless black death? Now that Mr. Poitier and Mr. Belafonte have shot up all the racists in "Buck and the Preacher," have they all gone away? Can we really move into better neighborhoods and not be set on fire? Is there anybody who will lay me a $5 bet on it?

The past decade is a fairly good index of the odds at which you lay your money down.

Ten years ago in Queens, as black people like me moved into a neighborhood 20 minutes away from the Triborough Bridge, "for sale" signs shot up in front of white folks' houses like dandelions after a hot spring rain. And the black people smiled. "Goody, goody," said my neighbor. "Maybe we can push them on out to the sea. You think?"

Now I live in another neighborhood, 20 minutes away from the George Washington Bridge, and again the "for sale" signs are pushing up out of the ground. Fewer, perhaps, and for different reasons, perhaps. Still the Haitian lady and I smile at each other. "My, my," she says "they goin' on up to the hills? Seem like they just come from there." "The woods," I say. "They like to live in the woods." She nods with infinite understanding, then shrugs. The Haitians have already arranged for one mass in the church to be said in French, already have their own newspaper, stores, community center. That's not movement. That's progress.

But the decade has other revelations. Ten years ago, young, bright, energetic blacks were sought out, pursued and hired into major corporations, major networks, and onto the staffs of newspapers and national magazines. *Many survived that courtship, some even with their souls intact.* Newscasters, corporate lawyers, marketing specialists, journalists, production managers, plant foremen, college deans. But many more spend a lot of time on the telephone these days, or at the typewriter preparing résumés, which they send out (mostly to friends now) with little notes attached: "Is there anything you know of?" Or they think there is a good book in the story of what happened to them, the great hoax that was played on them. They are right, of course, about the hoax, for many of them were given elegant executive jobs with the work drained out. Work minus power. Work minus decision-making. Work minus dominion. Affirmative Action Make Believe that a lot of black people *did* believe because they also believed that the white people in those nice offices were not like the ones in the general store or in the plumbers' union—that they were fundamentally kind, or fair, or something. Anything but the desperate prisoners of economics they turned out to be, holding on to their dominion with a tenacity and sang-froid that can only be described as Nixonian. So the bright and the black (architects, reporters, vice-presidents in charge of public relations) walk the streets right along with that astounding 38 percent of the black teen-aged female work force that does not have and never has had a job. So the black female college graduate earns two-thirds of what a white male high-school dropout earns. So the black people who put everything into community-action programs supported by Government funds have found themselves bereft of action, bereft of funds, and all but bereft of community.

This decade has been rife with disappointment in practically every place where we thought we saw permanent change: Hostos, CUNY, and the black-studies departments that erupted like minivolcanoes on campuses all over the nation; easy integrations of public-school systems; acceleration of promotion in factories and businesses. But now when we describe what has happened we cannot do it without using the verbs of upheaval and destruction: Open admission *closes;* minority-student quotas *fall* or *discontinue;* salary gaps between blacks and whites *widen;* black-studies departments *merge.* And the only growth black people can count on is in the prison population and the unemployment line. Even busing, which used to be a plain, if emotional, term at best, has now taken on an adjective normally reserved for rape and burglary—it is now called "forced" busing.

All of that counts, but I'm not sure that in the long haul it matters. Maybe Ardelia Willis had the best idea. One sees signs of her vision and the fruits of her prophecy in spite of the dread-lock statistics. The trees *are* walking, albeit slowly and quietly and without the fanfare of a cross-country run. It seems that at last black people have abandoned our foolish dependency on the Government to do the work that we once thought all of its citizenry would be delighted to do. Our love affair with the Federal Government is over. We misjudged the ardor of its attention. We thought its majority constituency would *prefer* having their children grow up among happy, progressive, industrious, contented black children rather than among angry, disenchanted and dangerous ones. That the profit motive of industry alone would keep us employed and therefore spending, and that our poverty was bad for business. We thought landlords wanted us to have a share in our neighborhoods and therefore love and care for them. That city governments wanted us to control our schools and therefore preserve them.

We were wrong. And now, having been eliminated from the lists of urgent national priorities, from TV documentaries and the platitudes of editorials, black people have chosen, or been forced to seek safety from the white man's promise, but happily not under a bed. More and more there is the return to Ardelia's ways: the exercise of the will, the recognition of obstacles as only that—obstacles, not fixed stars. Black judges are fixing appropriate rather than punitive bail for black "offenders" and letting the rest of the community of jurisprudence scream. Young black women are leaving plush Northern jobs to sit in their living rooms and teach black children, work among factory women and spend months finding money to finance the college education of young blacks. Groups of blacks are buying huge tracts of land in the South and cutting off entirely the dependency of whole communities on grocery chains. For the first time, significant numbers of black people are returning or migrating to the South to focus on the acquisition of land, the transferral of crafts and skills, and the sharing of resources, the rebuilding of neighborhoods.

16   In the shambles of closing admissions, falling quotas, widening salary gaps and merging black-studies departments, builders and healers are working quietly among us. They are not like the heroes of old, the leaders we followed blindly and upon whom we depended for everything, or the blacks who had accumulated wealth for its own sake, fame, medals or some public acknowledgment of success. These are the people whose work is real and pointed and clear in its application to the race. Some are old and have been at work for a long time in and out of the public eye. Some are new and just finding out what their work is. But they are unmistakably the natural aristocrats of the race. The ones who refuse to imitate, to compromise, and who are indifferent to public accolade. Whose work is free or priceless. They take huge risks economically and personally. They are not always popular, even among black people, but they are the ones whose work black people respect. They are the healers. Some are nowhere near the public eye: Ben Chavis, preacher and political activist languishing now in North Carolina prisons; Robert Moses, a pioneering activist; Sterling Brown, poet and teacher; Father Al McKnight, land reformer; Rudy Lombard, urban sociologist; Lerone Bennett, historian; C.L.R. James, scholar; Alyce Gullattee, psychologist and organizer. Others are public legends: Judge Crockett, Judge Bruce Wright, Stevie Wonder, Ishmael Reed, Miles Davis, Richard Pryor, Muhammad Ali, Fannie Lou Hamer, Eubie Blake, Angela Davis, Bill Russell. . . .

17   But a complete roll-call is neither fitting nor necessary. They know who they are and so do we. They clarify our past, make livable our present and are certain to shape our future. And since the future is where our immortality as a race lies, no overview of the state of black people at this time can ignore some speculation on the only ones certain to live it—the children.

18   They are both exhilarating and frightening, those black children, and a source of wonderment to me. Although statistics about black teen-age crime and the "failure" of the courts to gut them are regularly printed and regularly received with outrage and fear, the children I know and see, those born after 1960, do not make such great copy. They are those who have grown up with nothing to prove to white people, whose perceptions of themselves are so new, so different, so focused they appear to me to be either magnificent hybrids or throwbacks to the time when our ancestors were called "royal." They are the baby sisters of the

sit-in generation, the sons of the neighborhood blockbusters, the nephews of jailed revolutionaries, and a huge number who have had college graduates in their families for three and four generations. I thought we had left them nothing to love and nothing to want to know. I thought that those who exhibited some excitement about their future had long ago looked into the eyes of their teachers and were either saddened or outraged by the death of possibility they found there. I thought that those who were interested in the past had looked into the faces of their parents and seen betrayal. I thought the state had deprived them of a land and the landlords and banks had deprived them of a turf. So how is it that, with nothing to love, nothing they need to know, landless, turfless, minus a future and a past, these black children look us dead in the eye? They seem not to know how to apologize. And even when they are wrong they do not ask for forgiveness. It is as though they are waiting for us to apologize to them, to beg their pardon, to seek their approval. What species of black is this that not only does not choose to grovel, but doesn't know how? How will they keep jobs? How will they live? Won't they be killed before they reproduce? But they are unafraid. Is it because they refuse to see the world as we did? Is it because they have rejected both land and turf to seek instead a world? Maybe they finally got the message that we had been shouting into their faces; that they *live* here, *belong* here on this planet earth and that it is *theirs*. So they watch us with the eyes of poets and carpenters and musicians and scholars and other people who know who they are because they have invented themselves and know where they are going because they have envisioned it. All of which would please Ardelia—and John Solomon, too, I think. After all, he did hold on to his violin.

Meaning and Idea

1. Summarize the grandfather's thinking about the progress of black people. Summarize the grandmother's thinking. How do they compare? Whose thinking does the writer favor?

2. What is the background of each of the grandparents?

3. How does Morrison compare the status and conditions of blacks from the sixties with those in the seventies? What is her point in making that comparison? Why does she call the "prisoners of economics" *Nixonian?* How does this section fit in with her overall historical comparison?

4. On the first list of "the ones whose work black people respect," how many names do you recognize? Do you think Morrison meant those names to be recognizable? What is her point?

Language, Form, Structure

1. What is Morrison's thesis in this essay? Does she ever state it exactly? If so, where? If not, how can you tell what her main point is?

2. What is the initial comparison the writer develops? How does Morrison use it as the seed to develop a comparison in a larger context? What is that comparison?

3. How does Morrison use data in this essay? Give three examples and analyze each for its significance and use in the essay. What generalization do the data support?

4. How does Morrison use references to popular culture? Why are they effective? How do they influence the organization and coherence of the essay?

5. In the conclusion to this essay, the author makes use of a series of questions. What is their purpose? Does she mean for them to be answered? Why or why not? What tone do they create? How do they serve as a fitting conclusion to the essay?

6. Define the following words from the essay: predators; rancor; fastidious; succor; vertigo; solace; disparate; sang-froid; rife; albeit; accolade; grovel. Choose five of these terms and use them in sentences of your own.

Ideas for Writing

1. Write a comparison between your parents' and your own outlook on a key political, social, or historical issue. Attempt to blend objective data with vivid, sometimes metaphoric descriptions.

2. Write an essay in which you compare and contrast the advances made by African Americans in our society with what you believe still must be accomplished.

3. What is the relation between Morrison's intended audience and her style, outlook, choice of information, and use of language? She wrote this piece originally for *The New York Times Magazine.* How do you think her audience influenced her? How do you think her readers received the article? What significance is added by the fact that the article first appeared on the day of the U.S. Bicentennial—July 4, 1976? In your analysis make specific references to the text.

Everyday Use

Alice Walker

Born into a family of sharecroppers in Eatonton, Georgia, in 1944, Alice Walker later attended college at Spelman and Sarah Lawrence and was active in the civil rights movement. Now she regularly teaches at various universities and contributes to *Ms.* magazine. Of her several novels, *The Color Purple* won the Pulitzer Prize in 1983 and went on to become a popular film. The following selection comes from *In Love and Trouble: Stories of Black Women.*

Walker has said of herself and her work, "I am committed to exploring the oppressions, the insanities, the loyalties, and the triumphs of black women." "Everyday Use" is a gentle, revealing story of love, understanding, and heritage.

I will wait for her in the yard that Maggie and I made so clean and wavy yesterday afternoon. A yard like this is more comfortable than most people know. It is not just a yard. It is like an extended living room. When the hard clay is swept clean as a floor and the fine sand around the edges lined with tiny, irregular grooves anyone can come and sit and look up into the elm tree and wait for the breezes that never come inside the house.

Maggie will be nervous until after her sister goes: she will stand hopelessly in corners homely and ashamed of the burn scars down her arms and legs, eyeing her sister with a mixture of envy and awe. She thinks her sister has held life always in the palm of one hand, that "no" is a word the world never learned to say to her.

You've no doubt seen those TV shows where the child who has "made it" is confronted, as a surprise, by her own mother and father, tottering in weakly from backstage. (A pleasant surprise, of course: What would they do if parent and child came on the show only to curse out and insult each other?) On TV mother and child embrace and smile into each other's faces. Sometimes the mother and father weep, the child wraps them in her arms and leans across the table to tell how she would not have made it without their help. I have seen these programs.

Sometimes I dream a dream in which Dee and I are suddenly brought together on a TV program of this sort. Out of a dark and soft-seated limousine I am ushered into a bright room filled with many people. There I meet a smiling, gray, sporty man like Johnny Carson who shakes my hand and tells me what a fine girl I have. Then we are on the stage and Dee is embracing me with tears in her eyes. She pins on my dress a large orchid, even though she has told me once that she thinks orchids are tacky flowers.

In real life I am a large, big-boned woman with rough, man-working hands. In the winter I wear flannel nightgowns to bed and overalls during the day. I can kill and clean a hog as mercilessly as a man. My fat keeps me hot in zero weather. I can work all day, breaking ice to get water for washing. I can eat pork liver cooked over the open fire minutes after it comes steaming from the hog. One winter I knocked a bull calf straight in the brain between the eyes with a sledge hammer and had the meat hung up to chill before nightfall. But of course all this does not show on television. I am the way my daughter would want me to be: a hundred pounds lighter, my skin like a uncooked barley pancake. My hair glistens in the hot bright lights. Johnny Carson has much to do to keep up with my quick and witty tongue.

But that is a mistake. I know even before I wake up. Who ever knew a Johnson with a quick tongue? Who can even imagine me looking a strange white man in the eye? It seems to me I have talked to them always with one foot raised in flight, with my head turned in whichever way is farthest from them. Dee, though. She would always look anyone in the eye. Hesitation was no part of her nature.

"How do I look, Mama?" Maggie says, showing just enough of her thin body enveloped in pink skirt and red blouse for me to know she's there, almost hidden by the door.

"Come out into the yard," I say.

Have you ever seen a lame animal, perhaps a dog run over by some careless person rich enough to own a car, sidle up to someone who is ignorant enough to be kind to him? That is the way my Maggie walks. She has been like this, chin on chest, eyes on ground, feet in shuffle, ever since the fire that burned the other house to the ground.

Dee is lighter than Maggie, with nicer hair and a fuller figure. She's a woman now, though sometimes I forget. How long ago was it that the other house burned? Ten, twelve years? Sometimes I can still hear the flames and feel Maggie's arm sticking to me, her hair smoking and her dress falling off her in little black papery flakes. Her eyes seemed stretched open, blazed open by the flames reflected in them. And Dee, I see her standing off under the sweet gum tree she used to dig gum out of; a look of concentration on her face as she watched the last dingy gray board of the house fall in toward the red-hot brick chimney. Why don't you do a dance around the ashes? I'd wanted to ask her. She had hated the house that much.

I used to think she hated Maggie, too. But that was before we raised the money, the church and me, to send her to Augusta to school. She used to read to us without pity; forcing words, lies, other folks' habits, whole lives upon us two, sitting trapped and ignorant underneath her voice. She washed us in a river of make-believe, burned us with a lot of knowledge we didn't necessarily need to know. Pressed us to her with the serious way she read, to shove us away at just the moment, like dimwits, we seemed about to understand.

Dee wanted nice things. A yellow organdy dress to wear to her graduation from high school; black pumps to match a green suit she'd made from an old suit somebody gave me. She was determined to stare down any disaster in her efforts. Her eyelids would not flicker for minutes at a time. Often I fought off the temptation to shake her. At sixteen she had a style of her own: and knew what style was.

I never had an education myself. After second grade the school was closed down. Don't ask me why: in 1927 colored asked fewer questions than they do now. Sometimes Maggie reads to me. She stumbles along good-naturedly but can't see well. She knows she is not bright. Like good looks and money, quickness passed her by. She will marry John Thomas (who has mossy teeth in an earnest face) and then I'll be free to sit here and I guess just sing church songs to myself. Although I never was a good singer. Never could carry a tune. I was always better at a man's job. I used to love to milk till I was hoofed in the side in '49. Cows are soothing and slow and don't bother you, unless you try to milk them the wrong way.

I have deliberately turned my back on the house. It is three rooms, just like the one that burned, except the roof is tin; they don't make shingle roofs any more. There are no real windows, just some holes cut in the sides, like the portholes in a ship, but not round and not square, with rawhide holding the shutters up on the outside. The house is in a pasture, too, like the other one. No doubt when Dee sees it she will want to tear it down. She wrote me once that no matter where we "choose" to live, she will manage to come see us. But she will never bring her friends. Maggie and I thought about this and Maggie asked me, "Mama, when did Dee ever *have* any friends?"

She had a few. Furtive boys in pink shirts hanging about on washday after school. Nervous girls who never laughed. Impressed with her they worshiped the well-turned phrase, the cute shape, the scalding humor that erupted like bubbles in lye. She read to them.

When she was courting Jimmy T. she didn't have much time to pay to us, but turned all her faultfinding power on him. He *flew* to marry a cheap gal from a family of ignorant flashy people. She hardly had time to recompose herself.

When she comes I will meet—but there they are!

Maggie attempts to make a dash for the house, in her shuffling way, but I stay her with my hand. "Come back here," I say. And she stops and tries to dig a well in the sand with her toe.

It is hard to see them clearly through the strong sun. But even the first glimpse of leg out of the car tells me it is Dee. Her feet were always neat-looking, as if God himself had shaped them with a certain style. From the other side of the car comes a short, stocky man. Hair is all over his head a foot long and hanging from his chin like a kinky mule tail. I hear Maggie suck in her breath. "Uhnnnh," is what it sounds like. Like when you see the wriggling end of a snake just in front of your foot on the road. "Uhnnnh."

Dee next. A dress down to the ground, in this hot weather. A dress so loud it hurts my eyes. There are yellows and oranges enough to throw back the light of the sun. I feel my whole face warming from the heat waves it throws out. Earrings, too, gold and hanging down to her shoulders. Bracelets dangling and making noises when she moves her arm up to shake the folds of the dress out of her armpits. The dress is loose and flows, and as she walks closer, I like it. I hear Maggie go "Uhnnnh" again. It is her sister's hair. It stands straight up like the wool on a sheep. It is black as night and around the edges are two long pigtails that rope about like small lizards disappearing behind her ears.

"Wa-su-zo-Tean-o!" she says, coming on in that gliding way the dress makes her move. The short stocky fellow with the hair to his navel is all grinning and he follows up with "Asalamalakim, my mother and sister!" He moves to hug Maggie but she falls back, right up against the back of my chair. I feel her trembling there and when I look up I see the perspiration falling off her chin.

"Don't get up," says Dee. Since I am stout it takes something of a push. You can see me trying to move a second or two before I make it. She turns, showing white heels through her sandals, and goes back to the car. Out she peeks next with a Polaroid. She stoops down quickly and lines up picture after picture of me sitting there in front of the house with Maggie cowering behind me. She never takes a shot without making sure the house is included. When a cow comes nibbling around the edge of the yard she snaps it and me and Maggie *and* the house. Then she puts the Polaroid in the back seat of the car, and comes up and kisses me on the forehead.

Meanwhile Asalamalakim is going through the motions with Maggie's hand. Maggie's hand is as limp as a fish, and probably as cold, despite the sweat, and she keeps trying to pull it back. It looks like Asalamalakim wants to shake hands but wants to do it fancy. Or maybe he don't know how people shake hands. Anyhow, he soon gives up on Maggie.

"Well," I say. "Dee."

"No, Mama," she says. "Not 'Dee.' Wangero Leewanika Kemanjo!"

"What happened to 'Dee'?" I wanted to know.

"She's dead." Wangero said. "I couldn't bear it any longer being named after the people who oppress me."

"You know as well as me you was named after your aunt Dicie." I said. Dicie is my sister. She named Dee. We called her "Big Dee" after Dee was born.

"But who was *she* named after?" asked Wangero.

"I guess after Grandma Dee," I said.

"And who was she named after?" asked Wangero.

"Her mother," I said, and saw Wangero was getting tired. "That's about as far back as I can trace it," I said. Though, in fact, I probably could have carried it back beyond the Civil War through the branches.

"Well," said Asalamalakim, "there you are."

"Uhnnnh," I heard Maggie say.

"There I was not," I said, "before 'Dicie' cropped up in our family, so why should I try to trace it that far back?"

He just stood there grinning, looking down on me like somebody inspecting a Model A car. Every once in a while he and Wangero sent eye signals over my head.

"How do you pronounce this name?" I asked.

"You don't have to call me by it if you don't want to," said Wangero.   38

"Why shouldn't I?" I asked. "If that's what you want us to call you, we'll   39
call you."

"I know it might sound awkward at first," said Wangero.   40

"I'll get used to it," I said. "Ream it out again."   41

Well, soon we got the name out of the way. Asalamalakim had a name   42
twice as long and three times as hard. After I tripped over it two or three times
he told me to just call him Hakim-a-barber. I wanted to ask him was he a barber,
but I didn't really think he was, so I didn't ask.

"You must belong to those beef-cattle peoples down the road," I said.   43
They said "Asalamalakim" when they met you, too, but they didn't shake hands.
Always too busy: feeding the cattle, fixing the fences, putting up salt-lick shel-
ters, throwing down hay. When the white folks poisoned some of the herd the
men stayed up all night with rifles in their hands. I walked a mile and a half just
to see the sight.

Hakim-a-barber said, "I accept some of their doctrines, but farming and   44
raising cattle is not my style." (They didn't tell me, and I didn't ask, whether
Wangero [Dee] had really gone and married him.)

We sat down to eat and right away he said he didn't eat collards and pork   45
was unclean. Wangero, though, went on through the chitlins and corn bread, the
greens and everything else. She talked a blue streak over the sweet potatoes.
Everything delighted her. Even the fact that we still used the benches her daddy
made for the table when we couldn't afford to buy chairs.

"Oh, Mama!" she cried. Then turned to Hakim-a-barber. "I never knew   46
how lovely these benches are. You can feel the rump prints," she said, running
her hands underneath her and along the bench. Then she gave a sigh and her
hand closed over Grandma Dee's butter dish. "That's it!" she said. "I knew there
was something I wanted to ask you if I could have." She jumped up from the
table and went over in the corner where the churn stood, the milk in its clabber
by now. She looked at the churn and looked at it.

"This churn top is what I need," she said. "Didn't Uncle Buddy whittle it   47
out of a tree you all used to have?"

"Yes," I said.   48

"Uh huh," she said happily. "And I want the dasher, too."   49

"Uncle Buddy whittle that, too?" asked the barber.   50

Dee (Wangero) looked up at me.   51

"Aunt Dee's first husband whittled the dash," said Maggie so low you al-   52
most couldn't hear her. "His name was Henry, but they called him Stash."

"Maggie's brain is like an elephant's," Wangero said, laughing. "I can use   53
the churn top as a centerpiece for the alcove table," she said, sliding a plate over
the churn, "and I'll think of something artistic to do with the dasher."

When she finished wrapping the dasher the handle stuck out. I took it for a   54
moment in my hands. You didn't even have to look close to see where hands
pushing the dasher up and down to make butter had left a kind of sink in the

wood. In fact, there were a lot of small sinks; you could see where thumbs and fingers had sunk into the wood. It was beautiful light yellow wood, from a tree that grew in the yard where Big Dee and Stash had lived.

After dinner Dee (Wangero) went to the trunk at the foot of my bed and started rifling through it. Maggie hung back in the kitchen over the dishpan. Out came Wangero with two quilts. They had been pieced by Grandma Dee and then Big Dee and me had hung them on the quilt frames on the front porch and quilted them. One was in the Lone Star pattern. The other was Walk Around the Mountain. In both of them were scraps of dresses Grandma Dee had worn fifty and more years ago. Bits and pieces of Grandpa Jarrell's Paisley shirts. And one teeny faded blue piece, about the size of a penny matchbox, that was from Great Grandpa Ezra's uniform that he wore in the Civil War.   55

"Mama," Wangero said sweet as a bird. "Can I have these old quilts?"   56

I heard something fall in the kitchen, and a minute later the kitchen door slammed.   57

"Why don't you take one or two of the others?" I asked "These old things was just done by me and Big Dee from some tops your grandma pieced before she died."   58

"No," said Wangero. "I don't want those. They are stitched around the borders by machine."   59

"That's to make them last better," I said.   60

"That's not the point," said Wangero. "These are all pieces of dresses Grandma used to wear. She did all this stitching by hand. Imagine!" She held the quilts securely in her arms, stroking them.   61

"Some of the pieces, like those lavender ones, come from old clothes her mother handed down to her," I said, moving up to touch the quilts. Dee (Wangero) moved back just enough so that I couldn't reach the quilts. They already belonged to her.   62

"Imagine!" she breathed again, clutching them closely to her bosom.   63

"The truth is," I said, "I promised to give them quilts to Maggie, for when she marries John Thomas."   64

She gasped like a bee had stung her.   65

"Maggie can't appreciate these quilts!" she said. "She'd probably be backward enough to put them to everyday use."   66

"I reckon she would," I said. "God knows I been saving 'em for long enough with nobody using 'em. I hope she will!" I didn't want to bring up how I had offered Dee (Wangero) a quilt when she went away to college. Then she had told me they were old-fashioned, out of style.   67

"But they're *priceless!*" she was saying now, furiously, for she has a temper. "Maggie would put them on the bed and in five years they'd be in rags. Less than that!"   68

"She can always make some more," I said. "Maggie knows how to quilt."   69

Dee (Wangero) looked at me with hatred. "You just will not understand. The point is these quilts, *these* quilts!"   70

"Well," I said, stumped. "What would *you* do with them?"   71

"Hang them," she said. As if that was the only thing you *could* do with quilts.   72

Maggie by now was standing in the door. I could almost hear the sound   73
her feet made as they scraped over each other.

"She can have them, Mama," she said, like somebody used to never win-   74
ning anything, or having anything reserved for her. "I can 'member Grandma
Dee without the quilts."

I looked at her hard. She had filled her bottom lip with checkerberry snuff   75
and it gave her face a kind of dopey, hangdog look. It was Grandma Dee and
Big Dee who taught her how to quilt herself. She stood there with her scarred
hands hidden in the folds of her skirt. She looked at her sister with something
like fear but she wasn't mad at her. This was Maggie's portion. This was the
way she knew God to work.

When I looked at her like that something hit me in the top of my head and   76
ran down to the soles of my feet. Just like when I'm in church and the spirit of
God touches me and I get happy and shout. I did something I never had done before: hugged Maggie to me, then dragged her on into the room, snatched the
quilts out of Miss Wangero's hands and dumped them into Maggie's lap. Maggie just sat there on my bed with her mouth open.

"Take one or two of the others," I said to Dee.   77

But she turned without a word and went out to Hakim-a-barber.   78

"You just don't understand," she said, as Maggie and I came out to the car.   79

"What don't I understand?" I wanted to know.   80

"Your heritage," she said. And then she turned to Maggie, kissed her,   81
and said, "You ought to try to make something of yourself, too, Maggie. It's
really a new day for us. But from the way you and Mama still live you'd never
know it."

She put on some sunglasses that hid everything above the tip of her nose   82
and her chin.

Maggie smiled; maybe at the sunglasses. But a real smile, not scared.   83
After we watched the car dust settle I asked Maggie to bring me a dip of snuff.
And then the two of us sat there just enjoying, until it was time to go in the
house and go to bed.

Meaning and Idea

1. What are the essential features of the women's personalities—"I"
   (Momma), Maggie, and Dee (Wangero)? What features do they have in
   common? How are they different?

2. What is Maggie's reaction to the man who accompanies Dee? Why does she
   react as she does?

3. Why did Dee change her name? How do Momma and Maggie feel about
   this change? Why do they react as they do?

4. Wangero seems to reject much of her earlier life, yet she eagerly seeks to take with her objects from Momma's house. How do you account for her interest in the churn top, the dasher, and the handmade quilts?

5. Why does Momma refuse to give Wangero the quilts when she first asks? Why does Maggie agree to let them go, however? What does she mean by the line "I can 'member Grandma Dee without the quilts"?

6. Why does Momma hug Maggie? Momma makes this action seem as if it grew out of a religious epiphany. What made Momma feel as if the spirit of God had touched her? How does she finally resolve the issue of who gets the quilts? Why does she make the decision she makes?

Language, Form, Structure

1. This piece has many levels of comparison and contrast—between the two sisters, between Momma and each of her daughters, between the "new day" and the old ways for African Americans. Discuss the various elements of comparison here. How do the contrasting behaviors help you understand the characters?

2. How does Walker's use of language make us see how cruel Dee is as she leaves? How is the last paragraph, in its homey simplicity, a vindication of the life that Momma and Maggie live as opposed to the life Dee lives?

3. The word *Asalamalakim* is really a greeting. Is it also Wangero's friend's name? Why do you think that Momma uses the word as the man's name?

4. Discuss these phrases for their sensory diction and meaning: eyeing her sister with a mixture of envy and awe; man-working hands; mossy teeth in an earnest face; furtive boys in pink shirts; scalding humor that erupted like bubbles in lye.

Ideas for Writing

1. Think of two people you know who have different ways of dealing with their heritage and write a comparison-and-contrast essay about them.

2. Mothers and daughters, fathers and sons can often represent classical conflicts in their attitudes and behaviors toward each other. Write an essay about a mother and daughter or a father and son whom you know; show how they compare and contrast.

3. Write an essay in which you consider the characters in this fictional piece. How do they compare and contrast with each other? How has Walker succeeded through comparison and contrast strategies in making the characters alive and memorable for the reader?

CROSSOVER

1. Virginia Woolf in "Shakespeare's Gifted Sister," Amy Tan in "Two Kinds," and Alice Walker in "Everyday Use" all write about women, family, and the traditions that shape their lives. Write an essay that identifies the common elements of women's lives explored in at least two of these selections. Identify differences, too, in the authors' perspectives on women, family, and tradition.

2. Thomas Hardy in "The Ruined Maid" and William Shakespeare in "My Mistress' Eyes Are Nothing Like the Sun" both use comic elements to explore their female subjects. How effective is each of these poems as a comic statement? What elements make each one funny? What goals beyond the comic does each poem seem to reach for?

Chapter Six

■

CLASSIFICATION

INTRODUCTION TO CLASSIFICATION

As thinking animals we are forever dividing things up in our minds and putting them back together in new ways. Basic to much of this analytic thinking is the effort to classify myriad experiences and phenomena into meaningful categories. Related objects look clearer and more sensible when sorted into like groups.

Classification and Division

Classification usually works hand in hand with division (or analysis). In *division,* you break something down into discrete elements. In *classification,* you place like members of a group into categories. Generally, the intent of division is to take one large object, concept, or idea and split it so that its parts are clear. To understand the structure of a newspaper, you might divide it into departments—news, sports, advertising, human interest, and so on. The intent of classification is to identify groups by putting together items with common properties. You come closer to understanding newspaper advertisements if you look at specific examples of personal ads, want ads, department store ads, supermarket ads, and so on. Division breaks a large unit down into its pieces; classification builds groups up by collecting common examples.

Think of almost any subject and imagine where we would be without our well-honed habits of division and classification for mental sorting. Take the simple but necessary task of housekeeping, for example. Faced with items piled high during a busy week, we must turn to division and classification as an aid. We divide the items in our pile—clothing, books, papers, sports equipment, CDs, games. Then we put similar items together into a large category, building to a group identity, so to speak. Thus, a deflated soccer ball, a worn pair of Nikes, a catcher's mitt, two stained sweatbands, a surfboard—these specific objects help us create the category "sports equipment." Classifying our housekeeping objects even further, we can see other possibilities for groupings. Clothing falls into categories—dirty and clean, sports and dressy, daytime and evening, and so on. These categories can be even further split: You might classify the clean clothing, for example, into underwear, slacks, shirts; the dirty into nonwashable and washable; the washable into cold, warm, and hot or bleach and no bleach.

Grouping Ideas

Classification, in short, helps us order our lives, and this ordering can be either humble, as you saw above, or more lofty, as, for example, when we group countries by their economic or political systems, people by their learning styles or creative talents, or colleges by their courses of study. Through classification, we can make sensible groupings not only of our daily lives but also of the complex issues that emerge in every area of human activity and study. Indeed, without classification, advanced and systematic thinking could not exist. Chemists first divide the world into organic and inorganic objects and then proceed to subdivide each of those categories further. Biologists classify living things into large groups that are further subdivided to link common creatures. Literary critics classify writing—fiction, poetry, drama, essays—and then make smaller groups within the larger ones.

For a writer, in any area or discipline, classification is essential. Rich details, observations, and examples may be the writer's stock-in-trade, but through appropriate groupings, the writer can link ideas that otherwise might lose force.

READING CLASSIFICATION

As we read classification, we are reminded of the human invention involved in the undertaking. All the selections in this chapter eschew common categories and instead offer the reader fresh mental containers for classifying the various subjects at hand.

Malcolm Cowley's essay "The National Heartbeat: 'We-ness' and 'Me-ness' " allows us to see our age under a modern political microscope. Through his classification of twentieth-century politics as "me"-oriented or "we"-oriented, conservative and then progressive, a back-and-forth pendulum swing between two poles, Cowley helps us see our century as patterned and predict the tone of our next era. The two groups and the characteristics of their members enrich our understanding of contemporary politics. Judith Viorst's essay "Friends, Good Friends—and Such Good Friends" uses classification to help us view friendship from a fresh perspective. She categorizes women friends at varying levels of intensity.

Classification is a particularly powerful tool for helping us see the patterns and habits of political and social life. But through classification we also can come to an understanding of life's subtle meanings. Dylan Thomas's poem "Do Not Go Gentle into That Good Night" classifies dying men into types. Thomas shows the ways of men as they face death—wise men, good men, wild men, and grave men. By means of his classification, he brings us to a unique view—for his dying father and for us, the readers—of how to face the end of life. Phillip Lopate in "Modern Friendships" reviews classical opinions of friendship in order to establish a new taxonomy of the word for modern times, elucidating both relations and conditions of late-twentieth-century life.

The selections included in this chapter suggest the wide range of subjects that the strategy of classification can help illuminate, the fresh and novel categories we can use to help us see patterns in personal, public, and artistic life. The selections also demonstrate how writers use their fresh classifications to advance original theses, bringing complex categories to their persuasive purposes.

WRITING CLASSIFICATION

Much of what you are called on to write requires some classification—breaking down your subject into classes or groups of similar members. You want to write about a poem; well, then chances are that you will want to explore the *kind* of poem it is. Is it a sonnet, a ballad, a haiku? How can you classify it according to stanzaic form? Or you might try classifying the poem according to literary genre—epic, lyric, dramatic monologue—or according to subject—love poem, war poem, historical poem. You may do much more besides classifying the poem in your paper, certainly, but writing on almost any topic, in almost any discipline, you will see that classification plays an important role. And it is not just in determining where your subject stands—what class of thing it is—that you call on classification as a writer. Further analysis of your subject may compel you to make steady use of classification by grouping and categorizing your ideas and observations. In writing about a poem, let's say, you may prepare for the task by jotting down your many thoughts as you read. But then you use a rudimentary classification system to help you sort your many thoughts into different groups: thoughts on imagery, thoughts on word choice, thoughts on characters in the poem perhaps. And then within each of these groups you may find yourself using classification again. In discussing word choice you may classify into denotative meanings (dictionary meanings) and connotative meanings (the meanings that have clustered about word through usage), or Latinate and Anglo-Saxon words, or abstract and concrete words, and so on—classifying within each of your categories.

Because categorization is a much-used tool in thinking and writing, it is worthwhile to practice writing classification. Again, as with writing of any kind, in preparing the classification paper you will draw on many of the writer's strategies—description, exemplification, and so on. In this writing exercise, however, you will use classification as the controlling strategy. But as with any strategy, your purpose should be to advance a point or position, to use rhetorical technique to develop a coherent thesis.

PURPOSE AND AUDIENCE

Classification by definition reflects an act of individual judgment. People, chemicals, flora, and fauna do not come into the world neatly fitting into categories; *people* put them into categories in order to make better sense of them and make the world more orderly through these understandings.

Exploring a Topic

You must make many decisions as you think about exploring a topic through classification. Do you want to be funny or serious? Do you want to criticize or to persuade? Classification is an able tool and lends itself to many purposes. You want to write about your family, let's say. Well, classifying family members into ranters, ravers, whimperers, and pouters—categorizing their behavior when hurt or angry—will help you develop your thoughts along a comic vein, think about your family in humorous terms, and make your reader laugh. But perhaps it's a very serious matter to you when your family members are angry or hurt. Well, then you will classify them very differently: You'll discuss those in your family who hold their anger in and those who let their anger go. How you classify depends on how you see your subject.

The Need for Planning

Readers naturally take to classification because readers, being human, like to see the world made comprehensible and like to see the sorts of arrangements others can make. But without sufficient planning and invention on the part of the writer, classification, like comparison, can grow tedious. Beware, then, of papers whose ideas are merely informational, with little point of view expressed. An essay with the following thesis risks boring the reader terribly: "My teachers fall into three categories: those with degrees in science, those with degrees in the humanities, and those with degrees in the social sciences." True, some lively description of teachers and their habits might make such a thesis come to life. But if the writer settles simply for cataloguing information in this clinical way, readers, unless they are especially interested in the subject, will soon lose interest. How much more engaging, then, to build your own special perception into your classification. "My teachers fall into three categories: friend, mother-surrogate, confessor." Or if you're using a common classification scheme to group them—science, humanities, social science, say—then chances are that you can heighten your reader's attention if you build a point of view into your thesis. "Here at Dovery College my teachers in major academic areas—science, humanities, social science—operate from the same educational assumption: that writing is learning and learning is writing." As we said, a reader with a special interest in or knowledge of a subject may be tolerant or even enthusiastic about a classification essay that is purely informational. But your own lively perspective will add a unique tone to the essay and will engage your audience. Be sure, then, to think about your audience and its relation to your subject, as well as your own relation to the subject, as you prepare your classification essay.

PROCESS

Establishing a Principle for Classification

Your first step in designing an essay in classification is to select the principle by which you will classify. Many subjects you might choose to write about lend themselves to varied classification systems. You want to write a classification essay on microcomputers, let's say. You should decide whether you want to classify by price, make, power, availability of software, compatibility, or what have you. Produce a thesis statement that expresses both your topic and your attitude toward it. Once you've decided on the principle that goes best with your interests, as well as your audience's knowledge and interest, stick with this principle as you develop your paper. Keep your categories discrete and do not overlap them. Classifying microcomputers as low-priced, mainframe, medium-priced, microcomputers, IBMs, and high-priced would reflect confused thinking and would lead to a confusing paper.

Categories and Completeness

You must also be careful to be as complete as possible when you develop your various categories. A classification of urban transportation into automobiles and buses is clearly an incomplete classification. A complete classification would have to include trains, subways, and taxis as well. Although Cowley's two large groups are complex and original, you should be aware of the pitfalls in simplistic divisions into two groups only, these and everything else. Classifying films into the successful and the unsuccessful or foods into the nutritious and the non-nutritious creates categories too large and diffuse to be meaningful. A good rule of thumb to help you achieve a relatively complete classification system is to present at least three groups. Depending on your purpose, you might have to approach your topic exhaustively, omitting no categories whatsoever. And you should pay some attention to exceptions: Do examples exist that defy the orderly system you have created? To ignore them is to stack the deck, and an intelligent reader will mistrust you for it. If as you plan your classification paper you find you have too many categories to manage, then modify your subject so that you and your reader don't feel either overwhelmed by too much material or cheated by a big purpose not successfully developed.

When your categories are set, decide how you will arrange them in your paper. If you're classifying literary genres, will you move chronologically, referring as you name the groups to their origins in time? Will you present them by considering the simpler forms first and then the more complex? Or will you follow public sensibilities by organizing your categories from the least to the most popular forms?

Classifications require the writer to attend to a good deal at once. The effective classification is one whose sections get more or less equal attention. If you devote lots of space to one or two of your categories and skimp on another, your essay will be unsatisfactory in shape and consistency.

Writing classification demands rigorous thinking and careful planning. The rewards of this effort, however, are many, as you and your readers see a subject illuminated by this important reflective act.

STUDENT WRITING

In this classification essay the student writer draws on many of the techniques explained in this chapter. The annotations will help you see the elements that contribute to the paper's development.

Suppertime Pests

It's always the same time. Just when we're sitting down to eat. They want to sell you a new telephone service, or a magazine subscription, or a five-day cruise. They want you to enter a sweepstake that will win you cash, or airline tickets, or a Las Vegas spree. But whatever these nighttime callers are pushing, they fall into a few distinct styles: teasers, teachers, and preachers.[a] And identifying the approach each one takes is a step toward a safe escape.[b,c]

The telephone teasers[d] don't even engage you in conversation.[e] A tape calls you, not a live person. It says an important message is coming your way—don't move, just wait. If you don't stay put, you might lose out big time—a winning lottery ticket, a large inheritance from an unknown uncle, a notice that your son just made the National Honor Society. If you go back to your now cold meat loaf and peas,[f] you'll never know what you missed, but maybe your life will be less satisfying and substantial. The teaser turns the tables. He doesn't need you; you need him. As the taped music plays and you wait for the important message, you've been tricked and teased into thinking, "I have to know. Don't hang up."

Then there are the telephone teachers,[g] the solicitors who read from a lesson plan. Now and then they break to breathe noisily or clear their throats[h] and ask a question. "How much are you paying now for your phone service?" "How much do you spend for magazines at newsstand prices?" Like the worst teachers, they know the answers they want. No matter what you say, they go on for part two of their canned lesson. "How would you like to save money each month?" If you mumble, "Blah, blah, blah," or any such nonsense, they ignore you and say, "That's what I thought. And it's so easy. What credit card do you want to use?"

The telephone preachers[i] are much like the teachers. They also[j] talk a lot. But they rely on improvisation and inspiration. They want the best for you. If you follow their advice and buy what they're selling, life is going to be amazing. If you ask them questions, they tell you you're missing your big chance. If you say, "Can I call you back?" they say, "This offer is ending soon." If you say, "How soon?" they say in honey-coated tones, "You're my last call. I really want this for you. If you let this offer slip by, you'll really regret it."[k] The preacher, like the other telephone solicitors, is merely after the leather wallet in your back pocket.[n]

Teaser, teacher, preacher. Now[j] they all get the same response from me. "I'm glad you called. I have something to sell you!"[m] I say. If it's a teaser, I put down the phone, say, "Hold on," and go back to my meal. A telephone

[a] Subject, telephone solicitors, broken into three groups

[b] Thesis includes point of view: knowing the approach of each group helps you end their annoyance

[c] Purpose: to explain how, to escape solicitors, others can use these strategies

[d] First discrete category: telephone teasers

[e] Audience: people like the writer who are troubled by endless suppertime solicitors

[f] Sensory detail (sight)

[g] Second discrete category

[h] Sensory detail (sound)

[i] Last discrete category

[j] Transition

[k] Comparison and contrast strategies

[l] Process analysis throughout body paragraphs

[m] Use of spoken conversation enlivens humorous presentation

[n] Arrangement of categories: simplest group to most complex

°Conclusion clinches
the essay: humorous
tone contributes to
unity of paper

teacher? I read to her the contents of a cereal box to let her know how it feels to be talked and bored to death. If I hear the preacher, though, I simply read the same stuff, breaking now and then to say, "I want only the best for you." They take less and less time to hang up on me as I get better at my spiel.[1]

Somehow word must have gotten out across the land that it's not worth calling my house. Recently, our suppers have been pest-free. Maybe I should try to sell my approach. I can hear my pitch now: "Good evening. Tired of suppertime pest calls? Here for a limited time only is a plan to beat annoying solicitors at their own game."°

SUMMING UP: CLASSIFICATION

Reading Classification

- Working along with *division,* which means breaking something down into discrete elements, *classification* means placing like members of a group into categories.

- Identify the categories that the writer has established and try to determine why he or she has chosen those categories.

- Determine how the stated (or implied) thesis identifies the classification strategy.

- As you examine the classification piece, ask how the categories enlighten your understanding of the topic. Do the groupings help you understand complex issues?

Writing Classification

- Break your subject into classes or groups of similar members.

- Be aware that each group may lend itself to further classification.

- Decide on your purpose for classifying the topic you have chosen and convey that purpose either explicitly in a thesis sentence or by indirection as you explore the features of the topic.

- Be sure to express a point of view toward the topic and the classification strategy in order to avoid a merely informational paper with no embedded attitude or opinion about the essay's subject.

- Consider the audience's needs and interests: the elements of your writing that will engage the readers' interest in the topic you wish to develop through classification.

- Weighing your own interests and your audience's knowledge and interests, determine the principle by which you will develop your classification paper and stick with that principle as you develop it.

- Keep your established categories discrete and do not overlap them.

- Be sure that your categories present a complete classification scheme for the topic: Do not omit any categories that are essential for the paper's proper development.

- Beware of simplistic categories that produce groupings too large or diffuse; aim for at least three groups for a relatively complete classification system.

- Pay attention to the possibilities of exceptions to your classification scheme and treat the exceptions honestly for your readers.

- Avoid a classification scheme that produces too many categories; modify your subject if you find that you have too many groups.

- As you develop your draft, determine an appropriate method of grouping the categories you have established.

- Treat the various categories with more or less equal attention; avoid skimping on details in one category as you provide a great deal of information in another.

Friends, Good Friends— and Such Good Friends

Judith Viorst

A prolific author, writing stories for children as well as light verse for adults, Judith Viorst (1936–) became nationally known with her first book, *It's Hard to Be Hip over Thirty and Other Tragedies of Married Life* (1970). She followed that success with *How Did I Get to be Forty and Other Atrocities* (1984) and *Forever Fifty and Other Negotiations.* She continues to publish a monthly column in *Redbook,* where she is a contributing editor. With its carefully detailed portraits of people, Viorst's writing often focuses on her own family and her married life. She has said, "Someone once remarked to me that if I hadn't gotten married, I might have written the great American novel, but I think if I hadn't gotten married, maybe I wouldn't have written anything." In addition to humorous poetry Viorst has written one novel, the mystery *Murdering Mr. Monti,* and a book about mourning, *Necessary Losses* (1986), which draws on psychoanalytical theory to offer advice on dealing with grief.

This piece shows Viorst's light humor at its best. Her truthful observations are carefully couched in a light engaging style.

W omen are friends, I once would have said, when they totally love   1
and support and trust each other, and bare to each other the secrets of their souls,
and run—no questions asked—to help each other, and tell harsh truths to each
other (no, you can't wear that dress unless you lose ten pounds first) when harsh
truths must be told.

Women are friends, I once would have said, when they share the same af-   2
fection for Ingmar Bergman, plus train rides, cats, warm rain, charades, Camus,
and hate with equal ardor Newark and Brussels sprouts and Lawrence Welk and
camping.

In other words, I once would have said that a friend is a friend all the way,   3
but now I believe that's a narrow point of view. For the friendships I have and
the friendships I see are conducted at many levels of intensity, serve many different functions, meet different needs and range from those as all-the-way as the
friendship of the soul sisters mentioned above to that of the most nonchalant and
casual playmates.

Consider these varieties of friendship: 4

1. Convenience friends. These are women with whom, if our paths weren't   5
crossing all the time, we'd have no particular reason to be friends: a next-door
neighbor, a woman in our car pool, the mother of one of our children's closest
friends or maybe some mommy with whom we serve juice and cookies each
week at the Glenwood Co-op Nursery.

Convenience friends are convenient indeed. They'll lend us their cups and silverware for a party. They'll drive our kids to soccer when we're sick. They'll take us to pick up our car when we need a lift to the garage. They'll even take our cats when we go on vacation. As we will for them.   6

But we don't, with convenience friends, ever come too close or tell too much; we maintain our public face and emotional distance. "Which means," says Elaine, "that I'll talk about being overweight but not about being depressed. Which means I'll admit being mad but not blind with rage. Which means that I might say that we're pinched this month but never that I'm worried sick over money."   7

But which doesn't mean that there isn't sufficient value to be found in these friendships of mutual aid, in convenience friends.   8

2. Special-interest friends. These friendships aren't intimate, and they needn't involve kids or silverware or cats. Their value lies in some interest jointly shared. And so we may have an office friend or a yoga friend or a tennis friend or a friend from the Women's Democratic Club.   9

"I've got one woman friend," says Joyce, "who likes, as I do, to take psychology courses. Which makes it nice for me—and nice for her. It's fun to go with someone you know and it's fun to discuss what you've learned, driving back from the classes." And for the most part, she says, that's all they discuss.   10

"I'd say that what we're doing is *doing* together, not being together," Suzanne says of her Tuesday-doubles friends. "It's mainly a tennis relationship, but we play together well. And I guess we all need to have a couple of playmates."   11

I agree.   12

My playmate is a shopping friend, a woman of marvelous taste, a woman who knows exactly *where* to buy *what,* and furthermore is a woman who always knows beyond a doubt what one ought to be buying. I don't have the time to keep up with what's new in eyeshadow, hemlines and shoes and whether the smock look is in or finished already. But since (oh, shame!) I care a lot about eyeshadow, hemlines and shoes, and since I don't *want* to wear smocks if the smock look is finished, I'm very glad to have a shopping friend.   13

3. Historical friends. We all have a friend who knew us when . . . maybe way back in Miss Meltzer's second grade, when our family lived in that three-room flat in Brooklyn, when our dad was out of work for seven months, when our brother Allie got in that fight where they had to call the police, when our sister married the endodontist from Yonkers and when, the morning after we lost our virginity, she was the first, the only, friend we told.   14

They years have gone by and we've gone separate ways and we've little in common now, but we're still an intimate part of each other's past. And so whenever we go to Detroit we always go to visit this friend of our girlhood. Who knows how we looked before our teeth were straightened. Who knows how we talked before our voice got un-Brooklyned. Who knows what we ate before we learned about artichokes. And who, by her presence, puts us in touch with an earlier part of ourself, a part of ourself it's important never to lose.   15

"What this friend means to me and what I mean to her," says Grace, "is having a sister without sibling rivalry. We know the texture of each other's lives. She remembers my grandmother's cabbage soup. I remember the way her uncle played the piano. There's simply no other friend who remembers those things."

4. Crossroads friends. Like historical friends, our crossroads friends are important for *what was*—for the friendship we shared at a crucial, now past, time of life. A time, perhaps, when we roomed in college together; or worked as eager young singles in the Big City together; or went together, as my friend Elizabeth and I did, through pregnancy, birth and that scary first year of new motherhood.

Crossroads friends forge powerful links, links strong enough to endure with not much more contact than once-a-year letters at Christmas. And out of respect for those crossroads years, for those dramas and dreams we once shared, we will always be friends.

5. Cross-generational friends. Historical friends and crossroads friends seem to maintain a special kind of intimacy—dormant but always ready to be revived—and though we may rarely meet, whenever we do connect, it's personal and intense. Another kind of intimacy exists in the friendships that form across generations in what one woman calls her daughter-mother and her mother-daughter relationships.

Evelyn's friend is her mother's age—"but I share so much more than I ever could with my mother"—a woman she talks to of music, of books and of life. "What I get from her is the benefit of her experience. What she gets—and enjoys—from me is a youthful perspective. It's a pleasure for both of us."

I have in my own life a precious friend, a woman of 65 who has lived very hard, who is wise, who listens well; who has been where I am and can help me understand it; and who represents not only an ultimate ideal mother to me but also the person I'd like to be when I grow up.

In our daughter role we tend to do more than our share of self-revelation; in our mother role we tend to receive what's revealed. It's another kind of pleasure—playing wise mother to a questing younger person. It's another very lovely kind of friendship.

6. Part-of-a-couple friends. Some of the women we call our friends we never see alone—we see them as part of a couple at couples' parties. And though we share interests in many things and respect each other's views, we aren't moved to deepen the relationship. Whatever the reason, a lack of time or—and this is more likely—a lack of chemistry, our friendship remains in the context of a group. But the fact that our feeling on seeing each other is always, "I'm *so* glad she's here" and the fact that we spend half the evening talking together says that this too, in its own way, counts as a friendship.

(Other part-of-a-couple friends are the friends that came with the marriage, and some of these are friends we could live without. But sometimes, alas, she married our husband's best friend; and sometimes, alas, she *is* our husband's best friend. And so we find ourself dealing with her, somewhat against our will, in a spirit of what I'll call *reluctant* friendship.)

7. Men who are friends. I wanted to write just of women friends, but the women I've talked to won't let me—they say I must mention man-woman friendships too. For these friendships can be just as close and as dear as those that we form with women. Listen to Lucy's description of one such friendship:

"We've found we have things to talk about that are different from what he talks about with my husband and different from what I talk about with his wife. So sometimes we call on the phone or meet for lunch. There are similar intellectual interests—we always pass on to each other the books that we love—but there's also something tender and caring too."

In a couple of crises, Lucy says, "he offered himself for talking and for helping. And when someone died in his family he wanted me there. The sexual, flirty part of our friendship is very small, but *some*—just enough to make it fun and different." She thinks—and I agree—that the sexual part, though small, is always *some,* is always there when a man and a woman are friends.

It's only in the past few years that I've made friends with men, in the sense of a friendship that's *mine,* not just part of two couples. And achieving with them the ease and the trust I've found with women friends has value indeed. Under the dryer at home last week, putting on mascara and rouge, I comfortably sat and talked with a fellow named Peter. Peter, I finally decided, could handle the shock of me minus mascara under the dryer. Because we care for each other. Because we're friends.

8. There are medium friends, and pretty good friends, and very good friends indeed, and these friendships are defined by their level of intimacy. And what we'll reveal at each of these levels of intimacy is calibrated with care. We might tell a medium friend, for example, that yesterday we had a fight with our husband. And we might tell a pretty good friend that this fight with our husband made us so mad that we slept on the couch. And we might tell a very good friend that the reason we got so mad in that fight that we slept on the couch had something to do with that girl who works in his office. But it's only to our very best friends that we're willing to tell all, to tell what's going on with that girl in his office.

The best of friends, I still believe, totally love and support and trust each other, and bare to each other the secrets of their souls, and run—no questions asked—to help each other, and tell harsh truths to each other when they must be told.

But we needn't agree about everything (only 12-year-old girl friends agree about *everything*) to tolerate each other's point of view. To accept without judgment. To give and to take without ever keeping score. And to *be* there, as I am for them as they are for me, to comfort our sorrows, to celebrate our joys.

Meaning and Idea

1. How has Viorst's idea of what a friend is changed over time? What did it used to be? What has it become?

2. How does Viorst characterize relations between men and women?

3. What does Viorst mean when she say that friendships "serve many different functions"?

Language, Form, Structure

1. What is Viorst's purpose in writing this essay? Who is her intended audience? How does she use classification?

2. What is the effect of Viorst's use of quotations from her friends as evidence? What do these quotations add to the essay?

3. Define the following words and use each one in an original sentence: ardor; nonchalant; sibling; calibrate.

Ideas for Writing

1. Do you agree with Viorst's comment that men and women can be good friends even if there will always be a "sexual, flirty" part of the friendship? Write an argumentative essay to answer this question.

2. Invent a classification system similar to Viorst's for one of the following groups: relatives, lovers, coworkers.

3. Which parts of this essay are funny? Which parts are serious? Write an essay analyzing how humor strengthens and deepens Viorst's essay.

The Girls in Their Summer Dresses

Irwin Shaw

Irwin Shaw (1913–1984) was a novelist, short story writer, playwright, and screenplay writer who was born in Brooklyn, New York, and was educated at Brooklyn College. James Gindin observed that his works "combine sharp commentary and sensitive observation" about the changing social scene, politics, and violence. Shaw was alternately considered a pop writer and a serious writer, and his talents and ironic sense ran the gamut in such works as *Rich Man, Poor Man* (1970), *Nightwork* (1975), and *Beggarman, Thief* (1977).

Irwin Shaw's simple yet lasting "The Girls in Their Summer Dresses" is set in the New York City of the 1930s but could easily pertain to a modern couple. Notice how Shaw develops various levels of affection and response.

*F*ifth Avenue was shining in the sun when they left the Brevoort.   1
The sun was warm, even though it was February, and everything looked like Sunday morning—the buses and the well-dressed people walking slowly in couples and the quiet buildings with the windows closed.

Michael held Frances' arm tightly as they walked toward Washington   2
Square in the sunlight. They walked lightly, almost smiling, because they had slept late and had a good breakfast and it was Sunday. Michael unbuttoned his coat and left it flap around him in the mild wind.

"Look out," Frances said as they crossed Eighth Street. "You'll break   3
your neck."

Michael laughed and Frances laughed with him.   4

"She's not so pretty," Frances said. "Anyway, not pretty enough to take a   5
chance of breaking your neck."

Michael laughed again. "How did you know I was looking at her?"   6

Frances cocked her head to one side and smiled at her husband under the   7
brim of her hat. "Mike, darling," she said.

"O.K.," he said. "Excuse me."   8

Frances patted his arm lightly and pulled him along a little faster toward   9
Washington Square. "Let's not see anybody all day," she said. "Let's just hang around with each other. You and me. We're always up to our neck in people, drinking their Scotch or drinking our Scotch; we only see each other in bed. I want to go out with my husband all day long. I want him to talk only to me and listen only to me."

"What's to stop us?" Michael asked.   10

"The Stevensons. They want us to drop by around one o'clock and they'll   11
drive us into the country."

"The cunning Stevensons," Mike said. "Transparent. They can whistle. 12
They can go driving in the country by themselves."

"Is it a date?" 13

"It's a date." 14

Frances leaned over and kissed him on the tip of the ear. 15

"Darling," Michael said, "this is Fifth Avenue." 16

"Let me arrange a program," Frances said. "A planned Sunday in New 17
York for a young couple with money to throw away."

"Go easy." 18

"First let's go to the Metropolitan Museum of Art," Frances suggested, be- 19
cause Michael had said during the week he wanted to go. "I haven't been there
in three years and there're at least ten pictures I want to see again. Then we can
take the bus down to Radio City and watch them skate. And later we'll go down
to Cavanagh's and get a steak as big as a blacksmith's apron, with a bottle of
wine, and after that there's a French picture at the Filmarte that everybody
says—say, are you listening to me?"

"Sure," he said. He took his eyes off the hatless girl with dark hair, cut 20
dancer-style like a helmet, who was walking past him.

"That's the program for the day," Frances said flatly. "Or maybe you'd 21
just rather walk up and down Fifth Avenue."

"No," Michael said. "Not at all." 22

"You always look at other women," Frances said "Everywhere. Every 23
damn place we go."

"Now, darling," Michael said, "I look at everything. God gave me eyes 24
and I look at women and men and subway excavations and moving pictures and
the little flowers in the field. I casually inspect the universe."

"You ought to see the look in your eyes," Frances said, "as you casually 25
inspect the universe on Fifth Avenue."

"I'm a happily married man." Michael pressed her elbow tenderly. "Exam- 26
ple for the whole twentieth century—Mr. and Mrs. Mike Loomis. Hey, let's
have a drink," he said, stopping.

"We just had breakfast." 27

"Now listen, darling," Mike said, choosing his words with care, "it's a 28
nice day and we both felt good and there's no reason why we have to break it
up. Let's have a nice Sunday."

"All right. I don't know why I started this. Let's drop it. Let's have a 29
good time."

They joined hands consciously and walked without talking among the 30
baby carriages and the old Italian men in their Sunday clothes and the young
women with Scotties in Washington Square Park.

"At least once a year everyone should go to the Metropolitan Museum of 31
Art," Frances said after a while, her tone a good imitation of the tone she used at
breakfast and at the beginning of their walk. "And it's nice on Sunday. There're
a lot of people looking at the pictures and you get the feeling maybe Art isn't on
the decline in New York City, after all—"

"I want to tell you something," Michael said very seriously. "I have not touched another woman. Not once. In all five years." 32

"All right," Frances said. 33

"You believe that, don't you?" 34

"All right." 35

They walked between the crowded benches, under the scrubby city-park trees. 36

"I try not to notice it," Frances said, "but I feel rotten inside, in my stomach, when we pass a woman and you look at her and I see that look in your eye and that's the way you looked at me the first time. In Alice Maxwell's house. Standing there in the living room, next to the radio, with a green hat on and all those people." 37

"I remember the hat," Michael said. 38

"The same look," Frances said. "And it makes me feel bad. It makes me feel terrible." 39

"Sh-h-h, please, darling, sh-h-h." 40

"I think I would like a drink now," Frances said. 41

They walked over to a bar on Eighth Street, not saying anything, Michael automatically helping her over curbstones and guiding her past automobiles. They sat near a window in the bar and the sun streamed in and there was a small, cheerful fire in the fireplace. A little Japanese waiter came over and put down some pretzels and smiled happily at them. 42

"What do you order after breakfast?" Michael asked. 43

"Brandy, I suppose," Frances said. 44

"Courvoisier," Michael told the waiter. "Two Courvoisiers." 45

The waiter came with the glasses and they sat drinking the brandy in the sunlight. Michael finished half his and drank a little water. 46

"I look at women," he said. "Correct. I don't say it's wrong or right. I look at them. If I pass them on the street and I don't look at them, I'm fooling you, I'm fooling myself." 47

"You look at them as though you want them," Frances said, playing with her brandy glass. "Every one of them." 48

"In a way," Michael said, speaking softly and not to his wife, "in a way that's true. I don't do anything about it, but it's true." 49

"I know it. That's why I feel bad." 50

"Another brandy," Michael called. "Waiter, two more brandies." 51

He sighed and closed his eyes and rubbed them gently with his fingertips. "I love the way women look. One of the things I like best about New York is the battalions of women. When I first came to New York from Ohio that was the first thing I noticed, the million wonderful women, all over the city. I walked around with my heart in my throat." 52

"A kid," Frances said. "That's a kid's feeling." 53

"Guess again," Michael said. "Guess again. I'm older now, I'm a man getting near middle age, putting on a little fat and I still love to walk along Fifth Avenue at three o'clock on the east side of the street between Fiftieth and 54

Fifty-seventh Streets. They're all out then, shopping, in their furs and their crazy hats, everything all concentrated from all over the world into seven blocks—the best furs, the best clothes, the handsomest women, out to spend money and feeling good about it."

The Japanese waiter put two drinks down, smiling with great happiness.   55

"Everything is all right?" he asked.   56

"Everything is wonderful," Michael said.   57

"If it's just a couple of fur coats," Frances said, "and forty-five dollar hats—"   58

"It's not the fur coats. Or the hats. That's just the scenery for that particu-   59
lar kind of woman. Understand," he said, "you don't have to listen to this."

"I want to listen."   60

"I like the girls in the offices. Neat, with their eyeglasses, smart, chipper,   61
knowing what everything is about. I like the girls on Forty-fourth Street at lunchtime, the actresses, all dressed up on nothing a week. I like the salesgirls in the stores, paying attention to you first because you're a man, leaving lady customers waiting. I got all this stuff accumulated in me because I've been thinking about it for ten years and now you've asked for it and here it is."

"Go ahead," Frances said.   62

"When I think of New York City, I think of all the girls on parade in the   63
city. I don't know whether it's something special with me or whether every man in the city walks around with the same feeling inside him, but I feel as though I'm at a picnic in this city. I like to sit near the women in the theatres, the famous beauties who've taken six hours to get ready and look it. And the young girls at the football games, with the red cheeks, and when the warm weather comes, the girls in their summer dresses." He finished his drink. "That's the story."

Frances finished her drink and swallowed two or three times extra. "You   64
say you love me?"

"I love you."   65

"I'm pretty, too," Frances said. "As pretty as any of them."   66

"You're beautiful," Michael said.   67

"I'm good for you," Frances said, pleading. "I've made a good wife, a   68
good housekeeper, a good friend. I'd do any damn thing for you."

"I know," Michael said. He put his hand out and grasped hers.   69

"You'd like to be free to—" Frances said.   70

"Sh-h-h."   71

"Tell the truth." She took her hand away from under his.   72

Michael flicked the edge of his glass with his finger. "O.K.," he said gen-   73
tly. "Sometimes I feel I would like to be free."

"Well," Frances said, "any time you say."   74

"Don't be foolish." Michael swung his chair around to her side of the table   75
and patted her thigh.

She began to cry silently into her handkerchief, bent over just enough so   76
that nobody else in the bar would notice. "Someday," she said, crying, "you're going to make a move."

Michael didn't say anything. He sat watching the bartender slowly peel a   77
lemon.

"Aren't you?" Frances asked harshly. "Come on, tell me. Talk. Aren't you?"   78

"Maybe," Michael said. He moved his chair back again. "How the hell do   79
I know?"

"You know," Frances persisted. "Don't you know?"   80

"Yes," Michael said after a while, "I know."   81

Frances stopped crying then. Two or three snuffles into the handkerchief   82
and she put it away and her face didn't tell anything to anybody. "At least do me
one favor," she said.

"Sure."   83

"Stop talking about how pretty this woman is or that one. Nice eyes, nice   84
breasts, a pretty figure, good voice." She mimicked his voice. "Keep it to yourself. I'm not interested."

Michael waved to the waiter. "I'll keep it to myself," he said.   85

Frances flicked the corners of her eyes. "Another brandy," she told the   86
waiter.

"Two," Michael said.   87

"Yes, Ma'am, yes, sir," said the waiter, backing away.   88

Frances regarded Michael coolly across the table. "Do you want me to call   89
the Stevensons?" she asked. "It'll be nice in the country."

"Sure," Michael said. "Call them."   90

She got up from the table and walked across the room toward the tele-   91
phone. Michael watched her walk, thinking what a pretty girl, what nice legs.

Meaning and Idea

1. Into what categories does Michael classify women? Does his energetic
   classification of women make Michael a male chauvinist, or is it just an
   indication of his general appreciation for the opposite sex and for life in
   general, as he claims? Explain your opinion.

2. To what social class do these characters belong? How do you know?

3. In what ways does Frances classify her relation with Michael?

4. What sort of relationship exists between Frances and Michael?

Language, Form, Structure

1. By what method does Michael classify women? Does he follow any
   system?

2. What is the significance of the title of this story? Could it have been named
   just as easily "The Girls in the Offices," or "The Salesgirls in the Stores," or
   "The Girls on Forty-fourth Street at Lunchtime?" Why or why not?

3. At one point the Japanese waiter is described as "smiling with great happiness." What types or levels of happiness does Shaw deal with in the story?

4. In what ways can you read this narrative fiction as classification?

5. Look up and write definitions for the following words: excavations; scrubby; battalions; accumulated; mimicked.

Ideas for Writing

1. Write a few paragraphs in which you classify the members of the opposite sex in your school.

2. Select a single emotion and write a classification of the levels of your reactions to it. You might choose jealousy, fear, love, hate, anxiety, or some other emotion important to you.

3. With whom, Frances or Michael, do you think Shaw's sympathies lie most? Why? What elements of the writing give you this opinion?

Do Not Go Gentle into That Good Night

Dylan Thomas

Dylan Thomas (1914–1953), one of the most flamboyant modern poets, was born in Swansea, Wales, the son of a schoolteacher. However, Thomas was not particularly enamored of school and chose instead the life of a writer, publishing his first volume of poems at the age of 20. In 1936, he began a turbulent and dramatic marriage with Caitlin MacNamara, from whom he was often separated in order to give reading and lecture tours in the United States. Thomas is also known for his drama and prose, among which are the voiceplay *Under Milkwood* and the delightful *A Child's Christmas in Wales.* Thomas was an excessive drinker, and his alcoholism finally caused his death. Outside the Chelsea Hotel, where he often stayed in New York City, there is a plaque posted to his memory.

"Do Not Go Gentle into That Good Night" was written in 1952 on the occasion of Thomas's father's final illness and just one year before Thomas's own death. In the poet's categorization of the ways in which different types of men face death, we discern a poignant plea to his father.

*D*o not go gentle into that good night,
Old age should burn and rave at close of day;
Rage, rage against the dying of the light.

Though wise men at their end know dark is right,
Because their words had forked no lightning they   5
Do not go gentle into that good night.

Good men, the last wave by, crying how bright
Their frail deeds might have danced in a green bay,
Rage, rage against the dying of the light.

Wild men who caught and sang the sun in flight,   10
And learn, too late, they grieved it on its way
Do not go gentle into that good night.

Grave men, near death, who see with blinding sight
Blind eyes could blaze like meteors and be gay,
Rage, rage against the dying of the light.   15

And you, my father, there on the sad height,
Curse, bless, me now with your fierce tears, I pray.
Do not go gentle into that good night.
Rage, rage against the dying of the light.

Meaning and Idea

1. Whom is the speaker addressing in this poem? How is the address different in stanzas 1 and 6? Why?

2. Into what categories does Thomas classify men who are near death? How are they different from one another? How well do these classifications present a full spectrum of types of people? By what principle do you think Thomas made his selection of categories? Why?

3. What does Thomas ask from his dying father? Is there more than one way to interpret his request? Why does he ask for what he does?

Language, Form, Structure

1. This poem is written according to an intricate French structural form called the *villanelle*. Without actually diagramming that form, explain in your own words how Thomas uses structure as an organizing technique in this poem. What effect does it produce?

2. What is the irony in the use of the word *grave* in line 13? How is that irony achieved? Why do you think Thomas uses irony here?

3. What is the overall purpose of this poem? How well does Thomas fulfill that purpose? How does classification assist that purpose?

4. Select any words that are not familiar to you from this poem and write definitions for them.

Ideas for Writing

1. Write a short classification in which you group different types of reactions to an important natural event of your choosing, such as birth, maturation, or death. Address your writing to a specific person for a specific reason.

2. Write a classification essay about different types of people in love. Be sure to include reasons you think they fit into certain categories.

3. In the Author's Prologue to the *Collected Poems of Dylan Thomas* (1957), Thomas writes, "I read somewhere of a shepherd who, when asked why he made from within Fairy rings, ritual observances to the moon to protect his flocks, replied: 'I'd be a damn' fool if I didn't!' These poems, with all their crudities, doubts, and confusions, are written for the love of man and in praise of God, and I'd be a damn' fool if they weren't." Analyze "Do Not Go Gentle into That Good Night" in light of Thomas's stated purpose. Do you see "crudities, doubts, and confusions"? In what way is the poem for the love of man and in praise of God?

Naming of Parts

Henry Reed

Although Henry Reed wrote only two volumes of poetry, his earlier one, *A Map of Verona* (1946), is characterized by a fine combination of feeling and form. The volume is divided into four sections. The first, "Naming of Parts," deals with World War II. Reed's observation is sharp and ironic, and his theme is the futility of war. Born in 1914 in Birmingham, England, Henry Reed was a freelance journalist and teacher. He is best known for his ironic and amusing dramas and radio plays produced by the BBC. His more recent volume of poetry is *Lessons of the War* (1970). He died in 1986.

As you read Henry Reed's "Naming of Parts," play close attention to how the poet intertwines two classifications of simultaneous activities. This poem is a poignant example of Reed's own opinions about war and its activities.

*T*oday we have naming of parts. Yesterday,
We had daily cleaning. And tomorrow morning,
We shall have what to do after firing. But today,
Today we have naming of parts. Japonica
Glistens like coral in all of the neighboring gardens,   5
     And today we have naming of parts.

This is the lower sling swivel. And this
Is the upper sling swivel, whose use you will see,
When you are given your slings. And this is the piling swivel,
Which in your case you have not got. The branches   10
Hold in the gardens their silent, eloquent gestures,
     Which in our case we have not got.

This is the safety-catch, which is always released
With an easy flick of the thumb. And please do not let me
See anyone using his finger. You can do it quite easy   15
If you have any strength in your thumb. The blossoms
Are fragile and motionless, never letting anyone see
     Any of them using their finger.

And this you can see is the bolt. The purpose of this
Is to open the breech, as you see. We can slide it   20
Rapidly backwards and forwards: we call this
Easing the spring. And rapidly backwards and forwards
The early bees are assaulting and fumbling the flowers:
     They call it easing the Spring.

They call it easing the Spring: it is perfectly easy   25
If you have any strength in your thumb: like the bolt,
And the breech, and the cocking-piece, and the point of balance,
Which in our case we have not got; and the almond-blossom
Silent in all of the gardens and the bees going backwards and forwards,
     For today we have naming of parts.   30

Meaning and Idea

1. How does Reed categorize experience in this poem into the "gun world" and the "living world"? Briefly describe the basis of each. What is the relation between the two?

2. What three divisions of activity appear in the first stanza? How does the poet follow through on each division?

3. What is Reed's attitude toward the activities of the training camp? Support your answer with specific references from the poem.

4. To what does the word *parts* in the title refer?

Language, Form, Structure

1. How many speakers are there in this poem? Who are they? How are they different? Where does one voice end and the other begin? Would you call this poem a dialogue? Why or why not?

2. How is time used as a classifying principle in this poem? What are the time periods dealt with?

3. What is the theme of this poem? What is its tone? How do the two affect each other?

4. How is the last stanza structurally different from the others? For what purpose?

5. Define these terms: Japonica; swivel; slings; fragile; assaulting; breech.

Ideas for Writing

1. Classify the various kinds of activities involved in a familiar task. Try to include—in a subtle way—your feelings about the task.

2. Reed's poem is a subtle attack on guns. Write an essay on the role—good or bad—of firearms in today's culture.

3. *Double entendre,* a French term meaning "double meaning," identifies a word or expression that simultaneously carries two equally valid meanings and may be used to create irony. How is *double entendre* used in this poem? How does it affect your response to the theme of the poem?

Ecclesiastes

Ecclesiastes is the twenty-first book of the Old Testament. It was originally thought to be composed by Solomon, but scholars now place its writing ca. 300–160 B.C.

Ecclesiastes can be read as a philosophical essay whose theme is that all life needs to be lived happily to the fullest because "all is vanity." The certainty of death, the necessities of wisdom and mercy, and ultimate respect for God's judgments form its philosophical core.

Chapter 3 emphasizes acceptance of the "natural rhythm" of the universe along with enjoyment of one's labors as God's ultimate gift.

CHAPTER 3

*T*o every thing there is a season, and a time to every purpose under the heaven:

2   A time to be born, and a time to die; a time to plant, and a time to pluck up that which is planted;

3   A time to kill, and a time to heal; a time to break down, and a time to build up;

4   A time to weep, and a time to laugh; a time to mourn, and a time to dance;

5   A time to cast away stones, and a time to gather stones together; a time to embrace, and a time to refrain from embracing;

6   A time to get, and a time to lose; a time to keep, and a time to cast away;

7   A time to rend, and a time to sew; a time to keep silence, and a time to speak;

8   A time to love, and a time to hate; a time of war, and a time of peace.

9   What profit hath he that worketh in that wherein he laboureth?

10   I have seen the travail, which God hath given to the sons of men to be exercised in it.

11   He hath made every thing beautiful in his time: also he hath set the world in their heart, so that no man can find out the work that God maketh from the beginning to the end.

12   I know that there is no good in them, but for *a man* to rejoice, and to do good in his life.

13   And also that every man should eat and drink, and enjoy the good of all his labour, it *is* the gift of God.

14   I know that, whatsoever God doeth, it shall be for ever: nothing can be put to it, nor any thing taken from it: and God doeth *it,* that *men* should fear before him.

15   That which hath been is now; and that which is to be hath already been; and God requireth that which is past.

16   And moreover I saw under the sun the place of judgment, *that* wickedness *was* there; and the place of righteousness, that iniquity *was* there.

17   I said in mine heart, God shall judge the righteous and the wicked: for *there is* a time there for every purpose and for every work.

18   I said in mine heart concerning the estate of the sons of men, that God might manifest them, and that they might see that they themselves are beasts.

19   For that which befalleth the sons of men befalleth beasts; even one thing befalleth them: as the one dieth, so dieth the other; yea, they have all one breath; so that a man hath no preeminence above a beast: for all *is* vanity.

20   All go unto one place; all are of the dust, and all turn to dust again.

21   Who knoweth the spirit of man that goeth upward, and the spirit of the beast that goeth downward to the earth?

22   Wherefore I perceive that *there is* nothing better, than that a man should rejoice in his own works; for that *is* his portion: for who shall bring him to see what shall be after him?

Meaning and Idea

1. How, according to this chapter, did God order man's relation to time? What attitude about daily life should derive from that relation?

2. According to the text, are negative emotions and actions permissible? If so, when and why?

Language, Form, Structure

1. This chapter divides into two structural units. Where does the division take place? What is the change? Why does it occur?

2. Verses 1 through 8 give examples of the "natural flow" of life. Do these examples follow any special patterning or classification? Try to group them into general categories.

3. Define these terms: refrain; rend; travail.

Ideas for Writing

1. Write a classification of your various emotional ups and downs of the past few years.

2. Write an essay in which you analyze and explain from your perspective the first line of Ecclesiastes.

3. This text derives from the traditional King James translation of the Bible. Yet, within the past 25 years or so many modernized versions of the Bible have appeared—versions that update syntax, try to eliminate the male-oriented language, deal with cultural sensitivities, and so on. How do you feel about the old language versus the new? How do you feel about updated versions of the Bible in general? Why? If possible, find a modified text of this chapter and use specific comparisons to support your opinion. Write an essay to address these questions.

The Plight of the High-Status Woman

Barbara Dafoe Whitehead

Barbara Dafoe Whitehead (1944–), the younger sister of the actor Willem Dafoe, was born in Minnesota and received a Ph.D. from the University of Chicago. She burst into public notice with the article "Dan Quayle Was Right" in 1993, a piece later selected as one of the 10 most influential magazine articles of the decade. Not strictly speaking a defense of the vice president's attack on the television drama "Murphy Brown's" portrayal of a lead character choosing single motherhood, Whitehead's piece builds a strong case around a simple thesis—divorce is very destructive to children. In 1997 she published *The Divorce Culture,* in which she argued that the current high rates of divorce and abandonment stem from the valorization of individual economic and social freedom over social responsibility. Whitehead is currently codirector of the National Marriage Project.

Whitehead is known for casting a wide net in her search for evidence. In her book on divorce, for instance, she cites social science studies, Emily Post etiquette books, and Disney's movie *Dumbo.* The current selection is an examination of what Whitehead calls a new literary category, "dump literature," and an argument that these books represent a real social trend in young women's prospects for a traditional marriage.

Women's tastes in popular reading have long favored two kinds of romances. One is the romance of falling in love and making a brilliant marriage. This centuries-old staple traces the progress of true love from wooing to wedding, through all the confusions and complications along the way. The other is more contemporary and appears prominently in women's magazines, especially those aimed at educated women in the Baby Boom generation. It is the romance of finding a job and making a brilliant career. Here the progress is from first job to first six-figure salary. Complications arise in this narrative as well, but it ends happily with the acquisition of an executive title, a great wardrobe, and a bicoastal social life. What the two romances have in common is the optimistic and essentially liberal faith that a young woman can get what she wants through the shrewd exercise of her own intelligence, talents, and discerning judgment.

Now, however, a vastly different kind of popular literature is emerging. It is written for and about the privileged members of a new generation. These young women, the highly educated daughters of educated Baby Boomers, are in their twenties and thirties, living and working on their own. Compared with earlier generations, they spend a long time in the mating market, and thus face prolonged exposure to the vicissitudes of love, including multiple breakups, fears of sexually transmitted disease, and infertility anxieties. They must also go through a prolonged period of higher education and career apprenticeship in order to establish themselves in a demanding job market. During these years they may be laid off, downsized, or fired at least once or twice. Neither their love life nor their work life is settled or secure.

The new literature reflects these dual realities. Like traditional women's stories, it deals with themes of love and work, often interweaving the two, but it breaks sharply with the romantic view of both. The defining theme in this literature isn't finding the dream guy or landing the great job but precisely the opposite. It's getting dumped—by a boyfriend or a boss or both. What's more, these books challenge the idea that a young woman blessed with talent and education, and filled with desire and ambition, can get what she wants.

The purest statement of the signature theme in this literature can be found in a batch of self-help books published over the past few years, with titles such as *Dumped!; He Loved Me, He Loves Me Not; The Heartbreak Handbook; Getting Over Him; Exorcising Your Ex; How to Heal the Hurt by Hating;* and *The Woman's Book of Revenge.* There is also a *Complete Idiot's Guide to Handling a Breakup.* But this theme is not limited to self-help literature. It crosses over into other genres. Suzanne Yalof's *Getting Over John Doe* is a mini-memoir. Candace Bushnell's *Sex and the City* is a collection of her columns in the *New York Observer.* Perhaps the most thorough treatment of the theme is found in recent coming-of-age fiction such as Melissa Bank's critically acclaimed *The Girls' Guide to Hunting and Fishing,* Amy Sohn's *Run Catch Kiss,* Kate Christensen's *In the Drink,* and Laura Zigman's *Animal Husbandry.*

Like Jane Austen's Emma, the young women in these four books are handsome, clever, and rich in educational advantage (a good education is the contemporary equivalent of propertied wealth). After graduating from elite colleges they move to Manhattan, find minuscule apartments, and seek their fortunes. Eventually they land jobs in the glamorous media or entertainment industry. But their jobs are low-level and short-term; they are temps, part-timers, and freelancers. What's more, their employment prospects don't improve as time goes on: instead of moving up the career ladder, they get stuck at the level of the temp job. Far from making brilliant careers, they forever remain Girl Fridays.

Their love lives aren't much more successful. They go out with attractive, high-profile men, but these men are not looking for a lifelong mate—they're already encumbered by a wife or a live-in girlfriend, or they have weird habits (wearing mouse slippers to bed) or "multiple substance issues." Far from making brilliant marriages, these smart, funny, talented women forever remain girlfriends or ex-girlfriends.

Consider Claudia Steiner, the twenty-nine-year-old protagonist of *In the Drink.* A Swarthmore graduate, she has spent nine post-college years in New York City in low-level jobs (receptionist, dog walker, phone-sex scriptwriter, temp, waitress, housecleaner, and temp again) when she lands an $18-an-hour position as a personal assistant to and ghostwriter for a celebrity author of mystery romances. Her boss, Jackie del Castellano, turns out to be egotistical and tyrannical; she insists on pretending that Claudia, who is turning Jackie's literary straw into best-selling gold, is merely providing a fresh insight or two. What's more, Jackie routinely yells at, humiliates, and mistreats Claudia, and finally dumps her.

Claudia's home life isn't much better. She lives alone in a "rathole on an airshaft," eats takeout, and drinks too much. She says, "I was like a tiny version of the city itself; all my systems were a welter of corruption and neglect." And her love life is a mess. Although she is desperately in love with William, her childhood friend, she can't find the "bridge between friendship and romance." Instead she falls into and out of relationships that follow a predictable course: "bantering dive-bar pick-up, drunken sex, a rushed exchange of phone numbers afterwards on a subway platform, then other nights with more dive-bar bantering and drunken sex." 8

Bosses and boyfriends behave a lot alike in the novels. They make nice to you (ever so briefly). Then they dump you. The bosses are invariably vain, capricious, self-centered, and hard-shelled women, not mentors but tormentors. In *The Girls' Guide to Hunting and Fishing,* Jane Rosenal is a rising star in her publishing company until Mimi Howlett, her new boss, arrives. Mimi demotes Jane from the promising position of associate book editor to de facto personal assistant. She also relentlessly criticizes Jane's professional work while generously offering her tips on how to improve her appearance. 9

Jobs go from bad to worse following a firing. After Ariel Steiner, the protagonist in *Run Catch Kiss,* is dumped from her freelance job as a sex columnist and from her temp job in a Manhattan publishing company, she slides from a temp job in a bank in Queens to a part-time job in Brooklyn before hitting bottom with a waitressing job at a twelve-table restaurant in the Village. (Her salary plummets from a high of $18 an hour to a low of $5.50 an hour plus tips.) Jane Rosenal languishes as a temp worker in a bank. 10

Boyfriends look good on paper—they're a mostly upscale crowd of writers, publishers, artists, fund managers, and investment bankers—but they turn out to be cruel, careless, self-absorbed, socially clueless, and sexually inept. What's more, as prospective mates they're virtually indistinguishable. 11

In the traditional romance there was one special guy for every special girl. The special girl found her special guy by administering a set of means and morals tests and then using her powers of discernment to pick him out of the pack. Dump literature rejects this premise. It takes the opposing view—that men are all the same. "I've gone out with the short, fat, and ugly," says a woman journalist in *Sex and the City,* "and it doesn't make any difference. They're just as unappreciative and self-centered as the good-looking ones." In short, the existence of many men doesn't guarantee the existence of many choices. There's just One Guy. Take him or leave him. More precisely, take him and he'll leave you. 12

When it comes to ending a relationship, male behavior is entirely predictable. According to dump literature, it's over when he says (pick one): a) "I think maybe we should cool things for a while," b) "I've been doing a lot of thinking," c) "God, this week is going to be terrible . . . I'm completely swamped," or d) "It's not you, it's me." 13

Once dumped, however, the ex-girlfriends and ex-Girl Fridays don't get downhearted. They get even. In these books the functional equivalent of romantic passion is revenge, served up fast and hot. The self-help books reject the therapeutic approach of grieving over a loss, which was popular in an earlier generation of books aimed mainly at divorcing couples. The best therapy, many of them advise, is to work through your grief on his property. Since many contemporary breakups involve a household as well as a relationship, the revenge schemes focus on destroying or defacing his stuff, including his car and clothing. Some of this is intended as mere fantasy, or played for laughs. But some scenarios recur so frequently—obsessively calling his answering machine and driving past his place, shredding his pictures or clothes, getting mutual friends to spy on him—that it is hard not to assume that they have been battle-tested.

For the characters in the novels, writing is the best revenge. As one observes, "It's the ultimate revenge fantasy. You get rich and famous writing about something you're already obsessed with." In *Run Catch Kiss,* Ariel Steiner takes revenge on the disgusting men she goes out with by lampooning them in her popular sex column. After her boyfriend dumps her, Jane Goodall, the protagonist in *Animal Husbandry,* turns to animal research for evidence on why men flee. She invents a theory based on the observation that a bull will ditch an old cow as soon as a new cow appears, and then gets a job writing about her "Old-Cow–New-Cow" theory as a pseudonymous science columnist for a men's magazine. Bosses are likewise targets for revenge. In a twist on the writing-as-revenge tactic, Claudia Steiner strikes back by unwriting: she erases the disk containing the text of her boss's nearly completed book.

Revenge is psychologically expedient, but it does not accomplish lasting personal transformation, much less social change. What is striking is how little this literature protests the cycle of temping and dumping and how little hope it holds out for an end to it. This is all the more surprising because these books are about young women blessed by all the advantages that education, fond parents, and a good therapist can provide. Nevertheless, the challenge for these women is not to avoid, let alone alter, the bleak disjunctions of life but merely to survive them—to get over them and move on.

In a world so blindly indifferent to individual merit and mettle a woman's chief psychological resource is humor, and her only form of activism is to laugh it off and get back in the game. Despite its resignation, this literature is hardly weary or despondent. It is full of riffs, spoofs, quips, and mordant observations about men, women, and their mating and relating problems. The most appealing element of this humor is not its acidulous portrait of men and bosses but its unsparing view of women's weaknesses and self-deceptions. "I couldn't get enough of the most unsuitable men," one character says. Another explains why she and her female boss were attracted to each other: "She was desperate, and I was available."

However, an undercurrent of anxiety runs through the hilarity. After all, what is funny at twenty-five might be less so at thirty-five. Some of the characters are haunted by a vision of themselves in the future, living alone in a dark studio apartment, eating out of an open refrigerator, and earning a meager wage stuffing envelopes at home. And although the fiction resorts to the expedient of the happy ending, the girl-gets-guy resolutions that some employ are thoroughly unconvincing and entirely at odds with everything that has come before.

Of course, no one believes that dump literature offers a documentary portrait of today's educated young women. In its depiction of work it draws heavily on the experience of the authors (themselves young), who, like aspiring actors, may have taken part-time or temp jobs in order to devote themselves more fully to their craft. Theirs is a very narrow slice of work life, hardly representative of the experience of the many post-college single women who enjoy far greater success in their careers than these fictional characters. Nor can the sex lives of these women be taken as typical. Few young women spend every night at clubs or have sex, drunken or otherwise, with a string of partners. What does ring true, however, is the depiction of what might be called the plight of the high-status woman. [19]

Given the high divorce rate, today's young women cannot rely on marriage for economic security. Even if they aspire to marriage (and according to survey research, most do), they have to be ready and able to support themselves with their own earnings. This has meant ever-increasing education beyond high school. For women pursuing high-status professions the schooling can extend several years beyond college, well into their twenties. Them, for as much as another decade, such women must invest heavily in developing their careers. Indeed, women on the make adopt the same priorities as men on the make. Work is in the foreground, love in the middle distance or the background. Neither men nor women have the time or a pressing desire for marriage, especially when they can get some marriagelike benefits without it. So they put it off and enter into relationships that offer some combination of sex, companionship, convenience, and economies of scale. [20]

By the time high-status single men and women reach their early thirties, however, their marriage prospects begin to diverge. Men's educational and career achievements enhance their marriageability and increase the pool of prospective mates, because men tend to marry women of similar or lesser education, and the supply at or below their achievement level is large. For women of the same age and education the opposite is the case: high-status women tend to seek husbands of higher levels of education and achievement, and their lofty status decreases the pool of eligible mates. For men, age is no barrier to attracting women. A few gray hairs can be sexy. For women, age is no asset. A few gray hairs can send a woman racing to the colorist. [21]

Moreover, intragender competition can be fierce. High-status women find themselves in competition not only with other high-status women but also with younger women of lesser education, in lower occupations. The classic example is thirtyish female physicians who, having finished their rigorous training, are ready for marriage. They find themselves up against slightly younger residents and interns along with a large pool of twenty-something nurses and other health professionals. Since the nurses and the physical therapists are in careers that can [22] be disrupted and then picked up again, they may be more willing than the female physicians to stay home and raise children while their husbands pursue careers. This, too, can be a source of competitive disadvantage for the female physicians.

By this stage in life single women of talent and accomplishment begin to 23 grasp the principle that life is unfair in at least one key domain. Men may be able to pursue their careers singlemindedly during their twenties and postpone marriage until their thirties without compromising their fertility or opportunities to find a suitable mate, but women cannot. Just at the moment when they are ready to slow down and share the pleasures of life with similarly successful mates, they look around and find that many of the most desirable men are already taken. What is left is an odd assortment: married men who want a girlfriend on the side; divorced men with serious financial, child-custody, or ex-wife problems; and single men who invite suspicion simply because they're still single. These mating patterns lead to a plaint familiar among upscale single women in their thirties: "There are no good men left."

Thus the career strategy now favored by well-educated young women, in 24 part to establish their own economic viability as a cushion against the likelihood of an eventual divorce, exacts a maddening cost of its own: it makes it less likely that they will marry in the first place. This is a classic case of what is known as goods in conflict.

Taken separately, most of the dump books can be read as entertainments; 25 taken together, however, they suggest that an important and recent change is occurring in the lives of educated young women. The romance of love and marriage took its inspiration from a long-standing mating system, but the defining institutions of the old system are breaking down. Courtship is dead. Marriage is in decline. A new mating system is emerging, with its own complications and confusions, including the conflict that faces high-status women. These books are field reports on the new rules of engagement—and disengagement.

Meaning and Idea

1. What does Whitehead mean by her title? What type of woman is she most concerned with? What types of women does she exclude from her analysis?

2. How does Whitehead describe the traditional types of popular women's literature? What kinds of stories does this literature tell? What presuppositions lie behind it?

3. How does Whitehead describe the kind of women's literature now emerging? How is it different from previous books? What new assumptions underlie this new type? What social or economic forces have created this new type of literature?

4. What challenges, according to Whitehead, face a professional woman searching for a mate? How are these challenges different for a professional man? What is the result?

Language, Form, Structure

1. What is Whitehead's thesis?

2. What kind of evidence does Whitehead offer in support of her argument? What objections does she anticipate? How does she address those objections?

3. Whitehead spends roughly half of her essay describing the characteristics of "dump literature" and the second half making more general statements about American culture. How does the system of classification she develops in the first half support her arguments in the second half? How does dividing the essay in this way make her piece stronger?

4. Define the following words and then choose five to use in original sentences: genre; minuscule; encumbered; welter; protagonist; lampoon; expedient; mettle; acidulous; plaint.

Ideas for Writing

1. Do you agree with Whitehead when she writes in paragraph 25, "Courtship is dead. Marriage is in decline"? Write an essay in which you argue either for or against this position, using your personal experience and evidence from popular culture.

2. Write an essay in which you classify the types of romance in today's television shows. You might want to organize your essay according to the classifications dominant in each different type of television show: sitcoms, dramas, soap operas, and other genres you would like to discuss.

3. Write an essay in which you analyze Whitehead's use of classification. Are the categories she develops discrete? Do her examples fit the categories she develops? Does her use of classification support her thesis?

The Plot Against People

Russell Baker

Russell Baker was born in Virginia in 1925. First with the *Baltimore Sun* and then with *The New York Times,* Baker has been a newspaper man and columnist his entire life. As a young reporter he worked his way up to the prestigious position of Washington correspondent but then decided that that coveted job did not suit him. Washington reporting, he later said, was like "sit[ting] in a confined space, listening to my colleagues breathe." Baker's reputation for informative and lively writing earned him a column in 1962. Called "Observer," the column was soon nationally syndicated and won the Pulitzer Prize in 1979. True to Baker's wide interests, "Observer" is devoted not only to skewering pompous or overblown politicians and political figures but also to broader cultural commentary, satirizing Super Bowl Sunday, for example, or the Miss America pageant. Baker's writing has always been motivated by a strong sense of ethics and a sense of rage at journalists who compromise their ethics. He has also written about his childhood in a pair of memoirs, *Growing Up* (1982) and *Good Times* (1989).

"The Plot Against People" shows the lighter side of this hard-nosed reporter, but the ethical sense of concern for our culture is still present. Who exactly is being satirized in this piece? It is not the inanimate objects.

*I*nanimate objects are classified scientifically into three major categories—those that don't work, those that break down and those that get lost.

The goal of all inanimate objects is to resist man and ultimately to defeat him, and the three major classifications are based on the method each object uses to achieve its purpose. As a general rule, any object capable of breaking down at the moment when it is most needed will do so. The automobile is typical of the category.

With the cunning typical of its breed, the automobile never breaks down while entering a filling station with a large staff of idle mechanics. It waits until it reaches a downtown intersection in the middle of the rush hour, or until it is fully loaded with family and luggage on the Ohio turnpike.

Thus it creates maximum misery, inconvenience, frustration and irritability among its human cargo, thereby reducing its owner's life span.

Washing machines, garbage disposals, lawn mowers, light bulbs, automatic laundry dryers, water pipes, furnaces, electrical fuses, television tubes, hose nozzles, tape recorders, slide projectors all are in league with the automobile to take their turn at breaking down whenever life threatens to flow smoothly for their human enemies.

Many inanimate objects, of course, find it extremely difficult to break down. 6 Pliers, for example, and gloves and keys are almost totally incapable of breaking down. Therefore, they have had to evolve a different technique for resisting man.

They get lost. Science has still not solved the mystery of how they do it, 7 and no man has ever caught one of them in the act of getting lost. The most plausible theory is that they have developed a secret method of locomotion which they are able to conceal the instant a human eye falls upon them.

It is not uncommon for a pair of pliers to climb all the way from the cellar 8 to the attic in its single-minded determination to raise its owner's blood pressure. Keys have been known to burrow three feet under mattresses. Women's purses, despite their great weight, frequently travel through six or seven rooms to find hiding space under a couch.

Scientists have been struck by the fact that things that break down virtu- 9 ally never get lost, while things that get lost hardly ever break down.

A furnace, for example, will invariably break down at the depth of the first 10 winter cold wave, but it will never get lost. A woman's purse, which after all does have some inherent capacity for breaking down, hardly ever does; it almost invariably chooses to get lost.

Some persons believe this constitutes evidence that inanimate objects are 11 not entirely hostile to man, and that a negotiated peace is possible. After all, they point out, a furnace could infuriate a man even more thoroughly by getting lost than by breaking down, just as a glove could upset him far more by breaking down than by getting lost.

Not everyone agrees, however, that this indicates a conciliatory attitude 12 among inanimate objects. Many say it merely proves that furnaces, gloves and pliers are incredibly stupid.

The third class of objects—those that don't work—is the most curious of 13 all. These include such objects as barometers, car clocks, cigarette lighters, flashlights and toy-train locomotives. It is inaccurate, of course, to say that they never work. They work once, usually for the first few hours after being brought home, and then quit. Thereafter, they never worked again.

In fact, it is widely assumed that they are built for the purpose of not 14 working. Some people have reached advanced ages without ever seeing some of these objects—barometers, for example—in working order.

Science is utterly baffled by the entire category. There are many theories 15 about it. The most interesting holds that the things that don't work have attained the highest state possible for an inanimate object, the state to which things that break down and things that get lost can still only aspire.

They have truly defeated man by conditioning him never to expect any- 16 thing of them, and in return they have given man the only peace he receives from inanimate society. He does not expect his barometer to work, his electric locomotive to run, his cigarette lighter to light or his flashlight to illuminate, and when they don't it does not raise his blood pressure.

He cannot attain that peace with furnaces and keys, and cars and women's 17 purses as long as he demands that they work for their keep.

Meaning and Idea

1. Into what categories does Baker divide inanimate objects? What characterizes each category?

2. What connotations does the word *plot* in the title of the piece suggest to you? What does the title add to the essay?

3. How does Baker suggest that the conflict between people and inanimate objects is solved by the category of objects that don't work?

Language, Form, Structure

1. What is the source of humor in this piece? How does Baker sustain the joke over the course of the essay? What kind of development is there in this piece?

2. Analyze the last sentence of the essay. How does this sentence fit into the essay as a whole? How does it provide the essay with an effective conclusion?

3. Define the following words and use them in original sentences: inanimate; plausible; inherent; conciliatory; barometer.

Ideas for Writing

1. Baker uses personification, the technique of attributing human characteristics to an inanimate object, to structure his essay. Write a short essay describing the personality of a particular object with which you are familiar. Be sure not only to give that object a personality but also to make clear how that personality affects your relation with the object.

2. Baker wrote this essay in 1968, years before the advent of the personal computer and the cellular phone. Cellular phones, beepers, laptop computers, and other consumer electronics constitute a type of inanimate object that Baker doesn't consider—things that get lost, break, *and* refuse to work. Write an update to Baker's essay, fitting these new objects into his categories or proposing a new category to accommodate them.

3. Baker repeatedly insists that his classifications are "scientific" or come from scientists. What do these claims add to the essay? Write an essay analyzing the comment Baker is making on science and scientists.

The National Heartbeat:
"We-ness" and "Me-ness"

Malcolm Cowley

Malcolm Cowley (1898–1989) was a literary critic, poet, editor, and social historian. He is well known for his studies of the Lost Generation of American expatriate writers in the 1920s, *Exiles' Return* (1934) and *A Second Flowering* (1973). As editor of the liberal *New Republic,* he organized the 1932 Bonus Expeditionary Force to march to President Hoover's doorstep during the Great Depression to demand army pensions.

"The National Heartbeat: 'We-ness' and 'Me-ness' " carries into the 1980s Cowley's 60-plus-year history of alert social criticism. As you read, pay attention to his social and cultural classifications and how they differ from what he describes as the mainstream opinions.

So it has been more or less agreed that America is turning right. One pictures a disciplined army of 200 million persons, not counting toddlers, all, as at a word of command, executing a right face and marching off into John Wayne country.

I should question whether there has been any such unanimity, but undoubtedly there has been a change in mood and direction. Liberals now admit to being qualmish about big government. Conservatives are shouting hallelujah! as they band into national lobbies. The watchword in education is "back to basics." College students, those barometers of the future—if one learns to read the dials—have stopped being rebels; instead they plug for marks, worry about finding jobs after graduation, and one reads that their favorite course is Accounting.

But after the turbulent age group of the 1960's, isn't that what might have been expected? Another age group has appeared with its own standards of the good life, and these were pretty certain to be in conflict with the standards of the group that preceded it.

Age groups and the part they have played in American culture—or indeed in any culture—are a subject that has seldom been thoroughly discussed. It first attracted my attention when I was working on the literary records of the so-called Lost Generation. Soon I noted that this was only one of several "generations" in 20th-century American literature. Then I observed that the same phenomenon of conflicting age groups appeared in other fields—art, music, science, public affairs—and was finally mirrored in the general mood of the country. Each new group had its own likes, dislikes, and aspirations, its own "consciousness" or sense of life, and this it tried to impose on older groups and on the future.

But was "generation" the right word for those successive groups? They seemed to come forward at much shorter intervals than the 30-year span of a biological generation. American commentators have preferred to speak in terms of decades, thereby adopting a numerical scheme that lends itself to simple adjectives: the Roaring 20's, the Depression 30's (which were not depressed), the silent or shameful 50's, the rebellious 60's. I noted, however, that this counting by tens doesn't often correspond to the true date either for an age group or for changes in the dominant mood.

I decided to make a chronological table, based on what I remembered or had learned about our century. The result was something like this:

1904–1918: The Age of Reform. Muckrakers, labor novelists, Bull Moose, and finally a crusade to make the world safe for democracy.

1919–1930: The Jazz Age. Wall Street follies, the fast buck, bathtub gin, "The Great Gatsby," expatriation, the crash of '29.

1931–1945: The Depression. Bread lines, the New Deal, Spain, "The Grapes of Wrath," The Hitler-Stalin Pact, and finally the great war that was not a crusade.

1946–1960: The Silent Generation. Security, "making it," the baby boom, the cold war, Joe McCarthy, the New Critics.

1961–1973: The Youth Rebellion. Freedom marches, pot, rock music, "Make love, not war," Vietnam, "The March on the Pentagon," Watergate.

Others might choose different dates for the beginning and end of each period (except when the change in mood was abrupt and unmistakable, as at the end of the two world wars). More often there was a gradual transition, as when the Silent Generation of the 1950's made way for the Youth Rebellion. Did the 60's really begin with John F. Kennedy's Inaugural Address ("Ask what you can do for your country") or only with the bitter news of his assassination? And what about movements like Women's Liberation that have already spanned two eras?

One could argue at length about such questions, but I think that two or three facts might become apparent from my little chart. The first is that there have been five distinct periods—or six, counting the present era—since the turn of the century.

They have lasted for an average of a little less than 15 years, or half the span of a human generation. Finally, one notes that the dominant mood of the country has gone from one extreme to another, and back again, so that periods 30 years apart bear some resemblance to each other. The Old Left of the 1930's fathered the New Left of the 1960's. Now, in the late 1970's, we have the New Right, just as in the late 1940's.

Right . . . left . . . right. Hearing those words so often, we picture the country as following the swing of a giant pendulum. The real process, however, is rather an expansion and contraction of interests on the part of influential minorities. "We-ness" and "me-ness" are the two key words. During an expansive period, the general attention is turned outward to broad issues affecting "us," the nation or the world. The leftists are loud and confident. During a contractive period, attention is focused on "my" success in a stable society. The voices we hear are those of conservatives.

One period has followed another in an immensely slow heartbeat rhythm of diastole followed by systole. The Age of Reform, the Depression, the Youth Rebellion of the 1960's—all those were expansive periods. In each case they were succeeded by a contractive period: the Jazz Age, the Silent Generation, and now the "me" years after Watergate.   16

Of course those alternations were shaped by external events, including wars, a depression, and the baby boom. I believe, however, that they also reveal an inner logic and sequence. Perhaps the guiding concept here is disillusionment. The spokesmen for an expansive period are disillusioned when their dream of the future is shattered by such events as the Treaty of Versailles (1919) or the Hitler-Stalin Pact of 1939. A contractive period, with its hunger for personal achievement, or simply for money, leads to another type of disillusionment, this time connected with stress, alienation, corruption, and nervous breakdown. That was what happened toward the end of the Jazz Age, and it may soon happen again, if we can trust college reports.   17

And then what is to be expected? Putting on my tall, conical wizard's hat and acting the part of an aged seer, I prophesy that some time in the middle 1980's there will be another reaction from me-ness into we-ness, another cresting and falling wave of popular idealism. I don't know what form it will take, since that will depend on events in the world and the nation, but I am sure it is coming.   18

Meaning and Idea

1. What is Cowley's basic premise in this essay? What is the focus of his evaluation of the changes that have taken place over the years?

2. What is Cowley's opinion of the American political climate of the 1980s? What examples does he offer to support his opinion? What does he say about how college students of that era fit into this political climate?

3. What does the author mean in paragraph 1 by the phrase "marching off into John Wayne country"? Explain in your own words the meaning of the complete metaphor in the second sentence.

4. What did Cowley mean by *we-ness* and *me-ness?* Why does he identify them as "the two key words" (paragraph 15)?

5. What did Cowley predict would take place in the mid-1980s? Since we have already passed that time, do you see any evidence of his predictions having come true? How would you characterize Cowley's overall political stance? Do you classify him as a pessimist or an optimist? Why?

Language, Form, Structure

1. According to Cowley, by what classification scheme have most American commentators on culture identified America's consciousness of the

twentieth century? What is Cowley's scheme of classification? How is his scheme different? On what basis does he decide to make his categories?

2. Name the special *connotations* that the author applies to the following words or expressions: right; barometers; consciousness; generation; New Left; New Right.

3. How does this essay combine classification with process analysis? Identify and briefly summarize two process analyses used in this essay.

4. Cowley makes use of numerous allusions to political, social, and cultural events. From each of the eras listed on his chart covering the period 1904–1973, choose and explain one fully.

5. Look up the following words in a dictionary and then use each in a sentence: unanimity; qualmish; turbulent; aspirations; expatriation; contractive; diastole; systole; seer; prophesy.

Ideas for Writing

1. Write a classification of the various cliques or social groups in your school. In your prewriting, be sure to decide on basic principles of classification by which to describe the groups.

2. Write a short classification of either "givers" *or* "takers" among social or cultural groups in evidence today in America. Include at least three categories.

3. Do you agree with Cowley's basic division of the ages by means of the "we-ness" and "me-ness" factors? Write a further classification of these two groups based on your own observations. Into which group would you place yourself? Into which group would you place the majority of students in your school? Why?

Modern Friendships

Phillip Lopate

Born in 1943 in Jamaica Heights, New York, Phillip Lopate has written two books of poetry and one novel and has taught in the Teachers and Writers Collaborative in New York public schools for several years. *Being with Children* is about his time spent in the classroom. This selection is from *Joie de Vivre,* a book of essays published in 1990.

His examination and classification of friendships are of, by, and for his own time. The parameters for and kinds of friendships he discusses are contemporary, and he points out the ways friendship has changed over the years through his many allusions and direct references.

*I*s there anything left to say about friendship after so many great essayists have picked over the bones of the subject? Probably not. Aristotle and Cicero, Seneca and Montaigne, Bacon and Samuel Johnson, Hazlitt, Emerson, and Lamb have all taken their cracks at it; since the ancients, friendship has been a sort of examination subject for the personal essayist. It is partly the very existence of such wonderful prior models that lures the newcomer to follow in the others' footsteps, and partly a self-referential aspect of the genre, since the personal essay is itself an attempt to establish a friendship on the page between writer and reader. 1

Friendship has been called "love without wings," implying a want of lyrical afflatus. On the other hand, the Stoic definition of love ("Love is the attempt to form a friendship inspired by beauty") seems to suggest that friendship came first. Certainly a case can be made that the buildup of affection and the yearning for more intimacy, without the release of sexual activity, keeps friends in a state of sweet-sorrowful itchiness that has as much romantic quality as a love affair. We know that a falling-out between two old friends can leave a deeper and more perplexing hurt than the ending of a love affair, perhaps because we are more pessimistic about the latter's endurance from the start. 2

Our first attempted friendships are within the family. It is here we practice the techniques of listening sympathetically and proving that we can be trusted, and learn the sort of kindness we can expect in return. I have a sister, one year younger than I, who often took care of me when I was growing up. Once, when I was about fifteen, unable to sleep and shivering uncontrollably with the start of a fever, I decided in the middle of the night to go into her room and wake her. She held me, performing the basic service of a friend—presence—and the chills went away. 3

There is something tainted about these family friendships, however. This same sister, in her insecure adolescent phase, told me: "You love me because I'm related to you, but if you were to meet me for the first time at a party, you'd think I was a jerk and not worth being your friend." She had me in a bind: I had 4 no way of testing her hypothesis. I should have argued that even if our bond was not freely chosen, our decision to work on it had been. Still, we are quick to dismiss the partiality of our family members when they tell us we are talented, cute, or lovable; we must go out into the world and seduce others.

It is just a few short years from the promiscuity of the sandbox to the tormented, possessive feelings of a fifth grader who has just learned that his best and only friend is playing at another classmate's house after school. There may be worse betrayals in store, but probably none is more influential than the sudden fickleness of an elementary school friend who has dropped us for someone more popular after all our careful, patient wooing. Often we lose no time inflicting the same betrayal on someone else, just to ensure that we have got the victimization dynamic right.

What makes friendships in childhood and adolescence so poignant is that we need the chosen comrade to be everything in order to rescue us from the gothic inwardness of family life. Even if we are lucky enough to have several companions, there must be a Best Friend, knightly dubbed as though victor of an Arthurian tournament.

I clung to the romance of the Best Friend all through high school, college, and beyond, until my university circle began to disperse. At that point, in my mid-twenties, I also "acted out" the dark competitive side of friendship that can exist between two young men fighting for a place in life and love, by doing the one unforgivable thing: sleeping with my best friend's girl. I was baffled at first that there was no way to repair the damage. I lost this friendship forever, and came away from that debacle much more aware of the amount of injury that friendship can and cannot sustain. Perhaps I needed to prove to myself that friendship was not an all-permissive, resilient bond, like a mother's love, but something quite fragile. Precisely because Best Friendship promotes such a merging of identities, such seeming boundarylessness, the first major transgression of trust can cause the injured party to feel he is fighting for his violated soul against his darkest enemy. There is not much room to maneuver in a best friendship between unlimited intimacy and unlimited mistrust.

Still, it was not until the age of thirty that I reluctantly abandoned the Best Friend expectation and took up a more pluralistic model. At present, I cherish a dozen friends for their unique personalities, without asking that any one be my soul-twin. Whether this alteration constitutes a movement toward maturity or toward cowardly pragmatism is not for me to say. It may be that, in refusing to depend so much on any one friend, I am opting for self-protection over intimacy. Or it may be that, as we advance into middle age, the life problem becomes less that of establishing a tight dyadic bond and more one of making our way in a broader world, "society." Indeed, since Americans have so indistinct a notion of society, we often try to put friendship networks in its place. If a certain intensity is lost in the pluralistic model of friendship, there is also the gain of being able to experience all of one's potential, half-buried selves, through witnessing the spectacle of the multiple fates of our friends. Since we cannot be polygamists in our conjugal life, at least we can do so with friendship. As it happens, the harem of friends, so tantalizing a notion, often translates into feeling pulled in a dozen different directions, with the guilty sense of having disappointed everyone a little. It is also a risky, contrived enterprise to try to make one's friends behave in a friendly manner toward each other: if the effort fails one feels obliged to mediate; if it succeeds too well, one is jealous.

Whether friendship is intrinsically singular and exclusive, or plural and democratic, is a question that has vexed many commentators. Aristotle distinguished three types of friendship in *The Nicomachean Ethics:* "friendship based on utility," such as businessmen cultivating each other for benefit; "friendship based on pleasure," like young people interested in partying; and "perfect friendship." The first two categories Aristotle calls "qualified and superficial friendships," because they are founded on circumstances that could easily change; the last, which is based on admiration for another's good character, is more permanent, but also rarer, because good men "are few." Cicero, who wrote perhaps the best treatise on friendship, also insisted that what brings true friends together is "a mutual belief in each other's goodness." This insistence on virtue as a precondition for true friendship may strike us as impossibly demanding: who, after all, feels himself good nowadays? And yet, if I am honest, I must admit that the friendships of mine which have lasted longest have been with those whose integrity, or humanity, or strength to bear their troubles I continue to admire. Conversely, when I lost respect for someone, however winning he otherwise remained, the friendship petered away almost immediately. "Remove respect from friendship," said Cicero, "and you have taken away the most splendid ornament it possesses."

Montaigne distinguished between friendship, which he saw as a once-in-a-lifetime experience, and the calculating worldly alliances around him, which he thought unworthy of the name. In paying tribute to his late friend Etienne de la Boetie, Montaigne wrote: "Having so little time to last, and having begun so late, for we were both grown men, and he a few years older than I, it could not lose time and conform to the pattern of mild and regular friendships, which need so many precautions in the form of long preliminary association. Our friendship has no other model than itself, and can be compared only with itself. It is not one special consideration, nor two, nor three, nor four, nor a thousand: it is I know not what quintessence of all this mixture, which, having seized my whole will, led it to plunge and lose itself in his; which, having seized his whole will, led it to plunge and lose itself in mine, with equal hunger, equal rivalry. . . . So many coincidences are needed to build up such a friendship that it is a lot if fortune can do it once in three centuries." This seems a bit high hat: since the sixteenth century, our expectations of friendship may have grown more plebeian. Even Emerson, in his grand romantic essay on the subject, allowed as how he was not up to the Castor-and-Pollux standard: "I am not quite so strict in my terms, perhaps because I have never known so high a fellowship as others." Emerson contents himself with a circle of intelligent men and women, but warns us not to throw them together: "You shall have very useful and cheering discourse at several times with two several men, but let all three of you come together, and you shall not have one new and hearty word. Two may talk and one may hear, but three cannot take part in a conversation of the most sincere and searching sort."

Friendship is a long conversation. I suppose I could imagine a nonverbal friendship revolving around shared physical work or sport, but for me, good talk is the point of the thing. Indeed, the ability to generate conversation by the hour is the most promising indication, during its uncertain early stages, that a possible friendship will take hold. In the first few conversations there may be an exaggeration of agreement, as both parties angle for adhesive surfaces. But later on, trust builds through the courage to assert disagreement, through the tactful acceptance that differences of opinion will have to remain.

Some view like-mindedness as both the precondition and product of friendship. Myself, I distrust it. I have one friend who keeps assuming that we see the world eye-to-eye. She is intent on enrolling us in a flattering aristocracy of taste, on the short "we" list against the ignorant "they"; sometimes I do not have the strength to fight her need for consensus with my own stubborn disbelief in the existence of any such inner circle of privileged, cultivated sensibility. Perhaps I have too much invested in a view of myself as idiosyncratic to be eager to join any coterie, even a coterie of two. What attracts me to friends' conversation is the give-and-take, not necessarily that we come out at the same point.

"Our tastes and aims and views were identical—and that is where the essence of a friendship must always lie," wrote Cicero. To some extent, perhaps, but then the convergence must be natural, not, as Emerson put it, "a mush of concession. Better be a nettle in the side of your friend than his echo." And Francis Bacon observed that "the best preservative to keep the mind in health is the faithful admonition of a friend."

Friendship is a school for character, allowing us the chance to study in great detail and over time temperaments very different from our own. These charming quirks, these contradictions, these nobilities, these blind spots of our friends we track not out of disinterested curiosity: we must have this information before knowing how far we may relax our guard, how much we may rely on them in crises. The learning curve of friendship involves, to no small extent, filling out this picture of the other's limitations and making peace with the results. (With one's own limitations there may never be peace.) Each time I hit up against a friend's inflexibility I am relieved as well as disappointed: I can begin to predict, and arm myself in advance against repeated bruises. I have one friend who is always late, so I bring a book along when I am to meet her. If I give her a manuscript to read and she promises to look at it over the weekend, I start preparing myself for a month-long wait.

Not that one ever gives up trying to educate the friend to one's needs. I approach such matters experimentally: sometimes I will pride myself in tactfully circumventing the friend's predicted limitation, even if it means relinquishing all hope of getting the response I want; at other times I will confront a problem with intentional tactlessness, just to see if any change is still possible.

I have a dear old friend, Richard, who shies away from personal confidences. Years go by without my learning anything about his love life, and he does not encourage the baring of my soul either, much as I like that sort of thing. But we share so many other interests and values that that limitation seems easily borne, most of the time. Once, however, I found myself in a state of emotional despair; I told him I had exhausted my hopes of finding love or success, that I felt suicidal, and he changed the topic, patently embarrassed. I was annoyed both at his emotional rigidity and at my own stupidity—after all, I'd enough friends who ate up this kind of confessional talk, why foist on Richard what I might have predicted he couldn't, or wouldn't, handle? For a while I sulked, annoyed at him for having failed me, but I also began to see my despair through his eyes as melodramatic, childish petulance, and I began to let it go. As it happened, he found other ways during our visit to be so considerate that I ended up feeling better, even without our having had a heart-to-heart talk. I suppose the moral is that a friend can serve as a corrective to our insular miseries simply by offering up his essential otherness.

Though it is often said that with a true friend there is no need to hold anything back ("A friend is a person with whom I may be sincere. Before him I may think aloud," wrote Emerson), I have never found this to be entirely the case. Certain words may be too cruel if spoken at the wrong moment—or may fall on deaf ears, for any number of reasons. I also find with each friend, as they must with me, that some initial resistance, restlessness, psychic weather must be overcome before that tender ideal attentiveness may be called forth. 17

I have a good friend, Charlie, who is often very distracted whenever we first get together. If we are sitting in a cafe he will look around constantly for the waiter, or be distracted by a pretty woman or the restaurant's cat. It would be foolish for me to broach an important subject at such moments, so I resign myself to waiting the half hour or however long it takes until his jumpiness subsides. Or else I draw this pattern grumpily to his attention. Once he has settled down, however, I can tell Charlie virtually anything, and he me. But the candor cannot be rushed. It must be built up to with the verbal equivalent of limbering exercises. 18

The Friendship Scene—a flow of shared confidences, recognitions, humor, advice, speculation, even wisdom—is one of the key elements of modern friendships. Compared to the rest of life, this ability to lavish one's best energies on an activity utterly divorced from the profit motive and free from the routines of domination and inequality that affect most relations (including, perhaps, the selfsame friendship at other times) seems idyllic. The Friendship Scene is by its nature not an everyday occurrence. It represents the pinnacle, the fruit of the friendship, potentially ever-present but not always arrived at. Both friends' dim yet self-conscious awareness that they are wandering conversationally toward a goal that they have previously accomplished but which may elude them this time around creates a tension, an obligation to communicate as sincerely as possible, like actors in an improvisation exercise struggling to shape their baggy material into some climactic form. This very pressure to achieve "quality" communication may induce a sort of inauthentic epiphany, not unlike what happens sometimes in the last ten minutes of a psychotherapy session. But a truly achieved Friendship Scene can be among the best experiences life has to offer. 19

I remember one such afternoon when Michael, a close writer-friend, and I [20] met at a cafeteria on a balmy Saturday in early spring and talked for three and a half hours. There were no outside time pressures that particular afternoon, a rare occurrence for either of us. At first we caught up with our latest business, the sort of items that might have gone into a biweekly bulletin sent to any number of acquaintances. Then gradually we settled into an area of perplexing unresolved impressions. I would tell Michael about A's chance, seemingly hostile remark toward me at a gathering, and he would report that the normally ebullient B looked secretly depressed. These were the memory equivalents of food grains stuck in our teeth, which we were now trying to free with our tongues: anecdotal fragments I was not even sure had any point, until I started fashioning them aloud for Michael's interest. Together we diagnosed our mutual acquaintances, each other's character, and, from there, the way of the world. In the course of our free associations we eventually descended into what was really bothering us. I learned he was preoccupied with the fate of an old college friend who was dying of AIDS, he, that my father was in poor health and needed two operations. We had touched bottom—mortality—and it was reassuring to settle there awhile. Gradually we rose again, drawn back to the questions of ego and career, craft and romance. It was, as I've said, a pretty day, and we ended up walking through a new mall in Houston, gawking at the window displays of that bland emporium with a reawakened curiosity about the consumer treats of America, our attentions turned happily outward now that we had dwelt long enough in the shared privacies of our psyches.

Contemporary urban life, with its tight schedules and crowded appointment [21] books, has helped to shape modern friendship into something requiring a good deal of intentionality and pursuit. You phone a friend and make a date a week or more in advance; then you set aside an evening, like a tryst, during which to squeeze in all your news and advice, confession and opinion. Such intimate compression may add a romantic note to modern friendships, but it also places a strain on the meeting to yield a high quality of meaning and satisfaction, closer to art than life, thereby increasing the chance for disappointment. If I see certain busy or out-of-town friends only once every six months, we must not only catch up on our lives but convince ourselves within the allotted two hours together that we still share a special affinity, an inner track to each other's psyches, or the next meeting may be put off for years. Surely there must be another, saner rhythm to friendship in rural areas—or maybe not? I think about "the good old days" when friends would go on walking tours through England together, when Edith Wharton would bundle poor Henry James into her motorcar and they'd drive to the South of France for a month. I'm not sure my friendships could sustain the strain of travel for weeks at a time, and the truth of the matter is that I've gotten used to this urban arrangement of serial friendship "dates," where the pleasure of the rendezvous is enhanced by the knowledge that it will only last, at most, six hours. If the two of us don't happen to mesh that day (always a possibility)—well, it's only a few hours; and if it should go beautifully, one needs an escape hatch from exaltation as well as disenchantment. I am capable of only so much intense, exciting communication before I start to fade; I come to these encounters equipped with a six-hour oxygen tank. Is this an evolutionary pattern of modern friendship, or only a personal limitation?

Perhaps because I conceive of the modern Friendship Scene as a some- 22 what theatrical enterprise, a one-act play, I tend to be very affected by the "set," so to speak. A restaurant, a museum, a walk in the park through the zoo, even accompanying a friend on shopping errands—I prefer public turf where the stimulation of the city can play a backdrop to our dialogue, feeding it with details when inspiration flags. True, some of the most cherished friendship scenes have occurred around a friend's kitchen table. The problem with restricting the date to one another's houses is that the entertaining friend may be unable to stop playing the host, or may sink too passively into his or her surroundings. Subtle struggles may also develop over which domicile should serve as the venue.

I have a number of *chez moi* friends, friends who always invite me to come 23 to their homes while evading offers to visit mine. What they view as hospitality I see as a need to control the *mise-en-scène* of friendship. I am expected to fit in where they are most comfortable, while they play lord of the manor, distracted by the props of decor, the pool, the unexpected phone call, the swirl of children, animals, and neighbors. Indeed, *chez moi* friends often tend to keep a sort of open house, so that in going over to see them—for a *tête-à-tête,* I had assumed—I will suddenly find their other friends and neighbors, whom they have also invited, dropping in all afternoon. There are only so many Sundays I care to spend hanging out with a friend's entourage before becoming impatient for a private audience.

Married friends who own their own homes are much more apt to try to 24 draw me into their domestic fold, whereas single people are often more sensitive about establishing a discreet space for the friendship to occur. Perhaps the married assume that a bachelor like myself is desperate for home cooking and a little family life. I have noticed that it is not an easy matter to pry a married friend away from mate and milieu. For married people, especially those with children, the home often becomes the wellspring of all their nurturing feelings, and the single friend is invited to partake in the general flow. Maybe there is also a certain tendency on their parts to kill two birds with one stone: they don't see enough of their spouse and kids, and figure they can visit with you all at the same time. And maybe they need one-on-one friendship less, hampered as they are by responsibilities that no amount of camaraderie or discussion can change. Often friendship in these circumstances is not even a pairing, but a mixing together of two sets of parents and children willy-nilly. What would the ancients say about this? In Rome, according to Bacon, "the whole senate dedicated an altar to Friendship, as to a goddess. . . ." From my standpoint, friendship is a jealous goddess. Whenever a friend of mine marries, I have to fight to overcome the feeling that I am being "replaced" by the spouse. I don't mind sharing a friend with his family milieu—in fact I like it, up to a point—but eventually I must get the friend alone, or else, as a bachelor at a distinct power disadvantage, I risk becoming a mere spectator of familial rituals instead of a key player in the drama of friendship.

A person living alone usually has more control over his or her schedule, hence more energy to give to friendship. If anything, the danger is of investing too much emotional energy in one's friends. When a single person is going through a romantic dry spell he or she often tries to extract the missing passion from a circle of friends. This works only up to a point: the frayed nerves of protracted celibacy can lead to hypersensitive imaginings of slights and rejections, during which times one's platonic friends seem to come particularly into the line of fire.

Today, with the partial decline of the nuclear family and the search for alternatives to it, we also see attempts to substitute the friendship web for intergenerational family life. Since psychoanalysis has alerted us to regard the family as a minefield of unrequited love, manipulation, and ambivalence, it is only natural that people may look to friendship as a more supportive ground for relation. But in our longing for an unequivocally positive bond, we should beware of sentimentalizing friendship, as saccharine "buddy" movies or certain feminist novels do, of neutering its problematic, destructive aspects. Besides, friendship can never substitute for the true meaning of family: if nothing else, it will never be able to duplicate the family's wild capacity for concentrating neurosis.

In short, friends can't be your family, they can't be your lovers, they can't be your psychiatrists. But they can be your friends, which is plenty. For, as Cicero tells us, "friendship is the noblest and most delightful of all the gifts the gods have given to mankind." And Bacon adds: "it is a mere and miserable solitude to want true friends, without which the world is but a wilderness. . . ."

When I think about the qualities that characterize the best friendships I've known, I can identify five: rapport, affection, need, habit, and forgiveness. Rapport and affection can only take you so far; they may leave you at the formal, outer gate of goodwill, which is still not friendship. A persistent need for the other's company, for their interest, approval, opinion, will get you inside the gates, especially when it is reciprocated. In the end, however, there are no substitutes for habit and forgiveness. A friendship may travel for years on cozy habit. But it is a melancholy fact that unless you are a saint you are bound to offend every friend deeply at least once in the course of time. The friends I have kept the longest are those who forgave me for wronging them, unintentionally, intentionally, or by the plain catastrophe of my personality, time and again. There can be no friendship without forgiveness.

Meaning and Idea

1. Why is Lopate's essay called "Modern Friendships"? What distinction is he drawing?

2. What are Lopate's categories for friendship?

3. What are Lopate's categories for the qualities most important to friendship?

4. Lopate feels that we learn how to create and keep friendships. He also notes that it is sometimes necessary to behave differently with different kinds of

friends. What has he learned, in fact, do you think? Where did he get his first lessons? Did he always know how? Which classical authors does Lopate attend to the most? What does he think about their observations and classifications of friendship?

Language, Form, Structure

1. Especially throughout the first part of his essay, Lopate acknowledges and cites famous writers who have dealt with the topic of friendship or have been "great friends." Does he always completely agree with these others? How is he *using* them?

2. What does the writer achieve by opening his essay with a question?

3. What is the thesis in this essay?

4. The first section of the essay categorizes previous opinions on the topic relative to the writer's own. The second discusses kinds of friendships he has known or had. The third section specifically examines kinds of modern friendships. How is this developing structure useful for Lopate's overall theme?

5. Define the following words and use each one in a sentence: afflatus; stoic; poignant; gothic; debacle; permissive; pluralistic; pragmatism; dyadic; polygamists; conjugal; intrinsically; quintessence; plebeian; coterie; nettle; admonition; borne; foist; petulance; broach; candor; idyllic; epiphany; ebullient.

Ideas for Writing

1. Using classification as the main organizing principle, write an essay called "Modern _____." Fill in the blank with a term of your choice: *love, jobs, students, automobiles, films,* or the like.

2. Write your own essay called "Modern Friendships," using a classification scheme to develop your ideas.

3. Identify the three parts of Lopate's essay and discuss each section's success or quality in relation to his thesis.

CROSSOVER

1. Henry Reed's "Naming of Parts" (this chapter) and Wilfred Owen's "Dulce Et Decorum Est" (Chapter Nine) rivet the reader's attention on the destructiveness of war. Write an essay that considers the elements in each poem that most effectively convey the antiwar message.

2. Write an essay in which you compare and contrast the different views of friendship expressed by Judith Viorst in "Friends, Good Friends—and Such Good Friends" and Phillip Lopate in "Modern Friendships."

Chapter Seven

■

CAUSAL ANALYSIS

INTRODUCTION TO CAUSAL ANALYSIS

Thinking about causes—what produces something—and about effects—what something produces—is an activity both natural and necessary to human life. Questions like, "Why did I do that?" "What happened because I did that?" and "What might happen if I do that?" reflect both our instinctive curiosity and our desire to learn from experience—to explain or control life from our judgments of the past or from our anticipation of the future. Indeed, it is hard to think of an hour passing when our minds are not engaged in causal thinking. The whistling we hear: Is that the kettle, the wind, the radio? That pulsing headache: Is it an emerging cold, tension over an exam, eyestrain, or the day's humidity? And what will result from the headache? Will we miss work, fail a test, finally replace lost eye-glasses, shop for a dehumidifier?

Not surprisingly, great writing throughout history reflects the basic human habit of seeking explanations for why things happen and what occurs after they happen. In almost every culture, early myths explore why the world began and why its inhabitants, human and nonhuman alike, got to be the way they are. Philosophers from Aristotle on have dealt with causal thinking—what it is, how to do it best, how to avoid its traps. For Aristotle and then for the medieval philosophers who built on his thinking, there existed a taxonomy of causes— *efficient* cause, *material* cause, *formal* cause, *final* cause, to name but a few. For ages, most thinkers saw a *necessary* connection between causes and effects, a connection finally controlled by power from a divine source. In the eighteenth century, however, the philosopher David Hume painted a universe as a place of accidents and coincidences, not of absolute connections between causes and effects. Hume helped to change markedly a long-accepted view of causation. By the twentieth century, the philosopher Bertrand Russell declared the idea of cause a "relic of bygone days."

The stance of writers like Russell may be extreme and inaccurate, but it is valuable, for it cautions us away from fast and smug interpretations of why things happen. Essential as it is, the whole undertaking of causal thinking can be treacherous. Rushing to judgment, we can assign the wrong cause to an event or point to an effect that is no more than a coincidence. Chances are that the notion of causality will be with us for as long as humans think critically about events, but going slowly and carefully as we think about why things happen and what follows when something happens seems the only right way to reach sound and useful judgments. The imaginative writer delves steadily and deeply into causes and effects. The great writer eschews snap judgments, tracing the possibilities for why things occur or for the effects of occurrences, and inviting readers to use their own faculties to validate proposed causes and results.

READING CAUSAL ANALYSIS

Read a tale to a child, and the child asks, "Why? Then what?" These questions remain steady ones as we read throughout our lives. In great writing we find minds searching for why things happen—why wars start, why marriages last or fail, why people give up or endure, why kingdoms and civilizations crumble or advance. And great writing takes up the questions beyond these: What happens as a result of certain conditions—*after* wars begin, *after* marriages end, *after* men or women survive, *after* kingdoms fall. What happens then?

The selections in this chapter allow you to see both impulses at work—the search back into causes and the search forward from events into effects.

Reading causation in the masters, we are encouraged to see the subtlety of explanations that guide us away from pat interpretations. Indeed, in the hands of great writers, causal analysis is often more an *asking* or a *suggesting* than a certain *stating* of causes and (or) effects. Edwin Arlington Robinson's poem "Richard Cory" never tells the reader, "This is why Richard Cory killed himself"; rather, the poet lays out details and patterns that invite the reader to speculate *why*.

Reading causal analyses can teach us much as we approach our own thinking and writing. Great writers remind us to approach the whole undertaking of causation with care, to avoid the quick and facile explanations that lead to error, and to find the explanations that can open our eyes to past events and future possibilities. Yet these writers also help us thrill to the speculation about causes and effects, how these unite in a chain of interactions, what might have occurred had one small event not led to another and another and another. Jack London's famous story "To Build a Fire," though it is a simple narrative, will intensify your view of how incidents can link to produce tragic results.

WRITING CAUSAL ANALYSIS

Causal thinking is central to much writing. Again and again, students receive assignments whose major task is the identification and explanation of the cause of a particular phenomenon, the effects of the phenomenon, or both. History courses might ask you to examine in writing the causes or results of a war. Literature courses might ask you to write on causes or effects of character, events, or places. Science courses might ask you to reflect again and again on events leading to or resulting from some occurrence—how a compound forms from two elements in a test tube, say, or the consequences of unchecked atmospheric pollution.

Causal analysis is the dominant undertaking of a good portion of academic assignments and an important contributor to still more. Most writers undertaking a comprehensive analysis of a subject will pay attention to causality even if their major concerns lie elsewhere. Explaining how to establish a new lawn, for example, a writer might lay out the consequences of too little watering or too much fertilizer and would therefore be drawing cause and effect into a paper whose main intent was process analysis. In a comparison between two unequally successful socialist economic systems, you certainly would explore for your readers the causes for the failures of one and the gains of the other. Causal analysis, then, is something you must master as a writer in order to investigate many topics in many fields and must learn to approach with slow and deliberate thinking beforehand.

PURPOSE AND AUDIENCE

Causes or Effects?

While many causal assignments will require you to discuss causes *and* effects, many will require that you decide for yourself on one or the other. Often, then, the first step in clarifying purpose for your causal writing is to determine which you will be considering—causes or effects. Do you want to consider what led up to an event or phenomenon, or do you want to consider what came after it? Furthermore, what you decide to focus on in causal analysis will depend to a great extent on your interests and your point of view. The causes assigned to the same event—World War II, for example—will differ depending on the orientation of the person doing the analysis. A psychologist or a psychologically oriented person may stress the *Übermensch* mentality of the Third Reich. An economist or economically oriented person might stress the striving for control of world capital. A political scientist or someone interested in the study of government might stress the clash of nations or the political orientations of their leaders. All these approaches may be valid. Usually, important events, such as wars, stem from many conditions and occurrences.

Scope and Audience

Aside from orientation, you must take into account the scope of discussion within that orientation. Generally the causes leading to something are many and connected, as are the results. You must decide whether you wish to consider far-off causes, immediate causes, underlying causes, or precipitating events. And for results, too, do you wish to write of immediate or far-reaching results, the most important or the least expected? Will you show that causes or effects usually ascribed to an occurrence are simply wrong or inaccurate? If you decide which kinds of causes and effects you wish to include, you will be able to write with much greater purpose and direction.

In part, your audience may determine both the point of view and the scope you adopt. Does your audience have some special interest or intellectual approach? Does it know a good deal about the subject? If so, do you wish to deepen or instead to challenge their knowledge? Explaining the results of a new gene-splicing technique in a journal for geneticists requires one strategy; explaining it to the educated but not nearly so specialized readership of *Omni* or *Scientific American* requires quite another. Although a writer could assume avid interest from both audiences, the range of materials included in essays to each group would differ drastically. And imagine how those two essays would differ from a piece on the causal analysis of gene splicing in the Sunday magazine section of your local newspaper.

PROCESS

Prewriting for Your Causal Analysis

To help you think about your purpose in causal analysis, use prewriting strategies to produce a sequence of the events or phenomena involved in the topic you're interested in. If you are uncertain about whether you wish to write about causes, effects, or both, try to draft your time line so that your sequence stretches *back* through events and *forward* through results. Then look over your time line or sequential list and decide what interests you most—what *caused* an event or phenomenon, what resulted from an event or phenomenon, or both. As you look over your page, ask yourself if you have jotted down many causes, for example, that are psychological in nature. If so, that may tell you something about what you wish to stress in your analysis. Use your sequential list as a rough outline and cross out the items that seem uninteresting or illogical and add other items that might make for a fuller discussion. Suppose you've decided to write about the reasons you and your boyfriend broke up last month. You see as you look at your prewriting that the major problem was a raw competitiveness that underlay the relationship despite its passion and mutual respect. You see, too, that you've listed anxiety over pressure to marry as another cause for the end of the relationship. Well, then, the items you've included about your different tastes in clothing, food, and good times and your different intellectual interests (you're a business major, he's a poet) may not be relevant in this paper. But you might add another item—the psychological stress caused by your frequent separations.

Logical Writing

Once you've decided on your focus—causes, effects, or both—and have roughly outlined and revised possible causes and/or effects, you are ready to look even more critically at your analysis. Causality is an extremely valuable tool for a writer, but without sufficient care, we all too often can fall into illogical thinking, assigning cause or effect when there is neither. Therefore, you want to review your list of possible causes and effects for problems in logic. Have you called something an effect just because it happened after something else? Have you called something a cause because something else just happens to follow it? Because it snowed the day you got an A on your calculus final, it does not logically follow that the A *resulted* from the snow or that the snow *caused* the A grade. The two events have nothing logically to do with each other. Logicians call this error in logic *post hoc, ergo propter hoc* (after this, therefore because of this), and you must be on the lookout for this fallacy as you prepare to write. Also, make sure that you have provided a reasonable number of causes and/or effects in your analysis. At times, a single cause or effect is all the writer wishes to convey, but more often than not, several causes and/or several results make for a more enlightened discussion. In truth, causation is not a simple affair, and a whole chain of events and conditions precedes and follows almost any event.

When you're ready to write, if you wish to focus on effects, you will most likely start with a brief statement of *cause* and then move on to the main concern of your paper—effects of that cause. If, in contrast, you're primarily interested in discussing effect, then you will do well to start your paper by briefly identifying and explaining the causes leading to this effect. If you're doing both—an ambitious undertaking in a short essay—then identify your phenomenon at the start of the paper and discuss causes and effects in separate sections to avoid confusing the two. A well-wrought thesis statement that identifies your topic and your intended approach to it will guide your course as you produce your drafts.

The care and attention you give to planning a paper of causal analysis are worth the effort. Causal thinking is vital, helping us to explain past events and learn for the future. The well-reasoned causal analysis can teach much to both the writer and the reader.

Mixing Rhetorical (Modes)

Once again we remind you not to follow any particular rhetorical strategy slavishly. In other words, keep in mind the value of mixing methods as your topic demands it. In the instance, referred to in a previous paragraph, of writing about a breakup with a boyfriend, you certainly saw the opportunity for applying exemplification in the essay's development (see Chapter Three). A list of causes, if translated into body paragraphs, would bring the attendant choices for writing through examples—how to arrange the examples, which to expand with significant details, how to use transitions—even though the controlling rhetorical strategy here is causation. Certainly narrative and description can play a role in an essay rooted in causation. Comparison and contrast and classification may contribute to your essay. Definition can help you illuminate unclear terms or establish with great precision some aspect that you want to highlight in a word's meaning. And, as you will see in Chapter Nine, a strong written argument regularly draws on causes and effects for logical presentation. In other words, as you consider thesis, audience, and purpose, be open to using a range of rhetorical methods in your essay.

STUDENT WRITING

In the essay below the student writer attempts to explain why the poem "Dream Deferred" by Langston Hughes (see page 426 in this chapter) has had an effect on him. The annotations highlight the causal strategies, among others, that help the writer make his point.

The Impact of "Dream Deferred"

In the first line of "Dream Deferred" Langston Hughes asks and answers a question about human frustration: What happens to a dream when it's postponed? The rest of the poem is a series of possible answers. The poet's choices in sentence structure, language, and style produced a very strong effect on me.[a,b]

First,[c] the use of questions caused me to stop and think.[b] Had Hughes just said that it's not good to frustrate people, I might not have read on. But the question grabbed me. It's general. I have dreams too. What if my dreams were snuffed out? I read on. Each of Hughes's answers follows, and each is in the form of a question. Here again, the choice of an interrogative and not a declarative sentence caused me to buy in. I'm not being preached at. Hughes gave me choices. His use of questions really made me think about answers.

Then too[c] Hughes's figurative language caused me to give serious thought to the results of frustration. In almost every case the possibilities are expressed in similes. These similes caused me to experience a deferred dream as a picture (dried up raisin, festering sore, crusted sweet, sagging load) and even a smell (rotten meat), not an abstraction.[e] But the last possibility is not a simile but a metaphor. Hughes doesn't ask if it explodes *like* a bomb. The fact that the last line didn't say "like" after five previous questions that did made me think, This is the one he wants me to notice especially.[d]

Finally,[c] and most important to my way of thinking, the placement of lines on the page affected me. That last possible answer is separated from all the other possible answers, and it appears in italics.[e] Certainly this forces you to give it extra attention. The only other line that is separated from the body of the poem is the first one, which asks the main question. This fact caused me to put these two lines together in my mind. The very serious question of the first line finds the most serious answer in the last line. The fact that each of these is only on one line and the other questions take up two lines each also caused me to pay special attention.[f]

These things, I believe, work together to make the poem "Dream Deferred" a moving and challenging work. In just eleven lines the poem shows the endless frustration of having to put your dreams aside. In images that strike like bullets,[g] Hughes, a black man, spells out the failed desires of us all, but particularly those of many black people held back by racism, economics, living conditions, and unfair laws. One cannot fail to hear echoes of Hughes in Dr. Martin Luther King, Jr.'s, famous "I Have a Dream" speech. King sets forth bold dreams; Hughes tells what happens when they're put off for another day.[h]

[a]Thesis: states general reasons for the poem's effect on the writer; essay will stress causes

[b]Use of exemplification: sentence structure, language, style

[c]Transition

[d]Audience awareness: summaries and quotations inform those who did not read poem and highlight key areas of attention for those who did

[e]Specific details from poem to support assertions

[f]Arrangement of details: most important last

[g]Figurative language: "images that strike like bullets"

[h]Conclusion goes beyond mere summary

SUMMING UP: CAUSAL ANALYSIS

Reading Causal Analysis

- Causal analysis means determining the reason something happened or the consequences or effects of an event.

- Weigh the writer's arguments and explanations to be sure that the writer does not rush to judgment, assigning incorrect causes or pointing to effects that are no more than coincidences.

- If the writer presents a chain of events, determine whether they seem logical and how the events interlink to produce the result being analyzed.

- Identify ways the writer has suggested or asked about causes or effects, as opposed to stating them absolutely.

- From the details and patterns in the writing, speculate on your own about the causes and effects of issues presented by the writer.

- Ascertain whether the writer has stated clearly the causes and (or) effects she intends to explore in the paper.

Writing Causal Analysis

- Use prewriting to consider carefully the causes and effects of your chosen topic.

- Consider whether you want to stress causes or effects and determine the scope of your intended presentation.

- List the sequence of events or phenomena involved in the topic you're considering and use the list as a rough outline.

- When you have decided on your focus—causes, effects, or both—produce a thesis statement that identifies the topic and your intended approach to it.

- Examine your drafts for appropriate logic and beware of logical fallacies.

- Provide a sufficient number of causes or effects to make your point acceptable to the reader.

The Myth of Sisyphus

Albert Camus

Albert Camus was born in Algeria in 1913 and won the 1957 Nobel Prize for literature. He was killed in a car accident in 1960. He worked in many genres and was first published during the Nazi occupation of France while he was a resistance fighter in the French underground. With the release in 1942 of both *The Stranger* and *The Myth of Sisyphus* (the essay from which the following reading is taken), he instantly gained a reputation.

Camus found Sisyphus the prototypical absurd human being. The writer explores several issues surrounding the myth, but the unexplainable causes for Sisyphus's fate, and by extension humanity's, are his primary concern.

The gods had condemned Sisyphus to ceaselessly rolling a rock to the top of a mountain, whence the stone would fall back of its own weight. They had thought with some reason that there is no more dreadful punishment than futile and hopeless labor.

If one believes Homer, Sisyphus was the wisest and most prudent of mortals. According to another tradition, however, he was disposed to practice the profession of highwayman. I see no contradiction in this. Opinions differ as to the reasons why he became the futile laborer of the underworld. To begin with, he is accused of a certain levity in regard to the gods. He stole their secrets. Aegina, the daughter of Aesopus, was carried off by Jupiter. The father was shocked by that disappearance and complained to Sisyphus. He, who knew of the abduction, offered to tell about it on condition that Aesopus would give water to the citadel of Corinth. To the celestial thunderbolts he preferred the benediction of water. He was punished for this in the underworld. Homer tells us also that Sisyphus had put Death in chains. Pluto could not endure the sight of his deserted, silent empire. He dispatched the god of war, who liberated Death from the hands of her conqueror.

It is said also that Sisyphus, being near to death, rashly wanted to test his wife's love. He ordered her to cast his unburied body into the middle of the public square. Sisyphus woke up in the underworld. And there, annoyed by an obedience so contrary to human love, he obtained from Pluto permission to return to earth in order to chastise his wife. But when he had seen again the face of this world, enjoyed water and sun, warm stones and the sea, he no longer wanted to go back to the infernal darkness. Recalls, signs of anger, warnings were of no avail. Many years more he lived facing the curve of the gulf, the sparkling sea, and the smiles of earth. A decree of the gods was necessary. Mercury came and seized the impudent man by the collar and, snatching him from his joys, led him forcibly back to the underworld, where his rock was ready for him.

You have already grasped that Sisyphus is the absurd hero. He *is,* as much ₄ through his passions as through his torture. His scorn of the gods, his hatred of death, and his passion for life won him that unspeakable penalty in which the whole being is exerted toward accomplishing nothing. This is the price that must be paid for the passions of this earth. Nothing is told us about Sisyphus in the underworld. Myths are made for the imagination to breathe life into them. As for this myth, one sees merely the whole effort of a body straining to raise the huge stone, to roll it and push it up a slope a hundred times over; one sees the face screwed up, the cheek tight against the stone, the shoulder bracing the clay-covered mass, the foot wedging it, the fresh start with arms outstretched, the wholly human security of two earth-clotted hands. At the very end of his long effort measured by skyless space and time without depth, the purpose is achieved. Then Sisyphus watches the stone rush down in a few moments toward that lower world whence he will have to push it up again toward the summit. He goes back down to the plain.

It is during that return, that pause, that Sisyphus interests me. A face that ₅ toils so close to stones is already stone itself! I see that man going back down with a heavy yet measured step toward the torment of which he will never know the end. That hour like a breathingspace which returns as surely as his suffering, that is the hour of consciousness. At each of those moments when he leaves the heights and gradually sinks toward the lairs of the gods, he is superior to his fate. He is stronger than his rock.

If this myth is tragic, that is because its hero is conscious. Where would ₆ his torture be, indeed, if at every step the hope of succeeding upheld him? The workman of today works every day in his life at the same tasks, and this fate is no less absurd. But it is tragic only at the rare moments when it becomes conscious. Sisyphus, proletarian of the gods, powerless and rebellious, knows the whole extent of his wretched condition: it is what he thinks of during his descent. The lucidity that was to constitute his torture at the same time crowns his victory. There is no fate that cannot be surmounted by scorn.

If the descent is thus sometimes performed in sorrow, it can also take ₇ place in joy. This word is not too much. Again I fancy Sisyphus returning toward his rock, and the sorrow was in the beginning. When the images of earth cling too tightly to memory, when the call of happiness becomes too insistent, it happens that melancholy rises in man's heart: this is the rock's victory, this is the rock itself. The boundless grief is too heavy to bear. These are our nights of Gethsemane. But crushing truths perish from being acknowledged. Thus, Oedipus at the outset obeys fate without knowing it. But from the moment he knows, his tragedy begins. Yet at the same moment, blind and desperate, he realizes that the only bond linking him to the world is the cool hand of a girl. Then a tremendous remark rings out: "Despite so many ordeals, my advanced age and the nobility of my soul make me conclude that all is well." Sophocles' Oedipus, like Dostoevsky's Kirilov, thus gives the recipe for the absurd victory. Ancient wisdom confirms modern heroism.

One does not discover the absurd without being tempted to write a manual ⁸ of happiness. "What! by such narrow ways—?" There is but one world, however. Happiness and the absurd are two sons of the same earth. They are inseparable. It would be a mistake to say that happiness necessarily springs from the absurd discovery. It happens as well that the feeling of the absurd springs from happiness. "I conclude that all is well," says Oedipus, and that remark is sacred. It echoes in the wild and limited universe of man. It teaches that all is not, has not been, exhausted. It drives out of this world a god who had come into it with dissatisfaction and a preference for futile sufferings. It makes of fate a human matter, which must be settled among men.

All Sisyphus' silent joy is contained therein. His fate belongs to him. His ⁹ rock is his thing. Likewise, the absurd man, when he contemplates his torment, silences all the idols. In the universe suddenly restored to its silence, the myriad wondering little voices of the earth rise up. Unconscious, secret calls, invitations from all the faces, they are the necessary reverse and price of victory. There is no sun without shadow, and it is essential to know the night. The absurd man says yes and his effort will henceforth be unceasing. If there is a personal fate, there is no higher destiny, or at least there is but one which he concludes is inevitable and despicable. For the rest, he knows himself to be the master of his days. At that subtle moment when man glances backward over his life, Sisyphus returning toward his rock, in that slight pivoting he contemplates that series of unrelated actions which becomes his fate, created by him, combined under his memory's eye and soon sealed by his death. Thus, convinced of the wholly human origin of all that is human, a blind man eager to see who knows that the night has no end, he is still on the go. The rock is still rolling.

I leave Sisyphus at the foot of the mountain! One always finds one's bur- ¹⁰ den again. But Sisyphus teaches the higher fidelity that negates the gods and raises rocks. He too concludes that all is well. This universe henceforth without a master seems to him neither sterile nor futile. Each atom of that stone, each mineral flake of that nightfilled mountain, in itself forms a world. The struggle itself toward the heights is enough to fill a man's heart. One must imagine Sisyphus happy.

Meaning and Idea

1. What is Sisyphus's fate—how did the gods punish him? What is his guilt, and what is the severity of his crime? Is there justification for the severity of his punishment, do you think? Why? What does Camus note is the "breathingspace" for his hero.

2. Camus states that the rock has a victory, but which has the ultimate victory, the rock or Sisyphus? According to Camus, why is this so? What does he mean when he says, "There is no fate that cannot be surmounted by scorn" (paragraph 6) and "But crushing truths perish from being acknowledged" (paragraph 7)?

3. What is an absurd hero, according to Camus? Why does he say that Sisyphus fits that category? What other heroes, either real or in literature, would you call absurd?

4. How does Sisyphus compare to the modern workman? What does Camus say that they have in common, and when does he note that each is the most tragic?

Language, Form, Structure

1. What is Camus's thesis here?

2. What is the essential cause-and-effect element that structures the essay? What other causes and effects do you note?

3. Why does Camus make a number of references to classical mythology? What do they contribute to the essay?

4. Comment on the final paragraph. What is the meaning of the sentence "One always finds one's burden again"? With what impression does Camus leave the reader at the end? Explain your answer.

5. Define the following words and use each one in a sentence: futile; levity; citadel; benediction; dispatched; chastise; impudent; absurd; proletarian; lucidity; surmounted; Gethsemane; myriad; despicable.

Ideas for Writing

1. Write an essay about the cause-and-effect relation between an action you performed and a punishment that followed from it. Explain whether you felt the punishment was unjust.

2. Camus writes, "They [the gods] had thought with some reason that there is no more dreadful punishment than futile and hopeless labor." Write an essay in which you analyze that statement. Do you agree with it? Why? How do work programs in modern prison systems reflect Camus's beliefs?

3. Write an essay in which you examine the classical references in "The Myth of Sisyphus," particularly the references to the myths in paragraph 2 and the Oedipus story. How do these myths contribute to Camus's piece?

The Story of an Hour

Kate Chopin

Kate Chopin (1851–1904) was reared primarily by her Creole mother and great-grandmother in St. Louis. In her late teens, Chopin married, and she moved to New Orleans with her cotton broker husband. After he died, following 14 years of marriage, Chopin started life again with her six children. She began her literary career with stories about Creole life, heavily influenced by Maupassant. Her short pieces were published in various magazines, establishing her reputation firmly. *The Awakening* (1899), a forward-thinking novel about the sexual awakening and need for self-fulfilment of a wife, is considered Chopin's masterpiece.

In this short, short narrative Kate Chopin traces the ironic causal relations of fate and its strange twists. As you read, look for various levels of meaning and how they affect the causal development of the story.

*K*nowing that Mrs. Mallard was afflicted with a heart trouble, great care was taken to break to her as gently as possible the news of her husband's death. 1

It was her sister Josephine who told her, in broken sentences, veiled hints that revealed in half concealing. Her husband's friend Richards was there, too, near her. It was he who had been in the newspaper office when intelligence of the railroad disaster was received, with Brently Mallard's name leading the list of "killed." He had only taken the time to assure himself of its truth by a second telegram, and had hastened to forestall any less careful, less tender friend in bearing the sad message. 2

She did not hear the story as many women have heard the same, with a paralyzed inability to accept its significance. She wept at once, with sudden, wild abandonment, in her sister's arms. When the storm of grief had spent itself she went away to her room alone. She would have no one follow her. 3

There stood, facing the open window, a comfortable, roomy armchair. Into this she sank, pressed down by a physical exhaustion that haunted her body and seemed to reach into her soul. 4

She could see in the open square before her house the tops of trees that were all aquiver with the new spring life. The delicious breath of rain was in the air. In the street below a peddler was crying his wares. The notes of a distant song which some one was singing reached her faintly, and countless sparrows were twittering in the eaves. 5

There were patches of blue sky showing here and there through the clouds that had met and piled above the other in the west facing her window. 6

She sat with her head thrown back upon the cushion of the chair quite motionless, except when a sob came up into her throat and shook her, as a child who has cried itself to sleep continues to sob in its dreams. 7

She was young, with a fair, calm face, whose lines bespoke repression and even a certain strength. But now there was a dull stare in her eyes, whose gaze was fixed away off yonder on one of those patches of blue sky. It was not a glance of reflection, but rather indicated a suspension of intelligent thought.

There was something coming to her and she was waiting for it, fearfully. What was it? She did not know; it was too subtle and elusive to name. But she felt it, creeping out of the sky, reaching toward her through the sounds, the scents, the color that filled the air.

Now her bosom rose and fell tumultuously. She was beginning to recognize this thing that was approaching to possess her, and she was striving to beat it back with her will—as powerless as her two white slender hands would have been.

When she abandoned herself a little whispered word escaped her slightly parted lips. She said it over and over under her breath. "Free, free, free!" The vacant stare and the look of terror that had followed it went from her eyes. They stayed keen and bright. Her pulses beat fast, and the coursing blood warmed and relaxed every inch of her body.

She did not stop to ask if it were not a monstrous joy that held her. A clear and exalted perception enabled her to dismiss the suggestion as trivial.

She knew that she would weep again when she saw the kind, tender hands folded in death; the face that had never looked save with love upon her, fixed and gray and dead. But she saw beyond that bitter moment a long procession of years to come that would belong to her absolutely. And she opened and spread her arms out to them in welcome.

There would be no one to live for during those coming years; she would live for herself. There would be no powerful will bending her in that blind persistence with which men and women believe they have a right to impose a private will upon a fellow-creature. A kind intention or a cruel intention made the act seem no less a crime as she looked upon it in that brief moment of illumination.

And yet she had loved him—sometimes. Often she had not. What did it matter! What could love, the unsolved mystery, count for in face of this possession of self-assertion which she suddenly recognized as the strongest impulse of her being.

"Free! Body and soul free!" she kept whispering.

Josephine was kneeling before the closed door with her lips to the keyhole, imploring for admission. "Louise, open the door! I beg; open the door—you will make yourself ill. What are you doing, Louise? For heaven's sake open the door."

"Go away, I am not making myself ill." No; she was drinking in a very elixir of life through that open window.

Her fancy was running riot along those days ahead of her. Spring days, and summer days, and all sorts of days that would be her own. She breathed a quick prayer that life might be long. It was only yesterday she had thought with a shudder that life might be long.

She arose at length and opened the door to her sister's importunities. There was a feverish triumph in her eyes, and she carried herself unwittingly like a goddess of Victory. She clasped her sister's waist, and together they descended the stairs. Richards stood waiting for them at the bottom.   20

Some one was opening the front door with a latchkey. It was Brently Mallard who entered, a little travel-stained, composedly carrying his grip-sack and umbrella. He had been far from the scene of accident, and did not even know there had been one. He stood amazed at Josephine's piercing cry; at Richards' quick motion to screen him from the view of his wife.   21

But Richards was too late.   22

When the doctors came they said she had died of heart disease—of joy that kills.   23

Meaning and Idea

1. What potential cause-and-effect sequence is averted by the action described in the opening sentence? Is it really averted after all?

2. How are Mrs. Mallard's immediate reactions to the news of her husband's death different from the norm? What are her subsequent reactions?

3. What is the "something" that was "coming to her and she was waiting for"? How is it possible to read that "something" on more than one level?

4. How does Mrs. Mallard's attitude change after she starts repeating the words—and emotions—"Free, free, free"? What is she free of?

5. What ultimately kills Mrs. Mallard?

Language, Form, Structure

1. Identify three distinct instances of cause and effect in this story. Explain how they relate to one another.

2. How does Chopin's physical description of Mrs. Mallard prepare readers for her exuberance at the sense of new freedom she experiences after her husband's "death"?

3. What are the ironies of this story? To what extent does any one take precedence over the others?

4. What view of marriage is expressed in this story? Whose view of marriage is it—Mrs. Mallard's or the narrator's? Explain your answer.

5. Explain the meanings of the following expressions in this story: veiled hints; hastened to forestall; all aquiver; crying his wares; coursing blood; exalted perception; blind persistence; moment of illumination.

Ideas for Writing

1. Write a causal analysis which explains a sudden change in attitude toward something that recently happened to you. Take into account both immediate and deep-seated causes.

2. Write an essay to analyze why Mrs. Mallard died. Draw on particulars of the story when appropriate.

3. Write an essay on the technique of Chopin's story, particularly the relation between narrative and causation as writing strategies.

Why I Write

George Orwell

George Orwell (1903–1950) was the pseudonym of Eric Blair, the English essayist, novelist, and journalist who was perhaps best known for his scathing political fictions *Animal Farm* (1945) and *1984* (1949). His life was as fascinating as his works: He was born in India, was educated at Eton, served in Burma from 1922 to 1927, and was wounded while fighting with the International Brigade during the Spanish Civil War.

Orwell was a master of the autobiographical essay. While his works and his life indicate a leaning toward political issues, in the following selection he states that such themes are not his primary interests as a writer. Orwell's view of the cause-and-effect relations in his work reveals much about his craft.

*F*rom a very early age, perhaps the age of five or six, I knew that when I grew up I should be a writer. Between the ages of about seventeen and twenty-four I tried to abandon this idea, but I did so with the consciousness that I was outraging my true nature and that sooner or later I should have to settle down and write books.

I was the middle child of three, but there was a gap of five years on either side, and I barely saw my father before I was eight. For this and other reasons I was somewhat lonely, and I soon developed disagreeable mannerisms which made me unpopular throughout my schooldays. I had the lonely child's habit of making up stories and holding conversations with imaginary persons, and I think from the very start my literary ambitions were mixed up with the feeling of being isolated and undervalued. I knew that I had a facility with words and a power of facing unpleasant facts, and I felt that this created a sort of private world in which I could get my own back for my failure in everyday life. Nevertheless the volume of serious—i.e., seriously intended—writing which I produced all through my childhood and boyhood would not amount to half a dozen pages. I wrote my first poem at the age of four or five, my mother taking it down to dictation. I cannot remember anything about it except that it was about a tiger and the tiger had "chair-like teeth"— a good enough phrase, but I fancy the poem was a plagiarism of Blake's "Tiger, Tiger." At eleven, when the war of 1914–18 broke out, I wrote a patriotic poem which was printed in the local newspaper, as was another, two years later, on the death of Kitchener. From time to time, when I was a bit older, I wrote bad and usually unfinished "nature poems" in the Georgian style. I also, about twice, attempted a short story which was a ghastly failure. That was the total of the would-be serious work that I actually set down on paper during all those years.

However, throughout this time I did in a sense engage in literary activities. To begin with there was the made-to-order stuff which I produced quickly, easily and without much pleasure to myself. Apart from school work, I wrote *vers d'occasion,* semi-comic poems which I could turn out at what now seems to me astonishing speed—at fourteen I wrote a whole rhyming play, in imitation of Aristophanes, in about a week—and helped to edit school magazines, both printed and in manuscript. These magazines were the most pitiful burlesque stuff that you could imagine, and I took far less trouble with them than I now would with the cheapest journalism. But side by side with all this, for fifteen years or more, I was carrying out a literary exercise of a quite different kind: this was the making up of a continuous "story" about myself, a sort of diary existing only in the mind. I believe this is a common habit of children and adolescents. As a very small child I used to imagine that I was, say, Robin Hood, and picture myself as the hero of thrilling adventures, but quite soon my "story" ceased to be narcissistic in a crude way and became more and more a mere description of what I was doing and the things I saw. For minutes at a time this kind of thing would be running through my head: "He pushed the door open and entered the room. A yellow beam of sunlight, filtering through the muslin curtains, slanted on to the table, where a match-box, half open, lay beside the inkpot. With his right hand in his pocket he moved across to the window. Down in the street a tortoiseshell cat was chasing a dead leaf," etc., etc. This habit continued till I was about twenty-five, right through my non-literary years. Although I had to search, and did search, for the right words, I seemed to be making this descriptive effort almost against my will, under a kind of compulsion from outside. The "story" must, I suppose, have reflected the styles of the various writers I admired at different ages, but so far as I remember it always had the same meticulous descriptive quality.

When I was about sixteen I suddenly discovered the joy of mere words, i.e., the sounds and associations of words. The lines from *Paradise Lost*— 4

> So hee with difficulty and labour hard
> Moved on: with difficulty and labour hee.

which do not now seem to me so very wonderful, sent shivers down my backbone; and the spelling "hee" for "he" was an added pleasure. As for the need to describe things, I knew all about it already. So it is clear what kind of books I wanted to write, in so far as I could be said to want to write books at that time. I wanted to write enormous naturalistic novels with unhappy endings, full of detailed descriptions and arresting similes, and also full of purple passages in which words were used partly for the sake of their sound. And in fact my first completed novel, *Burmese Days,* which I wrote when I was thirty but projected much earlier, is rather that kind of book.

I give all this background information because I do not think one can assess a writer's motives without knowing something of his early development. His subject matter will be determined by the age he lives in—at least this is true in tumultuous, revolutionary ages like our own—but before he ever begins to write he will have acquired an emotional attitude from which he will never completely escape. It is his job, no doubt, to discipline his temperament and avoid getting stuck at some immature stage, or in some perverse mood: but if he escapes from his early influences altogether, he will have killed his impulse to 5 write. Putting aside the need to earn a living, I think there are four great motives for writing, at any rate for writing prose. They exist in different degrees in every writer, and in any one writer the proportions will vary from time to time, according to the atmosphere in which he is living. They are:

1. Sheer egoism. Desire to seem clever, to be talked about, to be remembered after death, to get your own back on grown-ups who snubbed you in childhood, etc., etc. It is humbug to pretend that this is not a motive, and a strong one. Writers share this characteristic with scientists, artists, politicians, lawyers, soldiers, successful businessmen—in short, with the whole top crust of humanity. The great mass of human beings are not acutely selfish. After the age of about thirty they abandon individual ambition—in many cases, indeed, they almost abandon the sense of being individuals at all—and live chiefly for others, or are simply smothered under drudgery. But there is also the minority of gifted, willful people who are determined to live their own lives to the end, and writers belong in this class. Serious writers, I should say, are on the whole more vain and self-centered than journalists, though less interested in money. 6

2. Aesthetic enthusiasm. Perception of beauty in the external world, or, on the other hand, in words and their right arrangement. Pleasure in the impact of one sound on another, in the firmness of good prose or the rhythm of a good story. Desire to share an experience which one feels is valuable and ought not to be missed. The aesthetic motive is very feeble in a lot of writers, but even a pamphleteer or a writer of textbooks will have pet words and phrases which appeal to him for nonutilitarian reasons; or he may feel strongly about typography, width of margins, etc. Above the level of a railway guide, no book is quite free from aesthetic considerations. 7

3. Historical impulse. Desire to see things as they are, to find out true facts and store them up for the use of posterity. 8

4. Political purpose—using the word "political" in the widest possible sense. Desire to push the world in a certain direction, to alter other people's ideas of the kind of society that they should strive after. Once again, no book is genuinely free from political bias. The opinion that art should have nothing to do with politics is itself a political attitude. 9

It can be seen how these various impulses must war against one another, and how they must fluctuate from person to person and from time to time. By nature—taking your "nature" to be the state you have attained when you are first adult—I am a person in whom the first three motives would outweigh the fourth. In a peaceful age I might have written ornate or merely descriptive books, and might have remained almost unaware of my political loyalties. As it is I have been forced into becoming a sort of pamphleteer. First I spent five 10 years in an unsuitable profession (the Indian Imperial Police, in Burma), and then I underwent poverty and the sense of failure. This increased my natural hatred of authority and made me for the first time fully aware of the existence of the working classes, and the job in Burma had given me some understanding of the nature of imperialism: but these experiences were not enough to give me an accurate political orientation. Then came Hitler, the Spanish civil war, etc. By the end of 1935 I had still failed to reach a firm decision. I remember a little poem that I wrote at that date, expressing my dilemma:

A happy vicar I might have been
Two hundred years ago,
To preach upon eternal doom
And watch my walnuts grow;

But born, alas, in an evil time,
I missed that pleasant haven,
For the hair has grown on my upper lip
And the clergy are all clean-shaven.

And later still the times were good,
We were so easy to please,
We rocked our troubled thoughts to sleep
On the bosoms of the trees.

All ignorant we dared to own
The joys we now dissemble;
The greenfinch on the apple bough
Could make my enemies tremble.

But girls' bellies and apricots,
Roach in a shaded stream,
Horses, ducks in flight at dawn,
All these are a dream.

It is forbidden to dream again;
We maim our joys or hide them;
Horses are made of chromium steel
And little fat men shall ride them.

I am the worm who never turned,
The eunuch without a harem;
Between the priest and the commissar
I walk like Eugene Aram;

And the commissar is telling my fortune
While the radio plays,
But the priest has promised an Austin Seven,
For Duggie always pays.

I dreamed I dwelt in marble halls,
And woke to find it true;
I wasn't born for an age like this;
Was Smith? Was Jones? Were you?

The Spanish war and other events in 1936–7 turned the scale and thereafter I knew where I stood. Every line of serious work that I have written since 1936 has been written, directly or indirectly, *against* totalitarianism and *for* democratic socialism, as I understand it. It seems to me nonsense, in a period like our own, to think that one can avoid writing of such subjects. Everyone writes of them in one guise or another. It is simply a question of which side one takes and what approach one follows. And the more one is conscious of one's political bias, the more chance one has of acting politically without sacrificing one's aesthetic and intellectual integrity.

What I have most wanted to do throughout the past ten years is to make 11 political writing into an art. My starting point is always a feeling of partisanship, a sense of injustice. When I sit down to write a book, I do not say to myself, "I am going to produce a work of art." I write it because there is some lie that I want to expose, some fact to which I want to draw attention, and my initial concern is to get a hearing. But I could not do the work of writing a book, or even a long magazine article, if it were not also an aesthetic experience. Anyone who cares to examine my work will see that even when it is downright propaganda it contains much that a full-time politician would consider irrelevant. I am not able, and I do not want, completely to abandon the world view that I acquired in childhood. So long as I remain alive and well I shall continue to feel strongly about prose style, to love the surface of the earth, and to take a pleasure in solid objects and scraps of useless information. It is no use trying to suppress that side of myself. The job is to reconcile my ingrained likes and dislikes with the essentially public, nonindividual activities that this age forces on all of us.

It is not easy. It raises problems of construction and of language, and it 12 raises in a new way the problem of truthfulness. Let me give just one example of the cruder kind of difficulty that arises. My book about the Spanish civil war, *Homage to Catalonia,* is, of course, a frankly political book, but in the main it is written with a certain detachment and regard for form. I did try very hard in it to tell the whole truth without violating my literary instincts. But among other things it contains a long chapter, full of newspaper quotations and the like, defending the Trotskyists who were accused of plotting with Franco. Clearly such a chapter, which after a year or two would lose its interest for any ordinary reader, must ruin the book. A critic whom I respect read me a lecture about it. "Why did you put in all that stuff?" he said. "You've turned what might have been a good book into journalism." What he said was true, but I could not have done otherwise. I happened to know, what very few people in England had been allowed to know, that innocent men were being falsely accused. If I had not been angry about that I should never have written the book.

In one form or another this problem comes up again. The problem of lan-   13
guage is subtler and would take too long to discuss. I will only say that of late years
I have tried to write less picturesquely and more exactly. In any case I find that by
the time you have perfected any style of writing, you have always outgrown it. *Animal Farm* was the first book in which I tried, with full consciousness of what I was
doing, to fuse political purpose and artistic purpose into one whole. I have not written a novel for seven years, but I hope to write another fairly soon. It is bound to be
a failure, every book is a failure, but I do know with some clarity what kind of book
I want to write. Looking back through the last page or two, I see that I have made it
appear as though my motives in writing were wholly public-spirited. I don't want to
leave that as the final impression. All writers are vain, selfish, and lazy, and at the
very bottom of their motives there lies a mystery. Writing a book is a horrible, exhausting struggle, like a long bout of some painful illness. One would never undertake such a thing if one were not driven on by some demon whom one can neither
resist nor understand. For all one knows that demon is simply the same instinct that
makes a baby squall for attention. And yet it is also true that one can write nothing
readable unless one constantly struggles to efface one's own personality. Good
prose is like a windowpane. I cannot say with certainty which of my motives are
the strongest, but I know which of them deserve to be followed. And looking back
through my work, I see that it is invariably where I lacked a *political* purpose that I
wrote lifeless books and was betrayed into purple passages, sentences without
meaning, decorative adjectives, and humbug generally.

Meaning and Idea

1. What is Orwell's opinion of "purple passages"? What exactly does he
   mean? What has he always wished his own writing could be like? He says
   that "by the time you have perfected any style of writing, you have always
   outgrown it." What does he mean? When he wrote this essay, how long had
   it been since he had written a novel?

2. What, according to Orwell, are the four great motives for writing? How
   does he feel about paying excessive attention to any one category? What
   does he mean by the claim that in terms of his own interests, "the first three
   motives would outweigh the fourth"? How does this self-analysis serve the
   cause-and-effect themes of the essay?

3. Orwell says, "The opinion that art should have nothing to do with politics is
   itself a political attitude." Do you agree? Why or why not? How in fact may
   art be seen as political?

Language, Form, Structure

1. What is Orwell's thesis here? State it in your own words. How does the
   essay fit the rhetorical category of causal analysis? What are the various
   causes and effects explored here?

2. What is the effect of the writer's looking at his own work with a highly critical eye?

3. What is the effect of Orwell's long opening narrative? How does it contribute to the thesis? How does it engage the reader's attention?

4. What aspects of language, style, form, and structure in this piece explain to you Orwell's status as a brilliant essayist?

5. Define the following words and use each one in a sentence: posterity; narcissistic; meticulous; arresting; snubbed; drudgery; aesthetic; typography; imperialism; dissemble; guise; integrity; reconcile; efface.

Ideas for Writing

1. Write an essay that explores the cause-and-effect relations that have led to your own choice of a career or those of someone close to you. Be sure to use an initial, framing narrative; then a listing of emphases you have decided upon; and, finally, further elaboration.

2. Orwell feels that everyone and everything is always political. Do you agree? Write a causation essay that considers why everyone is or is not political.

3. Reexamine Orwell's essay and write one of your own exploring the relation between his statement that he is not inherently political and the fact that all his work is overtly political. How can Orwell assert one position and behave in the opposite way? Search the essay and cite evidence to support your point.

Dream Deferred

Langston Hughes

Langston Hughes (1902–1967) was one of America's foremost poets, essayists, dramatists, and fiction writers, whose self-proclaimed desire as a writer was "to explain and illuminate the Negro condition in America." After being elected class poet in grammar school
in Lincoln, Illinois, Hughes first gained adult fame as a poet when he was a busboy at a
hotel in Washington, D.C. He left some poems by the plate of the poet Vachel Lindsay,
who fortunately recognized his talent.

"Dream Deferred" has become one of Langston Hughes's best-known poems, especially
during the racially turbulent 1960s. In this poem he asks—and perhaps answers—what
the results of aspirations unfulfilled are.

*W*hat happens to a dream deferred?

Does it dry up
like a raisin in the sun?
Or fester like a sore—
And then run?
Does it stink like rotten meat?   5
Or crust and sugar over—
like a syrupy sweet?

Maybe it just sags
like a heavy load.   10

Or does it explode?

Meaning and Idea

1. What do you think is the "dream" in this poem? What cause-and-effect
   relationship is implied concerning this dream?

2. Remembering that Hughes was among the foremost writers about the
   modern black experience in America, how does this poem relate to that
   experience as you know it? What "message" is carried by the poem?

Language, Form, Structure

1. Identify the similes and metaphors in this poem. How effective are they? Do
   you see a logic to their placement in the poem? What effect does the final

metaphor have, coming where it does? Would a simile have been as powerful? Why?

2. The poem is a sequence of questions. What effect does this have on the reader? Would the poem be as effective if it were built on a series of declarative statements? Why?

3. What is the effect of the rhymes in the poem—sun/run; meat/sweet; load/explode?

4. Make sure you know the meaning of *deferred* and *fester.*

Ideas for Writing

1. Write a short causal analysis about the effects of a time when you "put off" something. Were the results positive or negative? Did they occur naturally, or were they forced?

2. Write an essay in response to the question in line 1 of the poem.

3. As we noted, Hughes arranges this poem as a series of questions. Write an essay in which you identify what in the writing—choice of language, tone, arrangement on the page, and so on—gives either an implicit or an explicit answer to these questions?

Richard Cory

Edwin Arlington Robinson

Edwin Arlington Robinson (1869–1935), who was described by critic Allen Tate in 1933 as "the most famous of living American poets," led a life of two greatly contrasting halves. Born and reared in a bleak Maine town, he had a depressing childhood. He later devoted himself to his writing, but was often penniless and alcoholic, relying on friends and, at one point, on President Theodore Roosevelt for subsistence. In 1921, his *Collected Poems* was unexpectedly well received, and in rapid succession Robinson won the Pulitzer Prize three times, as well as an honorary degree from Yale University.

"Richard Cory" is one of the best-known modern poems; Simon and Garfunkel's early song with the same title rephrases the poem and puts it to music. In the poem, Robinson surprises us with the result of a life seemingly headed in one direction but taking a sharp turn in an opposite one.

Whenever Richard Cory went down town,
We people on the pavement looked at him:
He was a gentleman from sole to crown,
Clean favored, and imperially slim.

And he was always quietly arrayed,   5
And he was always human when he talked;
But still he fluttered pulses when he said,
"Good-morning," and he glittered when he walked.

And he was rich—yes, richer than a king—
And admirably schooled in every grace: 10
In fine, we thought that he was everything
To make us wish that we were in his place.

So on we worked, and waited for the light,
And went without the meat, and cursed the bread;
And Richard Cory, one calm summer night,   15
Went home and put a bullet through his head.

Meaning and Idea

1. Before his suicide, what sort of person did Richard Cory appear to be? Was he a fair person? Arrogant? What was his social position? What were the townspeople's impressions of him?

2. Who is the narrator of this poem? What is his opinion of Richard Cory? To whom does he address the poem? What is the occasion of this poem?

3. What do you make of Richard Cory's act of suicide? Why do you think he did it? Was it to be expected from the preceding stanzas? Why or why not?

4. Explain the meaning of lines 13–14:

So on we worked, and waited for the light,
And went without the meat, and cursed the bread;

Who are the "we"? What is "the light"? Why do the "we" curse the bread?

Language, Form, Structure

1. *Situational irony* occurs when the results of a situation do not match our expectations of the outcome. How is "Richard Cory" an example of situational irony?

2. According to the poem, is there any cause-and-effect relation between the townspeople's impressions of Richard Cory and his suicide? If so, what is it? Is it direct or indirect?

3. A number of descriptive words or phrases in this poem suggest royalty of a regal nature. Identify these and explain how each of them contributes to our understanding of Richard Cory and/or the speaker.

4. Define the following words as they are used in the poem: sole; crown; grace. Why do you think Robinson chose each of these words instead of possible synonyms?

Ideas for Writing

1. If you know personally of a suicide or a suicide attempt, try to write a causal analysis explaining it. If you have no direct knowledge of a suicide, choose another tragic event you know of and explain what caused it.

2. Choose someone in your school or social group who is greatly admired. Write a causal analysis of the reasons for this admiration.

3. The narrator describes the events of this poem from a retrospective (after-the-fact) point of view. How does that point of view affect his descriptions of Richard Cory? How might the narrative have been different in its feeling and focus if this poem took place before the suicide or if there were no suicide? You may want to try your hand at writing a second version of the poem from either of those points of view. Your version may be prose if you wish.

When My Love Swears That She Is Made of Truth

William Shakespeare

Although William Shakespeare (1564–1616) is considered the world's greatest English-language playwright, some critics feel that his poetry alone would have brought him great fame. He began publishing poetry in 1593, around the same time as his earliest plays, and the 154 poems in his *Sonnets,* published in 1609, are considered his greatest poetic achievement. The sonnets, as do the plays, deal with love and death and with time's effects on each one, but of course in much more compressed form. Shakespeare was born in Stratford-on-Avon, England, and spent a good deal of his time in London as a playwright-actor before retiring and eventually dying in his hometown.

The full range of Shakespeare's 154 sonets, written in the 1590s, deals with the universals of change, time, and death, as well as the means by which art and love afford ways for us to face these universals. In "When My Love Swears That She Is Made of Truth," one of Shakespeare's 25 "Dark Lady" sonnets, he explores the cause-and-effect relations between truth and love.

When my love swears that she is made of truth,
I do believe her, though I know she lies,
That she might think me some untutored youth,
Unlearned in the world's false subtleties.
Thus vainly thinking that she thinks me young,   5
Although she knows my days are past the best,
Simply I credit her false-speaking tongue;
On both sides thus is simple truth supprest.
But wherefore says she not she is unjust?
And wherefore say not I that I am old?   10
Oh, love's best habit is in seeming trust,
And age in love loves not to have years told:
Therefore I lie with her and she with me,
And in our faults by lies we flattered be.

Meaning and Idea

1. Is the speaker of this poem young or old? Is he younger or older than his beloved? How do you know?

2. Lines 9 and 10 ask two questions about the main conditions analyzed in this poem. In more modern English, the questions are: "Why doesn't she say

she's unjust?" and "Why don't I say that I'm old?" Answer the two questions on the basis of your reading of the poem.

3. What, according to the poem, are the causes for lying between lovers? What is the relationship between the causes and effects of lying?

Language, Form, Structure

1. Explain the meaning of the seeming contradiction of line 2. How else does Shakespeare use contradictions as an explanatory technique in this poem?

2. How is the word *lie* used as a *double entendre* (double meaning) in this poem?

3. What is the effect of Shakespeare's writing, "When my love swears that she *is made of truth*" rather than ". . . that she *is telling the truth*"? How are the two wordings different? How does the actual wording contribute to the meaning of the poem?

Ideas for Writing

1. Tell about the last lie—or the most important lie—you told. Analyze the reasons for your lying and the effects of it.

2. Write a short causal analysis explaining the main basis of a love (or a close friendship) in which you have recently been involved. Because of this basis, did the relationship work better or worse?

3. Shakespeare's sonnet deals with *lying* and *lovers*. In a short paper, identify the truths in the poem that seem to you most lasting and universal.

To Build a Fire

Jack London

Jack London (1876–1916), who was born to a poor family in San Francisco, built his reputation as an adventurer, a journalist, and, most important, a fiction writer. Many of his
brutally realistic stories derive from his gold-seeking exploits in the Yukon Territory and
reflect his socialist ideals. Among his novels are *The Call of the Wild* (1903), *The Sea-
Wolf* (1904), *The Iron-Heel* (1907), and *Martin Eden* (1909). At the age of 40, London
committed suicide through an overdose of narcotics.

By weaving a series of cause-and-effect relations, Jack London patterns an overall, very
basic, and very frightening causal development. "To Build a Fire" is an analysis of imagination and survival, instinct and practicality.

Day had broken cold and gray, exceedingly cold and gray, when   1
the man turned aside from the main Yukon trail and climbed the high earthbank,
where a dim and little-travelled trail led eastward through the fat spruce timber-
land. It was a steep bank, and he paused for breath at the top, excusing the act to
himself by looking at his watch. It was nine o'clock. There was no sun nor hint
of sun, though there was not a cloud in the sky. It was a clear day, and yet there
seemed an intangible pall over the face of things, a subtle gloom that made the
day dark, and that was due to the absence of sun. This fact did not worry the
man. He was used to the lack of sun. It had been days since he had seen the sun,
and he knew that a few more days must pass before that cheerful orb, due south,
should just peep above the sky line and dip immediately from view.

The man flung a look back along the way he had come. The Yukon lay a   2
mile wide and hidden under three feet of ice. On top of this ice were as many
feet of snow. It was all pure white, rolling in gentle undulations where the ice
jams of the freeze-up had formed. North and south, as far as his eye could see, it
was unbroken white, save for a dark hairline that curved and twisted from
around the spruce-covered island to the south, and that curved and twisted away
into the north, where it disappeared behind another spruce-covered island. This
dark hairline was the trail—the main trail—that led south five hundred miles to
the Chilcoot Pass, Dyea, and salt water; and that led north seventy miles to Daw-
son, and still on to the north a thousand miles to Nulato, and finally to
St. Michael, on Bering Sea, a thousand miles and half a thousand more.

But all this—the mysterious, far-reaching hairline trail, the absence of sun   3
from the sky, the tremendous cold, and the strangeness and weirdness of it all—
made no impression on the man. It was not because he was long used to it. He
was a newcomer in the land, a *chechaquo,* and this was his first winter. The
trouble with him was that he was without imagination. He was quick and alert in
the things of life, but only in the things, and not in the significances. Fifty de-

grees below zero meant eighty-odd degrees of frost. Such fact impressed him as being cold and uncomfortable, and that was all. It did not lead him to meditate upon his frailty as a creature of temperature, and upon man's frailty in general, able only to live within certain narrow limits of heat and cold; and from there on it did not lead him to the conjectural field of immortality and man's place in the universe. Fifty degrees below zero stood for a bite of frost that hurt and that must be guarded against by the use of mittens, ear flaps, warm moccasins, and thick socks. Fifty degrees below zero was to him just precisely fifty degrees below zero. That there should be anything more to it than that was a thought that never entered his head.

As he turned to go on, he spat speculatively. There was a sharp, explosive crackle that startled him. He spat again. And again, in the air, before it could fall to the snow, the spittle crackled. He knew that at fifty below spittle crackled on the snow, but this spittle had crackled in the air. Undoubtedly it was colder than fifty below—how much colder he did not know. But the temperature did not matter. He was bound for the old claim on the left fork of Henderson Creek, where the boys were already. They had come over across the divide from the Indian Creek country, while he had come the roundabout way to take a look at the possibilities of getting out logs in the spring from the islands in the Yukon. He would be in to camp by six o'clock; a bit after dark, it was true, but the boys would be there, a fire would be going, and a hot supper would be ready. As for lunch, he pressed his hand against the protruding bundle under his jacket. It was also under his shirt, wrapped up in a handkerchief and lying against the naked skin. It was the only way to keep the biscuits from freezing. He smiled agreeably to himself as he thought of those biscuits, each cut open and sopped in bacon grease, and each enclosing a generous slice of fried bacon.

He plunged in among the big spruce trees. The trail was faint. A foot of snow had fallen since the last sled had passed over, and he was glad he was without a sled, travelling light. In fact, he carried nothing but the lunch wrapped in the handkerchief. He was surprised, however, at the cold. It certainly was cold, he concluded, as he rubbed his numb nose and cheekbones with his mittened hand. He was a warm-whiskered man, but the hair on his face did not protect the high cheekbones and the eager nose that thrust itself aggressively into the frosty air.

At the man's heels trotted a dog, a big native husky, the proper wolf dog, gray-coated and without any visible or temperamental difference from its brother, the wild wolf. The animal was depressed by the tremendous cold. It knew that it was no time for travelling. Its instinct told it a truer tale than was told to the man by the man's judgment. In reality, it was not merely colder than fifty below zero; it was colder than sixty below, than seventy below. It was seventy-five below zero. Since the freezing point is thirty-two above zero, it meant that one hundred and seven degrees of frost obtained. The dog did not know anything about thermometers. Possibly in its brain there was no sharp consciousness of a condition of very cold such as was in the man's brain. But the brute had its instinct. It experienced a vague but menacing apprehension that subdued it and made it slink along at the man's heels, and that made it question eagerly every unwonted movement of the man as if expecting him to go into camp or to seek shelter somewhere and build a fire. The dog had learned fire, and it wanted fire, or else to burrow under the snow and cuddle its warmth away from the air.

The frozen moisture of its breathing had settled on its fur in a fine powder of frost, and especially were its jowls, muzzle, and eyelashes whitened by its crystalled breath. The man's red beard and mustache were likewise frosted, but more solidly, the deposit taking the form of ice and increasing with every warm, moist breath he exhaled. Also, the man was chewing tobacco, and the muzzle of ice held his lips so rigidly that he was unable to clear his chin when he expelled the juice. The result was that a crystal beard of the color and solidity of amber was increasing its length on his chin. If he fell down it would shatter itself, like glass, into brittle fragments. But he did not mind the appendage. It was the penalty all tobacco chewers paid in that country, and he had been out before in two cold snaps. They had not been so cold as this, he knew, but by the spirit thermometer at Sixty Mile he knew they had been registered at fifty below and at fifty-five.

He held on through the level stretch of woods for several miles, crossed a wide flat of nigger heads, and dropped down a bank to the frozen bed of a small stream. This was Henderson Creek, and he knew he was ten miles from the forks. He looked at his watch. It was ten o'clock. He was making four miles an hour, and he calculated that he would arrive at the forks at half-past twelve. He decided to celebrate that event by eating his lunch here.

The dog dropped in again at his heels, with a tail drooping discouragement, as the man swung along the creek bed. The furrow of the old sled trail was plainly visible, but a dozen inches of snow covered the marks of the last runners. In a month no man had come up or down that silent creek. The man held steadily on. He was not much given to thinking, and just then particularly he had nothing to think about save that he would eat lunch at the forks and that at six o'clock he would be in camp with the boys. There was nobody to talk to; and, had there been, speech would have been impossible because of the ice muzzle on his mouth. So he continued monotonously to chew tobacco and to increase the length of his amber beard.

Once in a while the thought reiterated itself that it was very cold and that he had never experienced such cold. As he walked along he rubbed his cheekbones and nose with the back of his mittened hand. He did this automatically, now and again changing hands. But, rub as he would, the instant he stopped his cheekbones went numb, and the following instant the end of his nose went numb. He was sure to frost his cheeks; he knew that, and experienced a pang of regret that he had not devised a nose strap of the sort Bud wore in cold snaps. Such a strap passed across the cheeks, as well, and saved them. But it didn't matter much, after all. What were frosted cheeks? A bit painful, that was all; they were never serious.

Empty as the man's mind was of thoughts, he was keenly observant, and he noticed the changes in the creek, the curves and bends and timber jams, and always he sharply noted where he placed his feet. Once, coming around a bend, he shied abruptly, like a startled horse, curved away from the place where he had been walking, and retreated several paces back along the trail. The creek he knew was frozen clear to the bottom—no creek could contain water in that arctic winter—but he knew also that there were springs that bubbled out from the hillsides and ran along under the snow and on top of the ice of the creek. He knew that the coldest snaps never froze these springs, and he knew likewise their danger. They were traps. They hid pools of water under the snow that might be three inches deep, or three feet. Sometimes a skin of ice half an inch thick covered them, and in turn was covered by the snow. Sometimes there were alternate layers of water and ice skin, so that when one broke through he kept on breaking through for a while, sometimes wetting himself to the waist.

That was why he had shied in such panic. He had felt the give under his feet and heard the crackle of a snow-hidden ice skin. And to get his feet wet in such a temperature meant trouble and danger. At the very least it meant delay, for he would be forced to stop and build a fire, and under its protection to bare his feet while he dried his socks and moccasins. He stood and studied the creek bed and its banks, and decided that the flow of water came from the right. He reflected awhile, rubbing his nose and cheeks, then skirted to the left, stepping gingerly and testing the footing for each step. Once clear of the danger, he took a fresh chew of tobacco and swung along at his four-mile gait.

In the course of the next two hours he came upon several similar traps. Usually the snow above the hidden pools had a sunken, candied appearance that advertised the danger. Once again, however, he had a close call; and once, suspecting danger, he compelled the dog to go on in front. The dog did not want to go. It hung back until the man shoved it forward, and then it went quickly across the white, unbroken surface. Suddenly it broke through, floundered to one side, and got away to firmer footing. It had wet its forefeet and legs, and almost immediately the water that clung to it turned to ice. It made quick efforts to lick the ice off its legs, then dropped down in the snow and began to bite out the ice that had formed between the toes. This was a matter of instinct. To permit the ice to remain would mean sore feet. It did not know this. It merely obeyed the mysterious prompting that arose from the deep crypts of its being. But the man knew, having achieved a judgment on the subject, and he removed the mitten from his right hand and helped tear out the ice particles. He did not expose his fingers more than a minute, and was astonished at the swift numbness that smote them. It certainly was cold. He pulled on the mitten hastily, and beat the hand savagely across his chest.

At twelve o'clock the day was at its brightest. Yet the sun was too far south on its winter journey to clear the horizon. The bulge of the earth intervened between it and Henderson Creek, where the man walked under a clear sky at noon and cast no shadow. At half-past twelve, to the minute, he arrived at the forks of the creek. He was pleased at the speed he had made. If he kept it up, he would certainly be with the boys by six. He unbuttoned his jacket and shirt and drew forth his lunch. The action consumed no more than a quarter of a minute, yet in that brief moment the numbness laid hold of the exposed fingers. He did not put the mitten on, but, instead, struck the fingers a dozen sharp smashes against his leg. Then he sat down on a snow-covered log to eat. The sting that followed upon the striking of his fingers against his leg ceased so quickly that he was startled. He had had no chance to take a bite of biscuit. He struck the fingers repeatedly and returned them to the mitten, baring the other hand for the purpose of eating. He tried to take a mouthful, but the ice muzzle prevented. He had forgotten to build a fire and thaw out. He chuckled at his foolishness, and as he chuckled he noted the numbness creeping into the exposed fingers. Also, he noted that the stinging which had first come to his toes when he sat down was already passing away. He wondered whether the toes were warm or numb. He moved them inside the moccasins and decided that they were numb.

He pulled the mitten on hurriedly and stood up. He was a bit frightened. 15 He stamped up and down until the stinging returned into the feet. It certainly was cold, was his thought. That man from Sulphur Creek had spoken the truth when telling how cold it sometimes got in the country. And he had laughed at him at the time! That showed one must not be too sure of things. There was no mistake about it, it *was* cold. He strode up and down, stamping his feet and threshing his arms, until reassured by the returning warmth. Then he got out matches and proceeded to make a fire. From the undergrowth, where high water of the previous spring had lodged a supply of seasoned twigs, he got his firewood. Working carefully from a small beginning, he soon had a roaring fire, over which he thawed the ice from his face and in the protection of which he ate his biscuits. For the moment the cold of space was outwitted. The dog took satisfaction in the fire, stretching out close enough for warmth and far enough away to escape being singed.

When the man had finished, he filled his pipe and took his comfortable 16 time over a smoke. Then he pulled on his mittens, settled the ear flaps of his cap firmly about his ears, and took the creek trail up the left fork. The dog was disappointed and yearned back toward the fire. This man did not know cold. Possibly all the generations of his ancestry had been ignorant of cold, of real cold, of cold one hundred and seven degrees below freezing point. But the dog knew; all its ancestry knew, and it had inherited the knowledge. And it knew that it was not good to walk abroad in such fearful cold. It was the time to lie snug in a hole in the snow and wait for a curtain of cloud to be drawn across the face of outer space whence this cold came. On the other hand, there was no keen intimacy between the dog and the man. The one was the toil slave of the other, and the only caresses it had ever received were the caresses of the whip lash and of harsh and menacing throat sounds that threatened the whip lash. So the dog made no effort to communicate its apprehension to the man. It was not concerned in the welfare of the man; it was for its own sake that it yearned back toward the fire. But the man whistled, and spoke to it with the sound of whip lashes, and the dog swung in at the man's heels and followed after.

The man took a chew of tobacco and proceeded to start a new amber 17 beard. Also, his moist breath quickly powdered with white his mustache, eyebrows, and lashes. There did not seem to be so many springs on the left fork of the Henderson, and for half an hour the man saw no signs of any. And then it happened. At a place where there were no signs, where the soft, unbroken snow seemed to advertise solidity beneath, the man broke through. It was not deep. He wet himself halfway to the knees before he floundered out to the firm crust.

He was angry, and cursed his luck aloud. He had hoped to get into camp with the boys at six o'clock, and this would delay him an hour, for he would have to build a fire and dry out his footgear. This was imperative at that low temperature—he knew that much; and he turned aside to the bank, which he climbed. On top, tangled in the underbrush about the trunks of several small spruce trees, was a highwater deposit of dry firewood—sticks and twigs, principally, but also larger portions of seasoned branches and fine dry last year's grasses. He threw down several large pieces on top of the snow. This served for a foundation and prevented the young flame from drowning itself in the snow it otherwise would melt. The flame he got by touching a match to a small shred of birch bark that he took from his pocket. This burned even more readily than paper. Placing it on the foundation, he fed the young flame with wisps of dry grass and with the tiniest dry twigs. [18]

He worked slowly and carefully, keenly aware of his danger. Gradually, as the flame grew stronger, he increased the size of the twigs with which he fed it. He squatted in the snow, pulling the twigs out from their entanglement in the brush and feeding directly to the flame. He knew there must be no failure. When it is seventy-five below zero, a man must not fail in his first attempt to build a fire—that is, if his feet are wet. If his feet are dry, and he fails, he can run along the trail for half a mile and restore his circulation. But the circulation of wet and freezing feet cannot be restored by running when it is seventy-five below. No matter how fast he runs, the wet feet will freeze the harder. [19]

All this the man knew. The old-timer on Sulphur Creek had told him about it the previous fall, and now he was appreciating the advice. Already all sensation had gone out of his feet. To build the fire he had been forced to remove his mittens, and the fingers had quickly gone numb. His pace of four miles an hour had kept his heart pumping blood to the surface of his body and to all the extremities. But the instant he stopped, the action of the pump eased down. The cold of space smote the unprotected tip of the planet, and he, being on that unprotected tip, received the full force of the blow. The blood of his body recoiled before it. The blood was alive, like the dog, and like the dog it wanted to hide away and cover itself up from the fearful cold. So long as he walked four miles an hour, he pumped that blood, willy-nilly, to the surface; but now it ebbed away and sank down into the recesses of his body. The extremities were the first to feel its absence. His wet feet froze the faster, and his exposed fingers numbed the faster, though they had not yet begun to freeze. Nose and cheeks were already freezing, while the skin of all his body chilled as it lost its blood. [20]

But he was safe. Toes and nose and cheeks would be only touched by the frost, for the fire was beginning to burn with strength. He was feeding it with twigs the size of his finger. In another minute he would be able to feed it with [21] branches the size of his wrist, and then he could remove his wet footgear, and, while it dried, he could keep his naked feet warm by the fire, rubbing them at first, of course, with snow. The fire was a success. He was safe. He remembered the advice of the old-timer on Sulphur Creek, and smiled. The old-timer had been very serious in laying down the law that no man must travel alone in the Klondike after fifty below. Well, here he was; he had had the accident; he was alone; and he had saved himself. Those old-timers were rather womanish, some of them, he thought. All a man had to do was to keep his head, and he was all right. Any man who was a man could travel alone. But it was surprising, the rapidity with which his cheeks and nose were freezing. And he had not thought his fingers could go lifeless in so short a time. Lifeless they were, for he could scarcely make them move together to grip a twig, and they seemed remote from his body and from him. When he touched a twig, he had to look and see whether or not he had hold of it. The wires were pretty well down between him and his finger ends.

All of which counted for little. There was the fire, snapping and crackling and promising life with every dancing flame. He started to untie his moccasins. They were coated with ice; the thick German socks were like sheaths of iron halfway to the knees; and the moccasin strings were like rods of steel all twisted and knotted as by some conflagration. For a moment he tugged with his numb fingers, then, realizing the folly of it, he drew his sheath knife. 22

But before he could cut the strings, it happened. It was his own fault or, rather, his mistake. He should not have built the fire under the spruce tree. He should have built it in the open. But it had been easier to pull the twigs from the brush and drop them directly on the fire. Now the tree under which he had done this carried a weight of snow on its boughs. No wind had blown for weeks, and each bough was fully freighted. Each time he had pulled a twig he had communicated a slight agitation to the tree—an imperceptible agitation, so far as he was concerned, but an agitation sufficient to bring about the disaster. High up in the tree one bough capsized its load of snow. This fell on the boughs beneath, capsizing them. This process continued, spreading out and involving the whole tree. It grew like an avalanche, and it descended without warning upon the man and the fire, and the fire was blotted out! Where it had burned was a mantle of fresh and disordered snow. 23

The man was shocked. It was as though he had just heard his own sentence of death. For a moment he sat and stared at the spot where the fire had been. Then he grew very calm. Perhaps the old-timer on Sulphur Creek was right. If he had only had a trail mate he would have been in no danger now. The trail mate could have built the fire. Well, it was up to him to build the fire over again, and this second time there must be no failure. Even if he succeeded, he would most likely lose some toes. His feet must be badly frozen by now, and there would be some time before the second fire was ready. 24

Such were his thoughts, but he did not sit and think them. He was busy all the time they were passing through his mind. He made a new foundation for a fire, this time in the open, where no treacherous tree could blot it out. Next he 25 gathered dry grasses and tiny twigs from the high-water flotsam. He could not bring his fingers together to pull them out, but he was able to gather them by the handful. In this way he got many rotten twigs and bits of green moss that were undesirable, but it was the best he could do. He worked methodically, even collecting an armful of the larger branches to be used later when the fire gathered strength. And all the while the dog sat and watched him, a certain yearning wistfulness in its eyes, for it looked upon him as the fire provider, and the fire was slow in coming.

When all was ready, the man reached in his pocket for a second piece of birch bark. He knew the bark was there, and, though he could not feel it with his fingers, he could hear its crisp rustling as he fumbled for it. Try as he would, he could not clutch hold of it. And all the time, in his consciousness, was the knowledge that each instant his feet were freezing. This thought tended to put him in a panic, but he fought against it and kept calm. He pulled on his mittens with his teeth, and threshed his arms back and forth, beating his hands with all his might against his sides. He did this sitting down, and he stood up to do it; and all the while the dog sat in the snow, its wolf brush of a tail curled around warmly over its forefeet, its sharp wolf ears pricked forward intently as it watched the man. And the man, as he beat and threshed with his arms and hands, felt a great surge of envy as he regarded the creature that was warm and secure in its natural covering.

After a time he was aware of the first faraway signals of sensation in his beaten fingers. The faint tingling grew stronger till it evolved into a stinging ache that was excruciating, but which the man hailed with satisfaction. He stripped the mitten from his right hand and fetched forth the birch bark. The exposed fingers were quickly going numb again. Next he brought out his bunch of sulphur matches. But the tremendous cold had already driven the life out of his fingers. In his effort to separate one match from the others, the whole bunch fell in the snow. He tried to pick it out of the snow, but failed. The dead fingers could neither touch nor clutch. He was very careful. He drove the thought of his freezing feet, and nose, and cheeks, out of his mind, devoting his whole soul to the matches. He watched, using the sense of vision in place of that of touch, and when he saw his fingers on each side of the bunch, he closed them—that is, he willed to close them, for the wires were down, and the fingers did not obey. He pulled the mitten on the right hand, and beat it fiercely against his knee. Then, with both mittened hands, he scooped the bunch of matches, along with much snow, into his lap. Yet he was no better off.

After some manipulation he managed to get the bunch between the heels of his mittened hands. In this fashion he carried it to his mouth. The ice crackled and snapped when by a violent effort he opened his mouth. He drew the lower jaw in, curled the upper lip out of the way, scraped the bunch with his upper teeth in order to separate a match. He succeeded in getting one, which he dropped on his lap. He was no better off. He could not pick it up. Then he devised a way. He picked it up in his teeth and scratched it on his leg. Twenty times he scratched before he succeeded in lighting it. As it flamed he held it with his teeth to the birch bark. But the burning brimstone went up his nostrils and into his lungs, causing him to cough spasmodically. The match fell into the snow and went out.

The old-timer on Sulphur Creek was right, he thought in the moment of controlled despair that ensued: after fifty below, a man should travel with a partner. He beat his hands, but failed in exciting any sensation. Suddenly he bared both hands, removing the mittens with his teeth. He caught the whole bunch between the heels of his hands. His arm muscles not being frozen enabled him to press the hand heels tightly against the matches. Then he scratched the bunch along his leg. It flared into flame, seventy sulphur matches at once! There was no wind to blow them out. He kept his head to one side to escape the strangling fumes, and held the blazing bunch to the birch bark. As he so held it, he became aware of sensation in his hand. His flesh was burning. He could smell it. Deep down below the surface he could feel it. The sensation developed into pain that grew acute. And still he endured it, holding the flame of the matches clumsily to the bark that would not light readily because his own burning hands were in the way, absorbing most of the flame. 29

At last, when he could endure no more, he jerked his hands apart. The blazing matches fell sizzling into the snow, but the birch bark was alight. He began laying dry grasses and the tiniest twigs on the flame. He could not pick and choose, for he had to lift the fuel between the heels of his hands. Small pieces of rotten wood and green moss clung to the twigs, and he bit them off as well as he could with his teeth. He cherished the flame carefully and awkwardly. It meant life, and it must not perish. The withdrawal of blood from the surface of his body now made him begin to shiver, and he grew more awkward. A large piece of green moss fell squarely on the little fire. He tried to poke it out with his fingers, but his shivering frame made him poke too far, and he disrupted the nucleus of the little fire, the burning grasses and tiny twigs separating and scattering. He tried to poke them together again, but in spite of the tenseness of the effort, his shivering got away with him, and the twigs were hopelessly scattered. Each twig gushed a puff of smoke and went out. The fire provider had failed. As he looked apathetically about him, his eyes chanced on the dog, sitting across the ruins of the fire from him, in the snow, making restless, hunching movements, slightly lifting one forefoot and then the other, shifting its weight back and forth on them with wistful eagerness. 30

The sight of the dog put a wild idea into his head. He remembered the tale of the man, caught in a blizzard, who killed a steer and crawled inside the carcass, and so was saved. He would kill the dog and bury his hands in the warm body until the numbness went out of them. Then he could build another fire. He spoke to the dog, calling it to him; but in his voice was a strange note of fear that frightened the animal, who had never known the man to speak in such way before. Something was the matter, and its suspicious nature sensed danger—it knew not what danger, but somewhere, somehow, in its brain arose an apprehension of the man. It flattened its ears down at the sound of the man's voice, and its restless, hunching movements and the liftings and shiftings of its forefeet be- 31 came more pronounced; but it would not come to the man. He got on his hands and knees and crawled toward the dog. The unusual posture again excited suspicion, and the animal sidled mincingly away.

The man sat up in the snow for a moment and struggled for calmness. 32
Then he pulled on his mittens, by means of his teeth, and got upon his feet. He glanced down at first in order to assure himself that he was really standing up, for the absence of sensation in his feet left him unrelated to the earth. His erect position in itself started to drive the webs of suspicion from the dog's mind; and when he spoke peremptorily, with the sound of whip lashes in his voice, the dog rendered its customary allegiance and came to him. As it came within reaching distance the man lost his control. His arms flashed out to the dog, and he experienced genuine surprise when he discovered that his hands could not clutch, that there was neither bend nor feeling in the fingers. He had forgotten for the moment that they were frozen and that they were freezing more and more. All this happened quickly, and before the animal could get away, he encircled its body with his arms. He sat down in the snow, and in this fashion held the dog, while it snarled and whined and struggled.

But it was all he could do, hold its body encircled in his arms and sit there. 33
He realized that he could not kill the dog. There was no way to do it. With his helpless hands he could neither draw nor hold his sheath knife nor throttle the animal. He released it, and it plunged wildly away, with tail between its legs, and still snarling. It halted forty feet away and surveyed him curiously, with ears sharply pricked forward.

The man looked down at his hands in order to locate them, and found 34
them hanging on the ends of his arms. It struck him as curious that one should have to use his eyes in order to find out where his hands were. He began threshing his arms back and forth, beating the mittened hands against his sides. He did this for five minutes, violently, and his heart pumped enough blood up to the surface to put a stop to his shivering. But no sensation was aroused in the hands. He had an impression that they hung like weights on the ends of his arms, but when he tried to run the impression down, he could not find it.

A certain fear of death, dull and oppressive, came to him. This fear 35
quickly became poignant as he realized that it was no longer a mere matter of freezing his fingers and toes, or of losing his hands and feet, but that it was a matter of life and death with the chances against him. This threw him into a panic, and he turned and ran up the creek bed along the old, dim trail. The dog joined in behind and kept up with him. He ran blindly, without intention, in fear such as he had never known in his life. Slowly, as he plowed and floundered through the snow, he began to see things again—the banks of the creek, the old timber jams, the leafless aspens, and the sky. The running made him feel better. He did not shiver. Maybe, if he ran on, his feet would thaw out; and, anyway, if he ran far enough, he would reach camp and the boys. Without doubt he would lose some fingers and toes and some of his face; but the boys would take care of him, and save the rest of him when he got there. And at the same time there was another thought in his mind that said he would never get to the camp and the

boys; that it was too many miles away, that the freezing had too great a start on him, and that he would soon be stiff and dead. This thought he kept in the background and refused to consider. Sometimes it pushed itself forward and demanded to be heard, but he thrust it back and strove to think of other things.

It struck him as curious that he could run at all on feet so frozen that he could not feel them when they struck the earth and took the weight of his body. He seemed to himself to skim along above the surface, and to have no connection with the earth. Somewhere he had once seen a winged Mercury, and he wondered if Mercury felt as he felt when skimming over the earth. [36]

His theory of running until he reached camp and the boys had one flaw in it: he lacked the endurance. Several times he stumbled, and finally he tottered, crumpled up, and fell. When he tried to rise, he failed. He must sit and rest, he decided, and next time he would merely walk and keep on going. As he sat and regained his breath, he noted that he was feeling quite warm and comfortable. He was not shivering, and it even seemed that a warm glow had come to his chest and trunk. And yet, when he touched his nose or cheeks, there was no sensation. Running would not thaw them out. Nor would it thaw out his hands and feet. Then the thought came to him that the frozen portions of his body must be extending. He tried to keep this thought down, to forget it, to think of something else; he was aware of the panicky feeling that it caused, and he was afraid of the panic. But the thought asserted itself, and persisted, until it produced a vision of his body totally frozen. This was too much, and he made another wild run along the trail. Once he slowed down to a walk, but the thought of the freezing extending itself made him run again. [37]

And all the time the dog ran with him, at his heels. When he fell down a second time, it curled its tail over its forefeet and sat in front of him, facing him, curiously eager and intent. The warmth and security of the animal angered him, and he cursed it till it flattened down its ears appeasingly. This time the shivering came more quickly upon the man. He was losing in his battle with the frost. It was creeping into his body from all sides. The thought of it drove him on, but he ran no more than a hundred feet, when he staggered and pitched headlong. It was his last panic. When he had recovered his breath and control, he sat up and entertained in his mind the conception of meeting death with dignity. However, the conception did not come to him in such terms. His idea of it was that he had been making a fool of himself, running around like a chicken with its head cut off—such was the simile that occurred to him. Well, he was bound to freeze anyway, and he might as well take it decently. With this new-found peace of mind came the first glimmerings of drowsiness. A good idea, he thought, to sleep off to death. It was like taking an anesthetic. Freezing was not so bad as people thought. There were lots worse ways to die. [38]

He pictured the boys finding his body next day. Suddenly he found himself with them, coming along the trail and looking for himself. And, still with them, he came around a turn in the trail and found himself lying in the snow. He did not belong with himself any more, for even then he was out of himself, standing with the boys and looking at himself in the snow. It certainly was [39] cold, was his thought. When he got back to the States he could tell the folks what real cold was. He drifted on from this to a vision of the old-timer on Sulphur Creek. He could see him quite clearly, warm and comfortable, and smoking a pipe.

"You were right, old hoss; you were right," the man mumbled to the old-timer of Sulphur Creek.   40

Then the man drowsed off into what seemed to him the most comfortable and satisfying sleep he had ever known. The dog sat facing him and waiting. The brief day drew to a close in a long, slow twilight. There were no signs of a fire to be made, and, besides, never in the dog's experience had it known a man to sit like that in the snow and make no fire. As the twilight drew on, its eager yearning for the fire mastered it, and with a great lifting and shifting of forefeet, it whined softly, then flattened its ears down in anticipation of being chidden by the man. But the man remained silent. Later the dog whined loudly. And still later it crept close to the man and caught the scent of death. This made the animal bristle and back away. A little longer it delayed, howling under the stars that leaped and danced and shone brightly in the cold sky. Then it turned and trotted up the trail in the direction of the camp it knew, where were the other food providers and fire providers.   41

Meaning and Idea

1. Where does this story take place? Briefly describe the physical environment. Where is the protagonist headed? What does he imagine awaits him at the end of his journey? What is the reality of that ending?

2. At a number of points in this story, the man welcomes pain. Identify three such instances. Why does he welcome the pain? What condition is he fighting off?

3. What is "the advice of the old-timer on Sulphur Creek"? What was the man's attitude toward this advice? Did it prove to be correct or incorrect advice?

4. What is the man's attitude toward the dog that's with him? How does it change in the course of the story? What is the man's "last resort" use for the dog? Why is it impossible for him to follow through on this?

Language, Form, Structure

1. What is the overall cause-and-effect relationship in this story? This story is made up of many smaller causal relationships that contribute to the overall larger one. Identify 10 of these smaller relationships.

2. Discuss the significance of the sentence, "The trouble with him was that he was without imagination" (paragraph 3). How does the character flaw implied here become a cause of the man's death?

3. Throughout this story, London writes of both the man's and the dog's knowledge about the cold. Identify a few of those passages. How does London's comparison of the two different experiences (of the man and the dog) advance the main point of the story? What is this main point?

4. Explain the final line of the story. Is the final line really an expression of the dog's consciousness? How and what does it reveal about London's attitude about survival? What is the relation of that line to the earlier comment about the man's lack of imagination?

5. Write definitions for the following words: frailty; conjectural; appendage; reiterated; pang; conflagration; excrutiating; acute; nucleus; peremptorily; allegiance; drowsed.

Ideas for Writing

1. Write a causal analysis of an unfortunate result of someone's stubbornness. Attempt to build the overall causal relationship through a series of smaller ones.

2. Analyze the reasons behind a recent decision by the government with which you disagree. Make the effects the basis for your disagreement.

3. Throughout "To Build a Fire" the main character remains nameless; he is only "the man." Perhaps less important, the dog also remains simply "the dog." Write a short commentary about the causes and effects of namelessness in this story.

The He Hormone

Andrew Sullivan

Born in England in 1963 and educated at Oxford, Andrew Sullivan earned a Ph.D. at Harvard. He became the editor of *The New Republic* in 1991. In 1995 he published *Virtually Normal: An Argument about Homosexuality,* in which he takes issue with views on homosexuality ranging from the "prohibitionist" attitudes of the far right to the treatment of homosexuality as a civil rights issue by the left. Each of these positions he finds lacking in crucial ways.

Sullivan is a writer who defies political categorization. Although he sees his social views as extremely liberal, his iconoclastic refusal to stop questioning assumptions and his suspicion of bureaucratic solutions often diverge from mainstream liberal orthodoxy. This is particularly true in "The He Hormone," which explicitly challenges a range of commonplace assumptions about the role of biology in culture and identity.

*I*t has a slightly golden hue, suspended in an oily substance and injected in a needle about half as thick as a telephone wire. I have never been able to jab it suddenly in my hip muscle, as the doctor told me to. Instead, after swabbing a small patch of my rump down with rubbing alcohol, I push the needle in slowly until all three inches of it are submerged. Then I squeeze the liquid in carefully, as the muscle often spasms to absorb it. My skin sticks a little to the syringe as I pull it out, and then an odd mix of oil and blackish blood usually trickles down my hip.

I am so used to it now that the novelty has worn off. But every now and again the weirdness returns. The chemical I am putting in myself is synthetic testosterone: a substance that has become such a metaphor for manhood that it is almost possible to forget that it has a physical reality. Twenty years ago, as it surged through my pubescent body, it deepened my voice, grew hair on my face and chest, strengthened my limbs, made me a man. So what, I wonder, is it doing to me now?

There are few things more challenging to the question of what the difference between men and women really is than to see the difference injected into your hip. Men and women differ biologically mainly because men produce 10 to 20 times as much testosterone as most women do, and this chemical, no one seriously disputes, profoundly affects physique, behavior, mood and self-understanding. To be sure, because human beings are also deeply socialized, the impact of this difference is refracted through the prism of our own history and culture. But biology, it is all too easy to forget, is at the root of this process. As more people use testosterone medically, as more use testosterone-based steroids in sports and recreation and as more research explores the behavioral effects of this chemical, the clearer the power of that biology is. It affects every aspect of our society, from high divorce rates and adolescent male violence to the exploding cults of bodybuilding and professional wrestling. It helps explain, perhaps better than any other single factor, why inequalities between men and women remain so frustratingly resilient in public and private life. This summer, when an easy-to-apply testosterone gel hits the market, and when more people experience the power of this chemical in their own bodies, its social importance, once merely implicit, may get even harder to ignore.

My own encounter with testosterone came about for a simple medical reason. I am H.I.V.-positive, and two years ago, after a period of extreme fatigue and weight loss, I had my testosterone levels checked. It turned out that my body was producing far less testosterone than it should have been at my age. No one quite knows why, but this is common among men with long-term H.I.V. The usual treatment is regular injection of artificial testosterone, which is when I experienced my first manhood supplement. 4

At that point I weighed around 165 pounds. I now weigh 185 pounds. My collar size went from a 15 to a 17 ½ in a few months; my chest went from 40 to 44. My appetite in every sense of that word expanded beyond measure. Going from napping two hours a day, I now rarely sleep in the daytime and have enough energy for daily workouts and a hefty work schedule. I can squat more than 400 pounds. Depression, once a regular feature of my life, is now a distant memory. I feel better able to recover from life's curveballs, more persistent, more alive. These are the long-term effects. They are almost as striking as the short-term ones. 5

Because the testosterone is injected every two weeks, and it quickly leaves the bloodstream, I can actually feel its power on almost a daily basis. Within hours, and at most a day, I feel a deep surge of energy. It is less edgy than a double espresso, but just as powerful. My attention span shortens. In the two or three days after my shot, I find it harder to concentrate on writing and feel the need to exercise more. My wit is quicker, my mind faster, but my judgment is more impulsive. It is not unlike the kind of rush I get before talking in front of a large audience, or going on a first date, or getting on an airplane, but it suffuses me in a less abrupt and more consistent way. In a word, I feel braced. For what? It scarcely seems to matter. 6

And then after a few days, as the testosterone peaks and starts to decline, the feeling alters a little. I find myself less reserved than usual, and more garrulous. The same energy is there, but it seems less directed toward action than toward interaction, less toward pride than toward lust. The odd thing is that, however much experience I have with it, this lust peak still takes me unawares. It is not like feeling hungry, a feeling you recognize and satiate. It creeps up on you. It is only a few days later that I look back and realize that I spent hours of the recent past socializing in a bar or checking out every potential date who came vaguely over my horizon. You realize more acutely than before that lust is a chemical. It comes; it goes. It waxes; it wanes. You are not helpless in front of it, but you are certainly not fully in control. 7

Then there's anger. I have always tended to bury or redirect my rage. I once thought this an inescapable part of my personality. It turns out I was wrong. Late last year, mere hours after a T shot, my dog ran off the leash to forage for a 8 chicken bone left in my local park. The more I chased her, the more she ran. By the time I retrieved her, the bone had been consumed, and I gave her a sharp tap on her rear end. "Don't smack your dog!" yelled a burly guy a few yards away. What I found myself yelling back at him is not printable in this magazine, but I have never used that language in public before, let alone bellow it at the top of my voice. He shouted back, and within seconds I was actually close to hitting him. He backed down and slunk off. I strutted home, chest puffed up, contrite beagle dragged sheepishly behind me. It wasn't until half an hour later that I realized I had been a complete jerk and had nearly gotten into the first public brawl of my life. I vowed to inject my testosterone at night in the future.

That was an extreme example, but other, milder ones come to mind: losing my temper in a petty argument; innumerable traffic confrontations; even the occasional slightly too prickly column or e-mail flame-out. No doubt my previous awareness of the mythology of testosterone had subtly primed me for these feelings of irritation and impatience. But when I place them in the larger context of my new testosterone-associated energy, and of what we know about what testosterone tends to do to people, then it seems plausible enough to ascribe some of this increased edginess and self-confidence to that biweekly encounter with a syringe full of manhood. 9

Testosterone, oddly enough, is a chemical closely related to cholesterol. It was first isolated by a Dutch scientist in 1935 from mice testicles and successfully synthesized by the German biologist Adolf Butenandt. Although testosterone is often thought of as the definition of maleness, both men and women produce it. Men produce it in their testicles; women produce it in their ovaries and adrenal glands. The male body converts some testosterone to estradiol, a female hormone, and the female body has receptors for testosterone, just as the male body does. That's why women who want to change their sex are injected with testosterone and develop male characteristics, like deeper voices, facial hair and even baldness. The central biological difference between adult men and women, then, is not that men have testosterone and women don't. It's that men produce much, much more of it than women do. An average woman has 40 to 60 nanograms of testosterone in a deciliter of blood plasma. An average man has 300 to 1,000 nanograms per deciliter. 10

Testosterone's effects start early—really early. At conception, every embryo is female and unless hormonally altered will remain so. You need testosterone to turn a fetus with a Y chromosome into a real boy, to masculinize his brain and body. Men experience a flood of testosterone twice in their lives: in the womb about six weeks after conception and at puberty. The first fetal burst primes the brain and the body, endowing male fetuses with the instinctual knowledge of how to respond to later testosterone surges. The second, more familiar adolescent rush—squeaky voices, facial hair and all—completes the process. Without testosterone, humans would always revert to the default sex, which is female. The Book of Genesis is therefore exactly wrong. It isn't women who are made out of men. It is men who are made out of women. Testosterone, to stretch the metaphor, is Eve's rib. 11

The effect of testosterone is systemic. It engenders both the brain and the body. Apart from the obvious genital distinction, other differences between men's and women's bodies reflect this: body hair, the ratio of muscle to fat, upper-body strength and so on. But testosterone leads to behavioral differences as well. Since it is unethical to experiment with human embryos by altering hormonal balances, much of the evidence for this idea is based on research conducted on animals. A Stanford research group, for example, as reported in Deborah Blum's book "Sex on the Brain," injected newborn female rats with testosterone. Not only did the female rats develop penises from their clitorises, but they also appeared fully aware of how to use them, trying to have sex with other females with merry abandon. Male rats who had their testosterone blocked after birth, on the other hand, saw their penises wither or disappear entirely and presented themselves to the female rats in a passive, receptive way. Other scientists, theorizing that it was testosterone that enabled male zebra finches to sing, injected mute female finches with testosterone. Sure enough, the females sang. Species in which the female is typically more aggressive, like hyenas in female-run clans, show higher levels of testosterone among the females than among the males. Female sea snipes, which impregnate the males, and leave them to stay home and rear the young, have higher testosterone levels than their mates. Typical "male" behavior, in other words, corresponds to testosterone levels, whether exhibited by chromosomal males or females.

Does this apply to humans? The evidence certainly suggests that it does, though much of the "proof" is inferred from accidents. Pregnant women who were injected with progesterone (chemically similar to testosterone) in the 1950's to avoid miscarriage had daughters who later reported markedly tomboyish childhoods. Ditto girls born with a disorder that causes their adrenal glands to produce a hormone like testosterone rather than the more common cortisol. The moving story, chronicled in John Colapinto's book "As Nature Made Him," of David Reimer, who as an infant was surgically altered after a botched circumcision to become a girl, suggests how long-lasting the effect of fetal testosterone can be. Despite a ruthless attempt to socialize David as a girl, and to give him the correct hormonal treatment to develop as one, his behavioral and psychological makeup was still ineradicably male. Eventually, with the help of more testosterone, he became a full man again. Female-to-male transsexuals report a similar transformation when injected with testosterone. One, Susan/Drew Seidman, described her experience in The Village Voice last November. "My sex-drive went through the roof," Seidman recalled. "I felt like I had to have sex once a day or I would die. . . . I was into porn as a girl, but now I'm *really* into porn." For Seidman, becoming a man was not merely physical. Thanks to testosterone, it was also psychological. "I'm not sure I can tell you what makes a man a man," Seidman averred. "But I know it's not a penis."

The behavioral traits associated with testosterone are largely the cliché-ridden ones you might expect. The Big T correlates with energy, self-confidence, competitiveness, tenacity, strength and sexual drive. When you talk to men in testosterone therapy, several themes recur. "People talk about extremes," one man in his late 30's told me. "But that's not what testosterone does for me. It makes me think more clearly. It makes me think more positively. It's my Saint Johnswort." A man in his 20's said: "Usually, I cycle up the hill to my apartment in 12th gear. In the days after my shot, I ride it easily in 16th." A 40-year-old executive who took testosterone for bodybuilding purposes told me: "I walk into a business meeting now and I just exude self-confidence. I know there are lots of other reasons for this, but my company has just exploded since my treatment. I'm on a roll. I feel capable of almost anything."

When you hear comments like these, it's no big surprise that strutting pea- 15 cocks with their extravagant tails and bright colors are supercharged with testosterone and that mousy little male sparrows aren't. "It turned my life around," another man said. "I felt stronger—and not just in a physical sense. It was a deep sense of being strong, almost spiritually strong." Testosterone's antidepressive power is only marginally understood. It doesn't act in the precise way other antidepressants do, and it probably helps alleviate gloominess primarily by propelling people into greater activity and restlessness, giving them less time to think and reflect. (This may be one reason women tend to suffer more from depression than men.) Like other drugs, T can also lose potency if overused. Men who inject excessive amounts may see their own production collapse and experience shrinkage of their testicles and liver damage.

Individual effects obviously vary, and a person's internal makeup is af- 16 fected by countless other factors—physical, psychological and external. But in this complex human engine, testosterone is gasoline. It revs you up. A 1997 study took testosterone samples from 125 men and 128 women and selected the 12 with the lowest levels of testosterone and the 15 with the highest. They gave them beepers, asked them to keep diaries and paged them 20 times over a four-day period to check on their actions, feelings, thoughts and whereabouts. The differences were striking. High-testosterone people "experienced more arousal and tension than those low in testosterone," according to the study. "They spent more time thinking, especially about concrete problems in the immediate present. They wanted to get things done and felt frustrated when they could not. They mentioned friends more than family or lovers."

Unlike Popeye's spinach, however, testosterone is also, in humans at least, 17 a relatively subtle agent. It is not some kind of on-off switch by which men are constantly turned on and women off. For one thing, we all start out with different base-line levels. Some women may have remarkably high genetic T levels, some men remarkably low although the male-female differential is so great that no single woman's T level can exceed any single man's, unless she, or he, has some kind of significant hormonal imbalance. For another, and this is where the social and political ramifications get complicated, testosterone is highly susceptible to environment. T levels can rise and fall depending on external circumstances—short term and long term. Testosterone is usually elevated in response to confrontational situations—a street fight, a marital spat, a presidential debate—or in highly charged sexual environments, like a strip bar or a pornographic Web site. It can also be raised permanently in continuously combative environments, like war, although it can also be suddenly lowered by stress.

Because testosterone levels can be measured in saliva as well as in blood, [18] researchers like Alan Booth, Allan Mazur, Richard Udry and particularly James M. Dabbs, whose book "Heroes, Rogues and Lovers" will be out this fall, have compiled quite a database on these variations. A certain amount of caution is advisable in interpreting the results of these studies. There is some doubt about the validity of onetime samples to gauge underlying testosterone levels. And most of the studies of the psychological effects of testosterone take place in culturally saturated environments, so that the difference between cause and effect is often extremely hard to disentangle. Nevertheless, the sheer number and scale of the studies, especially in the last decade or so, and the strong behavioral correlations with high testosterone, suggest some conclusions about the social importance of testosterone that are increasingly hard to gainsay.

Testosterone is clearly correlated in both men and women with psychologi- [19] cal dominance, confident physicality and high self-esteem. In most combative, competitive environments, especially physical ones, the person with the most T wins. Put any two men in a room together and the one with more testosterone will tend to dominate the interaction. Working women have higher levels of testosterone than women who stay at home, and the daughters of working women have higher levels of testosterone than the daughters of housewives. A 1996 study found that in lesbian couples in which one partner assumes the male, or "butch," role and another assumes the female, or "femme," role, the "butch" woman has higher levels of testosterone than the "femme" woman. In naval medical tests, midshipmen have been shown to have higher average levels of testosterone than plebes. Actors tend to have more testosterone than ministers, according to a 1990 study. Among 700 male prison inmates in a 1995 study, those with the highest T levels tended to be those most likely to be in trouble with the prison authorities and to engage in unprovoked violence. This is true among women as well as among men, according to a 1997 study of 87 female inmates in a maximum security prison. Although high testosterone levels often correlate with dominance in interpersonal relationships, it does not guarantee more social power. Testosterone levels are higher among blue-collar workers, for example, than among white-collar workers, according to a study of more than 4,000 former military personnel conducted in 1992. A 1998 study found that trial lawyers—with their habituation to combat, conflict and swagger—have higher levels of T than other lawyers.

The salient question, of course, is, How much of this difference in ag- [20] gression and dominance is related to environment? Are trial lawyers naturally more testosteroned, and does that lead them into their profession? Or does the experience of the courtroom raise their levels? Do working women have naturally higher T levels, or does the prestige of work and power elevate their testosterone? Because of the limits of researching such a question, it is hard to tell beyond a reasonable doubt. But the social context clearly matters. It is even possible to tell who has won a tennis match not by watching the game, but by monitoring testosterone-filled saliva samples throughout. Testosterone levels rise for both players before the match. The winner of any single game sees his T production rise; the loser sees it fall. The ultimate winner experiences a postgame testosterone surge, while the loser sees a collapse. This is true even for people watching sports matches. A 1998 study found that fans backing the winning side in a college basketball game and a World Cup soccer match saw their testosterone levels rise; fans rooting for the losing teams in both games saw their own T levels fall. There is, it seems, such a thing as vicarious testosterone.

One theory to explain this sensitivity to environment is that testosterone was originally favored in human evolution to enable successful hunting and combat. It kicks in, like adrenaline, in anticipation of combat, mental or physical, and helps you prevail. But a testosterone crash can be a killer too. Toward the end of my two-week cycle, I can almost feel my spirits dragging. In the event of a just-lost battle, as Matt Ridley points out in his book "The Red Queen," there's a good reason for this to occur. If you lose a contest with prey or a rival, it makes sense not to pick another fight immediately. So your body wisely prompts you to withdraw, filling your brain with depression and self-doubt. But if you have made a successful kill or defeated a treacherous enemy, your hormones goad you into further conquest. And people wonder why professional football players get into postgame sexual escapades and violence. Or why successful businessmen and politicians often push their sexual luck.

Similarly, testosterone levels may respond to more long-term stimuli. Studies have shown that inner-city youths, often exposed to danger in high-crime neighborhoods, may generate higher testosterone levels than unthreatened, secluded suburbanites. And so high T levels may not merely be responses to a violent environment; they may subsequently add to it in what becomes an increasingly violent, sexualized cycle. (It may be no accident that testosterone-soaked ghettos foster both high levels of crime and high levels of illegitimacy.) In the same way, declines in violence and crime may allow T levels to drop among young inner-city males, generating a virtuous trend of further reductions in crime and birth rates. This may help to explain why crime can decline precipitously, rather than drift down slowly, over time. Studies have also shown that men in long-term marriages see their testosterone levels progressively fall and their sex drives subsequently decline. It is as if their wives successfully tame them, reducing their sexual energy to a level where it is more unlikely to seek extramarital outlets. A 1993 study showed that single men tended to have higher levels of testosterone than married men and that men with high levels of testosterone turned out to be more likely to have had a failed marriage. Of course, if you start out with higher T levels, you may be more likely to fail at marriage, stay in the sexual marketplace, see your testosterone increase in response to this and so on.

None of this means, as the scientists always caution, that testosterone is directly linked to romantic failure or violence. No study has found a simple correlation, for example, between testosterone levels and crime. But there may be a complex correlation. The male-prisoner study, for example, found no general above-normal testosterone levels among inmates. But murderers and armed robbers had higher testosterone levels than mere car thieves and burglars. Why is this not surprising? One of the most remarkable, but least commented on, social statistics available is the sex differential in crime. For decades, arrest rates have shown that an overwhelmingly disproportionate number of arrestees are male. Although the sex differential has narrowed since the chivalrous 1930's, when the male-female arrest ratio was 12 to 1, it remains almost 4 to 1, a close echo of the testosterone differential between men and women. In violent crime, men make up an even bigger proportion. In 1998, 89 percent of murders in the United States, for example, were committed by men. Of course, there's a nature-nurture issue here as well, and the fact that the sex differential in crime has decreased over this century suggests that environment has played a part. Yet despite the enormous social changes of the last century, the differential is still 4 to 1, which suggests that underlying attributes may also have a great deal to do with it.

This, then, is what it comes down to: testosterone is a facilitator of risk— physical, criminal, personal. Without the influence of testosterone, the cost of these risks might seem to far outweigh the benefits. But with testosterone charging through the brain, caution is thrown to the wind. The influence of testosterone may not always lead to raw physical confrontation. In men with many options it may influence the decision to invest money in a dubious enterprise, jump into an ill-advised sexual affair or tell an egregiously big whopper. At the time, all these decisions may make some sort of testosteroned sense. The White House, anyone? [24]

The effects of testosterone are not secret; neither is the fact that men have far more if it than women. But why? As we have seen, testosterone is not synonymous with gender; in some species, it is the female who has most of it. The relatively new science of evolutionary psychology offers perhaps the best explanation for why that's not the case in humans. For neo-Darwinians, the aggressive and sexual aspects of testosterone are related to the division of labor among hunter-gatherers in our ancient but formative evolutionary past. This division— men in general hunted, women in general gathered—favored differing levels of testosterone. Women need some testosterone—for self-defense, occasional risk-taking, strength—but not as much as men. Men use it to increase their potential to defeat rivals, respond to physical threats in strange environments, maximize their physical attractiveness, prompt them to spread their genes as widely as possible and defend their home if necessary. [25]

But the picture, as most good evolutionary psychologists point out, is more complex than this. Men who are excessively testosteroned are not that attractive to most women. Although they have the genes that turn women on— strong jaws and pronounced cheekbones, for example, are correlated with high testosterone—they can also be precisely the unstable, highly sexed creatures that childbearing, stability-seeking women want to avoid. There are two ways, evolutionary psychologists hazard, that women have successfully squared this particular circle. One is to marry the sweet class nerd and have an affair with the college quarterback: that way you get the good genes, the good sex and the stable home. The other is to find a man with variable T levels, who can be both stable and nurturing when you want him to be and yet become a muscle-bound, [26] bristly gladiator when the need arises. The latter strategy, as Emma Bovary realized, is sadly more easily said than done.

So over millennia, men with high but variable levels of testosterone were the ones most favored by women and therefore most likely to produce offspring, and eventually us. Most men today are highly testosteroned, but not rigidly so. We don't have to live at all times with the T levels required to face down a woolly mammoth or bed half the village's young women. We can adjust so that our testosterone levels make us more suitable for co-parenting or for simply sticking around our mates when the sexual spark has dimmed. Indeed, one researcher, John Wingfield, has found a suggestive correlation in bird species between adjustable testosterone levels and males that have an active role to play in rearing their young. Male birds with consistently high testosterone levels tend to be worse fathers; males with variable levels are better dads. So there's hope for the new man yet. 27

From the point of view of men, after all, constantly high testosterone is a real problem, as any 15-year-old boy trying to concentrate on his homework will tell you. I missed one deadline on this article because it came three days after a testosterone shot and I couldn't bring myself to sit still long enough. And from a purely genetic point of view, men don't merely have an interest in impregnating as many women as possible; they also have an interest in seeing that their offspring are brought up successfully and their genes perpetuated. So for the male, the conflict between sex and love is resolved, as it is for the female, by a compromise between the short-term thrill of promiscuity and the long-term rewards of nurturing children. Just as the female does, he optimizes his genetic outcome by a stable marriage and occasional extramarital affairs. He is just more likely to have these affairs than a woman. Testosterone is both cause and effect of this difference. 28

And the difference is a real one. This is so obvious a point that we sometimes miss it. But without that difference, it would be hard to justify separate sports leagues for men and women, just as it would be hard not to suspect judicial bias behind the fact that of the 98 people executed last year in the United States, 100 percent came from a group that composes a little less than 50 percent of the population; that is, men. When the discrepancy is racial, we wring our hands. That it is sexual raises no red flags. Similarly, it is not surprising that 55 percent of everyone arrested in 1998 was under the age of 25—the years when male testosterone levels are at their natural peak. 29

It is also controversial yet undeniable that elevating testosterone levels can be extremely beneficial for physical and mental performance. It depends, of course, on what you're performing in. If your job is to whack home runs, capture criminals or play the market, then testosterone is a huge advantage. If you're a professional conciliator, office manager or teacher, it is probably a handicap. Major League Baseball was embarrassed that Mark McGwire's 1998 season home-run record might have been influenced by his use of androstenedione, a legal supplement that helps increase the body's own production of testosterone. But its own study into andro's effects concluded that regular use of it clearly 30 raises T levels and so improves muscle mass and physical strength, without serious side effects. Testosterone also accelerates the rate of recovery from physical injury. Does this help make sense of McGwire's achievement? More testosterone obviously didn't give him the skill to hit 70 home runs, but it almost certainly contributed to the physical and mental endurance that helped him do so.

Since most men have at least 10 times as much T as most women, it therefore makes sense not to have coed baseball leagues. Equally, it makes sense that women will be underrepresented in a high-testosterone environment like military combat or construction. When the skills required are more cerebral or more endurance-related, the male-female gap may shrink, or even reverse itself. But otherwise, gender inequality in these fields is primarily not a function of sexism, merely of common sense. This is a highly controversial position, but it really shouldn't be. Even more unsettling is the racial gap in testosterone. Several solid studies, published in publications like Journal of the National Cancer Institute, show that black men have on average 3 to 19 percent more testosterone than white men. This is something to consider when we're told that black men dominate certain sports because of white racism or economic class rather than black skill. This reality may, of course, feed stereotypes about blacks being physical but not intellectual. But there's no evidence of any trade-off between the two. To say that someone is physically gifted is to say nothing about his mental abilities, as even N.F.L. die-hards have come to realize. Indeed, as Jon Entine points out in his new book, "Taboo," even the position of quarterback, which requires a deft mix of mental and physical strength and was once predominantly white, has slowly become less white as talent has been rewarded. The percentage of blacks among N.F.L. quarterbacks is now twice the percentage of blacks in the population as a whole.

But fears of natural difference still haunt the debate about gender equality. Many feminists have made tenacious arguments about the lack of any substantive physical or mental differences between men and women as if the political equality of the sexes depended on it. But to rest the equality of women on the physical and psychological equivalence of the sexes is to rest it on sand. In the end, testosterone bites. This year, for example, Toys "R" Us announced it was planning to redesign its toy stores to group products most likely to be bought by the same types of consumers: in marketing jargon, "logical adjacencies." The results? Almost total gender separation. "Girl's World" would feature Easy-Bake Ovens and Barbies; "Boy's World," trucks and action figures. Though Toys "R" Us denied that there was any agenda behind this—its market research showed that gender differences start as young as 2 years old—such a public outcry ensued that the store canceled its plans. Meanwhile, Fox Family Channels is about to introduce two new, separate cable channels for boys and girls, boyzChannel and girlzChannel, to attract advertisers and consumers more efficiently. Fox executives told The Wall Street Journal that their move is simply a reflection of what Nielsen-related research tells them about the viewing habits of boys and girls: that, "in general terms, girls are more interested in entertainment that is relationship-oriented," while boys are "more action-oriented." T anyone? After more than two decades of relentless legal, cultural and ideological attempts to negate sexual difference between boys and girls, the market has turned around and shown that very little, after all, has changed.

Advocates of a purely environmental origin for this difference between the sexes counter that gender socialization begins very early and is picked up by subtle inferences from parental interaction and peer pressure, before being reinforced by the collective culture at large. Most parents observing toddlers choosing their own toys and play patterns can best judge for themselves how true this is. But as Matt Ridley has pointed out, there is also physiological evidence of very early mental differences between the sexes, most of it to the advantage of girls. Ninety-five percent of all hyperactive kids are boys; four times as many boys are dyslexic and learning-disabled as girls. There is a greater distinction between the right and left brain among boys than girls, and worse linguistic skills. In general, boys are better at spatial and abstract tasks, girls at communication. These are generalizations, of course. There are many, many boys who are great linguists and model students, and vice versa. Some boys even prefer, when left to their own devices, to play with dolls as well as trucks. But we are talking of generalities here, and the influence of womb-given testosterone on those generalities is undeniable.

Some of that influence is a handicap. We are so used to associating testosterone with strength, masculinity and patriarchal violence that it is easy to ignore that it also makes men weaker in some respects than women. It doesn't correlate with economic power: in fact, as we have seen, blue-collar workers have more of it than white-collar workers. It gets men into trouble. For reasons no one seems to understand, testosterone may also be an immune suppressant. High levels of it can correspond, as recent studies have shown, not only with baldness but also with heart disease and a greater susceptibility to infectious diseases. Higher levels of prostate cancer among blacks, some researchers believe, may well be related to blacks' higher testosterone levels. The aggression it can foster and the risks it encourages lead men into situations that often wound or kill them. And higher levels of testosterone-driven promiscuity make men more prone to sexually transmitted diseases. This is one reason that men live shorter lives on average than women. There is something, in other words, tragic about testosterone. It can lead to a certain kind of male glory; it may lead to valor or boldness or impulsive romanticism. But it also presages a uniquely male kind of doom. The cockerel with the brightest comb is often the most attractive and the most testosteroned, but it is also the most vulnerable to parasites. It is as if it has sacrificed quantity of life for intensity of experience, and this trade-off is a deeply male one.

So it is perhaps unsurprising that those professions in which this trade-off is most pronounced—the military, contact sports, hazardous exploration, venture capitalism, politics, gambling—tend to be disproportionately male. Politics is undoubtedly the most controversial because it is such a critical arena for the dispersal of power. But consider for a moment how politics is conducted in our society. It is saturated with combat, ego, conflict and risk. An entire career can be lost in a single gaffe or an unexpected shift in the national mood. This ego-driven roulette is almost as highly biased toward the testosteroned as wrestling. So it makes some sense that after almost a century of electorates made up by as many women as men, the number of female politicians remains pathetically small in most Western democracies. This may not be endemic to politics; it may have more to do with the way our culture constructs politics. And it is not to say that women are not good at government. Those qualities associated with low testosterone—patience, risk aversion, empathy—can all lead to excellent governance. They are just lousy qualities in the crapshoot of electoral politics.

If you care about sexual equality, this is obviously a challenge, but it need not be as depressing as it sounds. The sports world offers one way out. Men and women do not compete directly against one another; they have separate tournaments and leagues. Their different styles of physical excellence can he appreciated in different ways. At some basic level, of course, men will always be better than women in many of these contests. Men run faster and throw harder. Women could compensate for this by injecting testosterone, but if they took enough to be truly competitive, they would become men, which would somewhat defeat the purpose. 36

The harder cases are in those areas in which physical strength is important but not always crucial, like military combat or manual labor. And here the compromise is more likely to be access but inequality in numbers. Finance? Business? Here, where the testosterone-driven differences may well be more subtly psychological, and where men may dominate by discrimination rather than merit, is the trickiest arena. Testosterone-induced impatience may lead to poor decision-making, but low-testosterone risk aversion may lead to an inability to seize business opportunities. Perhaps it is safest to say that unequal numbers of men and women in these spheres is not prima facie evidence of sexism. We should do everything we can to ensure equal access, but it is foolish to insist that numerical inequality is always a function of bias rather than biology. This doesn't mean we shouldn't worry about individual cases of injustice; just that we shouldn't be shocked if gender inequality endures. And we should recognize that affirmative action for women (and men) in all arenas is an inherently utopian project. 37

Then there is the medical option. A modest solution might be to give more women access to testosterone to improve their sex drives, aggression and risk affinity and to help redress their disadvantages in those areas as compared with men. This is already done for severely depressed women, or women with hormonal imbalances, or those lacking an adequate sex drive, especially after menopause. Why not for women who simply want to rev up their will to power? Its use needs to be carefully monitored because it can also lead to side effects, like greater susceptibility to cancer, but that's what doctors are there for. And since older men also suffer a slow drop-off in T levels, there's no reason they should be cold-shouldered either. If the natural disadvantages of gender should be countered, why not the natural disadvantages of age? In some ways, this is already happening. Among the most common drugs now available through Internet doctors and pharmacies, along with Viagra and Prozac, is testosterone. This summer, with the arrival of AndroGel, the testosterone gel created as a medical 38 treatment for those four to five million men who suffer from low levels of testosterone, recreational demand may soar.

Or try this thought experiment: what if parents committed to gender equity opted to counteract the effect of testosterone on boys in the womb by complementing it with injections of artificial female hormones? That way, structural gender difference could be eradicated from the beginning. Such a policy would lead to "men and women with normal bodies but identical feminine brains," Matt Ridley posits. "War, rape, boxing, car racing, pornography and hamburgers and beer would soon be distant memories. A feminist paradise would have arrived." Today's conservative cultural critics might also be enraptured. Promiscuity would doubtless decline, fatherhood improve, crime drop, virtue spread. Even gay men might start behaving like lesbians, fleeing the gym and marrying for life. This is a fantasy, of course, but our increasing control and understanding of the scientific origins of our behavior, even of our culture, is fast making those fantasies things we will have to actively choose to forgo.   39

But fantasies also tell us something. After a feminist century, we may be in need of a new understanding of masculinity. The concepts of manliness, of gentlemanly behavior, of chivalry have been debunked. The New Age bonding of the men's movement has been outlived. What our increasing knowledge of testosterone suggests is a core understanding of what it is to be a man, for better and worse. It is about the ability to risk for good and bad; to act, to strut, to dare, to seize. It is about a kind of energy we often rue but would surely miss. It is about the foolishness that can lead to courage or destruction, the beauty that can be strength or vanity. To imagine a world without it is to see more clearly how our world is inseparable from it and how our current political pieties are too easily threatened by its reality.   40

And as our economy becomes less physical and more cerebral, as women slowly supplant men in many industries, as income inequalities grow and more highly testosteroned blue-collar men find themselves shunted to one side, we will have to find new ways of channeling what nature has bequeathed us. I don't think it's an accident that in the last decade there has been a growing focus on a muscular male physique in our popular culture, a boom in crass men's magazines, an explosion in violent computer games or a professional wrestler who has become governor. These are indications of a cultural displacement, of a world in which the power of testosterone is ignored or attacked, with the result that it reemerges in cruder and less social forms. Our main task in the gender wars of the new century may not be how to bring women fully into our society, but how to keep men from seceding from it, how to reroute testosterone for constructive ends, rather than ignore it for political point-making.   41

For my part, I'll keep injecting the Big T. Apart from how great it makes me feel, I consider it no insult to anyone else's gender to celebrate the uniqueness of one's own. Diversity need not mean the equalization of difference. In fact, true diversity requires the acceptance of difference. A world without the unruly, vulnerable, pioneering force of testosterone would be a fairer and calmer, but far grayer and duller, place. It is certainly somewhere I would never want to live. Perhaps the fact that I write this two days after the injection   42 of another 200 milligrams of testosterone into my bloodstream makes me more likely to settle for this colorful trade-off than others. But it seems to me no disrespect to womanhood to say that I am perfectly happy to be a man, to feel things no woman will ever feel to the degree that I feel them, to experience the world in a way no woman ever has. And to do so without apology or shame.

Meaning and Idea

1. What are the immediate effects of an injection of testosterone, as described by Sullivan? What are the longer-term effects?

2. List some of the social problems that Sullivan suggests might be explained by differing levels of testosterone. Which of these do you find the most convincing? Which do you find the least convincing?

3. What are some of the negative effects of high levels of testosterone?

4. What, according to Sullivan, would the world be like if the levels of testosterone in men and women were equal?

Language, Form, Structure

1. Choose two or three of the social problems that Sullivan suggests may be heavily influenced by testosterone. Reread carefully the evidence he provides. How convincing is his argument? How does he treat the possibility of other causes?

2. Reread the first paragraph of Sullivan's essay. How is this paragraph different from the rest of the piece? How does it serve as a good introduction to the essay? Why do you think that Sullivan chose to begin "The He Hormone" with this image?

3. Define the following words: physique; refracted; garrulous; satiate; aver; salient; vicarious; gaffe; utopian; secede.

Ideas for Writing

1. According to Sullivan, what characteristics make a man manly? Write an essay in which you discuss your personal reactions to Sullivan's characterization of a "man." Do you agree with his definition? Would you add other characteristics?

2. Write an essay in which you analyze a social problem and argue for a single, strongest cause.

3. Do you find Sullivan's thesis convincing? Write an essay in which you take a strong position attacking or defending Sullivan's thesis and conclusion. Either way, provide a clear evaluation of Sullivan's evidence.

Smart Bombs

Patricia J. Williams

Patricia J. Williams was born in 1951 and grew up in heavily segregated Boston. She received her M.A. from Wellesley College and went on to earn a J.D. from Harvard Law School in 1975. Remembering Harvard, Williams has said, "My abiding recollection of being a student at Harvard Law School is the sense of being invisible." This sense of the pervasiveness of racism has animated her writing. Williams often is thought of as a radical for her politics and style, and her books, *The Alchemy of Race and Rights* (1991) and *The Rooster's Egg: On the Persistence of Prejudice* (1995), are dissections of the uneasy relations between blacks and whites in America. Both books collect essays on current issues from the Clarence Thomas hearings of the early 1990s to the rise of shock radio shows. Williams taught in the City University system in New York City until 1991, when she moved to Columbia University.

In "Smart Bombs," as in all of her writing, Williams draw on her own experiences to illustrate points of law and philosophy.

*T*here was quite an astonishing little item in the paper recently about the sort of thing that makes me glad I grew up in the inner city: i.e., the national proliferation of "assassination games" among mostly white, suburban, middle- and upper-class youth. High school students across the country, even in the wake of Littleton, organize mock war games as a rite of passage or of spring. "A.P. Assassination" is what one school in exclusive Westport, Connecticut, calls the hunting season that begins right after advanced placement testing. For approximately three weeks students track one another around town with toy guns. (At one school five car crashes were attributed to the chase.) The student left standing after this grueling process of elimination "wins." One exuberant 18-year-old who aspires to be a physics professor dismissed criticism as politically correct overreaction and likened the game to "playing cowboys and Indians." (No Indians were apparently available for comment.)

It began to dawn on me why all those kids in Colorado could go on and on about how "normal" Eric Harris and Dylan Klebold were. I began to appreciate why the authorities might find it hard to pick out any further suspects from a student body whose poetic sensibility is suffused with the metaphors of blood lust. (Although if "assassination games" were played in the inner city, I wonder whether those same authorities wouldn't have cordoned off entire neighborhoods—remember the 3,000 policemen who showed up for Khallid Muhammad's Million Youth March in Harlem? I suspect they'd have gone door to door strip-searching anyone who blinked the wrong way. I think of the long, tragic history of what happens to minority kids who wave toy guns in public. I think about Dylan Klebold tootling around town in his BMW with its trunk full of bombs, and I can't help thinking about the black dentist in New Jersey who was stopped by the highway patrol more than a hundred times over four years before he finally traded in his BMW for something more drably utilitarian.) Perhaps the power of "the normative" to induce moral blind spots can be appreciated for its depth and complexity only when the world for some reason gets turned upside down.

The last time I can remember so much national soul-searching was around the Jeffrey Dahmer case. Dahmer, as you will recall, murdered and cannibalized at least seventeen men, mostly black, Hispanic or Asian, in Milwaukee. As in the Littleton case, there was lots of evidence that Dahmer had expressed intense hatred for very specific categories of humanity, particularly blacks and gays, yet, again as in Littleton, a kind of randomized, free-enterprise denial tended to diffuse the significance of that. As one commentator on the Dahmer case put it, "only" ten of his victims were black. Or, as one Milwaukee resident put it, "He could have hated women, he could have hated whites, he just happened to hate men." 3

This is not to say that the criminal acts of Klebold, Harris or Dahmer were in any way "normal." But it is intriguing that all of them were able to render their criminality invisible by operating within the lacunae of larger, socialized denial. Clever criminals will always do their worst. But a society enables those criminals when it allows itself to be predictably and collectively dumb about certain things, when it succumbs to the kinds of stereotypes that are barely noticed because "everyone thinks that." 4

Jeffrey Dahmer, for example, escaped suspicion for as long as he did because his bizarre, outsized hatreds were located in areas where a lot of saner people also lodge their little hostilities. Dahmer was on probation for child molestation, yet the social workers who were supposed to do home visits had missed that shrine of bones in his living room because they were afraid—not of him but of visiting the inner-city neighborhood where he lived. Most of Dahmer's victims were gay men, a community against which the national campaign of beating, disappearance and murder is so out of control that more than a dozen missing gay men in one city were not enough to alert anyone to the fact that a serial killer might be on the loose. One 14-year-old Laotian victim, who had escaped despite being drugged, naked and bleeding, was actually returned to Dahmer's apartment by the police after Dahmer told them the incident was a domestic dispute between the boy and himself. (Even in the face of repeated follow-up calls from worried neighbors, police issued casual assurances that the boy was an "adult.") Finally, there were charges that the police discounted calls from the women of the mostly black neighborhood who had complained repeatedly and urgently about everything from the smell emanating from Dahmer's apartment to his public drunkenness. 5

In retrospect, what is remarkable is the amount of official energy that went into denying the evidence that was right under everyone's nose. The Dahmer case was the product of a struggle among competing understandings held by communities with very different ideas of what is legitimate. Dahmer's status within those communities says a lot about those in power and those not— 6

Dahmer as white man deemed legitimate in a largely black neighborhood; as gay man deemed exotically licentious in a world of heterosexist, militarily modeled police; and as child molester in a world that sexualizes children relentlessly. Dahmer's ability to fool rested solidly upon the socialized proclivities of those in positions of institutional power for seeing only their own expectations and then lending those expectations a stupid degree of veracity. It depended on a strong presumption about adult Asian men as soft, effeminate, exotic, sexualized and perpetually childlike; of blacks as dangerous; and of women, particularly black women, as hysterical and unbelievable.

We will find out more about what happened at Columbine High as time goes on. And I'm sure the young physicist from Westport will one day make his mother proud by developing some very smart bombs indeed. In the meantime, we need to take a good, hard look at the diversity in what we call "common" sense. 7

Meaning and Idea

1. According to Williams, why did the police return the Laotian boy to Dahmer? What point does she claim that incident proves about the police?

2. How does Williams contrast the treatment of the assassination game in the white suburbs with the treatment of threats of violence in the inner city?

3. Comment on Williams's statement in paragraph 4 that "a society enables those criminals when it allows itself to be predictably and collectively dumb about certain things." What is her basic argument? To what "things" is she referring?

Language, Form, Structure

1. What is Williams's thesis?

2. Williams ends the essay by claiming that "we need to take a good, hard look at the diversity in what we call 'common' sense." What does she anticipate we will find if we follow her advice? How does the ironic tone of these words add to her argument?

3. Williams leaps from the assassination game, to the Columbine killings, to Jeffrey Dahmer. What is the basic cause that she sees linking these disparate events? Where does she make that connection?

4. Define the following words and then use each one in an original sentence: exuberant; suffused; lacunae; emanating; veracity.

Ideas for Writing

1. Williams writes anticipating an emotional reaction to her words, either a cheer of agreement or an angry denial. Write an essay detailing your personal reaction to her essay. Which parts of the essay were most effective in causing a reaction in you?

2. Write an augmentative essay about a hotly debated current issue. Try to identify an underlying cause.

3. Write an essay analyzing the title of Williams's piece, "Smart Bombs." How is this title appropriate to her essay? What does it add to her argument?

CROSSOVER ▬▬▬▬▬▬▬▬▬▬▬▬▬▬▬▬▬▬▬▬▬▬▬

1. In this chapter, Kate Chopin, Langston Hughes, Edwin Arlington Robinson, and Jack London all write about the tragic effects of particular situations. Choose two or three of these selections and write an essay that identifies and explains the major insight that each piece offers about the outcomes of conditions or actions. Draw on particular passages to develop your points. Which insight seems truest to you? Why?

2. Kate Chopin in "The Story of an Hour" and Langston Hughes in "Dream Deferred" bring thinking about gender and racial conditions, respectively, to bear on their works. What understanding about oppression do the two selections share? How does each piece develop the details of oppression and its effects to make its powerful point? How do the points differ? Write your views on these issues in a well-supported essay.

including description, narration, exemplification, process analysis, comparison and contrast, causal analysis, and classification. All good definitions, like all good expository writing in any mode, come most alive when they advance a particular point of view or thesis. Exploring accrued meanings of words and terms, the writer advances a persistent point.

Writing Definition

This chapter provides opportunities for practice in the various kinds of definitions explained in the previous section, but for the most part you'll be concentrating here on writing the extended definition. It's a useful activity to practice; the extended definition has many applications, whether you're developing a laboratory report, a research paper, a short story or a poem, a business report, or an article for the school newspaper. In one sense, an extended definition is easy to write, for it allows you a great deal of freedom to choose from many different rhetorical patterns. In another sense, the task of defining can be rather complicated, especially if you are writing about an abstract term that is rich in connotative meanings. As usual, your purpose, thesis, and intended audience will help you shape the scope and direction of your definition.

PURPOSE AND AUDIENCE

Finding Your Topic

Choosing a word to define, like choosing any topic for any writing task, demands considerable thought and attention at the outset. How will you select a word or phrase from the hundreds of thousands available in our language? As you think about the various possibilities, as you choose and reject words in an effort to find the one you want to write about, be sure to consider what you intend to do with the term once you select it. Of course it should be one that interests you (for whatever reason)—*love,* perhaps, *heroism, sitcoms, machismo, literacy,* the term *media explosion* or *brotherhood of man* or *a good daughter,* the expression "Have a good day" or "Cool it!"—but unless you're clear on your reasons for writing, you risk a diffuse and fuzzy presentation.

An eye toward purpose will help you shape your topic as you consider some possibilities for your definition. If you selected an abstract term like *love,* for example, you'd soon be lost without some serious thought about why you were writing on this word. You might want to *indicate its particular characteristics* as a human emotion as opposed to other, related emotions, like *affection* or *passion.* Here you might choose to dwell on only one essential quality for the term. You might want to *teach* about the various psychological or philosophical definitions of love that key thinkers have used over the last century. You might want to write an *amusing* piece on the foibles of love or a piece that *argues* that love in the 1990s is a vanishing phenomenon. You might want to *explain* the meaning of Christian love.

Why and for Whom?

Your topic is bound to sharpen as your own particular interest in the word interacts with your ideas about purpose. You might feel that the word *love* is too all-encompassing. Perhaps you want to zero in on a particular feature of love. Is your purpose to explore the nonromantic, nonphysical love that one human being, a stranger even, can show toward another? Are you interested in the sexual dimensions of love—man for woman, woman for man, man for man, woman for woman? Are you interested in love of country and its wrenching sacrifices in wartime? Are you interested in the sanctification of love through marriage and its connections to religious ritual? Any one of those approaches would lead you down a path quite different from any other. You might ultimately decide on a different but related term, one better suited to your purpose, like *brotherly love,* say, or *patriotism, fidelity, puppy love,* or *homosexuality.* Whatever your term and your purpose, a sharp thesis will enrich your writing. What is your position about your word or term and the thinking and associations surrounding it? Is romantic love, for example, a natural gift, or an invented trap? Is brotherly love a wondrous social ideal, an impossible goal, or both? A clear and original thesis will help you expand your definition with direction and energy.

Consider, too, your audience's expectations as you shape your topic. Try to imagine the group of readers you want to aim for. A sense of audience will help you determine an appropriate level of language and idiom, of course, but it also will help you focus your definition so that your purpose matches the audience's needs and expectations. Suppose you wanted to define *puppy love,* the adolescent condition of infatuation. You'd take one approach if your intended audience were a group of teenagers you wanted to amuse. You'd use words and present ideas familiar to this age group, and you'd explain any terms you thought the readers would not know, even, perhaps, one as basic to your definition as *infatuation.* Surely your jokes would be jokes that adolescents could appreciate. However, if your audience were a group of puzzled parents of junior high school–age children whom you wanted to instruct about the value of puppy love in an adolescent's maturation, your approach would be quite different. In either case, readers would expect to know the distinguishing features of the concept so that they could recognize it easily.

It's a familiar point, the interaction of audience, purpose, and topic. You want to give these issues careful attention every time you write.

PROCESS

Getting Started

In advance of writing, spend as much time as you can afford deciding on your topic, but don't be surprised if the process of limiting and shaping it continues beyond your early prewriting efforts and through a draft or two. You do have many options, and you want to explore them in depth before you finally decide on any one. A good place to start as a stimulus for ideas is an unabridged dictionary. The range of denotative meanings of a word certainly will simulate further thought. What has the dictionary excluded? How does the lexical meaning compare with connotative meanings? Depending on your topic, you might wish to consult one of the specialized dictionaries, like the 13-volume *Oxford English Dictionary* (OED), Eric Partridge's *Dictionary of Slang and Unconventional English,* or H. W. Fowler's *A Dictionary of Modern English Usage.* A dictionary of synonyms like *Roget's International Thesaurus* can show you a galaxy of words and concepts related to your topic.

Varied Rhetorical Strategies

We said earlier that for your extended definition you can use any of the various rhetorical strategies explained in other chapters of this book, and we want to examine that point a bit further by looking once again at the topic *puppy love.* You'll benefit greatly if you weigh your rhetorical options thoughtfully. You might investigate the meaning of the phrase by *describing* your kid sister's suffering in her most recent infatuation with the high school varsity quarterback. You might *narrate* a firsthand definition of puppy love, based on recollections of the moment your heart leapt at the sight of the green-eyed blonde who joined your tenth-grade algebra class at midsemester. You might build toward a definition as you *explain the process* of falling in love for an adolescent. To offer a specialized text-based definition, you might provide *examples* of characters drawn from children's literature who fall in love in their early teens. For some fun with wordplay you might develop *comparative* or *contrasting* definitions—puppy love with a person's love for puppies, say, or with puppies' love for each other; or, more seriously, you might contrast puppy love with mature love. You might *classify* the various types of puppy love you've observed and so create a multitextured definition. You might *argue* that puppy love is another manifestation of teenage hysteria or peer pressure or emotional immaturity or adult emulation. You might try to *persuade* what you perceive as a reluctant audience of health education teachers to cover puppy love in their courses of study for high school students. For any of these approaches you could draw on your own personal experiences; your readings in fiction, periodicals, and reference books; or the films or television programs you have seen. The possibilities are far-reaching—we have presented only a few here, of course—and considered along with purpose and audience, the rhetorical strategies provide fruitful areas of exploration in this assignment.

Advancing Your Definition

No matter which approach you take, you should be prepared to make your definition clear and specific; to set it off from what may be related but, for your paper, extraneous meanings; and to provide adequate details to make your point comprehensible. You may have to rely on *negation;* often a reader will best understand what your word means if you say what the word does not mean. When Emerson complains in his essay "Gifts" in this chapter that "Rings and other jewels are not gifts, but apologies for gifts," he startles us with a negative view that few of us hold. Negation, however, helps him move toward an equally surprising affirmation: "The only gift," he insists "is a portion of thyself. Thou must bleed for me."

Some writers of definition like to explore the *etymological features* of a term as a technique for developing meanings. Where did the word originate? How has its meaning changed historically? Yet another technique for constructing a concrete definition is to use an *analogy.* By showing your reader point by point how your topic is like something else, you can illustrate the unknown in terms of the known. Analogies can make concrete what may otherwise be hard to visualize. If you tried to define a *singles bar,* for example, by drawing a careful analogy between it and a supermarket or department store where people shop around before settling on a desirable product, you'd be helping readers who had never seen a singles bar to picture the scene with all its tensions, seriousness, and humor.

It seems fitting here to consider a definition. According to *The American Heritage Dictionary,* to *define* means "to state the precise meaning of (a word or sense of a word, for example); to describe the nature or basic qualities of; to delineate the outline or form of; to specify distinctly; to serve to distinguish; characterize." Your emphasis should be precision, clarity, and specificity—all just challenges for practicing writers.

STUDENT WRITING

In this introduction to a student writer's definition essay, note how he attempts to place a familiar term in a new light. The annotations point to successful strategies in writing a definition paper.

He Who Can, Teaches

[a]Word to be defined identified early in the paper

[b]Audience awareness: writer provides familiar dictionary meaning and then challenges it to explain the need for an extended definition

[c]Quotation establishes another reason for the writer's topic choice

Just what is a good teacher?[a] The *American Heritage Dictionary*'s sterile definition is not much help. Certainly a teacher is more than simply "one who teaches, esp. a person hired to teach."[b] George Bernard Shaw's stinging comment—"He who can, does. He who cannot, teaches"—damns the teaching profession with negativity and incompetence.[c] As the child and sibling of teachers, and as a teacher myself, I believe that to define the word, one must look at the positive qualities in examples set by outstanding instructors.

Where do we find these examples? In building a valid definition of *teacher,* I want to consider two portrayed in the media (admittedly highly idealized portraits) and one I have met in my life as a student. Mr. Chips in James Hilton's 1934 novel *Goodbye Mr. Chips* and

Mr. Holland in the 1995 film *Mr. Holland's Opus,*[d] written by Patrick Sheane Duncan, have many qualities that contribute to the word's meaning.[e] And my ninth-grade instructor, Mrs. Ruiz, by the way she dealt with us reluctant algebra students in Public School 24, also showed many traits that are essential to a valid definition.[f] By identifying the characteristics of excellence in these three educators, I will provide a positive meaning of *teacher* to challenge Shaw's mean-spirited observation.[g]

[d]Citations of book and film tell readers what to expect

[e]Development through comparison and contrast implied

[f]Writer will draw on cases and quotations from these sources as supporting details

[g]Thesis: writer will redefine the word *teacher* by identifying qualities in fictional and real instructors

SUMMING UP: DEFINITION

Reading Definitions

- As a sustained rhetorical strategy, definition—usually *extended definition*—means providing for a word or concept precise meanings beyond dictionary wording in order to produce clear and sharply focused ideas in a new or special context.

- As you read, identify the meanings of words and terms by looking for language and punctuation clues—such as paired commas, dashes, parentheses, italics, quotation marks, the words *that is* or *means.*

- Be aware of any restrictive meanings the writer may produce, that is, meanings considerably narrowed from a range of dictionary definitions, and determine whether you can accept the restrictive definition.

- Consider whether the writer has completely redefined the word or concept and whether you can accept the meaning for a new but valid perspective.

- Determine the elements of any carefully structured definitions.

- Explore the features of the extended definition, considering personal, subjective, even idiosyncratic meanings provided by the writer.

- Consider the various other rhetorical strategies the writer may have used to advance the extended definition. Find evidence of description, narration, exemplification, process analysis, comparison and contrast, causal analysis, and classification.

Writing Definitions

- Prepare to write an extended definition by choosing a word or concept that interests you and decide how you will explore it rhetorically in your paper. Use an unabridged dictionary as a good starting point for ideas.

- Give careful thought to the word you choose and be clear on your reasons for writing. For example, you might indicate a term's particular characteristics, teach something about its various and contradictory elements, argue some specialized quality of the term, or simply explain through examples a forgotten dimension of the word.

- Appraise your audience to determine the appropriate level of language and idiom and to focus your definition toward the audience's expectations.

- Use prewriting to limit and shape your topic as much as you can, but expect the process of refining the definition to extend throughout the writing of your drafts.

- Weigh your rhetorical options carefully and consider which strategies—description perhaps, or comparison or classification, to name just three of the many explored in this book—can help you best develop your topic.

- Develop a well-focused thesis statement that names the term you wish to define and indicates your special focus.

- Present an appropriate kind and level of detail to support the elements of your definition; use sensory detail, statistics, cases, quotations, or paraphrases to build your definition.

- Consider the value of using one of these definition strategies to help you develop your paper:
  - negation
  - etymological features
  - analogy

Gifts

Ralph Waldo Emerson

Ralph Waldo Emerson (1803–1882), born into a family of Puritan clergy in Boston, was a Unitarian minister at Boston's Old North Church from 1829 to 1832. But he left the ministry because of his distrust of established creeds and his growing belief that an individual's intuition, drawn from nature, is the highest form of knowledge. With this personal philosophy already taking shape, Emerson traveled to Europe, where he met Thomas Carlyle, Samuel Taylor Coleridge, and William Wordsworth, all of whom greatly influenced Emerson and his contributions to the literary and philosophical movement of transcendentalism. Emerson was at the core of this movement—along with Thoreau, Alcott, and Fuller—which flourished in New England between 1836 and 1860.

Emerson was a noted lecturer as well as a poet and essayist. His writings include *Nature* (1836), his *Journals* (kept since his Harvard undergraduate days), his *Essays* (1841, 1844), and *Poems* (1847), as well as articles in the magazine *The Dial,* which he edited for two years.

In "Gifts" Emerson defines a term which is usually thought of as being a material object. Yet he skillfully combines the spiritual with the material in what is ultimately a prescription for allowing others to "feel you and delight in you all the time."

Gifts of one who loved me,—
'Twas high time they came;
When he ceased to love me,
Time they stopped for shame.

*I*t is said that the world is in a state of bankruptcy, that the world owes the world more than the world can pay, and ought to go into chancery, and be sold. I do not think this general insolvency, which involves in some sort all the population, to be the reason of the difficulty experienced at Christmas and New Year, and other times, in bestowing gifts; since it is always so pleasant to be generous, though very vexatious to pay debts. But the impediment lies in the choosing. If, at any time, it comes into my head, that a present is due from me to somebody, I am puzzled what to give, until the opportunity is gone. Flowers and fruits are always fit presents; flowers, because they are a proud assertion that a ray of beauty outvalues all the utilities of the world. These gay natures contrast with the somewhat stern countenance of ordinary nature: they are like music heard out of a workhouse. Nature does not cocker us: we are children, not pets: she is not fond: everything is dealt to us without fear or favor, after severe universal laws. Yet these delicate flowers look like the frolic and interference of love and beauty. Men used to tell us that we love flattery, even though we are not deceived by it, because it shows that we are of importance enough to be courted. Something like that pleasure, the flowers give us: what am I to whom these sweet hints are addressed? Fruits are acceptable gifts, because they are the flower of commodities, and admit of fantastic values being attached to them. If a man should send to me to come a hundred miles to visit him, and should set before me a basket of fine summer-fruit, I should think there was some proportion between the labor and the rewards.

For common gifts, necessity makes pertinences and beauty every day, and one is glad when an imperative leaves him no option, since if the man at the door have no shoes, you have not to consider whether you could procure him a paint box. And as it is always pleasing to see a man eat bread, or drink water, in the house or out of doors, so it is always a great satisfaction to supply these first wants. Necessity does everything well. In our condition of universal dependence, it seems heroic to let the petitioner be the judge of his necessity, and to give all that is asked, though at great inconvenience. If it be a fantastic desire, it is better to leave to others the office of punishing him. I can think of many parts I should prefer playing to that of the Furies. Next to things of necessity, the rule for a gift, which one of my friends prescribed, is, that we might convey to some person that which properly belonged to his character, and was easily associated with him in thought. But our tokens of compliment and love are for the most part barbarous. Rings and other jewels are not gifts, but apologies for gifts. The only gift is a portion of thyself. Thou must bleed for me. Therefore the poet brings his poem; the shepherd, his lamb; the farmer, corn; the miner, a gem; the sailor, coral and shells; the painter, his picture; the girl, a handkerchief of her own sewing. This is right and pleasing, for it restores society in so far to its primary basis, when a man's biography is conveyed in his gifts, and every man's wealth is an index of his merit. But it is a cold, lifeless business when you go to the shops to buy me something, which does not represent your life and talent, but a goldsmith's. This is fit for kings, and rich men who represent kings, and a false state of property, to make presents of gold and silver stuffs, as a kind of symbolical sin-offering, or payment of black-mail. 2

The law of benefits is a difficult channel, which requires careful sailing, or rude boats. It is not the office of a man to receive gifts. How dare you give them? We wish to be self-sustained. We do not quite forgive a giver. The hand that feeds us is in some danger of being bitten. We can receive anything from love, for that is a way of receiving it from ourselves: but not from any one who assumes to bestow. We sometimes hate the meat which we eat, because there seems something of degrading dependence in living by it. 3

> Brother, if Jove to thee a present make,
> Take heed that from his hands thou nothing take.

We ask the whole. Nothing less will content us. We arraign society, if it do not give us besides earth, and fire, and water, opportunity, love, reverence, and objects of veneration.

He is a good man, who can receive a gift well. We are either glad or sorry at a gift, and both emotions are unbecoming. Some violence, I think, is done, some degradation borne, when I rejoice or grieve at a gift. I am sorry when my indepen- 4 dence is invaded, or when a gift comes from such as do not know my spirit, and so the act is not supported; and if the gift pleases me overmuch, then I should be ashamed that the donor should read my heart, and see that I love his commodity and not him. The gift, to be true, must be the flowing of the giver unto me, correspondent to my flowing unto him. When the waters are at level, then my goods pass to him, and his to me. All his are mine, all mine his. I say to him, How can you give me this pot of oil, or this flagon of wine, when all your oil and wine is mine, which belief of mine this gift seems to deny? Hence the fitness of beautiful, not useful things for gifts. This giving is flat usurpation, and therefore when the beneficiary is ungrateful, as all beneficiaries hate all Timons, not at all considering the value of the gift, but looking back to the greater store it was taken from, I rather sympathize with the beneficiary, than with the anger of my lord Timon. For, the expectation of gratitude is mean, and is continually punished by the total insensibility of the obliged person. It is a great happiness to get off without injury and heart-burning, from one who has had the ill luck to be served by you. It is a very onerous business, this of being served, and the debtor naturally wishes to give you a slap. A golden text for these gentlemen is that which I so admire in the Buddhist, who never thanks, and who says, "Do not flatter your benefactors."

The reason of these discords I conceive to be, that there is no commensurability between a man and any gift. You cannot give anything to a magnanimous person. After you have served him, he at once puts you in debt by his magnanimity. The service a man renders his friend is trivial and selfish, compared with the service he knows his friend stood in readiness to yield him, alike before he had begun to serve his friend, and now also. Compared with that goodwill I bear my friend, the benefit it is in my power to render him seems small. Besides, our action on each other, good as well as evil, is so incidental and at random, that we can seldom hear the acknowledgments of any person who would thank us for a benefit, without some shame and humiliation. We can rarely strike a direct stroke, but must be content with an oblique one; we seldom have the satisfaction of yielding a direct benefit, which is directly received. But rectitude scatters favors on every side without knowing it, and receives with wonder the thanks of all people.

I fear to breathe any treason against the majesty of love, which is the genius and god of gifts, and to whom we must not affect to prescribe. Let him give kingdoms or flower-leaves indifferently. There are persons, from whom we always expect fairy tokens; let us not cease to expect them. This is prerogative, and not to be limited by our municipal rules. For the rest, I like to see that we cannot be bought and sold. The best of hospitality and of generosity is also not in the will but in fate. I find that I am not much to you; you do not need me; you do not feel me; then am I thrust out of doors, though you proffer me house and lands. No services are of any value, but only likeness. When I have attempted to join myself to others by services, it proved an intellectual trick,—no more. They eat your service like apples, and leave you out. But love them, and they feel you, and delight in you all the time.

Meaning and Idea

1. According to Emerson, what is the greatest cause of difficulty in gift-giving? How can that difficulty be overcome?

2. What is Emerson's attitude about the best source for gifts? What does he mean by "The only gift is a portion of thyself"?

3. Why are beautiful things more "fit" as gifts than useful things are?

4. According to Emerson, what is the greatest of all possible gifts? What is the most exalted basis for gift-giving? Why?

Language, Form, Structure

1. Throughout the essay, Emerson continually limits the scope of his definition of *gifts* until he arrives at one critical basis for all gift-choosing and -giving. Trace the process of limitation and identify the conclusion which derives from it.

2. What is the relation in this essay among gift-choosing, gift-giving, and gift-receiving? How do Emerson's discussions of these three categories amount to a definition of *gifts?*

3. What metaphor does Emerson create for gift-giving? How does it help define the term *gifts?*

4. Identify two sections where Emerson uses exemplification to limit the definition.

5. Write definitions for Emerson's use of the following words: chancery; vexations; impediment; countenance; imperative; veneration; onerous; commensurability; rectitude; prerogative.

Ideas for Writing

1. Choose a term that can have both spiritual and materialistic meanings (*wealth, success,* or *marriage,* for example) and write a definition which blends the two values and shows their relationship to each other.

2. Define the term *generosity.* Focus on either material or spiritual generosity—or both.

3. One critic writes of Emerson's contribution that the philosopher developed "the doctrine of self-reliance, a spirit of optimism, and defiance of tradition and authority: for to the extent that all men are godlike . . . they must trust themselves, can overcome evil, and should regard their fellow men as equal." Write a paper in which you explore the validity of this comment in regard to "Gifts."

A Tree. A Rock. A Cloud.

Carson McCullers

Carson McCullers (1917–1967), born in Columbus, Georgia, was an American fiction writer who often focused on an individual's sense of isolation and loneliness in the midst of a malevolent or uncaring society. Her stories were so finely wrought as to lend themselves easily to dramatizations; *The Member of the Wedding* (1946) was made into a play in 1950, and Edward Albee in 1963 dramatized McCullers's novella *The Ballad of the Sad Café* (1951). Her best-known, earlier work is *The Heart Is a Lonely Hunter* (1940).

A tree, a rock, and a cloud are in this story both the end points of disillusionment and the starting points of love. McCullers's characterization and setting skillfully play against the ultimate happiness (or unhappiness?) she wants to define.

*I*t was raining that morning, and still very dark. When the boy   1
reached the streetcar café he had almost finished his route and he went in for a cup of coffee. The place was an all-night café owned by a bitter and stingy man called Leo. After the raw, empty street the café seemed friendly and bright: along the counter there were a couple of soldiers, three spinners from the cotton mill, and in a corner a man who sat hunched over with his nose and half his face down in a beer mug. The boy wore a helmet such as aviators wear. When he went into the café he unbuckled the chin strap and raised the right flap up over his pink little ear; often as he drank his coffee someone would speak to him in a friendly way. But this morning Leo did not look into his face and none of the men were talking. He paid and was leaving the café when a voice called out to him:

'Son! Hey Son!'   2

He turned back and the man in the corner was crooking his finger and   3
nodding to him. He had brought his face out of the beer mug and he seemed suddenly very happy. The man was long and pale, with a big nose and faded orange hair.

'Hey Son!'   4

The boy went toward him. He was an undersized boy of about twelve,   5
with one shoulder drawn higher than the other because of the weight of the paper sack. His face was shallow, freckled, and his eyes were round child eyes.

'Yeah Mister?'   6

The man laid one hand on the paper boy's shoulders, then grasped the   7
boy's chin and turned his face slowly from one side to the other. The boy shrank back uneasily.

'Say! What's the big idea?'   8

The boy's voice was shrill; inside the café it was suddenly very quiet.   9

The man said slowly: 'I love you.'   10

All along the counter the men laughed. The boy, who had scowled and si-   11
dled away, did not know what to do. He looked over the counter at Leo, and Leo
watched him with a weary, brittle jeer. The boy tried to laugh also. But the man
was serious and sad.

'I did not mean to tease you, Son,' he said. 'Sit down and have a beer with   12
me. There is something I have to explain.'

Cautiously, out of the corner of his eye, the paper boy questioned the men   13
along the counter to see what he should do. But they had gone back to their beer
or their breakfast and did not notice him. Leo put a cup of coffee on the counter
and a little jug of cream.

'He is a minor,' Leo said.   14

The paper boy slid himself up onto the stool. His ear beneath the upturned   15
flap of the helmet was very small and red. The man was nodding at him soberly.
'It is important,' he said. Then he reached in his hip pocket and brought out
something which he held up in the palm of his hand for the boy to see.

'Look very carefully,' he said.   16

The boy stared, but there was nothing to look at very carefully. The man   17
held in his big, grimy palm a photograph. It was the face of a woman, but
blurred, so that only the hat and the dress she was wearing stood out clearly.

'See?' the man asked.   18

The boy nodded and the man placed another picture in his palm. The   19
woman was standing on a beach in a bathing suit. The suit made her stomach
very big, and that was the main thing you noticed.

'Got a good look?' He leaned over closer and finally asked: 'You ever   20
seen her before?'

The boy sat motionless, staring slantwise at the man. 'Not so I know of.'   21

'Very well.' The man blew on the photographs and put them back into his   22
pocket. 'That was my wife.'

'Dead?' the boy asked.   23

Slowly the man shook his head. He pursed his lips as though about to   24
whistle and answered in a long-drawn way: 'Nuuu—' he said. 'I will explain.'

The beer on the counter before the man was in a large brown mug. He did   25
not pick it up to drink. Instead he bent down and, putting his face over the rim,
he rested there for a moment. Then with both hands he tilted the mug and
sipped.

'Some night you'll go to sleep with your nose in a mug and drown,' said   26
Leo. 'Prominent transient drowns in beer. That would be a cute death.'

The paper boy tried to signal to Leo. While the man was not looking he   27
screwed up his face and worked his mouth to question soundlessly: 'Drunk?'
But Leo only raised his eyebrows and turned away to put some pink strips of
bacon on the grill. The man pushed the mug away from him, straightened himself, and folded his loose crooked hands on the counter. His face was sad as he
looked at the paper boy. He did not blink, but from time to time the lids closed
down with delicate gravity over his pale green eyes. It was nearing dawn and the
boy shifted the weight of the paper sack.

'I am talking about love,' the man said. 'With me it is a science.'   28

The boy half slid down from the stool. But the man raised his forefinger, and   29 there was something about him that held the boy and would not let him go away.

'Twelve years ago I married the woman in the photograph. She was my   30 wife for one year, nine months, three days, and two nights. I loved her. Yes . . .' He tightened his blurred, rambling voice and said again: 'I loved her. I thought also that she loved me. I was a railroad engineer. She had all home comforts and luxuries. It never crept into my brain that she was not satisfied. But do you know what happened?'

'Mgneeow!' said Leo.   31

The man did not take his eyes from the boy's face. 'She left me. I came in   32 one night and the house was empty and she was gone. She left me.'

'With a fellow?' the boy asked.   33

Gently the man placed his palm down on the counter. 'Why naturally,   34 Son. A woman does not run off like that alone.'

The café was quiet, the soft rain black and endless in the street outside.   35 Leo pressed down the frying bacon with the prongs of his long fork. 'So you have been chasing the floozie for eleven years. You frazzled old rascal!'

For the first time the man glanced at Leo. 'Please don't be vulgar. Besides,   36 I was not speaking to you.' He turned back to the boy and said in a trusting and secretive undertone: 'Let's not pay any attention to him. O.K.?'

The paper boy nodded doubtfully.   37

'It was like this,' the man continued. 'I am a person who feels many   38 things. All my life one thing after another has impressed me. Moonlight. The leg of a pretty girl. One thing after another. But the point is that when I had enjoyed anything there was a peculiar sensation as though it was laying around loose in me. Nothing seemed to finish itself up or fit in with the other things. Women? I had my portion of them. The same. Afterwards laying around loose in me. I was a man who had never loved.'

Very slowly he closed his eyelids, and the gesture was like a curtain drawn   39 at the end of a scene in a play. When he spoke again his voice was excited and the words came fast—the lobes of his large, loose ears seemed to tremble.

'Then I met this woman. I was fifty-one and she always said she was   40 thirty. I met her at a filling station and we were married within three days. And do you know what it was like? I just can't tell you. All I had ever felt was gathered together around this woman. Nothing lay loose in me any more but was finished up by her.'

The man stopped suddenly and stroked his long nose. His voice sank   41 down to a steady and reproachful undertone: 'I'm not explaining this right. What happened was this. There were these beautiful feelings and loose little pleasures inside me. And this woman was something like an assembly line for my soul. I run these little pieces of myself through her and I come out complete. Now do you follow me?'

'What was her name?' the boy asked.   42

'Oh,' he said. 'I called her Dodo. But that is immaterial.'   43

'Did you try to make her come back?'   44

The man did not seem to hear. 'Under the circumstances you can imagine   45
how I felt when she left me.'

Leo took the bacon from the grill and folded two strips of it between a   46
bun. He had a gray face, with slitted eyes, and a pinched nose saddled by faint
blue shadows. One of the mill workers signaled for more coffee and Leo poured
it. He did not give refills on coffee free. The spinner ate breakfast there every
morning, but the better Leo knew his customers the stingier he treated them. He
nibbled his own bun as though he grudged it to himself.

'And you never got hold of her again?'   47

The boy did not know what to think of the man, and his child's face was   48
uncertain with mingled curiosity and doubt. He was new on the paper route; it
was still strange to him to be out in the town in the black, queer early morning.

'Yes,' the man said. 'I took a number of steps to get her back. I went   49
around trying to locate her. I went to Tulsa where she had folks. And to Mobile.
I went to every town she had ever mentioned to me, and I hunted down every
man she had formerly been connected with. Tulsa, Atlanta, Chicago, Cheehaw,
Memphis . . . For the better part of two years I chased around the country trying to lay hold of her.'

'But the pair of them had vanished from the face of the earth!' said Leo.   50

'Don't listen to him,' the man said confidentially. 'And also just forget   51
those two years. They are not important. What matters is that around the third
year a curious thing begun to happen to me.'

'What?' the boy asked.   52

The man leaned down and tilted his mug to take a sip of beer. But as he   53
hovered over the mug his nostrils fluttered slightly; he sniffed the staleness of
the beer and did not drink. 'Love is a curious thing to begin with. At first I
thought only of getting her back. It was a kind of mania. But then as time went
on I tried to remember her. But do you know what happened?'

'No,' the boy said.   54

'When I laid myself down on a bed and tried to think about her my mind   55
became a blank. I couldn't see her. I would take out her pictures and look. No
good. Nothing doing. A blank. Can you imagine it?'

'Say Mac!' Leo called down the counter. 'Can you imagine this bozo's   56
mind a blank!'

Slowly, as though fanning away flies, the man waved his hand. His green   57
eyes were concentrated and fixed on the shallow little face of the paper boy.

'But a sudden piece of glass on a sidewalk. Or a nickel tune in a music   58
box. A shadow on a wall at night. And I would remember. It might happen in a
street and I would cry or bang my head against a lamppost. You follow me?'

'A piece of glass . . .' the boy said.   59

'Anything. I would walk around and I had no power of how and when to   60
remember her. You think you can put up a kind of shield. But remembering
don't come to a man face forward—it corners around sideways. I was at the
mercy of everything I saw and heard. Suddenly instead of me combing the

countryside to find her she begun to chase me around in my very soul. *She* chasing *me,* mind you! And in my soul.'

The boy asked finally: 'What part of the country were you in then?'   61

'Ooh,' the man groaned. 'I was a sick mortal. It was like smallpox. I con-   62 fess, Son, that I boozed. I fornicated. I committed any sin that suddenly appealed to me. I am loath to confess it but I will do so. When I recall that period it is all curdled in my mind, it was so terrible.'

The man leaned his head down and tapped his forehead on the counter.   63 For a few seconds he stayed bowed over in this position, the back of his stringy neck covered with orange furze, his hands with their long warped fingers held palm to palm in an attitude of prayer. Then the man straightened himself; he was smiling and suddenly his face was bright and tremulous and old.

'It was in the fifth year that it happened,' he said. 'And with it I started   64 my science.'

Leo's mouth jerked with a pale, quick grin. 'Well none of we boys are get-   65 ting any younger,' he said. Then with sudden anger he balled up a dishcloth he was holding and threw it down hard on the floor. 'You draggle-tailed old Romeo!'

'What happened?' the boy asked.   66

The old man's voice was high and clear: 'Peace,' he answered.   67

'Huh?'   68

'It is hard to explain scientifically, Son,' he said. 'I guess the logical explana-   69 tion is that she and I had fleed around from each other for so long that finally we just got tangled up together and lay down and quit. Peace. A queer and beautiful blankness. It was spring in Portland and the rain came every afternoon. All evening I just stayed there on my bed in the dark. And that is how the science come to me.'

The windows in the streetcar were pale blue with light. The two soldiers   70 paid for their beers and opened the door—one of the soldiers combed his hair and wiped off his muddy puttees before they went outside. The three mill workers bent silently over their breakfasts. Leo's clock was ticking on the wall.

'It is this. And listen carefully. I meditated on love and reasoned it out. I   71 reasoned it out. I realized what is wrong with us. Men fall in love for the first time. And what do they fall in love with?'

The boy's soft mouth was partly open and he did not answer.   72

'A woman,' the old man said. 'Without science, with nothing to go by,   73 they undertake the most dangerous and sacred experience in God's earth. They fall in love with a woman. Is that correct, Son?'

'Yeah,' the boy said faintly.   74

'They start at the wrong end of love. They begin at the climax. Can you   75 wonder it is so miserable? Do you know how men should love?'

The old man reached over and grasped the boy by the collar of his leather   76 jacket. He gave him a gentle little shake and his green eyes gazed down unblinking and grave.

'Son, do you know how love should be begun?'   77

The boy sat small and listening and still. Slowly he shook his head. The   78 old man leaned closer and whispered:

'A tree. A rock. A cloud.'   79

It was still raining outside in the street: a mild, gray, endless rain. The mill   80
whistle blew for the six o'clock shift and the three spinners paid and went away.
There was no one in the café but Leo, the old man, and the little paper boy.

'The weather was like this in Portland,' he said. 'At the time my science   81
was begun. I meditated and I started very cautious. I would pick up something
from the street and take it home with me. I bought a goldfish and I concentrated
on the goldfish and I loved it. I graduated from one thing to another. Day by day
I was getting this technique. On the road from Portland to San Diego————'

'Aw shut up!' screamed Leo suddenly. 'Shut up! Shut up!'   82

The old man still held the collar of the boy's jacket; he was trembling and   83
his face was earnest and bright and wild. 'For six years now I have gone around
by myself and built up my science. And now I am a master. Son, I can love anything. No longer do I have to think about it even. I see a street full of people and
a beautiful light comes in me. I watch a bird in the sky. Or I meet a traveler on
the road. Everything, Son. And anybody. All stranger and all loved! Do you realize what a science like mine can mean?'

The boy held himself stiffly, his hands curled tight around the counter   84
edge. Finally he asked: 'Did you ever really find that lady?'

'What? What say, Son?'   85

'I mean,' the boy asked timidly, 'have you fallen in love with a woman   86
again?'

The old man loosened his grasp on the boy's collar. He turned away and   87
for the first time his green eyes had a vague and scattered look. He lifted the
mug from the counter, drank down the yellow beer. His head was shaking
slowly from side to side. Then finally he answered: 'No, Son. You see that is the
last step in my science. I go cautious. And I am not quite ready yet.'

'Well!' said Leo. 'Well well well!'   88

The old man stood in the open doorway. 'Remember,' he said. Framed   89
there in the gray damp light of the early morning he looked shrunken and seedy
and frail. But his smile was bright. 'Remember I love you,' he said with a last
nod. And the door closed quietly behind him.

The boy did not speak for a long time. He pulled down the bangs on his   90
forehead and slid his grimy little forefinger around the rim of his empty cup.
Then without looking at Leo he finally asked:

'Was he drunk?'   91

'No,' said Leo shortly.   92

The boy raised his clear voice higher. 'Then was he a dope fiend?'   93

'No.'   94

The boy looked up at Leo, and his flat little face was desperate, his voice   95
urgent and shrill. 'Was he crazy? Do you think he was a lunatic?' The paper
boy's voice dropped suddenly with doubt. 'Leo? Or not?'

But Leo would not answer him. Leo had run a night café for fourteen   96
years, and he held himself to be a critic of craziness. There were the town

characters and also the transients who roamed in from the night. He knew the manias of all of them. But he did not want to satisfy the questions of the waiting child. He tightened his pale face and was silent.

So the boy pulled down the right flap of his helmet and as he turned to leave he made the only comment that seemed safe to him, the only remark that could not be laughed down and despised: 97

'He sure has done a lot of traveling.'   98

Meaning and Idea

1. What does the story attempt to define?

2. How old is the boy in this story? What does he do? Approximately what area of the country is the setting for this story? How do you know?

3. What is the man's "science"? Is it really an exact measure of things? Look at the line where he says the woman was his wife for "one year, nine months, three days, and two nights." Does that exactitude derive from scientific thought or from something else?

4. Has the man ever really given up his love for his wife? Where does he state a specific answer to that question? Do you know the answer before he says it? How?

5. Why does the man choose to tell this story to the boy rather than to the other adult patrons in the café? Does he really "love" the boy? Why does he tell him he does?

Language, Form, Structure

1. How would you characterize the boy's attitude toward the man? How does it serve the definition being formulated?

2. Why is the name of the man's wife "immaterial"? If he loved her so deeply, why wouldn't he say her name? What is the effect of that omission on the definition?

3. How does McCullers use process analysis to develop the definition in this story? In the process of love, how is "A tree. A rock. A cloud." the correct starting point?

4. What purpose does Leo serve in this story? What is his attitude toward the man? How does it serve as a contrast to the man? How does that contrast contribute to the definition?

5. Look up and define the following words from the story; then use each one in an original sentence: scowled; sidled; transient; floozie; undertone; immaterial; mania; tremulous.

Ideas for Writing

1. Write your own definition of *love,* arranging the definition in three stages: the beginning point of love, the point at which you know for sure, the point at which you are satisfied.

2. Write a definition for *loneliness.* Use experience as the main basis for your definition; in other words, try to avoid abstraction.

3. McCullers's great strength as a writer is her ability to evoke a rich human sensibility, to treat emotionally fragile people who are lonely and love-starved, and to honor individualism and sensitivity. To what degree does "A Tree. A Rock. A Cloud." support that judgment? In your essay response, make specific references to the text.

Femininity

Susan Brownmiller

Susan Brownmiller began her writing career as a journalist for the *Village Voice* and *Newsweek*. Born in 1935 in Brooklyn, New York, she was educated at Cornell and at the Jefferson School of Social Science. Her book *Against Our Will: Men, Women, & Rape* (1975) explores the women's movement and male-female relations. She founded Women Against Pornography in the late 1970s.

In this selection from *Femininity* (1984), Brownmiller examines the biological and cultural origins of her topic as she attempts to define the term and provide a frame for understanding it. In so doing, she illuminates both her theme and her approach.

We had a game in our house called "setting the table" and I was Mother's helper. Forks to the left of the plate, knives and spoons to the right. Placing the cutlery neatly, as I recall, was one of my first duties, and the event was alive with meaning. When a knife or a fork dropped to the floor, that meant a man was unexpectedly coming to dinner. A falling spoon announced the surprise arrival of a female guest. No matter that these visitors never arrived on cue, I had learned a rule of gender identification. Men were straight-edged, sharply pronged and formidable, women were softly curved and held the food in a rounded well. It made perfect sense, like the division of pink and blue that I saw in babies, an orderly way of viewing the world. Daddy, who was gone all day at work and who loved to putter at home with his pipe, tobacco and tool chest, was knife and fork. Mommy and Grandma, with their ample proportions and pots and pans, were grownup soup spoons, large and capacious. And I was a teaspoon, small and slender, easy to hold and just right for pudding, my favorite dessert.

Being good at what was expected of me was one of my earliest projects, for not only was I rewarded, as most children are, for doing things right, but excellence gave pride and stability to my childhood existence. Girls were different from boys, and the expression of that difference seemed mine to make clear. Did my loving, anxious mother, who dressed me in white organdy pinafores and Mary Janes and who cried hot tears when I got them dirty, give me my first instruction? Of course. Did my doting aunts and uncles with their gifts of pretty dolls and miniature tea sets add to my education? Of course. But even without the appropriate toys and clothes, lessons in the art of being feminine lay all around me and I absorbed them all: the fairy tales that were read to me at night, the brightly colored advertisements I pored over in magazines before I learned to decipher the words, the movies I saw, the comic books I hoarded, the radio soap operas I happily followed whenever I had to stay in bed with a cold. I loved being a little girl, or rather I loved being a fairy princess, for that was who I thought I was.

As I passed through a stormy adolescence to a stormy maturity, femininity   3
increasingly became an exasperation, a brilliant, subtle esthetic that was baf-
flingly inconsistent at the same time that it was minutely, demandingly concrete,
a rigid code of appearance and behavior defined by do's and don't-do's that
went against my rebellious grain. Femininity was a challenge thrown down to
the female sex, a challenge no proud, self-respecting young woman could afford
to ignore, particularly one with enormous ambition that she nursed in secret, alternately feeding or starving its inchoate life in tremendous confusion.

"Don't lose your femininity" and "Isn't it remarkable how she manages to   4
retain her femininity?" had terrifying implications. They spoke of a bottom-line
failure so irreversible that nothing else mattered. The pinball machine had registered "tilt," the game had been called. Disqualification was marked on the forehead of a woman whose femininity was lost. No records would be entered in her
name, for she had destroyed her birthright in her wretched, ungainly effort to
imitate a man. She walked in limbo, this hapless creature, and it occurred to me
that one day I might see her when I looked in the mirror. If the danger was so
palpable that warning notices were freely posted, wasn't it possible that the
small bundle of resentments I carried around in secret might spill out and place
the mark on my own forehead? Whatever quarrels with femininity I had I kept to
myself; whatever handicaps femininity imposed, they were mine to deal with
alone, for there was no women's movement to ask the tough questions, or to
brazenly disregard the rules.

Femininity, in essence, is a romantic sentiment, a nostalgic tradition of im-   5
posed limitations. Even as it hurries forward in the 1980s, putting on lipstick and
high heels to appear well dressed, it trips on the ruffled petticoats and hoop-
skirts of an era gone by. Invariably and necessarily, femininity is something that
women had more of in the past, not only in the historic past of prior generations,
but in each woman's personal past as well—in the virginal innocence that is replaced by knowledge, in the dewy cheek that is coarsened by age, in the "inherent nature" that a woman seems to misplace so forgetfully whenever she steps
out of bounds. Why should this be so? The XX chromosomal message has not
been scrambled, the estrogen-dominated hormonal balance is generally as biology intended, the reproductive organs, whatever use one has made of them, are
usually in place, the breasts of whatever size are most often where they should
be. But clearly, biological femaleness is not enough.

Femininity always demands more. It must constantly reassure its audience   6
by a willing demonstration of difference, even when one does not exist in nature, or it must seize and embrace a natural variation and compose a rhapsodic
symphony upon the notes. Suppose one doesn't care to, has other things on her
mind, is clumsy or tone-deaf despite the best instruction and training? To fail at
the feminine difference is to appear not to care about men, and to risk the loss of
their attention and approval. To be insufficiently feminine is viewed as a failure
in core sexual identity, or as a failure to care sufficiently about oneself, for a
woman found wanting will be appraised (and will appraise herself) as mannish
or neutered or simply unattractive, as men have defined these terms.

We are talking, admittedly, about an exquisite esthetic. Enormous pleasure can be extracted from feminine pursuits as a creative outlet or purely as relaxation; indeed, indulgence for the sake of fun, or art, or attention, is among femininity's great joys. But the chief attraction (and the central paradox, as well) is the competitive edge that femininity seems to promise in the unending struggle to survive, and perhaps to triumph. The world smiles favorably on the feminine woman: it extends little courtesies and minor privilege. Yet the nature of this competitive edge is ironic, at best, for one works at femininity by accepting restrictions, by limiting one's sights, by choosing an indirect route, by scattering concentration and not giving one's all as a man would to his own, certifiably masculine, interests. It does not require a great leap of imagination for a woman to understand the feminine principle as a grand collection of compromises, large and small, that she simply must make in order to render herself a successful woman. If she has difficulty in satisfying femininity's demands, if its illusions go against her grain, or if she is criticized for her shortcomings and imperfections, the more she will see femininity as a desperate strategy of appeasement, a strategy she may not have the wish or the courage to abandon, for failure looms in either direction.

It is fashionable in some quarters to describe the feminine and masculine principles as polar ends of the human continuum, and to sagely profess that both polarities exist in all people. Sun and moon, yin and yang, soft and hard, active and passive, etcetera, may indeed be opposites, but a linear continuum does not illuminate the problem. (Femininity, in all its contrivances, is a very active endeavor.)

What, then, is the basic distinction? The masculine principle is better understood as a driving ethos of superiority designed to inspire straightforward, confident success, while the feminine principle is composed of vulnerability, the need for protection, the formalities of compliance and the avoidance of conflict—in short, an appeal of dependence and good will that gives the masculine principle its romantic validity and its admiring applause.

Femininity pleases men because it makes them appear more masculine by contrast; and, in truth, conferring an extra portion of unearned gender distinction on men, and unchallenged space in which to breathe freely and feel stronger, wiser, more competent, is femininity's special gift. One could say that masculinity is often an effort to please women, but masculinity is known to please by displays of mastery and competence while femininity pleases by suggesting that these concerns, except in small matters, are beyond its intent. Whimsy, unpredictability and patterns of thinking and behavior that are dominated by emotion, such as tearful expressions of sentiment and fear, are thought to be feminine precisely because they lie outside the established route to success.

If in the beginnings of history the feminine woman was defined by her physical dependency, her inability for reasons of reproductive biology to triumph over the forces of nature that were the tests of masculine strength and power, today she reflects both an economic and emotional dependency that is still considered "natural," romantic and attractive. After an unsettling fifteen years in which many basic assumptions about the sexes were challenged, the economic disparity did not disappear. Large numbers of women—those with small children, those left high and dry after a mid-life divorce—need financial support. But even those who earn their own living share a universal need for connectedness (call it love, if you wish). As unprecedented numbers of men abandon their sexual interest in women, others, sensing opportunity, choose to demonstrate their interest through variety and a change in partners. A sociological fact of the 1980s is that female competition for two scarce resources—men and jobs—is especially fierce.

So it is not surprising that we are currently witnessing a renewed interest 12 in femininity and an unabashed indulgence in feminine pursuits. Femininity serves to reassure men that women need them and care about them enormously. By incorporating the decorative and the frivolous into its definition of style, femininity functions as an effective antidote to the unrelieved seriousness, the pressure of making one's way in a harsh, difficult world. In its mandate to avoid direct confrontation and to smooth over the fissures of conflict, femininity operates as a value system of niceness, a code of thoughtfulness and sensitivity that in modern society is sadly in short supply.

There is no reason to deny that indulgence in the art of feminine illusion can 13 be reassuring to a woman, if she happens to be good at it. As sexuality undergoes some dizzying revisions, evidence that one is a woman "at heart" (the inquisitor's question) is not without worth. Since an answer of sorts may be furnished by piling on additional documentation, affirmation can arise from such identifiable but trivial feminine activities as buying a new eyeliner, experimenting with the latest shade of nail color, or bursting into tears at the outcome of a popular romance novel. Is there anything destructive in this? Time and cost factors, a deflection of energy and an absorption in fakery spring quickly to mind, and they need to be balanced, as in a ledger book, against the affirming advantage.

Meaning and Idea

1. What is Brownmiller's definition of femininity? Discuss how she defines it.

2. How does Brownmiller use history to explore her subject? What bearing does that history have on today's quest for femininity?

3. What value does femininity have for men, according to the writer?

4. How does Brownmiller ultimately feel about femininity? What is her thesis? Is this thesis surprising? Why?

Language, Form, Structure

1. In the first part of the essay, Brownmiller often uses vivid descriptions of her childhood to show how she was instructed in the ways of femininity. The table-setting game, the white organdy pinafores, the Mary Janes, and

other elements lead up to her statement that it seems "biological femaleness is not enough." What is the effect of drawing on these personal examples of behavior?

2. What rhetorical strategies does the writer use to build her definition?

3. Brownmiller's ultimate position in the essay is one of tolerance and even appreciation for femininity. How convincingly does she develop this view? What support does she offer? Cite particular passages.

4. Define the following words and use each one in a sentence: formidable; capacious; esthetic; inchoate; palpable; rhapsodic; continuum; appeasement; ethos; whimsy; frivolous; fissures.

Ideas for Writing

1. Look back into your own past and think about the first memories you have of masculinity or femininity. Use these memories as an introduction to create an essay about where you stand on these issues today and why.

2. How should *they* act, and why do you think so? Write a definition essay in which you clarify the parameters that you feel the opposite gender *should* fulfill, and in so doing build to a definition of the opposite sex.

3. Write an essay in which you weigh the success of Brownmiller's essay. How does Brownmiller use complexities and contradictions?

Claiming the Self: The Cripple as American Man

Leonard Kriegel

Leonard Kriegel (1933–) earned his B.A. from Hunter College and his Ph.D from New York University; for many years he served on the English faculty of The City College of the City University of New York. His work has appeared in *Best American Essays* and in *The O'Henry Awards Prize Stories*. Recipient of both the Guggenheim and Rockefeller Fellowships, Kriegel lives and works in New York.

In "Claiming the Self," Kriegel considers his own experience as a "cripple" (a word he defiantly insists on) and a man, and the relation between the two.

I am not a physician; I am not a psychologist; I am not a sociologist; indeed, I do not work in any aspect of health care. But I am a man who has lived all but eleven of his years here on earth as a cripple, a word I prefer to the euphemistic "handicapped" or "disabled," each of which does little more than further society's illusions about illness and accident and the effects of illness and accident. For to be "disabled" or "handicapped" is to deny oneself the rage, anger, and pride of having managed to survive as a cripple in America. If I know nothing else, I know that I have endured—and I know the price I have paid for that endurance.

As a writer and as a teacher of literature, I believe that the essence of what we like to call the human condition is each individual's struggle to claim a self, to create an *I* stamped with his own distinct individuality. This affirmation of the self is what we seek in biography and autobiography. It may exist beyond our capacity to create it, beyond our habits and virtues and will—but not beyond our need. I have never met a man or woman who did not want to stake a claim to an identifiable *I*.

Of course, it is a tentative claim, existing within the confines of a world in which we are never truly at home. Our capacities as individuals are always being tested. Everywhere we go, we seek to affirm the separate self, the identifiable *I* who possesses the strength and courage to withstand whatever tests lie in wait. Although it may be immodest to state it openly, the truth is that no one has a greater right to claim that *I* than a man who has wrested his sense of a separate identity from the very condition that threatened to declare his life as a man at an end. And however self-conscious and embarrassed I am about saying it, no one has a better right to claim that his sense of himself as a man has been seized from adversity than the cripple does.

Cripples are forced to affirm their existence and claim selfhood by pushing beyond those structures and categories their condition has created. On one level, this is what all men and women try to do. But in a culture that places such importance on the physical—however uncomfortable it may be with the actual body—the cripple's insistence on getting beyond the restrictions imposed by physical limitations is the kind of violent joining together of forces pulling in opposite directions that is characteristic of modern life.

It would be the most absurd nonsense to suggest that the cripple is envied by other Americans seeking to claim the *I*. No one *wants* to find himself the victim of disease or accident—no one, at least, who is rational. Anyone contemplating the prospect of spending the rest of his life in a wheelchair would exchange that fate for a normal pair of legs without a moment's hesitation. Ask me to give up the most visible symbols of being a cripple—in my case, the braces and crutches on which I walk—and I will jump at the chance. To insist on our capacity, to be willing to face the everyday risks that a cripple must confront simply to meet the world, to enjoy the sense of triumph that an *earned* mobility bestows—we can accept all this and yet hunger after what we lack. We can believe in our capacity to face whatever has to be faced; we can assume that we have paid a price for the existence we claim that others might not have been able to pay; we can think of ourselves as having confronted our fate even with such grandiose metaphors as Jacob wrestling with his angel. The one thing cripples cannot afford to do is to assume the luxury of lying to themselves.

Cripples are second-class citizens only because they are conscious of nothing so much as of the barriers the outside world places in their way. My hungers are invariably personal; the joys not tasted are joys not tasted *by me*. However simplistic my desires may seem to others, their significance is multiplied a thousand times by an imagination that knows what they are but has not been able to possess them. However absurd and childish they are as desires, I reach out and touch them in my imagination alone. And they are not abstract. They are available to any of those the distinguished social psychologist Erving Goffman labeled the "normals." That *they* should be able to touch them so easily, so unconsciously, infuriates me. For my life as a cripple tells me that a man should earn the self he claims. However successful I may be in the eyes of the world—and I certainly am, to use a phrase that should be burned out of the vocabulary, a man who has "overcome his handicap"—I am always measuring what I have against what I want. How do I tell the normals that I still dream about being able to run on the beach with my young sons (both of them long since grown adults), that I sometimes lie awake at night thinking about swinging a baseball bat again, that even as I visualize what I would do were I suddenly given the legs of a normal I know that what I want to do would seem stupid and banal in his normal eyes? I want to kick a football, jump rope, ride a bike, climb a mountain—not a mountain as metaphor but a real honest-to-god mountain—ride a horse. I want to make love differently; I want to drive differently; I want to know my sons differently. In short, I want to know the world as the normal is privileged to know it.

These are not great feats, not even for the imagination to conjure up. They do not call for special skills or training. But they are what *I* want—what I have never tasted or else tasted so long ago that the memories have become one with the desire, locked in a permanent embrace. And such memories frame all that is absent from my life.

People struggle not only to define themselves but to avoid being defined by others. But to be a cripple is to learn that one can be defined from outside. Our complaint against society is not that it ignores our presence but that it ignores our reality, our sense of ourselves as humans brave enough to capture our destinies against odds that are formidable. Here is where the cripple and society war with each other. If we were satisfied to be held up for compassion, to be infantilized on telethons, we would discover that this America has a great deal of time for us, a great deal of room for us in a heart open to praise for its own generosity. We are not, like Ellison's black man, invisible in America. But the outline of the shadow we cast has been created not by us but by those who will find a way to see what they want to see rather than what is there. In what we call literature, as well as in popular culture, we are what others make of us. In literature as demonic as Shakespeare's Richard III or as wooden as Lawrence's Clifford Chatterley, on television as bathetic as the stream of smiling children paraded before our eyes as if their palsy were Jerry Lewis's reason for living, what we invariably discover is that our true selves, our own inner lives, have been auctioned off so that we can be palatable rather than real. We can serve the world as victim or demon, the object of its charity or its terror. But the only thing we can be certain of is that the world would prefer to turn a blind eye and a deaf ear to our real selves—and that it will do precisely that until we impose those selves on the world.

Years ago, this recognition led me to write an essay entitled "Uncle Tom and Tiny Tim: Some Reflections on the Cripple as Negro." But the situation of the cripple in American society today seems to me considerably less grim than I described it in 1969. Tiny Tim is not the only image the cripple calls forth. The self wrested from adversity is a far more attractive image to be offered to society and ourselves.

And yet, society is more than a bit dubious about that image's validity. For if it honors what it sees as our suffering, it retreats before our need to define our inner lives, to speak of who and what we are. Society continues to need the ability to define us if it is to be comfortable with us. In its own eyes, it is society that defines our authenticity. I remember that when I returned at the age of thirteen from a two-year rehabilitation stay in a state home, my mother was immediately asked by the neighborhood chairman of the March of Dimes campaign (this was in 1946, before the introduction of the Salk vaccine) to go from door to door to collect in the campaign's annual fund drive. It seemed somehow natural: My mother possessed a kind of subaltern authenticity, for she was the mother of a cripple. Her presence at the door was supposed to remind our normal neighbors that their charity had been *earned.* Any other individual going from door to door would not have seemed as believable.

And the truth is that my mother *was* more effective, for she, along with our neighbors, assumed her authenticity. For the next forty years, long after the disease that had crippled me had been wiped out as a threat by the development of the Salk and Sabin vaccines, my mother made her annual door-to-door pilgrimage for the March of Dimes. Her "success" as a collector of charity was directly attributable to the sense our neighbors had that she was "the genuine article." Indeed, the kind of fund-raising she was doing mixes the comic and the bathetic, and it remains characteristic of efforts of such groups as the Shriners to support hospitals. The Shriners sponsor an annual all-star college football game that displays the salable talents of college athletes while giving everyone—sponsors, hospital executives, fans, professional football scouts, and players—a substantial charity fix. "Let strong legs run so that weak legs can walk" is the game's slogan. I can think of no better illustration of how society defines cripples as their condition. And it does this through the simple strategy of remaining purposely oblivious to the feelings it inspires in them. A child who thinks of himself or herself as an object for the charity of others has been defined as dependent. Only a considerable act of defiance can possibly save that child from the fate of being permanently dependent. In January, 1968, vacationing in Florida with my wife and two small children, I drove past a large shopping center. Strung out in huge black letters against a white marquee was a sign: "Help Cripple Kids! See Stalin's Limousine! Donation: $1.00."

Now, this is the kind of material Nathanael West or Woody Allen might have done justice to, for it is genuinely funny, a most human denial of the human. But it is also a definition of cripples from outside, one that remains the most formidable obstacle in their path as they push toward defining the self. They want to realize all that they can make out of their situation. Society, in turn, wants them to make it feel good. Even the act of reaching out for a real self is a challenge to what society tells cripples is their proper due. Their task is not only to claim a self but also to refuse to allow their pain to be marketed. The authenticity they must insist on is one that each person alone can create—not the cripple's nurses, not the doctors, not the teachers, not the social workers. For no one knows what his existence costs him as he does. No one has lived with the intimacy of his fears as he has. And no one understands better that the self's reality can be taken from the self's resistance. Better if Stalin's limo were laughed out of existence. Better if "Jerry's kids" forced Jerry to understand the immense psychological destructiveness of his telethons. Better if hospitals were viewed as a right to be paid for, not by charity, but by a rational society.

Part of me still hungers to perform those banal tasks that define the normal for all of us. But another part of me—perhaps the braver part—insists that the mark of a man is to acknowledge that he has been formed by the very accidents that have made him what he is. Perhaps the task of those of us who are crippled is to face honestly what the normal can choose to ignore, to take a chance on a conscious existence pulled from the remnants of disease or accident. Our condition is intense, our isolation massive. Society views us as both pariah and victim. We are pitied, shunned, labeled, classified, analyzed, and categorized. We are packed in the spiritual ice of a sanitized society in the hope that we can somehow be dealt with in some even more sanitized society of the future. Society will *permit* us anything, except the right to be what we can become. And yet without that right we cannot extricate ourselves from the role of supplicants for society's largesse.

If society is uncomfortable with us, it is not uncomfortable with what it can do for us. That shopping center sign was created for the same audience at whose doors my mother knocked. Those Jerry Lewis telethons are responded to by men and women who believe they are deeply concerned with "Jerry's kids." Those well-meaning Shriners in their silly hats interviewed at halftime do not intend to tamper with the cripple's need to establish a self. Accident and disease bring out the charitable in other men. They also bring out the sanctimonious and self-righteous in other men. What cripples discover they share is not a physical condition—the differences among them are far more pronounced than the differences between white and black, Jew and Gentile, German and Italian—so much as it is the experience of having been categorized by the normal world. For the normals, we possess a collective presence. For if cripples prove themselves capable of defining their own lives, then what excuse can normals offer for their failure? If cripples break with the restrictions placed upon their existence and insist that they will be what they have earned the right to be, then where does that leave the normals?

I do not wish to suggest that anyone is "better" for having suffered disease or disability. Nonsense does not cease being nonsense when it is cloaked in metaphysics or theology. All I mean is that cripples have no choice but to attempt to establish the terms and the boundaries of their existence, and that they should recognize that in choosing to do this they are going to offend those normals who have an interest in cripples remaining what they want to perceive. Only by turning stigma into strength can cripples avoid the categorization the normal world insists on thrusting upon them. "This is where I am because here is where I have placed myself." Only through scrupulous self-scrutiny can we hold up the ragged ends of our own existence and insist that the normals match our honesty with their own. In a mendacious time, during which what it really takes to become an authentic self has been buried beneath one or another variation on doing one's own thing, the cripple who chooses to be honest can at least keep faith with his wound.

Having already witnessed the power of chance and accident, cripples know that if the reconciliation of their needs with the world's actualities can lead to maturity, it can also lead to madness and despair and even suicide. Under the best of circumstances, maturity is not permanent. But when its necessity is dictated by disease or accident it is not only temporary, it is also what one is condemned to live with. Indeed, it can be said of cripples that they are condemned to adulthood. Every step one takes, every breath one draws, every time one makes love, crosses a street, drives a car, one lives out the terms of the adult's argument with responsibility for the self. The image of what one was or could have been smashes against the reality of what one is. And if one has accepted the rules of the game, then the sin of pride beckons—pride in performance, pride in one's capacity.

For there is a point at which the living on an everyday basis with that internal enemy who, as Ernest Becker wrote, unremittingly "threatens danger" leads to a certain haughtiness, perhaps even to a barely concealed sense of superiority to normals who have not been called upon to prove their selfhood. Our dirty little secret is the pride we may feel in a performance designed to impose the self on the world. For someone who has matched his or her will against possible destruction, the normal's frame of reference can seem comic, even banal, in the rhetoric it employs and the strategies it assumes. One who lives his daily life on intimate terms with pain can only listen in amazement to a sportscaster praising the courage of an athlete earning a great deal of money on enduring his "aching" knees.

But it is always within the power of the normals to diminish the cripples' sense of their own reality. We are, after all, trapped by the accoutrements of our existence. An individual may choose to create an authentic self out of defiance of accident or disease, but he cannot remake the truth of his condition. It is what it is. No matter what demands he makes upon himself, dead legs do not run and blind eyes do not see. The cripple can make of his injury an acquisition; he can transform his handicap into a symbol of endurance; he can formulate his very existence as an act of defiance. But he cannot change what has happened to him. He must recognize that his life is to be different in its essentials from the life of the normal person. He has learned to look on stigmatization itself as something he has earned. He comes to recognize that he has truly been set apart.

The process of recognition has been beautifully voiced in a poem by Karl Shapiro. The poem is about a soldier's loss of his leg during the Second World War. At first the soldier struggles to accept the loss of part of his body. The soldier discovers that he must learn to adapt to life without the leg even as the life he possesses is transformed into an act of defiance of the loss.

> Later, as if deliberately, his fingers
> Begin to explore the stump. He learns
>   shape
> That is comfortable and tucked in
>   like a sock.
> This has a sense of humor, this can
>   despise
> The finest surgical limb, the dignity
>   of limping,
> The nonsense of wheelchairs. Now he
>   smiles to the wall:
> The Amputation becomes an acquisition.

But the soldier in "The Leg" will ultimately discover that even such hard-won acquisitions can be taken away by the society that insists on defining who he is, a society that will remain intent on shrinking his reality by insisting on its right to define the limits of his space, the boundaries of his quest for a self. And the effort to live honestly will pinch his sense of his own courage and test his ability to live on his own terms. For what we remember remains embedded in what we are—and in what we once were.

Meaning and Idea

1. What reasons does Kriegel give for preferring the word *cripple* to the more socially acceptable *handicapped* (or, more recently, *differently abled*)?

2. Explain Kriegel's statement, "The only thing cripples cannot afford to do is assume the luxury of lying to themselves." Why does he choose the term *luxury?*

3. What does Kriegel mean when he says that "no one has a better right to claim that his sense of himself has been seized from adversity than the cripple does"?

4. Why is Kriegel's mother so successful in raising money for the March of Dimes? How does Kriegel react to this?

5. Why does Kriegel characterize Jerry Lewis's telethons as being responsible for an "immense psychological destructiveness"?

6. In the poem, what is the "shape" that the soldier discovers? How is that shape important in converting the "Amputation" into an "acquisition"?

Language, Form, Structure

1. Despite his careful arguments and psychological and philosophical vocabulary, Kriegel's essay is full of emotions. List instances where Kriegel's emotions become clear and comment on how those emotions make the essay more affecting, more persuasive, or more illuminating.

2. Why does Kriegel italicize the word *earned* in paragraph 5?

3. How does Kriegel use the word *define* in this essay? What power does the ability to define carry? What is Kriegel trying to define or redefine?

4. Define the following words and then choose five of them and use each one in an original sentence: euphemism; tentative; immodest; grandiose; palsy; palatable; subaltern; marquee; sanctimonious; mendacious; accoutrement.

Ideas for Writing

1. In a short piece explore your own personal reactions to this essay. How do Kriegel's arguments leave you feeling?

2. Compare a common euphemism with the word that it is meant to replace. Write an essay about the two words, noting both what is lost in choosing to use the euphemism and what is gained.

3. Write an essay in which you analyze Kriegel's use of the term *normals* to refer to those who retain full use of the body. What effect on his reader is he trying to accomplish by adding this definition to his essay?

The Naked and the Nude

Robert Graves

Robert Graves, born in 1895 near London, gained a reputation as a novelist, poet, and literary critic. Graves saw considerable action as a member of the Royal Welsh Fusiliers in World War I, during which time he befriended the poet Siegfried Sassoon. After the war, he studied at Oxford, where he later taught. Graves's novel *I, Claudius* (1934) is familiar to British and American television audiences as the basis for a critically acclaimed public television series. His war memoir *Good-bye to All That* (1929) is a haunting chronicle of the physical and social destruction of World War I. *The White Goddess* (1948), Graves's "historical grammar of poetic myth," delves into the matriarchal basis of history and artistic creation. Graves died in 1985.

In reading Graves's "The Naked and the Nude" pay special attention to the ways in which the poet separates, then synthesizes, the denotative and connotative values of two seemingly similar words.

*F*or me, the naked and the nude
(By lexicographers construed
As synonyms that should express
The same deficiency of dress
Or shelter) stand as wide apart   5
As love from lies, or truth from art.

Lovers without reproach will gaze
On bodies naked and ablaze;
The hippocratic eye will see
In nakedness, anatomy;   10
And naked shines the Goddess when
She mounts her lion among men.

The nude are bold, the nude are sly
To hold each treasonable eye.
While draping by a showman's trick   15
Their dishabille in rhetoric,
They grin a mock-religious grin
Of scorn at those of naked skin.

The naked, therefore, who compete
Against the nude may know defeat;
Yet when they both together tread   20
The briary pastures of the dead,
By Gorgons with long whips pursued,
How naked go the sometime nude!

Meaning and Idea

1. Check a dictionary to find the denotation of the word *naked*. What, according to Graves, does the word *naked* connote? What details does he offer to show what he means by the word? What do lines 11–12 mean?

2. What is the denotation of the word *nude?* What images support the connotation Graves is trying to present for the word?

3. How do the two compare? Explain the last stanza in your own words.

Language, Form, Structure

1. The first stanza of the poem establishes Graves's main point. What is that point? What is the purpose of the statement in parentheses in lines 2–5? Why is the language there so much more formal and scholarly than the language in the rest of the stanza? What in general is the tone of the poem?

2. Graves's definitions progress through a series of images. Which images are the most vivid? Why does he use exemplification to define the words? How does the repetition of the words *naked* and *nude* serve as a transitional device? What other transitional devices are apparent?

3. In stanza 2 Graves explains what he means by *naked,* and in stanza 3 what he means by *nude.* Then in stanza 4 he presents the two words together. How do you think this organizational pattern serves the meaning of the poem? Why does he choose comparison and contrast as a strategy for defining the words? What is the surprise in the last line?

4. What are the "briary pastures of the dead"? What is Graves's purpose in using the phrase "dishabille in rhetoric"? Check your dictionary for the meanings of the following words: lexicographers; deficiency; hippocratic; Gorgon.

Ideas for Writing

1. Write a paragraph in which you define the words *naked* and *nude* with images based on your own connotations for the words.

2. Select any two synonyms that have similar denotations but different connotations and write an essay in which you explore the definitions of those words. Provide details in order to make your meanings of the words clear.

3. Write a paragraph in which you comment upon Graves's use of language in this poem. Consider, for example, his choice of words. Why does he select *deficiency* (line 4) instead of *lack? Gaze* (7) instead of *stare? Mount* (12) instead of *climb? Bold* instead of *daring* or *brave?* You might also comment on Graves's use of nouns and verbs, his use of classical references (lines 11–12 and 24), and his use of rhyme, rhythm, and meter.

A Politician

e. e. cummings

Born in Cambridge, Massachusetts, in 1894, e.e. cummings took his B.A. and M.A. degrees at Harvard, lived in Paris in the 1920s, and then settled in New York's bohemian Greenwich Village. His travels spurred him to write the semifictional, semisociological *The Enormous Room* (1922) and *Eimi* (1933). He is best known, however, for his poetry, for his whimsical play with typography and syntax, as well as for his near abhorrence of capital letters (he did not use capitals even for his name). He died in New Hampshire in 1962.

Notice how in this very brief poem cummings manages to evoke various levels of meaning.

a politician is an arse upon
which everyone has sat except a man

Meaning and Idea

1. What is an *arse?* Why does cummings choose this spelling and pronunciation over the more common one?

2. What can you say about the poet's attitude toward politicians? Do his feelings seem to be general or specific? Explain.

Language, Form, Structure

1. What are the various meanings of the word *arse* in this poem? Explain how "everyone" can have sat on this arse, but not one man has. What various levels of meaning of *man* are implied?

2. Explain the metaphorical structure of this definition.

Ideas for Writing

1. Write an essay in which you define the word *politician.* Draw on your personal experiences or on what you have read or observed about politicians. Be specific.

2. Select a profession and write a series of two-line definitions of it, following cummings's plan.

3. Write a few paragraphs in which you respond to the seeming simplicity of cummings's statement. Do you think this definition is sufficient? Do you think it is a poem? Explain your responses.

I Want a Wife

Judy Brady

Born in 1937 in San Francisco, Judy Brady attended the University of Iowa, graduating with a bachelor's degree in painting in 1962. A longtime activist in progressive social movements, Brady credits the women's liberation movement of the 1960s with raising her awareness of political issues and women's rights. Aside from numerous magazine articles, Brady has edited *1 in 3: Women with Cancer Confront an Epidemic,* an account of the politics of cancer motivated by her own struggle with the disease. Brady still lives in San Francisco and earns her living as a secretary.

"I Want a Wife" was first published in the inaugural issue of *Ms.* magazine and has been reprinted frequently since that time. In 1991 it was reprinted as "Why I [Still] Want a Wife." Written after 11 years of marriage but before her own separation, Brady's definition of *wife* is that of one who has long lived that role.

I belong to that classification of people known as wives. I am A Wife. And, not altogether incidentally, I am a mother.

Not too long ago a male friend of mine appeared on the scene fresh from a recent divorce. He had one child, who is, of course, with his ex-wife. He is looking for another wife. As I thought about him while I was ironing one evening, it suddenly occurred to me that I, too, would like to have a wife. Why do I want a wife?

I would like to go back to school so that I can become economically independent, support myself, and, if need be, support those dependent upon me. I want a wife who will work and send me to school. And while I am going to school I want a wife to take care of my children. I want a wife to keep track of the children's doctor and dentist appointments. And to keep track of mine, too. I want a wife to make sure my children eat properly and are kept clean. I want a wife who will wash the children's clothes and keep them mended. I want a wife who is a good nurturant attendant to my children, who arranges for their schooling, makes sure that they have an adequate social life with their peers, takes them to the park, the zoo, etc. I want a wife who takes care of the children when they are sick, a wife who arranges to be around when the children need special care, because, of course, I cannot miss classes at school. My wife must arrange to lose time at work and not lose the job. It may mean a small cut in my wife's income from time to time, but I guess I can tolerate that. Needless to say, my wife will arrange and pay for the care of the children while my wife is working.

I want a wife who will take care of *my* physical needs. I want a wife who will keep my house clean. A wife who will pick up after my children, a wife who will pick up after me. I want a wife who will keep my clothes clean, ironed, mended, replaced when need be, and who will see to it that my personal things are kept in their proper place so that I can find what I need the minute I need it. I want a wife who cooks the meals, a wife who is a *good* cook. I want a wife who will plan the menus, do the necessary grocery shopping, prepare the meals, serve them pleasantly, and then do the cleaning up while I do my studying. I want a wife who will care for me when I am sick and sympathize with my pain and loss of time from school. I want a wife to go along when our family takes a vacation so that someone can continue to care for me and my children when I need a rest and change of scene.

I want a wife who will not bother me with rambling complaints about a wife's duties. But I want a wife who will listen to me when I feel the need to explain a rather difficult point I have come across in my course of studies. And I want a wife who will type my papers for me when I have written them.   5

I want a wife who will take care of the details of my social life. When my wife and I are invited out by friends, I want a wife who will take care of the babysitting arrangements. When I meet people at school that I like and want to entertain, I want a wife who will have the house clean, will prepare a special meal, serve it to me and my friends, and not interrupt when I talk about things that interest me and my friends. I want a wife who will have arranged that the children are fed and ready for bed before my guests arrive so that the children do not bother us. I want a wife who takes care of the needs of my guests so that they feel comfortable, who makes sure that they have an ashtray, that they are passed the hors d'oeuvres, that they are offered a second helping of the food, that their wine glasses are replenished when necessary, that their coffee is served to them as they like it. And I want a wife who knows that sometimes I need a night out by myself.   6

I want a wife who is sensitive to my sexual needs, a wife who makes love passionately and eagerly when I feel like it, a wife who makes sure that I am satisfied. And, of course, I want a wife who will not demand sexual attention when I am not in the mood for it. I want a wife who assumes the complete responsibility for birth control, because I do not want more children. I want a wife who will remain sexually faithful to me so that I do not have to clutter up my intellectual life with jealousies. And I want a wife who understands that *my* sexual needs may entail more than strict adherence to monogamy. I must, after all, be able to relate to people as fully as possible.   7

If, by chance, I find another person more suitable as a wife than the wife I already have, I want the liberty to replace my present wife with another one. Naturally, I will expect a fresh, new life; my wife will take the children and be solely responsible for them so that I am left free.   8

When I am through with school and have a job, I want my wife to quit working and remain at home so that my wife can more fully and completely take care of a wife's duties.   9

My God, who *wouldn't* want a wife?   10

Meaning and Idea

1. List some of the duties that a wife is supposed to take care of.

2. Comment on the use of italics in paragraphs 4, 7, and 10.

3. Which of the wife's needs are mentioned in the essay, and, specifically, how are they to be treated?

Language, Form, Structure

1. What kind of progression structures Brady's essay? How does the essay or the reader's response to it change as it continues?

2. Look at the last sentence again. How is this sentence different from the preceding essay? How does it relate to the rest of the piece? What would Brady have lost if she had omitted this sentence?

3. How is this essay an argument? What is its thesis? What is its supporting evidence?

4. Define the following words and use each one in a sentence: nurturant; hors d'oeuvres; replenished; adherence; monogamy.

Ideas for Writing

1. Write an argumentative essay using many repetitions of the same key word or phrase. You might choose to use irony, as Brady does, but you might also choose to use your repetitions to add gravity, sorrow, or another emotion.

2. This essay was first published in 1971. Many things have changed since then. Write an essay in which you discuss the extent to which Brady's criticism is still relevant. What new problems have arisen that she does not anticipate?

3. Write an essay in which you discuss Brady's use of irony. Why is irony particularly effective for the argument Brady is making?

Poetry

Marianne Moore

Marianne Moore (1887–1972) was born near St. Louis a year before another famous American poet, T. S. Eliot, was born there. Moore and her mother later moved to Carlisle, Pennsylvania, where she attended the Metzger Institute, and then took her degree at Bryn Mawr College. She originally considered being a painter but abandoned that pursuit to try writing poetry and to teach stenography at a U.S. Indian School from 1911 to 1915. In 1918, she moved to New York City, where she worked as a tutor and as an assistant in the New York Public Library and where she became one of the most ardent Brooklyn Dodgers fans. For three years, Moore edited *The Dial,* an established literary review of the time.

"Poetry" is a classic example of Marianne Moore's straightforward style of poetry. She defines for us that most elusive of terms, effecting a synthesis of the abstract and the concrete, which she considered so vital.

I, too, dislike it: there are things that are important beyond
    all this fiddle.
Reading it, however, with a perfect contempt for it, one
    discovers in
it after all, a place for the genuine.
  Hands that can grasp, eyes
  that can dilate, hair that can rise
    if it must, these things are important not because a

high-sounding interpretation can be put upon them but
    because they are
useful. When they become so derivative as to become
    unintelligible,
the same thing may be said for all of us, that we
    do not admire what
    we cannot understand: the bat
      holding on upside down or in quest of something to

eat, elephants pushing, a wild horse taking a roll, a tireless
    wolf under
a tree, the immovable critic twitching his skin like a
    horse that feels a flea, the base-
ball fan, the statistician—
    nor is it valid
      to discriminate against 'business documents and

5

10

15

school-books'; all these phenomena are important. One
      must make a distinction
   however: when dragged into prominence by half poets,
      the result is not poetry,
  nor till the poets among us can be
    'literalists of
    the imagination'—above
      insolence and triviality and can present

for inspection, imaginary gardens with real toads in them,
      shall we have
  it. In the meantime, if you demand on the one hand,
  the raw material of poetry in
    all its rawness and
    that which is on the other hand
      genuine, then you are interested in poetry.

(line numbers: 20, 25, 30)

Meaning and Idea

1. What is the "it" of stanza 1? What is "all this fiddle"? What is "the genuine"?

2. Summarize in your own words Marianne Moore's definition of poetry. What ideal combination of elements makes up genuine poetry? How is the image "imaginary gardens with real toads in them" an example of this ideal combination?

3. What do you suppose Moore meant by "half poets"?

4. What is Moore's attitude toward critics? Do you think that she was expressing her feelings about critics in general or about one specific critic? Why?

Language, Form, Structure

1. How would you characterize Moore's poem—as essentially concrete or abstract? Why? Which is more important to Moore?

2. How is the technique of exemplification important to stanzas 2 and 3? What is exemplified in each? What examples are offered?

3. For whom did Moore intend this definition? How do you know? How does her audience affect her style here?

4. The phrases "business documents and school-books" and "literalists of the imagination" refer to writings by two of the world's greatest writers— Tolstoy and Yeats. What value do such references add to Moore's definition of poetry?

5. Be sure you understand how Moore uses the following words: dilate; derivative; quest; phenomena; insolence; triviality.

Ideas for Writing

1. Write a definition of the term *satisfaction.* Distinguish between abstract and concrete manifestations of the term, and integrate them to form your definition.

2. Write your own prose definition of *poetry.* You may use references to specific poems or poets, or you may make your definition more general in nature.

3. In the final edition of her *Collected Poems,* Moore ended this poem at the word *genuine* in line 3. What do you think of that version of the poem? Why do you think she might have first ended the poem at that point? Is it as effective as a definition (or as a poem) in that severely abridged version? Write an essay in which you compare the two versions.

The Insufficiency of Honesty

Stephen L. Carter

"To be black and an intellectual in America is to live in a box," Stephen Carter begins his most prominent book, *Reflections of an Affirmative Action Baby* (1991). A thorough and fiercely independent thinker, Carter has a reputation for taking on the orthodoxies of both the political left and the right. Born in Harlem in 1954, Carter earned a B.A. from Stanford University in 1976 and a J.D. from Yale Law School in 1979. After receiving his degree, he clerked for Supreme Court Justice Thurgood Marshall, worked for a Washington law firm, and then, in 1982, returned to Yale to teach.

Honesty and *integrity* are frequently used as if they were synonymous. Yet, Carter points out, this is far from the case. In fact, a careful definition of the two terms suggests that being one frequently conflicts with being the other.

A couple of years ago I began a university commencement address by telling the audience that I was going to talk about integrity. The crowd broke into applause. Applause! Just because they had heard the word "integrity": that's how starved for it they were. They had no idea how I was using the word, or what I was going to say about integrity, or, indeed, whether I was for it or against it. But they knew they liked the idea of talking about it.

Very well, let us consider this word "integrity." Integrity is like the weather: Everybody talks about it but nobody knows what to do about it. Integrity is that stuff that we always want more of. Some say that we need to return to the good old days when we had a lot more of it. Others say that we as a nation have never really had enough of it. Hardly anybody stops to explain exactly what we mean by it, or how we know it is a good thing, or why everybody needs to have the same amount of it. Indeed, the only trouble with integrity is that everybody who uses the word seems to mean something slightly different.

For instance, when I refer to integrity, do I mean simply "honesty"? The answer is no; although honesty is a virtue of importance, it is a different virtue from integrity. Let us, for simplicity, think of honesty as not lying; and let us further accept Sissela Bok's definition of a lie: "any intentionally deceptive message which is *stated.*" Plainly, one cannot have integrity without being honest (although, as we shall see, the matter gets complicated), but one can certainly be honest and yet have little integrity.

When I refer to integrity, I have something very specific in mind. Integrity, as I will use the term, requires three steps: discerning what is right and what is wrong; acting on what you have discerned, even at personal cost; and saying openly that you are acting on your understanding of right and wrong. The first criterion captures the idea that integrity requires a degree of moral reflectiveness. The second brings in the ideal of a person of integrity as steadfast, a quality that includes keeping one's commitments. The third reminds us that a person of integrity can be trusted.

The first point to understand about the difference between honesty and integrity is that a person may be entirely honest without ever engaging in the hard work of discernment that integrity requires: She may tell us quite truthfully what she believes without ever taking the time to figure out whether what she believes is good and right and true. The problem may be as simple as someone's foolishly saying something that hurts a friend's feelings; a few moments of thought would have revealed the likelihood of the hurt and the lack of necessity for the comment. Or the problem may be more complex, as when a man who was raised from birth in a society that preaches racism states his belief in one race's inferiority as a fact, without ever really considering that perhaps this deeply held view is wrong. Certainly the racist is being honest—he is telling us what he actually thinks—but his honesty does not add up to integrity.

Telling Everything You Know

A wonderful epigram sometimes attributed to the filmmaker Sam Goldwyn goes like this: "The most important thing in acting is honesty; once you learn to fake that, you're in." The point is that honesty can be something one *seems* to have. Without integrity, what passes for honesty often is nothing of the kind; it is fake honesty—or it is honest but irrelevant and perhaps even immoral.

Consider an example. A man who has been married for fifty years confesses to his wife on his deathbed that he was unfaithful thirty-five years earlier. The dishonesty was killing his spirit, he says. Now he has cleared his conscience and is able to die in peace.

The husband has been honest—sort of. He has certainly unburdened himself. And he has probably made his wife (soon to be his widow) quite miserable in the process, because even if she forgives him, she will not be able to remember him with quite the vivid image of love and loyalty that she had hoped for. Arranging his own emotional affairs to ease his transition to death, he has shifted to his wife the burden of confusion and pain, perhaps for the rest of her life. Moreover, he has attempted his honesty at the one time in his life when it carries no risk; acting in accordance with what you think is right and risking no loss in the process is a rather thin and unadmirable form of honesty.

Besides, even though the husband has been honest in a sense, he has now twice been unfaithful to his wife: once thirty-five years ago, when he had his affair, and again when, nearing death, he decided that his own peace of mind was more important than hers. In trying to be honest he has violated his marriage vow by acting toward his wife not with love but with naked and perhaps even cruel self-interest.

As my mother used to say, you don't have to tell people everything you know. Lying and nondisclosure, as the law often recognizes, are not the same thing. Sometimes it is actually illegal to tell what you know, as, for example, in the disclosure of certain financial information by market insiders. Or it may be unethical, as when a lawyer reveals a confidence entrusted to her by a client. It may be simple bad manners, as in the case of a gratuitous comment to a colleague on his or her attire. And it may be subject to religious punishment, as when a Roman Catholic priest breaks the seal of the confessional—an offense that carries automatic excommunication.

In all the cases just mentioned, the problem with telling everything you know is that somebody else is harmed. Harm may not be the intention, but it is certainly the effect. Honesty is most laudable when we risk harm to ourselves; it becomes a good deal less so if we instead risk harm to others when there is no gain to anyone other than ourselves. Integrity may counsel keeping our secrets in order to spare the feelings of others. Sometimes, as in the example of the wayward husband, the reason we want to tell what we know is precisely to shift our pain onto somebody else—a course of action dictated less by integrity than by self-interest. Fortunately, integrity and self-interest often coincide, as when a politician of integrity is rewarded with our votes. But often they do not, and it is at those moments that our integrity is truly tested.

Error

Another reason that honesty alone is no substitute for integrity is that if forthrightness is not preceded by discernment, it may result in the expression of an incorrect moral judgment. In other words, I may be honest about what I believe, but if I have never tested my beliefs, I may be wrong. And here I mean "wrong" in a particular sense: The proposition in question is wrong if I would change my mind about it after hard moral reflection.

Consider this example. Having been taught all his life that women are not as smart as men, a manager gives the women on his staff less-challenging assignments than he gives the men. He does this, he believes, for their own benefit: He does not want them to fail, and he believes that they will if he gives them tougher assignments. Moreover, when one of the women on his staff does poor work, he does not berate her as harshly as he would a man, because he expects nothing more. And he claims to be acting with integrity because he is acting according to his own deepest beliefs.

The manager fails the most basic test of integrity. The question is not whether his actions are consistent with what he most deeply believes but whether he has done the hard work of discerning whether what he most deeply believes is right. The manager has not taken this harder step.

Moreover, even within the universe that the manager has constructed for himself, he is not acting with integrity. Although he is obviously wrong to think that the women on his staff are not as good as the men, even were he right, that would not justify applying different standards to their work. By so doing he betrays both his obligation to the institution that employs him and his duty as a manager to evaluate his employees.

The problem that the manager faces is an enormous one in our practical politics, where having the dialogue that makes democracy work can seem impossible because of our tendency to cling to our views even when we have not examined them. As Jean Bethke Elshtain has said, borrowing from John Courtney Murray, our politics are so fractured and contentious that we often cannot even reach *disagreement*. Our refusal to look closely at our own most cherished principles is surely a large part of the reason. Socrates thought the unexamined life not worth living. But the unhappy truth is that few of us actually have the time for constant reflection on our views—on public or private morality. Examine them we must, however, or we will never know whether we might be wrong.

None of this should be taken to mean that integrity as I have described it presupposes a single correct truth. If, for example, your integrity-guided search tells you that affirmative action is wrong, and my integrity-guided search tells me that affirmative action is right, we need not conclude that one of us lacks integrity. As it happens, I believe—both as a Christian and as a secular citizen who struggles toward moral understanding—that we *can* find true and sound answers to our moral questions. But I do not pretend to have found very many of them, nor is an exposition of them my purpose here.   17

It is the case not that there aren't any right answers but that, given human fallibility, we need to be careful in assuming that we have found them. However, today's political talk about how it is wrong for the government to impose one person's morality on somebody else is just mindless chatter. *Every* law imposes one person's morality on somebody else, because law has only two functions: to tell people to do what they would rather not or to forbid them do what they would.   18

And if the surveys can be believed, there is far more moral agreement in America than we sometimes allow ourselves to think. One of the reasons that character education for young people makes so much sense to so many people is precisely that there seems to be a core set of moral understandings—we might call them the American Core—that most of us accept. Some of the virtues in this American Core are, one hopes, relatively noncontroversial. About 500 American communities have signed on to Michael Josephson's program to emphasize the "six pillars" of good character: trustworthiness, respect, responsibility, caring, fairness, and citizenship. These virtues might lead to a similarly noncontroversial set of political values: having an honest regard for ourselves and others, protecting freedom of thought and religious belief, and refusing to steal or murder.   19

Honesty and Competing Responsibilities

A further problem with too great an exaltation of honesty is that it may allow us to escape responsibilities that morality bids us bear. If honesty is substituted for integrity, one might think that if I say I am not planning to fulfill a duty, I need not fulfill it. But it would be a peculiar morality indeed that granted us the right to avoid our moral responsibilities simply by stating our intention to ignore them. Integrity does not permit such an easy escape.   20

Consider an example. Before engaging in sex with a woman, her lover tells her that if she gets pregnant, it is her problem, not his. She says that she   21 understands. In due course she does wind up pregnant. If we believe, as I hope we do, that the man would ordinarily have a moral responsibility toward both the child he will have helped to bring into the world and the child's mother, then his honest statement of what he intends does not spare him that responsibility.

This vision of responsibility assumes that not all moral obligations stem from consent or from a stated intention. The linking of obligations to promises is a rather modern and perhaps uniquely Western way of looking at life, and perhaps a luxury that only the well-to-do can afford. As Fred and Shulamit Korn (a philosopher and an anthropologist) have pointed out, "If one looks at ethnographic accounts of other societies, one finds that, while obligations everywhere play a crucial role in social life, promising is not preeminent among the sources of obligation and is not even mentioned by most anthropologists." The Korns have made a study of Tonga, where promises are virtually unknown but the social order is remarkably stable. If life without any promises seems extreme, we Americans sometimes go too far the other way, parsing not only our contracts but even our marriage vows in order to discover the absolute minimum obligation that we have to others as a result of our promises.

That some societies in the world have worked out evidently functional structures of obligation without the need for promise or consent does not tell us what *we* should do. But it serves as a reminder of the basic proposition that our existence in civil society creates a set of mutual responsibilities that philosophers used to capture in the fiction of the social contract. Nowadays, here in America, people seem to spend their time thinking of even cleverer ways to avoid their obligations, instead of doing what integrity commands and fulfilling them. And all too often honesty is their excuse.

Meaning and Idea

1. What do you think is Carter's purpose in writing this piece? Where does he state that purpose most clearly?

2. What distinction does Carter make between the definition of *honesty* and the definition of *integrity?*

3. According to Carter, how can a person be honest without having integrity? How can a person have integrity but not necessarily be completely honest?

4. List three of the test cases that Carter explores. What principle does each case illustrate?

Language, Form, Structure

1. Evaluate the subheadings that Carter uses to organize his essay. How do they relate to the text? How does this method of organization add to the essay?

2. Reread the last two sentences of Carter's essay. Why is this an effective conclusion? How do these comments differ from the rest of the essay? How do they clarify his points? What do they add to the essay as a whole?

3. In addition to definition, Carter uses narration, comparison, and other modes to structure his essay. Find and identify examples.

4. Define the following words and use each one in a sentence: criterion; discernment; laudable; berate; fallibility.

Ideas for Writing

1. Think about an event in your life where you or someone you know had to make a choice between being honest and hurting someone else or being dishonest and protecting that person. Write an essay about that experience in the light of Carter's essay. Would he have approved of your response? Why or why not?

2. Write your own definition of the word *moral*. Cite several difficult examples of moral or immoral behavior to clarify your definition.

3. Write an essay in which you evaluate the success of Carter's essay. Is he successful in making his distinction clear? Is he successful in making larger points about American culture?

Complexion

Richard Rodriguez

Richard Rodriguez was born in San Francisco in 1944 and held a variety of jobs, including janitor, before becoming a full-time writer in 1981, a transition which was facilitated by the publication and positive reception of *Hunger of Memory: The Education of Richard Rodriguez* in 1982. He has received a Fullbright fellowship and a National Endowment for the Humanities fellowship. Rodriguez's work often chronicles his (and others') alienation from his own culture; he has led a strong campaign against affirmative action, which he views as yet another form of cultural alienation. He claims George Orwell as his prose model.

In this selection from *Hunger of Memory: The Education of Richard Rodriguez,* the author defines for us what is essentially an objective, physical term. However, the nature of his personal definition of the physical takes us beneath the surface to the emotional roots of the term.

*C*omplexion. My first conscious experience of sexual excitement   1
concerns my complexion. One summer weekend, when I was around seven years old, I was at a public swimming pool with the whole family. I remember sitting on the damp pavement next to the pool and seeing my mother, in the spectators' bleachers, holding my younger sister on her lap. My mother, I noticed, was watching my father as he stood on a diving board, waving to her. I watched her wave back. Then saw her radiant, bashful, astonishing smile. In that second I sensed that my mother and father had a relationship I knew nothing about. A nervous excitement encircled my stomach as I saw my mother's eyes follow my father's figure curving into the water. A second or two later, he emerged. I heard him call out. Smiling, his voice sounded, buoyant, calling me to swim to him. But turning to see him, I caught my mother's eye. I heard her shout over to me. In Spanish she called through the crowd: 'Put a towel on over your shoulders.' In public, she didn't want to say why. I knew.

That incident anticipates the shame and sexual inferiority I was to feel in   2
later years because of my dark complexion. I was to grow up an ugly child. Or one who thought himself ugly. (*Feo.*) One night when I was eleven or twelve years old, I locked myself in the bathroom and carefully regarded my reflection in the mirror over the sink. Without any pleasure I studied my skin. I turned on the faucet. (In my mind I heard the swirling voices of aunts, and even my mother's voice, whispering, whispering incessantly about lemon juice solutions and dark, *feo* children.) With a bar of soap, I fashioned a thick ball of lather. I began soaping my arms, I took my father's straight razor out of the medicine cabinet. Slowly, with steady deliberateness, I put the blade against my flesh, pressed it as close as I could without cutting, and moved it up and down across

my skin to see if I could get out, somehow lessen, the dark. All I succeeded in doing, however, was in shaving my arms bare of their hair. For as I noted with disappointment, the dark would not come out. It remained. Trapped. Deep in the cells of my skin.

Throughout adolescence, I felt myself mysteriously marked. Nothing else about my appearance would concern me so much as the fact that my complexion was dark. My mother would say how sorry she was that there was not money enough to get braces to straighten my teeth. But I never bothered about my teeth. In three-way mirrors at department stores, I'd see my profile dramatically defined by a long nose, but it was really only the color of my skin that caught my attention.

I wasn't afraid that I would become a menial laborer because of my skin. Nor did my complexion make me feel especially vulnerable to racial abuse. (I didn't really consider my dark skin to be a racial characteristic. I would have been only too happy to look as Mexican as my light-skinned older brother.) Simply, I judged myself ugly. And, since the women in my family had been the ones who discussed it in such worried tones, I felt my dark skin made me unattractive to women.

Thirteen years old. Fourteen. In a grammar school art class, when the assignment was to draw a self-portrait, I tried and I tried but could not bring myself to shade in the face on the paper to anything like my actual tone. With disgust then I would come face to face with myself in mirrors. With disappointment I located myself in class photographs—my dark face undefined by the camera which had clearly described the white faces of classmates. Or I'd see my dark wrist against my long-sleeved white shirt.

I grew divorced from my body. Insecure, overweight, listless. On hot summer days when my rubber-soled shoes soaked up the heat from the sidewalk, I kept my head down. Or walked in the shade. My mother didn't need anymore to tell me to watch out for the sun. I denied myself a sensational life. The normal, extraordinary, animal excitement of feeling my body alive—riding shirtless on a bicycle in the warm wind created by furious self-propelled motion—the sensations that first had excited in me a sense of my maleness, I denied. I was too ashamed of my body. I wanted to forget that I had a body because I had a brown body. I was grateful that none of my classmates ever mentioned the fact.

I continued to see the *braceros,* those men I resembled in one way and, in another way, didn't resemble at all. On the watery horizon of a Valley afternoon, I'd see them. And though I feared looking like them, it was with silent envy that I regarded them still. I envied them their physical lives, their freedom to violate the taboo of the sun. Closer to home I would notice the shirtless construction workers, the roofers, the sweating men tarring the street in front of the house. And I'd see the Mexican gardeners. I was unwilling to admit the attraction of their lives. I tried to deny it by looking away. But what was denied became strongly desired.

In high school physical education classes, I withdrew, in the regular company of five or six classmates, to a distant corner of a football field where we smoked and talked. Our company was composed of bodies too short or too tall, all graceless and all—except mine—pale. Our conversation was usually witty. (In fact we were intelligent.) If we referred to the athletic contests around us, it was with sarcasm.

With savage scorn I'd refer to the "animals" playing football or baseball. It would have been important for me to have joined them. Or for me to have taken off my shirt, to have let the sun burn dark on my skin, and to have run barefoot on the warm wet grass. It would have been very important. Too important. It would have been too telling a gesture—to admit the desire for sensation, the body, my body.

Fifteen, sixteen. I was a teenager shy in the presence of girls. Never dated. Barely could talk to a girl without stammering. In high school I went to several dances, but I never managed to ask a girl to dance. So I stopped going. I cannot remember high school years now with the parade of typical images: bright drive-ins or gliding blue shadows of a Junior Prom. At home most weekend nights, I would pass evenings reading. Like those hidden, precocious adolescents who have no real-life sexual experiences, I read a great deal of romantic fiction. 'You won't find it in your books,' my brother would playfully taunt me as he prepared to go to a party by freezing the crest of the wave in his hair with sticky pomade. Through my reading, however, I developed a fabulous and sophisticated sexual imagination. At seventeen, I may not have known how to engage a girl in small talk, but I had read *Lady Chatterley's Lover.*

It annoyed me to hear my father's teasing: that I would never know what 'real work' is; that my hands were so soft. I think I knew it was his way of admitting pleasure and pride in my academic success. But I didn't smile. My mother said she was glad her children were getting their educations and would not be pushed around like *los pobres.* I heard the remark ironically as a reminder of my separation from *los braceros.* At such times I suspected that education was making me effeminate. The odd thing, however, was that I did not judge my classmates so harshly. Nor did I consider my male teachers in high school effeminate. It was only myself I judged against some shadowy, mythical Mexican laborer—dark like me, yet very different.

Language was crucial. I knew that I had violated the ideal of the *macho* by becoming such a dedicated student of language and literature. *Machismo* was a word never exactly defined by the persons who used it. (It was best described in the 'proper' behavior of men.) Women at home, nevertheless, would repeat the old Mexican dictum that a man should be *feo, fuerte, y formal.* 'The three F's,' my mother called them, smiling slyly. *Feo* I took to mean not literally ugly so much as ruggedly handsome. (When my mother and her sisters spent a loud, laughing afternoon determining ideal male good looks, they finally settled on the actor Gilbert Roland, who was neither too pretty nor ugly but had looks 'like a man.') *Fuerte,* 'strong,' seemed to mean not physical strength as much as inner strength, character. A dependable man is *fuerte. Fuerte* for that reason was a characteristic subsumed by the last of the three qualities, and the one I most often considered—*formal.* To be *formal* is to be steady. A man of responsibility, a good provider. Someone *formal* is also constant. A person to be relied upon in adversity. A sober man, a man of high seriousness.

I learned a great deal about being *formal* just by listening to the way my father and other male relatives of his generation spoke. A man was not silent necessarily. Nor was he limited in the tones he could sound. For example, he could tell a long, involved, humorous story and laugh at his own humor with high-pitched giggling. But a man was not talkative the way a woman could be. It was permitted a woman to be gossipy and chatty. (When one heard many voices in a room, it was usually women who were talking.) Men spoke much less rapidly. And often men spoke in monologues. (When one voice sounded in a crowded room, it was most often a man's voice one heard.) More important than any of this was the fact that a man never verbally revealed his emotions. Men did not speak about their unease in moments of crisis or danger. It was the woman who worried aloud when her husband got laid off from work. At times of illness or death in the family, a man was usually quiet, even silent. Women spoke up to voice prayers. In distress, women always sounded quick ejaculations to God or the Virgin; women prayed in clearly audible voices at a wake held in a funeral parlor. And on the subject of love, a woman was verbally expansive. She spoke of her yearning and delight. A married man, if he spoke publicly about love, usually did so with playful, mischievous irony. Younger, unmarried men more often were quiet. (The *macho* is a silent suitor. *Formal.*)

At home I was quiet, so perhaps I seemed *formal* to my relations and other 13 Spanish-speaking visitors to the house. But outside the house—my God!—I talked. Particularly in class or alone with my teachers, I chattered. (Talking seemed to make teachers think I was bright.) I often was proud of my way with words. Though, on other occasions, for example, when I would hear my mother busily speaking to women, it would occur to me that my attachment to words made me like her. Her son. Not *formal* like my father. At such times I even suspected that my nostalgia for sounds—the noisy, intimate Spanish sounds of my past—was nothing more than effeminate yearning.

High school English teachers encouraged me to describe very personal feel- 14 ings in words. Poems and short stories I wrote, expressing sorrow and loneliness, were awarded high grades. In my bedroom were books by poets and novelists— books that I loved—in which male writers published feelings the men in my family never revealed or acknowledged in words. And it seemed to me that there was something unmanly about my attachment to literature. Even today, when so much about the myth of the *macho* no longer concerns me, I cannot altogether evade such notions. Writing these pages, admitting my embarrassment or my guilt, admitting my sexual anxieties and my physical insecurity, I have not been able to forget that I am not being *formal.*

So be it. 15

Meaning and Idea

1. In the incident by the swimming pool when the author is 12, why does his mother tell him to put a towel over his shoulders? Why does she say it in Spanish? What was the effect of the comment on Rodriguez?

2. What two expected results of his dark complexion did Rodriguez not fear? Why? What result did he fear most? How does he develop that fear?

3. What does Rodriguez mean when he says he was *feo?* What were the effects of the author's considering himself *feo* during his adolescence? What were the longer-lasting effects?

4. How does Rodriguez compare himself to the *braceros,* construction workers, and Mexican gardeners? Why does he envy them?

5. What is Rodriguez's definition of *machismo?* What were the "three F's"? How did Rodriguez arrive at his own definition of each? How did he see himself in relation to the "three F's"? What is his present view of himself in relation to them?

Language, Form, Structure

1. What is the main term defined in this essay? How does Rodriguez use various lesser definitions to build up support for the whole definition? Why does the author define both English and Spanish words? How does he connect them?

2. What is the connection between the use of language and the definition of character traits or feelings according to this essay? Explain fully at least two examples.

3. In the paragraph that begins, "Thirteen years old. Fourteen," Rodriguez writes about his class photographs. He says: "I located myself . . . my dark face undefined by the camera." What is the meaning of the word *undefined* here? How does it relate to the overall definitional context of this essay?

4. How does Rodriguez use narration as an integral part of his definition? How does he arrange his narrations?

5. Write definitions for these words from the essay: buoyant; menial; vulnerable; precocious; pomade; effeminate; subsumed.

Ideas for Writing

1. Write an extended definition of the term *cultural* or *racial stereotype.* You may choose to focus on the stereotypes you know about your own cultural or racial group and develop your definition through personal narrative.

2. Write a definition of the term *ugly.* Use negation as your main development technique.

3. At the end of this essay, Rodriguez writes:

> Writing these pages, admitting my embarrassment or my guilt, admitting my sexual anxieties and my physical insecurity, I have not been able to forget that I am not being *formal.*

Do you feel that men exposing their emotions so publicly in writing is "unmanly," as Rodriguez fears it may be? Do you feel Rodriguez's writing in this essay is in any way effeminate? On a broader scale, do you feel there are appropriate differences in subject and tone in writing for male and female writers? Why? Explore these issues in an analytic essay.

CROSSOVER

1. Susan Brownmiller in "Femininity" and Richard Rodriguez in "Complexion" explore stereotypical thinking and its effect on individual development. Write an essay on the ways the two writers deal with stereotypes. What commonalities exist between the two pieces about how the culture transmits traditional gender ideas? What insights are unique to each piece?

2. Leonard Kriegel in "Claiming the Self: The Cripple as American Man" and Robert Graves in "The Naked and the Nude" consider words that are often taken as synonyms. Write an essay in which you compare the points made in the works about how we use language.

Chapter Nine

■

ARGUMENTATION AND PERSUASION

INTRODUCTION TO ARGUMENTATION AND PERSUASION

We devote a good deal of our daily thinking and talking time to reasoning, often reasoning with someone or other to convince the person to believe something that we ourselves believe or to take a particular action we believe necessary. X is the best place to go; Y is the worst choice for mayor; plan B is the most reasonable solution to problem Z; course 1 is the only valid course to follow. In writing, too, we take positions and defend them, and this undertaking, stemming in the most formal sense from ancient Greek oratory, we call *argumentation.*

Although some logicians make a precise distinction between arguing and persuading, the two frequently work together. Strictly speaking, the essence of *argumentation* is a coolly rational presentation of statement and support, eschewing emotional appeals and prejudicial language and aiming instead for a person's intellectual faculty. The arguer's goal is to get you to agree. *Persuasion,* on the other hand, reaches for feelings; based in logic, too, it usually aims to arouse emotion, even passion, so that you act. The persuader's goal is to get you to agree—and then to do something about it. When you say "You're right" to a friend who marshals statistics—batting averages, win-loss records, runs batted in—to convince you that the Dodgers are a better team than the Cubs, he's won the argument. When you buy a new breakfast cereal because of a 30-second commercial spot on television, you're not only convinced, you're convinced strongly enough to take action.

Good written argumentation and persuasion, designed to appeal to reasonable readers, will be grounded in reason. The writer asserts something, takes a position (when stated formally, this is often called the *proposition*), and then advances this position point by point. But like effective argumentation in life, written argumentation usually provides more than direct logical proof. Readers and writers alike are complex creatures, feeling and thinking at once. No wonder, then, that throughout history, writers have developed argumentative approaches to convince readers both through reasoning and through emotional evocation.

READING ARGUMENTATION AND PERSUASION

From early literature to modern novels, stories, dramas, and essays, argumentation abounds. From Job's remonstrance to God to the polemics of Brecht, Lawrence, and Woolf in the twentieth century, we note lively evidence of the impulse to argue well so that others see important issues as we do.

Swaying the Mind and Heart

Effective argumentation not only will move the reader through logic but will move the reader to "feel" the writer's position as well. In effective argumentative essays the writer may draw on a whole arsenal of strategies—comparison, classification, causation, description, narration, and so on. A sharp anecdote, a lambent sensory description, an explanation of ghastly or wonderful effects, an extended analogy, an apt comparison—all these can help persuade the reader to accept the writer's particular position or point of view. But fiction writers, poets, dramatists, and satirists also employ argumentation and persuasion. The essayist may dwell more on aspects of logic and the imaginative writer more on emotional appeals, but the good writer in any genre will draw on techniques that sway both intellect and emotions, yoking in the work both sense and sensibility. Indeed, writers from Aristotle to Austen to T. S. Eliot have recommended this joining in life and in literature.

In this chapter, Swift's satire, "A Modest Proposal," argues against popular policy and attitudes toward Ireland not by saying outright, "The British treatment of Ireland should be altered," but by using a variety of expository techniques that move us not only intellectually but emotionally. His comparison of babies to livestock, for example, to be bred, killed, "stewed, roasted, baked, or boiled," and put on the table for dinner alarms the reader, convincing us of the *narrator's* lunacy and of the *writer's* good sense. Point by point, Swift has his speaker argue for the wisdom of killing babies as a solution to "the Irish problem," and through well-chosen details, examples, facts and figures—"I compute that Dublin would take off annually about twenty thousand carcasses, and the rest of the kingdom (where they will be sold somewhat cheaper) the remaining eighty thousand"—makes readers see British proposals to maintain domination of impoverished Ireland as cruelty and madness in the name of reason and logic. Indeed, the whole superlogical structure of Swift's satire encourages in the reader an *emotional* acceptance of the victims and an *emotional* aversion to the oppressor. The "Proposal" encourages the reader to say, "No more proposals, no more propositions. Just kindness, just love."

Good argumentation, then, can move not only our minds but also our hearts. Perhaps the most remarkable balance between logic and emotion in literature resides in Marvell's "To His Coy Mistress," one of the poems in this chapter. The poet appeals to his mistress's reason so that she'll accept his propositions, yet his language, fraught with subtle sensuality, aims for emotional appeal ("The grave's a fine and private place, / But none, I think, do there embrace"). The speaker's objective is to persuade his demure lady through reason and feeling to love him now, not later. He wants action, and he wants it today!

Strategies in Argumentation

As we read argumentation, we can see, too, the choices of logical strategies. Will the writer start with a proposition and then support it point by point, or will the writer lay down points and let the proposition emerge? The former approach we call *deduction;* the latter, *induction.* Martin Luther King, Jr., in the "I Have a Dream" speech, works deductively; he comes right out with his proposition, which his entire speech then supports through example, analysis of causes and effects, and so on. Swift's essay, in contrast, works inductively. Readers, after experiencing the *speaker's* proposition, supporting details, and calculations, grasp on their own the *writer's* proposition—a rejection of the basic assumptions laid down in the "Proposal."

While reading argumentation, then, we can observe a rich play of the writer's options. Chekhov uses the principles of argumentation to achieve very funny effects in his play "A Marriage Proposal." But even in humorous writing we can see the wide range of possibilities for argumentative ploys. To get us to embrace a proposition, writers will use a variety of dramatic and expository techniques. They may appeal to our reason and to our emotions, probably both. Writers may work deductively, guiding us from proposition to support, or inductively from detail and example until their handiwork frames the larger proposition. In short, reading argumentation provides a blueprint of strategies in logic that have already been used to win many readers and that remain useful as we ourselves write to argue or persuade.

WRITING ARGUMENTATION AND PERSUASION

The ancient Greeks developed certain rules that strictly governed formal argumentation and debate, and orators and writers followed those rules for centuries. Today we tend to approach argumentation with fewer rules. Still, it is useful to keep certain guidelines in mind as you develop your own argumentative essays and to keep certain thoughts in mind even before you select your topic. Argumentation will require a good deal of you—your most careful reasoning, an energetic marshaling of support, extreme sensitivity to the emotional issues of your topic, and exact use of language. The first question you want to ask yourself is, "What issue do I care strongly enough about to be able to take an emphatic position on?" This is no occasion for reticence; you must take a stand and stick by it. Also, before you choose your topic, you'll want to ask yourself, "What do I know about?" You don't necessarily want your first argumentation papers to end up being extensive research undertakings, and so a topic that you not only care about but also know something about will be a good place to start.

PURPOSE AND AUDIENCE

Achieving the Goals of Argumentation

Argumentative essays have as their goal the logical presentation of ideas in order to convince the reader of a sound point of view. A further purpose may be to get their readers to act once they accept the essay's proposition. In either case, you want to take readers with you from proposition to supporting points to conclusion. And to do so you must think carefully about *who* your readers are, what they know, and what information, data, illustrations, or other supporting details are likely to get them to think as you do. Your level of usage, your choice of vocabulary, and your tone and style all must serve your ultimate purpose. To argue against the excessive use of living animals for scientific experiments, you might present readers with a dispassionate paper that lays out statistics and cases drawn from reliable sources. Numbers have their own drama, and a careful, rational presentation could win over your readers. If your purpose were to recruit demonstrators for a march in Washington next month to support the Animal Protection League, you might spark your essay with your own bias, individualizing the cases, emphasizing the particular suffering of animals in selected examples, and exhorting your readers with emotionally charged language to meet you on the steps of the Capitol.

One point to keep in mind is that readers are, more often than not, rational people. You will want, then, to build a sound argument and to avoid name-calling that might alienate your audience. As you develop your proposition, try for a statement that will respect your audience's diversity. If you say that anyone who doesn't support school busing is "a Nazi and a right-wing hoodlum," you will prevent any readers inclined toward opposing busing from reading your essay with an open mind.

Of course, certain audiences tend to be in agreement on certain subjects. But more often than not, an academic audience—generally your main readership—holds diverse views. As you write, try to imagine what a reader with opposing views might say. An excellent strategy is to include these opposing views somewhere in your essay and either acknowledge their viability before you go on to make your own points or refute them one by one. This *refutation,* a requirement in classical argumentation, is still useful for persuading readers on the other side or for convincing readers sitting on the fence. As for readers who agree with your position, the refutation and the good argumentation in general can help them test their beliefs and sharpen and strengthen their thinking.

Weighing Your Audience

As you prepare to write, think about the knowledge level of your readers. If they know very little about the subject, then your argument will have to cover some very basic points. What is *vivisection?* What is its history in the American scientific community? What are other options for researchers? If, however, your readers are specialists on your topic, then you will need to pitch your essay to their high level, avoid telling them what they already know, and include sophisticated thinking and information.

Think of your audience as you organize the points that support your proposition. If you put your strongest points first, most readers will lose interest as the essay moves on to weaker arguments. If you put all your strong points last, the readers may never be interested enough to get to them. A balanced strategy is to put your second strongest point first, then proceed to your less strong points, and end your argument with your strongest point—the point you most want your readers to remember.

Being especially clear about your own purpose and about your audience is critical as you develop essays designed to change minds.

PROCESS

Identify the issue you want to write about. Consider the matters raised in the selections in this chapter. If you have trouble identifying a strong belief or conviction, look at a news magazine or a newspaper. Study editorial pages;

read a political column; listen to a commentator's opinion on radio or television. No doubt your thinking on different matters will perk up even if it's just to *oppose* what you read or hear. Once you've chosen a topic that you care about and perhaps even know a good deal about, you can turn to developing your argument.

From Topic to Proposition

First, you must shape your topic into a proposition, the thesis statement in argumentation. Whether the logical plan of your essay is deductive or inductive, you will need a clear statement of proposition to work with. As you know, not every essay states its thesis outright—writers sometimes leave you to figure it out on your own—but a clear statement of proposition helps a reader straight off to determine where the essay intends to go. Even an inductive essay can benefit from such a statement at the end so that readers can check their perceptions against the writer's. At any rate, a clear idea of the main position that the essay will assert directs you as you plan and as you write. An argumentative essay builds on a strong proposition (Y must be upheld; B should be abolished). Write your proposition and edit any language that could bait or alienate your audience.

Prewrite on your topic in order to generate the major points of your argument. Even the most fair-minded proposition needs strong supporting points in order for readers to accept it fully. Through jottings, lists, freewriting—whatever technique works for you—generate the points that will hold up your position. And before you write, generate examples, facts, figures, descriptions that make each point convincing and alive.

Looking at Logic

Also before you write, check your argument for logic. Logic, of course, plays a part in most writing, but in argumentation it plays an especially important role. If your logic is faulty, reasonable readers will reject your entire premise, however worthy it in itself may be. Look to see that your essay does not oversimplify complicated matters. Consider cautiously, for example, the value of calling for an end to all biological investigations that employ living animals. Many advances in human health care have followed such experimentation, and you may lose readers if you overlook the advantages stemming from such scientific research. Also, look to see that your conclusions logically follow the proposition and its supporting points. The Latin phrase *non sequitur,* meaning "doesn't follow," refers to a statement that does not logically follow another statement, although we intend it to. "Opposing vivisection will improve the lot of helpless animals everywhere" risks being a *non sequitur* if you do not develop the issues in your paper carefully. What about the cruelty inflicted on pets in some households? What about animals abandoned every September as resort areas close down all over America and families return home? Look as well to see that the authorities you invoke are truly authorities. Your brother's report of outrageous experiments with frogs in a summer camp nature program would not convince anyone that vivisection abuse is widespread throughout the scientific community. Another way to strengthen the logic of your position is to make sure that you've argued the issues and have not just attacked people connected with your "opposition." Such a personal attack is called *ad hominem,* from the Latin for "to the person." The *ad hominen* approach is easy to turn to in argumentation involving us emotionally, but readers can easily dismiss it as beside the point.

Language Aids

Good logic can work for you, and so can good language. Solid argumentation relies on good writing. As you write and as you edit, try for the most alive language and the most alive examples and descriptions. The well-turned phrase will attract your readers' attention and incline them toward your position more than will dull phrases or repetitive syntax. Fresh figurative language, sensory description, lively comparisons, lively examples—all the rhetorical devices that you have at your command as a writer—will serve you well as you argue for your proposition, making logical and emotional appeals to your reader.

In arguing, it's easy to overdo the use of transitions by linking ideas frequently with logical connectors—*therefore, thus, and so, as a result, then, consequently,* and many others like them. These transitions are useful certainly to connect points here and there, but the logic in a well-reasoned essay has its own flow that requires few guideposts. In most cases readers will know on their own when point A follows point B intelligently and will not need the added push of *therefore.*

Finally, the conclusion of your argumentative essay is particularly important. It's what readers "hear" last, and it often can clinch or lose their support. There are no hard-and-fast rules for concluding argumentation. In a fairly long paper, a restatement of your proposition, one that presents your point with fresh language, will impress readers with what is most important in the essay without being boring. But you won't want to stop there in every case. Your conclusion might set a new frame of reference by generalizing from your stated proposal to an even larger, more relevant issue. Your conclusion can help readers apply your generalization in a broader context than the immediate concerns of your essay.

Throughout your college career and on the job, your skills at argumentation will serve you well. Spend time here in practicing these skills: presenting your points honestly, avoiding the overstatement of emotional appeals, and weighing the logic of your positions carefully.

STUDENT WRITING

As you read this essay, note the student writer's uses of argumentation strategies, which the annotations in the margin highlight for your attention. Look especially for logical presentation as the writer tries to convince you to accept her point of view. Look also for the range of rhetorical strategies the writer uses.

Pornography and Women

[a]Audience awareness: definition of pornography so that readers know what this writer means specifically by the term

[b]Proposition (thesis): pornography degrades women

[c]Logic draws on deduction: proposition is stated, and points refute or support it

[d]Consideration of opposing views, treated fairly, in a substantial paragraph

[e]Speaker's exact words add substance and interest to the example

[f]Transition

[g]Specific cases to support opposition point of view

[h]Effective transition to previous paragraph

[i]Writer returns to proposition established in opening paragraph

[j]Logical connector: "as a result"

Pornography intends to cause sexual excitement by showing erotic behavior.[a] We observe pornography in various forms, such as novels, magazines, photographs, and triple-X-rated movies. Mostly it is women displayed in pornography for the pleasure of men. By its very nature, pornographic material completely degrades the women of our society.[b]

Yet many people feel that pornography is not degrading. Pornography is a million-dollar industry, and many young women choose it for easy money.[c] Publishers of such magazines as *Playboy, Hustler,* and *Penthouse* do not believe that having nude women on their pages is "wrong" or degrading. After all, in now classic "nudie" photographs, Marilyn Monroe, the great movie queen, displayed her body to millions.

On the television show "Good Morning America," to take another example,[d] a reporter asked a young porn star if she thought she was doing anything wrong in her films. She replied, "I'm not ashamed of my body and I have nothing to hide."[e] In fact, some feminists and their supporters believe that women should be able to do whatever they want with their bodies and that the choice to show sexual activity in public is the ultimate act of freedom.[f] From the enormous numbers of people who purchase pornographic material, we can assume that many think the degradation of women is an issue not worth considering.[g]

Although some people show a lack of concern for women in pornography,[h] most civilized societies feel that pornography is extremely degrading. Pornographers are considered outcasts.[i] In a well-publicized case a few years back, for example, women police officers posed for nude pictures. As a result, the women were either suspended or fired from their jobs.[j] Normal citizens have little respect for such displays and do not tolerate this kind of behavior from people in respectable positions in our society.

Another case of values versus pornography that now has pretty much vanished from the public eye involved the megastar Vanessa Williams, who was Miss America in 1983. Because she posed in nude pictures before she won the title, she was stripped of her crown. The Miss America position represents traditional values of feminine honor; no woman who takes her clothes off for public viewing could reflect those values. Perhaps Williams was flattered to think that her naked body would stimulate men all over the country. Yet[f] she was misled by the idea still held by many men that, aside from the kitchen, a woman's place is in the bedroom. Penthouse magazine gives the title "Pet of the Month" to a woman who will share her nude body in erotic photographs for male readers. Such women are foolish to consider the term "Pet" an honor. It is perfectly normal for a woman to share her body, but with someone she loves—and not the whole world![k]

    In spite of all the money, supposed thrills, and glamour in the pornography industry, it is a dangerous business.[l] Many crimes are associated with pornography.[m] There are perverts and rapists who enact on unwilling women in the streets what they see in X-rated movies or snapshots. There are sexual crimes against children, who are forced to pose before cameras. Young female runaways, drug addicts, prostitutes, and mentally ill women often turn to pornography for security and money. Our whole culture is affected negatively when we accept the sexual exploitation of women because we pay for the violence and crime attached to it. If pornography is freedom for the individual, that freedom makes a prison for the rest of the society![n]

[k]Exemplification: Most important example in the paragraph placed last

[l]Effective transition to conclusion

[m]Specific instances to support writer's assertion that pornography degrades women

[n]Conclusion clinches argument: writer examines consequences of pornography in the society at large (use of causation strategies)

SUMMING UP: ARGUMENTATION AND PERSUASION

Reading Argumentation and Persuasion

Argumentation is a rational presentation that takes a position and defends it without excessive emotional appeals and that is aimed at a person's intellectual faculty; *persuasion,* also based in logic, intends to arouse emotion to compel an action. Often argumentation and persuasion work together.

- Determine the elements in the selection that appeal to your intellect and your emotion.
- Determine the writer's assertion or position, often called the *proposition.*
- Consider how the writer advances her position point by point.
- Identify the various rhetorical strategies—narration, comparison, definition, causation, and others surely—that the writer uses to advance his argument.
- Weigh the uses of induction and deduction.

Writing Argumentation and Persuasion

- Choose a topic about which you can take a stand and stick by it; that is, determine an issue that you care strongly enough about to take an emphatic position on.

- Be prepared to use your most careful reasoning and exact language, to present your most convincing details, and to show extreme sensitivity to the emotional issues of your topic.

- Take readers logically from your proposition to supporting points to your conclusion.

- Evaluate who your readers are, what they know about the topic, and what information, data, illustrations, or other supporting details are likely to get them to think as you do.

- Honor the diversity of your audience by considering what a reader with opposing views on your topic would say, and then address those views.

- Weigh the arrangement of the points in your arguments, ending with your strongest point.

- Develop your proposition, a thesis statement that indicates the main position of the essay and that directs you as you plan and write the essay.

- Use prewriting to help generate the major points in your argument: jottings, lists, freewriting—these activities can help you develop the early stages of your argument.

- Check your essay for adherence to logic; avoid *oversimplifying, non sequiturs,* and *ad hominem* arguments.

- As you edit, pay particular attention to language, aiming for clear, alive examples.

- Do not overdo the use of logical connectors as transitions.

- Produce a conclusion that clinches your argument.

I Have a Dream

Martin Luther King, Jr.

Martin Luther King, Jr. (1929–1968), was born in Atlanta, Georgia, the son of a Baptist minister. King followed his father's lead into the ministry and soon became known for his inspiring oratorical abilities. He became the most prominent leader of the early civil rights movement in the United States: In 1955, he organized the year-long successful boycott of the segregated Montgomery, Alabama, bus system; he subsequently organized and led the Southern Christian Leadership Council, which promoted other boycotts, marches, and demonstrations in favor of civil rights for blacks. King was an instrumental organizer of the 1963 March on Washington and the 1965 voter-registration drive in Selma, Alabama. Staunchly devoted to Gandhian-style nonviolent resistance, the Reverend Dr. King received the 1968 Nobel Prize for Peace. In 1968, he was assassinated.

On August 28, 1963, nearly a quarter of a million people of all races converged on Washington, D.C., to take part in the historic March on Washington at the height of the American civil rights movement. In front of the Lincoln Memorial, on the one-hundredth anniversary of the Emancipation Proclamation, the Reverend Dr. Martin Luther King, Jr., delivered the spellbinding "I Have a Dream" speech, in which he outlined his vision of a better, more peaceful country.

Five score years ago, a great American, in *whose symbolic shadow we stand,* signed the Emancipation Proclamation. This momentous decree came as a great beacon light of hope to millions of Negro slaves who had been seared in the flames of withering injustice. It came as a joyous daybreak to end the long light of captivity.

But one hundred years later, we must face the tragic fact that the Negro is still not free. One hundred years later, the life of the Negro is still sadly crippled by the manacles of segregation and the chains of discrimination. One hundred years later, the Negro lives on a lonely island of poverty in the midst of a vast ocean of material prosperity. One hundred years later, the Negro is still languishing in the corners of American society and finds himself an exile in his own land. So we have come here today to dramatize an appalling condition.

In a sense we have come to our nation's capital to cash a check. When the architects of our republic wrote the magnificent words of the Constitution and the Declaration of Independence, they were signing a promissory note to which every American was to fall heir. This note was a promise that all men would be guaranteed the unalienable rights of life, liberty, and the pursuit of happiness.

It is obvious today that America has defaulted on this promissory note in-   4
sofar as her citizens of color are concerned. Instead of honoring this sacred obligation, America has given the Negro people a bad check; a check which has
come back marked "insufficient funds." But we refuse to believe that the bank
of justice is bankrupt. We refuse to believe that there are insufficient funds in
the great vaults of opportunity of this nation. So we have come to cash this
check—a check that will give us upon demand the riches of freedom and the security of justice. We have also come to this hallowed spot to remind America of
the fierce urgency of *now*. This is no time to engage in the luxury of cooling off
or to take the tranquilizing drugs of gradualism. *Now* is the time to make real the
promises of Democracy. *Now* is the time to rise from the dark and desolate valley of segregation to the sunlit path of racial justice. *Now* is the time to open the
doors of opportunity to all of God's children. *Now* is the time to lift our nation
from the quicksands of racial injustice to the solid rock of brotherhood.

It would be fatal for the nation to overlook the urgency of the moment and   5
to underestimate the determination of the Negro. This sweltering summer of the
Negro's legitimate discontent will not pass until there is an invigorating autumn
of freedom and equality. 1963 is not an end, but a beginning. Those who hope
that the Negro needed to blow off steam and will now be content will have a
rude awakening if the nation returns to business as usual. There will be neither
rest nor tranquility in America until the Negro is granted his citizenship rights.
The whirlwinds of revolt will continue to shake the foundations of our nation
until the bright day of justice emerges.

But there is something that I must say to my people who stand on the   6
warm threshold which leads into the palace of justice. In the process of gaining
our rightful place we must not be guilty of wrongful deeds. Let us not seek to
satisfy our thirst for freedom by drinking from the cup of bitterness and hatred.
We must forever conduct our struggle on the high plane of dignity and discipline. We must not allow our creative protest to degenerate into physical violence. Again and again we must rise to the majestic heights of meeting physical
force with soul force. The marvelous new militancy which has engulfed the
Negro community must not lead us to a distrust of all white people, for many of
our white brothers, as evidenced by their presence here today, have come to realize that their destiny is tied up with our destiny and their freedom is inextricably
bound to our freedom. We cannot walk alone.

And as we walk, we must make the pledge that we shall march ahead. We   7
cannot turn back. There are those who are asking the devotees of civil rights,
"When will you be satisfied?" We can never be satisfied as long as the Negro is
the victim of the unspeakable horrors of police brutality. We can never be satisfied as long as our bodies, heavy with the fatigue of travel, cannot gain lodging
in the motels of the highways and the hotels of the cities. We cannot be satisfied
as long as the Negro's basic mobility is from a smaller ghetto to a larger one.
We can never be satisfied as long as a Negro in Mississippi cannot vote and a
Negro in New York believes he has nothing for which to vote. No, no, we are

not satisfied, and we will not be satisfied until justice rolls down like waters and righteousness like a mighty stream.

I am not unmindful that some of you have come here out of great trials and tribulations. Some of you have come fresh from narrow jail cells. Some of you have come from areas where your quest for freedom left you battered by the storms of persecution and staggered by the winds of police brutality. You have been the veterans of creative suffering. Continue to work with the faith that un-earned suffering is redemptive.   8

Go back to Mississippi, go back to Alabama, go back to South Carolina, go back to Georgia, go back to Louisiana, go back to the slums and ghettos of our northern cities, knowing that somehow this situation can and will be changed. Let us not wallow in the valley of despair.   9

I say to you today, my friends, that in spite of the difficulties and frustra-tions of the moment I still have a dream. It is a dream deeply rooted in the American dream.   10

I have a dream that one day this nation will rise up and live out the true meaning of its creed: "We hold these truths to be self-evident; that all men are created equal."   11

I have a dream that one day on the red hills of Georgia the sons of former slaves and the sons of former slaveowners will be able to sit down together at the table of brotherhood.   12

I have a dream that one day even the state of Mississippi, a desert state sweltering with the heat of injustice and oppression, will be transformed into an oasis of freedom and justice.   13

I have a dream that my four little children will one day live in a nation where they will not be judged by the color of their skin but by the content of their character.   14

I have a dream today.   15

I have a dream that one day the state of Alabama, whose governor's lips are presently dripping with the words of interposition and nullification, will be transformed into a situation where little black boys and black girls will be able to join hands with little white boys and white girls and walk together as sisters and brothers.   16

I have a dream today.   17

I have a dream that one day every valley shall be exalted, every hill and mountain shall be made low, the rough places will be made plain, and the crooked places will be made straight, and the glory of the Lord shall be revealed, and all flesh shall see it together.   18

This is our hope. This is the faith with which I return to the South. With this faith we will be able to hew out of the mountain of despair a stone of hope. With this faith we will be able to transform the jangling discords of our nation into a beautiful symphony of brotherhood. With this faith we will be able to work together, to pray together, to struggle together, to go to jail together, to stand up for freedom together, knowing that we will be free one day.   19

This will be the day when all of God's children will be able to sing with   20
new meaning

> My country, 'tis of thee,
> Sweet land of liberty,
>   Of thee I sing:
> Land where my fathers died,
> Land of the pilgrims' pride,
> From every mountain-side
>   Let freedom ring.

And if America is to be a great nation this must become true. So let free-   21
dom ring from the prodigious hilltops of New Hampshire. Let freedom ring
from the mighty mountains of New York. Let freedom ring from the heightening
Alleghenies of Pennsylvania!

Let freedom ring from the snowcapped Rockies of Colorado!   22

Let freedom ring from the curvaceous peaks of California!   23

But not only that; let freedom ring from Stone Mountain of Georgia!   24

Let freedom ring from Lookout Mountain of Tennessee!   25

Let freedom ring from every hill and molehill of Mississippi. From every   26
mountainside, let freedom ring.

When we let freedom ring, when we let it ring from every village and   27
every hamlet, from every state and every city, we will be able to speed up that
day when all of God's children, black men and white men, Jews and Gentiles,
Protestants and Catholics, will be able to join hands and sing in the words of
the old Negro spiritual, "Free at last! free at last! thank God almighty, we are
free at last!"

Meaning and Idea

1. Who is the "great American" to whom King refers at the opening of his
   speech? What was the Emancipation Proclamation?

2. What comparisons does King make between the conditions of blacks in
   1863 and 1963? Are these conditions always stated explicitly? What is the
   point of the comparison?

3. What examples does King offer of the daily conditions of blacks which lead
   him to the conclusion that satisfaction cannot be achieved "until justice rolls
   down like waters and righteousness like a mighty stream"? What does he
   mean by the term *satisfied* in this context?

4. What does King say about the relations between blacks and whites? What
   are the potential difficulties? What is his suggestion?

Language, Form, Structure

1. For what position is King arguing? Does he ever directly state a thesis for this speech? In a single sentence in your own words, state what his main proposition is. Is King's intention merely to convince the audience of his opinion, or does he also want to persuade them to take action? Explain your answer.

2. King uses numerous metaphors in the development of his argument. Which do you find the most impressive? Explain the extended metaphor (an *extended metaphor* sustains a figurative comparison through a number of related images) that begins with the first sentence of paragraph 3: "In a sense we have come to our nation's capital to cash a check."

3. What is the role of repetition in this speech? How does King use repetition to compound his opinions? How does he use it to move his argument forward?

4. One of the most impressive features of this speech is the full range of vision and audience that King demonstrates. How does he cover descriptive, geographic, and social range? How does he make his words appeal to the widest possible audience?

5. Toward the end of the speech, King introduces the litany of "Let freedom ring." Analyze the meaning and use of the transitional phrase "But not only that" in the middle of that section.

6. Make sure you know the meanings of the following words: manacles; languishing; degenerate; inextricably; wallow; interposition; nullification; exalted; prodigious. Select five for use in your own sentences.

Ideas for Writing

1. Write your own speech called "I Have a Dream" in which you strongly argue your position on a serious topic and propose a plan for action. Try to use language as dramatically as possible.

2. Do you believe that the dream expressed by Martin Luther King, Jr., in this speech can come true? Write an essay in which you take one side or the other of this question and argue for it convincingly.

3. As you know, Martin Luther King, Jr., like his father, was a Baptist minister. As such, he grew up on and practiced the art of stirring, emotional oratory. How is the language of this speech influenced by a "preacher style"? Do you feel it is effective as an essay alone, or is it written specifically to be orated? Explain your response.

A Modest Proposal

Jonathan Swift

Jonathan Swift (1667–1745) is rightfully afforded the title "greatest of English satirists." He was born in Dublin, Ireland, and was educated at Trinity College there. Swift was politically as well as literarily productive; originally a liberal Whig, he turned to Tory politics and wrote numerous political pamphlets. Appointed Dean of St. Patrick's Cathedral in Dublin in 1713, he remained at that post until 1736. His private life was secretive and somewhat complex. His *Journals to Stella* are a three-year series of letters to a young woman, Esther Johnson, whom he may or may not have secretly married. His early *Battle of the Books* and *Tale of a Tub* (1704) were satires on contemporary thought and religious excess. *Gulliver's Travels* (1726) and "A Modest Proposal" (1729) revealed the depth of Swift's social and political insights, along with his venomous satirical skills. He began experiencing terrifying bouts with mental illness around 1736, suffered a mental breakdown in 1741, and died four years later.

Next to *Gulliver's Travels,* "A Modest Proposal," written in 1729, is perhaps the best known among Jonathan Swift's writings. It was directed at the members of the British ruling class because of their oppressive treatment of the Irish. Clearly full of biting satire, this essay has its very serious side as well, easily discernible through a careful reading of Swift's seemingly outlandish argument.

*I*t is a melancholy object to those who walk through this great town   1
or travel in the country, when they see the streets, the roads, and cabin doors, crowded with beggars of the female-sex, followed by three, four, or six children, all in rags and importuning every passenger for an alms. These mothers, instead of being able to work for their honest livelihood, are forced to employ all their time in strolling to beg sustenance for their helpless infants, who, as they grow up, either turn thieves for want of work, or leave their dear native country to fight for the Pretender in Spain, or sell themselves to the Barbadoes.

I think it is agreed by all parties that this prodigious number of children in   2
the arms, or on the backs, or at the heels of their mothers, and frequently of their fathers, is in the present deplorable state of the kingdom a very great additional grievance; and therefore whoever could find out a fair, cheap, and easy method of making these children sound, useful members of the commonwealth would deserve so well of the public as to have his statue set up for a preserver of the nation.

But my intention is very far from being confined to provide only for the   3
children of professed beggars; it is of a much greater extent, and shall take in the whole number of infants at a certain age who are born of parents in effect as little able to support them as those who demand our charity in the streets.

As to my own part, having turned my thoughts for many years upon this   4
important subject, and maturely weighed the several schemes of other projec-

tors, I have always found them grossly mistaken in their computation. It is true, a child just dropped from its dam may be supported by her milk for a solar year, with little other nourishment; at most not above the value of two shillings, which the mother may certainly get, or the value in scraps, by her lawful occupation of begging; and it is exactly at one year old that I propose to provide for them in such a manner as instead of being a charge upon their parents or the parish, or wanting food and raiment for the rest of their lives, they shall on the contrary contribute to the feeding, and partly to the clothing, of many thousands.

There is likewise another great advantage in my scheme, that it will prevent those voluntary abortions, and that horrid practice of women murdering their bastard children, alas, too frequent among us, sacrificing the poor innocent babes, I doubt, more to avoid the expense than the shame, which would move tears and pity in the most savage and inhuman breast.

The number of souls in this kingdom being usually reckoned one million and a half, of these I calculate there may be about two hundred thousand couples whose wives are breeders; from which number I subtract thirty thousand couples who are able to maintain their own children, although I apprehend there cannot be so many under the present distresses of the kingdom; but this being granted, there will remain an hundred and seventy thousand breeders. I again subtract fifty thousand for those women who miscarry, or whose children die by accident or disease within the year. There only remain an hundred and twenty thousand children of poor parents annually born. The question therefore is, how this number shall be reared and provided for, which, as I have already said, under the present situation of affairs, is utterly impossible by all the methods hitherto proposed. For we can neither employ them in handicraft or agriculture; we neither build houses (I mean in the country) nor cultivate land. They can very seldom pick up a livelihood by stealing till they arrive at six years old, except where they are of towardly parts; although I confess they learn the rudiments much earlier, during which time they can however be looked upon only as probationers, as I have been informed by a principal gentlemen in the county of Cavan, who protested to me that he never knew above one or two instances under the age of six, even in a part of the kingdom so renowned for the quickest proficiency in that art.

I am assured by our merchants that a boy or girl before twelve years old is no salable commodity; and even when they come to this age they will not yield above three pounds, or three pounds and half a crown at most on the Exchange; which cannot turn to account either to the parents or the kingdom, the charge of nutriment and rags having been at least four times that value.

I shall now therefore humbly propose my own thoughts, which I hope will not be liable to the least objection.

I have been assured by a very knowing American of my acquaintance in London, that a young healthy child well nursed is at a year old a most delicious, nourishing, and wholesome food, whether stewed, roasted, baked or boiled; and I make no doubt that it will equally serve in a fricassee or a ragout.

I do therefore humbly offer it to public consideration that of the hundred and twenty thousand children, already computed, twenty thousand may be reserved for breed, whereof only one fourth part to be males, which is more than we allow to sheep, black cattle, or swine; and my reason is that these children are seldom the fruits of marriage, a circumstance not much regarded by our savages, therefore one male will be sufficient to serve four females. That the remaining hundred thousand may at a year old be offered in sale to the persons of quality and fortune through the kingdom, always advising the mother to let them suck plentifully in the last month, so as to render them plump and fat for a good table. A child will make two dishes at an entertainment for friends; and when the family dines alone, the fore or hind quarter will make a reasonable dish, and seasoned with a little pepper or salt will be very good boiled on the fourth day, especially in winter. 10

I have reckoned upon a medium that a child just born will weigh twelve pounds, and in a solar year if tolerably nursed increaseth to twenty-eight pounds. 11

I grant this food will be somewhat dear, and therefore very proper for landlords, who, as they have already devoured most of the parents, seem to have the best title to the children. 12

Infant's flesh will be in season throughout the year, but more plentiful in March, and a little before and after. For we are told by a grave author, an eminent French physician, that fish being a prolific diet, there are more children born in Roman Catholic countries about nine months after Lent than at any other season: therefore, reckoning a year after Lent, the markets will be more glutted than usual, because the number of popish infants is at least three to one in this kingdom; and therefore it will have one other collateral advantage, by lessening the number of Papists among us. 13

I have already computed the charge of nursing a beggar's child (in which list I reckon all cottagers, laborers, and four fifths of the farmers) to be about two shillings per annum, rags included: and I believe no gentleman would repine to give ten shillings for the carcass of a good fat child, which, as I have said, will make four dishes of excellent nutritive meat, when he hath only some particular friend or his own family to dine with him. Thus the squire will learn to be a good landlord, and grow popular among the tenants; the mother will have eight shillings net profit, and be fit for work till she produces another child. 14

Those who are more thrifty (as I must confess the times require) may flay the carcass; the skin of which artificially dressed will make admirable gloves for ladies, and summer boots for fine gentlemen. 15

As to our city of Dublin, shambles may be appointed for this purpose in the most convenient parts of it, and butchers we may be assured will not be wanting; although I rather recommend buying the children alive, and dressing them hot from the knife as we do roasting pigs. 16

A very worthy person, a true lover of his country, and whose virtues I highly esteem, was lately pleased in discoursing on this matter to offer a refinement upon my scheme. He said that many gentlemen of this kingdom, having of late destroyed their deer, he conceived that the want of venison might be well 17 supplied by the bodies of young lads and maidens, not exceeding fourteen years of age nor under twelve, so great a number of both sexes in every county being now ready to starve for want of work and service; and these to be disposed of by their parents, if alive, or otherwise by their nearest relations. But with due deference to so excellent a friend and so deserving a patriot, I cannot be altogether in his sentiments; for as to the males, my American acquaintance assured me from frequent experience that their flesh was generally tough and lean, like that of our schoolboys, by continual exercise, and their taste disagreeable; and to fatten them would not answer the charge. Then as to the females, it would, I think with humble submission, be a loss to the public, because they soon would become breeders themselves: and besides, it is not improbable that some scrupulous people might be apt to censure such a practice (although indeed very unjustly) as a little bordering upon cruelty; which, I confess, hath always been with me the strongest objection against any project, how well soever intended.

But in order to justify my friend, he confessed that this expedient was put [18] into his head by the famous Psalmanazar, a native of the island Formosa, who came from thence to London above twenty years ago, and in conversation told my friend that in his country when any young person happened to be put to death, the executioner sold the carcass to persons of quality as a prime dainty; and that in his time the body of a plump girl of fifteen, who was crucified for an attempt to poison the emperor, was sold to his Imperial Majesty's prime minister of state, and other great mandarins of the court, in joints from the gibbet, at four hundred crowns. Neither indeed can I deny that if the same use were made of several plump young girls in this town, who without one single groat to their fortunes cannot stir abroad without a chair, and appear at the playhouse and assemblies in foreign fineries which they never will pay for, the kingdom would not be the worse.

Some persons of a desponding spirit are in great concern about that vast [19] number of poor people who are aged, diseased, or maimed, and I have been desired to employ my thoughts what course may be taken to ease the nation of so grievous an encumbrance. But I am not in the least pain upon that matter, because it is very well known that they are every day dying and rotting by cold and famine, and filth and vermin, as fast as can be reasonably expected. And as to the younger laborers, they are now in almost as hopeful a condition. They cannot get work, and consequently pine away for want of nourishment to a degree that if at any time they are accidentally hired to common labor, they have not strength to perform it; and thus the country and themselves are happily delivered from the evils to come.

I have too long digressed, and therefore shall return to my subject. I think [20] the advantages by the proposal which I have made are obvious and many, as well as of the highest importance.

For first, as I have already observed, it would greatly lessen the number of [21] Papists, with whom we are yearly overrun, being the principal breeders of the nation as well as our most dangerous enemies; and who stay at home on purpose to deliver the kingdom to the Pretender, hoping to take their advantage by the absence of so many good Protestants, who have chosen rather to leave their country than to stay at home and pay tithes against their conscience to an Episcopal curate.

Secondly, the poorer tenants will have something valuable of their own, which by law may be made liable to distress, and help to pay their landlord's rent, their corn and cattle being already seized and money a thing unknown. 22

Thirdly, whereas the maintenance of an hundred thousand children, from two years old and upwards, cannot be computed at less than ten shillings a piece per annum, the nation's stock will be thereby increased fifty thousand pounds per annum, besides the profit of a new dish introduced to the tables of all gentlemen of fortune in the kingdom who have any refinement in taste. And the money will circulate among ourselves, the goods being entirely of our own growth and manufacture. 23

Fourthly, the constant breeders, besides the gain of eight shillings sterling per annum by the sale of their children, will be rid of the charge of maintaining them after the first year. 24

Fifthly, this food would likewise bring great custom to taverns, where the vinters will certainly be so prudent as to procure the best receipts for dressing it to perfection, and consequently have their houses frequented by all the fine gentlemen, who justly value themselves upon their knowledge in good eating; and a skillful cook, who understands how to oblige his guests, will contrive to make it as expensive as they please. 25

Sixthly, this would be a great inducement to marriage, which all wise nations have either encouraged by rewards or enforced by laws and penalties. It would increase the care and tenderness of mothers toward their children, when they were sure of a settlement for life to the poor babes, provided in some sort by the public, to their annual profit instead of expense. We should see an honest emulation among the married women, which of them could bring the fattest child to the market. Men would become as fond of their wives during the time of their pregnancy as they are now of their mares in foal, their cows in calf, or sows when they are ready to farrow; nor offer to beat or kick them (as is too frequent a practice) for fear of a miscarriage. 26

Many other advantages might be enumerated. For instance, the addition of some thousand carcasses in our exportation of barreled beef, the propagation of swine's flesh, and improvement in the art of making good bacon, so much wanted among us by the great destruction of pigs, too frequent at our tables, which are no way comparable in taste or magnificence to a well-grown, fat yearling child, which roasted whole will make a considerable figure at a lord mayor's feast or any other public entertainment. But this and many others I omit, being studious of brevity. 27

Supposing that one thousand families in this city would be constant customers for infants' flesh, besides others who might have it at merry meetings, particularly weddings and christenings, I compute that Dublin would take off annually about twenty thousand carcasses, and the rest of the kingdom (where probably they will be sold somewhat cheaper) the remaining eighty thousand. 28

I can think of no one objection that will possibly be raised against this pro- 29
posal, unless it should be urged that the number of people will be thereby much
lessened in the kingdom. This I freely own, and it was indeed one principal design in offering it to the world. I desire the reader will observe, that I calculate
my remedy for this one individual kingdom of Ireland and for no other that ever
was, is, or I think ever can be upon earth. Therefore let no man talk to me of
other expedients: of taxing our absentees at five shillings a pound: of using neither clothes nor household furniture except what is of our own growth and manufacture: of utterly rejecting the materials and instruments that promote foreign
luxury: of curing the expensiveness of pride, vanity, idleness, and gaming in our
women: of introducing a vein of parsimony, prudence, and temperance: of learning to love our country, in the want of which we differ even from Laplanders
and the inhabitants of Topinamboo: of quitting our animosities and factions, nor
acting any longer like the Jews, who were murdering one another at the very
moment their city was taken: of being a little cautious not to sell our country and
conscience for nothing: of teaching landlords to have at least one degree of
mercy toward their tenants: lastly, of putting a spirit of honesty, industry, and
skill into our shopkeepers; who, if a resolution could be now taken to buy only
our native goods, would immediately unite to cheat and exact upon us in the
price, the measure and the goodness, nor could ever yet be brought to make one
fair proposal of just dealing, though often and earnestly invited to it.

Therefore I repeat, let no man talk to me of these and the like expedients, 30
till he hath at least some glimpse of hope that there will ever be some hearty and
sincere attempt to put them in practice.

But as to myself, having been wearied out for many years with offering 31
vain, idle, visionary thoughts, and at length utterly despairing of success, I fortunately fell upon this proposal, which, as it is wholly new, so it hath something
solid and real, of no expense and little trouble, full in our own power, and
whereby we can incur no danger in disobliging England. For this kind of commodity will not bear exportation, the flesh being of too tender a consistence to
admit a long continuance in salt, although perhaps I could name a country which
would be glad to eat up our whole nation without it.

After all, I am not so violently bent upon my own opinion as to reject any 32
offer proposed by wise men, which shall be found equally innocent, cheap, easy,
and effectual. But before something of that kind shall be advanced in contradiction to my scheme, and offering a better, I desire the author or authors will be
pleased maturely to consider two points. First, as things now stand, how they
will be able to find food and raiment for an hundred thousand useless mouths
and backs. And secondly, there being a round million of creatures in human figure throughout this kingdom, whose sole subsistence put into a common stock
would leave them in debt two millions of pounds sterling, adding those who are
beggars by profession to the bulk of farmers, cottagers, and laborers, with their
wives and children who are beggars in effect; I desire those politicians who dislike my overture, and may perhaps be so bold to attempt an answer, that they
will first ask the parents of these mortals whether they would not at this day

think it a great happiness to have been sold for food at a year old in the manner I prescribe, and thereby have avoided such a perpetual scene of misfortunes as they have since gone through by the oppression of landlords, the impossibility of paying rent without money or trade, the want of common sustenance, with neither house nor clothes to cover them from the inclemencies of the weather, and the most inevitable prospect of entailing the like or greater miseries upon their breed forever.

I profess, in the sincerity of my heart, that I have not the least personal interest in endeavoring to promote this necessary work, having no other motive than the public good of my country, by advancing our trade, providing for infants, relieving the poor, and giving some pleasure to the rich. I have no children by which I can propose to get a single penny; the youngest being nine years old, and my wife past childbearing. 33

Meaning and Idea

1. Outline the six advantages Swift sees as the results of the enactment of his proposal. By what principle does he arrange them? What two types of "national profit" does he suggest?

2. How does the next to the last paragraph express Swift's genuine concern for the conditions of his native Ireland? What were some of those conditions?

3. What is the purpose of Swift's disclaimer at the end of the essay?

Language, Form, Structure

1. What is the main *proposition* of Swift's "modest proposal"? What are the *minor propositions?* (A *minor proposition* is a less generalized, though related, statement of opinion that supports the main proposition.)

2. The introduction in this essay spans a good many paragraphs. Identify the scope of the introduction. How does Swift begin establishing a fairly serious tone and purpose for his proposal? Where and how in the introduction does the reader begin to recognize the satire? (*Satire* is a literary form that uses wit, humor, irony, and sarcasm to criticize human behavior.) What satirical elements do you find in this essay?

3. Why does Swift repeatedly use words such as *modest, humbly,* and *sincerity?* Look up the etymology of the word *modest,* and check the *Oxford English Dictionary* for its various range of usages.

4. As in any well-written argumentation, Swift adequately deals with opposing arguments, although he does write: "I can think of no one objection that will possibly be raised against this proposal." What, in fact, is the purpose of his discussion of opposition arguments in this essay? What are some of the most important of these?

5. How does Swift use the "logic" of mathematics in support of his proposal?

6. *Logical fallacies* are errors in the logical development of an argument. What major logical fallacies do you discern in Swift's argument? Was he aware of them as well? How do you know?

7. Define the following words from "A Modest Proposal": alms; rudiments; liable; prolific; repine; deference; prudent; contrive; emulation; parsimony; inclemencies.

Ideas for Writing

1. Write a "modest proposal" of your own in which you use satire to argue about an important issue in society today. Make sure to deal with potential opposition arguments.

2. Write an argumentative essay in which you propose specific means by which political leaders could make life better in our country. Make your audience those leaders. Be sure to include some historical background to the present situation, as well as your vision of what future conditions will be if your proposal is adopted.

3. Check an unabridged dictionary or some other source for a complete definition of *satire*. Using the definition, comment on Swift's use of satire. How is it an effective tool in Swift's argument? Do you feel that satire makes his discussion of the Irish condition more or less effective than, say, a straightforward causal analysis? Do you find the satire in any way detrimental to your understanding of the issue, or do you find that it enhances your understanding? Explain with specific references to the text.

Unwanted Sex

Stephen Schulhofer

Stephen Schulhofer is currently the Julius Kreeger Professor of Law and Criminology and the director of the Center for Studies in Criminal Justice at the University of Chicago Law School. Schulhofer has written numerous articles in academic journals and is the author of a widely used textbook on criminal law. He has written and spoken on a wide variety of issues, including police interrogation, trial procedure, domestic violence, rape, sentencing policy, and the treatment of women in prison. He has also been a consultant to the U.S. Sentencing Commission, which mandates sentencing guidelines used by federal judges.

"Unwanted Sex" asserts that because current laws leave many loopholes in pursuing convictions for rape—saying "no" is not always sufficient to prove that a woman did not consent—we need to develop a new legal definition of rights based on what he calls "sexual autonomy." This would give people's right to refuse sex the same protections as their right to defend their property.

A young Illinois woman stopped to rest while biking along an isolated reservoir near the town of Carbondale. A stranger approached and struck up a conversation. After chatting with him for a few minutes, she got on her bicycle and started to leave. At that point the man, Joel Warren, put his hand on her shoulder. When she said, "No, I have to go now," he replied, "This will only take a minute. My girlfriend doesn't meet my needs." He added, "I don't want to hurt you."

Perhaps Warren only meant "We'll both enjoy this." But to the woman his comment sounded ominous, a hint of what he might do if she resisted him. In any event she had little time to consider nuances. Warren quickly lifted her up and carried her into the woods. He was six feet three inches tall and weighed 185 pounds. With no one else in sight, the young woman, who was only five feet two and weighed 100 pounds, did not attempt to scream or fight back, actions that she feared might prompt him to start choking or beating her. Once Warren had her hidden from view, he pulled off her pants, pushed up her shirt to expose her breasts, and subjected her to several acts of oral sex.

The police eventually identified Warren, prosecutors charged him with sexual assault, and a jury found him guilty. Yet an Illinois court set aside the conviction, saying that "the record is devoid of any attendant circumstances which suggest that complainant was compelled to submit." The year was 1983, but the court's approach remains very much with us.

Despite decades of public discussion and numerous statutory reforms before and since decisions like this one, the problem of defining and protecting our sexual boundaries has not been solved. The reasons are many. Sometimes statutes are highly protective but ineffectively enforced. Whatever the law may say, jurors often assume that it is neither abnormal nor harmful for a man to make aggressive physical advances to a silent, passive, or openly reluctant woman—literally to sweep her off her feet, pull off her clothes, and penetrate her, all without any explicit indication of her consent. Some jurors assume that women who submit to these advances really want the sexual contact, that they could easily resist if they didn't, or that it would be unfair to punish a man who, after all, was only doing what (so they may think) nature intended.

But attitudes like these are no longer universal. Our sexual culture has changed. Prosecutors sometimes file charges and juries sometimes convict in cases that would have been laughed out of court twenty or thirty years ago. Yet the law itself continues to pose obstacles, blocking enforcement and denying remedies even when juries are prepared to condemn defendants' conduct as outrageous. With its many gaps and limits, the law even tends to validate and reinforce the strands within our culture that persist in seeing aggressive male sexuality as a biological given that poses no problems. Outmoded standards are especially evident in criminal law, but other remedies have many of the same failings.

Criminal law's most obvious weak spot is its continuing vagueness—a surprise after all the effort devoted to reform. Standards remain extraordinarily murky, especially for determining when a man's behavior amounts to prohibited force or when a woman's conduct signals her consent. And where criminal law is murky, the benefit of the doubt usually goes to the defendant, in theory and often in practice. Acquittal rates are not noticeably lower for rape than they are for other serious felonies, but vague standards take their toll in other ways—deterring prosecutors from pursuing charges and deterring victims from filing complaints.

The number of cases affected is difficult to estimate, but a 1992 survey by researchers at the University of Chicago provides a chilling perspective on the problem. The survey found that 22 percent of American women felt they had been forced to have sex, yet only three percent of American men said they had ever forced a woman to have sex. After discounting the possibility that the men or the women had lied, or that a few men were responsible for forcing many different women, the researchers concluded that most of the men simply did not realize that their sexual partners were unwilling. The researchers wrote, "There seems to be not just a gender gap but a gender chasm in perceptions of when sex was forced."

But criminal-law rules are sometimes quite clear—especially when they *exclude* certain kinds of abuse. In the fall of 1988 a young Montana woman wrote an alarming letter to her school board. She claimed that two years earlier, during her senior year in high school, the school's principal had forced her to submit to intercourse by threatening to block her graduation. After an investigation by the county prosecutor, the principal was charged with two acts of "sexual intercourse without consent," a felony under Montana law.

Like many other cases of rape, indecent assault, or sexual harassment, the Montana case bristled with credibility questions. But the Montana Supreme

Court decided that the victim's story, even if true, could not support criminal charges. In Montana, as in most states, a sexual-assault charge normally requires proof that the abuser used physical force or threatened the victim with physical injury. Submission to avoid other kinds of harm is not enough to meet the statutory requirement of intercourse "without consent." The court itself was appalled by the narrow scope of the statute. The judges dismissed the case "with a good deal of reluctance," noting their "strong condemnation of the alleged acts," and adding, "If we could rewrite the statutes to [punish] the alleged acts . . . we would willingly do so."

In a situation like the one in Montana, the victim has a hard choice to make. An exceptionally self-possessed young woman might just tell her principal to get lost. But if she submits to the man's sexual demands, then as far as criminal law is concerned, she has consented.

Rape laws have moved far since the days when women were required to resist "to the utmost." Today "reasonable" resistance is supposed to be sufficient. In the more progressive states no resistance is required at all. But in nearly all states intimidation short of physical threats is still treated as if it were mere "persuasion." When it succeeds, courts will usually say that the victim "consented."

We have all heard of cases in which the police, judge, or jury refused to believe that a woman's "no" really meant no. But the problems run deeper: even when jurors are convinced that a woman was unwilling, unwillingness is not enough. In the face of clearly expressed objections, intercourse is still not considered rape or any other form of felonious assault unless the assailant used physical force or threatened bodily injury. And the law's definition of physical force remains extremely strict. The physical acts of lifting a woman up or pushing her onto a bed and accomplishing sexual penetration usually aren't enough. The "force" must be something beyond the acts involved in intercourse—something that physically "compels" the woman to submit.

Because nearly all states require proof of physical force in prosecutions for rape or sexual assault, many serious abuses are classified as "nonviolent" and penal sanctions are assumed to be inappropriate. The abuses are not really nonviolent, of course. It is more accurate to say that they don't involve what the law regards as the *required kind* of force. The force they do involve is seen as normal and therefore permissible.

When men use only the "right kind" of force, prosecutors seldom bother to file charges. But sometimes such cases are brought to court, often because of an aggravating element such as the youth of the victim. When prosecutors bring these cases, judges usually take the occasion to remind them that the force requirement will be strictly observed.

In a 1982 Mississippi case a fourteen-year-old girl I will call Sally was visiting her married sister, Elizabeth, who had recently separated from her husband, Dennis McQueen. One day Dennis stopped by Elizabeth's house and asked to take their two-year-old baby for a ride in his truck. Elizabeth did not want to leave Dennis alone with the baby, so she asked Sally to go along. When they returned, Sally was shaking and crying. She told her sister that Dennis had pulled off onto a deserted road and told her to get out of the truck. He told her to take off her clothes, lie down on the front seat, and put her legs up on his shoulders. Sally explained that she was scared of him because he had been drinking, and was afraid he was going to hurt her. She said she complied, crying throughout, as Dennis penetrated her and quickly had intercourse.

Because Mississippi then set the age of consent for intercourse at fourteen, Dennis McQueen was not charged with statutory rape. He was prosecuted for forcible rape, and the jury found him guilty. But the Mississippi Supreme Court set aside the conviction, because McQueen "did not threaten to injure [Sally], did not forcibly remove her from the truck, did not remove her clothes, and did not forcibly make her lie down in the truck." In 1992 an Ohio court reversed a similar conviction, invoking the same principle: no proof of physical force. [16]

When the victim is only fourteen, most states would be able to charge a man like McQueen with statutory rape. Earlier this year Mississippi raised its age of consent—to sixteen. But when a young woman reaches the age of sixteen, or in some states eighteen, statutory-rape charges are no longer possible; the man is likely to escape any criminal sanction. [17]

The narrow scope of contemporary criminal law becomes especially significant when a woman confronts sexual pressure from a man who holds professional power over her. Women face recurrent sexual demands from teachers, job supervisors, psychotherapists, doctors, and lawyers who misuse their authority to compel sexual submission. The best available estimates suggest that each year roughly a million working women are pressured to have sex with their job supervisors, and thousands (probably hundreds of thousands) of college women face unwanted sexual demands from their professors. Thousands more women submit each year to unwanted sex with their psychotherapists and physicians. Yet rape law offers no help in these situations, because the tactics the men use, though sometimes flagrantly coercive, are not physically violent. And civil suits, along with administrative penalties, often prove ineffective as well. Men who abuse their status or professional authority to coerce sexual compliance often face no significant sanctions. [18]

Karen (not her real name), the mother of three children, sought legal help to escape a troubled marriage. She hired a lawyer and paid him a $2,500 retainer. Later, distraught and insecure, she went to see him to discuss her case. He locked his office door, unzipped his pants, and asked her for oral sex. Convinced that he would drop her case and abandon her if she refused, Karen complied, and on two later occasions she submitted to his demands for intercourse. After several months she could no longer cope with the lawyer's sexual demands. She fired him and sued for malpractice. But in a 1990 decision an Illinois court said that she had no case, even if the lawyer had exploited her vulnerability and used his professional position to coerce her consent. The court ruled that lawyers can be held accountable for malpractice only when their misconduct has an adverse effect on their clients' *legal* problems. Emotional harm from coerced submission to repugnant sexual demands was, the court said, "insufficient"; the woman had no case because she "did not claim that her legal position in the divorce proceedings was harmed." [19]

Alcohol can add another dimension to the problem. A widely reported   20
1996 trial involved a woman in upstate New York who had been drinking heavily on a date and passed out in a restaurant bathroom. Her date, waiting for her
outside, fell asleep in his pickup truck. Meanwhile, five men carried the woman
from the bathroom to a booth, where they undressed her. All five then allegedly
raped her, left her in the booth, and returned to their beer and sandwiches.

The five men admitted the acts of intercourse, pleaded guilty to minor   21
misdemeanor charges, and were fined $840 each. But after a political uproar
over the leniency of the sentences, a special prosecutor managed to get the guilty
pleas set aside and brought the first of the defendants to trial on felony rape
charges. At the trial, *The New York Times* reported, the man's lawyer argued that
"if the woman had consumed enough alcohol to be helpless, as she testified,
then she could not be sure that she had not consented to sex." He didn't say, of
course, that the men should be sure that she *had* consented. Genuine willingness
on the part of the woman simply isn't required. The jury acquitted the man.

Criminal-law reforms often leave a false impression. For example, resis-   22
tance requirements have supposedly been restricted or abolished. But when a
woman says no, clearly and insistently, a man can still roll on top of her, remove
her clothes, and penetrate her, all without committing rape. The obstacle in such
a case is not conflicting versions of the truth or questions of credibility. The man
can admit to the facts, more or less with impunity. His conduct remains perfectly
legal, because he has not used what the law calls force—that is, physical power
in addition to the force that may be intrinsic to intercourse.

The upshot is that resistance requirements remain in effect even where the   23
law says they have been abolished. A woman's right to bodily integrity and sexual autonomy—her right to sexual choice—simply does not exist until she begins to scream or fight back physically.

Sexual-harassment suits provide an alternative for women who are co-   24
erced by tactics that stop short of physical force. It would be natural to assume
that sexual-harassment laws fill the gap left by criminal law's strict force requirement, because these laws are so often portrayed as exceedingly restrictive.
Vocal critics of these laws imply that they impose draconian sanctions on any
man who dares to use off-color language or express the slightest hint of sexual
interest in the presence of an exceptionally sensitive woman. In fact sexual-
harassment laws do nothing of the kind. On the contrary, they remain limited in
their coverage and effectiveness.

With few exceptions, sexual-harassment laws, state and federal, extend   25
protection only to employees and students. They are no help at all when a patient is pressured for sex by her doctor or when a client in a divorce proceeding
is coerced by a lawyer who threatens to stop working on her case if she won't
meet his sexual demands.

Even in the workplace, sexual-harassment laws are at best only partly effec-   26
tive. The laws apply if a supervisor or a professor is stupid enough to tell a woman
that he will hurt her career unless she submits to him. But sexual-harassment laws
often ignore the pressure that lurks beneath the surface of sexual demands from a

professor or a job supervisor. And even when an explicit threat can be proved, remedies are limited. The law permits civil damage suits against universities and companies, and such suits are often well publicized. What is less well known is that even when clear abuses are committed, the offender isn't personally liable for damages; sexual-harassment penalties apply only against the university or the business as an entity.

A series of Supreme Court decisions last spring made clear that women 27 subjected to sexual harassment can sue even when they have not been fired or denied a promotion. But at the same time the Court created new defenses that will permit many corporations and school districts to escape responsibility for harassment by their employees, and it left in place the rule that the employees themselves are not personally liable. President Bill Clinton's position in the Paula Jones suit is an exception, because a public official can be sued personally, under a separate set of federal laws, if he or she uses governmental power to violate a citizen's civil rights. However, the ordinary supervisor or teacher who uses his position to gain sexual favors usually incurs no civil or criminal liability, even for acts blatantly interfering with the sexual autonomy of a subordinate.

This gap in the law is puzzling, but not simple to fill. It is a daunting task 28 to define, clearly and specifically, what an appropriate system for protection of sexual autonomy should look like. It is not easy to set the boundaries for permissible conduct when positions of authority, threats, promises, alcohol, and abuses of trust have some effect on sexual interaction.

A prison guard's power clearly prevents an inmate from choosing freely 29 whether to accept *or* refuse a sexual proposal, but do we say the same about a college professor and a nineteen-year-old student taking his course? Do we say the same about a corporate vice-president and a junior executive working in another division? There are problems in such relationships, to be sure. But if sexual interaction is ruled legally out of bounds every time one of the parties has any possible source of power over the other, our opportunities to find companionship and sexual intimacy will shrink drastically. To create a legal barrier to every relationship not formed on the purely neutral ground of the singles bar or the church social would be pathetic and absurd.

A woman too drunk to stand up should not be expected to resist physically 30 or to protest explicitly—even if she downed all the drinks of her own accord and knew exactly what was in them. But do we say the same about a woman who has had just two or three drinks? Should we conclude that a woman's consent is invalid if she said "yes" because she was feeling relaxed and uninhibited after drinking a glass of wine? The law's willingness to find consent in cases of severe alcohol impairment should be considered intolerable, but a standard suggesting that rape occurred whenever alcohol played a part in sexual consent would be intolerable as well.

Respect for sexual autonomy requires safeguards against abuse and exploita- 31 tion. But—equally important—it requires that the law protect our freedom to seek emotional intimacy and sexual fulfillment with willing partners. Despite decades of discussion and years of ambitious feminist reforms, adequate protection of sexuality remains elusive, in part because freedom from unwanted sex and the freedom to seek mutually desired sex sometimes seem to be in tension. A workable notion of sexual autonomy appears to require compromises and balancing— the kind of chore that lawyers and academics often regard as a technical problem of "line-drawing." But the problem is neither simple nor unimportant. What is at stake is nothing less than women's bodily security and every person's right to control the boundaries of his or her own sexual experience.

Knowing Consent When We See It

Intercourse often "happens" after voluntary hugging, kissing, and sexual touching, without coercive threats but also without either of the parties ever saying "Yes, let's agree to have sex now." In one of the most frequent scenarios the woman remains silent and relatively passive; she may even push the man's hands away several times or say "No, don't." Traditional rape laws permit a defense of "consent," but they don't say what consent is. [32]

For many, the often-heard feminist view—that "no" means no—now seems obvious and uninteresting. In fact it is neither. By repeating the mantra " 'no' means no," anti-rape activists have sensitized many men and made some progress in changing assumptions about how women express interest in sex. But beneath the surface, in the messy, emotionally ambiguous real world of dating, petting, and sexual exploration, "no" doesn't always mean no. [33]

A 1988 survey of undergraduates at Texas A & M University presents a detailed look at this problem. More than 600 women were asked whether they had ever engaged in acts of token resistance when they really wanted to have sex. Thirty-nine percent of the women reported that they sometimes said no even though they "had every intention to and were willing to engage in sexual intercourse." Of the sexually experienced women, 61 percent said that they had done so. Though these women were willing to engage in intercourse eventually, they didn't necessarily want the men to disregard their "no" and force them to submit right away; many wanted their dates to wait or "talk me into it." But when a woman's "no" is equivocal, it means that her date, if he reads her intention correctly, should continue to press her for sex, perhaps in a physically assertive way. In fact, some of the women said that they told a date no because they "want[ed] him to be more physically aggressive." [34]

An obvious concern regarding this study is that the Texas A & M students may not be typical. The authors cautioned that the men tend to endorse gender roles that were prevalent in the 1950s. But subsequent studies elsewhere have reported strikingly similar findings, with no regional differences. A 1994 study of students at universities in Hawaii, Texas, and the Midwest found that 38 percent of the women sometimes said no when they meant yes. In a 1995 study at Penn State 37 percent of women reported having said no when they meant yes. For most women, most of the time, "no" does mean no. But sometimes it means "maybe" or "try harder." Sometimes, for some women, it means "get physical." [35]

Some supporters of rape-law reform prefer to set aside these empirical 36
findings. They probably fear that evidence of this sort will only reinforce society's willingness to tolerate male behavior that poses enormous risks for women.
But sexual ambivalence and miscommunication, though they undoubtedly exist,
do not automatically justify permissive legal standards. They need not dictate
impunity for men who ignore women's verbal protests. Indeed, it is precisely because of these inconvenient realities that legal requirements such as "consent"
and "reasonableness" solve so few of the difficulties.

The Search for Solutions

Despite their many disputes over theory and tactics, critics of existing rape law 37
largely agree in tracing its inadequacies to its overly narrow conception of force.
Protection of autonomy—a woman's right to make her own sexual choices—is
not ignored; it remains the ultimate goal and a frequent rhetorical theme. Yet
few reformers attempt to make autonomy or consent a formal legal requirement.

One reason is practical. Many anti-rape activists worry that evidence 38
about the victim's personal life might become relevant and that extensive cross-
examination of the victim might have to be permitted if legal proof focuses on
her state of mind rather than on the defendant's behavior. There is a more basic
point as well: a concern that autonomy simply has no meaning independent of
some notion of coercion. Through all the reform struggles of the past, reformers
and their critics alike shared the assumption that autonomy means—and can
only mean—freedom from force or duress.

As a result, most contemporary reformers stress autonomy only in their 39
rhetoric; they avoid making autonomous choice a formal requirement. Instead
the leading proposals for change urge two distinct but complementary reforms.
The first is to insist that "no" means no. The second aims to bridge the gaps in
existing legal protection by expanding traditional notions of force, coercion, or
duress. Both approaches have led the reform effort to unexpected dead ends.

The argument that a woman's "no" should always establish her unwilling- 40
ness remains intensely controversial. But even if that argument is accepted, as it
should be, it solves few of the problems. For example, a "no"-means-no rule
doesn't clarify the standards of behavior that should apply *after* the woman says
no. Is her "no" always final, or can a man ask again? Can he try to change her
mind—and if so, how? Those problems return us to the elusive question of what
should count as legally sufficient force. Winning legal recognition for the principle that "no" means no will not solve this puzzle.

Rape-law reformers have an answer. They hope to overcome the remaining 41
problems by extending the definition of "force" from physical violence to other
kinds of coercion. One obstacle here is the common practice of limiting rape
prosecutions to cases involving an explicit threat to use force. But shifting the
legal analysis to focus on implicit threats doesn't solve the problems; it only re-
states them. Courts still must identify some conduct that amounts to an unstated
threat. If the implicit-threat standard requires evidence tied to the defendant's

behavior at the time of the incident, verbal and physical details (flexing of the biceps, actual choking) will remain crucially important.

The problem is that even when implicit threats can count as force, the standard remains artificial because it focuses narrowly, in snapshot fashion, on specific comments and gestures made at the time of a rape incident. To escape that narrow focus, courts could consider the entire context, including the setting of the incident, the possibilities for running away or calling for help, the prior relationship between the parties, their relative size and strength, and so on.   42

This broader approach has clear advantages, but it poses a large problem. By shifting the force requirement from a man's threatening actions to his *capacity* to inflict harm, it makes the line between voluntary encounters and coercive sex hard to locate. If disparity in size, strength, and fighting ability is sufficient to establish force, then rape is implicit in most heterosexual relationships.   43

No court will permit a standard like this to extend to the limits of its logic, of course. The more serious concern is that a principle of this sort will seldom be used in practice. As long as the contextual approach fails to separate, in a roughly predictable way, what is legitimate from what is abusive, courts will bend over backward to ensure that men are not convicted of a serious offense unless they had fair warning that their conduct was criminal. Prosecutors, juries, and appellate courts will have no clear guidance and, much worse, no strong imperative to act. Underenforcement will be the all-too-foreseeable result.   44

Courts that accept the implicit-threat and inherent-capacity-to-harm standards keep those approaches within bounds by invoking a "reasonableness" limitation. An implicit threat or an intimidating capacity to inflict harm counts as force, and the woman does not have to resist physically—but her fears of injury must be considered "reasonable."   45

The reasonable-fear requirement seems a plausible limitation. Courts understandably consider it unfair to convict a man of rape when a woman who has cooperated in a sexual act has done so because of an unreasonable fear. Yet a reasonableness standard destroys most of the gains that the implicit-threat standard was supposed to achieve.   46

Reasonableness standards are common in law, and often work tolerably well, especially in highway driving and other areas of behavior in which norms of conduct are widely shared and moderately well understood. When norms are more controversial and stakes are high, as in the use of deadly force in self-defense, a general standard of reasonableness is seldom sufficient; the law uses elaborate rules to specify the kinds of threats that are serious enough to justify a lethal response, the circumstances that require the threatened person to shoot in defense rather than retreat, and so on.   47

In the case of sexual encounters, perceptions of danger can differ widely, and appropriate norms of behavior are intensely disputed. Our culture is at best ambivalent about whether a bit of physical aggression is attractive or unacceptable in male sexual initiatives. In these conditions a reasonableness standard doesn't just keep the implicit-threat approach within commonsense bounds. Instead it undercuts the effort to make traditional requirements of explicit force   48 more realistic. A reasonableness standard does little to challenge our culture's willingness to condone men's physically assertive sexual advances. And a reasonableness standard makes it all the more difficult to see why that culture—and the behavior it encourages—poses dangers for women.

As a result, the reasonableness standard leaves legal requirements almost   49 as narrow or unpredictable as they were before. Without some limitation, courts feel, reforms that extend force requirements from explicit to implicit threats and from actual conduct to inherent capabilities would have intolerable scope: they would render virtually all heterosexual sex coercive and therefore criminal. But with a limitation to "reasonable" fears, the move to include implicit threats and inherent capacities as forms of force ultimately achieves very little. The effort to stretch legal concepts of force cannot achieve what is needed—the recognition that sexual autonomy should be protected directly.

The Missing Entitlement—Sexual Autonomy

Sexual autonomy, like other rights, has two facets. The first is active—the right   50 to decide on the kind of life one wishes to live and the kinds of activities one wishes to pursue, including sexual interaction with others who are willing. The second is the reverse—the right to safeguard and exclude, the freedom to refuse to have sex with any person at any time, for any reason or for no reason at all.

Protection from coercion and the protection of autonomy are closely re-   51 lated and thus sometimes hard to tell apart. Existing rape laws and all the leading reform efforts add to this confusion by treating the two concerns as if they were two sides of the same coin. But the differences between them are crucial. Physical coercion interferes with autonomy, but many interferences with autonomy involve no coercion, physical or otherwise.

These distinctions are familiar when interests other than sexuality are at   52 stake. A person may take $100 from me by physical force, or he may take it by coercive but nonphysical threats—for example, if he threatens to spread false rumors that will ruin my business. A person may also get control over my property illegally without coercing me at all. He may take my $100 by stealth, or he may persuade me to give it to him by falsely promising something in return. In these cases his actions are illegal but not coercive. If our law of theft punished only coercive takings, we might try to say that takings by stealth or deception were in effect coercive—but we would know that the language was strained. The law of theft requires no such verbal contortions. It simply punishes takings by force (robbery), by coercive threats (extortion), by stealth (larceny), by breach of trust (embezzlement), and by deception (fraud and false pretenses). All these methods violate my rights because they impair—without adequate justification—my control over my property.

Much the same can be said for nearly all our most fundamental interests.   53 The law protects our control over our labor and our votes, our right to receive honest services from professionals, and our privacy, including confidential information about ourselves. Contexts are important, and the details of legal rights vary, but the general point holds: the law protects our autonomy in regard to these interests—our freedom to retain them or dispose of them however we may choose. It prohibits interference with meaningful choice by force, by stealth, and, usually, by breach of trust or deception. The law does not strain to say that all these interferences are coercive; it simply treats them as impermissible infringements on the liberty and self-determination to which every person is entitled.

Sexual autonomy is treated differently. Few of our other personal rights [54] and liberties—perhaps only our right to life itself—are as important as our right to decide whether and when we will become sexually intimate with another person. The emotional vulnerability and potential physical danger attached to sexual interaction make effective legal safeguards at least as important for sex as they are for the sale of land or the purchase of a used car. Strangely, in the list of fundamental entitlements that the law grants us as free and independent beings, sexual autonomy is somehow left out.

There is nothing intrinsic to sexuality that requires this constricted pattern [55] of protection. Violent threats are just one possible source of a defect in consent, and the law already recognizes a few others in the context of sexual relations. The best-known example is immaturity: the law has long prohibited consensual intercourse with a girl who is below the legally prescribed age of consent. The law likewise punishes acts of intercourse with a woman who is sleeping, unconscious, mentally incompetent, or unaware that a sexual act is being performed.

Traditionally, the law draws no formal distinction between cases of physi- [56] cal violence and exceptional cases like the ones just mentioned; all are classified as rape. Yet our terminology keeps force in the forefront. In ordinary language "rape" *means* the imposition of intercourse by force. The terminology influences assumptions about the proper scope of rape or assault, for judges, legislators, ordinary citizens, and committed anti-rape activists alike. Rather than asking whether certain sexual advances unjustifiably impair freedom of choice, we have asked only whether the conduct is so bad that it is equivalent to violent compulsion—whether it is tantamount to rape.

Sexual autonomy should not exist so precariously. Attention should no [57] longer focus exclusively on whether a man's behavior is aberrant, egregious, or potentially lethal. Instead the proper questions for debate are whether each participant in a sexual encounter had a meaningful opportunity to choose, and whether a meaningful choice was in fact made before sexual penetration occurred. In connection with criminal sanctions the law must also consider whether the defendant can fairly be considered culpable. But culpability cannot be confined to cases of aberrant physical violence; there is ample reason to find criminal responsibility when, for example, a man commits an act of sexual penetration *knowing* that he doesn't have the woman's consent.

Posing the issues in these terms will not by itself resolve them. Meaning- [58] ful choice and the limits of permissible interference with autonomy must be determined by paying close attention to contexts. We have to consider the dynamics of sexual interaction in different settings and the possible impairment of decision-making capabilities under different circumstances. We have to consider as well the possibility of significant differences between the scope of protection appropriate for sexuality and the scope of protection appropriate for other interests protected by current laws. But the issue must be framed in terms of sexual autonomy itself, not in terms of a futile search for something we can squeeze under the rubric of "force."

Once the focus of legal concern shifts from force to sexual autonomy, a much broader range of individual misconduct is called into question. When one person interferes with another person's ability to choose freely in a sexual encounter, legal intervention is appropriate even in the absence of force—just as it is when one person impairs another person's autonomy in relation to property rights, privacy, or other entitlements recognized by law. [59]

The starting point for any consideration of autonomy is the question of whether a person's consent is coerced. A focus on sexual autonomy enables us to distinguish legitimate inducements from threats or other sorts of pressure (sometimes in the form of offers) that should be criminally punishable. [60]

Without explicit threats or other improper inducements, freedom of choice can still be affected by the distribution of power in particular settings. For sexual relationships between men or women and their teachers, job supervisors, psychotherapists, doctors, dentists, and lawyers, legal restrictions are needed even in the absence of explicit threats. [61]

The capacity for meaningful choice can also be impaired by deception. Yet currently the law places no restrictions whatsoever on the use of fraudulent tactics to obtain consent to sex. Proposals for insisting on the same level of honesty in sexual exchange that we require as a matter of course in property transactions are usually dismissed as impractical or wildly out of touch with reality. At least in the case of egregiously deceptive inducements, the absence of legal sanctions is hard to justify. [62]

Even if a relationship is completely free of threats, deception, disparities of power, or breaches of trust, sexual contact obviously violates autonomy when one of the parties does not consent. But the question of what counts as an expression of consent is intensely contested: Does "no" always mean no? Is physical resistance necessary to make clear the absence of consent? And can we infer willingness from silence or ambivalence—from *not* saying no? [63]

Courts that find consent despite a verbal protest will inevitably find consent if the woman didn't protest or physically resist. But even courts and juries that treat a verbal no as sufficient to signal unwillingness are likely to consider a woman's silence equivalent to consent. Only a handful of states have taken the next step and insisted that consent to sex requires "affirmative and freely given permission." To most courts, a refusal to infer consent when a woman lies still and utters no protest is overly fastidious and wildly unrealistic. [64]

If a woman is unconscious or asleep, of course, her silence can't be equated with sexual willingness; a man who penetrates her will be guilty of rape. But when the woman is *able* to say no, the usual assumption is that if she remains silent, she must be willing; otherwise she would object. Or if she isn't [65] really willing, it is considered fair to treat her as if she were. Consent may be actual, or it may be a justified fiction. The episode on the Illinois bike path is just one of countless illustrations of this point of view. The court that reversed the man's sexual-assault conviction said that the woman's "failure to resist when it was within her power to do so conveys the impression of consent."

The soundness of requiring some protest is usually accepted without question. Yet it is by no means clear that women in such situations do have a fair chance to protest. The Illinois woman, for example, was a foot shorter and weighed eighty-five pounds less than her attacker, and was startled by a stranger in an isolated setting, with no one else in sight. Her silence might mean enthusiastic willingness, but it is *at least* equally likely that she was terrified and paralyzed by fear. [66]

The silence-means-consent assumption draws support even from some rape-law reformers. They worry that treating passivity or ambivalence as nonconsent will patronize women, who should be assumed to be capable of asserting their own wishes. But we seldom think it patronizing to insist on permission, not just silence, when the interests affected are ones that men can easily recognize. When a doctor asks if a patient wants a probe inserted into his rectum to check for tumors, the patient's silence is not assumed to indicate consent. The patient's willingness must be made explicit. Yet rape law doesn't require us to obtain actual permission for intercourse; it prohibits penetration only when there is clear evidence of *non*consent. [67]

An insistence on proof of unwillingness has a certain logic within the framework of existing law. It serves not only to ensure that potential lawbreakers have fair warning but also to keep the criminal prohibition focused on conduct involving force. A requirement of actual permission, however, would not shift the burden of proof to the defendant or require doubts to be resolved against him. A defendant could be convicted only if he knew he did not have the woman's affirmative permission or if he was criminally negligent in thinking that he did. But silence, ambiguous behavior, and the absence of a clearly expressed preference would be evidence that affirmative consent was absent; they would no longer suggest, as they do under present law, that a defendant did nothing wrong in forging ahead to intercourse. [68]

The significance of equivocal behavior should in effect be reversed. Equivocal behavior should reinforce prosecutors' claims that consent was absent, rather than serving (as under current law) to buttress defense claims that the woman never signaled her unwillingness. No standard can eliminate all factual uncertainty or swearing contests between witnesses. And some defendants would continue to avoid liability simply by telling elaborate lies. But facts that will often be quite clear—verbal protests, ambivalence, passivity, or silence— would by themselves be sufficient to establish an unambiguous offense against personal autonomy and an unambiguous basis for punishment. The important point is to shift the emphasis of the consent inquiry away from concern over whether the woman explicitly communicated her opposition. Sexual intimacy in- [69]

volves a profound intrusion on the physical and emotional integrity of the individual. Nothing less than positive willingness, clearly communicated, should ever count as consent.

In the few states—New Jersey, Wisconsin, Washington—where consent now means actual permission, not just the absence of protests, consent need not be in writing, of course. Permission can be communicated, these states' laws provide, by "actual words or conduct indicating freely given agreement to have sexual intercourse." Because body language can still count as an expression of consent, this approach (for better or worse) doesn't eliminate all the uncertainties of sexual communication. A world without ambiguity in erotic interaction might be a very dull place, after all. But ambiguity is also dangerous, especially for women who justifiably want the freedom to explore intimacy and sexual contact without losing their right to stop matters short of intercourse. 70

To minimize the risks, many reformers propose that nothing less than verbal permission—an explicit yes—should ever count as consent to intercourse. The drawbacks of such a rule are evident. If body language cannot be a legally effective way to express consent, many common modes of indicating a desire for intercourse will have to change radically, or—more likely—the verbal-permission requirement will simply be ignored by spouses, lovers, dating partners, and perhaps courts and juries as well. 71

To signal affirmative consent, body language must be unambiguous. Sexual petting does not in itself imply permission for intercourse, any more than does inviting a man in for coffee or permitting him to pay for dinner. A woman who engages in intense sexual foreplay should always retain the right to say no. If she doesn't say no, and if her silence is combined with passionate kissing, hugging, and sexual touching, it is usually sensible to infer actual willingness. A verbal-permission rule would reduce the risks of a possible misunderstanding in this situation, but at the cost of imposing a degree of formality and artificiality on human interactions in which spontaneity is especially important. 72

The verbal-yes rule thus seems many steps beyond the level of regulation that contemporary courts are likely to entertain. And a verbal-yes rule is not mandated by a commitment to respect sexual autonomy. The central point is that sexual intimacy must be chosen freely. The first priorities are to stop insisting on proof of the woman's opposition, and to stop requiring her to take actions clear enough to overcome the law's presumption that she is always interested in sex— at any time, in any place, with any person. The legal standard must move away from the demand for unambiguous evidence of her protests and insist instead that the man have affirmative indications that she chose to participate. So long as her choice is clearly expressed, by words or conduct, her right to control her sexuality is respected. 73

These important steps are not sufficient by themselves, however. In states that now require affirmative, "freely given" consent, the law still makes no effort to define which kinds of pressure prevent consent from being given 74 "freely." Experience under New Jersey's relatively progressive rule has demonstrated that when the concepts of force and coercion are left undefined, prosecutors continue to insist on evidence of physical intimidation. The law must stop equating force with physical violence.

Without this change of focus, clear-cut abuses will continue to slip   75
through the gaps in existing law. Men today are free, as in the Illinois case, to take advantage of strangers they accost in isolated settings. Lawyers in most states can exact sexual cooperation from clients who depend on them for essential help in divorce, child-custody, and criminal cases. A man in a bar or a fraternity house can get a woman drunk, undress her, and penetrate her before she can resist. In cases like these men continue to escape conviction by claiming that they never threatened physical violence and that the woman failed to make her unwillingness clear. Only when our laws and culture acknowledge the importance of affirmative, uncoerced permission will we afford women and men the right to control the boundaries of their own sexual lives. Until then sexual autonomy will remain the missing, unprotected entitlement.

Meaning and Idea

1. What laws does Schulhofer find inadequate? What specific cases, according to the writer, do the current laws allow to fall through the cracks? What solution does he propose for ameliorating this situation? How is the legal principle he proposes different from the current legal principle?

2. Schulhofer refers repeatedly to other reformers concerned with rape laws. What is his relation with those groups. On what grounds does he agree with them? On what grounds does he disagree with them?

3. Schulhofer repeatedly returns to the legal question of when a man's behavior during sex amounts to force. Why is this such a difficult question? Why is it important for the legal reforms Schulhofer is contemplating?

Language, Form, Structure

1. The opening three paragraphs of Schulhofer's essay tell a story. Why does he choose to begin his essay like this? How is this narrative an effective introduction to Schulhofer's argument? Why does he end this section with the date 1983?

2. How does the extended explanation in paragraph 53 of the way the law treats property crimes (larceny, extortion, and so on) help advance the writer's argument? Why is this comparison effective?

3. Schulhofer's essay provides many court cases, statistics, and results of expert studies. In what ways do these studies support his argument? Which ones are troublesome for him, and what does he do with "inconvenient" conclusions?

Ideas for Writing

1. In what ways do anti–sexual harassment laws and rules improve or inhibit relations between the sexes? Write an essay on whether you think sexual harassment laws and rules change the way you deal with your classmates or coworkers for the better or the worse. Do these codes of conduct make employees, students, and the public more comfortable in dealing with others? Do such laws simply define acceptable behavior, or do they confuse an issue that should resolve itself naturally?

2. Write an argumentative essay advancing your own proposal for reforming laws concerning rape. Explain how your solution will address the deficiencies in the legal system Schulhofer cites. Explain how it will improve upon Schulhofer's solutions.

3. As was noted above, Schulhofer provides both statistical evidence and case studies to back up his claims. This material offers not only coolly rational argumentation but also emotional prods for readers to support the legal reforms he proposes. Write an essay analyzing Schulhofer's use of examples to provoke a strong reaction in his readers.

To His Coy Mistress

Andrew Marvell

Andrew Marvell (1621–1678) is among the best known of the English metaphysical poets. He was a friend and assistant to John Milton, though he was somewhat more diplomatic and tolerant than his mentor. Marvell is best remembered for his biting wit and satire, some of it aimed directly at the Commonwealth, even though he remained a loyal member of Parliament until his death. Among his fine lyrical poetry are "The Garden," "Horatian Ode upon Cromwell's Return from Ireland," "The Nymph Complaining for the Death of her Faun," and "To His Coy Mistress."

Marvell makes an age-old argument the basis of this poem, but he gives it an energy and a universality that have earned for him respect and admiration from readers for over 300 years. As you read "To His Coy Mistress," pay special attention to Marvell's balance of subject, tone, and form in order to derive the full force of his argument.

*H*ad we but world enough, and time,
This coyness, lady, were no crime.
We would sit down, and think which way
To walk, and pass our long love's day.
Thou by the Indian Ganges' side   5
Shouldst rubies find; I by the tide
O Humber would complain. I would
Love you ten years before the Flood,
And you should, if you please, refuse
Till the conversion of the Jews.   10
My vegetable love should grow
Vaster than empires, and more slow;
An hundred years should go to praise
Thine eyes, and on thy forehead gaze;
Two hundred to adore each breast,   15
But thirty thousand to the rest;
An age at least to every part,
And the last age should show your heart.
For, lady, you deserve this state.
Nor would I love at lower rate.   20
        But at my back I always hear
Time's winged chariot hurrying near;
And yonder all before us lie
Deserts of vast eternity.
Thy beauty shall no more be found,   25

Nor, in thy marble vault, shall sound
My echoing song; then worms shall try
That long-preserved virginity,
And your quaint honor turn to dust,
And into ashes all my lust: 30
The grave's a fine and private place,
But none, I think, do there embrace.
      Now therefore, while the youthful hue
Sits on thy skin like morning dew,
And while thy willing soul transpires   35
At every pore with instant fires,
Now let us sport us while we may,
And now, like amorous birds of prey,
Rather at once our time devour
Than languish in his slow-chapped power.   40
Let us roll all our strength and all
Our sweetness up into one ball,
And tear our pleasures with rough strife
Thorough the iron gates of life.
Thus, though we cannot make our sun   45
Stand still, yet we will make him run.

Meaning and Idea

1. Why does the speaker call his mistress *coy?* How is her coyness a "crime" to him?

2. Of what is the speaker attempting to persuade his mistress? Approximately what age is the mistress?

3. How does the speaker use the element of time as a part of his argument?

4. The last two lines of the poem refer to a myth about Zeus, the Greek king of the gods: Zeus made the sun stand still so that his night of lovemaking with Alcmene would last all the longer. With that information, discuss the meaning of the last two lines of this poem.

Language, Form, Structure

1. What is the main point of the poem? Is it a poem about seduction, innocence, love, fleeting time, the mortality of the human race—any or all of these? Explain your answer.

2. Outline the three stages of the speaker's argument in his effort to convince his mistress. What transitions help Marvell connect the various argumentative strands?

3. What two contrasting views of seduction and sexuality does the speaker present? Which does he seem to prefer? Why?

4. Lines 29–32 form the end of the midpart of the speaker's argument. Would you say that his attitude has shifted from one of patience to one of slight sarcasm? Why? What words and phrases indicate his growing impatience? Do you feel he was *ever* really patient with his mistress? Why?

5. Marvell's use of language is extraordinary. Identify the most outstanding examples of original sensory images. Identify as many allusions as possible in the poem, especially in lines 5–20. Of what benefit to the argument are these allusions?

6. Identify and define at least five words that are new to you in this poem.

Ideas for Writing

1. Write an ironic argument in which you attempt to persuade a specific member of the opposite sex to take some specific course of action. In the beginning of your argument, pay close attention to the other person's point of view, then refute it before proposing your own plan of action.

2. Write a narration of a time when you convinced *yourself* to do something you thought you didn't want to do. Arrange your narration/argumentation chronologically.

3. One critic calls some of the lines in this poem "as fine an example as English poetry can show of wit blended with imagination." Write a paper in which you support this assessment of "To His Coy Mistress." Make specific references to the poem.

Dulce et Decorum Est

Wilfred Owen

Wilfred Owen (1893–1918) was among the English "war poets" of World War I, the most notable of whom was Siegfried Sassoon. Owen was born in Oswestry, England, and had a checkered education. He partially rejected Christianity in the midst of studying for the priesthood, then moved to Bordeaux, France. He returned to England in 1915 to enlist in the Manchester Regiment of the British Army. While recuperating in a hospital in Edinburgh, he met Sassoon, who encouraged Owen's poetry writing. Owen was killed a week before the Armistice in 1918, and his poems were published by Sassoon in 1920.

In "Dulce et Decorum Est" a young soldier pleads against the romanticization of war. The poet makes his case all the more convincing through the pointed contrast of his realistic description of a dying fellow soldier against an abstract and distant call to arms. The poem gains power from our knowledge that Owen died in that war. *Dulce et decorum est pro patria mori,* a line from Horace, a Roman poet who lived in the first century B.C., means "It is sweet and becoming to die for one's country."

*B*ent double, like old beggars under sacks,
Knock-kneed, coughing like hags, we cursed through sludge,
Till on the haunting flares we turned our backs,
And towards our distant rest began to trudge.
Men marched asleep. Many had lost their boots, 5
But limped on, blood-shod. All went lame, all blind;
Drunk with fatigue; deaf even to the hoots
Of gas-shells dropping softly behind.

Gas! GAS! Quick, boys!—An ecstasy of fumbling,
Fitting the clumsy helmets just in time, 10
But someone still was yelling out and stumbling
And flound'ring like a man in fire or lime.—
Dim through the misty panes and thick green light,
As under a green sea, I saw him drowning.

In all my dreams before my helpless sight 15
He plunges at me, guttering, choking, drowning.

If in some smothering dreams, you too could pace
Behind the wagon that we flung him in,
And watch the white eyes writhing in his face,
His hanging face, like a devil's sick of sin, 20

If you could hear, at every jolt, the blood
Come gargling from the froth-corrupted lungs
Bitter as the cud
Of vile, incurable sores on innocent tongues,—
My friend, you would not tell with such high zest   25
To children ardent for some desperate glory,
The old lie: *Dulce et decorum est*
Pro patria mori.

Meaning and Idea

1. Briefly describe, in your own words, the setting and action of this poem. How is the one soldier's experience different from the others'?

2. What are the "gas-shells" and the "Gas!" that Owen writes about? What war do those references clearly place this poem in?

3. How does Owen use the quotation from Horace to establish his own idea? Why does he call Horace's opinion "The old lie"? What attitude does that description express?

4. Explain the double meaning of line 4. What is the "distant rest"?

Language, Form, Structure

1. What would you say is the position Owen is arguing here? Who is being addressed in this poem? What clue does the "you" of line 17 provide? Is the intended audience fighting in the war as the narrator is? How are the narrator and the audience linked by dreams in this poem?

2. Given the narrative context of the poem, does *ecstasy* seem like a strange word choice in line 9? Why? Why does Owen use that word?

3. What descriptive details are most powerful in making Owen's argument? Comment on Owen's use of similes in this poem. Identify each one. How do they enhance the description of "Dulce et Decorum Est"?

4. Explain Owen's use of the following descriptions: blood-shod (line 6); helpless sight (line 15); desperate glory (line 26).

5. Make sure you know the meanings of the following words: hags; sludge; guttering; cud; vile; ardent.

The Smurfette Principle

Katha Pollitt

Katha Pollitt (1949–) was born in Brooklyn, New York, and lives and works in Manhattan. She received a B.A. from Radcliffe in 1972 and an M.F.A. in poetry from Barnard College. A poet who has been compared to Wallace Stevens, Pollitt served as poet in residence at Barnard and won the National Book Critics Circle Award for her first book of poetry, *Antarctica Traveler* (1982). Pollitt's articles appear regularly in *The Atlantic Monthly, Mother Jones, The New Yorker,* and *The Nation,* where she has been an associate editor. In 1994 she published *Reasonable Creatures: Essays on Women and Feminism.* Among the subjects *Reasonable Creatures* covers are the literary canon, "difference feminism," and the decision by journalists to disclose the victim's name in the rape trial of William Kennedy Smith.

Pollitt traces the concern for media representations of gender relations that underlie "The Smurfette Principle" to hearing her daughter repeat messages she would never have picked up at home. "Suddenly," she describes the experience, "it's like this little person is a radio station through which the culture is beaming itself."

*T*his Christmas, I finally caved in: I gave my 3-year-old daughter, Sophie, her very own cassette of "The Little Mermaid." Now, she, too, can sit transfixed by Ariel, the perky teen-ager with the curvy tail who trades her voice for a pair of shapely legs and a shot at marriage to a prince. ("On land it's much preferred for ladies not to say a word," sings the cynical sea witch, "and she who holds her tongue will get her man." Since she's the villain, we're not meant to notice that events prove her correct.)

Usually when parents give a child some item they find repellent, they plead helplessness before a juvenile filibuster. But "The Little Mermaid" was my idea. Ariel may look a lot like Barbie, and her adventure may be limited to romance and over with the wedding bells, but unlike, say, Cinderella or Sleeping Beauty, she's active, brave and determined, the heroine of her own life. She even rescues the prince. And that makes her a rare fish, indeed, in the world of preschool culture.

Take a look at the kids' section of your local video store. You'll find that features starring boys, and usually aimed at them, account for 9 out of 10 offerings. Clicking the television dial one recent week—admittedly not an encyclopedic study—I came across not a single network cartoon or puppet show starring a female. (Nickelodeon, the children's cable channel, has one of each.) Except for the crudity of the animation and the general air of witlessness and hype, I might as well have been back in my own 1950's childhood, nibbling Frosted Flakes in front of Daffy Duck, Bugs Bunny, Porky Pig and the rest of the all-male Warner Brothers lineup.

Contemporary shows are either essentially all-male, like "Garfield," or   4
are organized on what I call the Smurfette principle: a group of male buddies
will be accented by a lone female, stereotypically defined. In the worst car-
toons—the ones that blend seamlessly into the animated cereal commercials—
the female is usually a little-sister type, a bunny in a pink dress and hair ribbons
who tags along with the adventurous bears and badgers. But the Smurfette principle rules the more carefully made shows, too. Thus, Kanga, the only female
in "Winnie-the-Pooh," is a mother. Piggy, of "Muppet Babies," is a pint-size
version of Miss Piggy, the camp glamour queen of the Muppet movies. April,
of the wildly popular "Teen-Age Mutant Ninja Turtles," functions as a girl Friday to a quartet of male superheroes. The message is clear. Boys are the norm,
girls the variation; boys are central, girls peripheral; boys are individuals, girls
types. Boys define the group, its story and its code of values. Girls exist only in
relation to boys.

Well, commercial television—what did I expect? The surprise is that pub-   5
lic television, for all its superior intelligence, charm and commitment to worthy
values, shortchanges preschool girls, too. Mister Rogers lives in a neighborhood
populated mostly by middle-aged men like himself. "Shining Time Station" features a cartoon in which the male characters are train engines and the female
characters are passenger cars. And then there's "Sesame Street." True, the
human characters are neatly divided between the genders (and among the races,
too, which is another rarity). The film clips, moreover, are just about the only
place on television in which you regularly see girls having fun together: practicing double Dutch, having a sleep-over. But the Muppets are the real stars of
"Sesame Street," and the important ones—the ones with real personalities, who
sing on the musical videos, whom kids identify with and cherish in dozens of licensed products—are *all* male. I know one little girl who was so outraged and
heartbroken when she realized that even Big Bird—her last hope—was a boy
that she hasn't watched the show since.

Well, there's always the library. Some of the best children's books ever   6
written have been about girls—Madeline, Frances the badger. It's even possible
to find stories with funny, feminist messages, like "The Paper-bag Princess."
(She rescues the prince from a dragon, but he's so ungrateful that she decides
not to marry him, after all.) But books about girls are a subset in a field that includes a much larger subset of books about boys (12 of the 14 storybooks sin-
gled out for praise in last year's Christmas roundup in *Newsweek,* for instance)
and books in which the sex of the child is theoretically unimportant—in which
case it usually "happens to be" male. Dr. Seuss's books are less about individual
characters than about language and imaginative freedom—but, somehow or
other, only boys get to go on beyond Zebra or see marvels on Mulberry Street.
Frog and Toad, Lowly Worm, Lyle the Crocodile, all *could* have been female.
But they're not.

Do kids pick up on the sexism in children's culture? You bet. Preschoolers   7
are like medieval philosophers: the text—a book, a movie, a TV show—is more
authoritative than the evidence of their own eyes. "Let's play weddings," says

my little niece. We grownups roll our eyes, but face it: it's still the one scenario in which the girl is the central figure. "Women are *nurses,*" my friend Anna, a doctor, was informed by her then 4-year-old, Molly. Even my Sophie is beginning to notice the back-seat role played by girls in some of her favorite books. "Who's that?" she asks every time we reread "The Cat in the Hat." It's Sally, the timid little sister of the resourceful boy narrator. She wants Sally to matter, I think, and since Sally is really just a name and a hair ribbon, we have to say her name again and again.

The sexism in preschool culture deforms both boys and girls. Little girls learn to split their consciousness, filtering their dreams and ambitions through boy characters while admiring the clothes of the princess. The more privileged and daring can dream of becoming exceptional women in a man's world—Smurfettes. The others are being taught to accept the more usual fate, which is to be a passenger car drawn through life by a masculine train engine. Boys, who are rarely confronted with stories in which males play only minor roles, learn a simpler lesson: girls just don't matter much.

How can it be that 25 years of feminist social changes have made so little impression on preschool culture? Molly, now 6 and well aware that women can be doctors, has one theory: children's entertainment is mostly made by men. That's true, as it happens, and I'm sure it explains a lot. It's also true that, as a society, we don't seem to care much what goes on with kids, as long as they are reasonably quiet. Marshmallow cereal, junky toys, endless hours in front of the tube—a society that accepts all that is not going to get in a lather about a little gender stereotyping. It's easier to focus on the bright side. I had "Cinderella," Sophie has "The Little Mermaid"—that's progress, isn't it?

"We're working on it," Dulcy Singer, the executive producer of "Sesame Street," told me when I raised the sensitive question of those all-male Muppets. After all, the show has only been on the air for a quarter of a century; these things take time. The trouble is, our preschoolers don't have time. My funny, clever, bold, adventurous daughter is forming her gender ideas right now. I do what I can to counteract the messages she gets from her entertainment, and so does her father—Sophie watches very little television. But I can see we have our work cut out for us. It sure would help if the bunnies took off their hair ribbons, and if half of the monsters were fuzzy, blue—and female.

Meaning and Idea

1. List some of the specific programs Pollitt objects to. In each case, what is her criticism?

2. List some of the shows that Pollitt approves of. What about each individual show gives it value?

3. Define the "Smurfette principle." What examples does Pollitt give of that principle in action?

4. According to Pollitt, what is the effect—on girls and on boys—of the sexism in preschool culture?

5. What practical steps is Pollitt suggesting? What in particular drives her sense of urgency that these steps be taken?

6. In paragraph 9, Pollitt asks, "How can it be that 25 years of feminist social changes have made so little impression on preschool culture?" How does she answer this question?

Language, Form, Structure

1. What is the writer's thesis here?

2. Look back over the transitions Pollitt uses at the beginnings of her paragraphs. Pay particular attention to the *well* of paragraphs 5 and 6 and the questions that Pollitt asks to begin paragraphs 7 and 9. What do these transitions add to the essay? How do they change the essay's *tone?* What effect do you think Pollitt intended these transitions to have on the reader?

3. Look at the writer's use of irony in the last paragraph. At whose expense is it? Why do you think Pollitt uses irony here rather than a direct statement of criticism?

4. Define the following words and then use each one in a sentence: transfixed; filibuster; stereotype; peripheral.

Ideas for Writing

1. Which has more influence over a child's understanding of gender roles, the child's parent or the mass media? Write an essay in which you take a strong position one way or another and support that position with examples taken from Pollitt, your own experience, or other outside sources.

2. Pollitt's essay was written in 1991 and thus mentions several shows that have faded into obscurity. Do her points describe the current crop of preschool shows equally well? Write an essay in which you argue a position on this question. Be certain to refer specifically to the "Smurfette principle" and describe how current shows follow it or undermine it.

3. Read over the first two paragraphs of Pollitt's essay. For an essay that at times takes the position that there is really nothing good on television, this is a surprising introduction. Write an essay in which you analyze Pollitt's choice of introductions. How does this introduction relate to the rest of the essay? What does it add to the essay?

The Judgment

Franz Kafka

Born in Prague in 1883, Franz Kafka posthumously became one of the most respected writers of the twentieth century. His works are steeped in the anxiety, alienation, and indifference of the modern world, especially as they pertain to the relation between the individual and society. The author himself lived in the shadow of a strong-willed, patriarchal father, and the social structure of the family did not escape Kafka's eye.

He considered "The Judgment" (1913) an important story in his own work, though he saw few of his many, highly respected works published during his lifetime. He died of tuberculosis at the age of 41.

*I*t was a Sunday morning in the very height of spring. Georg Bende- 1 mann, a young merchant, was sitting in his own room on the first floor of one of a long row of small, ramshackle houses stretching beside the river which were scarcely distinguishable from each other except in height and coloring. He had just finished a letter to an old friend of his who was now living abroad, had put it into its envelope in a slow and dreamy fashion, and with his elbows propped on the writing table was gazing out of the window at the river, the bridge and the hills on the farther bank with their tender green.

He was thinking about his friend, who had actually run away to Russia 2 some years before, being dissatisfied with his prospects at home. Now he was carrying on a business in St. Petersburg, which had flourished to begin with but had long been going downhill, as he always complained on his increasingly rare visits. So he was wearing himself out to no purpose in a foreign country, the unfamiliar full beard he wore did not quite conceal the face Georg had known so well since childhood, and his skin was growing so yellow as to indicate some latent disease. By his own account he had no regular connection with the colony of his fellow countrymen out there and almost no social intercourse with Russian families, so that he was resigning himself to becoming a permanent bachelor.

What could one write to such a man, who had obviously run off the rails, a 3 man one could be sorry for but could not help? Should one advise him to come home, to transplant himself and take up his old friendships again—there was nothing to hinder him—and in general to rely on the help of his friends? But that was as good as telling him, and the more kindly the more offensively, that all his efforts hitherto had miscarried, that he should finally give up, come back home, and be gaped at by everyone as a returned prodigal, that only his friends knew what was what and that he himself was just a big child who should do what his successful and home-keeping friends prescribed. And was it certain, besides, that all the pain one would have to inflict on him would achieve its object? Perhaps it would not even be possible to get him to come home at all—he said himself that he was now out of touch with commerce in his native country—and then he would still be left an alien in a foreign land embittered by his friends' advice and more than ever estranged from them. But if he did follow their advice and then didn't fit in at home—not out of malice, of course, but through force of circumstances—couldn't get on with his friends or without them, felt humiliated, couldn't be said to have either friends or a country of his own any longer, wouldn't it have been better for him to stay abroad just as he was? Taking all this into account, how could one be sure that he would make a success of life at home?

For such reasons, supposing one wanted to keep up correspondence with 4
him, one could not send him any real news such as could frankly be told to the most distant acquaintance. It was more than three years since his last visit, and for this he offered the lame excuse that the political situation in Russia was too uncertain, which apparently would not permit even the briefest absence of a small businessman while it allowed hundreds of thousands of Russians to travel peacefully abroad. But during these three years Georg's own position in life had changed a lot. Two years ago his mother had died, since when he and his father had shared the household together, and his friend had of course been informed of that and had expressed his sympathy in a letter phrased so dryly that the grief caused by such an event, one had to conclude, could not be realized in a distant country. Since that time, however, Georg had applied himself with greater determination to the business as well as to everything else.

Perhaps during his mother's lifetime his father's insistence on having 5
everything his own way in the business had hindered him from developing any real activity of his own, perhaps since her death his father had become less aggressive, although he was still active in the business, perhaps it was mostly due to an accidental run of good fortune—which was very probable indeed—but at any rate during those two years the business had developed in a most unexpected way, the staff had had to be doubled, the turnover was five times as great, no doubt about it, farther progress lay just ahead.

But Georg's friend had no inkling of this improvement. In earlier years, 6
perhaps for the last time in that letter of condolence, he had tried to persuade Georg to emigrate to Russia and had enlarged upon the prospects of success for precisely Georg's branch of trade. The figures quoted were microscopic by comparison with the range of Georg's present operations. Yet he shrank from letting his friend know about his business success, and if he were to do it now retrospectively that certainly would look peculiar.

So Georg confined himself to giving his friend unimportant items of gos- 7
sip such as rise at random in the memory when one is idly thinking things over on a quiet Sunday. All he desired was to leave undisturbed the idea of the home town which his friend must have built up to his own content during the long interval. And so it happened to Georg that three times in three fairly widely separated letters he had told his friend about the engagement of an unimportant man to an equally unimportant girl, until indeed, quite contrary to his intentions, his friend began to show some interest in this notable event.

Yet Georg preferred to write about things like these rather than to confess   8
that he himself had got engaged a month ago to a Fräulein Frieda Brandenfeld, a
girl from a well-to-do family. He often discussed this friend of his with his fiancée and the peculiar relationship that had developed between them in their
correspondence. "So he won't be coming to our wedding," said she, "and yet I
have a right to get to know all your friends." "I don't want to trouble him," answered Georg, "don't misunderstand me, he would probably come, at least I
think so, but he would feel that his hand had been forced and he would be hurt,
perhaps he would envy me and certainly he'd be discontented and without being
able to do anything about his discontent he'd have to go away again alone.
Alone—do you know what that means?" "Yes, but may he not hear about our
wedding in some other fashion?" "I can't prevent that, of course, but it's unlikely, considering the way he lives." "Since your friends are like that, Georg,
you shouldn't ever have got engaged at all." "Well, we're both to blame for that;
but I wouldn't have it any other way now." And when, breathing quickly under
his kisses, she still brought out: "All the same, I do feel upset," he thought it
could not really involve him in trouble were he to send the news to his friend.
"That's the kind of man I am and he'll just have to take me as I am," he said to
himself, "I can't cut myself to another pattern that might make a more suitable
friend for him."

And in fact he did inform his friend, in the long letter he had been writing   9
that Sunday morning, about his engagement, with these words: "I have saved my
best news to the end. I have got engaged to a Fräulein Frieda Brandenfeld, a girl
from a well-to-do family, who only came to live here a long time after you went
away, so that you're hardly likely to know her. There will be time to tell you
more about her later, for today let me just say that I am very happy and as between you and me the only difference in our relationship is that instead of a
quite ordinary kind of friend you will now have in me a happy friend. Besides
that, you will acquire in my fiancée, who sends her warm greetings and will
soon write you herself, a genuine friend of the opposite sex, which is not without
importance to a bachelor. I know that there are many reasons why you can't
come to see us, but would not my wedding be precisely the right occasion for
giving all obstacles the go-by? Still, however that may be, do just as seems good
to you without regarding any interests but your own."

With this letter in his hand Georg had been sitting a long time at the writ-   10
ing table, his face turned towards the window. He had barely acknowledged,
with an absent smile, a greeting waved to him from the street by a passing acquaintance.

At last he put the letter in his pocket and went out of his room across a   11
small lobby into his father's room, which he had not entered for months. There
was in fact no need for him to enter it, since he saw his father daily at business
and they took their midday meal together at an eating house; in the evening, it
was true, each did as he pleased, yet even then, unless Georg—as mostly happened—went out with friends or, more recently, visited his fiancée, they always
sat for a while, each with his newspaper, in their common sitting room.

It surprised Georg how dark his father's room was even on this sunny   12
morning. So it was overshadowed as much as that by the high wall on the other
side of the narrow courtyard. His father was sitting by the window in a corner
hung with various mementoes of Georg's dead mother, reading a newspaper
which he held to one side before his eyes in an attempt to overcome a defect of
vision. On the table stood the remains of his breakfast, not much of which
seemed to have been eaten.

"Ah, Georg," said his father, rising at once to meet him. His heavy dress-   13
ing gown swung open as he walked and the skirts of it fluttered round him—
"My father is still a giant of a man," said Georg to himself.

"It's unbearably dark here," he said aloud.   14

"Yes, it's dark enough," answered his father.   15

"And you've shut the window, too?"   16

"I prefer it like that."   17

"Well, it's quite warm outside," said Georg, as if continuing his previous   18
remark, and sat down.

His father cleared away the breakfast dishes and set them on a chest.   19

"I really only wanted to tell you," went on Georg, who had been vacantly   20
following the old man's movements, "that I am now sending the news of my engagement to St. Petersburg." He drew the letter a little way from his pocket and
let it drop back again.

"To St. Petersburg?" asked his father.   21

"To my friend there," said Georg, trying to meet his father's eye.—In   22
business hours he's quite different, he was thinking, how solidly he sits here
with his arms crossed.

"Oh yes. To your friend," said his father, with peculiar emphasis.   23

"Well, you know, Father, that I wanted not to tell him about my engage-   24
ment at first. Out of consideration for him, that was the only reason. You know
yourself he's a difficult man. I said to myself that someone else might tell him
about my engagement, although he's such a solitary creature that that was hardly
likely—I couldn't prevent that—but I wasn't ever going to tell him myself."

"And now you've changed your mind?" asked his father, laying his enor-   25
mous newspaper on the window sill and on top of it his spectacles, which he
covered with one hand.

"Yes, I've been thinking it over. If he's a good friend of mine, I said to my-   26
self, my being happily engaged should make him happy too. And so I wouldn't put
off telling him any longer. But before I posted the letter I wanted to let you know."

"Georg," said his father, lengthening his toothless mouth, "listen to me!   27
You've come to me about this business, to talk it over with me. No doubt that
does you honor. But it's nothing, it's worse than nothing, if you don't tell me the
whole truth. I don't want to stir up matters that shouldn't be mentioned here.
Since the death of our dear mother certain things have been done that aren't
right. Maybe the time will come for mentioning them, and maybe sooner than
we think. There's many a thing in the business I'm not aware of, maybe it's not
done behind my back—I'm not going to say that it's done behind my back—I'm

not equal to things any longer, my memory's failing, I haven't an eye for so many things any longer. That's the course of nature in the first place, and in the second place the death of our dear mother hit me harder than it did you.—But since we're talking about it, about this letter, I beg you, Georg, don't deceive me. It's a trivial affair, it's hardly worth mentioning, so don't deceive me. Do you really have this friend in St. Petersburg?"

Georg rose in embarrassment. "Never mind my friends. A thousand friends wouldn't make up to me for my father. Do you know what I think? You're not taking enough care of yourself. But old age must be taken care of. I can't do without you in the business, you know that very well, but if the business is going to undermine your health, I'm ready to close it down tomorrow forever. And that won't do. We'll have to make a change in your way of living. But a radical change. You sit here in the dark, and in the sitting room you would have plenty of light. You just take a bite of breakfast instead of properly keeping up your strength. You sit by a closed window, and the air would be so good for you. No, Father! I'll get the doctor to come, and we'll follow his orders. We'll change your room, you can move into the front room and I'll move in here. You won't notice the change, all your things will be moved with you. But there's time for all that later, I'll put you to bed now for a little, I'm sure you need to rest. Come, I'll help you to take off your things, you'll see I can do it. Or if you would rather go into the front room at once, you can lie down in my bed for the present. That would be the most sensible thing." 28

Georg stood close beside his father, who had let his head with its unkempt white hair sink on his chest. 29

"Georg," said his father in a low voice, without moving. 30

Georg knelt down at once beside his father, in the old man's weary face he saw the pupils, over-large, fixedly looking at him from the corners of the eyes. 31

"You have no friend in St. Petersburg. You've always been a leg-puller and you haven't even shrunk from pulling my leg. How could you have a friend out there! I can't believe it." 32

"Just think back a bit, Father," said Georg, lifting his father from the chair and slipping off his dressing gown as he stood feebly enough, "it'll soon be three years since my friend came to see us last. I remember that you used not to like him very much. At least twice I kept you from seeing him, although he was actually sitting with me in my room. I could quite well understand your dislike of him, my friend has his peculiarities. But then, later, you got on with him very well. I was proud because you listened to him and nodded and asked him questions. If you think back you're bound to remember. He used to tell us the most incredible stories of the Russian Revolution. For instance, when he was on a business trip to Kiev and ran into a riot, and saw a priest on a balcony who cut a broad cross in blood on the palm of his hand and held the hand up and appealed to the mob. You've told that story yourself once or twice since." 33

Meanwhile Georg had succeeded in lowering his father down again and carefully taking off the woollen drawers he wore over his linen underpants and his socks. The not particularly clean appearance of this underwear made him reproach 34 himself for having been neglectful. It should have certainly been his duty to see that his father had clean changes of underwear. He had not yet explicitly discussed with his bride-to-be what arrangements should be made for his father in the future, for they had both of them silently taken it for granted that the old man would go on living alone in the old house. But now he made a quick, firm decision to take him into his own future establishment. It almost looked, on closer inspection, as if the care he meant to lavish there on his father might come too late.

He carried his father to bed in his arms. It gave him a dreadful feeling to notice that while he took the few steps towards the bed the old man on his breast was playing with his watch chain. He could not lay him down on the bed for a moment, so firmly did he hang on to the watch chain.   35

But as soon as he was laid in bed, all seemed well. He covered himself up and even drew the blankets farther than usual over his shoulders. He looked up at Georg with a not unfriendly eye.   36

"You begin to remember my friend, don't you?" asked Georg, giving him an encouraging nod.   37

"Am I well covered up now?" asked his father, as if he were not able to see whether his feet were properly tucked in or not.   38

"So you find it snug in bed already," said Georg, and tucked the blankets more closely round him.   39

"Am I well covered up now?" asked the father once more, seeming to be strangely intent upon the answer.   40

"Don't worry, you're well covered up."   41

"No!" cried his father, cutting short the answer, threw the blankets off with a strength that sent them all flying in a moment and sprang erect in bed. Only one hand lightly touched the ceiling to steady him.   42

"You wanted to cover me up, I know, my young sprig, but I'm far from being covered up yet. And even if this is the last strength I have, it's enough for you, too much for you. Of course I know your friend. He would have been a son after my own heart. That's why you've been playing him false all these years. Why else? Do you think I haven't been sorry for him? And that's why you had to lock yourself up in your office—the Chief is busy, mustn't be disturbed—just so that you could write your lying little letters to Russia. But thank goodness a father doesn't need to be taught how to see through his son. And now that you thought you'd got him down, so far down that you could set your bottom on him and sit on him and he wouldn't move, then my fine son makes up his mind to get married!"   43

Georg stared at the bogey conjured up by his father. His friend in St. Petersburg, whom his father suddenly knew too well, touched his imagination as never before. Lost in the vastness of Russia he saw him. At the door of an empty, plundered warehouse he saw him. Among the wreckage of his showcases, the slashed remnants of his wares, the falling gas brackets, he was just standing up. Why did he have to go so far away!   44

"But attend to me!" cried his father, and Georg, almost distracted, ran towards the bed to take everything in, yet came to a stop halfway.   45

"Because she lifted up her skirts," his father began to flute, "because she lifted her skirts like this, the nasty creature," and mimicking her he lifted his shirt so high that one could see the scar on his thigh from his war wound, "because she lifted her skirts like this and this you made up to her, and in order to make free with her undisturbed you have disgraced your mother's memory, betrayed your friend and stuck your father into bed so that he can't move. But he can move, or can't he?" 46

And he stood up quite unsupported and kicked his legs out. His insight made him radiant. 47

Georg shrank into a corner, as far away from his father as possible. A long time ago he had firmly made up his mind to watch closely every least movement so that he should not be surprised by any indirect attack, a pounce from behind or above. At this moment he recalled this long-forgotten resolve and forgot it again, like a man drawing a short thread through the eye of a needle. 48

"But your friend hasn't been betrayed after all!" cried his father, emphasizing the point with stabs of his forefinger. "I've been representing him here on the spot." 49

"You comedian!" Georg could not resist the retort, realized at once the harm done and, his eyes starting in his head, bit his tongue back, only too late, till the pain made his knees give. 50

"Yes, of course I've been playing a comedy! A comedy! That's a good expression! What other comfort was left to a poor old widower? Tell me—and while you're answering me be you still my living son—what else was left to me, in my back room plagued by a disloyal staff, old to the marrow of my bones? And my son strutting through the world, finishing off deals that I had prepared for him, bursting with triumphant glee and stalking away from his father with the closed face of a respectable businessman! Do you think I didn't love you, I, from whom you are sprung?" 51

Now he'll lean forward, thought Georg, what if he topples and smashes himself! These words went hissing through his mind. 52

His father leaned forward but did not topple. Since Georg did not come any nearer, as he had expected, he straightened himself again. 53

"Stay where you are, I don't need you! You think you have strength enough to come over here and that you're only hanging back of your own accord. Don't be too sure! I am still much the stronger of us two. All by myself I might have had to give way, but your mother has given me so much of her strength that I've established a fine connection with your friend and I have your customers here in my pocket!" 54

"He has pockets even in his shirt!" said Georg to himself, and believed that with this remark he could make him an impossible figure for all the world. Only for a moment did he think so, since he kept on forgetting everything. 55

"Just take your bride on your arm and try getting in my way! I'll sweep her from your very side, you don't know how!" 56

Georg made a grimace of disbelief. His father only nodded, confirming the truth of his words, towards Georg's corner. 57

"How you amused me today, coming to ask me if you should tell your ⁵⁸ friend about your engagement. He knows it already, you stupid boy, he knows it all! I've been writing to him, for you forgot to take my writing things away from me. That's why he hasn't been here for years, he knows everything a hundred times better than you do yourself, in his left hand he crumples your letters unopened while in his right hand he holds up my letters to read through!"

In his enthusiasm he waved his arm over his head. "He knows everything ⁵⁹ a thousand times better!" he cried.

"Ten thousand times!" said Georg, to make fun of his father, but in his ⁶⁰ very mouth the words turned into deadly earnest.

"For years I've been waiting for you to come with some such question! Do ⁶¹ you think I concern myself with anything else? Do you think I read my newspapers? Look!" and he threw Georg a newspaper sheet which he had somehow taken to bed with him. An old newspaper, with a name entirely unknown to Georg.

"How long a time you've taken to grow up! Your mother had to die, she ⁶² couldn't see the happy day, your friend is going to pieces in Russia, even three years ago he was yellow enough to be thrown away, and as for me, you see what condition I'm in. You have eyes in your head for that!"

"So you've been lying in wait for me!" cried Georg. ⁶³

His father said pityingly, in an offhand manner: "I suppose you wanted to ⁶⁴ say that sooner. But now it doesn't matter." And in a louder voice: "So now you know what else there was in the world besides yourself, till now you've known only about yourself! An innocent child, yes, that you were, truly, but still more truly have you been a devilish human being!—And therefore take note: I sentence you now to death by drowning!"

Georg felt himself urged from the room, the crash with which his father ⁶⁵ fell on the bed behind him was still in his ears as he fled. On the staircase, which he rushed down as if its steps were an inclined plane, he ran into his charwoman on her way up to do the morning cleaning of the room. "Jesus!" she cried, and covered her face with her apron, but he was already gone. Out of the front door he rushed, across the roadway, driven towards the water. Already he was grasping at the railings as a starving man clutches food. He swung himself over, like the distinguished gymnast he had once been in his youth, to his parents' pride. With weakening grip he was still holding on when he spied between the railings a motor-bus coming which would easily cover the noise of his fall, called in a low voice: "Dear parents, I have always loved you, all the same," and let himself drop.

At this moment an unending stream of traffic was just going over the bridge. ⁶⁶

Meaning and Idea

1. Describe the relations between Georg and his father, Georg and his friend in Russia, and Georg and his fiancée. Which of these relations seem normal to you? Which seem odd, at best?

2. What is Georg's fate? How do you explain the end of the story? Would you say that Georg's fate reflects his guilt? His father's dominance over him? His own mental instability? Defend your response.

3. What would you say is the theme of the story, the main point Kafka is trying to make here?

4. Sanity and insanity never lie too far beneath the surface in Kafka's works. Who in this story is sane, do you think? Who is insane? Why do you think so?

5. Why did Kafka choose the title "The Judgment" for his story? What conditions or events does the title refer to? Exactly what is being judged here, do you think?

Language, Form, Structure

1. What are the various elements of argument and persuasion here? How, for example, do argument and persuasion play a role in Georg's thoughts about telling his friend about the engagement? What elements of argument do you observe in Georg's conversation with his father? What, do you think, ultimately persuades Georg to take his final action at the bridge?

2. Kafka uses the strategy of comparison and contrast here to intensify the theme of the story. For example, how does the comparison between Georg's friend in St. Petersburg and Georg himself enrich your understanding of Georg? What elements of Georg's analysis of his friend actually apply to Georg too? What other comparisons and contrasts do you note?

3. What elements of description, particularly of the father and his environment, contribute to your understanding of his mental and physical state?

4. Define these words and use each one in an original sentence: ramshackle; latent; prodigal; estranged; mementos; plundered; remnants; grimace.

Ideas for Writing

1. Write an essay in which you present the arguments used by a family member to persuade you to do something you did not want to do.

2. What do you think are the obligations of a child to an aging parent? Write an essay in which you attempt to persuade the reader to take some course of action when it comes to dealing with a parent growing older, perhaps infirm, and unable fully to care for himself or herself.

3. Write an essay to convince your reader about the sanity of the characters in Kafka's story. Cite and analyze details from "The Judgment" to support your argument.

On Liberty

John Stuart Mill

John Stuart Mill (1806–1873), the Victorian British philosopher and economist, was one of the major influences on the direction of modern political, economic, and philosophical thought. Schooled in the utilitarianism of Jeremy Bentham and of his father, James Mill, John Stuart Mill liberalized that doctrine considerably. Mill's advocacy of *laissez-faire* economics is still highly touted, though Mill himself was an early advocate of such socialist movements as labor unions, women's rights, and farm cooperatives. His base of logic lay in induction and empiricism (the doctrine that all knowledge derives from experience) and can be found in such works as *Principles of Political Economy* (1848), *On Liberty* (1859), and *Utilitarianism* (1863).

"On Liberty" comes from Mill's *On Liberty; and Thoughts on Parliamentary Reform,* published in 1859. There are those who consider Mill's arguments in that collection the basis for liberal individualism, while others consider it the direct ancestor of the conservative *laissez-faire* doctrines of contemporary political leaders. In reading Mill's argument, postulate your own opinion about its contemporary importance and pay close attention to the structure of his argumentative development.

*T*he subject of this Essay is not the so-called Liberty of the Will, so unfortunately opposed to the misnamed doctrine of Philosophical Necessity; but Civil, or Social Liberty: the nature and limits of the power which can be legitimately exercised by society over the individual. A question seldom stated, and hardly ever discussed, in general terms, but which profoundly influences the practical controversies of the age by its latent presence, and is likely soon to make itself recognized as the vital question of the future. It is so far from being new, that, in a certain sense, it has divided mankind, almost from the remotest ages; but in the stage of progress into which the more civilized portions of the species have now entered, it presents itself under new conditions, and requires a different and more fundamental treatment.

The struggle between Liberty and Authority is the most conspicuous feature in the portions of history with which we are earliest familiar, particularly in that of Greece, Rome, and England. But in old times this contest was between subjects, or some classes of subjects, and the Government. By liberty, was meant protection against the tyranny of the political rulers. The rulers were conceived (except in some of the popular governments of Greece) as in a necessarily antagonistic position to the people whom they ruled. They consisted of a governing One, or a governing tribe or caste, who derived their authority from inheritance or conquest, who, at all events, did not hold it at the pleasure of the governed, and whose supremacy men did not venture, perhaps did not desire, to contest, whatever precautions might be taken against its oppressive exercise.

Their power was regarded as necessary, but also as highly dangerous; as a weapon which they would attempt to use against their subjects, no less than against external enemies. To prevent the weaker members of the community from being preyed upon by innumerable vultures, it was needful that there should be an animal of prey stronger than the rest, commissioned to keep them down. But as the king of the vultures would be no less bent upon preying on the flock than any of the minor harpies, it was indispensable to be in a perpetual attitude of defence against his beak and claws. The aim, therefore, of patriots was to set limits to the power which the ruler should be suffered to exercise over the community; and this limitation was what they meant by liberty. It was attempted in two ways. First, by obtaining a recognition of certain immunities, called political liberties or rights, which it was to be regarded as a breach of duty in the ruler to infringe, and which, if he did infringe, specific resistance, or general rebellion, was held to be justifiable. A second, and generally a later expedient, was the establishment of constitutional checks, by which the consent of the community, or of a body of some sort, supposed to represent its interest, was made a necessary condition to some of the more important acts of the governing power. To the first of these modes of limitation, the ruling power, in most European countries, was compelled, more or less, to submit. It was not so with the second; and, to attain this, or when already in some degree possessed, to attain it more completely, became everywhere the principal object of the lovers of liberty. And so long as mankind were content to combat one enemy by another, and to be ruled by a master, on condition of being guaranteed more or less efficaciously against his tyranny, they did not carry their aspirations beyond this point.

A time, however, came, in the progress of human affairs, when men ceased to think it a necessity of nature that their governors should be an independent power, opposed in interest to themselves. It appeared to them much better that the various magistrates of the State should be their tenants or delegates, revocable at their pleasure. In that way alone, it seemed, could they have complete security that the powers of government would never be abused to their disadvantage. By degrees this new demand for elective and temporary rulers became the prominent object of the exertions of the popular party, wherever any such party existed; and superseded, to a considerable extent, the previous efforts to limit the power of rulers. As the struggle proceeded for making the ruling power emanate from the periodical choice of the ruled, some persons began to think that too much importance had been attached to the limitation of the power itself. *That* (it might seem) was a resource against rulers whose interests were habitually opposed to those of the people. What was now wanted was, that the rulers should be identified with the people; that their interest and will should be the interest and will of the nation. The nation did not need to be protected against its own will. There was no fear of its tyrannizing over itself. Let the rulers be effectually responsible to it, promptly removable by it, and it could afford to trust them with power of which it could itself dictate the use to be made. Their power was but the nation's own power, concentrated, and in a form convenient for exercise. This mode of thought, or rather perhaps of feeling, was common among the last generation of European liberalism, in the Continental section of which it still apparently predominates. Those who admit any limit to what a government may do, except in the case of such governments as they think ought not to exist, stand out as brilliant exceptions among the political thinkers of the Continent. A similar tone of sentiment might by this time have been prevalent in our own country, if the circumstances which for a time encouraged it, had continued unaltered.

But, in political and philosophical theories, as well as in persons, success 4 discloses faults and infirmities which failure might have concealed from observation. The notion, that the people have no need to limit their power over themselves, might seem axiomatic, when popular government was a thing only dreamed about, or read of as having existed at some distant period of the past. Neither was that notion necessarily disturbed by such temporary aberrations as those of the French Revolution, the worst of which were the work of an usurping few, and which, in any case, belonged, not to the permanent working of popular institutions, but to a sudden and convulsive outbreak against monarchical and aristocratic despotism. In time, however, a democratic republic came to occupy a large portion of the earth's surface, and made itself felt as one of the most powerful members of the community of nations; and elective and responsible government became subject to the observations and criticisms which wait upon a great existing fact. It was now perceived that such phrases as "self-government," and "the power of the people over themselves," do not express the true state of the case. The "people" who exercise the power are not always the same people with those over whom it is exercised; and the "self-government" spoken of is not the government of each by himself, but of each by all the rest. The will of the people, moreover, practically means the will of the most numerous or the most active *part* of the people; the majority, or those who succeed in making themselves accepted as the majority; the people, consequently, *may* desire to oppress a part of their number; and precautions are as much needed against this as against any other abuse of power. The limitation, therefore, of the power of government over individuals loses none of its importance when the holders of power are regularly accountable to the community, that is, to the strongest party therein. This view of things, recommending itself equally to the intelligence of thinkers and to the inclination of those important classes in European society to whose real or supposed interests democracy is adverse, has had no difficulty in establishing itself; and in political speculations "the tyranny of the majority" is now generally included among the evils against which society requires to be on its guard.

Like other tyrannies, the tyranny of the majority was at first, and is still 5 vulgarly, held in dread, chiefly as operating through the acts of the public authorities. But reflecting persons perceived that when society is itself the tyrant—society collectively, over the separate individuals who compose it—its means of tyrannizing are not restricted to the acts which it may do by the hands of its political functionaries. Society can and does execute its own mandates: and if it issues wrong mandates instead of right, or any mandates at all in things with which it ought not to meddle, it practices a social tyranny more formidable than many kinds of political oppression, since, though not usually upheld by such extreme penalties, it leaves fewer means of escape, penetrating much more deeply into the details of life, and enslaving the soul itself. Protection, therefore, against the tyranny of the magistrate is not enough: there needs protection also against the tyranny of the prevailing opinion and feeling; against the tendency of society to impose, by other means than civil penalties, its own ideas and practices as rules of conduct on those who dissent from them; to fetter the development, and, if possible, prevent the formation, of any individuality not in harmony with its ways, and compel all characters to fashion themselves upon the model of its own. There is a limit to the legitimate interference of collective opinion with individual independence: and to find that limit, and maintain it against encroachment, is as indispensable to a good condition of human affairs, as protection against political despotism.

But though this proposition is not likely to be contested in general terms, the practical question, where to place the limit—how to make the fitting adjustment between individual independence and social control—is a subject on which nearly everything remains to be done. All that makes existence valuable to any one, depends on the enforcement of restraints upon the actions of other people. Some rules of conduct, therefore, must be imposed, by law in the first place, and by opinion on many things which are not fit subjects for the operation of law. What these rules should be, is the principal question in human affairs; but if we except a few of the most obvious cases, it is one of those which least progress has been made in resolving. No two ages, and scarcely any two countries, have decided it alike; and the decision of one age or country is a wonder to another. Yet the people of any given age and country no more suspect any difficulty in it, than if it were a subject on which mankind had always been agreed. The rules which obtain among themselves appear to them self-evident and self-justifying. This all but universal illusion is one of the examples of the magical influence of custom, which is not only, as the proverb says, a second nature, but is continually mistaken for the first. The effect of custom, in preventing any misgiving respecting the rules of conduct which mankind impose on one another, is all the more complete because the subject is one on which it is not generally considered necessary that reasons should be given, either by one person to others, or by each to himself. People are accustomed to believe, and have been encouraged in the belief by some who aspire to the character of philosophers, that their feelings, on subjects of this nature, are better than reasons, and render reasons unnecessary. The practical principle which guides them to their opinions on the regulation of human conduct, is the feeling in each person's mind that everybody should be required to act as he, and those with whom he sympathizes, would like them to act. No one, indeed, acknowledges to himself that his standard of judgement is his own liking; but an opinion on a point of conduct, not supported by reasons, can only count as one person's preference; and if the reasons, when given, are a mere appeal to a similar preference felt by other people, it is still only many people's liking instead of one. To an ordinary man, however, his own preference, thus supported, is not only a perfectly satisfactory reason, but the only one he generally has for any of his notions of morality, taste, or propriety, which are not expressly written in his religious creed; and his chief guide in the interpretation even of that. Men's opinions, accordingly, on what is laudable or blameable, are affected by all the multifarious causes which influence their wishes in regard to the conduct of others, and which are as numerous as those which determine their wishes on any other subject. Sometimes their reason—at other times their prejudices or superstitions: often their social affections, not seldom their anti-social ones, their envy or jealousy, their arrogance or contemptuousness: but most commonly, their desires or fears for themselves—their legitimate or illegitimate self-interest. Wherever there is an ascendant class, a large portion of the morality of the country emanates from its class interests, and its feelings of class superiority. The morality between Spartans and Helots, between planters and negroes, between princes and subjects, between nobles and roturiers, between men and women, has been for the most part the creation of these class interests and feelings: and the sentiments thus generated, react in turn upon the moral feelings of the members of the ascendant class, in their relations among themselves. Where, on the other hand, a class, formerly ascendant, has lost its ascendancy, or where its ascendancy is unpopular, the prevailing moral sentiments frequently bear the impress of an impatient dislike of superiority. Another grand determining principle of the rules of conduct, both in act and forbearance, which have been enforced by law or opinion, has been the servility of mankind towards the supposed preferences or aversions of their temporal masters, or of their gods. This servility, though essentially selfish, is not hypocrisy; it gives rise to perfectly genuine sentiments of abhorrence; it made men burn magicians and heretics. Among so many baser influences, the general and obvious interests of society have of course had a share, and a large one, in the direction of the moral sentiments: less, however, as a matter of reason, and on their own account, than as a consequence of the sympathies and antipathies which grew out of them: and sympathies and antipathies which had little or nothing to do with the interests of society, have made themselves felt in the establishment of moralities with quite as great force.

The likings and dislikings of society, or of some powerful portion of it, are thus the main thing which has practically determined the rules laid down for general observance, under the penalties of law or opinion. And in general, those who have been in advance of society in thought and feeling, have left this condition of things unassailed in principle, however they may have come into conflict with it in some of its details. They have occupied themselves rather in inquiring what things society ought to like or dislike, than in questioning whether its likings or dislikings should be a law to individuals. They preferred endeavouring to alter the feelings of mankind on the particular points on which they were themselves heretical, rather than make common cause in defence of freedom, with heretics generally. The only case in which the higher ground has been taken on principle and maintained with consistency, by any but an individual here and there, is that of religious belief: a case instructive in many ways, and not least so as forming a most striking instance of the fallibility of what is called the moral sense: for the *odium theologicum,* in a sincere bigot, is one of the most unequivocal cases of moral feeling. Those who first broke the yoke of what called itself the Universal Church, were in general as little willing to permit difference of religious opinion as that church itself. But when the heat of the conflict was over, without giving a complete victory to any party, and each church or sect was reduced to limit its hopes to retaining possession of the ground it already occupied; minorities, seeing that they had no chance of becoming majorities, were under the necessity of pleading to those whom they could not convert, for permission to differ. It is accordingly on this battlefield, almost solely, that the rights of the individual against society have been asserted on broad grounds of principle, and the claim of society to exercise authority over dissentients, openly controverted. The great writers to whom the world owes what religious liberty it possesses, have mostly asserted freedom of conscience as an indefeasible right, and denied absolutely that a human being is accountable to others for his religious belief. Yet so natural to mankind is intolerance in whatever they really care about, that religious freedom has hardly anywhere been practically realized, except where religious indifference, which dislikes to have its peace disturbed by theological quarrels, has added its weight to the scale. In the minds of almost all religious persons, even in the most tolerant countries, the duty of toleration is admitted with tacit reserves. One person will bear with dissent in matters of church government, but not of dogma; another can tolerate everybody, short of a Papist or a Unitarian; another, every one who believes in revealed religion; a few extend their charity a little further, but stop at the belief in a God and in a future state. Wherever the sentiment of the majority is still genuine and intense, it is found to have abated little of its claim to be obeyed.

In England, from the peculiar circumstances of our political history, though the yoke of opinion is perhaps heavier, that of law is lighter, than in most other countries of Europe; and there is considerable jealousy of direct interference, by the legislative or the executive power, with private conduct; not so much from any just regard for the independence of the individual, as from the still subsisting habit of looking on the government as representing an opposite interest to the public. The majority have not yet learnt to feel the power of the government their power, or its opinions their opinions. When they do so, individual liberty will probably be as much exposed to invasion from the government, as it already is from public opinion. But, as yet, there is a considerable amount of feeling ready to be called forth against any attempt of the law to control individuals in things in which they have not hitherto been accustomed to be controlled by it; and this with very little discrimination as to whether the matter is, or is not, within the legitimate sphere of legal control; insomuch that the feeling, highly salutary on the whole, is perhaps quite as often misplaced as well grounded in the particular instances of its application. There is, in fact, no recognized principle by which the propriety or impropriety of government interference is customarily tested. People decide according to their personal preferences. Some, whenever they see any good to be done, or evil to be remedied, would willingly instigate the government to undertake the business; while others prefer to bear almost any amount of social evil, rather than add one to the departments of human interests amenable to governmental control. And men range themselves on one or the other side in any particular case, according to this general direction of their sentiments; or according to the degree of interest which they feel in the particular thing which it is proposed that the government should do, or according to the belief they entertain that the government would, or would not, do it in the manner they prefer; but very rarely on account of any opinion to which they consistently adhere, as to what things are fit to be done by a government. And it seems to me that in consequence of this absence of rule or principle, one side is at present as often wrong as the other; the interference of government is, with about equal frequency, improperly invoked and improperly condemned.

The object of this Essay is to assert one very simple principle, as entitled   9
to govern absolutely the dealings of society with the individual in the way of compulsion and control, whether the means used be physical force in the form of legal penalties, or the moral coercion of public opinion. That principle is, that the sole end for which mankind are warranted, individually or collectively, in interfering with the liberty of action of any of their number, is self-protection. That the only purpose for which power can be rightfully exercised over any member of a civilized community, against his will, is to prevent harm to others. His own good, either physical or moral, is not a sufficient warrant. He cannot rightfully be compelled to do or forbear because it will be better for him to do so, because it will make him happier, because, in the opinions of others, to do so would be wise, or even right. These are good reasons for remonstrating with him, or reasoning with him, or persuading him, or entreating him, but not for compelling him, or visiting him with any evil in case he do otherwise. To justify that, the conduct from which it is desired to deter him, must be calculated to produce evil to some one else. The only part of the conduct of any one, for which he is amenable to society, is that which concerns others. In the part which merely concerns himself, his independence is, of right, absolute. Over himself, over his own body and mind, the individual is sovereign.

It is, perhaps, hardly necessary to say that this doctrine is meant to apply   10
only to human beings in the maturity of their faculties. We are not speaking of children, or of young persons below the age which the law may fix as that of manhood or womanhood. Those who are still in a state to require being taken care of by others, must be protected against their own actions as well as against external injury. For the same reason, we may leave out of consideration those backward states of society in which the race itself may be considered as in its nonage. The early difficulties in the way of spontaneous progress are so great, that there is seldom any choice of means for overcoming them; and a ruler full of the spirit of improvement is warranted in the use of any expedients that will attain an end, perhaps otherwise unattainable. Despotism is a legitimate mode of government in dealing with barbarians, provided the end be their improvement,

and the means justified by actually effecting that end. Liberty, as a principle, has no application to any state of things anterior to the time when mankind have become capable of being improved by free and equal discussion. Until then, there is nothing for them but implicit obedience to an Akbar or a Charlemagne, if they are so fortunate as to find one. But as soon as mankind have attained the capacity of being guided to their own improvement by conviction or persuasion (a period long since reached in all nations with whom we need here concern ourselves), compulsion, either in the direct form or in that of pains and penalties for noncompliance, is no longer admissible as a means to their own good, and justifiable only for the security of others.

It is proper to state that I forgo any advantage which could be derived to 11 my argument from the idea of abstract right, as a thing independent of utility. I regard utility as the ultimate appeal on all ethical questions; but it must be utility in the largest sense, grounded on the permanent interests of man as a progressive being. Those interests, I contend, authorize the subjection of individual spontaneity to external control, only in respect to those actions of each, which concern the interest of other people. If any one does an act hurtful to others, there is a prima facie case for punishing him, by law, or, where legal penalties are not safely applicable, by general disapprobation. There are also many positive acts for the benefit of others, which he may rightfully be compelled to perform; such as, to give evidence in a court of justice; to bear his fair share in the common defence, or in any other joint work necessary to the interest of the society of which he enjoys the protection; and to perform certain acts of individual beneficence, such as saving a fellow creature's life, or interposing to protect the defenceless against ill-usage, things which whenever it is obviously a man's duty to do, he may rightfully be made responsible to society for not doing. A person may cause evil to others not only by his actions but by his inaction, and in either case he is justly accountable to them for the injury. The latter case, it is true, requires a much more cautious exercise of compulsion than the former. To make any one answerable for doing evil to others, is the rule; to make him answerable for not preventing evil, is, comparatively speaking, the exception. Yet there are many cases clear enough and grave enough to justify that exception. In all things which regard the external relations of the individual, he is *de jure* amenable to those whose interests are concerned, and if need be, to society as their protector. There are often good reasons for not holding him to the responsibility; but these reasons must arise from the special expediencies of the case: either because it is a kind of case in which he is on the whole likely to act better, when left to his own discretion, than when controlled in any way in which society have it in their power to control him; or because the attempt to exercise control would produce other evils, greater than those which it would prevent. When such reasons as these preclude the enforcement of responsibility, the conscience of the agent himself should step into the vacant judgement-seat; and protect those interests of others which have no external protection; judging himself all the more rigidly, because the case does not admit of his being made accountable to the judgement of his fellow creatures.

But there is a sphere of action in which society, as distinguished from the ₁₂
individual, has, if any, only an indirect interest; comprehending all that portion
of a person's life and conduct which affects only himself, or if it also affects others, only with their free, voluntary, and undeceived consent and participation.
When I say only himself, I mean directly, and in the first instance: for whatever
affects himself, may affect others through himself; and the objection which may
be grounded on this contingency will receive consideration in the sequel. This,
then, is the appropriate region of human liberty. It comprises, first, the inward
domain of consciousness; demanding liberty of conscience, in the most comprehensive sense; liberty of thought and feeling; absolute freedom of opinion and
sentiment on all subjects, practical or speculative, scientific, moral, or theological. The liberty of expressing and publishing opinions may seem to fall under a
different principle, since it belongs to that part of the conduct of an individual
which concerns other people; but, being almost of as much importance as the
liberty of thought itself, and resting in great part on the same reasons, is practically inseparable from it. Secondly, the principle requires liberty of tastes and
pursuits; of framing the plan of our life to suit our own character; of doing as we
like, subject to such consequences as may follow: without impediment from our
fellow creatures, so long as what we do does not harm them, even though they
should think our conduct foolish, perverse, or wrong. Thirdly, from this liberty
of each individual, follows the liberty, within the same limits, of combination
among individuals; freedom to unite, for any purpose not involving harm to others: the persons combining being supposed to be of full age, and not forced or
deceived.

No society in which these liberties are not, on the whole, respected, is free, ₁₃
whatever may be its form of government; and none is completely free in which
they do not exist absolute and unqualified. The only freedom which deserves the
name, is that of pursuing our own good in our own way, so long as we do not attempt to deprive others of theirs, or impede their efforts to obtain it. Each is the
proper guardian of his own health, whether bodily, or mental and spiritual.
Mankind are greater gainers by suffering each other to live as seems good to
themselves, than by compelling each to live as seems good to the rest.

Meaning and Idea

1. What basic definition does Mill ascribe to the term *liberty?* How is that
   definition modified throughout the essay? On what "practical question"
   does Mill's argument about liberty hinge? What is the "principal question in
   human affairs"?

2. Trace the historical change in attitude toward rulers as outlined by Mill in
   this essay. Why did it occur?

3. According to Mill, why may it be necessary to limit the power of the
   majority opinion? What does he mean by "the tyranny of the majority"?

What, according to Mill, is the difference between the rights of society to persuade and to compel its citizens to act in certain ways? Which is preferable? What acts *may* be compelled? On what basis?

4. What is Mill's attitude toward the connection between religion and liberty?

5. What, according to Mill, is the relation between personal preference and rules of conduct or propriety? Which class has usually determined morality? What examples of this does he offer? Can you offer a few more examples from present-day societies?

Language, Form, Structure

1. Mill's first paragraph is almost a model introduction to argument because of the elements it includes. Analyze how Mill: (a) identifies the focus of the essay, (b) establishes a definition for his argument, (c) focuses on the contemporary importance of his discussion, and (d) provides a historical context for his argument. Also, identify any other element in the first paragraph that you feel is especially important.

2. The introduction to this chapter discusses the difference between *inductive* and *deductive* reasoning (see page 521). You may want to clarify your understanding of these terms further by looking in a dictionary, an encyclopedia, or a basic philosophy textbook. Would you characterize Mill's logic in this essay as primarily inductive or deductive? Explain.

3. Where does Mill place his thesis statement in this essay? Identify it. Why is it placed where it is?

4. Analyze Mill's use of transitions in this essay. Is it significant to the logical development that 3 of the essay's 13 paragraphs begin with the word *But?* How do the other transitions affect the development of Mill's argument?

5. What sentence signals the beginning of the essay's conclusion? How does Mill use *summary* as a part of his conclusion? What generalization does he derive from this summary?

6. Would you classify this piece more as an *argumentation* or a *persuasion* essay (see chapter introduction, pages 520–21)? Where does Mill include specific suggestions for action?

7. Check the meanings of the following words from the essay: infringe; efficaciously; superseded; axiomatic; despotism; formidable; fetter; multifarious; fallibility; tacit.

Ideas for Writing

1. Select an aspect of life over which you feel the government exerts too much—or too little—control. Write an argument in favor of reversing the

current trend. Be sure to include a blend of objective analysis and personal preference.

2. Write an argument for or against a greater voice by students in shaping the curriculum at your school. Include a discussion of the relation between students' goals at your school and the present curriculum's ability to fulfill those goals.

3. John Stuart Mill is known for advocating the doctrine of *laissez-faire* both in economics and in personal life. Very basically, *laissez-faire* means complete lack of, or at least minimal, government regulation. For further clarification, look up *laissez-faire* in an encyclopedia and pay close attention to how it relates to ideas about individualism.

    How is Mill's argument in "On Liberty" a reflection of *laissez-faire?* What do you think of this attitude? Is it applicable to the 2000s? How so?

A Marriage Proposal

Anton Chekhov

Anton Chekhov, born in 1860 and trained as a physician, is one of the most widely read and influential short story writers and dramatists of the modern era. During his lifetime, appreciative readers and audiences acknowledged and admired his innovations in both genres, and many of today's writers continue to be influenced by Chekov.

Chekhov was concerned with the personal and the ordinary, which resulted in works about his characters' psychologies more than their actions. Early in his career he wrote farcical, lighthearted material like the following one-act play. Here, as in much of Chekhov's work, the characters' behaviors, idiosyncrasies, and agendas are what really drive the narrative forward.

CHARACTERS

Stepán Stepánovich Choobookóv *a landowner.*

Natália Stepánovna, *his twenty-five-year-old daughter.*

Iván Vassílievich Lómov, Choobookóv's *neighbor, a healthy and well-fed, but terribly hypochondriac landowner.*

*T*he action takes place in the drawing room of Choobookóv's country house.

SCENE I

(Choobookóv and Lómov. *The latter enters, wearing tails and white gloves.*)

Choobookóv (*going over to welcome his guest*): Why, of all people! My old friend, Iván Vassílievich! How nice to see you! (*Shakes his hand.*) This really is a surprise, old boy. . . . How *are* you?

Lómov: Very well, thank you. And may I ask how *you* are?

Choobookóv: Not bad at all, old friend, with the help of your prayers and so on. . . . Please have a seat. . . . Now, really, it's not very nice of you to neglect your neighbors, my dear boy. And what are you all dressed up for? Morning coat, gloves, and so on! Are you off on a visit, old boy?

Lómov: No, I'm just calling on you, my esteemed neighbor.

Choobookóv: But why the morning coat, old friend? This isn't New Year's Day!

Lómov: Well, you see, the fact of the matter is . . . (*Takes his arm.*) I've burst in on you like this, Stepán Stepánovich, my esteemed neighbor, in order to ask a favor of you. I've already had the honor more than once of turning to you for help and you've always, so to speak, uh! . . . But forgive me, my nerves . . . I must have a sip of water, dear Stepán Stepánovich.

(*Drinks some water.*)

CHOOBOOKÓV (*aside*): He's after money. Fat chance! (*To* LÓMOV) What is it, my dear fellow?

LÓMOV: Well, you see, my Stepán dearovich, uh! I mean dear Stepánovich . . . uh! I mean, my nerves are in a terrible condition, which you yourself are so kind as to see. In short, you're the only one who can help me, although, of course, I've done nothing to deserve it and . . . and I don't even have the right to count on your help. . . .

CHOOBOOKÓV: Now, now; don't beat about the bush, old friend. Out with it! . . . Well?

LÓMOV: All right, here you are. The fact of the matter is, I've come to ask for your daughter Natália's hand in marriage.

CHOOBOOKÓV (*overjoyed*): My *dearest* friend! Iván Vassílievich. Could you repeat that—I'm not sure I heard right!

LÓMOV: I have the honor of asking—

CHOOBOOKÓV (*breaking in*): My oldest and dearest friend . . . I'm *so* delighted and so on. . . . Yes really, and all that sort of thing. (*Hugging and kissing him.*) I've been yearning for this for ages. It's been my constant desire. (*Sheds a tear.*) And I've always loved you like a son, you wonderful person, you. May God grant you love and guidance and so on, it's been my most fervent wish. . . . But why am I standing here like a blockhead? I'm dumbstruck by the sheer joy of it, completely dumbstruck. Oh, with all my heart and soul. . . . I'll go get Natália, and so on.

LÓMOV (*deeply moved*): Stepán Stepánovich, my esteemed friend, do you think I may count on her accepting me?

CHOOBOOKÓV: A handsome devil like you? How could she possibly resist? She's *madly* in love with you, don't worry, *madly,* and so on. . . . I'll call her right away.

(*Exit.*)

SCENE II

LÓMOV (*alone*): It's so cold . . . I'm shaking all over, like before a final exam. The important thing is to make up your mind. If you think about it too long, or waver, talk about it too much, and wait for the ideal woman or for true love, you'll never marry. . . . Brr! It's cold! Natália Stepánovna is an excellent housekeeper, she's not bad-looking, and she's got some education. . . . What more could I ask for? Oh, I'm so nervous, I can hear a buzzing in my ears. (*Drinks some water.*) It would be best for me to get married. . . . First of all, I'm thirty-five years old already—and that, as they say, is a critical age. And then, I have to start leading a steady and regular life. . . . I've got a heart condition, with palpitations all the time. . . . I've got an awful temper and I'm always getting terribly wrought up. . . . Even now, my lips are trembling and my right eyelid is twitching. . . . But the worst thing is when I try to sleep. The instant I get to bed and start dropping off, something *stabs* me in my left side—ungh! And it cuts right through my shoulder straight into my head—ungh! I jump like a lunatic, walk about a little, and then I lie down again, but the moment I start to doze off, I feel it in my side again—ungh! And it keeps on and on for at least twenty times. . . .

SCENE III

(NATÁLIA STEPÁNOVNA *and* LÓMOV.)

NATÁLIA (*entering*): Ah, it's you. And Papa said a customer had come for the merchandise. How do you do, Iván Vassílievich!

LÓMOV: How do you do, my esteemed Natália Stepánovna!

NATÁLIA: I'm sorry about my apron and not being dressed. . . . We're shelling peas for drying. Where've you been keeping yourself? Have a seat. . . . (*They sit down.*) Would you like a bite of lunch?

LÓMOV: Thank you so much, but I've already eaten.

NATÁLIA: Well, then have a cigarette. . . . The matches are over here. . . . The weather's magnificent today, but yesterday it rained so hard that the men couldn't do a thing all day long. How much hay did *you* get done? Can you imagine, I was so greedy that I had the whole meadow mown, and now I regret it, I'm scared that all my hay may rot. I should have waited. But what's this? I do believe you're wearing a morning coat! How original! Are you going to a ball or something? Incidentally, you're getting quite handsome. . . . But honestly, why are you all dolled up?

LÓMOV (*nervously*): You see, my esteemed Natália Stepánovna . . . the fact is I've made up my mind to ask you to listen to me. . . . Naturally you'll be surprised and even angry, but I . . . (*Aside.*) God, it's cold!

NATÁLIA: What is it? (*Pause.*) Well?

LÓMOV: I'll try to be brief. You are well aware, my esteemed Natália Stepánovna, that for a long time now, in fact since my childhood, I have had the honor of knowing your family. My late aunt and her husband, whose estate as you know I inherited, always held your father and your late mother in utmost esteem. The Lómov family and the Choobookóv family have always maintained extremely friendly, one might even say, intimate relations. Furthermore, as you know, my property borders on yours. Perhaps you will be so kind as to recall that my Ox Meadows run along your birch forest.

NATÁLIA: Excuse me for interrupting you. You said *"my* Ox Meadows." . . . Are they *yours?*

LÓMOV: Of course. . . .

NATÁLIA: Oh, come now! The Ox Meadows belong to us, not you!

LÁMOV: Oh no! They're mine, dear Natália Stepánovna.

NATÁLIA: That's news to me. How did they ever get to be yours?

LÓMOV: What do you mean? I'm talking about the Ox Meadows that are wedged in between your birch forest and the Burnt Marsh.

NATÁLIA: Exactly. . . . They're ours.

LÓMOV: No, you're mistaken, dear Natália Stepánovna—they're mine.

NATÁLIA: Do be reasonable, Iván Vassílievich! Since when have they been yours?

LÓMOV: Since when? They've always been ours, as far back as I can remember.

NATÁLIA: Excuse me, but this is too much!

LÓMOV: You can look at the documents, dear Natália Stepánovna. At one time, there *were* some quarrels about the Ox Meadows, you're quite right. But now, everyone knows they're mine. Why argue about it? If you will permit me to explain: my aunt's grandmother lent them to your paternal great-grandfather's peasants for an indefinite period and free of charge in return for their firing her bricks. Your great-grandfather's peasants used the Meadows free of charge for some forty years and began thinking of them as their own . . . and then after the Emancipation, when a statute was passed—

NATÁLIA: You've got it all wrong! Both my grandfather and great-grandfather regarded their property as reaching all the way to the Burnt Swamp— which means that the Ox Meadows were ours. What's there to argue about?—I don't understand. How annoying!

LÓMOV: I'll show you the documents, Natália Stepánovna.

NATÁLIA: No; you're joking or trying to tease me. . . . What a surprise! We've owned the land for practically three hundred years and now suddenly we're told it's not ours! I'm sorry, Iván Vassílievich, but I just can't believe my ears. Those Meadows don't mean a thing to me. The whole area probably doesn't come to more than forty acres, it's worth about three hundred rubles; but I'm terribly upset by the injustice of it all. You can say what you like, but I simply can't stand injustice.

LÓMOV: Please listen to me, I beseech you. Your paternal great-grandfather's peasants, as I have already had the honor of telling you, fired bricks for my aunt's grandmother. Now, my aunt's grandmother, wishing to do them a favor in return—

NATÁLIA: Grandfather, grandmother, aunt . . . I don't know *what* you're talking about! The Meadows are *ours,* and that's that.

LÓMOV: They're *mine!*

NATÁLIA: They're ours! You can keep arguing for two days, you can put on fifteen morning coats if you like, but they're ours, ours, ours! . . . I don't desire *your* property, but I don't care to lose mine. . . . Do as you like!

LÓMOV: I don't need the Meadows, Natália Stepánovna, but it's the principle of the thing. If you want, I'll *give* them to you.

NATÁLIA: It would be *my* privilege to give them to *you,* they're mine! . . . All this is rather odd—to put it mildly, Iván Vassílievich. Up till now we've always considered you a good neighbor and friend. Last year we let you borrow our threshing machine, and as a result we couldn't finish our own grain until November, and now you're treating us like Gypsies. You're *giving* me my own land. Excuse me, but that's not a neighborly thing to do! To *my* mind, it's impertinent, if you care to—

LÓMOV: Are you trying to tell me that I'm a land-grabber? Madam, I've never seized anyone else's property, and I won't allow anyone to *say* I have. . . . (*Hurries over to the carafe and drinks some water.*) The Ox Meadows are mine!

NATÁLIA: That's not true, they're ours.

LÓMOV: They're mine.

NATÁLIA: That's not true. I'll prove it to you! I'll send my men over to mow them this afternoon.

LÓMOV: What?!

NATÁLIA: My men will be there this afternoon!

LÓMOV: I'll kick them out!

NATÁLIA: You wouldn't dare!

LÓMOV: (*clutching at his heart*): The Ox Meadows are mine! Do you hear! Mine!

NATÁLIA: Stop shouting! Please! You can shout your lungs out in your own place, but I must ask you to control yourself here.

LÓMOV: Madam, if it weren't for these awful, excruciating palpitations and the veins throbbing in my temples, I'd speak to you in a totally different way! (*Shouting.*) The Ox Meadows are mine.

NATÁLIA: Ours!

LÓMOV: Mine!

NATÁLIA: Ours!

LÓMOV: Mine!

SCENE IV

(*Enter* CHOOBOOKÓV.)

CHOOBOOKÓV: What's going on? What's all the shouting about?

NATÁLIA: Papa, please tell this gentleman whom the Ox Meadows belong to. Us or him.

CHOOBOOKÓV (*to* LÓMOV): Why, the Meadows belong to us, old friend.

Lómov: But for goodness' sake, Stepán Stepánovich, how can that be? Can't *you* be reasonable at least? My aunt's grandmother lent the Meadows to your grandfather's peasants for temporary use and free of charge. His peasants used the land for forty years and got in the habit of regarding it as their own, but after the Land Settlement—

Choobookóv: Excuse me, old boy. . . . You're forgetting that our peasants didn't pay your grandmother and so on precisely *because* the Meadows were disputed and what not. . . . But now every child knows that they're ours. I guess you've never looked at the maps.

Lómov: I'll *prove* they're mine!

Choobookóv: You won't prove a thing, my boy.

Lómov: I will *so* prove it!

Choobookóv: My dear boy, why carry on like this? You won't prove a thing by shouting. I don't want anything of yours, but I don't intend to let go of what's mine. Why should I? If it comes to that, dear friend, if you mean to dispute my ownership of the Meadows, and so on, I'd sooner let my peasants have them than you. So there!

Lómov: I don't understand. What right do you have to give away other people's property?

Choobookóv: Allow me to decide whether or not I've got the right. Really, young man, I'm not accustomed to being spoken to in that tone of voice, and what not. I'm old enough to be your father, and I must ask you to calm down when you speak to me, and so forth.

Lómov: No! You're treating me like an idiot, and laughing at me. You tell me that *my* property is yours, and then you expect me to remain calm and talk to you in a normal fashion. That's not a very neighborly thing to do, Stepán Stepánovich. You're no neighbor, you're a robber baron.

Choobookóv: What?! What did you say, my good man?

Natália: Papa, have the men mow the Ox Meadows right now!

Choobookóv (*to* Lómov): What did you say, sir?

Natália: The Ox Meadows are our property, and I won't let anyone else have them. I won't, I won't, I won't!

Lómov: We'll see about that! I'll prove to you in court that they're mine.

Choobookóv: In court? My good man, you can take it to court, and what not. Go right ahead! I know you, you've just been waiting for a chance to litigate, and so on. You're a quibbler from the word go. Your whole family's nothing but a bunch of pettifoggers. All of them!

Lómov: I must ask you not to insult my family. The Lómovs have always been law-abiding folk. None of them was ever hauled into court for embezzlement the way your uncle was.

Choobookóv: Every last one of them was insane.

Natália: Every last one of them, every last one!

Choobookóv: Your grandfather drank like a fish, and the whole county knows that your youngest aunt, Nastasia, ran off with an architect, and what not—

LÓMOV: And your mother was a hunchback! (*Clutching at his heart.*) There's a twitching in my side. . . . My head's throbbing. . . . Oh, God. . . . Water!

CHOOBOOKÓV: And your father was a gambler and he ate like a pig!

NATÁLIA: And no one could beat your aunt at scandal-mongering.

LÓMOV: My left leg's paralyzed. . . . And you're a schemer. . . . Oooh! My heart! . . . And it's no secret to anyone that just before the elections you—There are stars bursting before my eyes. . . . Where's my hat?

NATÁLIA: Vermin! Liar! Brute!

CHOOBOOKÓV: You're a spiteful, double-dealing schemer! So there!

LÓMOV: Ah, my hat. . . . My heart. Where am I? Where's the door? Oooh! . . . I think I'm dying. . . . My foot's totally paralyzed. (*Drags himself to the door.*)

CHOOBOOKÓV (*calling after him*): And don't ever set your foot in my home again!

NATÁLIA: Go to court! Sue us! Just wait and see!

(LÓMOV *staggers out.*)

SCENE V

(CHOOBOOKÓV *and* NATÁLIA STEPÁNOVNA.)

CHOOBOOKÓV: He can go straight to hell, damn him! (*Walks about, all wrought up.*)

NATÁLIA: Isn't he the worst crook? Catch me trusting a good neighbor after this!

CHOOBOOKÓV: The chiseler! The scarecrow!

NATÁLIA: The monster! He not only grabs other people's property, he calls them names, to boot.

CHOOBOOKÓV: And that clown, that . . . freak had the colossal nerve to ask me for your hand in marriage, and so on. Can you imagine? He wanted to propose.

NATÁLIA: Propose?

CHOOBOOKÓV: Exactly! That's what he came for. To propose to you.

NATÁLIA: Propose? To me? Why didn't you *say* so?

CHOOBOOKÓV: And he got all dolled up in a morning coat. That pipsqueak. That upstart.

NATÁLIA: Propose? To me? Ohhh! (*Collapses into an armchair and wails.*) Bring him back. Get him. Ohh! Get him!

CHOOBOOKÓV: Get whom?

NATÁLIA: Hurry up, hurry! I feel sick. Bring him back. (*Hysterical.*)

CHOOBOOKÓV: What is it? What's wrong? (*Grabbing his head.*) This is awful! I'll shoot myself. I'll hang myself. They've worn me out.

NATÁLIA: I'm dying! Bring him back!

CHOOBOOKÓV: All right. Stop yelling!

(*Runs out.*)

NATÁLIA (*alone, wailing*): What've we done? Bring him back! Bring him back!

CHOOBOOKÓV (*running in*): He's coming and all that, goddamn him. Ughh! *You* talk to him, alone, I really don't feel like. . . .

NATÁLIA (*wailing*): Bring him back!

CHOOBOOKÓV (*shouting*): He's coming, I tell you. Oh God! What did I ever do to deserve a grown-up daughter? I'll cut my throat. I swear, I'll cut my throat. We insulted and abused him, and it's all your fault!

NATÁLIA: My fault? It was yours!

CHOOBOOKÓV: Now *I'm* the culprit!

(LÓMOV *appears at the French doors.* CHOOBOOKÓV *exits.*)

SCENE VI

(NATÁLIA *and* LÓMOV.)

LÓMOV (*entering, exhausted*): What horrible palpitations . . . my foot's gone numb . . . there's a jabbing in my side. . . .

NATÁLIA: My apologies, Iván Vassílievich, we got so worked up. . . . I do recall now that the Ox Meadows are actually *your* property.

LÓMOV: My heart's palpitating. . . . The Meadows *are* mine. . . . There are stars bursting in both my eyes.

(*They sit down.*)

NATÁLIA: We were wrong.

LÓMOV: It's the principle of the thing. . . . I don't care about the land, it's the principle of the thing—

NATÁLIA: Exactly, the principle. . . . Let's talk about something else.

LÓMOV: Particularly since I have proof. My aunt's grandmother let your paternal great-grandfather's peasants—

NATÁLIA: All right, all right. . . . (*Aside.*) I don't know how to go about it. . . . (*To* LÓMOV) Will you start hunting soon?

LÓMOV: Yes, for grouse, Natália Stepánovna. I think I shall begin after the harvest. Oh, have you heard what bad luck I had? My hound Guess— you know the one—he's gone lame.

NATÁLIA: What a pity! How did it happen?

LÓMOV: I don't know. He must have twisted his leg, or else some other dog bit him. . . . (*Sighs.*) My very best hound, not to mention the money! Why, I paid Mirónov a hundred and twenty-five rubles for him.

NATÁLIA: You overpaid him, Iván Vassílievich.

LÓMOV: I don't think so. It was very little for a wonderful dog.

NATÁLIA: Papa bought his dog Leap for eighty-five rubles, and Leap is vastly superior to your Guess.

LÓMOV: Leap superior to Guess? Oh, come now. (*Laughs.*) Leap superior to Guess!

NATÁLIA: Of course he is! I know that Leap is still young, he's not a full-grown hound yet. But for points and action, not even Volchanietsky has a better dog.

LÓMOV: Excuse me, Natália Stepánovna, but you're forgetting that he's pug-jawed, which makes him a poor hunting dog.

NATÁLIA: Pug-jawed? That's news to me.

LÓMOV: I can assure you, his lower jaw is shorter than his upper jaw.

NATÁLIA: Have you measured it?

LÓMOV: Indeed, I have. He'll do for pointing, of course, but when it comes to retrieving, he can hardly hold a cand—

NATÁLIA: First of all, our Leap is a pedigreed greyhound—he's the son of Harness and Chisel, whereas your Guess is so piebald that not even Solomon could figure out his breed. . . . Furthermore, he's as old and ugly as a broken-down nag—

LÓMOV: He may be old, but I wouldn't trade him for five of your Leaps. . . . The very idea! Guess is a real hound, but Leap. . . . Why argue? It's ridiculous. . . . Every huntsman's assistant has a dog like your Leap. At twenty-five rubles he'd be overpriced.

NATÁLIA: You seem to be possessed by some demon of contradiction, Iván Vassílievich. First you fancy that the Ox Meadows are yours, then you pretend that Guess is a better hound than Leap. If there's one thing I don't like it's a person who says the opposite of what he thinks. You know perfectly well that Leap is a hundred times better than . . . than that stupid Guess of yours. Why do you insist on denying it?

LÓMOV: You obviously must think, Natália Stepánovna, that I'm either blind or mentally retarded. Can't you see that your Leap has a pug jaw?

NATÁLIA: That's not true.

LÓMOV: A pug jaw.

NATÁLIA (*screaming*): That's not true.

LÓMOV: Why are you screaming, Madam?

NATÁLIA: Why are you talking such rubbish? It's exasperating! Your Guess is just about ready to be put out of his misery, and you compare him to Leap.

LÓMOV: Excuse me, but I can't keep on arguing like this. My heart's palpitating.

NATÁLIA: I've noticed that the sportsmen who argue most don't understand the first thing about hunting.

LÓMOV: Madam, pleeeease, keep quiet. . . . My heart's bursting. . . . (*Shouts.*) Keep quiet!

NATÁLIA: I won't keep quiet until you admit that Leap is a hundred times superior to your Guess!

LÓMOV: He's a hundred times *inferior*. Someone ought to shoot him. My temples . . . my eyes . . . my shoulder. . . .

NATÁLIA: No one has to wish that idiotic mutt of yours dead, because he's just skin and bones anyway.

LÓMOV: Keep quiet! I'm having heart failure!

NATÁLIA: I will *not* keep quiet!

SCENE VII

CHOOBOOKÓV (*entering*): What's going on now?

NATÁLIA: Papa, tell me, honestly and sincerely: which is the better dog—our Leap or his Guess?

LÓMOV: Stepán Stepánovich, I beseech you, just tell me one thing: is your Leap pug-jawed or isn't he? Yes or no?

CHOOBOOKÓV: So what! Who cares? He's still the best hound in the country, and what not.

LÓMOV: And my Guess isn't better? Tell me the truth.

CHOOBOOKÓV: Don't get all worked up, old boy. . . . Let me explain. . . . Your Guess *does* have a few good qualities. . . . He's pure-bred, he's got solid legs, he's well put together, and what not. But if you must know, my good man, your dog's got two basic faults: he's old, and his muzzle's too short.

LÓMOV: Excuse me, my heart's racing madly. . . . Let's examine the facts. . . . Please don't forget that when we were hunting in the Mapooskin Fields, my Guess ran neck and neck with the count's dog Waggy, while your Leap lagged behind by half a mile.

CHOOBOOKÓV: That was because the Count's assistant struck him with his riding crop.

LÓMOV: Naturally. All the other dogs were chasing the fox, but yours started running after sheep.

CHOOBOOKÓV: That's a lie! My dear boy, I fly off the handle easily, so please let's stop arguing. The man whipped him because people are always envious of everyone else's dogs. Yes, they're all filled with spite! And you, sir, are no exception. Why, the minute you notice that anyone else's dog is better than your Guess, you instantly start up something or other . . . and what not. I've got the memory of an elephant!

LÓMOV: And so do I.

CHOOBOOKÓV (*mimicking him*): "And so do I" . . . And what does your memory tell you?

LÓMOV: My heart's palpitating. . . . My foot's paralyzed. . . . I can't anymore. . . .

NATÁLIA (*mimicking*): "My heart's palpitating". . . . What kind of hunter are you anyway? You ought to be home in bed catching cockroaches instead of out hunting foxes. Palpitations! . . .

CHOOBOOKÓV: That's right, what kind of hunter are you? If you've got palpitations, stay home; don't go wobbling around the countryside on horseback. It wouldn't be so bad if you really hunted, but you only tag along in order to start arguments or meddle with other people's dogs, and what not. We'd better stop, I fly off the handle easily. You, sir, are not a hunter, and that's that.

Lómov: And you *are,* I suppose. The only reason *you* go hunting is to flatter the count and carry on your back-stabbing little intrigues. . . . Oh, my heart! . . . You schemer!

Choobookóv: Me, a schemer. (*Shouting.*) Shut up!

Lómov: Schemer!

Choobookóv: Upstart! Pipsqueak!

Lómov: You old fogy! You hypocrite!

Choobookóv: Shut up, or I'll blast you with a shot gun like a partridge.

Lómov: The whole county knows that—Oh, my heart!—your late wife used to beat you. . . . My leg . . . my temples . . . I see stars . . . I'm falling, falling. . . .

Choobookóv: And your housekeeper henpecks you all over the place!

Lómov: There, you see . . . my heart's burst! My shoulder's torn off. . . . Where's my shoulder? . . . I'm dying! (*Collapses into armchair.*) Get a doctor! (*Faints.*)

Choobookóv: Pipsqueak. Weakling. Windbag. I feel sick. (*Drinks some water.*) I feel sick.

Natália: What kind of hunter are you anyway? You don't even know how to sit in a saddle! (*To her father.*) Papa! What's the matter with him? Papa! Look, Papa! (*Screams.*) Iván Vassílievich! He's dead!

Choobookóv: I feel sick! . . . I can't breathe! . . . Air!

Natália: He's dead! (*Tugs at* Lómov's *sleeve.*) Iván Vassílievich! Iván Vassílievich! What've we done? He's dead. (*Collapses into easy chair.*) Get a doctor. (*She becomes hysterical.*)

Choobookóv: Oh! . . . What is it? What's wrong?

Natália (*moaning*): He's dead . . . he's dead!

Choobookóv: Who's dead? (*Glancing at* Lómov.) He really is dead! Oh, my God! Get some water! Get a doctor! (*Holds a glass to* Lómov's *mouth.*) Go ahead and drink! . . . He won't drink. . . . I guess he's dead and so on. . . . Why does everything have to happen to me? Why didn't I put a bullet through my head long ago? Why didn't I cut my throat? What am I waiting for? Give me a knife! Give me a gun!

(Lómov stirs.)

He's reviving, I think. . . . Drink some water! . . . That's right.

Lómov: Stars . . . fog . . . where am I?

Choobookóv: You two'd better hurry up and get married. . . . Dammit! She accepts. . . . (*Joins* Lómov's *hand with* Natália's.) She accepts. . . . My blessings and so forth. . . . Just do me a favor and leave me in peace.

Lómov: What? (*Getting up.*) Who?

Choobookóv: She accepts. Well? Kiss her and . . . the two of you can go straight to hell.

Natália (*moaning*): He's alive . . . I accept, I accept. . . .

Choobookóv: Kiss and make up.

LÓMOV: What? Who? (*Kisses* NATÁLIA.) *Enchanté.* . . . Excuse me, but what's going on? Oh yes, I remember. . . . My heart . . . stars . . . I'm very happy, Natália Stepánovna. (*Kisses her hands.*) My leg's paralyzed. . . .

NATÁLIA: I . . . I'm very happy, too. . . .

CHOOBOOKÓV: That's a load off my back. . . . Whew!

NATÁLIA: But. . . . all the same, why don't you finally admit that Guess isn't as good as Leap.

LÓMOV: He's much better.

NATÁLIA: He's worse.

CHOOBOOKÓV: The launching of marital bliss! Champagne!

LÓMOV: He's better.

NATÁLIA: Worse! Worse! Worse!

CHOOBOOKÓV (*trying to outshout them*): Champagne! Champagne!

Meaning and Idea

1. How does Choobookóv respond to the idea of Lómov's marrying Natália? How does Lómov feel? Why does he feel that way?

2. What interferes with Lómov's plans to propose marriage? Explain the issue of the Ox Meadows.

3. How does Natália react when she learns Lómov's intentions from her father? What is Chekhov saying about marriage here? What happens when Lómov is summoned back? Where does the conversation about Leap and Guess take Lómov and Natália?

4. How do Natália and Choobookóv react when Lómov collapses?

5. Explain the irony in Choobookóv's line "The launching of marital bliss!" Why does he call for champagne? How is that also ironic?

Language, Form, Structure

1. What elements of argument do you find in the play? Where do the arguments seem logical and rational? Where do they defy logic and rationality and turn into shouting matches?

2. What are the propositions about the Ox Meadows and the two dogs?

3. Identify lines of dialogue that seem highly typical of each character.

4. Where do the characters use narration? Exemplification? Comparison and contrast?

5. How does Chekhov achieve humor in this play?

6. Define the following words and use each one in a sentence: esteemed; fervent; palpitations; statute; beseech; threshing; impertinent; quibbler; pettifoggers; scandal-mongering; piebald; intrigues.

Ideas for Writing

1. Write a scene for a modern-day play version of "A Marriage Proposal." Draw your characters from people you know. Show a typical argument and how the two parties deal with it.

2. Write an essay in which you argue a position about marriage.

3. Write an essay in which you examine Chekhov's play as a farcical example of human behavior.

CROSSOVER ━━━━━━━━━━━━━━━━

1. Katha Pollitt in "The Smurfette Principle" and Barbara Dafoe Whitehead in "The Plight of the High-Status Woman" (Chapter Six) approach the idea of the modern girl and woman. What resonances do you note in their ideas? In their approach to the topic? How might you consider Whitehead's piece a challenge to Pollitt's? Write an essay exploring these questions.

2. Jonathan Swift in "A Modest Proposal" and John Stuart Mill in "On Liberty" explore freedom and oppression in specific historical instances. In an essay, identify the basic social beliefs that the two selections reflect. What unique point does each selection make? Which selection rallies you the most? Why?

Acknowledgments

Annie Dillard, "Mantis." From *Pilgrim at Tinker Creek,* by Annie Dillard. HarperCollins, 1974 by Annie Dillard. Reprinted by permission of Harper Collins Publishers Inc.

Barbara Ehrenreich, "What I've Learned from Men" *Ms.,* 1985. Reprinted by permission of Ms. Magazine, © 1985.

Ian Frazier, excerpt from *On the Rez.* Copyright © 2000 by Ian Frazier. Reprinted by permission of Farrar, Straus and Giroux, LLC.

Robert Frost, "Fire and Ice." From *The Poetry of Robert Frost,* edited by Edward Connery Lathem. Copyright 1923, 1928, © 1969 by Holt Rinehart & Winston. Copyright 1951, 1956 by Robert Frost. Reprinted by permission of Holt, Rinehart & Winston Publishers.

Adam Gopnik, "Like a King." Originally published in *The New Yorker,* January 31, 2000. © Adam Gopnik. Reprinted by permission.

Robert Graves, "The Naked and the Nude." From *Five Pens in Hand.* Copyright © 1958 by Robert Graves. Reprinted by permission of Doubleday & Co., Inc.

Seamus Heaney, "Digging." From *Opened Ground: Selected Poems 1966–1998* by Seamus Heaney. Copyright © 1998 by Seamus Heaney. Reprinted by permission of Farrar, Straus and Giroux, LLC.

Ernest Hemingway, "Camping Out." From *Dateline: Toronto,* edited by William White. Copyright © 1985 by Mary Hemingway, John Hemingway, Patrick Hemingway, and Gregory Hemingway. Reprinted with permission of Scribner, a division of Simon & Schuster, Inc.

Langston Hughes, "Dream Deferred." From *The Collected Poems of Langston Hughes* by Langston Hughes. Copyright © 1994 by The Estate of Langston Hughes. Used by permission of Alfred A. Knopf, a division of Random House, Inc.

Langston Hughes, "Salvation." From *The Big Sea,* by Langston Hughes. Copyright 1940 by Langston Hughes. Copyright renewed 1968 by Arna Bontemps and George Houston Bass. Reprinted by permission of Hill and Wang, a division of Farrar, Straus and Giroux, LLC.

James Joyce, "Araby." From *Dubliners* by James Joyce, copyright © 1916 by B. W. Heubsch. Definitive text copyright © 1967 by the Estate of James Joyce. Used by permission of Viking Penguin, a division of Penguin Putnam Inc.

Franz Kafka, "The Judgment." From *The Metamorphosis, The Penal Colony, and Other Stories* by Franz Kafka, translated by Willa and Edwin Muir. Copyright © 1948 by Schocken Books. Copyright renewed 1975 by Schocken Books. Reprinted by permission of Schocken Books, a division of Random House, Inc.

Alfred Kazin, excerpt from "The Kitchen." From *A Walker in the City,* copyright 1951 and renewed 1979 by Alfred Kazin, reprinted by permission of Harcourt, Inc.

Martin Luther King, Jr., "I Have a Dream." Reprinted by arrangement with the Estate of Martin Luther King, Jr. c/o Writers House as an agent for the proprietor. Copyright ©1963 by Martin Luther King. Copyright renewed 1991, Coretta Scott King.

Maxine Hong Kingston, "Family Ghosts." From *The Woman Warrior: Memoirs of a Girlhood among Ghosts,* by Maxine Hong Kingston. Copyright © 1975, 1976 by Maxine Hong Kingston. Reprinted by permission of Alfred A. Knopf, Inc.

Leonard Kriegel, "Claiming the Self: The Cripple as American Man." From *Falling into Life.* North Point Press, 1991. © Leonard Kriegel. Reprinted with permission of the author.

D.H. Lawrence, "The Rocking-Horse Winner." Copyright 1933 by the Estate of D.H. Lawrence, renewed © 1961 by Angelo Ravagli and C.M. Weekley, Executors of the Estate of Frieda Lawrence, from *Complete Short Stories of D.H. Lawrence* by D.H. Lawrence. Used by permission of Viking Penguin, a division of Penguin Putnam Inc.

Camara Laye, "The Gold Worker." From *The Dark Child* by Camara Laye, translated by James Kirkup, Ernest Jones, and Elaine Gottlieb. Copyright © 1954 and renewed © 1982 by Camara Laye. Reprinted by permission of Hill and Wang, a division of Farrar, Straus and Giroux, LLC.

Phillip Lopate, "Modern Friendships." From *Against Joie de Vie,* by Phillip Lopate. Poseidon Press. © Phillip Lopate, 1989.